T5-ACO-345

FUNCTIONAL MATHEMATICS FOR THE MENTALLY RETARDED

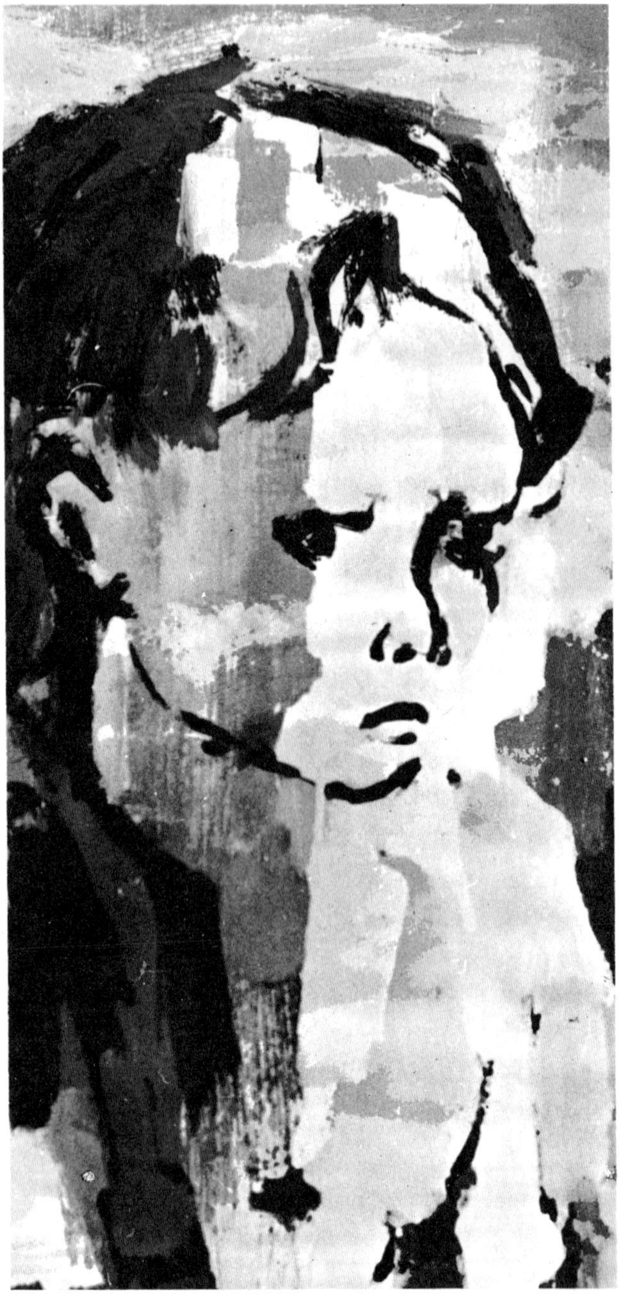

DANIEL L. PETERSON
Northern Arizona University
Flagstaff, Arizona

FUNCTIONAL MATHEMATICS FOR THE MENTALLY RETARDED

CHARLES E. MERRILL PUBLISHING COMPANY
A Bell & Howell Company   Columbus, Ohio

THE SLOW LEARNER SERIES
Edited by Newell C. Kephart

Published by
Charles E. Merrill Publishing Company
A Bell & Howell Company
Columbus, Ohio 43216

Copyright © 1973 by Bell & Howell Company. All rights reserved. No part of this book may be reproduced in any form, electronic or mechanical, including photocopy, recording, or any information storage and retrieval system without permission in writing from the publisher.

International Standard Book Number: 0-675-09097-0

Library of Congress Catalog Card Number: 70-188780

1 2 3 4 5 / 77 76 75 74 73

Printed in the United States of America

To My Mother and Father

Contents

	Foreword	XI
	Preface	XV
	Acknowledgements	XIX
chapter 1	The Mentally Retarded Child and Mathematics	1

The Mentally Retarded Child Defined, 1. Relevant Learning Characteristics, 4. Math Performance of the Educable Mentally Retarded, 10. Math Achievement of the Trainable Mentally Retarded, 12. Summary, 15. References, 16.

chapter 2	Constructing the Mathematics Curriculum	19

Obstacles to Achievement, 20. Mental Age as a Guide to Achievement, 20. Anticipated Grade Potential, 21. Multiple Criteria, 25. Achievement Level, 25. Achievement Discrepancy, 26. Functional Mathematics, 27. Objectives, 28. Principles of Adaptation, 32. Organizing for Instruction, 37. Modern Mathematics for the Retardate, 41. Curriculum Content, 46. Summary, 48. References, 49.

chapter 3   Early Childhood Mathematics Education   53

Ability Levels, 53. Objectives, 56. Form and Perception (Geometry), 58. Vocabulary Associated with Mathematics, 73. Number Symbols, 76. Cardinal Number, 81. Ordinal Number, 87. Measurement, 88. Money and Value, 90. Number Operations, 91. Summary, 92. Teaching Aids for Primary Mentally Retarded Children, 93. References, 96.

chapter 4   Primary Mathematics for the Mentally Retarded   99

Ability Levels, 100. Objectives, 101. Developmental Sequence of Mathematics Skills, 102. Form and Perception, 105. Vocabulary Associated with Mathematics, 115. Number Symbols, 119. Cardinal Number, 127. Ordinal Number, 143. Measurement, 149. Money and Value, 161. Number Operations, 171. Summary, 186. Teaching Aids for Primary Level Mentally Retarded Children, 187. References, 190.

chapter 5   Intermediate Mathematics for the Mentally Retarded   193

Ability Levels, 195. Objectives, 196. Developmental Sequence of Mathematical Skills, 197. Form and Perception, 200. The Kephart Training Activities, 208. The Frostig Program for the Development of Visual Perception, 211. Vocabulary Associated with Mathematics, 221. Number Symbols, 221. Cardinal Numbers, 229. Ordinal Numbers, 239. Measurement, 242. Money and Value, 263. Number Operations, 270. Summary, 292. Teaching Aids for Intermediate Level Mentally Retarded Children, 292. References, 296.

chapter 6   Pre-Adultation Junior High Mathematics   299

Ability Levels, 299. Objectives, 300. Developmental Sequence of Mathematics Skills, 301. Form and Perception, 305. Vocabulary Associated with Mathematics, 313. Number Symbols, 313. Cardinal and Ordinal Numbers, 315. Measurement, 322.

Money and Value, 332. Number Operations, 341. Summary, 367. Teaching Aids for Junior High Level Educable Mentally Retarded Children, 367. References, 372.

chapter 7   Mathematics for Adultation   375

Senior High Consumer-Vocational Mathematics, 375. Ability Levels, 376. Objectives, 377. Developmental Sequence of Mathematics Skills, 378. Form and Perception, 380. Vocabulary Associated with Mathematics, 381. Number Symbols, 382. Cardinal and Ordinal Numbers, 383. Measurement, 385. Money and Value, 407. Number Operations, 451. The Unit Approach to Vocational Mathematics Instruction, 451. Summary, 486. Teaching Aids for Senior High Level Educable Mentally Retarded Youth, 487. References, 501.

chapter 8   Mathematics for the Trainable Mentally Retarded   503

Specific Objectives for the Trainable Mentally Retarded, 506. Pre-Primary Mathematics for the Trainable Retarded, 508. Objectives for the Pre-Primary Level Trainable Mentally Retarded, 509. The Primary Mathematics Program for the Trainable Mentally Retarded, 515. Intermediate Program for the Trainable Mentally Retarded, 531. The Advanced Program for the Trainable Mentally Retarded, 557. Objectives for Advanced Level Trainable Mentally Retarded, 558. Summary, 576. Teaching Aids for Trainable Mentally Retarded Children, 577. References, 579.

chapter 9   The Evaluation of Pupil Progress in Mathematics   583

Interpreting the Psychometric Report, 584. Gathering Background Information, 587. Assessing Mathematical Achievement, 588. Constructing an Inventory, 595. Number Inventory for Educable Mentally Retarded Children, Pre-Primary Level, 603. Number Inventory for Educable Mentally Retarded Children, Primary Level, 611. Number Inventory for Educable Mentally Retarded Children, Intermediate Level, 623. Number Inventory for Educable Mentally Retarded Children, Junior High Level, 633. Number Inventory for Educable Mentally Retarded Children, Adultation Level, 643. Reporting to Parents, 658. Summary, 659. Evaluation Instruments, 659. References, 661.

Appendix 663

Index

FOREWORD

Since its inception, special education has had to wrestle with the problem of an adequate curriculum for the mentally retarded child. First attempts were very direct approaches: Since these children are slow they cannot be expected to learn as fast or as much as the typical child; therefore, we will teach them what we can and be satisfied. This approach led to the "watered down" curriculum. The mentally retarded were taught the same things in the same way as the regular classroom child but were allowed to progress more slowly, and endless repetition was used as the major teaching device. Although this approach relieved the child of the often frustrating pressures of the regular classroom situation, its results were unsatisfactory either to school personnel or to parents.

The pendulum then swung to a consideration of the ultimate goals of education for the mentally retarded. Stress was placed on the teaching of "skills of everyday life" and on as many vocational skills as it was thought the child could master. Often, these two approaches were combined so that minimum academic skills were worked toward at the same time that major stress was being placed on what were considered more practical skills.

Technology, however, advanced rapidly. Jobs and industrial tasks become increasingly complex, and, particularly, they began to be characterized by rapid change. The specific skills which had been taught these children were not adequate for such complex requirements, and the long arduous process of developing a new skill or work sequence was too slow for modern industrial technology. Workers were required to possess a greater fund of information and a greater repertory of skills and abilities than the programs for the mentally retarded were producing. As a result, the number of jobs on which such individuals could be placed became more and more limited. What seemed to be needed was a broader curriculum and more, not less, academic skill since academics, particularly mathematics, represent general methods of thinking about problems and situations.

In the meantime, the concept of differences in learning styles and atypical methods of processing data had been introduced to the educational profession. In its initial enthusiasm, special education workers conceived that anything could be taught to any child if only the proper methods were employed. A plethora of "methods for teaching the mentally retarded" began to appear. Some of these were well founded, but others were overdeveloped personal experiences based largely on wishful thinking.

The mentally retarded child is certainly different from other children, but the differences between individual children in the group are as great as the differences between the group as a whole and their "normal" peer groups. As a result, no one method has been found to possess magic qualities for the mentally retarded. Rather, a broad spectrum of methods adapted to the many needs of many children is required. Furthermore, these methods need to be aimed at the teaching of concepts which underlie the academic materials rather than at the mechanics of the academics themselves. Thus, the concept of method has been greatly enlarged and altered since its original introduction into special education.

The curriculum for the mentally retarded has had a long history and has profited from a vast number of experiences. It is never wise to throw out the learnings of the past because of their obvious inadequacies and start over anew. Rather, it is desirable to sift that which has proved useful from that which has proved transient, organize the useful, bring it together into a pattern, and augment it.

Such a task the author of the present volume has performed well in the specific area of the teaching of mathematics to the mentally retarded. Daniel Peterson has the audacity to introduce the "new math" to special education classes—a task which fills many a teacher of regular classes with anxiety. He takes great pains, however, to insure that the necessary concepts for each step are thoroughly learned before the mechanics of that step are introduced. Furthermore, he presents these basic concepts in a number of ways so that each child can find one method that is adequate for his learning style.

Peterson moves step by step through increasingly complex processes until he is able to present algebra and geometry. At each stage, however,

Foreword

he provides for an evaluation of the child's ability before proceeding to the next level. Thus, the limit of ability and slow rate of progress of the mentally retarded are recognized. The organization of his material is not designed in terms of that which is required by the development of theoretical mathematics, but, rather is planned for that which is required by the concepts and processes needed by the child in his everyday living and in his probable vocational pursuits. Thus, the practicality of the child's education is stressed.

Much more can be taught the mentally retarded than we are accustomed to think. With adequate presentations and with constant attention to basic concept learning and relevance to the child, various complex operations become possible for the retarded child to learn. It is not wise to divorce these learnings from traditional academic patterns since these patterns represent the way society and his peers think and react. If we separate his learning too much from these traditions, we widen the gap between him and his peers, and in so doing, lessen his chances of eventual success. The present volume presents an acceptable approach in the field of mathematics instruction.

NEWELL C. KEPHART

Glen Haven Achievement Center
Fort Collins, Colorado

Preface

Mathematics has long been included as an integral facet of the curriculum for mentally retarded children; however, several factors have suggested a need for placing greater emphasis on the content, teaching methodology, and evaluation of the mathematics curriculum for these children. One of the major purposes of this book is to identify those concepts and skills which will be needed by the mentally retarded when they reach adulthood and to outline a sequence of activities that will result in the mastery of such skills.

The modern mathematics movement has resulted in a dynamic reorganization of the curriculum even though as yet the full weight of its impact has not been felt. Traditionally, the average child has been thought to be "ready" for numbers when he reaches age five or six. However, studies have indicated that the preschool child masters some simple mathematical concepts well before his entrance into the first grade. In light of this finding, McDowell (1962, p. 433) has raised the following question:

> With today's trend moving curriculum to earlier grades—especially do we note this in mathematics—should we then, or should we not, introduce more profound concepts to kindergarteners in their incidental and planned mathematics activities?

Although McDowell was speaking of average children, the same question can be asked concerning the mentally retarded. Since more advanced concepts are being introduced to average children at increasingly earlier ages, shouldn't we also present mathematical concepts to the retarded sooner? The author has investigated this question and concluded that young mentally retarded children do possess mathematical knowledge at mental age levels as low as eighteen months. In this text, specific attention is given to mathematics programs designed for the early childhood education of the mentally retarded.

Modern mathematics has not only modified our view of *when* skills should be taught; it has also changed our thinking about *how* they should be taught. The traditional approach to mathematics for the retarded has placed undue emphasis on teaching rote computational skills because of a basic assumption that these children are incapable of grasping the central concepts and basic processes involved in arithmetic problem solving. On the other hand, because the underlying premise of modern mathematics is "teaching for understanding," the new mathematics is actually more a method of teaching than it is a new set of mathematical principles. The author holds the view that it is just as important for retarded children to understand what they are learning as it is for average children. The modern mathematics teaching model seems appropriate for both normal and retarded children.

A great deal of attention has been given in recent years to the perceptual-motor basis of academic learning, including mathematics. It will be shown later in this book that mathematics is a spatial task requiring significant visual-perceptual skills. Consequently, the organization of the mathematics curriculum in this book reflects the trend toward providing more perceptual background experiences for children.

It is generally accepted by those who work with the mentally retarded that the arithmetic portion of the curriculum should include those skills and concepts which the child needs in order to adapt maximally to his environment, yet there is little consensus as to precisely *what* these concepts are or *when* they should be taught.

It is also recognized that the task of constructing the mathematics curriculum for the mentally retarded is more intricate than is construction for nonhandicapped children. Kelly and Stevens (1950, p. 251) have discussed this problem at length and stated that:

> The task of construction of a curriculum for mentally retarded children is more complex than that for normal pupils because it is necessary to retain the basic elements in the curriculum for regular groups as well as adapt materials to the abilities of the special class.

This problem does not preclude teaching mathematical concepts and skills to mentally retarded children, but it does suggest that the typical

Preface xvii

arithmetic curriculum will not be suited to the special needs of these children. There is a need to adapt the regular program to fit the ability levels of mentally retarded children. Another major focus of this book will be to make these necessary adaptations.

Finally, it has been difficult for teachers of the mentally retarded to measure pupil progress in mathematics because of the lack of appropriate standardized achievement tests. Naturally, this shortcoming has also made it difficult to evaluate the effectiveness of the curriculum, methodology, and materials used in teaching mathematics to the retarded. Thus, an entire chapter of this volume is devoted to the topic of evaluation of mathematical skills for the mentally retarded.

THE SCOPE OF THIS TEXT

The purpose of this text is to provide the classroom teacher with a specific mathematics program for use with the mentally retarded. It has been pointed out that there is a need for material for younger children and that a modern mathematics approach should be pursued. There is also a need for greater emphasis on the perceptual-motor basis for mathematics. In addition, there is a need to identify specific functional goals and to structure a sequence of meaningful activities which will develop the problem-solving skills necessary to meet these goals. Further, there is a need to adapt what is useful from the regular mathematics curriculum to the needs of the mentally retarded and to develop adequate techniques of evaluation. This book attempts to answer the above stated needs.

Chapters 1 and 2 define the mentally retarded child and establish the guidelines for the development of the curriculum. Chapters 3 through 7 detail the objectives, teaching methods, and materials appropriate for educable mentally retarded children from preschool to adulthood. Chapter 8 presents the curriculum for the trainable mentally retarded while the processes of evaluation are given in Chapter 9.

DANIEL L. PETERSON

Northern Arizona University
Flagstaff, Arizona

Acknowledgements

The author gratefully acknowledges the following sources for permission to reproduce the photographs which appear in this volume:

Creative Playthings; Joey Enlow; Ideal School Toys; Instructional Materials for Exceptional Children, Continental Press, Elizabeth, Pennsylvania; Ohio State University Department of Special Education; Grace Schmittauer; Charles Sloane; SRA; Charlene Systma; Teaching Aids; and Teaching Resources.

chapter 1

The Mentally Retarded Child and Mathematics

THE MENTALLY RETARDED CHILD DEFINED

There is a great deal of confusion regarding the definition of mental retardation, and the wide array of terminology frequently obfuscates the pertinent issues. The teacher is apt to become perplexed by such terms as feebleminded, amentia, moron, mentally deficient, mentally handicapped, mentally retarded and slow learner. The attempt to unravel this clutter of labels can result in the neglect of mastering an understanding of the child.

It is important, then to understand that there is no great mystery or riddle to be solved. The retarded child is simply a child with below average general intelligence who has such difficulty in learning that he is significantly behind other children in developing social and academic skills. The mentally retarded child then is intellectually impaired. From a practical educational standpoint, mental retardation is an inability to think as quickly, reason as deeply, or remember as long. Usually retardation appears in early childhood, and in some instances, can be detected during infancy. The retarded child usually matures more slowly than his normal counterpart. He is apt to be later in learning to talk, delayed in walking, and awkward in his coordination. The school age mentally retarded child will have a history of academic failure and may have developed very annoying and disruptive patterns of classroom behavior. However, he has the same needs as a normal child for family, friends, recreation, community acceptance, school success, and vocational usefulness. He laughs and cries, bruises and mends, sings and dances, loves and feels rejection as any normal person does. In regard to psychological needs, the retarded child is normal and many retardates can achieve normality in adult living. The arbitrary label attached to such children is not nearly as vital as a knowledge of the nature of the impairment and its effect upon learning—for the purposes of this book, the learning of mathematics.

In order to properly understand the nature of the mentally retarded child one must appreciate the scope of the handicap. The following section will briefly discuss the two most widely used systems of classification.

CLASSIFYING THE MENTALLY RETARDED

The learning characteristics of the mentally retarded depend largely on two factors: (1) the degree of intellectual impairment, and (2) the learning and behavioral disorders associated with the retardation. During the last century the retarded were categorized as simpletons, fools, and idiots and more recently as morons, imbeciles, and idiots. Current educational terminology uses a similar classification system substituting the more palatable labels of educable, trainable, and custodial. The American Association on Mental Deficiency divides the retarded group into four categories by the degree of impairment as reflected by measured intelligence. Table 1.1 compares the educational trial with the system adopted by the AAMD.

TABLE 1.1
The Educational and American Association on Mental Deficiency Classification Systems

Educational Classification	IQ Range	American Association on Mental Deficiency Classification	IQ Range*
Low Average Learner	80-90	Borderline	70-84
Educable Mentally Retarded	50-79	Mild Retardation	55-69
Trainable Mentally Retarded	25-49	Moderate Retardation	40-54
Custodial Mentally Retarded	Below 25	Severe Retardation	25-39
		Profound Retardation	Below 25

*Based upon a standard deviation of 15.

An examination of the table shows that the major distinction between these two classifications lies in the inclusion of a moderately retarded category by the AAMD. That is, the low educable and high trainable retarded are combined into a category designated as the moderately retarded. The information in Table 1.1 indicates that the intellectual impairments of mentally retarded children range along a continuum from the very profound to mild retardation. The latter are scarcely distinguishable from the low average segment of the population, while the former represent the typical dependent institutional case. It is important to bear in mind, however, that by far the greatest number of retarded children are found in the borderline and mildly retarded ranges of intelligence. Of the six million retarded persons in the United States today, approximately one-third of one percent will need constant care for survival; another nine percent can undertake semi-productive endeavors in a protected environment; and the remaining ninety percent will be capable of absorption into the economic and social fabric of the community.

For the purpose of educational classification the terms educable and trainable mentally retarded have been utilized to distinguish between those students who are capable of significant academic accomplishments and eventual independent living as contrasted with those capable of only minimal academic achievement and semi-independent living. Custodial or dependent mentally retarded children are in need of a continuing sheltered environment as the severity of their handicap precludes even semi-independent living.

The present educational classification system, then, divides the mentally retarded children able to profit from education and training into two distinct groups with drastically different programs. This dichotomy contrasts with the AAMD classification which includes the moderate category. The moderately retarded classification overlaps both the trainable and educable groups in the educational classification system. The AAMD approach has the advantage of grouping together children who are capable of limited academic achievement. The traditional curriculum for trainable mentally retarded children emphasizes primarily socialization and other non-academic goals. In these programs, there is apt to be insufficient academic challenge for the moderately retarded. On the other hand, the conventional programs for educable mentally retarded place greater emphasis on academic goals. The moderately retarded children enrolled in these programs are likely to find the typical academic material too demanding. In academic potential the moderately mentally retarded are more of a homogeneous group than either the educable or trainable retarded. The author personally favors maintaining special programs for the moderately mentally retarded to deal with those children who fall in the gap between the educable and trainable classification.

Programs which provide for the borderline and high grade educable mentally retarded in the mainstream of regular elementary and secondary education are also encouraged. However, the concern in this book is with the mathematics curriculum for the mentally retarded and not specifically with administration and organization of special education. The position is taken that the moderately retarded children are capable of mastering elementary concepts of mathematics, and, therefore, mathematics should be incorporated into their curriculum to the extent that it can contribute to their daily lives. The teacher of trainable children should be alerted to the academic potential of her more capable students.

We are concerned, then, with both the educable and the trainable mentally retarded. Since the retarded youngsters have a great potential for learning, some general learning characteristics germane to mathematics instruction will be presented.

RELEVANT LEARNING CHARACTERISTICS

A comprehensive consideration of the learning characteristics of mentally retarded children is impractical due to the limitations of space. However, there are some learning characteristics so frequently attributed to the educable that a brief discussion is appropriate. This section of the book refers to the following characteristics: interpersonal relationships, short attention span, specific mathematics disability, language deficiency, creativity, memory and application, sex, socio-economic background, and interest and motivation.

INTERPERSONAL RELATIONS

The retarded child is generally quite aware of his immediate socio-economic climate. It is no more difficult for him than any other child to sense parental rejection, teacher hostility, peer antagonism, or social toleration. His self-concept is largely dependent upon the degree to which he is accepted by the important persons in his life. If he regards himself as an individual of considerable worth, he is more apt to approach a learning task with great confidence and thus improve his chance of success, while conversely feelings of inferiority can interfere with learning. The retarded child tends to respond to the reasonable expectations of those who surround him. If he is regarded as a person of dignity, capable of making real contributions, he will more likely be achieving in keeping with his potential. The retarded child's handicap evolving directly from limited intelligence is increased when learning problems which evolve from a deficient self-concept are superimposed on him. The teacher, as a major contact person, can be of immeasurable value in assisting the development of a healthy ego.

MYTH OF THE SHORT ATTENTION SPAN

Mentally retarded children are frequently accused of having a short attention span. Indeed, a significant number of mentally retarded children have a difficult time attending to specific tasks for long durations of time. However, a short attention span is frequently related to distasteful and difficult tasks. A lack of interest in an activity or task which is too difficult will result in a high rate of distractability even among average children. A mentally retarded child who has experienced repeated failures with mathematics will seek to avoid further failure. If the child anticipates failure, he will frequently avoid answering questions, completing worksheets, or engaging in group activities involving mathematics. He will seek every opportunity to avoid activities related to number concepts. This desire to circumvent distasteful tasks can easily be misinterpreted as short attention span. The teacher will on occasion discover retarded children who wander from their tasks rather easily even though the lesson is appropriate and they wish to sustain the activity. It is the writer's contention, however, that many retarded children are given the "short attention span" label when actually the curriculum is at fault. Caution must be exercised to be certain that the child is positively motivated and capable of doing the work. The teacher must not only structure activities within the interests and abilities of the student but also must select the most appropriate time of day for the activity and then insure that it can be completed within a reasonable amount of time. This will enable the student to leave the task with a feeling of satisfaction and a greater willingness to approach a similar activity again.

MATHEMATICS DISABILITY

It has been recognized for some time that a number of children have a specific problem with learning quantitative concepts and skills. Such terms as *acalculia* and *number blindness* have been used to describe the syndrome exhibited by these children. It is thought that the cause of the impairment in learning arithmetic is specific minimal brain damage or a subtle functional neurological disorder. It is not unusual for the severely and the moderately retarded to have suffered a degree of cortical damage serious enough to result in minimal cerebral dysfunction.

Mathematics is intrinsically involved with spatial fields and the processes of visual perception. It has been pointed out by Strauss (1951, pp. 28-53), Kephart (1960), and others, that even slight brain damage can result in severe perceptual impairments. These disturbances make it difficult for the child to accomplish even simple pre-academic tasks much less grasp more complex insights into such geometric concepts as closed and opened curves, configurations and forms, which constitute the beginnings of first grade mathematics. Children who display signs of perceptual and conceptual disorders are not necessarily brain damaged or mentally retarded. However, there are enough mentally retarded children of the type who experience difficulty in learning mathematics that it is appropriate to consider briefly the nature of the deficient visual perception as well as other characteristic behaviors of the neurologically impaired (brain damaged).

There are four characteristics which may be used to describe the behavior patterns of the neurologically handicapped.

Perceptual Impairments

Difficulties in visual perceptions first appear when the child is confronted with academic tasks. The child's world is egocentric—everything centers around him including his spatial world. The nonhandicapped child views objects as being near, far, above, below, behind, or in front of himself. The child with visual-perceptual problems will have difficulty in establishing coordinates in space and will be confused by such referents to position in space as *out, up, down, left, right,* and will confuse 14 and 41. *Eye-hand motor coordination* is another common deficiency. The child may experience considerable difficulty in learning to write his numbers. Another major facet of visual perception is figure-ground. The figure is that part of the visual field which is the center of the observer's focus and the ground is the surrounding areas. The child with a figure-ground disturbance has difficulty in sorting figure from ground as well as maintaining a focus on the figure. Serious difficulties in grouping, classifying, and selecting relevant details are the result.

Pathological Fixation

There are two characteristics of this pattern of behavior. First, the child tends to preseverate upon an object or an activity for relatively long periods of time; and, secondly, the child experiences difficulty in shifting from one object or activity to another. Such a child will pore over a single problem of addition for prolonged periods of time, or may solve a problem such as $5 + 1 = 6$ correctly but then answer subsequent problems as $4 + 1 = 6, 2 + 2 = 6$, etc.

Forced Responsiveness

Children with serious brain damage are easily distracted by extraneous stimuli. They will find it very difficult to work problems on the crowded pages of the typical arithmetic workbook. The busy colorful pictures used as illustrations in workbooks for the normal child simply distract the perceptually disturbed child from the task of problem solving. In addition such a child cannot resist punching the girl in front of him, gazing out the window at the trees, looking up at every incidental movement and sound in the classroom.

Deficient Self-Control

The behavior of the child can be typified as explosive, hyperactive, and erratic. He will be in constant motion, shuffling his feet, wringing his hands, looking about the room, and will seldom attend to his work.

The above descriptions do not characterize all of the children with a specific learning disability in mathematics. However, many of these children will exhibit some of the behavioral signs associated with perceptual impairments, pathological fixations, forced responsiveness, and deficient self-control.

It should be restated that specific math disabilities are not found among the majority of mentally retarded children. The teacher should simply be alerted to the possibility.

LANGUAGE DEFICIENCY

The degree of mental retardation is highly correlated with the degree of language impairment. The profoundly retarded seldom develop sufficient language skills to communicate in even simple sentences while the trainable retarded are capable of simple communications and marginal literacy. The educable mentally retarded develop language and speech skills adequate for ordinary conversation and reading and writing levels equivalent to grade three to five or in some cases even higher.

The severely retarded and the younger retardates are seriously handicapped in their ability to communicate. They need help in mastering elementary language skills. Ordinary conversation and directions should be made as simple and as brief as possible. These children will need particular assistance in learning the basic vocabulary associated with mathematics such as *middle, between, up,* as well as mathematical terms such as *add, borrow,* and *subtract.*

CREATIVITY

The children in these categories are not as able to profit from experience as their normal counterparts. This is related to their inability to synthesize, classify, transfer, generalize, and otherwise form concepts concerning their immediate environment. This frequently makes the retardate appear unimaginative, uninformed, and bored. The lack of breadth of interest and the limited scope of their creativity correlates with their ability to understand that which is going on about them. Retarded children are not innately uninterested and devoid of curiosity. Given proper exposure to their environment within their level of comprehension, they are capable of many learnings and insights. Knowledge and understanding are prerequisite to insight. The task of the teacher is to systematically guide these children to an ever-increasing understanding of their world. This approach will help develop creativity in retarded children.

MEMORY AND APPLICATION

Some educators have reasoned that the limited intelligence of the mentally retarded calls for limitations in our expectations of their achievement. This position is tenable; but it has often been overemphasized and used to the extreme. Research has indicated that mentally retarded children are capable of learning the complex motor and verbal skills consistent with their mental ages. There is some indication that overlearning for retardates results in retention comparable to normals of comparable mental ages (Klausmeier, 1960). Transfer does occur when transfer is specifically incorporated into the lesson, though not as readily as for normals. In other words, mentally retarded children are capable of rather complex learnings when sufficient repetition and motivation have been provided. They are able to retain and apply these skills and knowledge when transfer of training has been practiced. Teachers, therefore, must choose tasks which are appropriate for the child's present level of functioning, structure brief lessons, provide for overlearning, and provide for transfer. Under these circumstances, retardates can retain as much simple, rote, factual material as normals. The ability to utilize this information in unique situations may be less gratifying but nonetheless rewarding and valuable.

SEX

Thurstone (1960, pp. 7-15) found that on the *Stanford Achievement Tests* used with retardates, girls scored significantly higher than boys on arithmetic reasoning, while boys scored higher than girls on computation. Jacobs (1957, pp. 238-243) found that there was no significant difference among boys and girls on arithmetic scores as measured by the *California Achievement Tests*. Bensburg (1958, pp. 810-818) used an institutional sample and found that females matched with males on mental age and chronological age (mean chronological age of 18.8) were significantly superior to males in arithmetic. Klausmeier and others

(1960) found that girls have a higher total arithmetic achievement in relationship to capacity than do boys.

In general, the studies suggested female superiority on arithmetic reasoning while findings were at variance on arithmetic fundamentals. It should also be mentioned that there tend to be more boys than girls in special classes for the mentally retarded. However, this is probably due more to boys' aggressive reactions to failure than to any systematic sex differences in achievement.

SOCIO-ECONOMIC BACKGROUND

A suspected factor in the success or failure of children in mathematics is the socio-economic background of the child. Erickson (1958, pp. 287-93) found that the frequency of higher intelligence quotients was significantly greater in the higher socio-economic levels; but when arithmetic performance was equated to intelligence quotient ranges, there were no significant differences between the higher and lower socio-economic groups.

INTEREST AND MOTIVATION

It is almost axiomatic among special education teachers that mentally retarded children have a very negative attitude towards arithmetic. Most teachers would regard as the understatement of the decade the observation that mentally retarded children are not interested in mathematics. The retarded child typically has developed a distaste for mathematics and has learned a clever set of avoidance techniques. The teacher's announcement that it is time for the mathematics lesson is commonly greeted with pained facial expressions and an undercurrent of grumbling. The mathematics lesson leads to more broken pencils, misplaced workbooks, lost assignments and missing erasers than any other segment of the curriculum. These children are indeed intensely motivated in mathematics—but their motivation is to avoid anything to do with numbers.

The point is simple. Children are more apt to be interested in tasks in which they have experienced success, and less interested in tasks in which they have experienced failures. In other words, negative attitudes towards arithmetic are learned and positive attitudes towards arithmetic can be developed.

Some retarded children have repeatedly approached a learning task with anticipation of success, only to fail miserably. Experiences such as this encountered repeatedly over a period of years plunges the retarded child into a *defeat cycle,* which becomes self-perpetuating. Each defeat more strongly confirms the child's expectancies of failure. The learner who becomes involved in an instructional process believing he will fail undoubtedly does just that. It is not difficult to understand poor motivation and low interest levels under such circumstances.

MATH PERFORMANCE OF THE EDUCABLE MENTALLY RETARDED

Much of the research that has been done on arithmetic achievement among mentally retarded children has utilized a group of non-mentally handicapped children of comparable mental ages to test for similarities and differences.

One of the earliest researchers concerned with arithmetic achievement among the mentally retarded as contrasted to arithmetic achievement of normals of similar mental ability was Cruickshank (*Journal of Educational Research*, 1948, pp. 161-170). His investigation examined the assertion that mentally retarded children of a given mental age are not as successful in arithmetic as are normal children of similar mental ages because retarded children are unable to select the specific arithmetic elements needed in the solution of problems. Three kinds of problems were presented to both groups. The first problem consisted of the necessary facts with numerous extraneous information; the second problem presented only the needed facts; and the third problem was merely computational. It was found that:

1. Mentally retarded subjects were not as adept as normals in differentiating the needed from the unneeded facts.
2. Normal children are more successful than mentally retarded children in working problems freed from superfluous materials.
3. Mentally retarded children are more nearly like the normal in computational problems.
4. Retardates had difficulty in naming the process involved in solving a problem when it was given in printed form.

In a related study with the same groupings, Cruickshank (*American Journal of Mental Deficiency*, 1948, pp. 318-330) utilized the *Buswell-John Diagnostic Chart* for fundamentals in arithmetic and recorded errors made by retarded children as they worked on problems. He found that:

1. Retarded children made excessive use of primitive habits such as counting on fingers.
2. Retarded children demonstrated a lack of understanding of the processes of arithmetic.

3. Retarded children made numerous errors due to carelessness.
4. Retarded children committed many errors in reading.

On a companion study with the same retarded and normal groups, Cruickshank (1946, pp. 65-69) investigated the relationship of vocabulary comprehension to arithmetic achievement. The *Guy T. Buswell Vocabulary Test* with several modifications was administered to both the retarded group and the normal group. It was found that the mentally retarded boys were able to define forty-nine percent of the words, while the normals of the same mental age were able to define sixty-two percent. The inferior command of arithmetic terms for the retarded was most evident with the abstract terms of mathematics and least discernible with the easier arithmetic terms.

Finley (1962, pp. 281-286) studied the effect of varying the presentation of arithmetic problems to mentally retarded and normal subjects. Three experimental instruments embodying concrete, pictorial, and symbolic items were administered. The most striking result of the study was that neither group did as well on the concrete as on the pictorial or the symbolic tests. It was concluded that with the groups matched for mental age there was a significant difference in favor of the retarded group on the test of computational skills. The concrete test items tended to be more difficult for the retarded subjects than either the pictorial or symbolic test items, although the difference did not reach statistical significance. For normal subjects the pictorial items were significantly easier than either the concrete or symbolic test items.

Dunn (1954, pp. 7-99) compared twenty retarded and thirty normal children of comparable mental age in a public school and confirmed the finding of Cruickshank that there was no significant difference between the retarded and the normal group in arithmetic computation but that there was a significant difference in favor of the normals on arithmetic reasoning. Dunn additionally found that the retarded group worked twenty-four months below their mental age expectancy.

A few studies have been done comparing bright children with retardates.

Kolstoe (1954, pp. 161-168) conducted a study to determine if bright young children resemble dull older children of the same mental age. The findings indicated that with comparable mental ages, the additional factor of chronological ages was not significant.

Wilson (1926, pp. 43-53) compared regular-class dull normals and bright students of the same mental age. He found the dull group to be superior to the bright group on arithmetic as measured by the *Stanford Achievement Test*.

Klausmeier and others (1960) reported that on counting, addition, subtraction, and arithmetic problem solving the retarded acquired material graded to their level of difficulty more slowly than did average or bright students; however, there was no difference on the retention once it was learned. The authors concluded that the most important implication for teaching is that early assessment of arithmetic achievement is necessary in order to select learnings at the next high level.

In a study using bright and retarded groups, Merrill (1924, pp. 1-100) found that retardates perform at a lower level than normals on arithmetic fundamentals.

Burns (1911, pp. 57-61) reviewed the literature and reported that researchers agree that among other characteristics, educable mentally retarded children (1) demonstrate an impoverished arithmetic vocabulary, (2) do less well in abstract than concrete problems, (3) have less understanding of processes to be used on a problem, (4) are more apt to be careless, (5) are less successful in differentiating extraneous information from needed facts in problem solving, (6) have little concept of time, and (7) do better with addition and subtraction and need more training in multiplication and division.

The most significant research finding is that educable mentally retarded children perform in keeping with their mental age. There is general agreement in the literature contrasting educable retardates and normals of comparable mental ages that normals were superior in arithmetic reasoning. A lack of consensus was evident concerning skills in fundamentals. Some studies found no differences between the two groups; others gave evidence favoring retardates; and, still others found normals to achieve higher. Mentally retarded children appeared less adept in differentiating needed from superfluous facts, had an excess of primitive habits, demonstrated impoverished vocabularies, and were less capable readers.

MATH ACHIEVEMENT OF THE TRAINABLE MENTALLY RETARDED

Studies measuring the academic achievement of trainable mentally retarded children were limited in number. Most of the references to academic skills were made parenthetically to discussions of social and vocational skills.

Reynolds and Kiland (1963, pp. 151-152) evaluated four classes of trainable mentally retarded children with chronological ages from seven through twenty years. The chief assessment instruments were questionnaires and interviews. Parental and teacher reports indicated progress in special classes. The children learned only minimal skills in reading, writing, and arithmetic, but the report concluded that the children made considerable progress in self-help skills and socialization. The results of Guenther's (1956, pp. 1-50) investigation were in agreement with the above findings. However, Guenther expressed the need for measuring instruments to assess the academic potential of young trainable retardates.

Hudson (1960, pp. 8-49) conducted a study of the curriculum of trainable retarded. Although she was not specifically concerned with achievement, her results do have implications for the measurement of achievement. She observed instructional procedures in twenty-nine classrooms for two one-hundred-minute periods, and tabulated the following lesson categories in rank order of emphasis:

1. Language
2. Motor Development
3. Mental Development
4. Sensory Training
5. Music
6. Health and Safety
7. Social Studies
8. Arithmetic Concepts
9. Self-Help
10. Occupational Education
11. Socialization
12. Arts and Crafts
13. Dramatization
14. Science Concepts
15. Practical Arts

Her observations also revealed that language received the major amount of instructional time while arithmetic was allotted but a fraction of this time.

Goldstein (1956, pp. 4-28) investigated twenty-two classes for the trainable mentally retarded. Academic achievement tests were not administered; however, intelligence tests were given and social maturity scales, behavior check lists, and interviews with parents, teachers and school administrators were conducted. The major findings of the study denoted gains in behavior traits during the first year, but no gains during the second year, and more realistic parental concepts about pupil's abilities and limitations.

Hottel (1958, pp. 3-7) conducted a one-year study using two groups of twenty-one matched pairs of mental retardates. One group was enrolled in school while the other, serving as the control, remained at home. He concluded that in one year there were no significant differences between the experimental and control groups. However, when the groups were subdivided into low groups with an intelligence quotient from thirty to forty and high groups with intelligence quotients from forty to fifty, it was found that the high group in school had significantly better gains than both the low groups and the high groups at home. This led Hottel to recommend that the lower limit for special education classes be established at an intelligence quotient of forty.

Cain and Levine (1961, p. 244) conducted a study which merits mention for the systematic observations of the instructional programs for trainable mentally retarded children. Children living in the community made more progress than those living in an institution. Children not attending school made as much progress in social competency as those attending school. Instructional programs devoted little time to the development of social competency and much of the class time was given to non-instructional activities such as rest periods, recess, and free activities.

Silverstein, Auger, and Krudis (1964, pp. 419-424) tested forty-five boys and girls in a state institution to determine their understanding of three indefinite number terms; "a few," "most," and "a lot." Subjects were required to select beads from a tray in response to these terms. Results indicated that the subjects tested had concepts of indefinite number terms, but that this understanding was not related to their understanding of definite number concepts as measured by more conventional methods.

An extensive investigation of academic achievement of the trainable mentally retarded was conducted by Warren (1963, pp. 75-88). She studied the academic achievement of 177 pupils who had five or more years of school instruction and found:

> The median arithmetic achievement scores were between 1.2 and 1.5; none of the pupils seemed to be able to handle the more difficult processes; generally adding and subtracting single digit numbers was the maximal level of competence. Such concepts as borrowing, carrying, and adding columns were beyond these pupils' abilities. Discussions with some of the pupils indicated that they worked arithmetic problems by rote with little understanding of the concepts behind the additions and subtractions. Rote counting was much easier for them.
>
> It is apparent that generally the females tended to achieve at a slightly higher level than did males of the same ability level.

Most of the publications concerning the academic achievement of trainable mentally retarded children emphasized the developmental skills rather than formal tests of academic achievement. These observations indicated little academic progress, and pointed out that the teaching of arithmetic concepts received only slight amounts of instructional time. In reference to these studies Warren (1963, pp. 75-88) stated:

> One cannot deny the possibility that the studies that have been done might have found academic achievement in trainables if it had been measured, though chances seem remote. Another possibility, is that the children had not been given sufficient training to offer them the opportunity to achieve reading and arithmetic to the level of their potential.

The one study concerned with formal testing found that retardates were able to master a few fundamentals of arithmetic and grasp a few basic number concepts.

SUMMARY

In this chapter the mentally retarded child has been described as a normal youngster who has considerable difficulty with mathematics primarily due to low intelligence. However, it was indicated that mentally retarded children are susceptible to other problems which can restrict their capacities for mathematical achievement. It was indicated that educable mentally retarded children have a potential to learn mathematics at a level comparable to the third though fifth grade. This means that they are able to learn to use arithmetic computation in such activities as buying and selling, banking, making simple measurements, and filing income tax returns. The trainable mentally retarded are able to learn to use arithmetic at a level comparable to first and second grade. This means they are able to grasp some simple number concepts and complete some basic computations but will be unable to develop independently functioning skills.

REFERENCES

Bensburg, Gerard. "The Relationship of Academic Achievement of Mental Defectives to Mental Age, Sex, Institutionalization, and Etiology." *American Journal of Mental Deficiency* LXII (May, 1958): 810-18.

Burns, Paul C. "Arithmetic Fundamentals for the Educable Mentally Retarded." *American Journal of Mental Deficiency* LXVI (July, 1961): 57-61.

Cain, L. F. and Levine, S. A. *A Study of the Effects of Community and Institutional School Classes for Trainable Mentally Retarded Children.* Washington: U.S. Office of Education, 1961.

Cruickshank, William M. "Arithmetic Ability of Mentally Retarded Children, I." *Journal of Educational Research* XLII (November, 1948): 161-70.

Cruickshank, William M. "Arithmetic Vocabulary of Mentally Retarded Boys." *Exceptional Children* XIII (October, 1946): 65-69.

Cruickshank, William M. "Arithmetic Work Habits of Mentally Retarded Boys." *American Journal of Mental Deficiency,* LII (November, 1948): 318-30.

Dunn, Lloyd M. "A Comparison of the Reading Processes of Mentally Retarded Boys of the Same Mental Age." *Monograph of the Society for Research in Child Development, Inc.* XIX (1954): 7-99.

Erickson, Leland H. "Certain Ability Factors and Their Effect on Arithmetic Achievement." *Arithmetic Teacher* V (1958): 287-93.

Finley, Carment J. "Arithmetic Achievement in Mentally Retarded Children: The Effects of Presenting the Problem in Different Contexts." *American Journal of Mental Deficiency* LXII (September, 1962): 281-86.

Goldstein, Herbert. *Report Number Two on Study Projects for Trainable Mentally Handicapped Children.* Springfield, Illinois: Superintendent of Public Instruction, 1956.

Guenther, R. J. *Final Report of the Michigan Demonstration Research Project for Severely Retarded,* Bulletin. Lansing, Michigan: State Department of Public Instruction, 1956.

Hottel, J. V. *An Evaluation of Tennessee's Day Class Program for Severely Mentally Retarded Children: Final Report.* Nashville, Tennessee: Peabody College, 1958.

Hudson, Margaret. "An Exploration of Classroom Procedures for Teaching

Trainable Mentally Retarded Children." *CEC Research Monograph,* Series A, No. 2 Washington: 1960.

Jacobs, A. N. "A Study of Performance of Slow Learners in the Cincinnati Public Schools on Mental and Achievement Tests." *American Journal of Mental Deficiency* LXIII (September, 1957): 238-43.

Kelly, Elizabeth M., and Stevens, Harvey A. "Special Education for the Mentally Handicapped." *Special Education,* The Fifty-Ninth Yearbook of the National Society for the Study of Education, Part II. Chicago: The University of Chicago Press, 1950.

Kephart, Newell. *The Slow Learner in the Classroom,* 2d ed. Columbus, Ohio: Charles E. Merrill Books, Inc., 1971.

Klausmeier, H. H., *et. al. An Analysis of Learning Efficiency in Arithmetic of Mentally Retarded Children in Comparison with Children of Average and High Intelligence.* Project No. 266, Washington: U.S. Office of Education, 1960.

Kolstoe, Oliver P. "A Comparison of Mental Abilities of Bright and Dull Children of Comparable Mental Age." *Journal of Educational Psychology* XLV (October, 1954): 161-68.

McDowell, Louis K. "Number Concepts and Preschool Children." *The Arithmetic Teacher* IX (December, 1962): 433.

Merrill, Maud A. "On the Relation of Intelligence to Achievement in the Case of Mentally Retarded Children." *Comparative Psychology Monographs* II (1924): 1-100.

Peterson, Daniel L. "A Study of Mathematical Knowledge of Young Mental Retardates." Ph.D. dissertation, University of Missouri, 1967.

Reynolds, M. C., and Kiland, J. R. A Study of Public School Children with Severe Mental Retardation. In *Exceptional Children in the Schools,* Lloyd M. Dunn, ed. New York: Holt, Rinehart and Winston, Inc., 1963.

Silverstein, A. B. "The Meaning of Indefinite Number Terms for Mentally Retarded Children." *American Journal of Mental Deficiency* LXIX (November, 1964): 419-24.

Strauss, Alfred A., and Lehtinen, Laura E. *Psychopathology and Education of the Brain-Injured Child.* New York, Grune and Stratton, 1951.

Thurstone, Thelma G. *An Evaluation of Educating Mentally Handicapped Children in Special and Regular Classes,* Project 168. Washington: U.S. Office of Education, 1960.

Warren, Sue A. "Academic Achievement of Trainable Pupils with Five or More Years of Schooling." *The Training School Bulletin* (August, 1963): 75-88.

Wilson, F. T. "Some Achievement of Pupils of the Same Mental Age But Different Intelligence Quotients." *Journal of Educational Research* XIV (September, 1926): 43-53.

chapter 2

Constructing the Mathematics Curriculum

There has been much confusion regarding the place of mathematics in the curriculum for the mentally retarded. The problem has emerged in part from the comprehensive reorganization which has taken place in the "new" or "modern mathematics" programs in general education. Further, there is an on-going review of the total scope of the curriculum for the mentally retarded which brings the problem somewhat into focus.

It is generally accepted by those who work with the mentally retarded that the mathematics portion of the curriculum should include primarily those basic concepts which the children need in order to get along with their environment (Thresher, 1962, p. 766). However, there is little agreement on just what these concepts are, which of the concepts retarded children are able to learn, and how they should be taught.

This chapter presents, then, a frame of reference for the development of appropriate curricular content and methodology by dealing with these questions:

> What special problems confront the teacher of the mentally retarded in teaching mathematics?
>
> Is there any basis on which the teacher can predict the achievement potential of these children?
>
> What factors need to be considered in planning mathematics instruction for individual mentally retarded children?
>
> What mathematics necessary for independent living are within the capacities of mentally retarded youth?

Are there any principles for teaching mathematics to the mentally retarded which differ in emphasis or scope from those appropriate for teaching other children?

How should the teacher go about organizing for mathematics instruction?

Does modern mathematics have a place in the education of mentally retarded children?

OBSTACLES TO ACHIEVEMENT

There are a number of obstacles confronting the teacher as she approaches the task of constructing the mathematics curriculum. Foremost among these is the absence of well-designated commercial texts and materials for use with the retarded. Until this void is filled, the teacher of the retarded will continue to be responsible for the development of her own curriculum with only the benefit of those aids available to the teacher of the non-handicapped child. Herein lies the problem. There is a scarcity of references and materials. Obviously, the typical special education teacher does not have the time to prepare a sequential, continuous mathematics curriculum from scratch. This chapter will, then, indicate a practical procedure for adapting existing materials to use with mentally retarded children.

The mathematics curriculum for the mentally retarded is based primarily upon the child's potential for adult living. Such a prediction of adultation is made upon an assessment of the degree of intellectual impairment and the learning and behavioral problems associated with retardation. The actual construction of a mathematics curriculum should flow then from a study of the learning characteristics of the particular child under consideration. The results and implications of such a study guide the direction of the curriculum and determine reasonable expectancies.

MENTAL AGE AS A GUIDE TO ACHIEVEMENT

The question thus emerges, "How does the teacher initiate the processes of adapting and sequencing the mathematics curriculum? How can we determine the readiness of mentally retarded children for specific instruction?" To that end, both Zigler (1962, p. 160) and Dunn (1963, p. 62) stated that mental age is the single most important factor in predicting academic success for retarded children. There is considerable support for this point of view in the literature concerning mentally retarded youth.

Constructing the Mathematics Curriculum

Lewis (1954, pp. 321-331) determined that the more retarded tended to achieve above their mental age. Bensburg (1958, pp. 810-818) disclosed that the achievement of mentally retarded children was within one month of their mental age. Cruickshank (1948, pp. 161-170) found that with two groups of matched pairs of normals and retarded, arithmetic age corresponded closely with mental age. Dunn (1963, p. 62) reported that retarded children work within twenty-four months of their mental age in arithmetic reasoning, while Ring (1951, pp. 3-54) found them to work at the same level as their mental age in arithmetic fundamentals. Witty and McCafferty (1930, pp. 588-97) established that children in the educable retarded range were at mental age level expectancy in arithmetic reasoning.

There appears to be general agreement that retardates function close to their mental age in arithmetic achievement with evidence of performance at or above mental age capacity on arithmetic fundamentals and below on arithmetic reasoning. Mental age, then, may be utilized as the primary predictor of arithmetic achievement, modified in terms of environmental conditions and specific learning disorders which may underlie behavior.

ANTICIPATED GRADE POTENTIAL

It has been shown that the mentally retarded are capable of acquiring mathematics skills and concepts comparable to those attained by children of average intelligence of the same mental age when other significant factors are considered. In other words, from a knowledge of mental age span the teacher can predict the approximate grade level range at which a group of mentally retarded children might reasonably be expected to perform. The advantage of using mental age as a sole factor in the initial steps of predicting achievement range is that the teacher is able to obtain a reasonable estimate of mental age. The formula is shown below:

$$\text{Estimated Mental Age} = \frac{(\text{Intelligence Quotient}) \times (\text{Chronological Age})}{100}$$

The teacher can compare such a derived mental age to that of average children of a given grade level to estimate an anticipated level of functioning. A derived mental age of six would be comparable to first grade potential, a derived mental age of nine comparable to fourth grade potential, and so forth. Practically all mentally retarded children in special education have been tested with the *Stanford-Binet, Welschler Intelligence Scale for Children,* or equivalent individual intelligence tests. Since the results of the intelligence tests are typically recorded on the cumulative educational record, the teacher can easily estimate the mental age for each of her pupils and the mental age range for her class. An example may clarify the point.

Dennis is ten years old and has an IQ of 75. His mental age is seven years and six months. (MA = IQ × CA/100 = 75 × 10/100 = 7.5 = seven years six months). An IQ of 100 indicates that mental and chronological age are very nearly the same. Thus children in the first grade are typical six-year-olds with mental ages of six years while children in the second grade are typically seven-year-olds with mental ages of seven. Dennis with a mental age of seven years and six months would be like the second grader in terms of his mental ability, although chronologically he would be placed in the fifth grade. The anticipated grade potential for Dennis would be 2.5 grade level. This does not mean that Dennis functions intellectually precisely like the typical second grader of average intelligence. It simply indicates that in academic learning he will probably be able to master many of the skills usually taught in the second grade.

A simple short cut for calculating anticipated grade potential is to subtract five from the mental age. Using the formula for mental age given above, anticipated grade potential could be figured in this form:

$$AGP = \left(\frac{IQ \times CA}{100}\right) - 5*$$

Anticipated grade potential is restricted by all the limitations of intelligence testing. At best, it is a very primitive estimate of a child's capacity for learning. It does not tell the teacher where to begin instruction or warn her of possible obstacles to achievement. There are simply

---

*There will be times (for educable mentally retarded children eleven years and older) that the teacher's estimate of AGP will be more realistic if six is substituted for five. This is more conservative, but one of the problems with older educable mentally retarded children is starting instruction at too high a level. The teacher should not limit her expectations, but rather exercise caution in the initial planning stages.

TABLE 2.1
Estimated Mental Ages for Chronological Ages and IQ Scores

Chronological Ages

IQ	3	4	5	6	7	8	9	10	11	12	13	14	15	16
20			1.0	1.2	1.5	1.7	1.10	2.0	2.2	2.5	2.7	2.10	3.0	3.2
25			1.3	1.6	1.8	2.0	2.2	2.6	2.10	3.0	3.2	3.6	3.8	4.0
30	1.0	1.0	1.6	1.10	2.1	2.5	2.8	3.0	3.3	3.7	3.11	4.2	4.5	4.10
40	1.2	1.2	2.0	2.5	2.10	3.2	3.7	4.0	4.5	4.10	5.2	5.7	6.0	6.5
50	1.6	1.7	2.6	3.0	3.6	4.0	4.6	5.0	5.6	6.0	6.6	7.0	7.6	8.0
55	1.8	2.0	2.9	3.4	3.10	4.5	4.11	5.6	6.1	6.6	7.2	7.8	8.3	8.9
60	1.10	2.2	3.0	3.7	4.2	4.10	5.4	6.0	6.7	7.2	7.9	8.4	8.11	9.7
65	1.11	2.5	3.3	3.11	4.7	5.2	5.10	6.6	7.2	7.9	8.5	9.1	9.8	10.4
70	2.1	2.7	3.6	4.3	4.11	5.7	6.1	7.0	7.8	8.5	9.1	9.9	10.5	11.2
75	2.3	2.9	3.9	4.6	5.3	6.0	6.9	7.6	8.3	9.0	9.9	10.6	11.3	12.0
80	2.5	3.0	4.0	4.10	5.7	6.5	7.2	8.0	8.10	9.7	10.5	11.2	12.0	12.10
85	2.7	3.2	4.3	5.1	5.11	6.10	7.8	8.6	9.4	10.2	11.0	11.11	12.9	13.7
90	2.9	3.5	4.5	5.5	6.4	7.2	8.1	9.0	9.4	10.10	11.8	12.7	13.6	14.5
100	3.0	3.7	5.0	6.0	7.0	8.0	9.0	10.0	11.0	12.0	13.0	14.0	15.0	16+

Calculation Of Anticipated Grade Level

A child's anticipated grade potential (AGP) can be estimated from the above table. Refer to the appropriate IQ and CA and read the MA in the table. Subtract five for educable mentally retarded children with CA's to tens, and six for educable mentally retarded children with CA's eleven and above to obtain the AGP.

+2 = second grade   −1 = 4K   −3 = pre-nursery
+1 = first grade   −2 = nursery   −4 = infant level
 0 = 5k

too many variables for AGP to be an accurate predictor of individual performance. However, AGP does give the teacher initial guidance in the formulation of tentative hypotheses concerning reasonable expectancies for groups of children. When the teacher wishes to estimate the approximate grade equivalent range of an entire class these variables have a tendency to balance out. For example, if an intermediate teacher had a group of educable mentally retarded students (IQ 50-80) with chronological ages from ten years to twelve years, she could expect a range in anticipated grade potential from kindergarten AGP = 50 × 10/100 − 5 = grade 0 to third grade AGP = 80 × 12/100 − 6 = grade 3.6. She would probably have more students towards the higher IQ levels so the typical grade equivalents for her intermediate class would be about second and third grade. Nevertheless, there would be a number of children with anticipated grade performance at the first grade level and perhaps one or two children at the preschool level.

Table 2.1 indicates the estimated mental ages of children with chronological ages from three years to sixteen years and intelligence quotients from twenty to 100. A child's anticipated grade potential can be estimated by subtracting five or six from the mental age and interpreting the results as shown at the bottom of the table.

The major advantage to the anticipated grade potential formula then is its simplicity. The major disadvantage is the lack of preciseness. The AGP provides the teacher with a "ball park" figure. In the example, it means that all other things being equal Dennis could be expected to achieve at a second grade level. However, the special education teacher should resist the temptation to walk down to the second grade classroom, borrow a second grade arithmetic text, workbook, study sheets and proceed to instruct Dennis by following the second grade teacher's guide. The teacher would probably experience great disappointment in an attempt to teach Dennis mathematics in this way. Dennis does not have a chronological age of seven; he is ten years old. Counting ducks, balloons, and paper dolls might be appropriate for the second grader, but it would build resentment if tried with Dennis. There may be other differences. Let's assume that Dennis has experienced much failure in his early attempts to learn mathematics. His approach to the study of mathematics might be so negative that it predisposes him to continued failure. An initial prediction of first grade level might be more appropriate. Problems such as negative set and other problems previously discussed must be considered in assessing his potential for learning mathematics. The practice of assessing a mentally retarded child's potential for learning by considering a myriad of factors is called the multiple criteria. The estimation of potential for learning by the multiple criteria is basically a clinical judgment.

MULTIPLE CRITERIA

Obviously mental age and, therefore, anticipated grade potential cannot be the sole criteria for determining the specific curriculum for particular children. But it has been shown that the mental age range can prove a valuable guide in structuring general objectives for various age groups. Other factors which need to be considered in assessing a particular child's curricular needs depend not only upon mental age but also upon an array of variables.

The concept of mental age is superior to many other indices of achievement potential. However, used in isolation without references to mathematical achievement, chronological age, and specific learning disabilities and potential for independent adult living (as estimated by the degree of mental retardation), the concept of mental age can lead to inadequate curricular provisions. There are learning activities which may be appropriate for a child in terms of his mental age but be an insult to his social age. For example, asking an adolescent retardate to count the number of dollies in a playhouse would be pointless. A mentally retarded child might be capable of learning a particular concept which is typically taught to normal children of the same mental age as readiness for higher mathematics, but it would be senseless to require the retarded child to learn such a concept. A final example might be the application of second grade mathematics. The ten-year-old retarded child with different background experiences and daily activities will need to make different applications of the concepts he has learned than those of his younger seven-year-old mental age counterpart.

ACHIEVEMENT LEVEL

Once the teacher has made a clinical interpretation of the anticipated grade potential, she needs to assess the child's current level of functioning. The techniques of pupil evaluation are discussed in considerable detail in chapter nine, however, it is appropriate to comment briefly on assessment procedures at this point.

The usual approach with children of average intelligence is to use standardized mathematics tests. However, the special education teacher finds that many of these tests are completely inappropriate for use with the mentally retarded. The most useful standardized achievement tests available at this writing are the mathematics subtest of the *Peabody Individual Achievement Test* and the arithmetic subtest of the *Wide Range Achievement Test*. Both of these tests allow the teacher to make some determination of the child's grade level functioning as compared to children of average intelligence.

Frequently, discrepancies appear between the anticipated grade potential of a child and the child's actual level of achievement as measured by tests such as those mentioned above. The teacher must then ask herself the question, "Why?" In other words she has located a disparity between what she would expect the child to do in terms of mental age as modified by the multiple criteria when compared to the actual level of performance as measured on an achievement test.

ACHIEVEMENT DISCREPANCY

The multiple criteria states that the teacher must formulate long range curricular objectives with a rough knowledge of the child's potential in adulthood. The specific curriculum at any given level is derived from a study of the child, utilizing such data as IQ scores, achievement test results, and teacher observations. Anticipated grade potential when contrasted to actual test performance will at times indicate discrepancies between achievement and expectancy. The teacher must seek an explanation for this disparity.

The reasons for a given child's underachievement may be found in an examination of educational history. Premature school entrance, initial failure experiences, erratic attendance patterns, and a variety of other problems may account in part for the difficulties. In other cases the teacher will utilize diagnostic arithmetic tests which are designed to locate special academic problems. In complex instances, the teacher may need to look for more subtle causes of the learning problems. The child's difficulties may be related to minimal brain damage, visual perceptual problems, emotional difficulties and so on. In this case, the teacher will need to search for specific mathematical disabilities. Systematic observation and careful record keeping may reveal sources of difficulties which at first seem most unlikely. On many occasions, the teacher will need to have the help of other specialists such as the school psychologist, guidance counselor, and physician in finding causal factors and prescribing a remedial program.

In the example of Dennis, there was such a discrepancy. It appeared in that hypothetical case that the problem related to Dennis's negative attitudes and inadequate curricular experiences. The causes of Dennis's problems may run deeper, however, demanding that the teacher continue her search with professional assistance from allied fields. The important point to remember is that the task of the teacher is to continually assess the status of learning, compare it to potential, analyze discrepancies, and adjust the curriculum accordingly.

FUNCTIONAL MATHEMATICS

There are other pitfalls before the teacher as she constructs a functional curriculum. The mathematics appropriate for the mentally retarded is different from that appropriate for normals of similar mental ages in several ways. The basic differences lie in considerations of what, how, and when mathematical skills and concepts are taught.

First of all, there are certain concepts presented to normal children of a given mental age which are irrelevant for the mentally retarded child mainly because the concepts are taught as background for learning higher mathematics. The concepts of closed and open curves, graphs, and scale readings are examples of concepts which are superfluous to the long range needs and objectives of the retarded.

Secondly, certain skills and concepts are omitted from the curriculum of the non-handicapped child on the assumption that these have been learned through incidental experiences and maturation. Many of these basic concepts must be taught directly and not left to experiential background. For example, average children acquire a knowledge of such basic forms as circles, squares, and triangles in their daily experiences with typical household and play objects. Since retarded children do not profit as well from incidental experiences they will need special training in order to master such simple forms as circles and squares.

Thirdly, the vocational potential of the retarded child will demand certain mathematical skills and concepts beyond those typically learned by a normal child of a comparable mental age. For example, the adolescent male on work-study training assignment in a service station who functions at the second grade level in arithmetic may need an understanding far beyond that level. He may be required to understand the numbers printed on a tire that indicate the desired air pressure, compare a gauge reading to it, and then add air to the tires until the gauge and the tire markings agree. If the tire number indicated twenty pounds of pressure and the gauge read eighteen, he would then have to ascertain that he needed to add two pounds of pressure to make twenty. The second grade teacher might approach the same concept by using a completely different context. For example, she might say that with twenty children in the class there are eighteen glasses of milk. How many more glasses of milk are needed so that everyone has at least one? Both problems present the same operations, but the context is simply different. Again, the retarded child on the work-study program may need to make change, calculate overtime, understand payroll deductions, and have some insight into income tax. Such skills are not usually a part of the second grade mathematics curriculum.

Finally, in addition to the vocational demands for mathematical skills, the teacher must be aware of the social situations in which knowledge of specific number concepts becomes vital. These concepts often exceed the typical fourth or fifth grade level of mathematics achievement and even go beyond the sixth and seventh grade levels, which are considered the maximal grade level potential for the high educable retardates. The problems associated with recipes, sports' scores, advertising, directions, discounts, charge accounts, taxes, bills, and withholdings must be interpreted into relevant everyday skills. The teacher must attempt to develop the problem solving skills that these children need to functionally meet the ordinary demands of day to day living.

In summary, the teacher of the mentally retarded must be alerted to the unique features of the daily needs and life needs of her students and modify and adapt the mathematics curruculum accordingly. The ultimate criteria for including a concept or skill in the mathematics curriculum must not be its traditional use with normal children, but its functionality in the social-vocational adjustment of the retarded child. Functional mathematics, then is an instructional program that provides the mentally retarded youngster with the number skills necessary for independent living. It is important, therefore, to determine the mathematical skills which are prerequisite to self-sufficiency or semi-independence. These skills become the objectives for the mathematics program.

OBJECTIVES

The primary goal of the mathematics curriculum for the mentally retarded is to assist them in the development of skills necessary in conducting their everyday affairs. Most retardates in adult life will be called upon to use mathematics skills in buying and selling, maintaining records, making reports, performing simple measurements, handling money, and filing tax returns. However, a few will be unable to perform at such a high level and will be limited to very simple accomplishments. In this section we shall consider the objectives for independent living which in turn will guide the goals for the educable and trainable mentally retarded children.

OBJECTIVES FOR INDEPENDENT LIVING

It is helpful to consider the general arithmetic skills required for minimal socio-vocational adjustment before discussing the specific applications to the trainable and educable mentally retarded. The construction of the arithmetic curriculum for the mentally retarded should have socio-vocational utility as the determining factor.

Norton discussed the arithmetic skills needed by most people for success in everyday living (1936, p. 344). These included (1) addition and subtraction to no more than six places, (2) multiplication and division by no more than five places, (3) fractions of 1/2, 1/3, 1/5, 1/6, 1/8, 1/10, 1/100, (4) measurement by inches, feet, yards, miles, pints, quarts, gallons, pecks, bushels, ounces, pounds, tons, dozens, and gross, (5) the buying and selling of food and clothing, and (6) money management and banking.

Adams (1924) discussed the mathematics encountered in general reading of newspapers and periodicals. The author concluded that the reader of daily newspapers and periodicals would need to comprehend these concepts:

1. time—hour, day, week, month, year
2. number—house numbers, room numbers, telephone numbers
3. money—most frequent values were under $100.00
4. simple ratios
5. various units of measure
6. wide variety of mathematical expressions and terms
7. practical, as opposed to theoretical, problems

WHAT PEOPLE NEED TO KNOW ABOUT MATHEMATICS FOR EVERYDAY LIVING

The average person uses mathematics extensively in everyday living. The author asked seventy teachers to keep track of the various ways they used mathematics over a ten day period from January third to January thirteenth, 1970. They were specifically instructed to avoid listing mathematics used in their teaching or academic studies and to include only those uses significant to everyday living. The responses included relatively low level skills such as weighing on bathroom scales, dialing the telephone, setting the dial on the refrigerator, selecting channels on the television set, and addressing letters. The more complex uses included maintaining a checking account; making grocery, hardware and other purchases; paying household bills; measuring in cooking and sewing; calculating wages; and filing income tax returns. The reports did not lend themselves to formal analysis. However, the responses were categorized into the problems which were simply computational and those which involved arithmetic reasoning. The problems were then compared to mastery tests found in several elementary school arithmetic texts. Most of the problems submitted by these college students were comparable to material covered in third- and fourth-grade level arithmetic books. The interesting thing to note about this is that a relatively low level of computational and arithmetic reasoning skill is required to meet the everyday encounters of even college educated adults. This would seem to indicate that if mentally retarded children could learn mathematics at a level comparable to the third grade that they would be able to solve most of their everyday number problems. This is the approximate level of achievement potential predicted for educable mentally retarded children.

Similar results were found in an informal survey administered during the Spring of 1971. The author asked thirty-nine elementary and special education teachers to reflect upon the computational and arithmetic reasoning problems they had solved during a seven day period. They were then given the list of problems found in the Written Part of the Arithmetic Subtest, Level II, of the *Wide Range Achievement Test*. They were directed to check those problems which were similar to those which they had worked during the past week on their job and in their everyday activities. Subjects were given full credit for the Oral Part of the test but were not allowed to count problems they solved by resorting to mathematical tables, adding machines, calculators and so forth. The purpose was to determine the types of problems they actually worked over a period of seven days and not to measure their performance on the test. In other words, they were not given the test and they were not required to solve any problems. The subjects merely indicated the type of problem they had worked.

The scores of the group ranged from 13 to 22 with a mean slightly under 15. This would indicate a grade level range from 3.4 to 6.7 with a mean somewhat under 4.4. The typical problems checked as being similar to those worked by the subjects were limited to very simple addition, subtraction, multiplication, and division items. Very few worked the items such as converting feet to inches, decimals to percents, finding averages, figuring with fractions, dealing with the complement of angles and similar elementary mathematics problems. To the best of their recall, then, these subjects over a period of one week seemed to be dealing with numbers at about a fourth grade level.

The results of these surveys indicate that the mathematical knowledge required for independent adult living are somewhat like the number concepts and computational skills taught at the fourth grade level and below. The everyday problems encountered by adults in earning a living, managing an income, and functioning as a wise consumer can be resolved with computational skills at an elementary level. It has been shown elsewhere that mentally retarded children are able to learn mathematics at a level consistent with their mental ages, and that mental age predictions suggest a first- to third-grade level achievement potential for moderately retarded individuals and a third- to sixth-grade level for educable retarded individuals. It may be concluded that:

1. Many adults living self-sufficient lives are performing mathematical tasks at about a fourth-grade level.
2. Since educable mentally retarded children have the potential of functioning at fourth-grade level, they possess the potential for independent living in terms of mathematical abilities.
3. Since trainable mentally retarded children have the potential of functioning at a primary level, they possess the potential for semi-independent living in terms of mathematical abilities.

The construction of the mathematics curriculum for the mentally retarded then must reflect the skills such as those demanded by society for adult living. The objectives of the mathematics curriculum should emerge from the potential for independent adult living and the number skills prerequisite to that end.

OBJECTIVES FOR THE EDUCABLE MENTALLY RETARDED

The educable mentally retarded have needs which involve much more than merely teaching them to add, subtract, multiply, and divide. Such computational skills are of value only if applicable to the quantitative problems which arise in everyday living. It is important that emphasis be placed upon the socially significant aspects of the mathematics program. The ultimate goal of the mathematics program for the mentally retarded is to provide them with the skills to solve the daily problems they face in independent living. The mentally retarded will be handling money, figuring paychecks, calculating the cost of a half dozen eggs, or a quarter of a pound of hamburger. The mathematics curriculum must encompass counting, measuring, weighing, computing, budgeting, buying, selling, reading, estimating, and record keeping. Number concepts and fundamental skills unrelated to everyday life are meaningless for the retardate.

OBJECTIVES FOR THE TRAINABLE MENTALLY RETARDED

Obviously, the trainable mentally retarded will have needs quite different from those of the educable mentally retarded. These differences are reflected by the discrepancies between independent socio-vocational adjustment as contrasted with marginal special vocational adequacy. Indeed, there will be many aspects of the mathematics curriculum which are very similar. This is especially true for the high trainable and low educable children. For example, both will have a need to handle money. The trainable child's skill in this area will probably be limited to making change for a dollar and calculating the costs of simple purchases, or his earnings on piecework in a sheltered workshop. The educable mentally retarded adult will go much beyond this dealing with large sums such as automobile purchases, social security withholdings, and income taxes. The trainable adult will have needs to figure bus fare, tell time, the admission price to the theatre, dialing the telephone, selecting a TV channel, grouping, separating, classifying one-to-one correspondence, and simple record keeping as demanded in the typical daily routines and in a sheltered workshop setting.

PRINCIPLES OF ADAPTATION

It has been shown that mental age and other variables associated with academic learning can guide the teacher in planning mathematics instruction for the mentally retarded. A major distinction between the mathematics program for the mentally retarded and children of average intelligence is the difference in objectives. Mathematics must be functional for the mentally retarded. The principles which guide the construction of functional mathematics for the mentally retarded are similar to the principles of good teaching for all children. Some principles which apply to both mentally retarded children and children of average intelligence deserve special emphasis. In addition, there are some guidelines which are usually applicable only to the mentally retarded. A number of teaching principles which have specific implications for mathematics education of the mentally retarded follow.

Readiness. "Billy just can't do the work....Mary obviously is not ready for second grade work. John hasn't learned to read after three years in school, and I don't see how anyone could expect me to do anything with him." The notion of readiness can be construed to imply that a child is not able to profit from any type of academic instruction. What readiness means especially in reference to reading is that a preparation program usually needs to precede academic teaching. It should not preclude efforts to teach simply because a given child is unable to learn the skills that other children are learning. No matter where a child is functioning, he is ready for a next step. Every child is always ready for a step forward even though that step might be quite small. This is especially important to remember with mentally retarded children since there is such a drastic difference between their academic performance and that of children with unimpaired intelligence. If the teacher focuses upon this tremendous gap, it can seem as if the retarded will never be ready to learn anything. *Remember: All retarded children are always ready to learn something new.*

Patience. The teacher of children with average intelligence frequently marvels at the patience of the special education teacher. The author has overheard remarks similar to this one countless times: "I don't know how you are able to work with mentally retarded children. I just wouldn't have the patience." Actually, the contrary is more accurate. The special education teacher has to be very impatient. She must be constantly planning strategy to promote pupil progress. She must not be content to wait patiently in the face of nonachievement. Each time a child fails to make progress she must question why. It could be that her evaluation instruments are not sensitive enough. In this case, another method of measurement must be found. The lack of progress may be the result of ineffective teaching, inappropriate curriculum or insufficient materials. The teacher must constantly review the child's educational program, test for signs of growth, and above all be very impatient with herself when satisfactory progress is not shown.

Pity. "I feel so sorry for Freddy. Everything comes so hard to him." Such expressions of sympathy are acceptable only as long as the feelings which give rise to them do not interfere with teacher expectations. Frankly, the mentally retarded child does not need the teacher's pity. He needs her teaching skill to help him develop the competencies for independent living. Some mentally retarded children have had many devastating experiences, and certainly life has dealt them a cruel blow. Pampering the child does not equip him to compensate for his handicap. Only sound professional instruction can do that.

The Intermediate Step. Mentally retarded children are often unable to follow what appears to be the logical sequence of instruction. The concept which at first seems to follow another immediately may be beyond the grasp of the retarded child. He is in need of an intermediate step, a bridge from one concept to the next. Retardates learn through step by step teaching. However, lack of insight impedes progress along the usual logical continuum. They need simpler, shorter steps.

The Alternative to the Alternative. Closely related to the idea of the intermediate step is that of concept presentation. Frequently a concept will have to be presented in its simplest context in order to be understood by the retarded child. The teacher will need to search for a method of presentation which is comprehensible to the child. The child might be quite capable of mastering the concept but not in a context or form which the teacher has first presented. Even the third try may not be the charm. The teacher should be prepared to offer many approaches to the concept she wishes the children to learn.

The Strategic Retreat. The teacher will sometimes discover that she is presenting a concept which is beyond the student's present level. This is a corollary to the principle of alternatives above. That is, she may need to retreat to an increasingly simpler concept and basic elements until she finds the child's instructional level.

Vocabulary. The vocabulary associated with mathematics is often very different from that normally encountered in the traditional language arts program. Consequently new number terms and quantitative vocabulary must be systematically taught.

Individual Differences. Mentally retarded children, like normal children, will vary considerably among themselves in their rates of learning. The teacher will need to adapt instruction to these individual differences and the wide range of intellectual impairment. Some children will have gaps in their skills which need remediation. The teacher should structure the curriculum in keeping with the special disabilities and strengths of her particular students.

Practical Experience. The skills and concepts taught should reflect the student's present life needs. These children may be able to grasp the practical significance of a concept even though they do not comprehend the mathematical derivation for computation. The teacher needs to evaluate the functionality of the content in terms of the child's potential for adult living, and provide first-hand experiences with concepts and skills to be learned.

Motivation. A frequent complaint from teachers of mentally retarded children (especially those in the regular classroom) is that these children simply are not motivated. This characteristic may be spoken of as lack of drive and enthusiasm for school work. It is important that this misconception be put to rest. Mentally retarded children are just as motivated as any other group of children. It may well be that their motivation system is directed towards avoiding mathematics or other academic tasks which are threatening to them. But there is no absence of the desire to succeed and be well regarded by one's peers and adult figures. Indeed, every mentally retarded child seeks the admiration of his friends and the attention of his teachers. In most cases he is not able to receive this recognition through academic achievement so he may shy away from the arithmetic lesson and balk at instructional attempts. The teacher should not interpret this as laziness or native negativism, but rather it should be viewed as the child's endeavor to salvage his ego. Most teachers will be amazed at how a series of success experiences and positive reinforcements will modify a child's avoidance and negative behavior. *Remember: All mentally retarded children are highly motivated.*

Focus on a Target. There will be many aspects of the child's problem solving behavior which the teacher may wish to modify. The child may make a number of careless errors, he may waste precious time, he may be a discipline problem, or he may mirror write his numbers. The teacher should be precise about the behavior to be changed. "To improve Billy's attitude toward arithmetic" is not an objective that is easy to focus upon. The objective should be achievable, measurable, and simply stated so that both teacher and students can judge progress. In order for progress to be measurable, the objective must be stated in behavioral terms. "Billy, count a set of five marbles accurately," is achievable, measurable, and is simply stated in behavioral terms.

Consistency of Reward. This is essential to mentally retarded children. They must know that a given behavior will result in a specific consequence. If diligent effort on a child's part is rewarded with a profuse amount of attention on one day and completely ignored on another, the child will be less likely to remain attentive to the assigned task. Capricious and sporadic responses to the child's behavior will serve only to confuse the child and confirm his own erratic patterns of behavior.

Immediate Rewards. Immediate rewards are more desirable for mentally retarded children who are less future oriented. Delayed gratification may be effective with children of average intelligence, but rewards for retarded children should immediately follow the desired behavior. This way, there is no confusion in the child's mind concerning what is being rewarded.

Use Concrete Rewards. Mentally retarded children may not be reinforced in their learning merely by the self-satisfaction of skill acquisition. In some instances, the children may not know that they are making progress. Such children will benefit from concrete rewards such as candy, or a favorite book. Other children will respond to a token economy. A token may be any object which is used as a medium of exchange. For example, a token such as a plastic counter or paper script may be exchanged for free time to play with the number games in the mathematic corner. More subtle rewards, such as a smile or an appreciative nod are sufficient rewards for other children.

The Age Tripod. A major problem for the teacher of the mentally retarded is to present an arithmetic lesson at the child's ability level (mental age) which is of sufficiently high interest (social age) and peer prestige (chronological age). He must deal with all three ages at once.

Expectancies. The teacher needs to hold reasonable demands for the child to meet and slowly increase these expectancies as the child achieves.

Arithmetic Reasoning. Arithmetic reasoning should be emphasized at the functional level. Computational and rote learnings too often consume major portions of instructional time. In order for computational skills to be meaningful, they must be related to arithmetic reasoning and problem solving.

Drill. Rote learning should be tied to practical situations. All drill should be meaningful to the student. Computation should be tied to problem solving tasks. Busy work should be avoided, and basic principles and concepts should be emphasized rather than mere rote learnings. Blind memorization is as useless with the mentally retarded as it is with the normal children. When drill seems appropriate, the lessons should be brief, spaced, and related to social uses. This does not preclude systematic repetition and review. As indicated elsewhere, at the same difficulty level the same concepts can be given in different context with different application.

Integration. Mathematics instruction should be integrated with unit work and incidental teaching; however, the arithmetic lesson or mathematics project does have a specific place in the instructional program.

The Success Spiral. Many children come to the arithmetic lesson anticipating failure. They have become trapped in a defeat cycle. Each failure deflates their self-concepts, predisposes them to avoid the task or accept it half-heartedly, making additional failure even more likely. The teacher needs to establish a success spiral. One must begin where the child can experience success, reward freely, and move slowly until the anticipation of failure becomes anticipation of success. The defeat cycle then is reversed into a success spiral.

Abstract Problems. Retardates should not be expected to perform complex abstract problems. However, the teacher must develop the retardate's skill in handling simple abstract problems and assist the youngster in relating them to his immediate environment.

Emphasis on Processes. Educable retardates have less understanding of processes to be used in a problem situation than normal children and are more apt to guess. Consequently, the special education teacher needs to stress the diagnosing of problems, identifying essentials, and selecting appropriate procedures.

Carelessness. Mentally retarded children are not innately careless nor prone to technical errors. The instructor must be certain that the child *understands* the processes and provide for sufficient repetition and transfer. Such precautions will minimize errors of carelessness which may occur because of misunderstanding processes involved.

Regular Texts and Workbooks. The shortage of texts, workbooks, and other materials designed specifically for the retardate is well-known to the practitioner. The teacher is left with little alternative other than adapting materials designed for children with normal intelligence. The teacher of the retardate will be able to utilize much of these materials successfully if she properly adapts them to the specific characteristics of her students.

Word Problems. The mentally retarded child can perform word problems if the instructions have been meaningful. However, the arithmetic period is not the time to teach reading.

Attention Span. Most retarded children are capable of attending to attractive tasks at which they experience success for relatively long periods of time. A short attention span may simply reflect the inappropriateness of the mathematics lesson. It should be recognized that a few such children will be able to pursue the arithmetic lesson due to such factors as distractability and negative set.

Acalculia and Perceptual Deficits. Cerebral dysfunction, perceptual deficit, or brain damage may result in failure to learn arithmetic. When such cases occur, the teacher should provide appropriate perceptual-motor training and modify the movement to offset the tendencies toward psychological fixation, forced responsiveness, and deficient self-control.

ORGANIZING FOR INSTRUCTION

There are at least four possible patterns of organizing the mathematics for the instruction of trainable mentally retarded pupils: (1) specific mathematics lessons, (2) incidental mathematics instruction, (3) integration of mathematics within the total curriculum, and (4) the unit approach.

The specific mathematics lesson presented at a fixed time of the day is perhaps the most well-known approach. Most teachers will agree to the value of incidental and integrative teaching. Although the unit approach is the most frequently overlooked, it still holds the greatest potential for the development of functional number concepts and skills. The comparative roles of each of these four approaches, their advantages and limitations, will be discussed in the following sections.

SPECIFIC MATHEMATICS LESSON

The typical procedure in using the specific mathematics lesson is to schedule a portion of each day (usually twenty to forty minutes) as the arithmetic period. The teacher will have prepared a lesson geared to the developmental level of each student. On occasion, she will have specific commercial material for her use. However, it would be more common for her to present specific lessons, utilizing work sheets, to each student or group of students. The class will work as a whole during some arithmetic exercises such as "bingo" and other teaching games, and other certain topics lending themselves to group instruction such as computing tax or opening a savings account. The teacher should then prepare a lesson plan specific to the given objective, but which still provides for individual differences.

INCIDENTAL INSTRUCTION

Another approach frequently employed is incidental instruction. The teacher deliberately seeks opportunities to introduce, reinforce, or review a particular mathematics concept or skill. This technique is probably used at the preprimary and primary levels more than any other. The teacher might ask these youngsters, for example, to count the number of cookies, using one-to-one correspondence, or distribute milk (using one-to-one correspondence). There are, however, many advantages to using incidental instruction at the higher levels as well as at preprimary and primary levels.

The teacher should be cautioned that incidental instruction is quite opposite from accidental instruction. If a teacher seized upon every opportunity to utilize number and number related activities through incidental instruction, a very confused and disorganized mathematics curriculum would result. There are several principles which can serve as a guide to using the incidental approach:

1. Select occasions which emerge naturally. Do not force or manufacture situations.
2. Utilize periods which lend themselves to incidental teaching without distracting from the major activity or lesson in progress.
3. Concepts and skills selected should be related to the current mathematics objectives. Incidental teaching is not an end in itself.
4. It is just as important to follow principles of sequential, continuous instruction in incidental teachings as in any other approach.

Even the most sensitive teacher needs to anticipate and plan for events which lend themselves to incidental teaching, while at the same time making the best use of spontaneous situations which may also be used to advantage. Incidental instruction has its place, especially with young children. However, its greatest contribution will be found in providing for (1) the establishment of the need for a new idea or skill, (2) for application of a newly learned skill, and (3) for revision of an established skill. However, as every special education teacher realizes, mathematics cannot be taught exclusively by the incidental or informal technique.

INTEGRATION

There has been much written recently about the child-centered curriculum and the integration of subject matter through core programs. Upon close examination of programs which purport to be highly integrative, one finds that arithmetic (and other subjects as well) is in fact taught in a separated, systematic and orderly fashion. The desirability of integrating mathematics into other areas of the curriculum is self-apparent.

The nature of the arithmetic experiences to be offered in content fields will by necessity be determined by the scope of learning undertaken in these fields. For example, no well-designed program could conceivably avoid mathematical concepts and skills in the areas of language arts, science, and social studies. Most studies conducted on this problem have shown that the number of arithmetic terms and concepts used in other elementary school subjects is significant. The following is taken from an elementary reader:

> "Goodness me!" she said with a giggle. "I made a mistake, didn't I?" "Yes, you did!" replied Mr. Maple. "But it was a small one."
>
> Then all three of them began to laugh. George looked much nicer when he was not making faces. Mrs. Hall looked pleasanter when she was smiling, and Mr. Maple looked much better when he was not cross. "Here, son," he said, tapping George on the shoulder. "Here's a nickel and a dime. Go and buy yourself some candy."

Devault (1961, p. 186) discusses the problem of integration of mathematics in some detail. He cites the paragraph below from a social studies text which further illustrates the degree to which mathematics is already integrated into commercially published resources.

> Not many years ago there were few symphony orchestras in the United States. Today there are many, and quite a number of them may be heard over the air in regular weekly programs. The radio has accustomed more people than ever to the music of orchestras, and the United States has probably taken the first place as a nation of music lovers and music sponsors. Music has become a part of American life, and a large part of our recreation and entertainment is connected with music.

The author pointed out that in this relatively short selection the number of quantitative terms and concepts is extremely high. Of the eighty-eight words, eighteen percent (sixteen words) are quantitative in nature. Consequently, the teacher does not make the decision of whether she will integrate mathematics, but simply must decide how she will deal with the integration which already exists. She must, in addition, determine the degree to which she will integrate beyond this level and plan accordingly.

If a teacher pauses to explain or teach mathematical concepts during a social studies lesson, such as the one above, she may indirectly distract from the main goal of the lesson. Children of normal intelligence may be capable of tolerating such tangents, but such deviations may prove highly distressing to the mentally retarded. The mathematics curriculum can contribute to the successful implementation of other content areas by freeing students from annoying interruptions for learnings that might be better taught during the arithmetic period. Integration for review and application at the automatic level (as opposed to instructional level) would appear to be the most profitable approach to pursue.

UNIT METHOD

The unit approach to teaching retarded children has been clearly presented by such authors as Laura Jordan and Malinda Garton. As indicated in previous discussions above, mathematics may be taught incidentally or through integration into other content areas. The techniques and principles of incorporating mathematics instruction into units would parallel this discussion. The great value of mathematics as taught through units relates to motivation and functionality. Certainly, mathematics could easily be included in a unit such as "the weather." Reading scales, calculating differences, maintaining records could all be part of such a unit. However, it would be dangerous to assume that the unit approach could satisfy the demands for continuous and sequential mathematics instruction. An innovative unit approach would be to build a "mathematics unit" with other topics such as social studies, science, language arts and so on serving as related fields and skills. If the mathematics objectives were to determine the selection of the content from the area in such units, one would feel more assured about an orderly presentation. The reader will find two examples of the unit approach to vocational mathematics at the Senior High or adultation level in chapter 7.

MODERN MATHEMATICS FOR THE RETARDATE

If the concept of the "new" and "modern" mathematics has made some elementary teachers uneasy, it has literally terrified the teachers of the mentally retarded. The author overheard a principal comment to a teacher about teaching modern mathematics to the educable mentally retarded, "Well, if these kids can learn modern mathematics, they shouldn't be in your room!" What this principal failed to comprehend, and what many special education teachers do not grasp, is that modern mathematics is more a philosophy of instruction than a new content. It approaches the study of mathematics with emphasis on the importance of concepts, patterns, and relationships on the development of mathematical skills. This is precisely the major ingredient of mathematics for the mentally retarded—that in so far as possible these youngsters learn mathematical skills and concepts with sufficient understanding for application and transfer. The emphasis of the teaching is on process rather than rote learning.

Teachers tend to become confused by terms such as "set, intersection, identity, region, venn diagram" and so forth. Equally perplexing are such notations as:

$$< \quad \{c, d, e\}$$
$$\leftrightarrow \quad \sim$$
$$\neq \quad \geq$$

In part this is simply due to the teachers' unfamiliarity with such terms and notations. Perhaps the retardate would be equally confused by traditional terms if he had not been exposed to them throughout his educational experience. For example, terms such as "algorism, cardinal number, denominator, addend, place value," and notations such as

$$\times \quad -$$
$$\div \quad +$$
$$= \quad (3 \times 2)$$

might cause considerable confusion. All of this is not to indicate that mentally retarded children can learn the total sequence of modern mathematics any more than the traditional arithmetic approach suggests the possible mastering of advanced number skills and concepts. The position is simply taken that retarded children are just as capable of mastering numerical skills through the philosophy inherent in modern mathematics as through the basic assumption inherent in the traditional approach.

Further, the point of view of teaching for understanding, even to a limited degree, will result in improved ability in mental calculation and consequently improved use of mathematics in everyday life situations. This position guides the development of the curriculum in the following chapters.

There are a number of themes that run through the modern mathematics program from early childhood to the high school level. These strands will be introduced here and elaborated in later chapters.

Concept of Set

The teacher of the retarded child need not concern himself with set theory but rather direct his attention to a few simple concepts. He does need, however, to be somewhat familiar with the language of sets which is the primary step in constructing sequential and meaningful mathematical concepts.

The term "set" cannot be given a definition in the formal sense since it is a primary idea and cannot be reduced to simpler terms. For our purpose, it is convenient to think of a set as an obvious collection, group, or class of objects. A set is obvious when it is simple for the viewer to determine whether an object is or is not a part of the set. A collection of coins, a group of third graders, and a number of boys are some samples of sets. The objects within the set are called *members* or elements.

This concept of set will aid in the precise communication of mathematical knowledge. Teachers have taught through the use of groups of objects for years. It is not so much that the idea of set is a startling new idea but rather that the language associated with set enables the learner to deal with the most elementary ideas of mathematics in a way that is clear to him. This will help the child immensely in mastering the skills of correspondence and counting, the concepts of cardinal and ordinal numbers, actions with whole and fractional numbers, measurement, and geometry.

Natural Numbers

The preliminary skill to counting is one-to-one correspondence. As a young boy counts the number of children in a class to determine how many cartons of milk he should bring from the cafeteria, he is actually matching elements in two sets. One of these sets is the children and the other set is the number names. The last number named matched with the last child tells the boy how many cartons of milk he will need.

We regard these counting numbers as natural numbers. With young students we assume that each counting number is followed by a counting

Constructing the Mathematics Curriculum 43

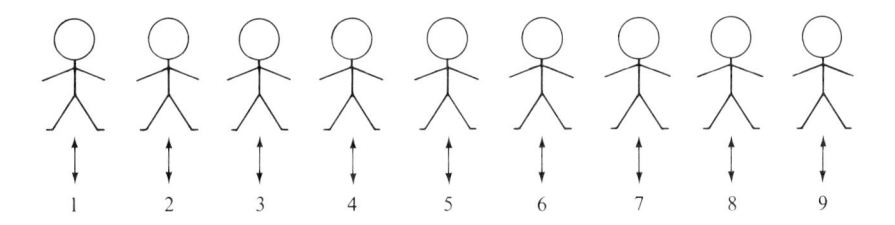

FIGURE 2.1

number that is one more than the number which preceded it. The counting numbers may be thought of as beginning at 1 and continuing to infinity.

Natural (counting) numbers = {1,2,3............}

In later chapters, cardinal number and ordinal number will also be considered.

Numerals Are Not Numbers

A number is a concept while a numeral is a symbolic representation of a concept. Just as the word *cat* is quite distinct from Billy's real live pet, so the symbol *8* is very much different from eightness. The name of the symbol is not nearly as significant as the meanings the symbol may represent. For example, the word *chair* may arouse such images as four leggedness, comfort, relaxation, sitting position, soft. The symbol 8 may also elicit such different meanings as 8, ½ × 16, 4 + 4, 2 × 4, 5 $\overline{)40}$. Progress will be much more rapid if the child is able to bring many meanings to a symbol.

It has been indicated previously that retarded children often fail to understand the processes of arithmetic. This deficit may be attributable in part to their failure to comprehend basic number concepts and to grasp the relationship of one operation to another. The development of the elementary number concepts which are the basis of number operations will proceed with less difficulty if the students understand the distinction between a number and a numeral.

Positional Notation

It is understandable that man elected to facilitate his ability to count by grouping objects in tens (one-to-one correspondence of objects to his number of fingers). The operations with numbers are founded on this group with ten and the multiples of ten. The numeral 17 represents one ten and seven ones, the numeral 217 represents two hundreds, one ten, and seven ones and so forth. In other words, in our decimal notation each digit has a place value. Each position contains only one digit in each series of numerals and that position determines its value. Thus, ours is a system of positional notation. The concepts of base 10 and place value are vital elements in the modern mathematics instructional program.

Basic Principles of Number Operations

Shortly after the child has mastered the initial concept of sets and has developed some skill in rational counting, he will be introduced to the processes of addition and subtraction. Later he will extend his competencies to multiplication and division. He will be guided to the discovery that subtraction is the inverse of addition and division is the reverse of multiplication. In order to perform these operations economically, he will be introduced to the commutative, associative, and distributive principles which are central to the modern mathematics program. These basic ideas will help him avoid a rigid, rote form of computation and problem solving. A grasp of these principles is essential if the youngster is ever going to gain an understanding of the common algorisms.

The commutative principle applies to the order of addition and multiplication. It can be observed that $2 + 1 = 3 = 1 + 2$ and that $3 \times 2 = 6 = 2 \times 3$.

The associative principle applies to grouping. When two or more numbers are added, or when two or more numbers are multiplied, the sum or product is unaffected by the grouping. For example:

$$(1 + 2) + 3 = 1 + (2 + 3)$$
$$(2 \times 3) \times 4 = 2 \times (3 \times 4)$$

The distributive principle is concerned with both addition and multiplication. It can be seen from the illustration below that either of the factors may be distributed through the use of addition.

$$\begin{aligned} 3 \times 12 &= 3 \times (10 + 2) \\ &= (3 \times 10) + (3 \times 2) \text{ and} \\ &= 30 + 6 \\ &= 36 \end{aligned}$$

$$3 \times 12 = (1 + 2) \times 12$$
$$= (1 \times 12) + (2 \times 12)$$
$$= 12 + 24$$
$$= 36$$

Number Patterns

2,3,5,4,5,7,___,___,___,

When you start with one and add the next number, what do you find?

$$1 + 2 = 3$$
$$2 + 3 = 5$$
$$3 + 4 = 7$$

Mathematical Sentences

Consider the problem, "Mary has one pencil and her mother gave her two more. How many pencils did Mary have altogether?" The pupil would "write" the problem

$$1 + 2 = ? \quad \text{or} \quad \begin{array}{r} 1 \\ +2 \\ \hline ? \end{array}$$

In one very real sense, the pupil has written a mathematical sentence. Modern mathematics introduces a frame to represent the unknown.

$$1 + 2 = \Box$$

The problem could be slightly modified by asking, "Mary's mother gave her two pencils. She has three altogether. How many pencils did she have in the first place?" The problem could be written in a mathematical sentence as: $\Box + 2 = 3$. Later, two unknowns might be introduced: $\Box \times \Box = 3$. In some instances problems are presented with two or more variables and the child is allowed to provide his own solutions.

$$\Box \times \triangle \times \bigcirc = 12$$

This type of an approach will encourage students to expand their understandings of the basic number properties and operations.

Other Modern Mathematics Ideas

The few simple ideas introduced here do not begin to exhaust the elements of a modern mathematics program. Themes such as identity elements, number lines, decimal notation, and geometry will be discussed later. Other strands such as functions, Cartesian coordinates, and factoring are omitted altogether as beyond the abilities of the mentally retarded. The decision to include some topics while excluding others was made on the basis of the contribution they can make to the child's present understanding, and how well they prepare him for continual progress.

CURRICULUM CONTENT

The content of the curriculum for the mentally retarded has been organized around eight mathematical categories for the purposes of this book (Peterson, 1967). It would seem appropriate at this time to define each of these and present the rationale for its selection.

Form and Perception

Such noted authors as Piaget (1965), Weaver (1963, p. 514), and Williams (1965, p. 261) have indicated that geometric shapes and forms should be an integral part of the mathematics curriculum even for very young children. Mastain and Nossoff (1966, pp. 32-37) have indicated that an organized pattern design of relationships is within the range of understanding of preschool children. The intention within this category is to improve the children's ability to perceive position in space and the spatial relationships of two or more objects. Further, training should be given in the elementary skills of visual-motor coordination as well as understandings of fundamental properties of spatial configurations.

Vocabulary Associated with Mathematics

It has been indicated in the preceding chapters that the vocabulary of mentally retarded children is deficient. Kirk (1962), Johnson (1951), and Stutler (1962, pp. 81-86) have suggested the need for the development of arithmetic vocabulary according to the needs and abilities of these children. Terms selected for presentation are basically referents to size, position, shape and quality; in addition, common terms also related to arithmetic processes and terms of business are included.

Number Symbols

Both Stutler (1962, pp. 81-86) and Williams (1965, p. 261) have indicated the need for naming and reproducing number symbols as prerequisite to developing arithmetic skills. In this category, the children are instructed in the recognition of number symbols, number names, and for the natural order of sequence.

Cardinal Numbers

Mastain and Nossoff (1966, pp. 32-37) again have suggested that an understanding of sets of objects is very important in early formation of number concepts. Weaver (1963, p. 514) has stressed the need for young children to associate numbers with sets of objects. Williams (1965, p. 261) regards sets as a significant strand throughout the mathematical concepts and abilities, such as indefinite numbers, correspondence of sets and numbers, set recognition, conservation of numbers through varying configuration of sets, and reproducing sets.

Ordinal Numbers

Coxford (1963, pp. 419-427) points out that an understanding of seriation is a significant element in the development of number concept. This category is aimed at the development of skills in seriation on the basis of some quality as well as a determination of position by assigning a number to a particular object in an ordered arrangement.

Measurement

A number of authors have illustrated the value of measurement concepts in the mathematics curriculum. Skills and concepts were selected for this section which represented the basic measures of time, calendar, weight, capacity, and length.

Money and Value

An effective review of the literature of arithmetic fundamentals for the mentally retarded, reported by Burns (1961, pp. 57-61), and a review of workbooks and research on arithmetic for young children, conducted by Stutler (1962, pp. 81-86), emphasize the worth of developing an understanding of money and value. The money and value portion of the curriculum seeks to improve the children's ability to recognize money values and conduct transactions involving the use of money as well as to discriminate the value of items of varying worth.

Number Operations and Problem Solving

A most obvious category of mathematics instruction is the process of computation and manipulation with numbers. Weaver (1963, p. 514) has reported on an experimental project which indicated that even very young children can successfully participate in number operations by simple joining and separating sets of objects. He encourages number operations as a major division of the curriculum. This category seeks to enhance children's abilities in combining and separating objects and the other basic operations of addition, subtraction, multiplication, and division. The ultimate objective of the mathematics program for the mentally retarded is to assist them in the organizing and assigning meaning to their environment so that they may more effectively deal with their day-to-day problems. Basic number concepts and abilities are necessary tools for the development of effective reasoning with all children, but most particularly with the mentally retarded.

SUMMARY

This chapter has presented a basic approach to constructing the mathematics curriculum. The entire thrust of the curriculum for the retarded child must be judged by its functionality. To a degree, this is true for the educational experiences of all children. The differences between the typical curriculum and that for the retarded revolves primarily around developmental learning capacities and adult achievement potential. These differences dictate an adjustment of objectives, a process of content adaptation, and a modification of instructional organization. The value of modern mathematics to such an approach should not be underestimated. Finally, a framework for the development of curriculum content has been indicated.

REFERENCES

Adams, H. W. "The Mathematics Encountered in General Reading of Newspapers and Periodicals." Master's Thesis, University of Chicago, 1924.

Bensburg, Gerard. "The Relationship of Academic Achievement of Mental Defective Mental Age, Sex, Institutionalization, and Etiology." *American Journal of Mental Deficiency* LXII (May, 1958): 810-18.

Burns, Paul C. "Arithmetic Fundamentals for the Educable Mentally Retarded." *American Journal of Mental Deficiency* LXVI (July, 1961): 57-61.

Benoitt, Paul E., and Valeno, Rita S. "Teaching Retarded Children to Tell Time." *Training School Bulletin* Vol. 59 (May, 1962): 22-26.

Chaney, C. M., and Kephart, N. C. *Motoric Adds to Perceptual Training.* Columbus, Ohio: Charles E. Merrill, 1968.

Coleman, Josephine K. "Just Plain Drill." *The Arithmetic Teacher* Vols. 4, 8 (December, 1961): 431-32.

Coxford, Arthur F. "The Effects of Instruction in the Stage Placement of Children in Piaget's Seriation Experiments." *The Arithmetic Teacher* XI (January, 1964): 4-9.

———. "Piaget: Number and Measurement." *The Arithmetic Teacher* X (November, 1963): 419-27.

Cruickshank, William M. "Arithmetic Ability of Mentally Retarded Children: I. Ability to Differentiate Extraneous Materials from Needed Arithmetic Facts." *Journal of Educational Research* XLII (November, 1948): 161-70.

Dunn, Lloyd M. (ed.) *Exceptional Children in the Schools.* New York: Holt, Rinehart and Winston, Inc., 1963.

Edwards, Alice D. "Arithmetic in Everyday Living." *Arithmetic Teacher* Vol. 9 (December, 1962): 453-58.

Hommes, Csanyi; Gonsales; and Rechs. *How to Use Contingency Contracting in the Classroom.* Champaign, Illinois: Research Press, 1969.

Kaleski, Lotte. "Arithmetic and the Brain Injured Child." *Arithmetic Teacher* Vol. IX, (May, 1962): 245-51.

Kirk, Samuel A. *Educating Exceptional Children.* Boston: Houghton-Mifflin Co., 1962.

Kirk, Samuel A. and Johnson, G. Orville. *Educating the Retarded Child.* Cambridge: Riverside Press, 1951.

Lewis, W. D. "The Relative Intellectual Achievement of the Mentally Gifted and Retarded Children." *Journal of Educational Psychology* XLV (April 1954): 321-31.

Mastain, Richard K., and Nossoff, Bernice C. "Mathematics in the Kindergarten." *The Arithmetic Teacher* XIII (January, 1966): 32-37.

Norton, John K., and Norton, Margaret. *A Foundation of Curriculum Building.* New York: Ginn and Company, 1963.

Peterson, Daniel L. "A Study of Mathematical Knowledge of Young Mental Retardates." Ed.D. dissertation, University of Missouri, 1967.

Piaget, Jean. *The Child's Conception of Number.* New York: W. Norton and Co., 1965.

Ring, S. B. "A Comparison of Achievement and Mental Ages of Ninety-eight Special Class Children." Master's thesis, Boston University, 1951.

Rosenberg, M. B. *Diagnostic Teaching.* Seattle: Special Child Publications, 1968.

Stephens, T. M. *Directive Teaching of Children with Learning and Behavioral Handicaps.* Columbus: Charles E. Merrill, 1970.

Stutler, Mary S. "Arithmetic Concepts in the First Grade." *The Arithmetic Teacher* IX (February, 1962): 81-86.

Trapp, E. Philip and Himelstein, Philip. Readings in *The Exceptional Child.* Edited by Edward Zigler. New York: Appleton-Century-Crofts, Inc., 1962.

Weaver, J. Fred. "The School Mathematical Study Group Project on Elementary School Mathematics, Grades K-3." *The Arithmetic Teacher* X (December, 1963): 514.

Williams, Alfred H. "Mathematical Concepts, Skills, and Abilities of Kindergarten Entrants." *The Arithmetic Teacher* XII (April, 1965): 261.

Witty, P. A. and McCafferty, E. "Attainment by Feebleminded Children." *Education* LII (November, 1930): 588-97.

Valett, R. E. *Effective Teaching.* Belmont, California: Fearon Publishers, 1970.

Valett, R. E. *Programming Learning Disabilities.* Belmont, California: Fearon Publishers, 1969.

Zigler, Edward. "Rigidity in the Feebleminded." *The Exceptional Child* New York, Appleton-Century-Crofts, Inc., 1962.

chapter 3

Early Childhood Mathematics Education

The beginnings of mathematical skills and understandings are being established long before the mentally retarded child enters the special education classroom. Even the most severely retarded child makes judgments throughout his daily routine which give ample evidence of the initiation of the reasoning process. For example, he estimates how high to raise his foot to climb the stairs, he judges the space needed to navigate his tricycle through a myriad of toys in the playroom, or he may be able to indicate which balloon is larger, which objects are too heavy to move, which child has the most candy, and what his age is. In viewing pictorial representations he is able to determine which ball is big, which animal is heavy, and which man is tall. He often can distinguish real from play money, identify a clock, discriminate letters from number symbols, and do some rote counting. The teacher of the mentally retarded child never starts from the beginning. The child comes to the special education classroom with some understandings and skills. The teacher's task is to assess these abilities, determine the next logical step, select an appropriate activity, and evaluate its effectiveness.

ABILITY LEVELS

The preprimary school program typically limits itself to three, four, and five year old children. It has been pointed out in previous chapters that mental age seems to be the most accurate basis on which to structure the mathematics curriculum for the mentally retarded. It is well then, to consider for a moment the mental age ranges which the teacher of preprimary retardates is liable to encounter. Table 3.1 indicates the mental ages for educable mentally retarded children up to and including mental age four.

TABLE 3.1

Mental Ages of Educable Mentally Retarded Children Chronological Ages 3, 4, 5

Chronological Ages	Intelligence Quotients						
	50	55	60	65	70	75	80
	Mental Ages						
3	1.6		1.9		2.1		2.5
4	2.0		2.5		2.9		3.2
5	2.6		3.0		3.6		4.0

It can be seen from the table that the range begins from a mental age of eighteen months for three year olds and proceeds to a mental age of four years for a five year old. The teacher, then could expect a range of developmental levels from infancy to 4K. Closer inspection reveals most four-and five-year-olds will be functioning at a nursery level.

In this chapter, the concern is primarily with educable mentally retarded children. However, it can be demonstrated from Table 3.2 on page 55 that the absolute mental age differences among children of superior, average, and subaverage intelligence is comparatively small at the preprimary years. The differences in mental ages become quite marked as the chronological ages increase. Consequently, it is much less complicated to discuss the mathematics program for a wide range of intellectual impairment during the period of early childhood education than it is in later school years. Furthermore, the assessment of intelligence for very young children and the predictability of achievement is not nearly as trustworthy as it is for older youngsters. For this reason, it is not unusual to find educable mentally retarded children in preschool programs for the trainable, and vice versa. It should not be surprising, then, that much of what is suggested for the early childhood education of the educable will also hold true for the trainable mentally retarded. Chapter 8 will treat the early childhood education of trainable retarded children separately, but the reader will note many similarities and some overlap with the suggested curriculum for the educable.

Early Childhood Mathematics Education 55

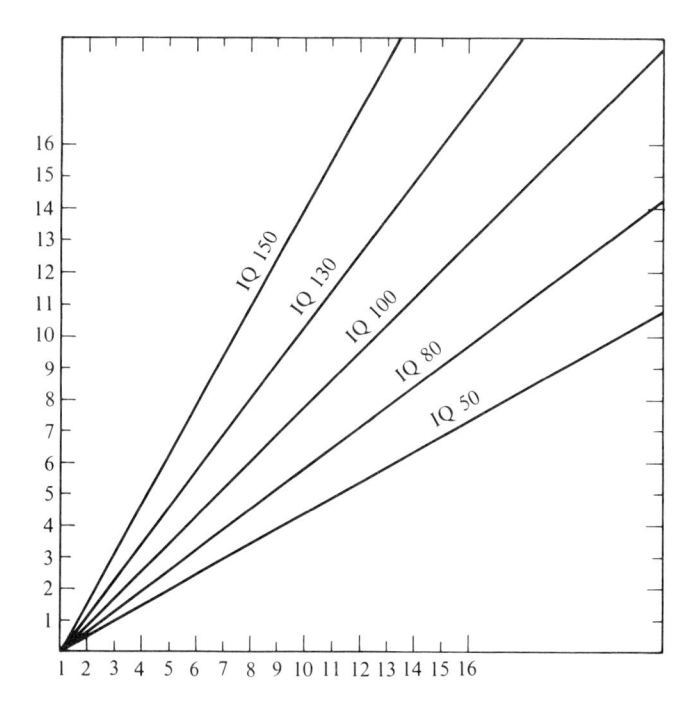

TABLE 3.2

Relative Difference in Mental Ages for Five IQ Levels for Increasing Chronological Ages

It is unlikely that the teacher of young mentally retarded children will be involved in the training of a child with a mental age of less than eighteen months. Indeed, most of her students will have mental ages of two and three years. It is doubtful that any training presented to a child under mental age eighteen months could truly be called mathematics instruction. Yet the normal child of eighteen months is an intricate intellectual dynamo with considerable perceptual motor skills. He is able to walk, run about, seat himself in a chair, go up and down stairs, and is capable of assisting in his own feeding. He understands many logical relationships, has an expressive vocabulary of about ten words, and is interested in pictures and books. The three-year-old educable mentally retarded child with an IQ of 50 will be functioning at this level and thus capable of participating in a limited mathematical curriculum. The five-year-old educable mentally retarded child with an IQ of 80 will be functioning at a four-year-old mental age level. Such a child can tell his own age, recognize small sets, count groups, write at least one numeral, identify measuring instruments and money, and use a wide array of vocabulary associated with mathematics. It would be folly to deprive such children of early mathematical and prenumber experiences which are so vital to their eventual mastery of functional mathematics.

The lower mental age children will be able to profit to a limited degree from all eight categories (see pages 57-58), but their program will center mostly around perception, form, and vocabulary development.

The following section presents the objectives for the preprimary educable program. Again the reader is reminded that many of the suggestions will also be applicable to the trainable mentally retarded. Obviously, modifications in the style of teaching and the expectancies of growth will develop as the teacher provides for individual differences.*

OBJECTIVES

The general objective of the mathematics program for preprimary age retarded children is the development of basic number awareness. Number concepts emerge from the perceptions children form of their own bodies and the external world which whirls about them. Nevertheless, the children will need assistance in gaining an understanding of how numbers can be utilized to structure their environment in a quantitative fashion. The teacher's task, then, is to guide the development of an adequate body-image, accurate perception of space and form, and beginning use of numbers in organizing the maze of objects and activities which comprise the human milieu.

More specifically many students will:

1. begin to develop elementary skills in visual-motor coordination as well as to gain understandings of fundamental properties of spatial configurations
2. continue to develop body-image and improve in the ability to perceive position in space, and the spatial relationship of two or more objects, as well as to discriminate forms
3. begin to develop a vocabulary associated with mathematics and continue to grow in the general vocabulary which is the framework for such learnings
4. begin to utilize some numbers in games and songs and do some rote counting
5. begin to develop some indefinite cardinal number concepts and limited rational counting.

---

*See Chapter 8.

Early Childhood Mathematics Education 57

6. begin to make some use of ordinal numbers, although unable to seriate or order objects
7. begin to recognize some measurement instruments and gain some understanding of gross measurements of calendar, weight, capacity and length
8. begin to recognize money as a medium of exchange and understand money value with the ability to conduct transactions involving the use of coins
9. begin to develop abilities in combining and separating groups as well as to perform some simple number operations

DEVELOPMENTAL SEQUENCE OF MATHEMATICAL SKILLS

The beginning mathematics curriculum for young retardates can be initiated with a program that includes geometry, vocabulary associated with mathematics, number symbols, cardinal numbers, measurement, money and value, and additive and subtractive action. The specifics of such a program, as stated earlier, will depend on (1) the degree of intellectual impairment, (2) specific disabilities associated with learning; and (3) the background experiences of the pupils. The teacher should be so familiar with the developmental sequence that she is able to capitalize on spontaneous situations which permit the incidental study of mathematics, as well as to create more structured situations which may be systematically introduced, repeated, and reviewed in order to provide for a well-balanced, continuous curriculum.

The teacher will need to maintain an accurate record of the concepts and skills achieved by each pupil and plan additional experiences accordingly. A simple checklist can be very useful for this purpose. This list can also serve the purpose of a curriculum guide by merely adding possible teaching procedures and evaluative techniques. The eight categories introduced in Chapter 2 are elaborated for the preprimary child in Table 3.3.

TABLE 3.3
Checklist of Mathematics for the Preprimary Retardate

1. *Form and Perception*
   Basic manipulative experiences with geometric forms such as rectangles, squares, circles, and triangles should be correlated with perceptual-motor training (body-image, space relations, laterality, directionality) and motor coordination (running, jumping, crawling, matching, sorting, using coordination boards, scribbling, reproducing lines and circles, identifying body parts, imitating movement, matching forms to pictures).

2. *Vocabulary Associated with Mathematics*

big	tallest	narrow	off	in	down
little	thick	middle	ahead	out of	inside
long	thin	top	behind	next to	outside
short	wide	bottom	beside	heavy	all
tall	bunch	on	group	up	

3. *Number Symbols*
   use of numbers in play through rote songs and games
   symbol recognition and discrimination of numbers
   rote counting to 4
   writing numerals 1 and 2
   repeating three digits
4. *Cardinal Numbers*
   recognizing indefinite numbers such as "most" and "few"
   one-to-one correspondence
   one too many
   reproducing 1, 2, 3, 4
   set recognition of 2, 3, 4
5. *Ordinal Numbers*
   first, last
6. *Measurement*
   recognition of common measuring instruments
   concepts of day, night, age, older, younger, capacity, most
   discrimination of something heavy
7. *Money and Value*
   recognition of comparative values
   identification of penny
   discrimination of money
   knowledge of money by use
8. *Number Operations and Problem Solving*
   Additive and subtractive actions
      combine and separate combinations to four
      how much are 1 + 1?
      single responses to single questions

FORM AND PERCEPTION (GEOMETRY)

Geometry is the branch of mathematics which deals with the measurement, properties, and relationships of points, lines, angles, surfaces, and solids in space. The beginning concepts of space emerge from the child's perception of his own body and of objects within his immediate environment. The child learns that he is small enough to crawl under a kitchen chair but too large to crawl under the couch, that he can jump safely from the third step of the staircase but not from the eighth, that the light switch is within his reach but that the ceiling light bulb is not.

From these initial experiences with space and geometric properties the concept of number develops. The child learns that ten buttons require more space than two; that the toy dump truck can accommodate a certain number of building blocks and no more; and that weight, length, and time are organized into measurable standard units. Such understandings of the world emanate slowly from visual, audio, kinesthetic and tactile perceptions. Eventual success in arithmetic and other academic tasks will depend to a large extent upon the degree to which the environment has nurtured the development of these perceptual skills. Numbers are utilized by the child to organize his spatial perceptions and give quantitative structure to his world. Arithmetic, then, is a visual-spatial problem. Mathematics deals with groups of objects and the characteristics of groups and grouping processes. If the child has not constructed an adequate space concept, he will experience difficulty in dealing with groups which exist in space. Thus the rudiments of geometry are the key to an adult understanding of the space environs in which man lives, as well as being basic to the development of number concept in young children.

The significance of perceptual-motor learnings to achievement in arithmetic has been documented by such noted authorities as Strauss (1951, pp. 28-53) and Kephart (1960). There is no need to replicate their work here; however, a brief review may clarify the relationship between motor development and the spatial skills upon which mathematical concepts are built.

BASIC PERCEPTUAL-MOTOR TASKS

Body Image

The infant's first perceptions of the exterior world egress from experiments with his own body. The knowledge he gains concerning his physical being becomes the referent around which he constructs an orderly world. Objects are viewed as near, far, large, small, tall, and short in reference to his own body. The infant experiences heat and cold, pain and pleasure, kinesthetic and tactile impressions of his body, visual images, impressions of bodily functions, audio impressions of his own movement and sounds and those of others. The aggregate of perceptions gradually amalgamates into a total self-picture, or body image. A defective and incomplete body image is the mental construct to which all impressions of the exterior world are referred for interpretation. Thus, a disturbance in body image will cause a misinterpretation and stimulate faulty action. For example, the child pedaling his tricycle through the garage may bump the family car as a result of a poor estimate of the space required for the passage of his tricycle which resulted from a failure to comprehend his own body size. Or an infant crawling under a coffee table may raise her head too soon as a result of underestimating the space required to permit her to stand erect.

Assisting the child in developing an adequate body image is not the sole task of the arithmetic teacher, if indeed, it can be agreed that it is her responsibility to any degree. Nevertheless, much of the curriculum generally presented in the nursery school is appropriate for the development of body image. Incidental play in a cardboard packing carton, maneuvering through a chain of barrels, playing dress-up before a mirror, are examples of the type of experiences which are helpful in the development of body image.

Visual-Motor Synchronisms

The beginning of visual perceptual learnings emerges from a coordination of motor and visual impressions. The infant moves his arms and legs within the visual field and rudimentary coordinations are formed. By the end of the fifth week after birth the infant can follow a moving object with his eyes and by the end of four months eyes and hands have become synchronized for purposeful behavior. The process of mastering *eye-hand coordination* continues through the preschool years and minimal proficiency is a prerequisite to readiness for academic learnings.

Suggested Activities for Initial Training in Form and Perception

It has been stated that mathematics is a perceptual and spatial skill which develops from the child's accurate development of his own body image. Following is a series of activities which will assist the child in developing adequate body image and subsequent physical-perceptual development which will enable him to mature in his grasp of form. These are merely suggestive and should be regarded as representative rather than comprehensive exercises.

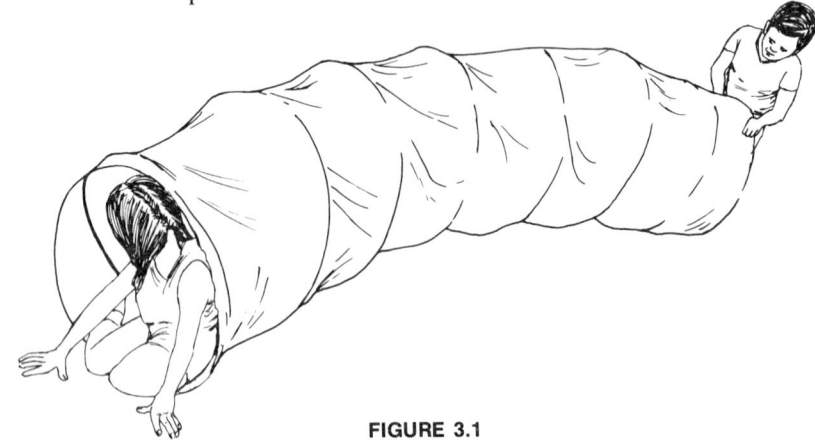

FIGURE 3.1

Early Childhood Mathematics Education 61

Tunnel Crawling. A very popular educational toy produced by a number of different companies is the "fun tunnel" or crawling maze. This imaginative, versatile device for active play may be set up either indoors or out. The maze is typically constructed out of wood, concrete blocks or bricks, and consists of two or more tunnels with numbered openings. It can be made to be adjustable in order to alter the path from the starting to finishing point. The canvas tunnel pictured in Figure 3.1 simply consists of a durable fabric secured to a spring steel frame. Children also enjoy building tunnels out of blocks. The child is encouraged to crawl through the opening from end to end. This will improve his kinesthetic response as well as assist him in the development of spatial relationship with respect to his own body size and position. Viewing and moving from one end to the other will help the child's depth perception as well.

FIGURE 3.2

Building Blocks. Building blocks such as those shown give the children a variety of opportunities to develop concepts of body image and gross motor coordination skills.

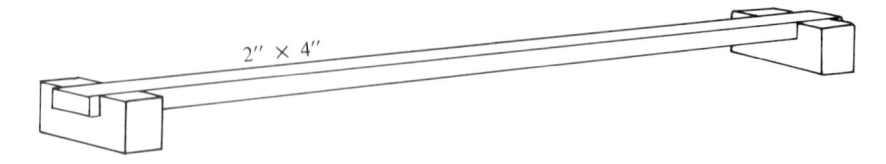

FIGURE 3.3. Walking Board made from a 2" × 4" with adjustments for both 2" and 4" walking surface.

Walking Board. Kephart (1960) has demonstrated the value of the walking board which is simply a modification of the familiar childhood exercise of walking a fence or the rails of a railroad track. A ten foot 2" x 4" is used. It is first laid with the wide side down on the floor, and later raised slightly off the floor. The child is taught to walk the board both backwards and forward in these positions. Preprimary retardates will probably progress no further than this, but the exercise can be made more difficult for older children by resting the beam on the narrow side and raising it from the floor. Some children will be unable to use the walking board due to poor coordination. In such cases, taped or painted lines on the floor can be substituted for the same purpose.

Climbing. An activity equally appealing to all children is climbing whether it be the family apple tree or a jungle gym. However, young retarded children may not be able to climb the usual outdoor challenges and thus a modified device may be necessary. Such a device (Dome Climber) is shown in Figure 3.4. Furthermore, with a sheet or blanket thrown over the top, the dome becomes a playhouse or hideaway.

FIGURE 3.4

Early Childhood Mathematics Education   63

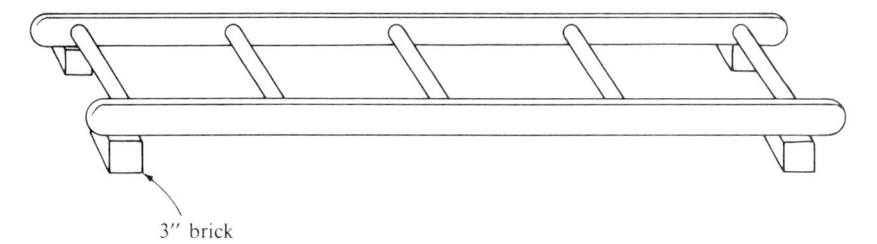

3" brick

Ladder Climbing and Stepping. For climbing, an ordinary handy-man's twelve foot to twenty foot ladder like those available in hardware departments may be used or a home-made ladder will do just as well. The ladder is first laid flat on the ground and the child is taught to place one foot before the other in separate, adjoining spaces. As the child improves in this skill, the ladder is raised slightly by resting it on a three inch brick. Gradually, the height may be increased to one-third the child's body height.

FIGURE 3.5

FIGURE 3.6

Stepping Tiles. Stepping tiles may be used to help the children improve their balance, gross motor coordination skills and their judgment of distances. Tiles are especially helpful because they are not raised off the floor and can easily be spaced to suit the child's stepping ability. This allows the teacher to concentrate on developing the sense of balance without depending on the children's strength as in climbing or introducing any fear of heights as in rope climbing. The teacher can approach the local floor covering dealer requesting vinyl floor tile samples 8" x 8" or larger. These can be placed in a variety of positions in the classroom. Initially, the child simply walks the arranged path, being careful not to step off the tiles. The game can be made more difficult by asking the children to step only on the tiles with the numeral 1, etc. Patterns of jumping can also add variety to the stepping tiles exercise.

Simon Says. A well-known game for young children can be used to teach the imitation of body movements and the location and names of body parts. The procedure is quite simple. The leader merely calls out such instructions as "Simon says hands up", etc. A command is to be followed only if the leader prefaces it with the remark "Simon says." When a child follows a command not so prefaced he is eliminated. The last remaining child wins the game and becomes the leader.

The Mail Box. This type of a device is especially helpful in developing gross motor and eye-hand motor coordination and form discrimination skills. The geometric shapes are relatively large and easy to handle so frustration is held to a minimum. There are many variations of this game, but the most well-known is the mail box. It consists of a container shaped and painted in the gay red, white and blue colors utilized by the post office. A set of geometric forms are provided which may be

Early Childhood Mathematics Education 65

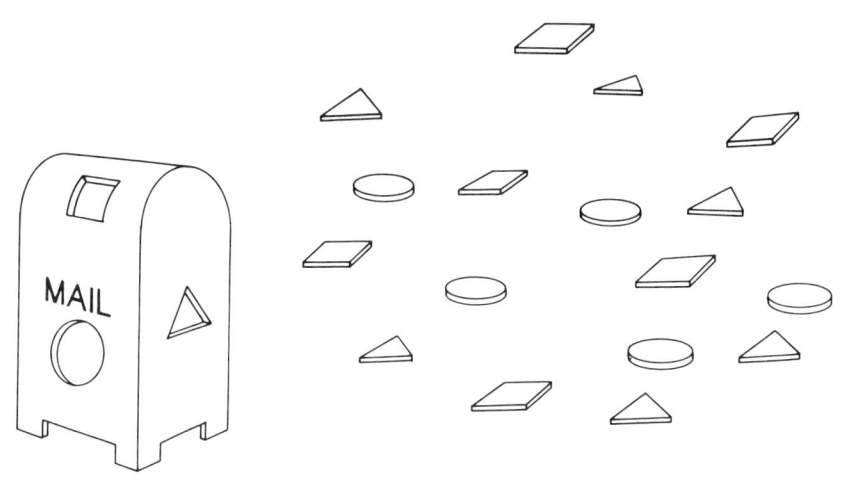

FIGURE 3.7

deposited in the mail box only if inserted into the slot of the same shape while held in the correct position.

FIGURE 3.8

FIGURE 3.8. There are a variety of self-correcting teaching aids similar to the one pictured here that can be used to teach the sets from one to five. Devices of this design are especially useful because they automatically demonstrate to the children the difference between cardinal and ordinal numbers. The children are encouraged to develop the ideas of sets and correspondence by playing with toys of this type.

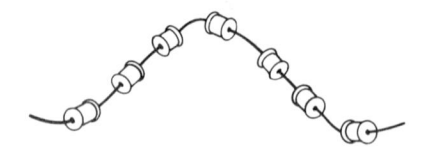

FIGURE 3.9

Spool Play. In this exercise, regular household empty spools or commercially available beads can be used. A variation of these are pop beads which are constructed of plastic and simply snap together and pop apart. The child begins simply by placing the beads on the string or snapping them together. A few children at this level may be able to arrange the beads in a pattern according to shape or color.

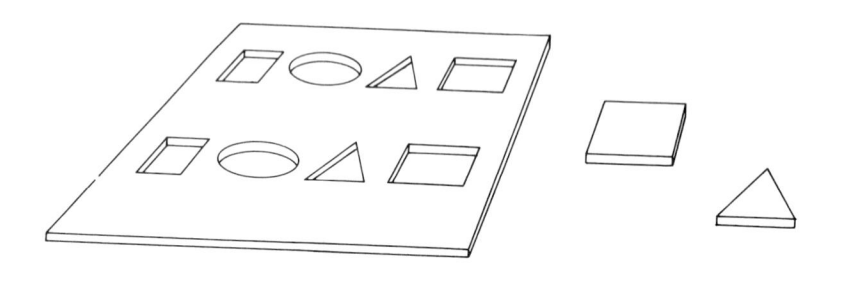

FIGURE 3.10

Coordination Board. Simple form boards such as the one shown in Figure 3.10 are will assist the children in refining their fine eye-hand motor skills. The shapes are thin and somewhat more difficult to manage than those used in the mail box. A typical coordination board would consist of eight color coded pieces, including two each of a circle, square, rectangle, and triangle. To begin, the teacher demonstrates the removal and replacement of one piece at a time. Then the child is asked to participate. It will not be long before the child will be removing all eight pieces simultaneously and replacing them in the same shape in the board.

Matching and Sorting Three Dimensional Shapes. Using pieces similar to those found in the coordination board ask the child to "find one like mine" as you show one form. A wide variety of objects such as large buttons and small buttons, spools, paper clips, and so forth can be used in sorting exercises. Set out a box with a number of such items

Early Childhood Mathematics Education 67

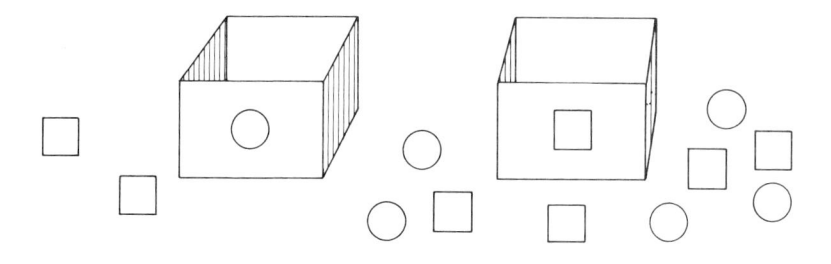

FIGURE 3.11

and instruct the child to place all the like objects (demonstrating and naming) like this in that box and all the like objects (again demonstrate and name) like this in the other box.

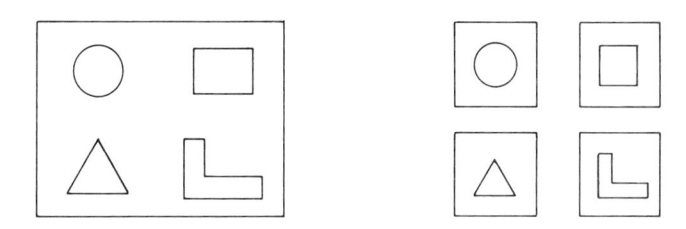

FIGURE 3.12

Form Discrimination Cards. In exercises of this type the child progresses from three dimensional shapes to geometric forms consisting of line drawings on tag board. This is a more difficult task for the children because they must rely totally upon visual clues without the automatic confirmation of their response provided by the form boards and mail box. The child is shown a response card with a number of geometric designs. The teacher asks the child to examine the figures on the card and then handing the child a stimulus card says "find one just like this one." The range of configuration and forms is limitless. These cards can be easily constructed by the teacher with a felt marker and white cardboard.

Dot-to-Dot Games. Even before the child can read numerals or has learned the natural order of numbers, dot-to-dot exercises are of value. They develop eye-hand motor coordination and the children's spatial perception. The illustration shows a technique of making a "happy face" simply by proceeding from one dot to the next. Similar exercises of

happy face   line   square   triangle

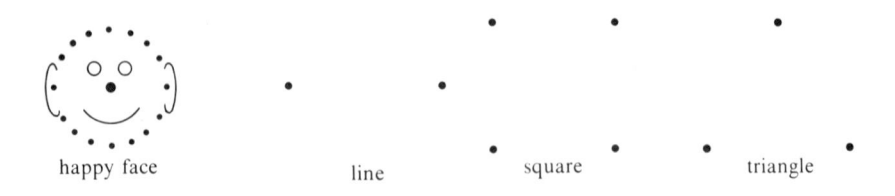

FIGURE 3.13

connecting dots to make straight lines, curves, or squares can be easily constructed.

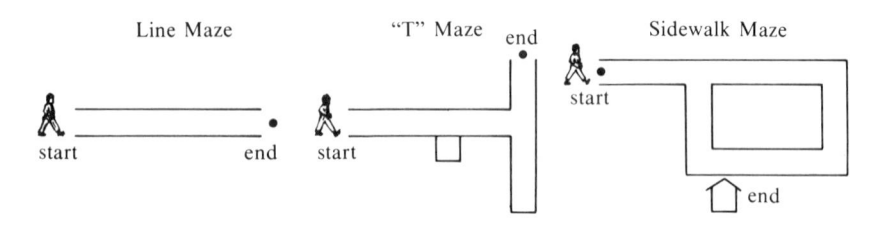

FIGURE 3.14

The Maze. The maze is used to strengthen the children's perception and fine motor coordination skills. The simplest maze requires the child to merely draw a straight line from one point to another within the confines of two parallel lines. The "T" maze and sidewalk maze are introduced next. For example, in using these instruct the child to take the little boy home by drawing a line with his crayon from the boy to the house, being careful not to get off the sidewalk.

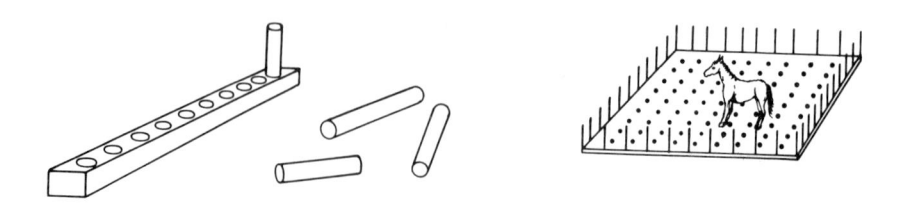

FIGURE 3.15

Peg Patterns. Peg boards are found in most kindergartens and nearly all primary classrooms for the mentally retarded. The manipulation of pegs provides another channel for refining perception coordination. A

Early Childhood Mathematics Education 69

series of holes are drilled in columns and rows (usually ten holes × ten holes). Pegs of five or six different colors are provided. The teacher begins by asking the child to remove the pegs from this board and place them in a random arrangement. A later step is to require that a certain pattern be imitated. A game can be made out of this by giving names to the pegs and using toys. For example, the teacher says, "See the horse. Build a fence so the horse will not run away." Marble boards are a variation of this aid.

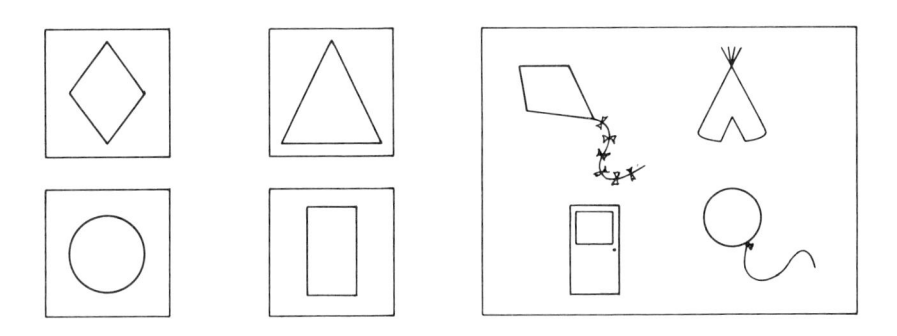

FIGURE 3.16

Forms to Pictures. A response card with different forms is presented to the child. Stimulus cards with pictures of the same general configurations as the forms are presented and the child matches the picture to the form. For example, have the child match a face to a circle, a kite to a diamond, a teepee to a triangle.

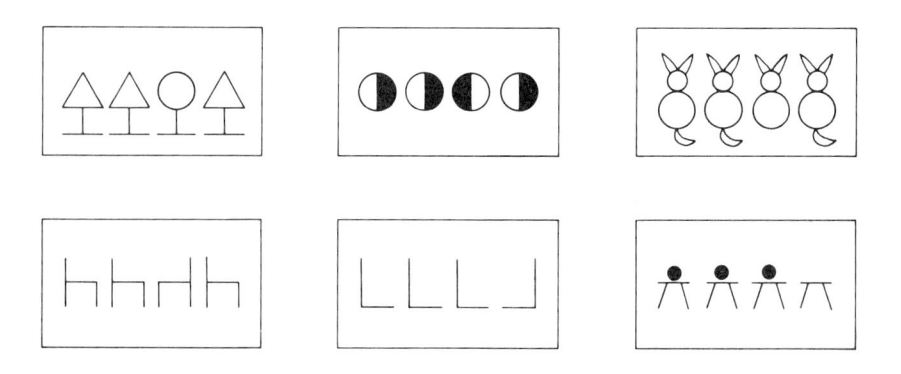

FIGURE 3.17

Dissimilar Forms. Working with quantities and numbers requires a recognition of like as well as unlike elements. This exercise will help the children develop visual discriminatory skills. Present the child with a series of plates with four pictures, one of which is different from the other three. "Here is a card with some pictures. See this one is not like the rest. Put your finger on the one not like the rest." Present subsequent cards and say, "Show me the one not like the others. Show me the one with your finger." The first plates should be simple, increasing in complexity as the child improves in discriminative skill.

FIGURE 3.18

Spatial Arrangements. With a collection of dime store toys, the teacher can train her youngsters in spatial arrangements. For example, the teacher places a small toy dog in front of a cardboard fence instructing the child to take his dog and fence and place them just like yours. The task can be made more difficult by adding more figures and increasing the complexity of the relative positions.

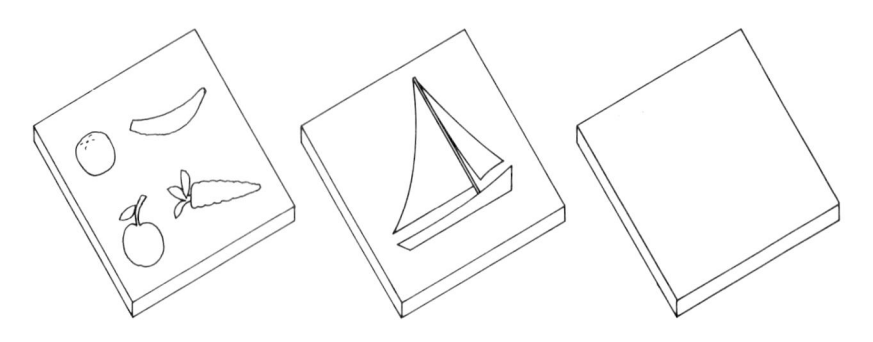

FIGURE 3.19

Early Childhood Mathematics Education 71

Puzzles. There are available an abundance of simple preschool puzzles ranging from single one piece wooden inlays to complex multi-piece interlocking types. These are designed to develop form perception and refine motor coordination. Preprimary children will usually not progress beyond six piece interlocking puzzles. Wooden, plastic, or those of other durable construction are recommended.

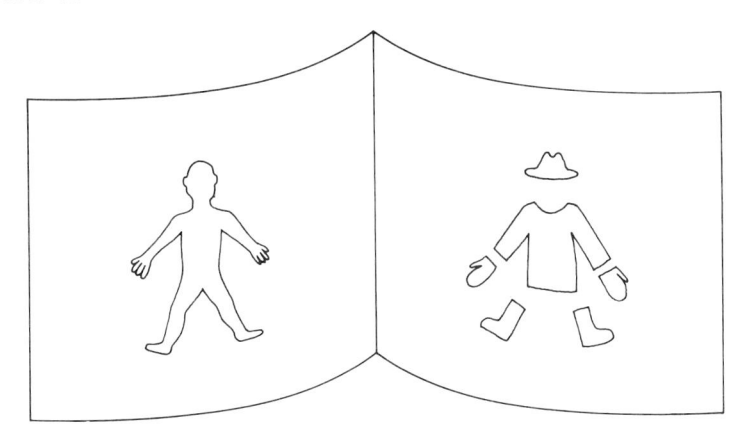

FIGURE 3.20

Punch-Outs, Stick'ems and Pastings. Most dime stores carry a variety of paper doll punch-out books. The people figures are made of cardboard and the clothes are printed on paper. Most are perforated to make their removal simple. Some newer books of this type have pictures which the child assembles by affixing the sub-parts to a master sheet.

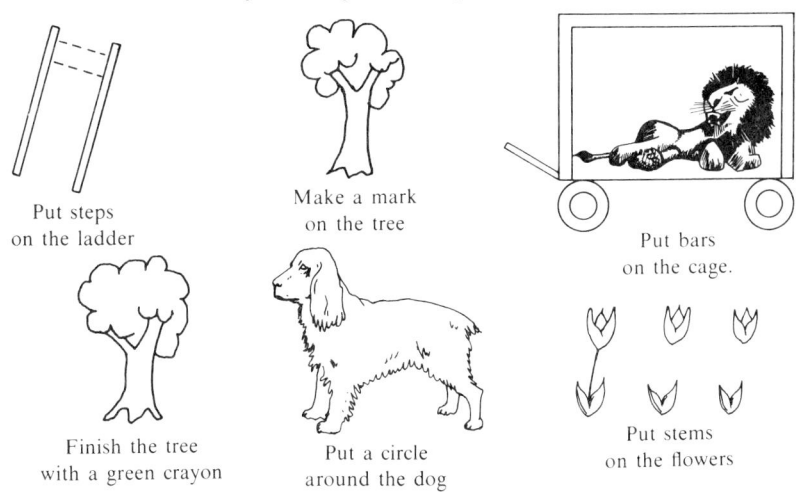

Put steps on the ladder

Make a mark on the tree

Put bars on the cage.

Finish the tree with a green crayon

Put a circle around the dog

Put stems on the flowers

FIGURE 3.21

Scribbles, Lines, Circles. The coordination of eye and hand is more enjoyable for the child when he discovers the crayon or pencil. Any mother of toddlers can attest to the child's delight at marking with bright color crayons over the bedroom walls! Marking lines on paper becomes a letter to grandmother while a circle on the chalkboard is really a "happy face." A number of examples are presented in Figure 3.21.

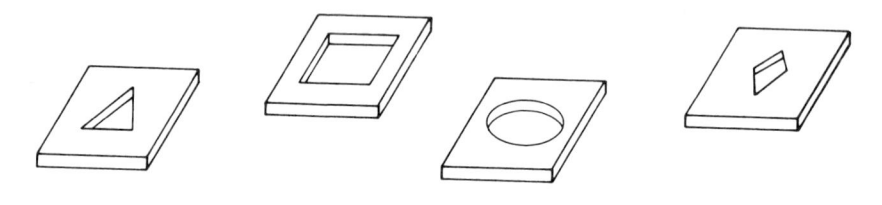

FIGURE 3.22

Tracing Forms. Another example of an eye-hand motor coordination task is tracing. The illustration in Figure 3.22 shows four forms. The child can be instructed to trace the form by holding his pencil or crayon against the outline as he moves along the configuration.

Finger Play. Finger play will foster development of eye-hand motor coordination and will help the children prepare for counting tasks by focusing their attention on the fingers as discrete digits. This will be particularly valuable as the children learn to enumerate sets of objects by counting on their fingers.

Most young children enjoy using finger play with popular rhymes. Here are several examples of traditional finger play activities which are especially suited for young mentally retarded children.

HICKORY, DICKORY, DOCK

Hickory Dickory, Dock!
  (Raise the left arm over the head to represent a tall clock.)
The mouse ran up the clock;
  (Raise right hand and imitate a mouse running up the clock.)
The clock struck one, and down he ran.
  (Clap hands as one is said.)
Hickory Dickory, Dock!

TWO LITTLE BLACKBIRDS

Two little blackbirds sitting on a hill.
  (Close fists, thumbs up.)

Early Childhood Mathematics Education   73

One named Jack and one named Jill,
  (Waggle thumbs.)
Fly away, Jack!
  (Move right hand behind back.)
Fly away, Jill!
  (Move left hand behind back.)
Come back, Jack!
  (Bring right hand in front.)
Come back, Jill!
  (Bring left hand in front.)
Two little blackbirds sitting on a hill,
  (Closed fists with thumbs up, bobbing in front of child.)
One named Jack and one named Jill.
  (Waggle thumbs.)

THIS LITTLE PIG

This little pig went to the market,
This little pig stayed home,
This little pig had roast beef,
This little pig had none.
This little pig cried wee, wee, wee,
  all the way home.

VOCABULARY ASSOCIATED WITH MATHEMATICS

The children initially will use terms related to quality and quantity which have no precise numerical significance. However, they will gradually begin to understand and use meaningful number vocabulary. At this level his terminology will relate to the use and comprehension of quantitative words such as all, big, little, up, down, heavy, and so forth. A suggested list is presented in Table 3.3. Emphasis should be placed upon experiences that demand number judgments in every day activities such as playing, eating, dressing, cleaning up, grouping, and measuring heights and weights.

PICTURES TO BUILD VOCABULARY

Pictures can be a valuable aid in teaching number related vocabulary. Line drawings such as the ones shown in Figure 3.23 are particularly useful because they avoid the clutter found in many picture books which may lead to perceptual confusions. As the pictures are shown to the children ask such questions as, "Which is the *big* balloon? Which is the little balloon? Which bird is *in* the cage? Which cage is *empty?* Which bird is *beside* the cage? What is *high* in the sky? What is *next to* the tree?"

FIGURE 3.23

More mature children and those without perceptual deficits will enjoy working with colorful, active pictures such as those found in childrens' books and popular magazines. Pictures of this type may be mounted on tag board and treated with a preservative. The advantage of these pictures over simple line drawings is that they are much more attractive and require no artistic ability on the part of the teacher. A collection including such pictures as *large* and *small* animals; *tall* and *short* buildings; *heavy* and *light* objects should be developed.

BODY IMAGE, MOVEMENT, AND VOCABULARY

It has been mentioned frequently that the body serves as the point of reference for spatial direction. Thus, using the body in the teaching of vocabulary related to such concepts as position, size, and shape is quite natural. The teachers might say to their students, "Watch me (raising her arms toward the ceiling). My hands are *up*. Put your hands *up*. Watch me (lowering her arms to her side). My hands are *down*." At this point the children can raise or lower their hands on verbal command without demonstration. Then follow such commands as "Girls' hands up, boys' hands down" and so forth. "Bill and Joe lift the box up. Sally put the flower down." "Put your hands *over* your heads, *under* your desks, *behind* your backs, *in* your pockets. *Open* your eyes, *close* your eyes," and so forth.

VOCABULARY BUILDING THROUGH SORTING, MATCHING
AND REPRODUCING

Sorting, grouping, matching and reproducing activities are also excellent techniques of developing the vocabulary associated with mathematics. Here are some examples.

Early Childhood Mathematics Education 75

Sorting Sticks. Have the children separate a box of sticks of two distinct lengths into two separate containers. "Place all the *long* sticks in this box and all the *short* sticks in that box." Prepare another collection of sticks of two distinct widths and have the children place all the *wide* pieces in one box and the *narrow* pieces in another. A similar activity could be developed for *thick* and *thin.*

Sorting Boxes. Collect a set of jewelry boxes and fill them with *light* and *heavy* contents. For example, put cotton in several boxes and sand in some others. Have the children separate the boxes by their weight. Using the same boxes, but being certain they are of different sizes, have the children sort them by size while ignoring the weight. "Put the *big* ones here and the *little* ones there."

Paper Dolls. Use paper dolls and clothes available at variety stores. Have the children place all the *big* clothes with the mommy doll and all the *little* clothes with the baby doll.

Rock Collections. Little boys especially enjoy playing with rocks. A rock collection may have specimens which are *large, small, heavy, light, thick,* and *thin.*

Reproducing Forms. Helping children reproduce relative shapes, sizes and positions is another approach. "Blow your red balloon *big.* Now make the blue one *little.* Make a *big* circle, then make a *small* one. Put a mark *on* the big circle, put a mark *inside* the little box, now put your pencil *down.*"

VOCABULARY BUILDING THROUGH WORKSHEETS

Worksheets with a range of illustrations such as the tall tree, narrow street, or thin man may be utilized. The teacher teaches the children to mark the appropriate item.

Mark the tall tree.

Mark the thin man.

PLAYING GAMES TO BUILD VOCABULARY

The children will delight in playing games that develop their vocabulary. There are a number of group activities which may be used. The game described here is a popular one with most preschoolers, called *Guess My Name*.

The children form a single circle around one blindfolded child in the center. The other children march around the child in a circle, singing the verse:

> I'm tall, so very tall,
> I'm short, so very short
> Sometimes I am tall;
> Sometimes I am short;
> Guess what I am now!

As the children walk and say "tall," "very tall," "short," or "very short," they stretch or stoop down to act out the adjective in question. At the end of the verse, the teacher signals the children in the circle to assume either a stretching or a stooping position. The child in the center then guesses which position the children are in. If he chooses correctly, he remains in the center; if not, he chooses another player to be in the circle.

NUMBER SYMBOLS

The child's use of numbers in play and routinized situations is not necessarily related to an understanding of numbers. Children enjoy using numbers well before they are ready to participate in the rational use of the numbers. The preschool age child will delight in a counting game even though his use of numbers is erroneous, such as "Ready? One, Three, Two, Jump!" The child may be able to discriminate between written letters and numerals. For example, he may be able to identify the numerals indicating page numbers, or to distinguish a group of numbers from groups of letters, configurations, and nonsense symbols printed on a card. The teacher will need to build upon the child's knowledge of number symbols in order to prepare him for the rational use of numbers.

A typical process for initiating a mastery of elemental number symbols is through simple games and rhythm activities. Rote auditory memory for numbers may be developed through a marching game. Ask the students to form a line and instruct them to march to the cadence of one, two, and to count aloud with you as they march. Later the count can be extended to a 1 - 2, 3 - 4 cadence. The students may be taught simple rhymes such as the popular:

ONE, TWO! BUCKLE YOUR SHOE

One, two! Buckle your shoe.
Three, four! Shut the door.
Five, six! Pick up sticks.
Seven, eight! Close the gate.
Nine, ten! Do it again.

ONE, TWO, THREE, FOUR

One, two, three, four
I buy candy at the store.
Five, six, seven, eight
Hurry home, can't be late.

One, two, three, four, five
I just caught a worm alive
Six, seven, eight, nine, ten
I just fed him to our hen.

ONE, TWO THREE, FOUR, FIVE

One, two, three, four, five,
I caught a hare alive;
Six, seven, eight, nine, ten,
I let her go again.

ONE FOR THE MONEY

One for the money, (Hold up one finger.)
Two for the show, (Hold up two fingers.)
Three to make ready, (Hold up three fingers.)
Four to go. (Hold up four fingers.)

Some children will readily learn to count by rote to five or ten with repetitive practice. Not infrequently parents have drilled their children at home, making this part of the teacher's task much easier.

Exercises which assist children in associating oral symbols with printed numerals would be another aspect of number symbol teaching.

The following lessons are suggested channels for achieving the objectives related to number symbols.

Number Symbol Recognition. The objective of this exercise is to teach youngsters the recognition and discrimination of number symbols. A simple card with four sets of configurations can easily be constructed and shown to the child. This will help the children improve visual

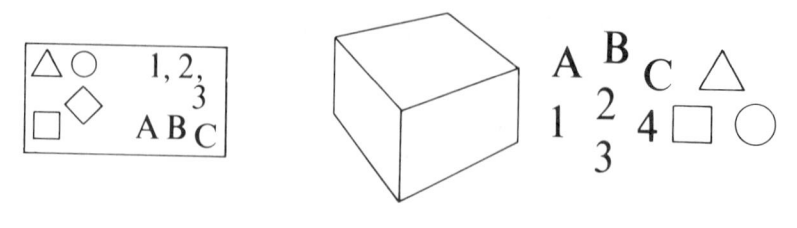

FIGURE 3.24

discrimination of forms and number symbols. A similar, but more complex, exercise requires the children to actively separate forms, letters, numerals, and nonsense configurations. The children can match, sort, or classify these according to their developmental levels. Some children may be limited to separating the numerals from the other symbols. The teacher would have these children place all the number symbols in the box and leave all the other symbols out of the box. Children at a more advanced stage may be able to sort the symbols by a more complex system. The teacher would have these children place all the letters in one group, all the numerals in a second group, all the geometric forms in a third group and the nonsense symbols into a fourth group.

Rhythm Train. Give the children two bamboo poles about ten to twelve inches in length (door molding, conduit pipe, or other light weight material will do). Have them line up in groups of two to five. Then say, "Now we are going to play choo, choo (train)." Swing the poles back and forth in cadence and have them count "One, two! Choo, choo!" or some rhyme such as "One, two, three, four: Hurry to the ice cream store."

Numerals to Oral Number Words. Using the same exercise as above, place large flash cards in front of the room. With a marker, point to the numerals as the child says them. Then, as a follow-up activity, merely hold the flash card and say, "What is the word for 3 (2,4,1)?" or "Show me the two, one, four, three."

Kinesthetics and Numerals. The children can engage in a wide range of kinesthetic movements or rhythms as they say their numbers. For example, "Clap your hands above your head when I say one; hands on your hips on two; hands on your toes on three; hands on your knees and straighten up on four. Ready—one, two, three, four!" Children can do other exercises and movements in a similar fashion; rotating trunks, swinging arms, marching in place or formation are but a few possibilities.

The Number Cards and Lines. Pass out cards or mimeographed papers with the numerals in random order. Have the child touch and say the

Early Childhood Mathematics Education

numbers. As a variation, have the youngsters cover one of the numbers of a fellow classmate's ordered number card. "Which number is covered?"

Numerals. A variety of aids may be used to help the children learn to write their numerals. Several of these ideas are illustrated below.

Numerals cut out of stiff tagboard

Have the children trace around the numeral and say the number simultaneously.

Numerals made with sandpaper

Have the children trace over the sandpaper numeral. Simply mount the numerals cut out of sheets of sandpaper on cards made of tagboard. This will enhance the children's kinesthetic sensations.

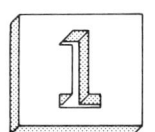

Numeral stencils

Have the children trace the numerals with a crayon using the stencil as an aid.

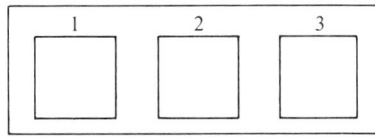

Numeral frames

Have the children write their numbers within the margins of a tagboard frame. Some children will need to trace over a numeral printed by the teacher, but the limits of the frame will be sufficient for most children.

80   *Early Childhood Mathematics Education*

1. milk
2. cookies
3. napkins
4. straws

FIGURE 3.25

Ferris Wheel. Using a ferris wheel, bicycle tire, roulette wheel or some other spinning device, have the children with the winning number match their cards to the wheel. Motivation can be added by saying such things as "*Three* can pass out the milk; *one* can take the attendance slip to the office," and so on.

Number Boxes. Small jewelry boxes may be obtained from local merchants or brought from home by the children. The teacher fills the boxes with sets of objects from one to three in number and prints the corresponding numeral on the bottom of the box. The children count the number of objects in each box and check their response by referring to the numeral written on the bottom. The variety of miniature toys and other interesting objects which may be hidden in the boxes make this a most delightful game for the children.

Concentration. The numerals from one through five are printed in bold black print on four 4" x 4" squares of plywood or tag board and placed face down on a table. The children gather around and one at a time turn up two cards. If the cards are identical, the child keeps them and gets another turn. If the cards are different, the cards are returned to the original face down position and the next student plays. Note that the name of the numerals need not be used, but rather the simple question, "Do they look alike?"

FIGURE 3.26

Number Puzzles. Numbers painted on plywood or tile squares may be cut with a jig saw into an appropriate number of pieces; the number one is uncut, the number two into two pieces, and the number three into three pieces, and the number four into four pieces. The children try to fit the appropriate pieces together.

CARDINAL NUMBER

The next step is to associate the rote numeral with a corresponding set.* This may be accomplished by asking the child to reproduce both definite and indefinite numbers. "Give me a *few* pieces of chalk; put two blocks here; make three marks on your paper." The child may be asked such questions as "How many sticks are on your desk? How many fingers am I holding up?" By asking the question "how many?" the teacher introduces cardinal numbers. Her purpose is to assist the child in the use of numbers as quantity. The concept of quantity involves relating groups of objects through a one-to-one correspondence with the natural order of numbers.

The understanding of quantity develops at an early age. The mother of an eighteen month-old can attest to the infant's skill in selecting the larger of two cookies. A two-year-old girl was observed by the author playing with a group of three beads. One of the beads was knocked out of her field of vision beside another toy. She noticed the bead was missing, thus indicating her recognititon of the total group. A five-year-old trainable mentally retarded youngster, known to the author, had a mental age of thirty months. He had a strong taste for stick pretzels. On one occasion, he was offered one pretzel and said, "No! More please!" One more pretzel was given and this time he responded, "Oh, please! Two bunch!" This youngster was well aware of the difference between one and many. Some concepts of set recognition had developed. The same youngster was able to distribute candy to his friends on the basis of one-to-one correspondence. Most preprimary age retardates will be able to select groups of one, two, three, and four from a larger collection of blocks and many will develop instantaneous set recognition up to four. In other words, these youngsters will develop a real awareness of oneness, twoness, threeness, and fourness.

The teacher will need a supply of materials and devices to assist her instruction. Most of the items can be collected from home or constructed in the classroom. The fortunate teacher may have access to an industrial arts class to assist with such projects. In developing such materials, several principles should be adhered to:

1. Is the device simple? A teaching aid should not require complex and lengthy discussion for young children.
2. Is it durable? Flimsy construction can result in "one shot" exercises. The aid should hold up under the abuses of busy little hands.
3. Does it have value for mathematics? The aid should promote understanding and be motivating. It must relate to a concept or skill which can be presented in a timely fashion in keeping with principles of sequence.
4. Is it practical? An aid that requires hours of planning and construction is not practical if the effort is not justified in terms of value derived.
5. Is it self-evaluative? Aids should be able to be used with a minimum of instruction and supervision. The device has more value to the teacher and pupil if the child can check the accuracy of his own response.
6. Is it motivating? Devices which are boring to children because of a lack of challenge are of little value even if they provide needed repetition and retraining.

Often, a number of inexpensive aids are given to teachers. The list is not exhaustive but does represent a sampling of desirable teaching aids. A later section in this chapter will present a list of recommended supplies not specifically mentioned in the nine categories of mathematical concepts and skills.

Counting Box (Number Box). The only way the children can advance their counting skills and number concepts is through lots of practice. A device for adding to the novelty of counting experiences is the counting box. The teacher should fill the box with a variety of stimulating toys and objects which help maintain the children's interest level. In this activity a cardboard box covered with contact paper with the dividers remaining is well-suited to the purpose; the shipping carton for baby foods is ideal. The teacher will then need to collect a host of objects for counting. Plastic sandwich bags may be used to store these items in the box's various compartments; and each compartment can be filled with a group of items which are identical for all the children in the class. The teacher will find this collection helpful in other areas besides mathematics. The greatest value of the arithmetic counting box is that is enables all of the youngsters to manipulate materials identical to the teacher's.

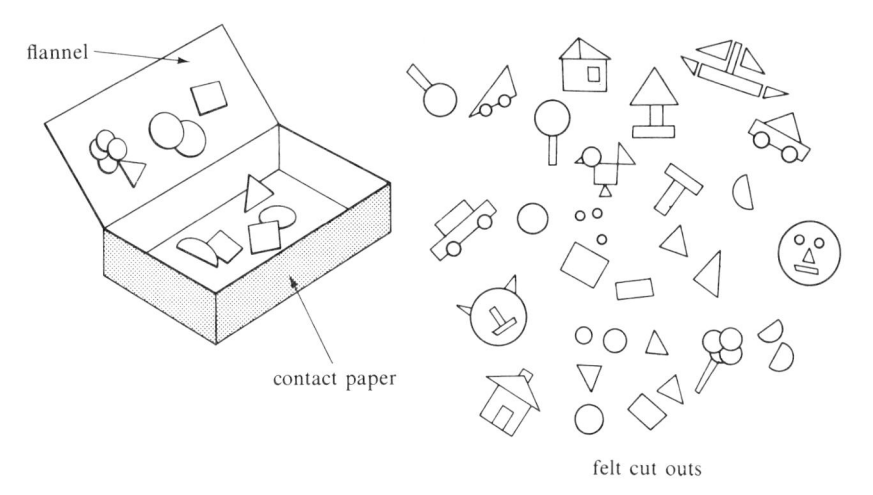

FIGURE 3.27

The Flannel Box. The use of the flannel board with the large number of commercially available cut-outs is well known. A variation of the flannel board is the flannel box. It is constructed out of a cigar box (or other sizes do just as well). The inside of the lid is covered with flannel and a variety of felt pieces are inside. As with the counting box the value is that *all* of the children can manipulate identical cut-outs in unison with the teacher's. The felt cut-outs should be constructed in multiples so that they are all the same.

Picture File. Children learn easily through pictures. A well-developed and maintained picture file is essential to effective teaching of the mentally retarded. The teacher should plan a collection of pictures which illustrate simple number ideas. At the preprimary level the pictures should present such concepts as many, few, more, one, two, and three. The picture file may also be used to build the children's vocabulary associated with mathematics. Samples would be pictures of a group of three children, a tall man and short lady, two ducks and one dog. Uncluttered pictures should be used in the initial phases of instruction, but more complex and colored pictures will be useful with more mature children. The picture file will serve as a teacher resource for bulletin boards, small group instruction and individualized tutoring. Some pictures will need to be mounted and others may easily be stored in file folders. Out-dated mail order catalogs, magazines, and posters are excellent sources of pictures.

Number Illustrations. Even with broad collections of concrete miniature objects (counting box), felt materials and pictures, the teacher will still

84   *Early Childhood Mathematics Education*

need to resort to her own drawings for flash cards and work sheets. A number of simple designs well within the capacity of the least talented artist are presented in Figure 3.28.

FIGURE 3.28

Early Childhood Mathematics Education 85

FIGURE 3.29

Number Book. Allow each child to build a number book which displays sets one through four, or as needed. The youngster can select the pictures from magazines, posters, and other sources; one apple, two wagons, and so forth.

One-to-One Correspondence. A muffin tin, egg carton, or similar container may be used. The child places one egg (or other object) in each space. Two, three, and four-to-one correspondence can be taught in a similar fashion.

Indefinite Number. A muffin tin or tray can be used for this exercise, too. The procedure is to instruct the youngster to "put a few in here . . . now more over there; take a few . . . take many; show me a few . . . show me many (using pictures or objects); which has many . . . few . . . more?"

Recognizing Two (Three, Four). Begin with sets of two. "This is two; you pick up two." Pictures can be collected and mounted. "How many in this one?" Additional sets can be handled in a similar fashion.

Counting Pan. A muffin tin can be used as a sorting game. The child is given a number of objects such as beans, nails, paper clips, miniature baby dolls. In each compartment a sign is placed as shown in Figure 3.30. The child fills each tin according to the directions. This will help develop the ability to count rationally and to produce sets accurately.

86   *Early Childhood Mathematics Education*

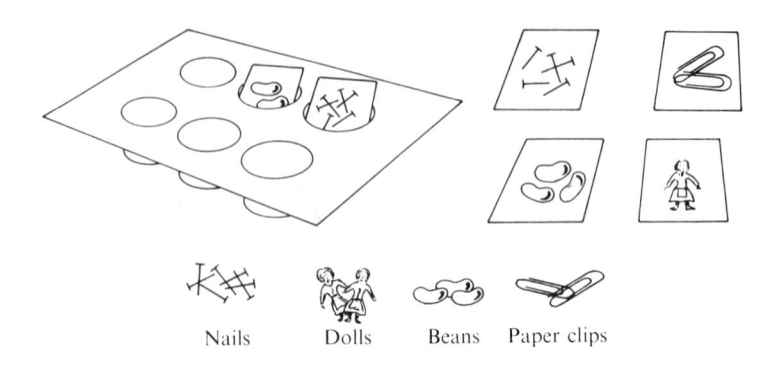

Nails   Dolls   Beans   Paper clips

FIGURE 3.30

FIGURE 3.31

Sorting Bins. This teaching aid is similar to the counting pan because it attempts to develop the idea of sets, but the use of pictures has the advantage of encouraging the children to recognize the number of a set as a whole without counting. To construct a sorting bin, use two pieces of one inch board and fasten them together at right angles with screws or small nails. Attach five pieces of masonite to serve as dividers. Construct a series of numeral cards from one to four. Make a series of set cards for each numeral.

Use illustrations like those shown on page 8,6. Place the numerals in slots above the partitions and have the children sort the cards placing the appropriate cards in the correct bins. Later the numerals may be placed out of order to give additional practice.

ORDINAL NUMBERS

Young children are easily confused by concepts of cardinal and ordinal numbers. Not only must youngsters learn to respond to the question, "How many?" but also to the question, "What position?" in an orderly arrangement of objects. If three objects in a row are counted from one end to another, object one and three are at the ends, and two is in the middle. The teacher should note that this is the ordinal use of number names. The idea of position can be expressed without using the terms *first, second, third,* and *fourth.* It is important that children learn early in their number experiences that position is relative to a starting point and some system of order.

It could reasonably be expected that some preprimary retarded children could master the use of the number names to indicate position at least to four. Further, many will be able to apply the terms *first, middle, last,* and *second* to ordered groups. More complex concepts of ordinal number should well be delayed for instruction at a more advanced level.

Incidental Teaching. Many opportunities will arise for the teacher to use ordinal number in incidental situations. "May, you be first in line today. Bill, will you wait to be last and turn off the light?"

Number Stories. Preprimary age children are very fond of simple stories. There are many elementary books which have major number concepts. A good example of this, appropriate to both preprimary and primary level is, *James and the Rain* (Kuskin, 1957). Jim starts out on a rainy day to find a game to play. First he meets a cow, then two ducks, three frogs, four birds and so forth. Such a story would permit simple illustration through the flannel board. It is the type of story that the children could learn and retell themselves. Teacher-made stories are likewise valuable and easily invented.

Object Arrangements. The counting box may easily be used for teaching ordinal number. A set of toy cars might be arranged on a race track. The teacher may ask the children, "What car is first? Which is last?"

Picture File. Pictures which illustrate relative positions are useful. "Which boy is in the middle? Show me who is second. Is the mommy last?"

Sequential Directions. In teaching this concept, one would begin with simple two-sequence directions but later could say to a child, "First put the pencil on my desk, next open the door, and then go sit in the red chair."

MEASUREMENT

The measurement category is highly related to other topics, and particularly to perception of form and development of vocabulary. The children will acquire and use vocabulary related to shape, size, capacity, distance, and time, with such words as: big, fat, little, long, round, high, cup, heavy, in, out.

Children of this age will begin to develop an understanding and awareness of variation in temperature. It is cold today, it was hot yesterday, it is freezing in the winter. They will begin to understand the uses of various measuring instruments; that weight can be read from the bathroom scales, that the temperature may be read from a thermometer, that time can be read from a clock. Appropriate concepts are, "There will be no school tomorrow. Your birthday is next week. John is five years old. This one is heavy."

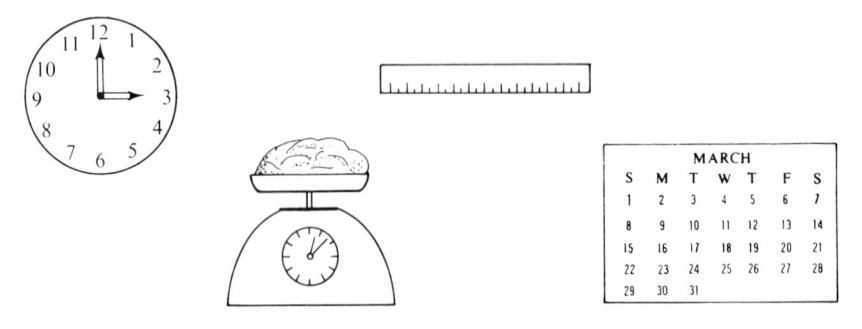

FIGURE 3.32

Identification of Measuring Instruments. Have children show you what tells us the time, where the calendar is, or the ruler.

Early Childhood Mathematics Education 89

FIGURE 3.33

Container Filling. The children will begin to develop some idea of capacity by playing with a variety of containers of different sizes and shapes. Some children may begin to discover the relationships between size, shape and capacity through simple manipulative activities. Water and sand are untidy contents from the teacher's point of view, but delightful from the children's perspective. Collect a variety of containers of different sizes and shapes. Have the children manipulate and pour with them.

Water and Sand Play. Two items which plague custodians but are of great value to preprimary children are the water box and the sand pile. The concepts of capacity can easily be incorporated into the children's play involving weighing and measuring.

Run, Jump, Throw. Have children measure the distance that youngsters jump, who ran the fastest, whose ball was thrown the farthest.

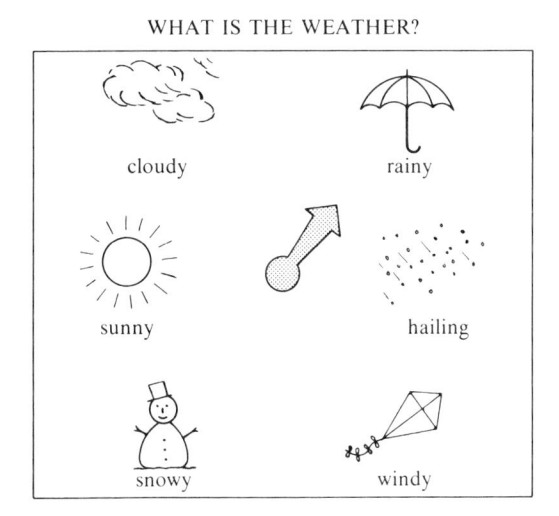

WHAT IS THE WEATHER?

cloudy   rainy

sunny   hailing

snowy   windy

FIGURE 3.34

Wall Thermometer. These are available commercially and can be adjusted by the children with the teacher's assistance. Generally, attention is merely given to the gross relation between the temperature and the thermometer. The illustration in Figure 3.34 is of a teacher-made weather indicator.

The Clock. Call attention to the clock and the relationship of it to various activities during the day. The teacher will use the clock to determine activities. "It is time for recess."

Books. Such books as *All Kinds of Time* (Behr, 1950) and *Mike Mulligan and His Steam Shovel* (Burton, 1939) can be meaningfully discussed if the teacher is careful not to impair the enjoyment of the stories by overemphasizing number words and concepts.

Calendar. An attractive caldendar should be pasted up on the wall and discussed in terms of days, dates, special holidays, birthdays, and celebrations.

MONEY AND VALUE

The vocabulary associated with money should be emphasized. Identification of a penny and the value of money as a medium of exchange is introduced. Such money experiences are provided as they become functional according to the child's skill level and level of maturity. In all activities with money, it is imperative that real coins be used at all times. Toy money is not an adequate substitute and serves to confuse the retardate since it lacks the appearance and genuine feel of the real thing. The ability to discriminate coins depends to a great extent upon the recognition of physical differences and the children should have ample opportunities to distinguish among them.

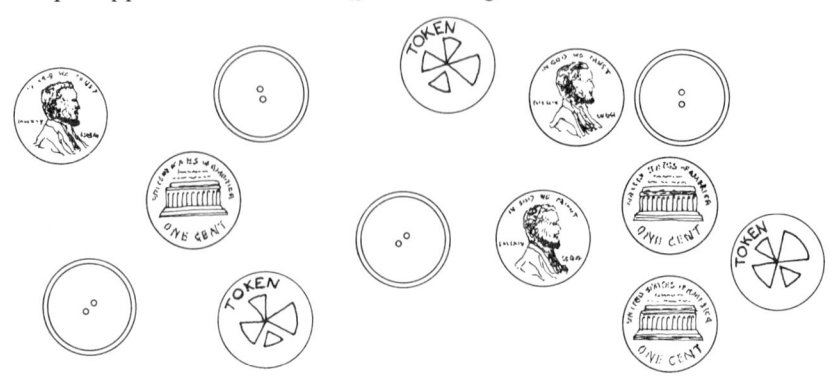

FIGURE 3.35

Money Discrimination. Give each child a collection of objects including some coins. "Put the money here and put the other things back in the box." The example in Figure 3.35 uses pennies, bus tokens, and buttons.

Penny Vending. Candy, gum, and charm vending machines are readily available to most youngsters in the supermarkets, drug stores, and other places of business frequented by children. The value of sticking a penny in such a machine is the immediate reward. Handing a penny to a clerk in exchange for a piece of candy may be interpreted by the child as simply a gift from the clerk. Inexpensive vending machines are commercially available for home or classroom use. Trinkets and miniature toys may be substituted for the candy and gum with which many machines come stocked.

Costs. Use frequent opportunities to discuss with the child the value of coins related to the cost of toys and gifts. In some situations, the children can actually buy their milk or lunch, thus understanding more fully the system of exchanging money for something tangible.

Play Store. The play store is a well-known teaching device for primary age children. However, the value for preprimary children should not be underestimated. As long as the games associated with the play store are kept simple, it can be quite valuable.

NUMBER OPERATIONS

Children of preprimary age will have only minimal experiences in number operations and problem solving. Much of what is presented will be in terms of sample questions and simple processes. This category will be emphasized at more advanced levels. However, some suggestions are given below for the limited amount of time the teacher would spend in actual number operations.

How Many More. Present the child with an egg carton or other partitioned device. Ask him to put one object in each section providing fewer objects than necessary. Then ask, "How many more do you need?" The exercise can be reversed by giving him an excess of objects and asking, "How many extra do you have?"

Separating. Some children will be ready to profit from operations with sets. For example, the teacher presents the child with a pile of three blocks. She then asks the child to give her two blocks from the pile. This sort of an activity not only reinforces the child's counting skills but is also lays the foundation for separating sets and subtraction. The number facts appropriate for preprimary instruction will probably be limited to these:

$$\begin{array}{cc} 2-1 & 3-2 \\ 3-1 & 4-2 \\ 4-1 & 4-3 \end{array}$$

Using the facts above construct simple problems as: "Give Judy three blocks from your pile."

Combining. A few children at the preprimary level may be able to enhance their number operations skills through exercises which emphasize the combination of sets. Here is an example. The teacher places two red blocks in the right hand of the child and holds one green in his hand. "How many blocks do you have? Good, you have two. How many do I have in my hand? Yes, I have one." The teacher then places the green block in the child's left hand making certain that both arms are beyond right angles to the child's body. Pointing to the left hand and then the right she asks, "How many in this hand. Good. There is one. How many in this hand? Fine. There are two." Then she moves the hands together at the midpoint of the child's body and says, "How many do you have altogether?" The teacher may have to count with the child to determine that there are three. Then the teacher says, "You see three is another name for two and one. Two and one are three."

A number of exercises of this type will assist the children in developing the basic ideas of sets and will make addition a much easier task. More advanced children will be able to respond to such direct questions as: "If Mary gives you one block and Bill gives you one block, how many blocks do you have?" The number facts appropriate at this level will typically include:

$$\begin{array}{cc} 1+1 & 2+1 \\ 1+2 & 2+2 \\ 1+3 & 3+1 \end{array}$$

SUMMARY

This chapter has presented the position that early childhood mathematics instruction for the mentally retarded is a viable concept. It has been indicated that even mentally retarded children come to the special education preprimary program with a vast array of quantitative perceptions and understanding of their spatial world. They have developed ideas of distance, time, shape, size and weight. These perceptions and knowledges are the basis for developing further number concepts. The major focus at this level has been on visual-perceptual skills and the acquisition of vocabulary although some attention was given to simple numerals. It was also emphasized that young children of widely varying intellectual capacities function more closely together at the preschool level than at later stages of development. It was indicated that during the early childhood years, there may be advantages in heterogeneous grouping of educable and trainable mentally retarded children. Included in the suggestions for the development of curricular materials at this level were a number of guidelines for the construction of teacher-made instructional aids.

TEACHING AIDS FOR PREPRIMARY MENTALLY RETARDED CHILDREN

The materials listed below are available at local stores and school supply firms.

PUB-LISHERS CODE	TITLE	DESCRIPTION
H-4	Pre-Number Readiness Kit	Manipulative materials plus unique worktext for pupils. This program contains five areas; seriation, form, logical sequence, spatial apperception and pattern.
C-11	Stepping Stones, Plastic pegboard and pegs, Number Learner	Manipulative items
P-8	Counting Cups	Set of forty-eight colorful plastic cups, which snap together to enable the child to build number concepts. They also encourage improved manual dexterity.
P-8	Self-Correcting Number Tray	Numbered squares from zero to nine in various colors. One side has raised numerals; the other sides, a cor-

PUB-LISHER CODE	TITLE	DESCRIPTION
		responding number of holes. These holes fit over corresponding pegs in the plastic tray to force the child to arrange numbers in consecutive order.
P-8	Rocker Balance Square	An 18″ × 18″ × 5″ wooden rocker for rhythmic balance activities. May be used in a sitting, kneeling or standing position.
P-8	Vestibular Board	60″ × 30″ board on rocker 12″ from floor. Permits stimulation of balance control from earliest developmental sequence of head righting in lying position through later stages of balance control in sitting, kneeling or standing position.
P-8	Barrel Roll	Barrel type apparatus for creative exploratory activities in rhythmic movement.
P-8	Circle Balance Discs	Six red and six blue 12″ rubber circles can be placed randomly and used for a variety of balancing activities.
P-8	Walk-On Numbers Kit	Consists of three different sets. Two sets are individual rubber stepping stones, one with domino-like number patterns, the other with numerals 1-10. The third is a ten foot long red vinyl mat with black numerals 0-20.

PUB-LISHER CODE	TITLE	DESCRIPTION
P-8	Balance Beam Set	Two six-foot beams which can be used in two widths (1⅝" or 3⅝") and four bases 6" high.
P-8	Bicycle Tire Set	Five tires provide imaginative running course for balance exercises, relays and obstacle courses.
P-8	Climbing Ladder	Two vertical wooden ladders support one horizontal overhead ladder. For climbing, crawling and hanging exercises.
Miscellaneous Sources	Obstacle Courses	Simple crawling obstacle courses help child to move his body by crawling in an integrated manner around and through objects in predetermined patterns.

straws	muffin tins
toothpicks	pegboards
cubes	magnetic board
balls	flannel board
beads	toy telephone
cartons	cash register
containers	blocks (large and small)
cups	cloth scraps
spoons	pictures
craft sticks	ladder
bottle caps	tiles
nails	mail box
hammer	jewelry boxes
paper bags	plywood forms
clocks	tagboard
watches	toy collections
timers	puzzles
bathroom scales	flash cards
cake pans	poster paper

REFERENCES

Behr, Harry. *All Kinds of Time.* New York: W. R. Scott, 1950.

Burton, V. L. *Mike Mulligan and His Steam Shovel.* Boston: Houghton Mifflin, 1939.

Feingold, Abraham. *Teaching Arithmetic to Slow Learners and Retarded.* New York: John Day Company, 1965.

Kephart, Newell. *The Slow Learner in the Classroom.* Columbus, Ohio: Charles E. Merrill Books, Inc., 1960.

Kuskin, Karla. *James and the Rain.* New York: Harper and Brothers, 1957.

Strauss, Alfred A., and Lehtinen, Laura E. *Psychopathology and Education of the Brain-Injured Child.* New York: Grune and Stratton, 1951.

chapter 4

Primary Mathematics for the Mentally Retarded

The children in the primary level may not have had the opportunity to attend a preprimary program. Headstart* and kindergarten are far from universal. This is true for children of normal intelligence as well as the mentally retarded. The concept of early childhood education for other categories of handicapped children is fairly well established especially for the blind, deaf, crippled, and cerebral palsied.

Unfortunately, the mentally retarded are not generally involved in such programs. This has occurred in part because of the overall deficiencies in program development, but also because of mistaken concepts concerning readiness. It has been reasoned that since children of normal intelligence are not ready for academics (i.e., reading, writing, arithmetic) until chronological age six, that the mentally retarded will be even older before they are ready. It is true that mentally retarded children will be chronologically older than six before they are ready to learn the concepts typically taught to first graders. However, this is not the same as saying that these children are not ready for simpler educational experiences prior to this time. Chapter 3 sought to outline in some detail what some of those simple mathematics concepts and skills are. Nonetheless, the special education teacher must face the reality that a number of her youngsters will come to the primary level without previous preschool experience and those who have had such experience may have

---

*Programs of early childhood education for disadvantaged preschoolers made available through the Office of Economic Opportunity.

been grouped with youngsters (and consequently exposed to curriculum) far advanced beyond their own achievement.

Another problem sometimes confronted by the primary teacher is that commonly children have not been identified as retarded upon school entrance. Consequently, many will have attended first, or even second grade before they are referred to special education. Such children will generally not only be delayed in achievement, but also will have developed strong negative feelings about academics in general and mathematics in particular. This set of circumstances means that the primary mathematics teacher will have to begin with concepts and skills generally allocated to the preprimary levels.

The important factor for the special education teacher to remember as she prepares the mathematics curriculum is that a few simple ideas provide the basis from which all mathematics develops. These basic ideas introduced in Chapter 3 include the concept of *one-to-one correspondence,* the concept of *groups* of objects and the number associated with each group, as well as the concept of *position* in an ordered arrangement of objects. These fundamental concepts are so elemental as to seem self-apparent, yet the retarded child will need continued practice and training to gain insight if he is to learn to use numbers effectively. At the primary level the teacher will continue to be concerned about the development of *vocabulary,* concepts of *measurement, money* and *problem solving.* Typically, the primary teacher will be charged with the task of developing the idea of numbers through ten. *No number greater than ten* should be introduced until the children have good control of these fundamentals. Attention can be given to greater numbers later, but retarded children should not be rushed. It is essential that the system of number naming in base ten numeration be carefully developed. It is less important to present the basic facts. Retarded children need ample time to learn the meaning of the first ten numbers.

ABILITY LEVELS

It can be seen from Table 4.1 that educable mentally retarded children of chronological ages six, seven and eight can be expected to possess MA's ranging from three years to six years and five months. The teacher should note that six-year-olds with IQ's up to 60 and seven year olds with IQ's up to 55, have mental ages below four. In other words, much of the content suggested for preprimary mental retardates will be appropriate for these youngsters. It can also be observed that since the upper level of the range includes children with mental ages of six and above, that one could anticipate equivalent achievement of about the first grade level. Some primary units have children with chronological ages as high as nine years and their achievement potential would be somewhat higher. The point to be made is that the levels of preprimary, primary and intermediate are not distinct but rather involve considerable overlap. The content suggested for the primary level, then, will be too difficult for some children and too simple for others. Mathematics is a sequential study and it is a simple matter to refer to lower or higher levels for individual children.

TABLE 4.1
Mental Ages of Mentally Retarded Children
Chronological Ages 6, 7, 8

IQ	6	7	8
50	3.0	3.6	4.0
55	3.4	3.10	4.5
60	3.7	4.2	4.10
65	3.11	4.7	5.2
70	4.3	4.11	5.7
75	4.6	5.3	6.0
80	4.10	5.7	6.5

OBJECTIVES

The children increase their awareness of the variety of number uses. There is a significant improvement in the ability to make use of number symbols, to count rationally, to work with sets, to understand measurement concepts, to name common geometric shapes, to understand specific arithmetic vocabulary, to handle money, and to use computation for the solving of problems. More specifically, many students will:

1. improve skills in visual-motor coordination as well as their understandings of the properties of spatial configurations
2. master the basic concepts of physical self; improve in the ability to perceive position in space and the spatial relationships of numbers of objects as well as discriminate more complex forms
3. develop a meaningful mathematical vocabulary especially qualitative and quantitative terms and those related to number operations, measurement, money, and form
4. make rational use of cardinal number and more advanced use of ordinal number including simple seriation

5. develop an understanding of the use of measurement concepts and devices including calendar, time by the half-hour, temperature, weight scales, and an introduction to the gross measures of capacity and length
6. improve skills in money usage, the recognition of coins, equivalencies, and the purchasing power of coins beyond the common candy and amusement purchases of the penny, nickel and dime
7. begin to understand and make use of the simple number facts of addition and subtraction up to ten with no regrouping
8. continue to develop simple problem solving and reasoning skills

DEVELOPMENTAL SEQUENCE OF MATHEMATICS SKILLS

The primary child becomes increasingly aware of the utility of numbers. He begins to gain insight into the use of numbers for such functions as age, street address, telephone, date, time, temperature. He learns to recognize common geometric shapes and name them properly. The idea that numbers relate to quantity becomes more fully developed and the ability to deal with groups to ten becomes fixed. Skills with measurement devices, money and related vocabulary continues to grow.

It has been mentioned previously that the major thrust of the preprimary program was in the development of perception and quantitative thinking. Before the teacher presents the concept of what is commonly called arithmetic, she must be certain that the children have sufficiently developed in perceptions and quantitative thinking; that is, the child must be able to perceive forms, groups, position in space and spatial relationships. He must be able to use the language of quantitative thinking. The ability to do rote counting and to recognize and understand a few written numbers is imperative before the teacher presents more advanced words. Finally, the development of skill in manipulating small sets of objects and instantaneous recognition of a few common patterned groups are basic to more advanced learnings. Once the child has achieved these basic fundamentals, he is ready for the content of the primary program. Table 4.2 outlines this content.

TABLE 4.2
Checklist for Primary Level Mathematics for Retardates

1. *Form and Perception*
    recognition of common geometric shapes (square, circle, rectangle, line, curve, star, ring, box)
    drawing lines, circles, and squares
    use of stencils to reproduce shapes

2. *Vocabulary Associated with Mathematics*

slow	in	pay	weight	center
high	out	buy	how many	cone
low	on	spend	as much as	hole
large	off	cost	as many as	float
small	many	price	fewer	the same as
heavy	few	and	more	how much
light	empty	add	fewer than	trace
early	full	take away	more than	whole
late	cupful	answer	spoonful	half
larger	glassful	cold	cup	group (set)
smaller	stamp	hot	enough	taller
top	penny	tardy	a short way	tallest
bottom	nickel	before	a long way	
far	half	after	for each	
near	whole	fast	round	
up	sell	temperature	cube	
down	save	day	flat	

3. *Number Symbols*
    rote counting to fifty
    reading number symbols to twenty
    reading number words to ten
    rote counting by 2s to ten and by 5s to twenty-five
    writing number symbols to twenty
    recognizing +, −, =, and ¢

4. *Cardinal Numbers*
    rational counting to twenty
    concepts of dozen, more than, less than, and equal
    relating number symbol to groups of objects through ten
    recognition of groups of objects through ten and ability to separate all possible subgroups
    instant recognition of sets two through five
    concepts of sets, equal sets, union of sets, empty set, cardinal number to set, one-to-one correspondence
    dozen, 1/2 dozen

5. *Ordinal Numbers*
    first   third   hours to twelve
    second   last   half hours to twelve

6. *Measurement*
    concepts of time for recess, lunch, play, school ending
    thermometer: hot, cold, warm
    clock: recognition of basic parts of a clock
              understanding terms such as hands and o'clock

associating activities with certain times
telling time by the hour (extension to half hour)
calendar: telling and reading numbers, names of days, of week and months of the year
ability to locate one's own birthday
linear: knowledge that ruler and yardstick are used for measuring
doing some non-standard measurements
recognizing longer, shorter, thick, thin, inch, foot
capacity
weight: recognizing scale, gross weight differences, ounce, cup, pound, pint, quart, and gallon

7. *Money and Value*
knowledge of the function of money
ability to name penny, nickel, dime, and quarter
concepts of equivalents of nickel and dime
use of money to make simple purchases such as vending machines, carnival rides, school lunches, bus fares, theater and other admissions

8. *Number Operations and Problem Solving*
knowledge of addition facts through ten

$\frac{1}{\underline{1}}$ $\frac{1}{\underline{2}}$ $\frac{2}{\underline{1}}$ $\frac{2}{\underline{2}}$ $\frac{1}{\underline{3}}$ $\frac{3}{\underline{1}}$ $\frac{2}{\underline{3}}$ $\frac{3}{\underline{2}}$ $\frac{3}{\underline{3}}$ $\frac{1}{\underline{4}}$ $\frac{4}{\underline{1}}$ $\frac{2}{\underline{4}}$ $\frac{4}{\underline{2}}$ $\frac{1}{\underline{5}}$ $\frac{5}{\underline{1}}$ etc.
 2   3   3   4   4   4   5   5   6   5   5   6   6   6   6

knowledge of subtraction facts through ten

$\frac{2}{\underline{1}}$ $\frac{3}{\underline{1}}$ $\frac{3}{\underline{2}}$ $\frac{4}{\underline{2}}$ $\frac{4}{\underline{1}}$ $\frac{4}{\underline{3}}$ $\frac{5}{\underline{2}}$ $\frac{5}{\underline{3}}$ $\frac{6}{\underline{3}}$ $\frac{5}{\underline{1}}$ $\frac{5}{\underline{4}}$ $\frac{6}{\underline{2}}$ $\frac{6}{\underline{1}}$ $\frac{6}{\underline{5}}$ etc.
 1   2   1   2   3   1   3   2   3   4   1   4   5   1

use of numbers to do such things as:
count children, cookies, straws, bottles of milk, etc.
tell age, address, and phone number
solve simple problems related to addition and subtraction facts

As indicated in Table 4.1, the primary teacher can expect to have a few youngsters in her class with mental ages as low as three. The teacher may be wary of having a child with such a low mental age in her charge. This concern can be easily alleviated by simply visiting with an average three year old for an hour or so. Such a youngster can repeat digits up to four lines from memory and has an expressive vocabulary of approximately 1,000 words. He can identify a host of pictures and name objects within complex pictures. He can relate happenings and announce his action. He uses verbs, pronouns, plurals, and adjectives. Such children can recognize groups of two, perform simple rote counting, and have some concept of cardinal numbers. The youngster at the lower end of the range, therefore, will achieve at a preprimary level. Much of what has been presented in Chapter 3 will be appropriate for these youngsters.

The upper range is a mental age of six. The teacher will be a little more at home with such a child. This youngster will have an anticipated grade equivalent of one.

$$\begin{aligned} AGP &= \frac{(IQ \times CA)}{100} - K \\ &= \frac{(80 \times 8)}{100} - 5 \\ &= \frac{640}{100} - 5 \\ &= 6.4 - 5 \\ &= 1.4 \end{aligned}$$

The typical six-year-old first grader has a sentence length of five words and he uses compound-complex sentence structure. Such a child knows most of the common opposites, can do counting to ten and can repeat four digits. Such youngsters are quite capable of extensive mathematical learnings.

These two examples (MA 3 and 6) represent the range. Most of the concepts and skills presented, therefore, should be approximately geared to kindergarten and first grade level.

Suggested activities for developing this sequence and achieving the objectives are presented below.

FORM AND PERCEPTION

The child continues to develop his visual-perceptual skills and improve his concept of form. As indicated in the checklist, the common shapes of boxes, squares, rectangles, curves, stars and rings are taught. The technique of discriminating, matching, sorting, and identifying introduced in Chapter 3 are applicable at the primary level although the task complexity is increased. Advanced perceptual-motor tasks such as reproducing lines, circles, and squares are taught. Suggested activities are given below.

Coordinating Lock Board. A painted wooden block 5" x 8" with a small lock, bolt-action slide fastener, door fastener and other items attached, provides fine motor coordination activities to open and close the pieces of hardware.

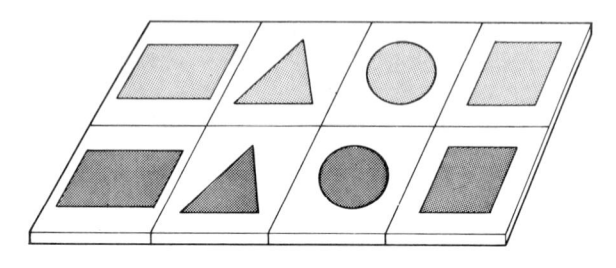

FIGURE 4.1

Geometric Form Boards. Geometric form boards are very popular educational toys sold in many large department and variety stores. The board generally includes matched pairs of rectangles, triangles, circles and squares painted so that each form is color coded to the correct placement. This device may be used for teaching form discrimination, form matching, colors, eye-hand motor coordination, and vocabulary. Here are some sample activities:

1. Remove one form from the board saying to the child, "Watch me. Now you put it back." As the child learns to do this remove two forms at a time, then three and so on until he can replace all of the forms.
2. Remove the one circle from the board saying, "Find another one like this one."
3. Place three forms in front of the child, one of which is different from the other two. "Which one is different?"
4. Arrange four forms in front of the child and hold a fifth shape in your hand which matches only one of the child's shapes. "Which of the ones that you have is just like mine?"
5. Show the child the red square saying "This is red, put it in the red space." Show the child the circle and say, "This is a circle. Show me another circle."

The Swirl. The swirl is a helpful aid in teaching balance and laterality. The object is for the child to walk from the box on the outside of the swirl to the dot on the inside of the circle without stepping off the line. The swirl is painted on concrete or another outdoor hard surface or

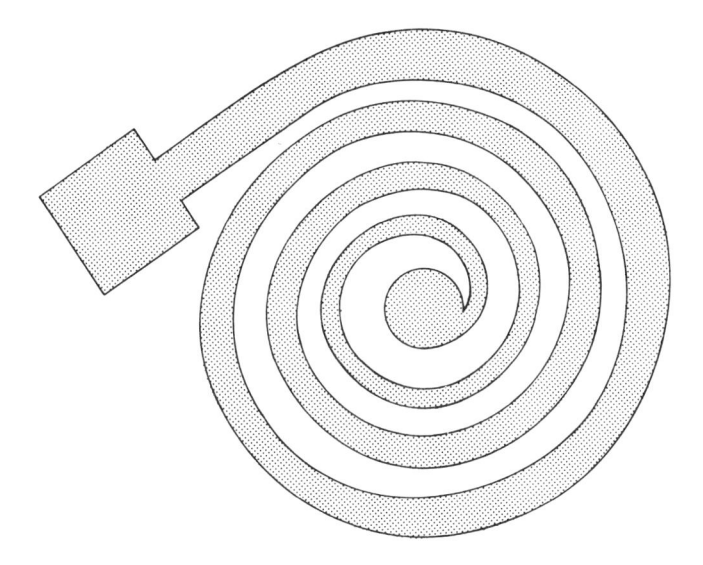

Primary Mathematics for the Mentally Retarded 107

FIGURE 4.2

on the gymnasium or classroom floor. If tempra paint is used it may be easily removed without permanently marking the floor. The swirl should be wide at the outside of the design and become narrower as the center dot is approached.

As the child walks to the center dot he is forced to step higher and higher on his toes as the line narrows. As it becomes increasingly more difficult for him to maintain his balance, he has to manipulate his legs

FIGURE 4.3

108   *Primary Mathematics for the Mentally Retarded*

and arms and control his body's center of gravity to keep from stepping off the line. These movements assist the child in improving his body image and especially in developing laterality. Experiences of this type help the child learn more about his own body and his spatial world. Such perceptions of space are a major facet of the background essential to developing mature concepts of position in space and spatial direction.

FIGURE 4.4

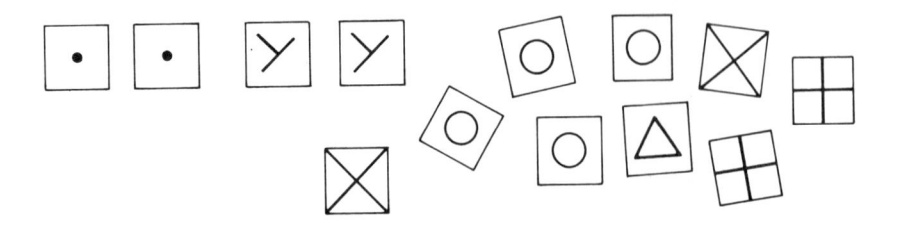

FIGURE 4.5

Configuration Cards. Cards may be used with a variety of configurations for matching, sorting, and so forth. This will aid the children in their development of visual discrimination and classification skills.

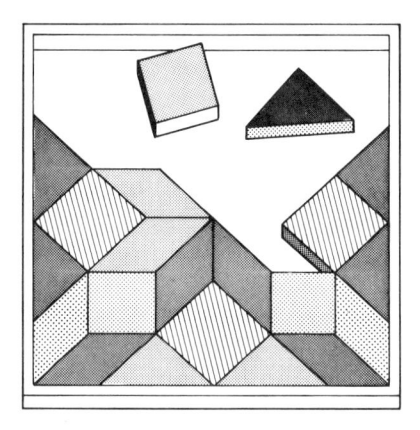

FIGURE 4.6

Parquetry Blocks. Sets of large parquetry puzzles as well as smaller sets of blocks are available in most dime stores. The objective of activities with parquetry blocks is to improve the child's visual-perception of forms through sorting, matching and designing.

Many sets of parquetry blocks come with patterns printed on paper for the child to duplicate with the blocks. In order to complete these designs, the child has to discriminate various shapes and to match pictorial forms with three dimension blocks. The teacher can help his students learn the names of the forms and express their creativity as they work with the blocks.

Miniature Toys. A collection of wooden and plastic miniature toys can be used for teaching spatial relations as well as sorting and matching. Figures of adults, children and infants are especially useful when combined with toy cars, houses, trees and so forth. Popular figures of pets and zoo animals add interest to the activities. Here are some suggestions which will improve the children's perception and skills in classifying.

1. Present the children with sets of objects in which one item does not belong. The teacher could use the Sesame Street song, *"One of These Things Is Not Like the Others"* to add interest. Ask the children to identify the toy which doesn't fit.
2. Arrange the toys in a diarama. Have the children follow directives such as, "Put the lion by the bear. Place the man by the women. Place the dog in front of the cat." The children can answer such questions as, "Which animal is taller? Show me the tallest tree?"

Magnetic Board. This device finds value beyond form and perception; however, its application to this area is obvious. The magnetic board provides opportunities to deal with shapes and designs as does the flannel board—however, the magnetic feature is a strong interest and motivating element. This is available at any school supply house.

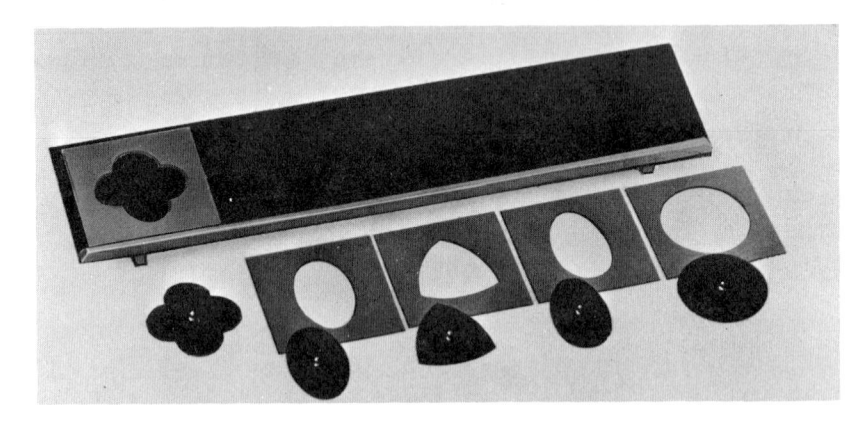

FIGURE 4.7a

FIGURE 4.7b

Metal Insets. This apparatus, available through Teaching Aids, aids in the development of eye-hand motor controls involved in copying designs. It consists of ten metal frames and insets. The child traces around the various shapes.

Basic Blocks. Primary children continue to enjoy and profit from block play. They will be challenged by unusual shapes. Their block collection should be expanded to include columns, triangles, arches, buttresses, half circles, as well as roof board and ramps.

Primary Mathematics for the Mentally Retarded 111

FIGURE 4.8

Blockmobiles. The blockmobiles not only help the children improve their ability to deal with a variety of forms and shapes but also serve as a valuable aid in developing the notions of cardinal number and operations with sets. The set consists of ten cars, two trucks, a bus, a

FIGURE 4.9

boat, a snap-together train, several trees, and peg people. The children should be given many opportunities to explore the shapes and make interesting patterns with blockmobiles.

Wood Hi-Sticks. Hi-sticks are designed to improve the children's body image and motor coordination. Once mastered, stilts are a source of real fun and a great self-confidence builder. When children learn to walk with them at the lower height, they turn the poles and graduate to the higher level.

FIGURE 4.10

Walk a Rail. Somewhat more advanced than the walking board mentioned in Chapter 3, it sits 8 inches off the ground and has a 2 inch wide top width. It may be purchased in sections five feet long. Practice on the walking board will develop balance and perceptions of laterality.

Jump Rope. The time tested game of jumping rope has great value in developing coordination and advanced body image.

Chalk Board. The most detailed discussion of chalk board training is presented by Kephart's (1971) book, *The Slow Learner in the Classroom.* He encourages using the chalkboard for the production of simultaneous circles, tracing, and reproduction. The reader is referred to this source.

Primary Mathematics for the Mentally Retarded   113

FIGURE 4.11

Hop Scotch. This is a very familiar game to youngsters which offers a fine opportunity to build perceptual-motor skills and body image.

Rhythms. Booklets on rhythmic activities and suggestions for marching, acting out stories, bouncing balls, and rhythms for holidays are available in popular department stores. Many of these activities are appropriate for primary retardates.

Hi-Q. This inexpensive and popular game stimulates reasoning and sequencing processes by providing a pegboard puzzle. Included are 38 plastic pegs, 6" x 6" plastic board, and rules. The game is available at popular department stores.

Puzzles. Puzzles are available through a wide sequence beginning with the simple ones indicated in Chapter 3, to more complex types suitable for primary level retardates. The puzzles can advance to ten or twenty interlocking pieces. Durable plastic or wooden puzzles are generally superior for such children. The children will advance their perception of space while enjoying the challenge of completing the puzzle.

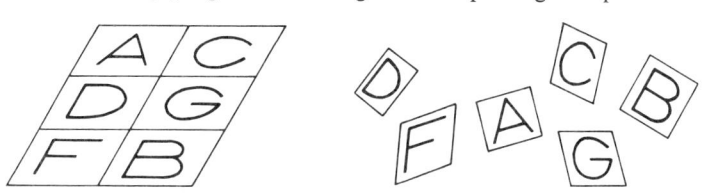

FIGURE 4.12

Matching Kits. Matching kits help the children improve their visual discrimination skills. These can be made by the pupils and/or the teacher. Latto or similar games may be used for motivation. Construct large cards as shown in Figure 4.12, and a group of smaller response cards which correspond. The first child to fill his card wins.

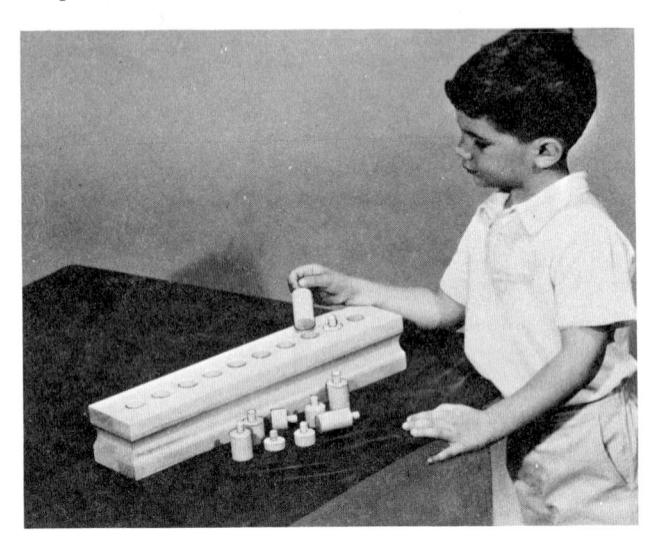

FIGURE 4.13

Cylinder Blocks. This aid is fashioned after Montessori. It improves visual perceptual skills and requires fairly advanced eye-hand motor coordination skills. It consists of four blocks with cavities each of which has a cylinder to fit in it. The aids are constructed of hardwood block and there is only one correct well for each cylinder. Thus, the child may work by himself. The cylinders are so versatile that the teacher will find many uses for them.

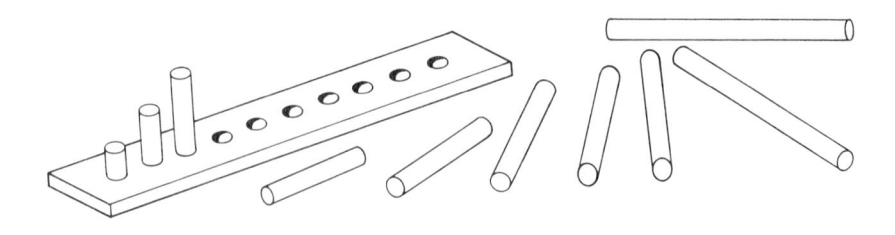

FIGURE 4.14

The Long Stair. This device calls upon the child to make the sharpest discrimination of size. Ten hardwood rods with equal cross-sections vary in length so that the ratio between the shortest and longest rod is 1:10.

FIGURE 4.15a

FIGURE 4.15b

Cabinet of Geometric Insets. The child is introduced to figures which show wide variation in form; as he masters these he is given series which show less divergence in shape and which call for finer distinctions. The apparatus not only develops visual perception, but utilizes the child's sense of touch to differentiate between forms.

VOCABULARY ASSOCIATED WITH MATHEMATICS

The importance of an adequate vocabulary does not diminish in the primary program. Words associated with mathematics are necessary not only for ordering one's environment in a quantitative fashion, but also for the expression of some ideas and the understanding of others. Particular focus must be placed on the meanings of words in the arithmetic context as opposed to other contents. Mentally retarded children will need much assistance in developing adequate word recognition with emphasis on the comprehension of familiar and new terms in the arithmetic sense.

Many words which are presented at the primary level have been a part of the mentally retarded child's vocabulary for some time, yet additional practice and insight will be necessary. For example "top" may be a toy that spins around; "cold" may refer to a cough and sickness; a quarter may simply be a "big nickel." A host of terms will need to be refined to finer meanings through careful definition by the teacher.

It should be noted at this point that number vocabulary will probably not be taught as an isolated aspect of the mathematics program, but will proceed concurrently with the presentation of number concepts. As new number experiences are planned, the teacher should list the key vocabulary words that need review and new words should be carefully and conscientiously controlled. Otherwise the teacher may find her students failing to learn a number concept not because the idea itself is beyond them but because they are unsure of the terminology. The arithmetic lesson must be sequentially planned for the orderly development of vocabulary so as to avoid such pitfalls. The misuse of words may be "cute" to adults (I want the *mostest* ice cream) but should be discouraged among retardates. Words found in the checklist for primary typify approaches which may be prepared by the teacher to develop the child's quantitative vocabulary.

It was suggested that the teacher begin at the preprimary level with the terms big and little (one balloon is big, the other is little). These two words are familiar even to the mentally retarded child. An understanding of other words of comparison can emerge naturally from their proper use. The teacher may introduce new objects compared by more mature terms such as large, small, and long. The children can expand such terms to the comparative forms; larger, bigger, smaller, longer, and fewer.

Objects and Pictures. The use of real, miniature, and concrete objects is recommended for teaching comparison terms. The number box, described in Chapter 3, would be most helpful. The picture file has equal applicability.

Classroom Comparisons. Compare two chalks, children, books, containers, and so forth, making such comparisons as:

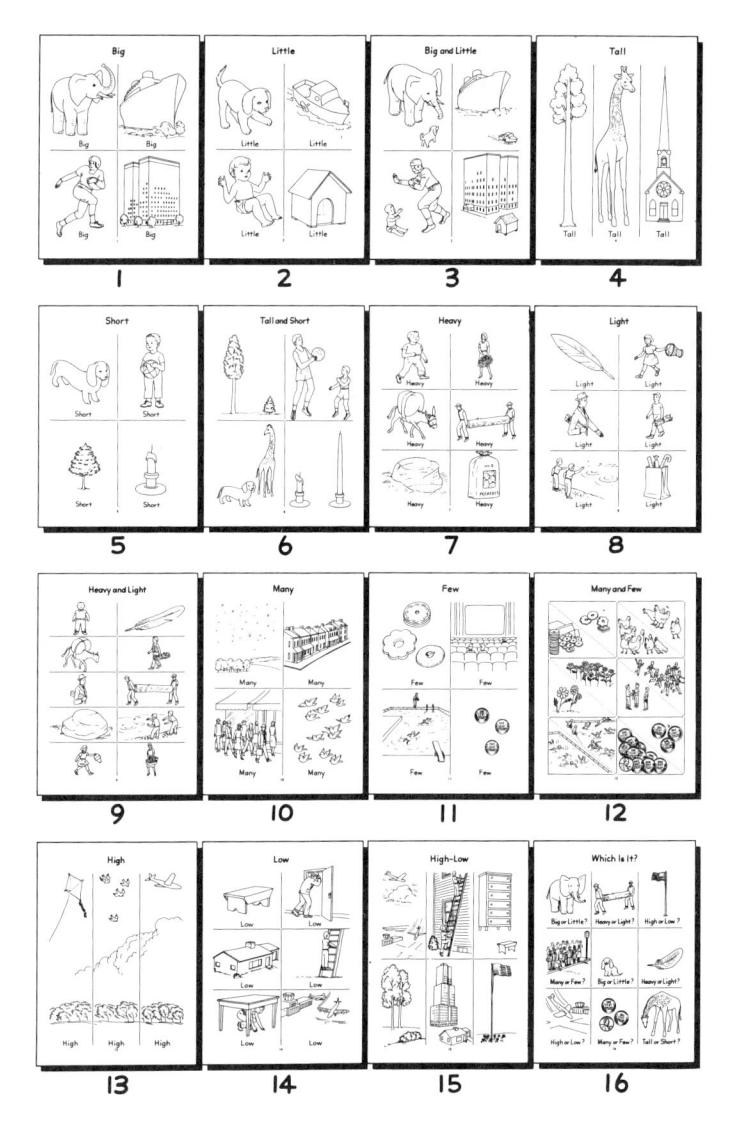

Primary Mathematics for the Mentally Retarded 117

FIGURE 4.16

One is smaller—one is larger
One is shorter—one is longer
One is empty—one is full

Directives. Concepts for terms such as "top," "bottom," "far," and "near" can be developed through simple directives such as: "Place your book on top of the desk; place your pencil in the bottom of the box; put the flower vase near the window."

Shelves and Stairs. A miniature set of stairs or shelves may be used to teach terms of relative position, using such directions as "Place the ball in the middle shelf and the jacks under the ball, put the girl doll on the top stair and the boy doll on the bottom one."

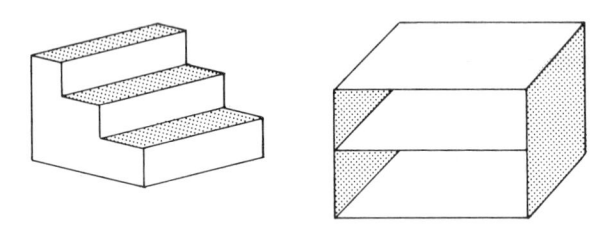

FIGURE 4.17

The Maze. The pencil and paper maze can be used to teach the youngster terms as near and far. Instruct your students to: "Draw a line to the house far away, put a mark (X) on the house near the boy."

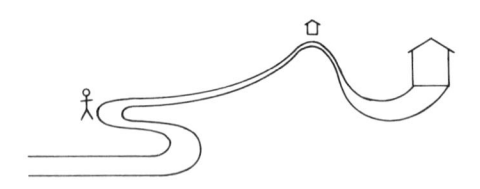

FIGURE 4.18

Discussions. The primary age retardate has a vocabulary sufficient to allow classroom discussion to be profitable for teaching arithmetic terms. Simple questions such as the following are instructive.
  Was anyone tardy today?
  Who was early for school?
  How much does a candy bar cost?
  What do we do right before lunch?

Incidental Teaching. Plan to use appropriate terms in games projects, and lessons which will reinforce words introduced in mathematics.

Number Book. The number scrapbook was first introduced at the preprimary level for teaching number symbols. However, it may also be used to teach vocabulary. Pictures cut from magazines and pasted into a scrapbook provide an ideal instructional aid. The illustrations should depict such comparative terms as many-few, half-whole, heavy-light. Each child should be provided with his own copy in order to enhance motivation and provide for individualized instruction.

The Worksheet. Mathematics worksheets for teaching vocabulary should be used sparingly. However, there are occasions when this approach is appropriate. The teacher must be careful that the children understand what they are to do and that the illustrations are clear and the pages uncluttered.

Chalkboard. Draw a house or tree on the chalkboard. Ask the children to place objects in relative positions—a bird on the tree, child in the house, or apple on the shortest branch.

Flannel Box. The use of a flannel box or board was presented in Chapter 3 and is still functional at the primary level. The manipulation and sorting of felt pieces assists the youngster in developing vocabulary. Felt pieces should include such items as circles, trees, spoons, cups, boxes, cubes, and so on. The children can work with displays which will teach concepts such as cupful, tallest, half, large and heavy. Refer to the vocabulary list on page 103.

NUMBER SYMBOLS

The use of number symbols at the primary level has almost always progressed to a stage where the child has developed considerable understanding. No longer is the child's number-play merely rote but rather to some degree is related to the rational use of numbers. By this time, the child will have a real understanding of numbers as high as four. He will have associated the expressive terms of one, two, three, four with the corresponding printed numerals 1, 2, 3, 4. However, the teacher cannot assume that since the child has learned some elementary concepts there is no longer concern for number symbols. True, the foundation built through the rational use of numbers under five makes it easier to introduce higher concepts of numbers; but the teacher must still remain aware of presenting new symbols. The number symbol "5," for example, may be introduced before the child has worked with sets of five. A child will probably always have rote skills before he is ready for genuine comprehension. Actually the temptation to accelerate the child's rote skills considerably beyond his real number concepts and level is great, yet must be resisted. A wide disparity between meaningless number symbols manipulation and understanding can easily confuse the retarded child; mislead his parents (and teachers) into over-estimating his level of mastery; clutter the curriculum; and force the teacher to unteach some poor habits.

Therefore, it is well that the teacher continue to control most judiciously the introduction of number symbols with the same vehemence and energy with which she controls vocabulary. The suggested scope of number symbols has been presented in Table 4.2.

Rote counting to fifty, counting by two's and five's may be taught in the incidental and game fashion indicated in Chapter 3. The teacher will make considerable use of finger plays, nursery rhymes, and games. The use of concrete items such as marbles, blocks, pencils, crayons, beans, counting sticks, and books help the child to rote count and lay the groundwork for rational enumeration.

Reading of number symbols to twenty and number words to ten should be presented simultaneously with teaching cardinal and ordinal numbers. The teacher will not find it difficult to design games such as lotto and bingo to give the child practice with these symbols.

Bulletin Boards with Simple Vocabulary Rhymes

Young children respond well to colorful bulletin boards and they find word games and rhymes delightful. Figure 4.19 shows some example bulletin boards and rhymes useful in teaching terms such as fall, fast, high, far, and tall.

My father is tall,
My brother is small;
And I'm in between
If you know what I mean.

It's very far
Up to a star.
It's very high
Up to the sky.

Primary Mathematics for the Mentally Retarded 121

It's easy as can be
To climb a little tree.
But if the tree is tall,
Watch out, or you might fall.

One day I saw a train go past
It made a noise and went so fast.
Then it was gone, and all around
I could not hear one tiny sound.

FIGURE 4.19

| 1 | 2 | 3 | 4 | 5 | 6 | 7 | 8 | 9 | 10 |

| 2 | 4 | 6 | 8 | 9 | 3 | 1 | 7 | 5 | 10 |

FIGURE 4.20

Number line (Ordered & Mixed). Cards are constructed with the numerals one to ten (or less) printed in bold manuscript. The children touch the symbols and say the words as they move along the line. A variation may be provided by presenting the children with individual number cards which are matched to the number line.

The Missing Number. A blank card can be used with the ordered numbered line. Cover a numeral and ask "Which one did I hide?" The children can use their individual cards in a like fashion. Place the cards in order. Remove cards and have the child replace them. Turn cards over and have child identify them.

The Mixed Up Train. A toy train (pictures or drawings do just as well) is placed before the child. Each car has a number from one to ten. The order is confused and the child is required to fix the train by putting the cars in proper sequence. To begin with, only two numerals are improperly ordered, but as the child gains in ordering skills, the sequence may be thoroughly mixed.

The Fish Pond. A rectangle is cut out of a cardboard carton leaving a frame in which to attach cellophane or other transparent materials. The sides are covered with contact paper. The interior is painted or lined with aqua or blue paper. Cellophane is added to give the effect of an aquarium. Fish are cut out of construction paper with the numerals one to ten affixed to them. A paper clip is attached. A magnet is attached to a pole. The child "fishes" and the fish are placed on the table in numerical order. The teacher may demonstrate the order before placing the fish in the tank.

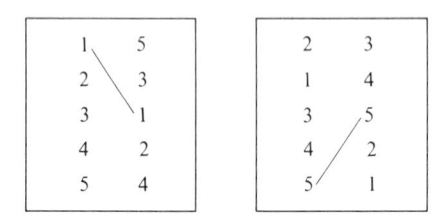

FIGURE 4.21

Matching sheets. "Draw a line between the ones which are the same."

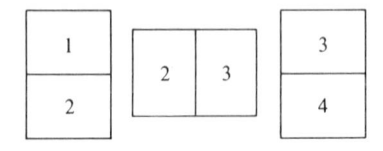

FIGURE 4.22

Number Dominoes. The use of dominoes is well-known. The teacher may construct simple dominoes from poster paper and use set patterns which are appropriate for the primary level.

Primary Number Book. Use ten sheets of newsprint for the interior pages and two sheets of colored construction paper for the cover. On the first page write the numeral "1" and illustrate it with a picture of

Primary Mathematics for the Mentally Retarded 123

FIGURE 4.23

one object cut from a magazine. On the adjacent page write the word "one" and illustrate it with another picture of one. Continue this process until the number ten has been reached.

Rhythms, Rhymes, Finger Plays, Songs. Children enjoy body movement, rhythms, and songs. This may be taken advantage of through such activities as the following.

Rhythms

Rhymes and rhythms may be used to introduce and reinforce counting by two's and five's.

2-4, 6-8-10!	2-4, 6-8-10!	5-10, 15-20
That was fun,	What a ball,	Joe the clown
do it again!	but now's the end.	was very funny.

5-10, 15-20	2-4, 6-8-10!
I like candy	That was fun,
fruit and honey.	do it again.

ONE POTATO

The players hold out their fists, and one player counts off the fists, his own included, with this rhyme. Each time he reaches the word "more" a fist is withdrawn and put behind its owner's back. Finally, only one fist is left.

> One potato, two potatoes,
> Three potatoes, four;
> Five potatoes, six potatoes,
> Seven potatoes. MORE

ONE, TWO

One, two, Buckle my shoe;
Three, four, Shut the door;
Five, six, Pick up sticks;
Seven, eight, Lay them straight;
Nine, ten, A good fat hen;
Eleven, twelve, Dig and delve;
Thirteen, fourteen, Maids a-courting;
Fifteen, sixteen, Maids in the Kitchen;
Seventeen, eighteen, Maids in waiting;
Nineteen, twenty, My plate's empty.

BA, BA, BLACK SHEEP

Ba, ba, black sheep,
Have you any wool?
Yes sir, no sire,
Three bags full.
One for my master,
And one for my dame,
But none for the little boy,
Who cries in the lane.

FIVE LITTLE SQUIRRELS

Five little squirrels sitting in a tree,
   (Hold left hand up, fingers limp from the wrist.)
This little squirrel says, "What do I see?"
   (Begin with thumb and hold up a finger as each squirrel is named.)
This little squirrel says, "I see a gun."
This little squirrel says, "Let us run."
This little squirrel says, "I'm not afraid."
This little squirrel says, "Let's hide in the shade."
Along came a man with a great big gun.
   (Right hand moves up as finger points in imitation of a gun.)
Bang! See those little squirrels run.
   (Clap hands and hide left hand.)

This rhyme may be used as instructional material for teaching the ordinals by substituting *first* through *fifth* for the word *this* at the beginning of the line.

MOTHER HEN AND CHICKENS

Point to each finger to indicate the *first, second, third,* etc. as the rhyme is repeated.

Said the first little chicken with a queer little squirm,
"I wish I could find a nice fat worm."
Said the second little chicken with an odd little shrug,
"I wish I could find a nice fat bug."
Said the third little chicken with a sigh of relief,
"I wish I could find a nice green leaf."
Said the fourth little chicken with a queer little squeal,
"I wish I could find some nice yellow meal."
"Now see here," said the mother hen from the green garden patch,
"If you want any breakfast, come here and scratch."

ONE, TWO, THREE

One, two, three,
I love coffee,
And Billy loves tea.

How good you be,
One, two, three
I love coffee,
And Billy loves tea.

THIS OLD MAN

This old man, he played one,
He played nick-nack on my drum;
Nick-nack paddy-whack, give a dog a bone,
This old man came rolling home.

This old man, he played three (tree)
This old man, he played four (door)
This old man, he played five (hive)
This old man, he played six (sticks)
This old man, he played seven (Devon)
This old man, he played eight (gate)
This old man, he played nine (line)
This old man, he played ten (hen)

Tracing. Cardboard and plastic numerals are available for sorting, matching, and noting differences. These items can likewise be used for tracing. The child says the number as he traces it.

Numeral Completion. The children at the primary level may already be able to write the numerals to four. Others will just be beginning. The teacher illustrates that one is like a stick; that two looks like a candy cane with a tail; that three looks like a butterfly's wing; that four is a tipped hat with a stick; that five has a hat and the bottom part of a three; that six is a down stroke with a circle at the bottom; that seven is a stick with a hat; that eight is a complete three or two circles; that nine is a circle with a stick; and that ten is a stick and a circle. The completion exercise might look like that in Figure 4.24.

FIGURE 4.24

The numerals 1, 3, 6, and 0 are omitted from the exercise since they do not readily lend themselves to completion. Ultimately the 1, 6, 8, and 0 should be taught as a continuous motion while the numerals 2, 3, 4, 5, 7, and 9 are made with interrupted motions.

The Three and Eight. The numerals 3 and 8 present specific obstacles for most retarded children. The use of disks, coins, or circles can be helpful. The coins may be glued onto cardboard and used for kinesthetic practice. A duplicated sheet with circles similarly placed is likewise of assistance.

The Lazy Eight. The construction of a "lazy eight," one circle placed on top of another, raises a question in some teachers' minds. Obviously, if the child appears as if he can master the regular one-motion eight, this is desirable. Some youngsters have great difficulty with this due to poor eye-hand motor coordination. The teacher must decide if the use of the lazy eight is worth the temporary convenience in light of the fact that unlearning and reteaching will be necessary later.

Writing the Numerals. The numerals should be practiced through a variety of exercises. The proper strokes are shown in Figure 4.25.

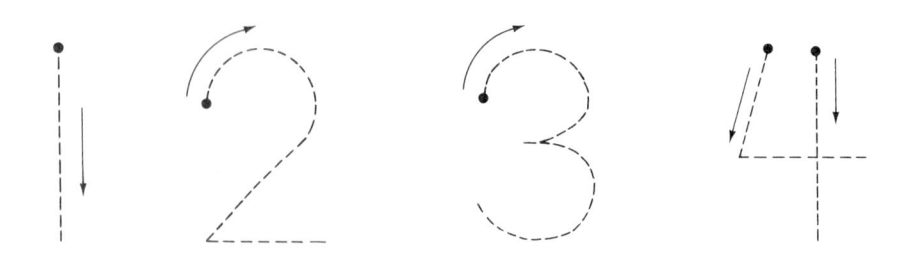

FIGURE 4.25

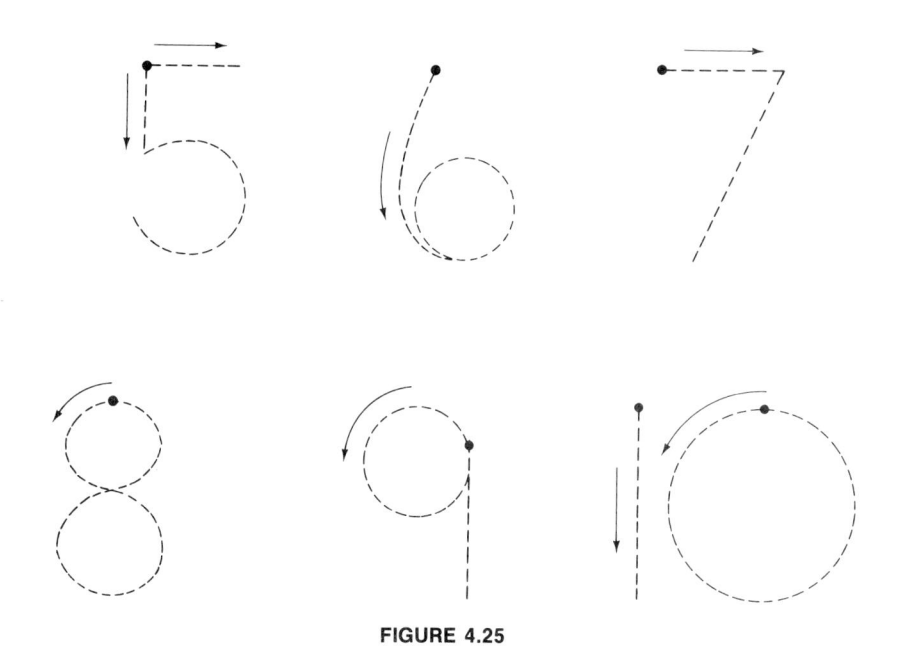

CARDINAL NUMBER

Many, though not all, children will come to the primary teacher with some skill in associating numbers with a corresponding group of objects. The teacher will attest to the children's skill in relating number symbols to sets up to ten. She will assist the youngsters in developing recognition of groups of objects through ten with emphasis on the ability to reproduce subsets of ten.

The importance of a solid understanding of cardinal numbers and sets cannot be over-emphasized. It is precisely this understanding that will be the foundation of the child's ability to compute and solve problems through the manipulation of number symbols. For this reason, some basic concepts relevant to a modern mathematics approach to teaching the mentally retarded will be discussed briefly. This text is not intended to present a course in modern mathematics. Such a task would consume a separate volume, and it is with this limitation in mind that the topics below are presented.

Concept of Sets. A precise definition of the term "set" is difficult simply because it is a self-apparent idea. For our purposes, a set may be thought of as a group, collection, or class of objects which may be easily identified.

That is, it is obvious to the viewer that objects are a group, and it can be decided without too much difficulty whether any object is included or excluded from the set. Mathematicians indicate a set by the use of braces. $A = \{A\ B\ C\}$ (Read as: A is the set whose elements are A, B, and C.)

The teacher will assist the children in learning that the sequence of listing the names of the members of the set is immaterial, as indicated by the "" symbol between the sets.

$$\{A,B,C\} = \{C,B,A\} = \{B,C,A\} = \{C,A,B\}$$

One-to-One Correspondence and Sets. One-to-one matching of objects is the prelude to counting. As soon as the child is capable of matching items in a definite order (one napkin to each pupil) he is counting. At this point, he needs to learn words and symbols in order to manipulate and communicate ideas of numbers. The concepts of "more than, less than" become inadequate for his needs. The child then is ready to develop a true concept of number. The Hindu Arabic numerals placed in one-to-one correspondence with a set of blocks is indicated below:

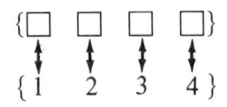

$$\{\square\ \square\ \square\ \square\}$$
$$\{1\ \ 2\ \ 3\ \ 4\ \}$$

Cardinal number up to this point has been thought of as simply the answer to the question "how many?" The illustration allows us to define cardinal number more precisely for our own thinking. Cardinal number is the number matched with the last element in a set—in this case four.

The concept of sets will be helpful as we approach the familiar processes of addition and subtraction later in the chapter. As background for this, the child must begin to experience the relationship between sets and the different ways of viewing a given set. For example, three is another name for two and one.

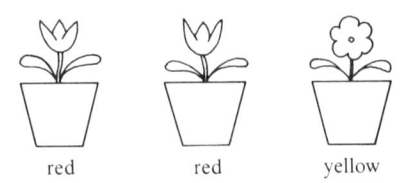

red   red   yellow

FIGURE 4.26

"How many flowers do we have? How many red ones? How many yellow ones? Instead of writing three, let's simply call this set of flowers two and one or (2 + 1). Two and one is another way of saying three."

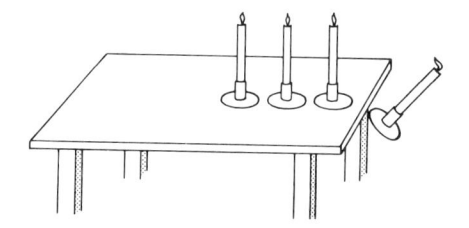

Primary Mathematics for the Mentally Retarded 129

FIGURE 4.27

There are four candles on the table. One fell off. You take away one or 4 − 1. How many do you have left? Another way of saying three is 4 − 1.

The following activities are a few techniques which may be used to develop this basic background.

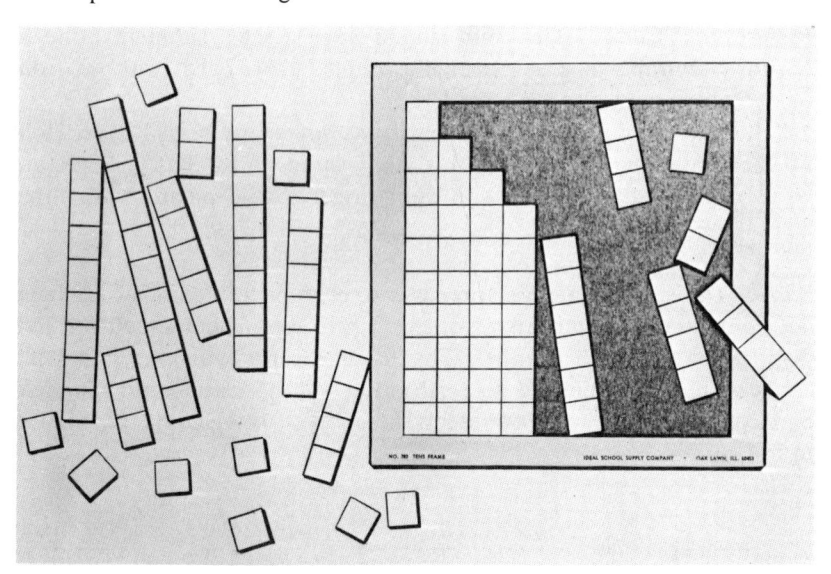

FIGURE 4.28

FIGURE 4.29

Equivalent Sets. Two counting sticks are bound together with one loose beside them. Another group of three identical counting sticks are also bound together. Have the child hold the single counting stick in his right hand, the set of two counting sticks in his left hand, leaving three counting sticks on the desk. The teacher holds up three duplicate counting sticks. How many do you have in your hands? How many in your right hand? How many in your left hand? One and two are three. Let's call the ones you are holding 1 + 2. How many on your desk? Let's call the ones on your desk 3. Do you have the same number in your hand as on your desk? So, 2 + 1 is another way of saying three.

Other equivalent sets may be shown in a similar fashion. Picture cards are a worthwhile aid.

Three hats are the same as 1 hat + 1 hat + 1 hat, which is the same as 2 hats + 1 hat.

Pictures and Cards. The child should have a set of numerals one to ten in his number box. A set of illustrated picture cards with set from one to ten should also be provided.

"Hold up the number card which shows how many birds I have. Hold up the picture card which has this many things in it." Put your picture cards on your desk. Point with your finger to the picture with three trees, two birds, one ball."

Sorting Decks. The teacher prepares a set of picture cards which have dot configurations and sets of objects up to ten. There should be five distinct sets for each number. That is, five cards with one item, five cards with two items and so forth. "Put all the cards with one item here, all the cards with two items here." The sets should be limited to the child's level.

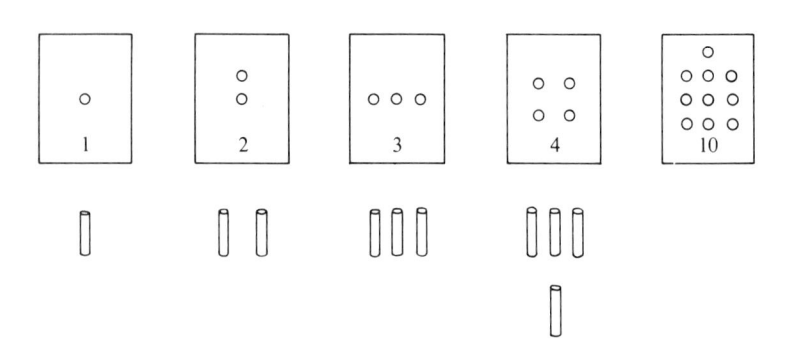

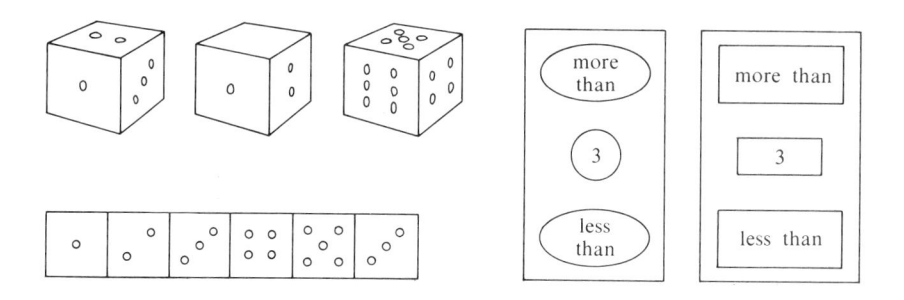

Primary Mathematics for the Mentally Retarded 131

FIGURE 4.30

Primary "More Than, Less Than" Game. Two or three children may play this game. Construct a rectangular game board with the numeral 3 in the center and the words "more than" and "less than" placed above and below the numeral. Use a cube with the domino patterns on the sides from one to five. There are two domino sets of three. This way each possibility of three, more than three, and less than three, will have equal probability. Each child is given a number of chips. He places some of his chips in one of the three circles. One child tosses the cube. If it turns up more than three, the child with a chip in that box wins all the chips. Begin with groups up to four and add the other sets as he appears ready.

Instantaneous Set Recognition. "We are going to play a game. I will flash a card with some pictures on it. You tell me how many objects are on the card. I am going to go very fast so you must watch carefully." Use large flash cards with domino patterns and pattern sets of pictures up through five.

More and Less Than. Distribute counting disks or other items to five children. Give the first child one, the second child two, and so on. Call the third child forward. "How many do you have? Which of you have less than he?" Select another child and proceed in a like manner.

More, Less Than, The Same As. Distribute picture cards. Give each child three containers or a cheese carton divided into three sections. Place the number three in the center section. "All the pictures which are the same as three place here. Those which are less than three put here (left section) and those which are more than three put here (right section)."

132   *Primary Mathematics for the Mentally Retarded*

FIGURE 4.31

Rational Counting. A muffin tin may be filled with groups of small objects up to twenty. The child counts the objects within each section. The total may be written on a folded piece of paper so the child may check himself.

Stick Man and Other Aids. A variety of teaching aids are available through commercial sources. Following are several aids which should be helpful to the special education teacher.

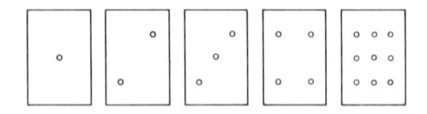

FIGURE 4.32

Number Peg Boards. Ten pieces of masonite about 5″ × 7″ are numbered one to ten. In the number one card, one hole is drilled, in the number two card two holes are drilled and so forth to ten. Teach the child to place a peg in the hole and say the number word aloud. Repeat the procedure for each set. (These boards are available commercially.)

Drawing. The primary age children will be able to draw some simple forms and pictures. This skill can be taken advantage of in their mathematics lessons. For example, give the children directions such as "On your paper draw five balls; make three boxes; draw one happy face."

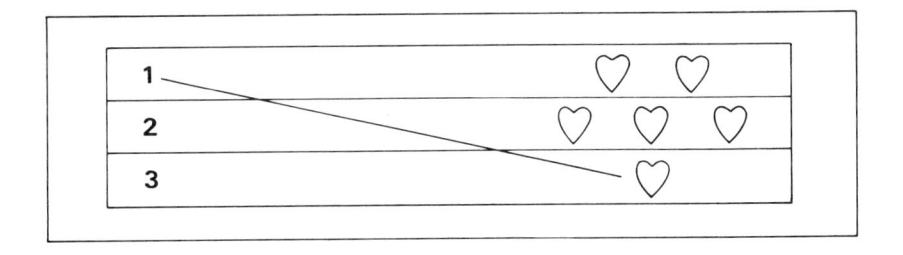

Primary Mathematics for the Mentally Retarded   133

FIGURE 4.33

Pictures to Numerals. Figure 4.33 presents an example of how the written number symbols and sets can be matched on easily constructed worksheets.

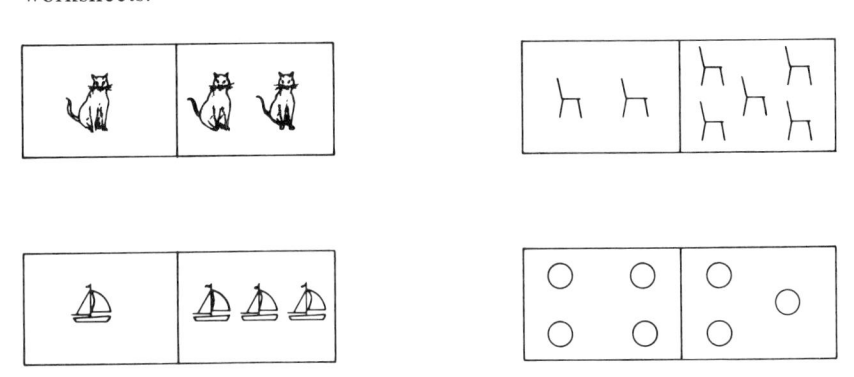

FIGURE 4.34

Which Is More? Which Is Less? A set of flash cards may be easily constructed on tagboard. On one side of the card illustrate a set and on the opposite side draw a non-equivalent set. Then ask the child, "Which is more? Point with your finger."

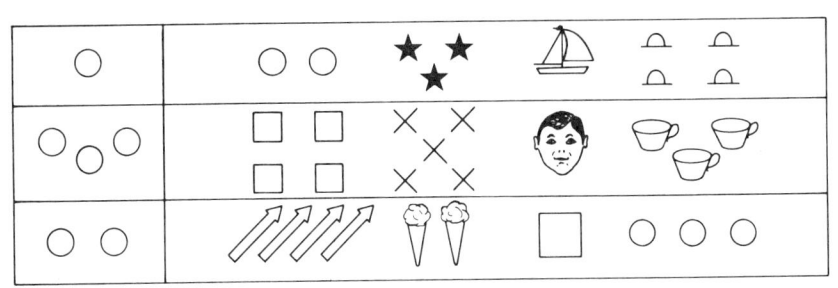

FIGURE 4.35

Which Is the Same? Make a worksheet that has five sets per line. Let the set on the left hand side of the page serve as the stimulus set and the other set serve as the response set. Tell the child, "You should place a mark on the picture that is the same number as the pictures you see here." After one or two demonstrations, there should be no problems in identifying the matching sets.

FIGURE 4.36

Counting Papers. Fig. 4.36 shows an illustration of a counting sheet that can be simply made.

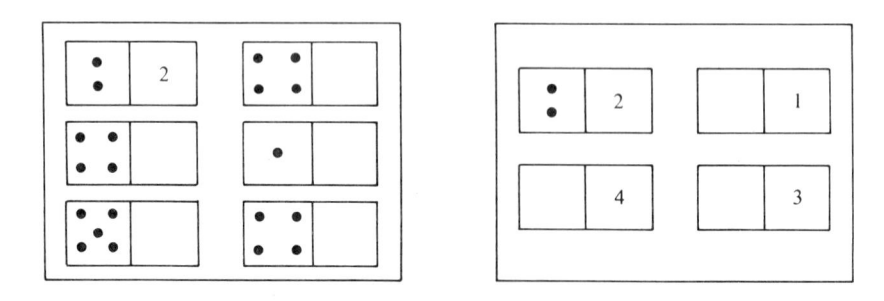

FIGURE 4.37

Domino Sheets. An illustration of two types of domino sheets is shown in Fig. 4.37. In the first example, the student writes the numeral in the space provided and in the second he reproduces a set corresponding to the numeral printed on the domino.

Primary Mathematics for the Mentally Retarded 135

1 or 2 3 or 5	5 or 4 1 or 3	2 or 4 3 or 1

FIGURE 4.38

Which Number Is More....Which Number Is Less. This activity is a variation of one presented earlier. In this case the numerals are used in lieu of unequal sets.

FIGURE 4.39

Flash Cards with Multiple Sets. In Fig. 4.39, the child can see five candles and six cherries. Yet there is one cake and two clusters of fruit. This type of study picture helps develop the child's idea of sets and operations on them. Present the card or picture and ask, "How many candles? And how many cakes? How many cherries? How many bunches of cherries?"

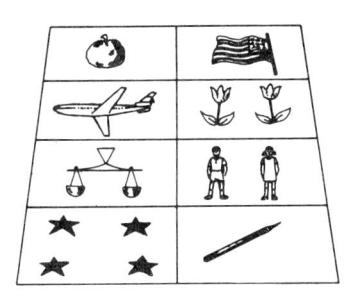

FIGURE 4.40

Picture Lotto. Construct a set of play and caller cards like those shown in Fig. 4.40. Each child is then given a player card and one child is elected caller. The caller has a quantity of cards turned face-down which correspond to the illustrations on the players' cards.

FIGURE 4.41

The caller turns up a card and calls "one flag." Each student who has one flag places a marker on his card. Next, two balloons might be called and each player with two balloons on his card would place a marker over the illustration of two balloons. The first child to cover all of the illustrations on his card wins and he becomes the caller for the next game.

FIGURE 4.42

Interlocking Puzzle Cards. A series of cards is constructed with a set on one part of the card and the appropriate numeral on the other part. The cards are then cut approximately in half so that only the proper matches will interlock. The pieces are scattered before the child and he is asked to put them together as they belong.

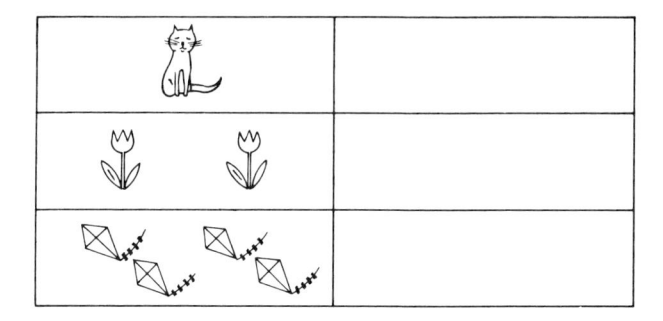

Primary Mathematics for the Mentally Retarded 137

FIGURE 4.43

Pictures and Reproductions. Prepare a sheet with a series of illustrations on one half of a page and a corresponding number of blank boxes on the other side of the paper. Show the children that in the box next to the picture with one object, they should draw one circle, that in the box next to the picture with two objects they should make two circles, and so on.

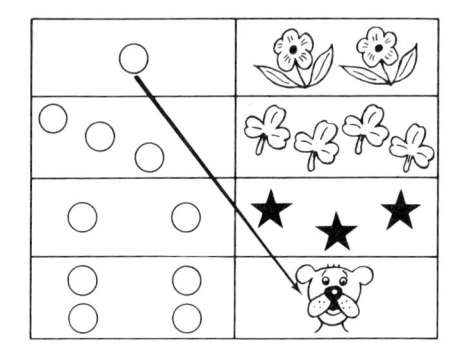

FIGURE 4.44

Match the Circles and Pictures. Divide a piece of paper in half vertically. On the left hand side draw a series of circles in random order and on the right hand side draw a number of illustrations corresponding to the sets of circles. Place them in such a fashion that the numbers of circles does not correspond to the number of items in the illustration next to it. Then demonstrate to the child how to draw connecting lines between the matching sets.

138 Primary Mathematics for the Mentally Retarded

FIGURE 4.45

Color the Pictures. Present the child with a series of illustrated sets. Have him color the objects according to your directions. "Color two flowers red and one flower blue."

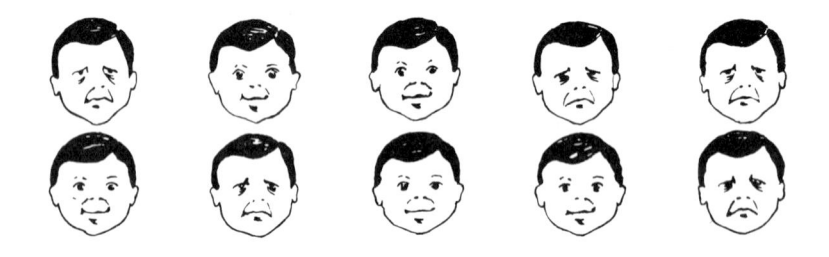

FIGURE 4.46

Marking. Prepare a sheet with happy and sad faces. Give the children a variety of instructions such as "Put a mark (X) on three sad faces. Put a mark on two happy faces."

Elephant Dance. One child is selected as the elephant trainer. Several children are chosen as circus elephants. The trainer hands each child a card with a number printed on it. Then the elephants march in a circle around the trainer until he calls a number. When a number is called all of the elephants stop and the child with the number that was called steps forward and taps his foot the same number of times as the numeral he holds. If he is correct he returns to his place in the circle, if not, he must stay in the circle with the trainer.

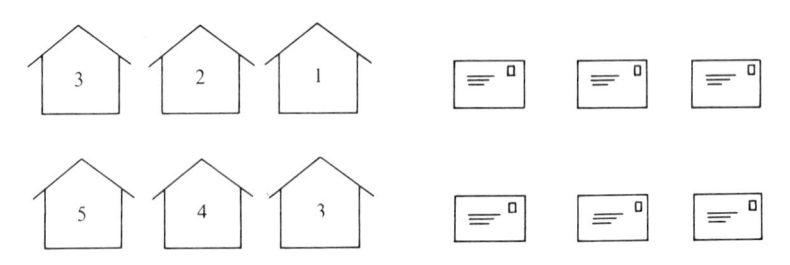

Primary Mathematics for the Mentally Retarded 139

FIGURE 4.47

Mailman. On a large piece of tagboard draw several rows of houses the same shape but slightly larger than a letter size envelope. A numeral is attached to each house with a paperclip. A child is selected for each street and is given cards constructed to look like letters. Each child delivers his mail by placing the proper number of letters at each house on his street.

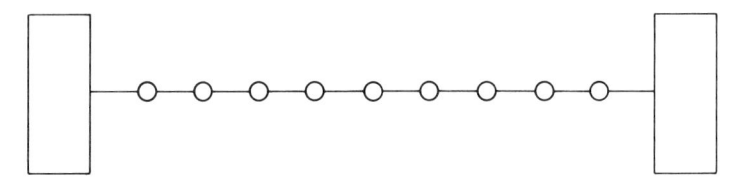

FIGURE 4.48

Bead Frame. Use a teacher-made number frame or commercial abacus to teach separating and combining sets. For example, ten may be shown as:

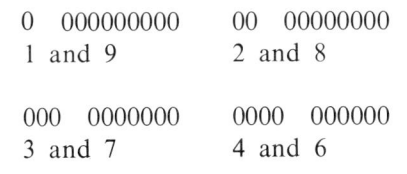

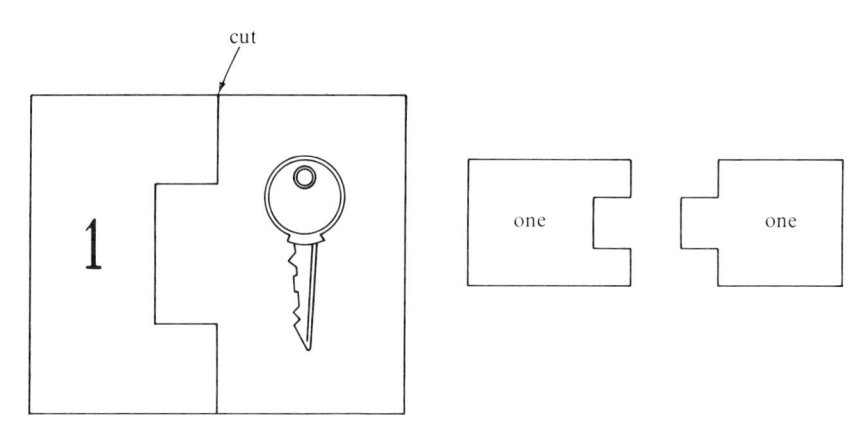

                0   000000000   00   00000000
                1 and 9   2 and 8

                000   0000000   0000   000000
                3 and 7   4 and 6

FIGURE 4.49

Interlocking Number Cards. These cards may be used individually by the children (a set could be made for each child by himself) to practice set and number recognition or the teacher could use them as flash cards in various ways. When children use them alone it is important that the children say the number's name when matching. They can be used alone either naming the number of objects, finding an example of the number, writing the word for the numeral or the number for the word or set. They may be made from posterboard and illustrated with line drawings or pictures cut from magazines.

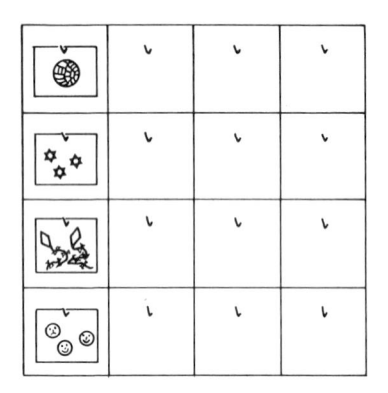

FIGURE 4.50

Picture Holder. For this game, divide a 24" x 36" of tagboard into sixteen sections. Use adhesive layers, paper clips or some other device to make a hook on which to hang picture cards. Make a series of 5" x 7" number cards by drawing or pasting sets of objects onto each one. The children are provided with cards and asked to match their cards to those the teacher has placed.

Another use of the picture holder is to teach "greater than—less than." Provide at least four blank cards. Place one card in the top space in column one. Ask the child to find a card with one less than (or one greater than) and place it in the top space in column two. If the number placed by the teacher in column one were four, the child would fill the entire first row. If the number had been one, the card in column two would have been blank. The teacher would thus proceed to the second row and begin another series.

Grab Bag. A paper bag is filled with cards with sets drawn or pictured as shown in the previous activity. Each child draws a card in turn and names the set. If correct, he keeps the card, if incorrect, he returns it to the grab bag. The child with the most cards is the winner.

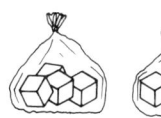

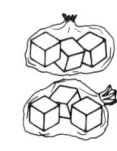

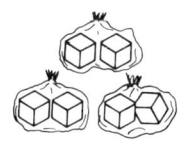

Primary Mathematics for the Mentally Retarded 141

FIGURE 4.51

Cubes. Cubes or other small objects may be sorted into polyethylene bags to indicate the various ways of representing sets. The example shows several ways of regarding the set of six.

The advantage of the polyethylene bag is that it illustrates the limits of the subsets. The example in Figure 4.51 shows a set of six counting cubes in one bag and three different ways of representing six by subsets. As shown in the illustration, other names for six are four and two, three and three, and two, two, and two.

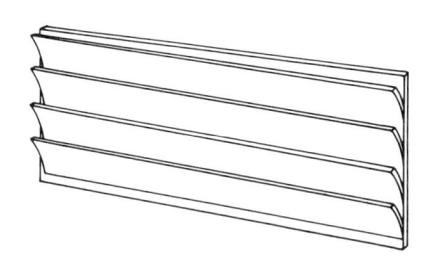

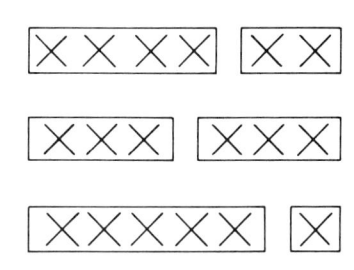

FIGURE 4.52

Pocket Charts. (room size and individual)
Use cards to show ways of making six.

Guess the Number. I am thinking of a number that is one more than five. Guess the number.

I am thinking of a number that is one greater than two. Guess the number.

Blindmen Guess. The object of this game is for a number of blindfolded children to guess the name of a classmate who is counting.

Strips of cloth are used as blindfolds. The children in the game are blindfolded and placed in a circle in such a manner that no one knows who is next to him. Then one of the children is selected to be "it". "It" moves to the center of the circle and begins to count beginning with the number one. The children take turns guessing until someone makes the correct choice. That person is the winner, and a new game begins.

142   *Primary Mathematics for the Mentally Retarded*

How Many in a Dozen? Another way to ask the question, "How many is twelve" is "How many in a dozen?" The worksheet below is one way to teach of ideas of dozen and one-half dozen.

Dozen
   Dozen eggs

½ Dozen oranges

6 Apples

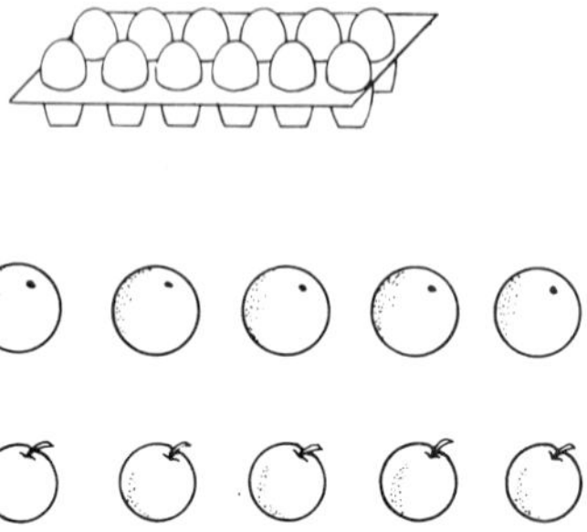

FIGURE 4.53

Another name for twelve is a dozen. Another name for six is a half-dozen. Write each of these another way.

        A dozen peaches   a half-dozen peaches

          six pears   twelve grapefruit

Dog Races. Each player selects a track and then takes turns spinning the dial. The dial should have more chances for the small numbers (five ones, four twos, three threes, two fours, and one five). The child

1	2	3	4	5	6	7	8	9	10	11	12	13
	spin again			fwd. 3				back 2				
		fwd. 3			back 2		spin again					WINNER
				spin again			fwd. 3		back 2			
		fwd. 3		back 2		spin again						

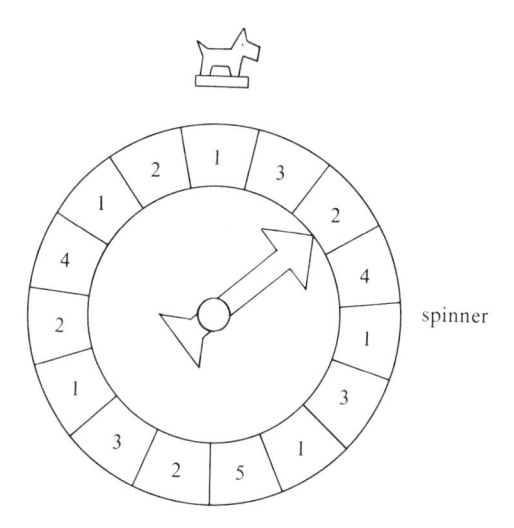

Primary Mathematics for the Mentally Retarded 143

FIGURE 4.54

advances the number of spaces indicated on the spinner. If he lands on a space with a bonus or a penalty, he follows the direction. The player whose dog reaches the thirteen spot first is selected the winner.

Ask, "Who is in the lead? How many ahead is he? John dialed two, he was on five. Five and two make seven. He has now gone seven spaces," etc.

ORDINAL NUMBER

As indicated in Chapter 3, the ordinal number is used to indicate position in series. When one counts a collection of objects to discover the cardinal number, the order in which the items are counted makes no difference in the result. However, when a number is used to indicate placement (the positional use), the order is significant. If one counts the set of pencils in Figure 4.55 from left to right, or vice versa, the six pencils are found. However, if one counts from left to right, pencil A is number one (first); but when one counts from right to left, pencil A is number six (sixth, last). Retarded children will need considerable experience in using ordinal number to learn that position is relative.

The primary teacher of the mentally retarded might expect the children to master the ordinals first, second, third, fourth, fifth and last. He should be able to use positional number to the same degree as cardinal number. That is, number ten may be used to indicate a set of ten as well as position ten.

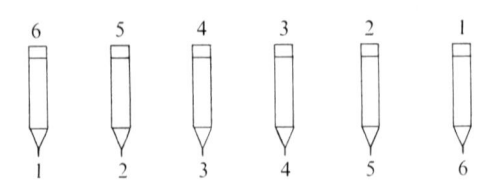

FIGURE 4.55

Incidental Teaching. The opportunities for incidental teaching do not diminish at the primary level. "The second row may leave for lunch first. Everyone take a number from the box, then line up in order. All right, who is number fifteen? You are last. Number fourteen, you are next to last."

The Number Before, After, Between. The children will need to learn the order of numbers through exercises which give practice in thinking of the number which comes before, after, or in between other numbers.

One approach is to use a sequence number card which has one or more numerals missing. Figure 4.56 shows some samples.

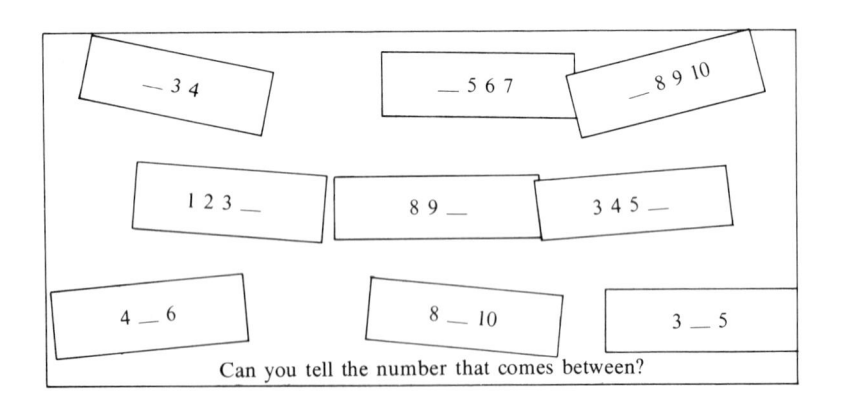

FIGURE 4.56

Another technique is to play a "thinking" game with the children. Say, "I am thinking of a number between eight and ten. What is the number? I am thinking of the number which comes before five. Can you tell me the number? What number comes after six?"

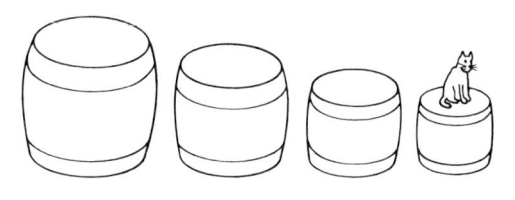

Primary Mathematics for the Mentally Retarded 145

FIGURE 4.57

Cat on the Barrel. Figure 4.57 shows a series of colorful plastic barrels decreasing in size with a toy cat attached to the smallest one. The student takes them apart (find the cat) by beginning with the large one first, but puts them back together (hide the cat) by beginning with the small one. The barrels may be put together and seriated. "Put the biggest one here, then the next largest in size until you get to the small one. Show me number two; where is number one?"

Three in a Row. Bring three children to the front of the room and line them in a row. Give the first child a card which says *first*, the second child a card which says *second*, and the third child a card which says *third*. "This is your new name. Now listen carefully, and when I call on you, I want you to do exactly as I tell you."

First, raise your hands.
Third, clap your hands.
Second, put your hands on your hips.

Will the second person touch your shoes?
Will the third person wave at the class?
Will the first person cross your feet?

I want the first person to take his seat.
Now will the second person take your seat?
Now the third person should sit down at his own desk.

The game may be repeated with a new group of three, and the terms *first*, *middle*, and *last* may be substituted if they seem appropriate.

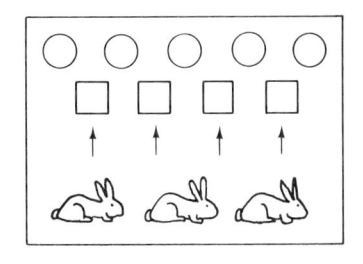

FIGURE 4.58

Worksheets. Put a mark (X) on the third ball; on the number two; on the last arrow; on the middle rabbit.

Nesting Wood Boxes. The children are challenged to fit one box inside the other, or to reverse them and pile them high. The blocks pictured in Figure 4.59 are constructed of natural hardwood with an orange finish. The children learn concepts of sequencing by size and volume as they build towers or fit the boxes inside each other.

FIGURE 4.59

Addresses and Telephone Numbers. The children will benefit from two special uses of ordinal number; namely, the address and the telephone number. Addresses may best be taught as a special use of ordinal number although the teacher may elect to teach telephone numbers in another context.

Dialing the Telephone

Learning to dial the telephone is a very practical non-computational use of number symbols. Although most telephone numbers have been converted to seven digits, some children's phones will still have the two letter prefix. Some telephones do not have dials but rather a rectangular punch board.

Write a telephone number on the chalk board. Have the children read it with you. Establish a rhythm in reading the numbers and include

Primary Mathematics for the Mentally Retarded 147

a pause between the exchange and the number. Give practice with both the three digit exchange as well as the exchange with a combination of letters and numerals.

FL3-1867
592-2094

Teach the children to write the numbers with a dash separating the exchange and the last four digits.

837-5482
594-2870

Reproduce the design of a telephone dial on a large piece of tagboard and mount it in the front of the room. Give each child a smaller reproduction of the same dial constructed from a four by five inch card. As you point to the letters and numbers on the demonstration card, ask the children to point to the corresponding letters and numbers on their own cards.

The next step is to practice dialing on a toy telephone.

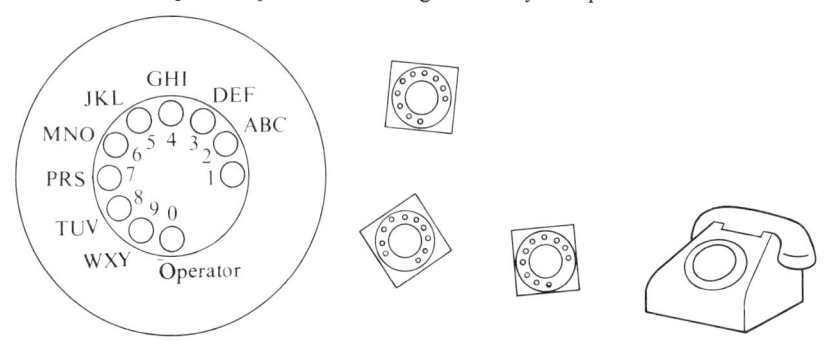

FIGURE 4.60

Help the children learn their own telephone numbers.

Learning Your Address

Another very practical application of numbers is the street address. Street addresses are actually ordinal numbers used to locate specific residences and businesses. A study of addresses not only will enhance the children's traveling skills but also show him a very useful application of ordinal numbers.

The teacher should prepare a list of the children's street addresses. The children will need ample practice in saying and writing their own street address until they are able to do both without assistance and from memory. Next the children should learn to read addresses through activities similar to the ones described in the following paragraph.

Reading Addresses

Construct a number of cards with street addresses on them. You might use the addresses of the children in class or use fictitious ones. Hold the cards up and have the children read them.

3715 Chestnut Street   1408 University Avenue   5 Slaughter Drive

Use a series of pictures which illustrate the name and number as illustrated. Give the children ample practice in reading the street as well as the house number.

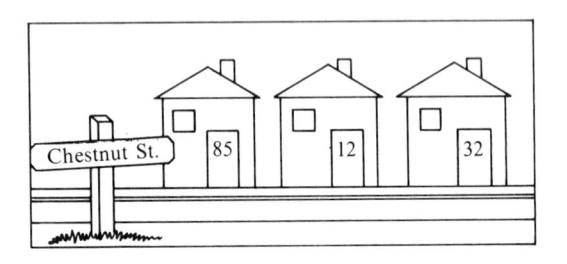

FIGURE 4.61

Make the children aware that apartments have numbers. Use illustrations like Figures 4.61 and 4.62 to give the children adequate practice.

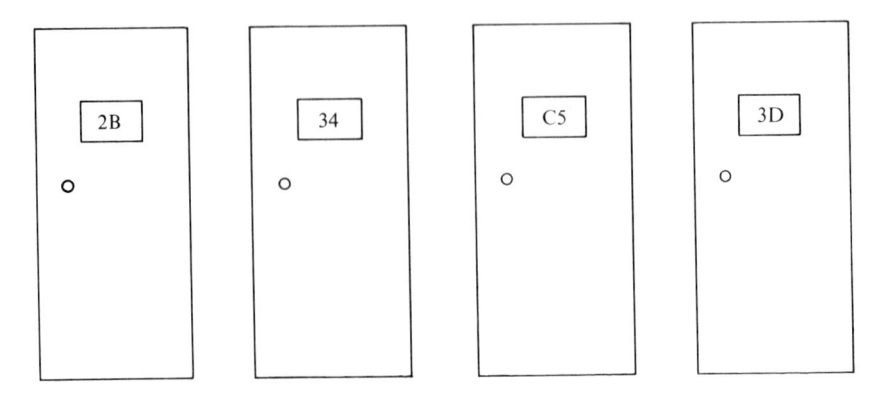

FIGURE 4.62

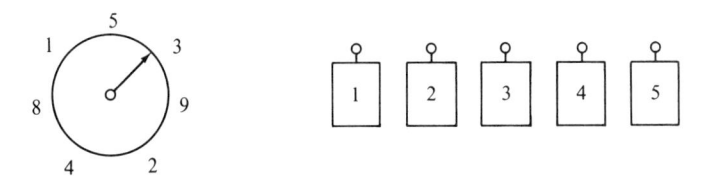

FIGURE 4.63

Spinner. The child spins the dial which will stop on a number. The child takes the card with that number. If a succeeding child lands on that same number, he forfeits his turn. The child with the most cards wins.

MEASUREMENT

The objective in the category for primary retardates is to develop an understanding of measurement concepts and devices. The skills will be related to dry and linear measures, weight, calendar, clock, and temperature.

At the primary level, it is not wise to introduce standard units such as inch or foot, but some idea of fixed comparison should develop. For example, Mary is shorter than Bill, while Henry is taller. Bill is the fixed unit for this comparison. It can be shown that one board is longer than another by placing sticks of equal length end to end by each board. Two sticks could be utilized to indicate that John's board is two sticks long, or that Jane's board is three sticks long. The boards might be measured by moving one stick from end to end and counting the number of times it is used. If a board were somewhat greater or less than a given number of units, the pupil would indicate that Mary's board is a little less than two sticks long, or John's a little more than three sticks long.

Names are given to such containers as cups, pints and quarts. Hour, pound, and temperature are introduced. The suggestions for accomplishing these ends are given below.

Telling Time

Learning to tell time is one of the most difficult measurement skills for mentally retarded children. The research reviewed in Chapter 1 indicated that these children have a poor sequence of time. When this deficit is coupled with the consideration of the complexity of the clock's number system, it is not surprising that they have problems. In spite of the difficulty encountered in learning to tell time, it is one of the most enjoyable and rewarding topics to teach. Children want to understand their environment, emulate adults, and are highly motivated by mechanical instruments. At a young age they learn to identify a clock and have a vague notion that it is something quite important. They see their parents and older children frequently referring to their wrist watches during the day. They enjoy listening to the "tick, tick", "bong, bong", "dong, dong", "cuckoo", and other fun sounds associated with the variety of time pieces. In short, their experiences with clocks help set the background for learning to tell time. However, if these children are to progress beyond regarding clocks as interesting toys, they must receive highly structured and sequential instruction. Teaching skills in visual-perception such as differentiating the big hand from the little hand, noting the significance of the positions of the hands, and perceiving the relationship between the two hands to the numerals, can tax the ingenuity of any teacher.

It is not unusual for primary mentally retarded children to have difficulty in developing such a fundamental visual-perceptual skill as laterality. These children do not find it easy to distinguish between was and saw, 12 and 21, and right from left. Consider the confusion they must experience in attempting to "read" the differences among the times in Figure 4.64.

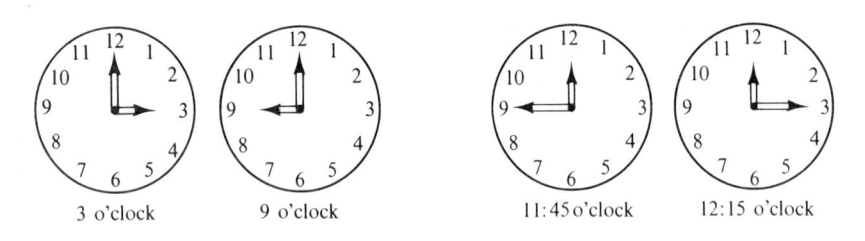

3 o'clock   9 o'clock   11:45 o'clock   12:15 o'clock

FIGURE 4.64

Even when the children overcome the obstacles of visual perception their problems are just beginning. They may learn that the big hand pointed to twelve and the little hand pointed to nine on a clockface means that it is nine o'clock. It is not so simple for them to understand that there are two nine o'clocks each day since each day has twenty-four hours. The twenty-four hours are not indicated on the clockface so that the children must be able to think of twenty-four hours as two sets of twelve. At nine o'clock in the evening, it is time to go to bed, while at nine o'clock in the morning it is time to go to school.

The author has observed that the teacher who does a good job in organizing and presenting instruction in the teaching of time is generally an excellent teacher in all facets of mathematics. This observation is

Primary Mathematics for the Mentally Retarded 151

not surprising when one reflects on the complexity of the teaching of time to the mentally retarded.

The children will have some background with concepts of time. They have had some experience with the ideas of "time for the school bus, time for lunch, time for recess" and so forth. They can locate the classroom clock and probably know where their clocks are at home. They probably have associated time with these instruments in some way. Activities related to experiences such as these should be continued. For example, ask the children, "Has your bus ever been late on a snowy day? Which comes first, time to go to school or time to eat breakfast? Who came to school before you this morning? Do you need more time to finish your milk?" Familiarize the children with some of the more common clocks. Present pictures of clocks and ask the children to tell about the clocks in their home or clocks they have seen elsewhere.

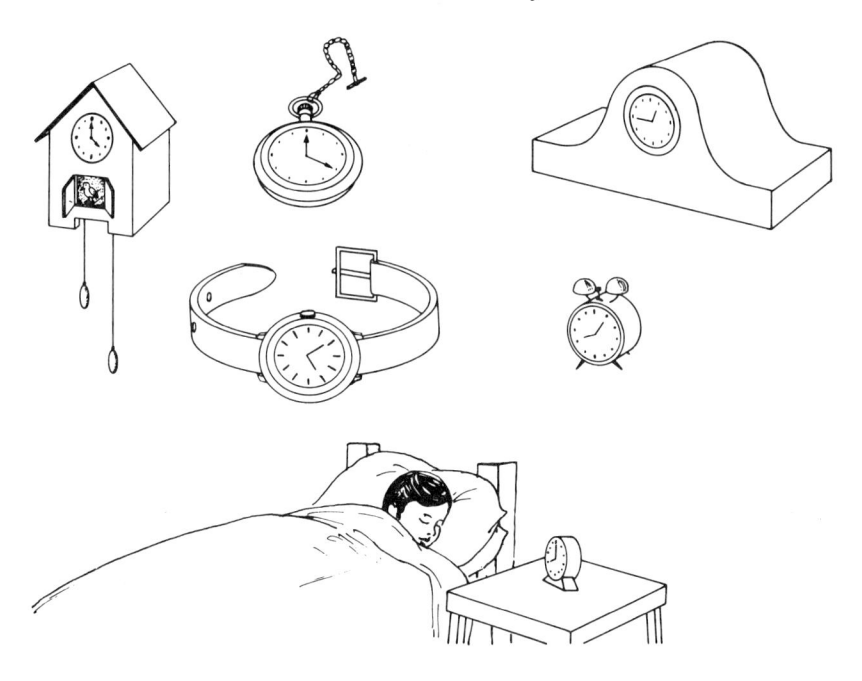

FIGURE 4.65

Present the face of the clock in a series of steps: (1) show a clock face with all the parts. Call attention to the circle, the numerals, and the hands. (2) Direct the children to watch as you construct a clock. "Here is the circle, now the numerals and then the hands are added." This can be demonstrated easily with transparencies, a series of sequential

152   *Primary Mathematics for the Mentally Retarded*

pictures, or it may be drawn on the chalk board in three steps. (3) Have the children construct their own clock by assembling a puzzle clock easily constructed out of posterboard. Draw a circle, then place the numerals and the hands to make a clock. Space each so that the clock can be cut into puzzle pieces as shown in Figures 4.66, 4.67 and 4.68.

Step (1) Discussion of parts of clock (whole to parts)

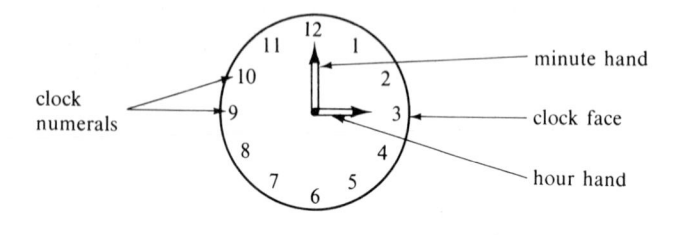

FIGURE 4.66

Step (2) Teacher demonstration of clock (parts to whole)

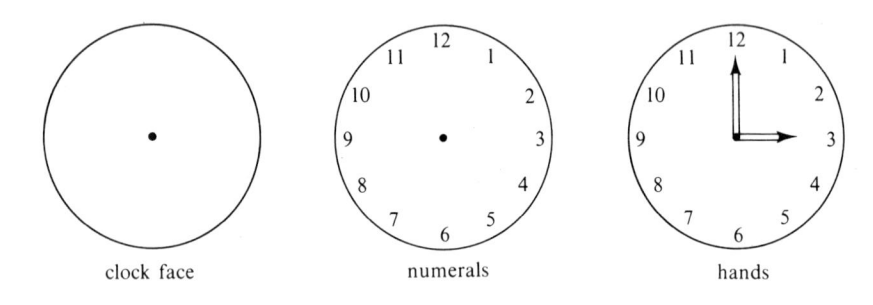

FIGURE 4.67

Step (3) Clock Puzzle: (whole to parts and parts to whole)

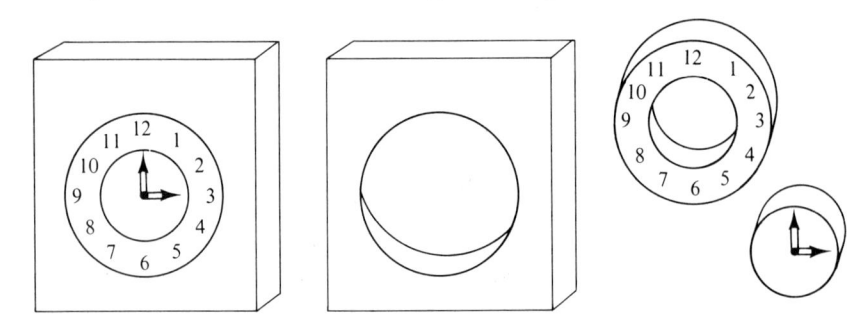

FIGURE 4.68

Primary Mathematics for the Mentally Retarded 153

The activities paralleling these demonstrations should include drawing circles, and marking them as clocks, identifying big and little hands, counting the numerals on the clock, and so forth.

Next use a simple clock made of tagboard, masonite, or plywood. These can be constructed although they are available from school supply companies at reasonable prices. The minute hand should be omitted at first, and when it is added it should be painted on or glued on pointing to the twelve. The hour hand should be adjustable. There should be a demonstration clock at least twelve inches square and all of the children should have an individual duplicate at their desk at least five inches square.

Hold the demonstration clock before the group and count, "one, two, three, four........twelve. See, the clock has twelve numbers. Put your finger on the one, on the six, etc. Watch, I am going to cover a number. Which one did I hide?"

Give the children their individual clocks. "Instead of pointing at the hour with your finger, use this marker. It is called the hour hand. Point to the eight. Now the clock says eight o'clock. Look carefully, I have moved the hour hand. Now the hour hand points to six o'clock. Now, I have moved the hour hand again. What time does the clock say now?" Always point the hour hand directly at the numeral. Have the children adjust their clocks to match yours exactly. They will learn to read the hour hand when it is between two numerals at a later date.

Primary Clock. Give the children two circles cut out of 11½" × 8" newsprint. "This circle is the face of the clock. See, it has numbers from one to twelve. The numbers tell us the hour. You make this second circle into the face of a clock by putting the numbers in the right places. The marks on the circle will help you place the numerals correctly."

Have the children construct a paper plate clock with the minute hand fixed at twelve and the hour hand movable. The hands should be made of different colors and should be labeled so that they are easily distinguishable. Give the children ample practice in naming all the parts of the clock, especially the hour hand.

The term *o'clock* should be presented as an easier way to say "on the clock." Rather than saying it is five on the clock, we say it is five o'clock.

Use the paper plate clock for this exercise. Instruct the children to *read the hour hand first.* The minute hand is always pointing to twelve when it is exactly on the hour.

"Now children, I am going to call the time exactly on an hour. You make your clocks say the hour that I say."

Clock Relay. Divide the class into several teams. Place a number of paper plate clocks on the chalk tray. Have the children form one relay line for each team. The first child in each line goes to the front of the room and picks up a card. The card has an hour written on it. The child goes to the clock and sets the clock to read the same as the card. Then he returns to his line and tags the next child who takes a card and sets the clock, etc. The first team through their set of cards wins.

Using Clocks to Teach About Time. A variety of clock faces and toy clocks are available through school supply firms which are designed to aid the teacher in presenting the basic ideas of time and reading of the clock. These teaching aids vary from the simple and inexpensive to the complex and costly. The teacher should have a collection of these in the room to make the study of the clock interesting and to help the children recognize a variety of clock face designs. With the aid of the toy clocks the teacher should lead discussion on such topics as the time of a favorite television show, recess, lunch, church services and other regularly scheduled events in the children's experiences.

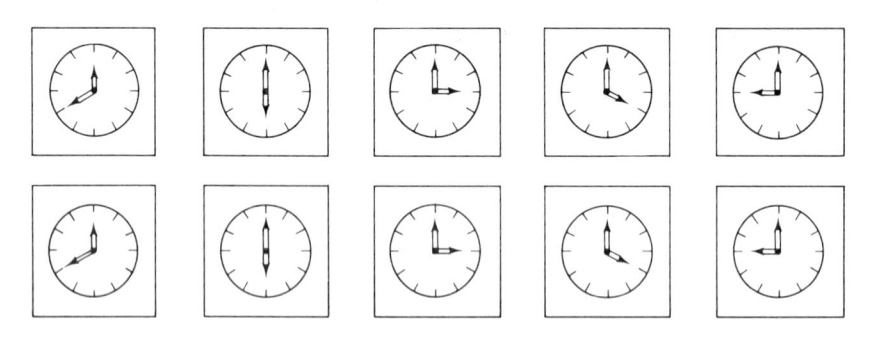

FIGURE 4.69

Matching Clocks Which Say the Same Time. Prepare five pairs of clocks with each pair showing an identical time. One set is needed for each child. Divide the cards among the children so that each child has a set of five matching pairs. The cards should be distributed in a random manner so that each child has mixed pairs. Have the children match the clocks with identical times.

Selecting the Correct Time. Distribute papers with clocks drawn on them like those shown in Figure 4.70. "What do you think we are going to do here? What time does this clock show? How do you know? Which

Primary Mathematics for the Mentally Retarded 155

number under the clock tells the correct time? Put a circle around the number which tells the time shown on the clock."

① 2 3   6 ⑦ 8   1 2 3   6 7 8   2 3 4

FIGURE 4.70

Make a mark with your pencil to show which clock is like the first one (Figure 4.71).

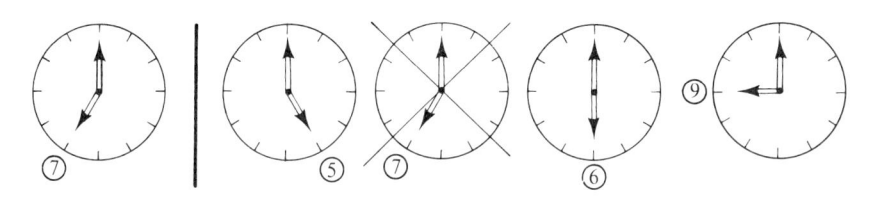

⑦   ⑤ ⑦   ⑥   ⑨

FIGURE 4.71

Mark with your pencil the clock which tells a different time (Figure 4.72).

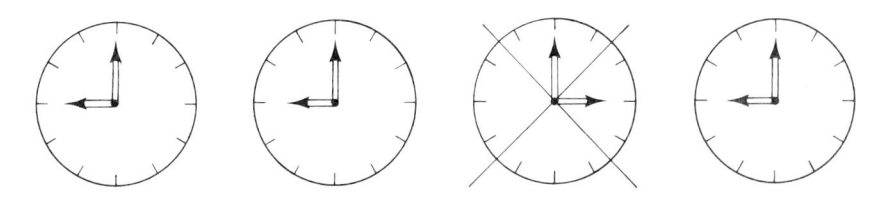

FIGURE 4.72

Making the Correct Time. Prepare a set of papers from a duplicating master with illustrated clocks complete except that the hour hands have been omitted. A numeral is written under each clock to indicate the time that the clock should show. "Look at these clocks. See in each

156   *Primary Mathematics for the Mentally Retarded*

clock the big hand is pointing to the twelve to show that we are talking about a time exactly on the hour. See the number three under the first clock. Draw an hour hand on the clock above the three so that the clock says three o'clock. For the rest of the clocks, read the number under the clock and make the clock above the number show that time."

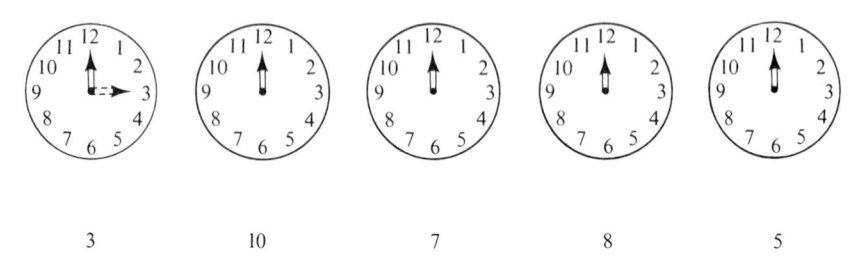

      3   10   7   8   5

FIGURE 4.73

Vary the exercises by having the children add both hands (Figure 4.74).

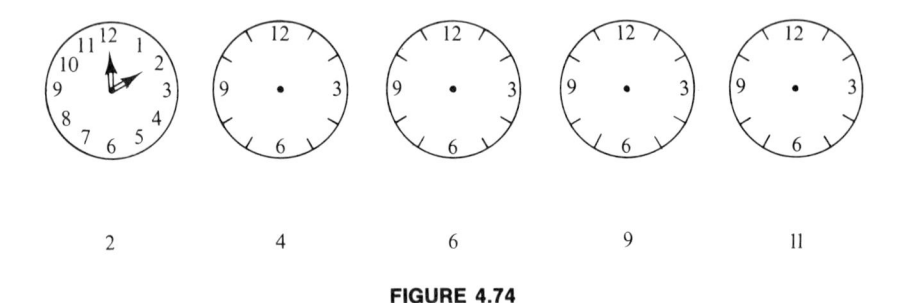

      2   4   6   9   11

FIGURE 4.74

Write the correct times in the spaces (Figure 4.75).

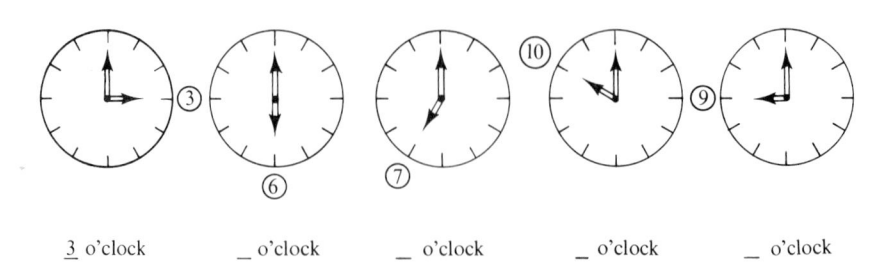

3 o'clock   _ o'clock   _ o'clock   _ o'clock   _ o'clock

FIGURE 4.75

Many other activities can be provided to help the children learn to tell time by the hour. The teacher should make these as interesting and

Primary Mathematics for the Mentally Retarded 157

pleasant as possible. Games should be utilized as well as practical situations. For example, allow the children to play card games with the matching sets of clocks described above. Give each child two, four, or six cards and have them draw from each other in the same way one does in "Old Maid" or "Authors." The one to draw the most pairs wins. One card could be marked midnight and the player who ends up with it could be turned into a "pumpkin" and sent to the "pumpkin chair" until the next game. Also, let the children set the alarm clock for "time to go to recess, time to stop working," etc. The activities and games are limited only by the teacher's imagination. The important consideration is that the children have daily experiences improving the concept of time and their skill in reading the clock and that they have concrete materials with which to work.

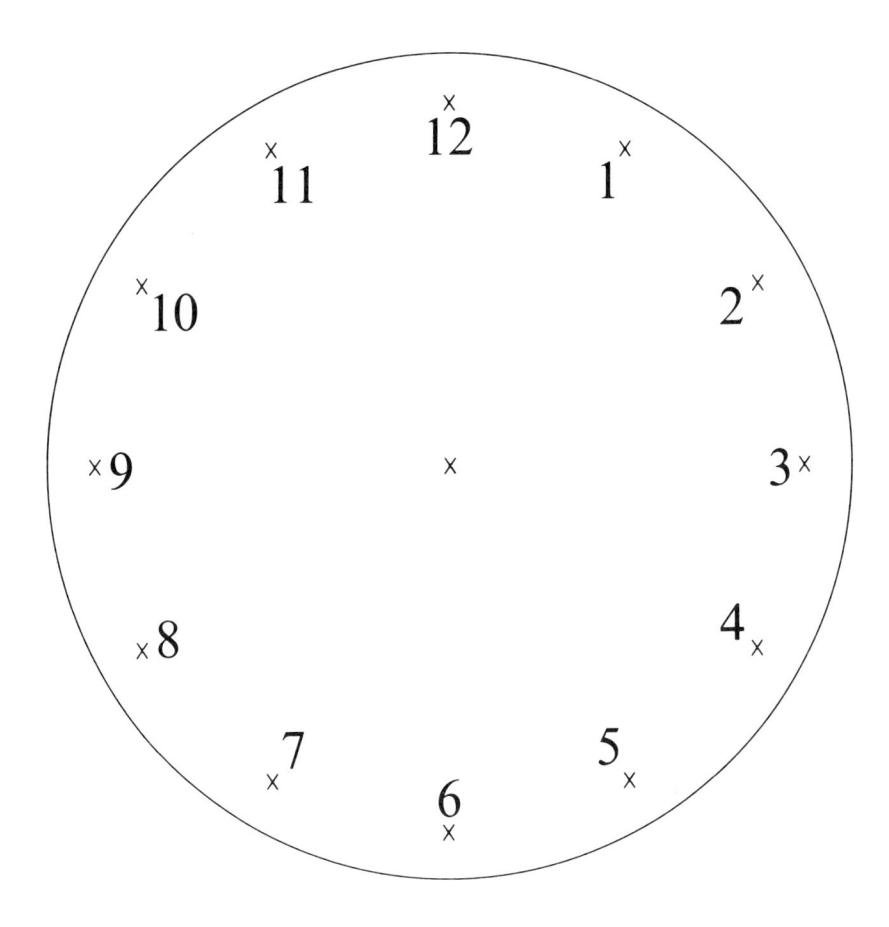

FIGURE 4.76

One needs a set of cards numbered one through twelve, a ruler, a demonstration clock with moveable hands. Set the numbered cards on the floor in a large circle in numerical order. Have twelve children sit behind a number. The rest of the class takes their chairs and sits behind the twelve children so they can see. A thirteenth child is chosen to go in the center of the circle. He is given a ruler to hold in one hand to distinguish the long hand and the short hand of a clock. The child will have his hands out in front of him, his eyes closed, and will turn around three times. When he stops the teacher will ask "What time is it?" The child who answers correctly will change the hands on the demonstration clock and then go into the center of the circle. The child who had previously been in the center of the circle will take the place of the the who had answered correctly.

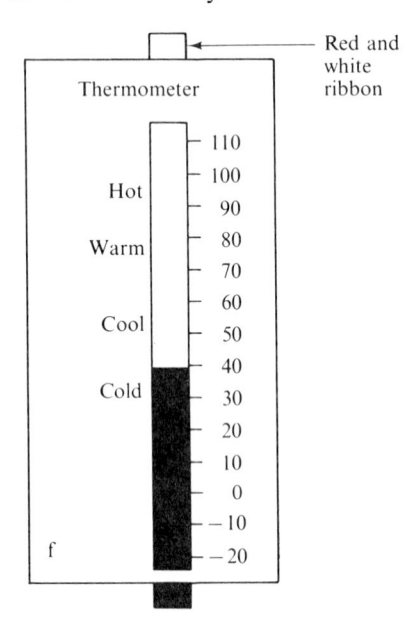

FIGURE 4.77

Reading the Thermometer

The disk thermometer was introduced at the preprimary level. The children are now ready for a more exact instrument. The terms hot, warm, cold and cool are used without the picture clues. A thermometer is constructed out of cardboard and a strip of red and white ribbon.

Through continued practice the children learn that if the red mark is low that it is cold and if it is high, it is hot.

A few children may be able to read some of the numerals.

	Month					
Sun	Mon	Tue	Wed	Thur	Fri	Sat

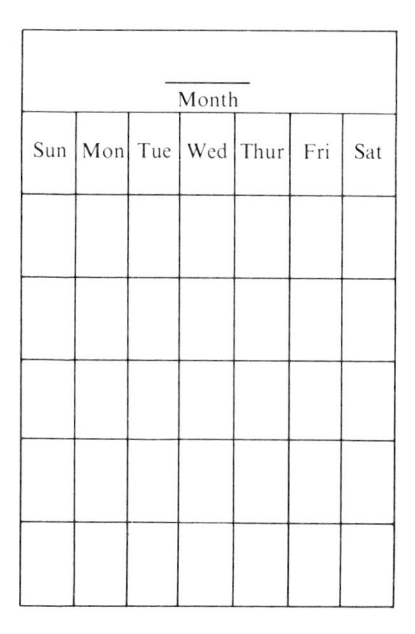

FIGURE 4.78

Reading the Calendar

The child gradually begins to understand that the calendar is related to time. He is taught to read the days of the week. The teacher assists the child in marking birthdays and other special events on the calendar. The child reads the day and date each day and they are written on the chalk board. The month is also noted. The child assists in the construction of the classroom calendar each month and/or makes his own.

Liquid Measures

The "cupful" is probably introduced first. "Bring a cup of water to water the flowers. How many cups of water will it take to make the Kool-Aid? How many cups of sugar did we use?" Pints and quarts are introduced through such common objects as milk cartons. The child will have only a generalized idea of relative size and capacity although the names are used.

Weight

The children go to the school nurse and are weighed in pounds. The teacher discusses the comparative weights. Pictures of different types

160   *Primary Mathematics for the Mentally Retarded*

of scales are shown. "Where have you seen a weight scales like this one Joan? Why do they have weight scales in the grocery?"

Linear Measures

The approach for teaching linear measure has been indicated in the introduction to this section. All of the children should be supplied with the standard ruler twelve inches and the classroom should have several yard sticks. In addition, nonstandard sticks, strings, shoelaces, etc. should be used to make comparisons of length and height.

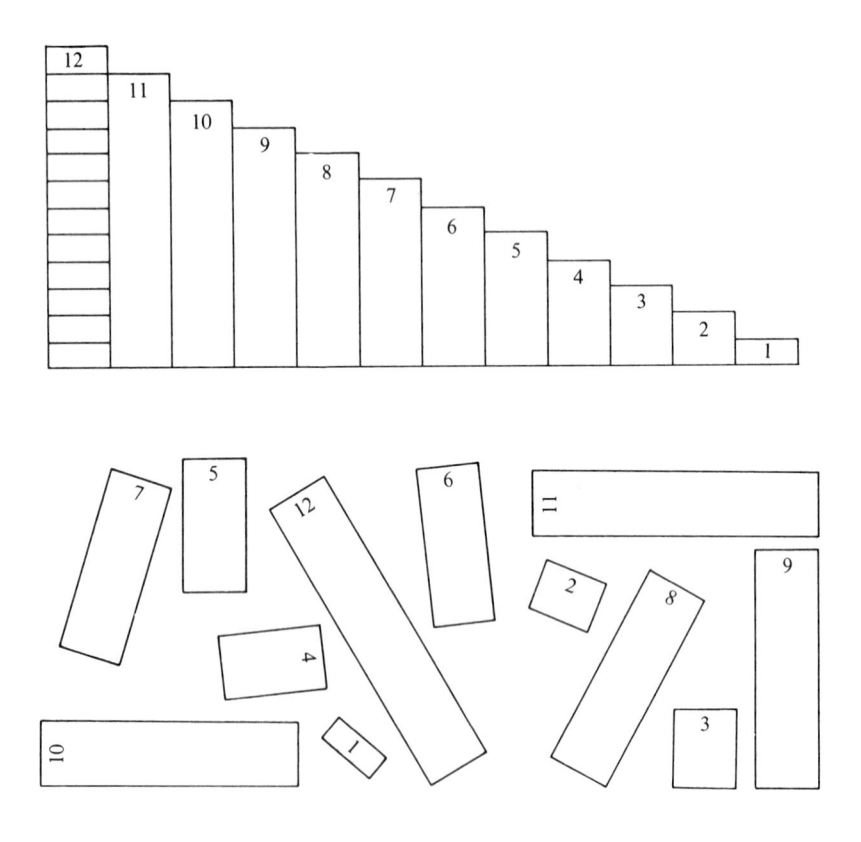

FIGURE 4.79

Construct two sets of boards ranging in length from one to twelve inches. Paint each a different color on one side and all the same color on the other.

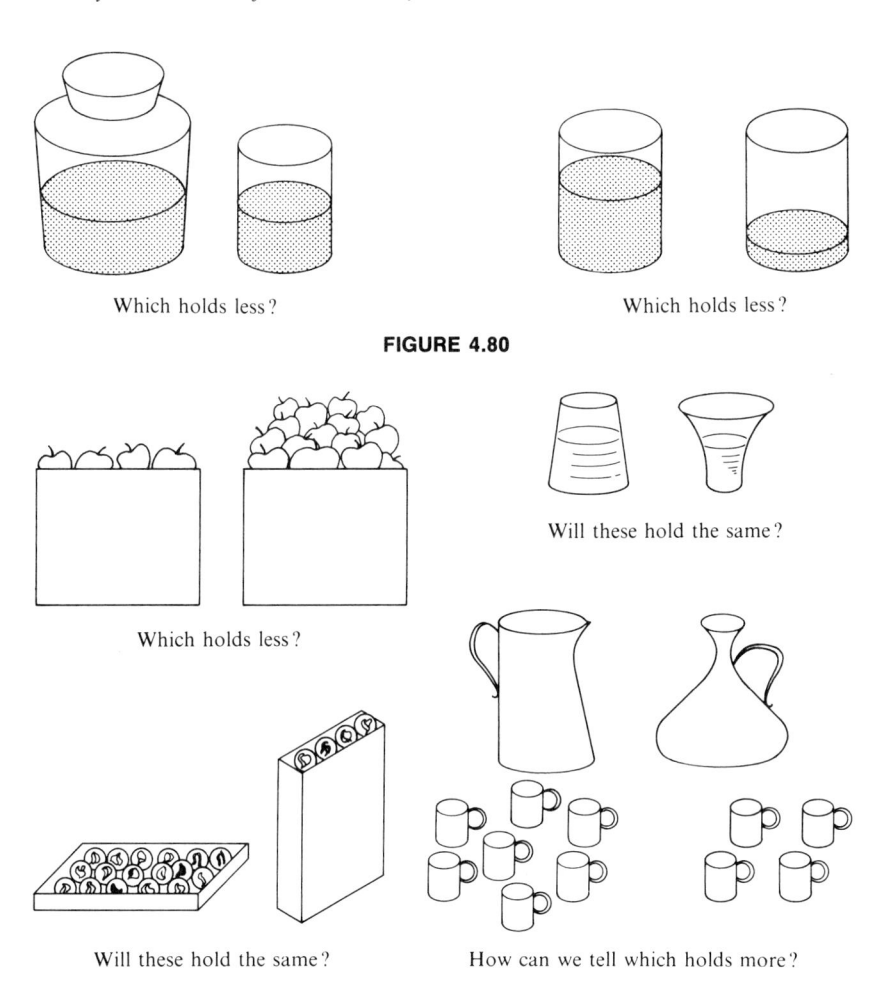

Primary Mathematics for the Mentally Retarded

Which holds less?   Which holds less?

FIGURE 4.80

Which holds less?

Will these hold the same?

Will these hold the same?   How can we tell which holds more?

FIGURE 4.81

MONEY AND VALUE

The child has already been introduced to some coins. He should continue to develop skill in the recognition of the penny, nickel, dime, and quarter. An awareness of the relative value of each coin will continue to increase. The equivalents of the coins are based upon groupings by fives (nickel and quarter) and grouping by tens (dime, half-dollar, dollar).

The symbol ¢ and the word "cents" are used. The primary age retardate will be able to determine the relative purchasing power of the penny, nickel and dime and learn the combinations of coins equivalent to the nickel and dime. One complicating factor in teaching the counting of coins other than pennies is that the coins themselves are not counted. It is the value the coin represents that is counted. Thus to "count" 1 nickel and 2 pennies means to determine the value of 5¢, 1¢, and 1¢. There are only three coins, but they represent the same value as 7 cents.

It should be restated here, that the use of toy money and worksheets picturing coins tend to confuse rather than aid the primary level retarded child.

At the primary level, all of the coins are reviewed, and the ¢ sign is introduced. The children are taught to count by pennies at first and later are taught to count pennies and nickels together. The equivalencies for a nickel and a dime are presented and the children are taught how to make simple purchases.

Barter as an Introduction to the Medium of Exchange

The teacher should be certain that the children have some idea of the different value of various items, and the use of money as a medium of exchange. Begin with common items such as cookies, marbles, suckers, tootsie rolls and so forth. Play some simple bartering games. Trade a vanilla cookie for a chocolate cookie. Have two children exchange a red marble for a blue marble. Discuss the trades as being fair since the items exchanged were essentially equivalent. Then make some inequitable exchanges. Trade one cookie for two cookies; one marble for two marbles and so forth. Discuss these trades as being unfair since two of any item is generally more valuable than one of the same item. Then discuss exchanges of items which are different but have the same approximate value; for example, a sucker for a tootsie roll. It will be apparent to the children that trades such as these are also fair.

The next step is to introduce trades of items of different value; for example suckers for a candy bar. Ask, "What would you rather have, a sucker or a candy bar? If you had a candy bar, would you be willing to trade it for one sucker? Two suckers? How many suckers would you trade your candy bar for?"

From activities such as these, the idea of relative value and exchange may be developed. Assume that a cookie, marble, sucker, piece of gum, and jawbreaker are all priced at 1¢. Have the children make a variety of trades with these items but also involve the penny. Trade one penny for one sucker. Is that a fair trade? Trade two pennies for one jawbreaker. Is that a fair trade?

Primary Mathematics for the Mentally Retarded 163

These introductory steps will help prepare the children for using money as a medium of exchange and for making simple common purchases.

Reviewing Coin Recognition

It is important that the children learn to differentiate the coins themselves before their relative value is taught. The activities used to teach these differences parallel those used in teaching form and perception. The names of the coins themselves have no special meaning. That is, there is nothing (at least for our purposes) in the word "nickel" that tells the children it is equivalent to five pennies and no clue in the word "dime" that tells the children it is equivalent to two nickels. Therefore, in the beginning, the term "5 cents" is preferred to "nickel"; "one cent" preferred to "penny"; and "ten cents" preferred to "dime". It will confuse the children at first to learn that the coins may be named in two different ways, but this understanding will be of immeasurable value in teaching equivalencies of coins and subsequently to making change.

The following activities will aid the children in discriminating among the coins and learning their names.

FIGURE 4.82

The Coin Boards. Coins are attached to squares of masonite with a strong glue. The first board has a penny, nickel, dime, and quarter glued to each corner with a fifty cent piece attached in the center. This will have many uses, and one should be constructed for each child. The first use is identification. The child simply learns the names of the coins and points to the proper coin as he says the name.

A penny, nickel, and a dime should be attached to masonite squares (one coin to each square). These will be used by the child to respond to questions by the teacher. "Show me a penny. Show me five cents. Which coin is the same as five cents?"

Identifying Coins by Touch. Give each child a set of coins in a bag or a box. Ask the children to select a coin just like yours. Use only two different types of coins at first but gradually include all the four basic coins.

Circles and Coins (sorting). Cut out a series of circles corresponding in diameter to the four coins. Have the children sort the circles. Give the children a collection of coins. Have them stack all the coins which are alike together.

Matching Circles and Coins. Give the children a set of coins and a corresponding set of circles. Have them put the coins and circles of the same size in one-to-one correspondence.

Identifying Coins by Size. Draw a series of circles on the chart board, or place cut-outs on the flannel or magnet board. Say, "Here are some circles which are exactly the size of the coins we have studied. Look at this circle. What coin is exactly the same size as this circle?"

Matching Coins. Give each child two sets of the four basic coins. Have the children place the two sets in one-to-one correspondence.

Finding the Circle Which Is Different. Use the flannel board to present a set of four circles. Three of the circles should be the same size as a penny and one should be the size of a nickel. Have the children point to the one that is different. This activity may be made into seat work for the more mature children by preparing a worksheet with a series of sets of circles representing the coins with one foil in each set.

Find the Circle Which Is the Same. Use the flannel board to present one circle and a set of four circles. The first circle will be the same size as one of the circles in the set of four. Have the children locate the circle in the group of four which is the same as the first circle.

Find the Coin Which Is Different. Present a set of four coins such as three pennies and a nickel. Ask the children, "Which one is different. Find the one which is not the same as the rest."

Find the Coin Which Is the Same. Show the children a set of four coins. Then show them one additional coin which is the same as one of the coins in the set. Have the children locate the coin in the set of four which is the same as the coin you are holding.

Learning to Count Money

Once the children have learned that money is a medium of exchange and are able to distinguish one coin from another, they are ready to learn to count money. They should begin by counting sets of pennies up to ten, and then count up to ten cents using the nickel as an equivalent of five cents. Some children will be able to extend their counting skills to twenty pennies and to use the dime as an equivalent of ten cents in the counting process. The teacher will probably not present any extension of counting beyond ten cents which involves using more than one coin of a value greater than one cent. The teacher will want to be certain that the children have a firm command of the combinations of ten cents before proceeding to more difficult concepts.

Begin by having the children count up to five cents. Provide ample opportunity for viewing five cents in a variety of ways. For example, other names for five cents are two cents and three cents; two cents and two cents and one cent; and so on.

Once the children are able to count sets of pennies to five, sets to ten should be introduced. Direct the children to indicate the set of five by a line or space as they reach six and above. This will help them when they begin to count up to ten cents with a combination of a nickel and pennies. Have them rename the set of six pennies as five pennies and one penny; the set of seven pennies as five pennies and two pennies; and continue in a similar fashion until they are able to rename the set of ten pennies as five pennies and five pennies.

FIGURE 4.83

Counting with the Nickel and Dime. Sets of coins six and above have been renamed by the children as a set of five pennies and a set of *n* pennies. The children who perform this renaming task satisfactorily should be introduced to the nickel as an equivalent value of five pennies. If the children have been taught that another name for the nickel is five cents, this will present no serious learning problem. Substitute the nickel for the set of five pennies telling the children that another name for the nickel is "five cents."

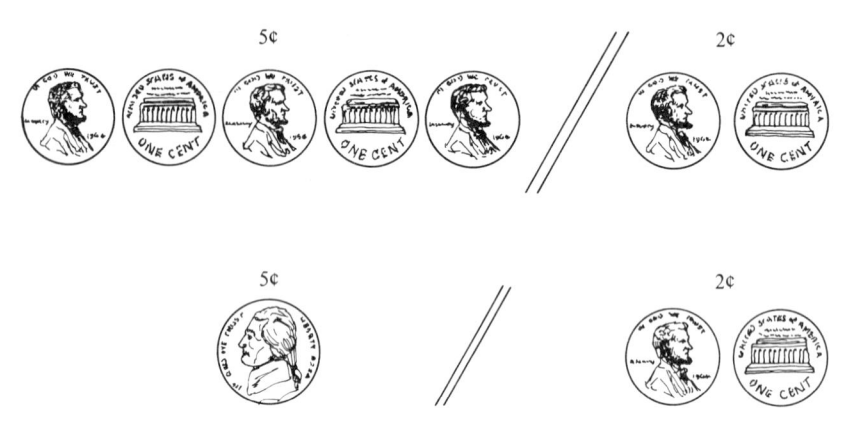

FIGURE 4.84

Give them a series of coin-counting problems with values of five cents to ten cents using sets of pennies and nickels. For example:

one nickel	two pennies
five pennies	two pennies
one nickel	four pennies
one nickel	three pennies
three pennies	one nickel

After the children have learned that a nickel is the equivalent of five cents and that a nickel and five pennies is equivalent to ten cents, they should be taught that two nickels equal ten cents.

The dime may then be shown as the equivalent of ten pennies, two nickels, and one nickel and five pennies. Counting coins beyond the value of ten cents should probably be reserved for the intermediate level. Demonstrate that the set of one dime may be renamed in a variety of ways such as:

Primary Mathematics for the Mentally Retarded

five cents and five cents
seven cents and three cents
two cents, three cents, and five cents

Since ten cents may be renamed in these ways, it is also true that ten cents may also be renamed:

one dime
two nickels
one nickel and five pennies
one nickel, two pennies, and three pennies

Count to twenty-five cents with the following combinations:

twenty-five pennies
one nickel, twenty pennies
one dime, fifteen pennies

Using Money as a Medium of Exchange

The children will be able to make simple purchases after they understand the value of the coins and the use of money as a medium of exchange. The following suggestions will be helpful in preparing the children for actual purchases outside the classroom.

The Money Box. The money box is retained by the teacher. She uses it to supply children with real money for their exercises and games. Approximately fifty cents per child should be available. The mother's club, the petty cash fund, and per child assessment are ways of supplying the box. Unhappily, on occasion, the teacher will be called upon to provide the funds herself. The uses of the money box are quite similar to that of the toy money box used in regular classrooms.

Common Purchases. The teacher collects a group of toys or other items that are ten cents in value or less. Candy bars and penny sticks are ideal. Although it is important that the coins be real, the teacher may find it more convenient to replace the chocolate with a wood block and the peppermint stick with a counting rod. "Put enough money on your desk to pay for this amount of candy." Shoelaces, crackerjacks, animal cookies, are examples of other low cost purchases.

Playstore. The preceding activity may be adapted by allowing one or two children to play clerk and others to be the customers. This method adds to elements of making and counting change.

Purchase Cards. The child is given a 12" x 12" card with pictures of items costing a penny to ten cents. By each picture (which is marked with a price tag), there is a space provided to place the correct amount. The child fills the spaces according to the cost of the purchase.

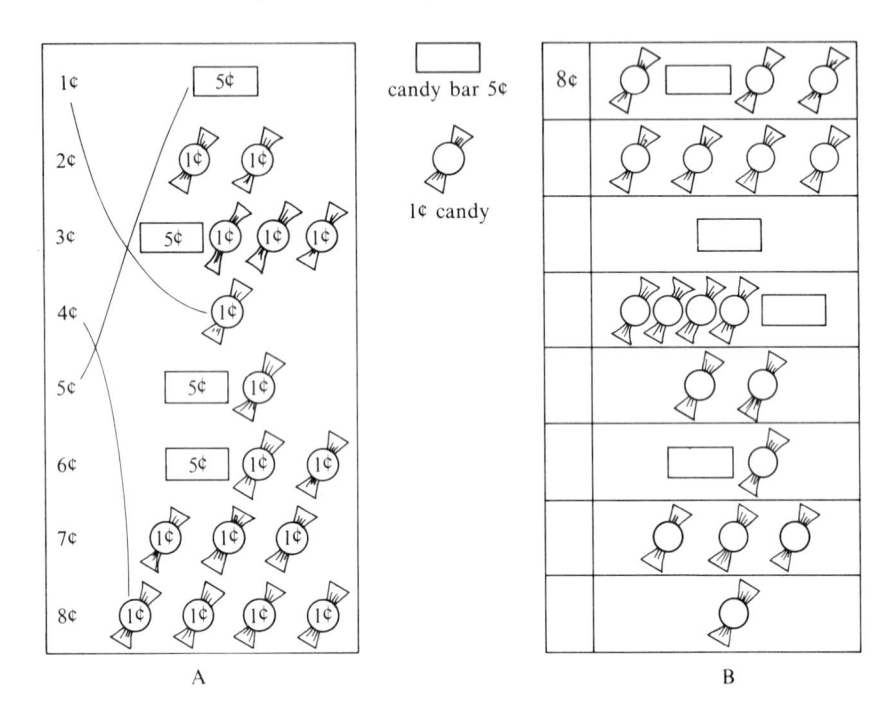

FIGURE 4.85

Worksheets. The reader has been cautioned to use worksheets in a most judicious fashion. Those prepared by the teacher should probably not attempt to illustrate the coins because it is quite difficult to reproduce pictures of the coins on school duplicating machines. However, some commercially printed materials use photographs of coins which are of a very high quality and are acceptable for seat work. Once the children have mastered the ¢ symbol, elementary worksheets such as the two examples shown in Figure 4.85 may be used.

Equivalents. "How many *cents* are in a nickel, a dime, a penny? Let's make an even trade. I'll give you a nickel and you give me ____ pennies. I'll give you a dime and you give me two ____. I'll give you ten pennies and you give me one ____."

Another Way-to-Say. "Another way to say a nickel is ____. Another way to say a dime is ____. Another way to say five cents is ____. Another way to say ten cents is ____. Another way to say seven cents is one nickel and ____."

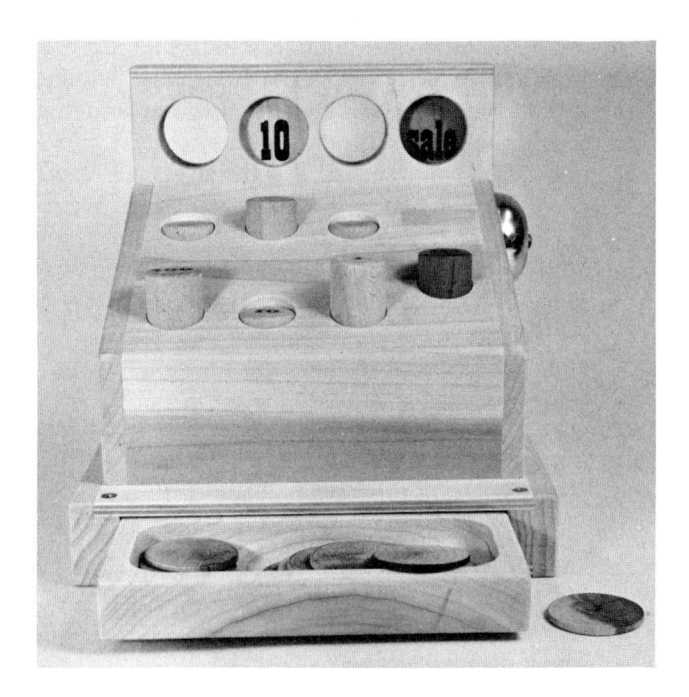

FIGURE 4.86

Making Change

It is easier to count than to add or subtract, so it should not be suprising that the children will be able to reproduce the correct combination of coins for amounts to twenty-five cents, but be unable to make change for amounts much smaller than this. It is simpler for the children to give a clerk one nickel and one penny for a six cent purchase than to make the correct change for a six cent purchase from a dime. Now that the children have learned to count groups of coins, they are ready for systematic instruction in making change.

The children must experience the need for making change. Give some of the children a nickel and several other children five pennies. Then "sell" each child a piece of candy costing two cents, by saying, "You give me two cents and I will give you this piece of candy." The children with the five pennies will be able to buy the candy, while the children with the nickels will not be able to exchange two cents for the candy. Ask the children, "What is another name for five pennies? (five cents). What is another name for a nickel? (five cents). Let's trade your nickel for five pennies. Now can you buy the candy? How many pennies do you have left? (three)." All of the children should then have a two cent piece of candy and three pennies. Next demonstrate another way to trade. Instead of exchanging the nickel for five pennies and then making the purchase, accept the nickel in trade for the two cent piece of candy and three pennies. The children will see through such exercises that they need not have the exact coins to make a purchase. When the coin they have is worth more than the item they purchase, the clerk will give them the difference between the cost of the item and their coin in change. Make certain the children understand the process of change.

Give me change for a nickel.
One nickel is a fair exchange for five pennies.
How much change do I get from a nickel when I spend two cents?
One nickel is a fair exchange for three pennies and a two cent piece of candy. The change in this case is three cents.

After much practice the children will be ready to learn to make change for the dime. At first, use only pennies in change, and add the nickel only after the children are at ease with change in pennies.

Coin	Cost of Item	Change
dime	three cents	seven pennies
dime	four cents	six pennies
dime	five cents	five pennies
dime	three cents	one nickel, two pennies
dime	four cents	one nickel, one penny
dime	five cents	one nickel

All of the activities suggested are designed to prepare the children for actual money transactions. Every opportunity to expose the children to realistic use of money should be utilized. Practical emphasis should be given to using money involving such situations as purchases from vending machines; paying for carnival rides; school lunches; bus fares; theatre and other admissions.

NUMBER OPERATIONS

The children in the primary level are now ready to deal more maturely with additive and subtractive action. Although the children at the preprimary level have been involved in combining and separating, the notational symbols and computational forms are not introduced until this level. In the author's opinion, one of the common errors committed by teachers of the retarded is the introduction of rote computation skills and the introduction of addition and subtraction too early. It has been observed for some time that retarded children are deficient in the understanding of the mathematical processes and in arithmetic reasoning. In order to combat this condition, it is advisable to postpone the teaching of computational addition and subtraction until the children have a firm basis upon which to build. It is also important that the computational skills and the number facts be presented in a way that is understood by the children. For this reason, a modern mathematics instructional program is advisable.

It is important that the teacher evaluate the children's conceptual level before proceeding. The children should:

1. know the number sequence
2. recognize the number symbols
3. write number symbols.

TEACHING ADDITION AND SUBTRACTION

The basis of number operations is the concept of set. Earlier in this chapter it was suggested that the concept of number be developed through tangible sets of real objects. In teaching the first two basic number operations (addition and subtraction) many concrete situations should be utilized including items mentioned previously: blocks, beads, pegs, craft sticks, toys, flannel boards and so forth. In teaching addition and subtraction at the primary level, we introduce the commutative property of addition, mathematical sentences, renaming, and subtraction as the inverse of addition.

Addition

A concept of set is vital to the understanding of the processes of addition. Yet, it is important to bear in mind the distinction between addition and set union. Addition is the operation performed on the cardinal numbers of disjoint sets which yields a single cardinal number called the sum. Set union is the process of joining the elements of two or more sets together to obtain a third set. For example, three boys plus three boys is equal to six boys. This is simple addition. But if the boys in the first group represent a committee composed of Dick, Dan, and Paul and the second group consists of a committee of Dick, John, and Tom, then the cardinal number of the union is not six but five. Dick is a member of both committees. This example should make it clear that the sum of the cardinal numbers of two sets and the cardinal number of two sets are different.

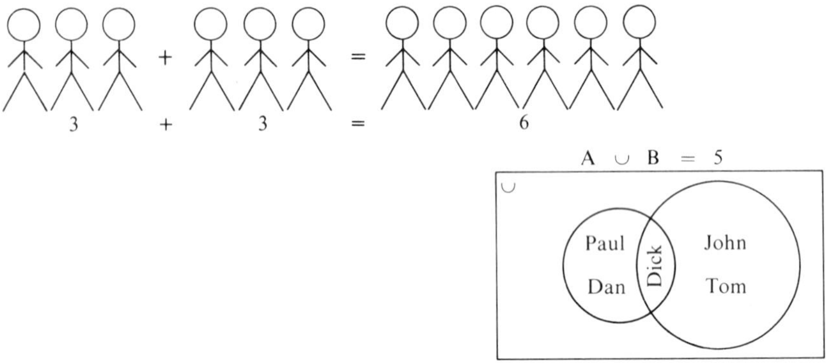

FIGURE 4.87

In the operation of addition, the numbers to be combined are called the addends. The addition operation is symbolized in vertical and horizontal forms:

$$a + b = s \quad \text{and} \quad \begin{array}{r} a \\ +b \\ \hline s \end{array}$$

where a and b represent the addends and s represents the sum. Retarded children will become easily confused by this fine distinction and will more readily develop an understanding of the process of addition by considering only the union of sets which have no common members (disjoint sets). In the case of the union of two disjoint sets the cardinal number of the two sets and the cardinal number of the union of the same two sets are equal.

It should be illustrated to the children that the addition of zero to any number is that number. That is $0 + 1$ is simply another name for 1 since $1 + 0 = 1$. In other words, *zero is the identity element for addition.* The understanding of this basic principle, leads to the understanding and knowledge of nineteen basic addition facts.

+	0	1	2	3	4	5	6	7	8	9
0	0	1	2	3	4	5	6	7	8	9
1	1									
2	2									
3	3									
4	4									
5	5									
6	6									
7	7									
8	8									
9	9									

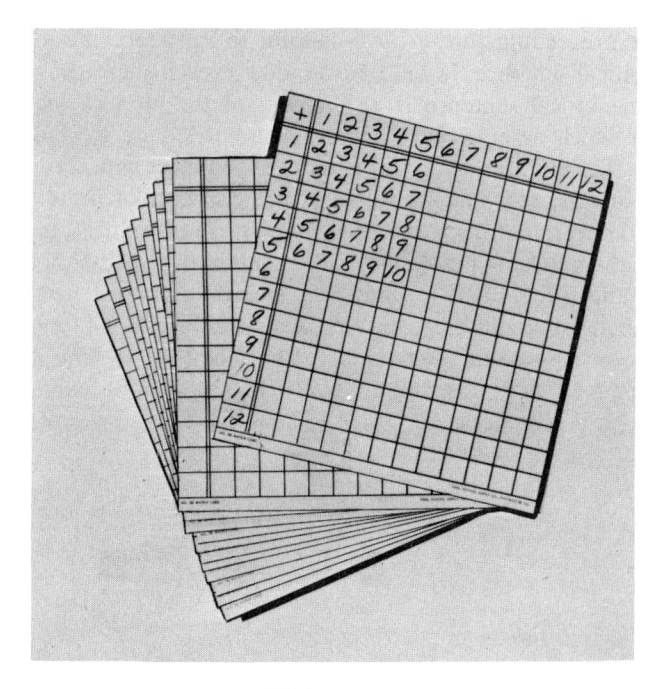

FIGURE 4.88

The children have had a great deal of practice with sets. They have learned that the expression one and one is another name for two; that the expression one and two is another name for three; and the expression one and three is another name for four. After dealing with many similar combinations, the children may be able to generalize that the sum of any number and one is the next larger counting number. This insight will make the meaning of the addition table truly meaningful.

+	0	1	2	3	4	5	6	7	8	9
0	0	1	2	3	4	5	6	7	8	9
1	1	2	3	4	5	6	7	8	9	10
2	2	3								
3	3	4								
4	4	5								
5	5	6								
6	6	7								
7	7	8								
8	8	9								
9	9	10								

Before proceeding further, it is helpful to introduce the idea of the mathematical sentence. It will be extended at each succeeding level but the mathematical sentence is an element of the modern mathematics program which deserves early inclusion in curriculum for the mentally retarded. The children have had lengthy experiences with sets of objects, equivalent sets, reproducing sets and the concepts of more than, less than, and fewer. In order to give new meaning to these ideas, the children need mathematical symbols just as the children need symbols (words) to read and write English sentences. The children will need symbols for numbers, sets, and elements (already introduced); symbols for relations (= ≠ <>) and symbols for operations (+, −). The illustration in Figure 4.89 shows how the work with sets can be expanded into mathematical sentences.

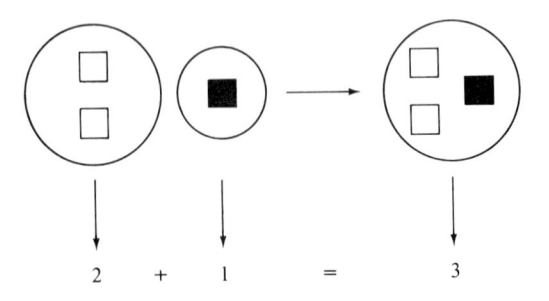

FIGURE 4.89

Primary Mathematics for the Mentally Retarded 175

The children have worked extensively with combining sets of objects. In the example, two blocks have been combined with one block to make a new set of three blocks. The children have already learned to think of two and one as another name for three, and now they will be shown a new way to talk about the process. The sets are represented by numbers and the process of their being joined together is indicated by a relation symbol (+). All mathematical sentences must follow this pattern. When a number is unknown we use the symbol ☐ and when the relationship is unknown we use the symbol ◯ as shown in these examples:

$$2 + \square = 4 \qquad 2 \bigcirc \square = 4$$

Some of the symbols which the retarded will need to become familiar with or which are of interest to the teacher are:

Operations		*Relations*		*Sets, Relations*	
+	addition	= ≠		∈	element of
−	subtraction	< ≮		∉	not element of
×	multiplication	> ≯		⊂	subset
÷	division	≤ ≥		⊄	not subset
∪	union			↔	equivalent to
∩	intersection	≦ ≧		↮	not equal to

It is not intended that these symbols be utilized by the children at this level, but only that the teacher be aware of them.

One of the major aspects of the modern mathematics curriculum is the teaching of the fundamental structure. The properties of number form this fundamental structure. The commutative property of addition is one example of the precise vocabulary which is emphasized in modern mathematics. The teacher of the mentally retarded will wisely refrain from this terminology but she will undoubtedly teach the children that the order of the addends does not affect the sum. The discovery of the commutative property as illustrated by this simple expression will reduce by fifty percent the number of basic addition facts to be learned.

$$1 + 2 = 2 + 1 = 3$$

The children will learn with practice that all other sums less than ten may be worked out in this manner.

```
3 + 2 = 3 + (1 + 1)        3 + 3 = 3 + (1 + 2)
      = (3 + 1) + 1              = (3 + 1) + 2
      = 4 + 1                    = 4 + (2)
      = 5                        = 4 + (1 + 1)
                                 = (4 + 1) + 1
                                 = 5 + 1
                                 = 6
```

If the child then learns that 9 + 1 = 10, then all sums equal to ten may be discovered and placed in the table which now appears like this:

```
+ | 0  1  2  3  4  5  6  7  8  9
0 | 0  1  2  3  4  5  6  7  8  9
1 | 1  2  3  4  5  6  7  8  9  10
2 | 2  3  4  5  6  7  8  9  10
3 | 3  4  5  6  7  8  9  10
4 | 4  5  6  7  8  9  10
5 | 5  6  7  8  9  10
6 | 6  7  8  9  10
7 | 7  8  9  10                etc.
```

The children should be given many experiences in what actually happens when two sets are joined together. Their previous work with sets has laid the background for this.

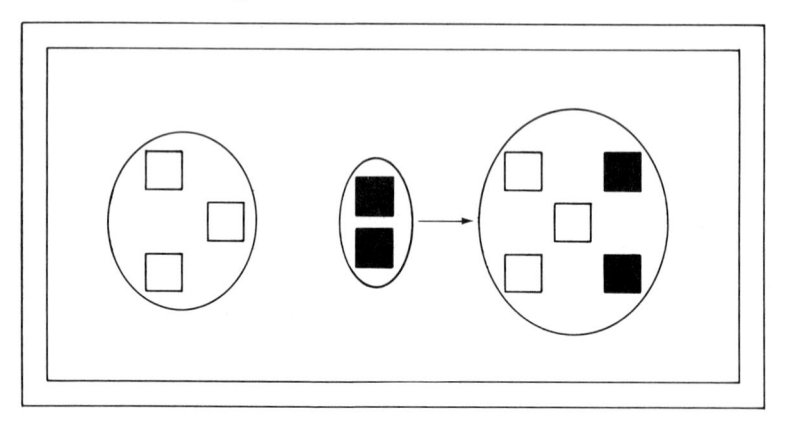

FIGURE 4.90

The symbol of operation, the numerals, and symbol of relationship are introduced in the mathematical sentence form as shown in Figure 4.91.

Primary Mathematics for the Mentally Retarded 177

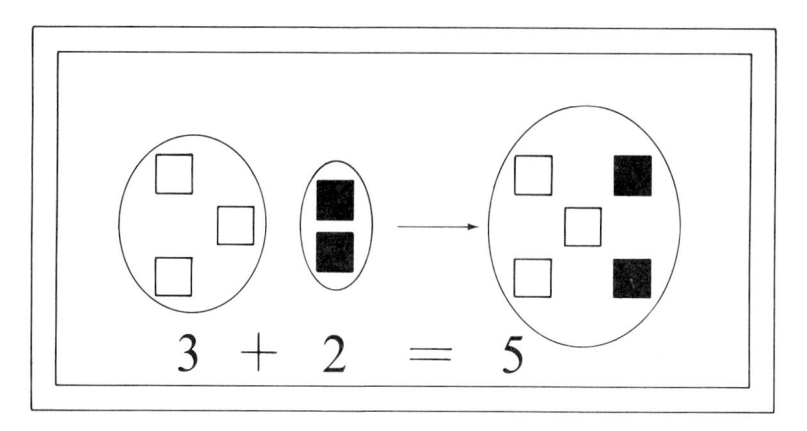

FIGURE 4.91

Further examples should be developed for use on the flannel or magnet board. Refer to the addition facts chart on page 180 for the complete list.

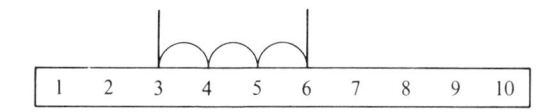

FIGURE 4.92

Number Line. Use the number line to illustrate addition. For example, 3 + 3 = __. Start with the numeral 3 and count to the right three spaces. The answer is shown on the number line as six.

FIGURE 4.93

Add with Beads. Use simple counting beads to solve addition problems.

☐ + 2 = 5   3 + ☐ = 5   3 + 2 = ☐

Use Pictures. How many fish altogether? How many big fish? How many little fish?

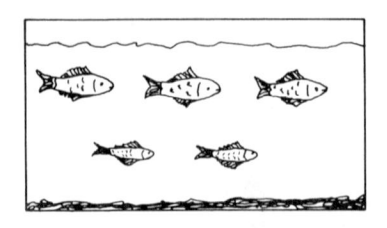

178   *Primary Mathematics for the Mentally Retarded*

FIGURE 4.94

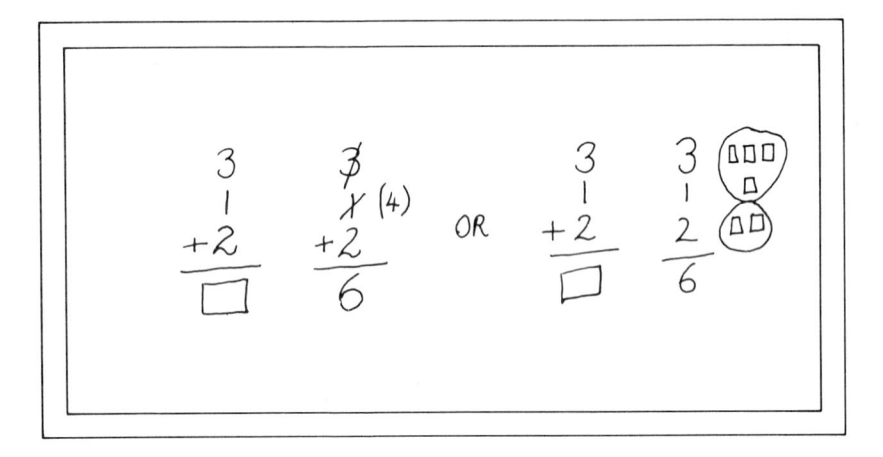

FIGURE 4.95

Column Addition.

$$\begin{array}{cccc} 3 & 4 & 2 & 2 \\ 1 & 1 & 1 & 1 \\ \underline{2} & \underline{1} & \underline{1} & \underline{2} \end{array}$$

Problems such as these should be introduced at the primary level. A complicating factor with the column addition of three or more numbers is the need for intermediate steps. Addition is a binary operation so, of course, only two numbers can be added at a time. Yet there are three numbers. In the example

$$\begin{array}{c} 3 \\ 1 \\ \underline{+2} \end{array}$$

Primary Mathematics for the Mentally Retarded

adding from the top the children must think (3 + 1) = 4; 4 + 2 = 6. Many retarded children will have difficulty with this because they are unable to think "4" without seeing the numeral "4". In the beginning then an aid similar to the ones presented here might be helpful.

Subtraction

Retarded children often have a great deal of trouble with subtraction. The difficulties may be reduced if the children have had proper experiences with sets and if subtraction is not introduced as a new process but rather as an operation closely related to addition. Subtraction does the opposite of addition. It takes apart or undoes what addition does, and is therefore referred to as the inverse operation of addition. It has already been shown that "addend + addend = sum." In addition we are looking for the missing sum while in subtraction we are looking for the missing addend. This simple illustration makes the point:

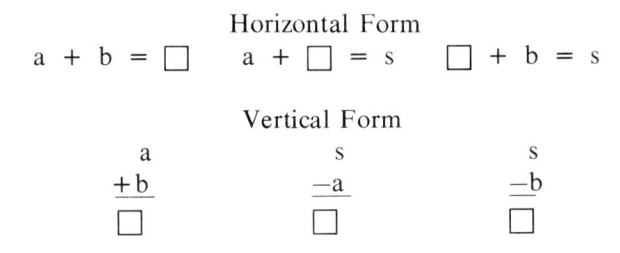

Horizontal Form

a + b = ☐   a + ☐ = s   ☐ + b = s

Vertical Form

$$\begin{array}{ccc} a & s & s \\ +b & -a & -b \\ \hline \square & \square & \square \end{array}$$

To show that subtraction is the inverse of addition present examples similar to this:

4 = 4

4 + 2 = 6

(4 + 2) − 2 = 4

4 ⟶ ○○○○

4 + 2 = 6 ⟶ ○○○○ and ○○

6 − 2 = 4 ⟶ ○○○○ ○○

4 ⟶ ○○○○

FIGURE 4.96

The most important thing to understand about subtraction is that when the children have learned the basic addition facts as shown in the preceding paragraphs *they already should know the subtraction facts.* The children know, for example, that 2 + 1 = 3. If they understand the inverse process, then, they know the answer to $2 + \square = 3$. The sentence $2 + \square = 3$ may be written $3 - 2 = \square$. To solve the problem in its first form the children reason, "addend + addend = sum or $2 + 1 = 3$." In the second form the children reason, "sum − addend = addend or $3 - 2 = 1$." In order to make this quite clear to the children, have them identify each number in the sentence.

$$2 + 1 = 3$$
addend addend sum
(missing)
(addition)

$$3 - 2 = 1$$
sum addend addend
(missing)
(subtraction)

Guide the children through the identification of each term in the sentence until they grasp the relationship between the facts and the two operations.

Related Facts for 3

Addition	Subtraction
1 + 2 = 3	3 − 1 = 2
2 + 1 = 3	3 − 2 = 1
0 + 3 = 3	3 − 0 = 3
3 + 0 = 3	3 − 3 = 0

Related Facts for 4

Addition	Subtraction
2 + 2 = 4	4 − 2 = 2
1 + 3 = 4	4 − 1 = 3
3 + 1 = 4	4 − 3 = 1
4 + 0 = 4	4 − 0 = 4
0 + 4 = 4	4 − 4 = 0

It is important that the children understand this relationship. After they have had practice with the related facts such as the threes and fours shown above, the mathematical sentence should be introduced with the placeholder (unknown symbol) $\square$. The children should learn to find the number for the missing addend called the *difference*. The number operation of finding the unknown addend is, of course, *subtraction*.

Mathematical Sentences
Related Facts for 3

Addition	Subtraction
1 + 2 = 3	3 − 1 = 2
□ + 2 = 3	3 − 2 = □
3 + □ = 3	3 − □ = 3
□ + 3 = 3	3 − 3 = □

Mathematical Sentences
Related Facts for 4

Addition	Subtraction
2 + 2 = 4	4 − 2 = 2
1 + □ = 4	4 − 1 = □
3 + □ = 4	4 − 3 = □
0 + □ = 4	4 − 0 = □
4 + □ = 4	4 − 4 = □

Since subtraction is the inverse operation, the properties that apply to addition are not applicable to subtraction. Subtraction is not commu-

Primary Mathematics for the Mentally Retarded 181

tative because the order in which two numbers are subtracted affects the difference.

$$1 + 2 = 2 + 1 \quad \text{commutative property of addition}$$
$$\text{but}$$
$$1 - 2 \neq 2 - 1 \quad \text{does not apply to subtraction}$$

Subtraction does not have an identity element since it is not possible to subtract a whole number from zero. (Of course, it is possible to subtract zero from zero and it is possible to subtract a whole number from zero but not in the set of whole numbers). The sentence $0 - 2 = \square$ is of only academic interest to the teacher and has no place in the instruction program at this level other than avoiding it as a problem.

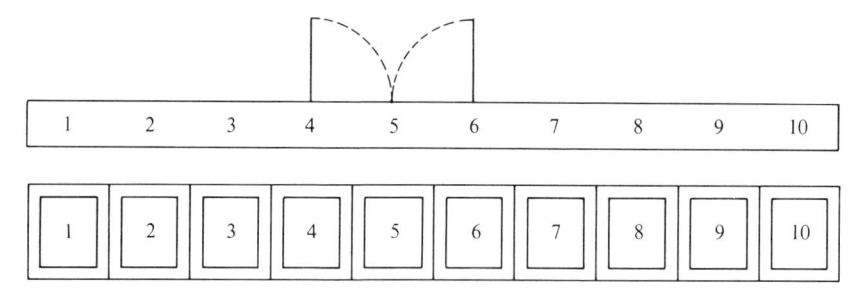

FIGURE 4.97

Number Line. Use the number line to illustrate subtraction. For example: $6 - 2 = \square$. Start with the numeral six on the number line and move two spaces to the left. The answer is shown on the number line as four. The number line may be printed on tagboard, painted on the floor, or made out of plastic covered number cards. The advantage of the latter is that the children may walk right on the line and that it may be easily removed and reused.

Subtraction—Sample Problems. The remainder concept:

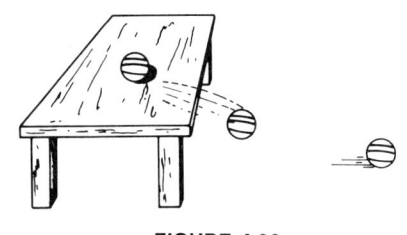

FIGURE 4.98

Mary had three balls on the table but two rolled off. How many were left on the table?

The additive concept:

FIGURE 4.99

Jerry has three cards, but needs five in order to play the game. How many more does he need?

The comparison concept:

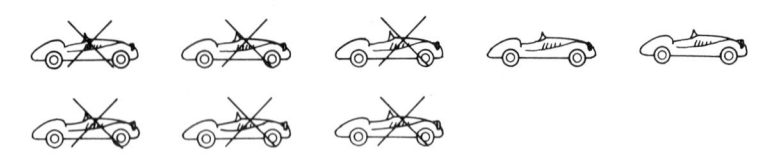

FIGURE 4.100

Kenny has three toy cars and Tom has five. Who has more? How many more does he have?

Subtract with beads: Find the number left.

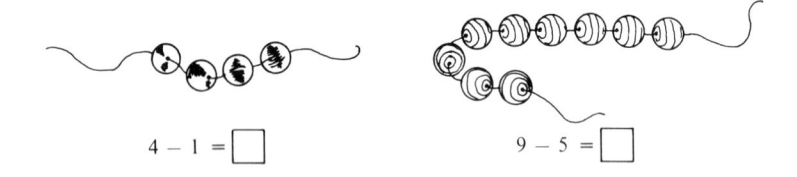

$4 - 1 = \square$ $9 - 5 = \square$

FIGURE 4.101

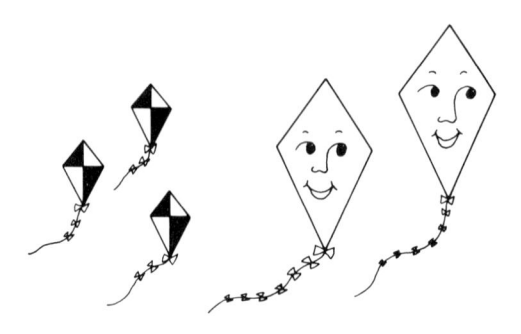

FIGURE 4.102

Primary Mathematics for the Mentally Retarded 183

Use pictures: How many kites altogether? How many small kites? How many big kites?

If someone took the small kites, how many would be left? 5 − 3 = ☐

If someone took only the big kites, how many would be left? 5 − 2 = ☐

Use dot patterns to illustrate sets and subtraction operation: Think of the many ways to name eight, and solve the problem in Figure 4.103.

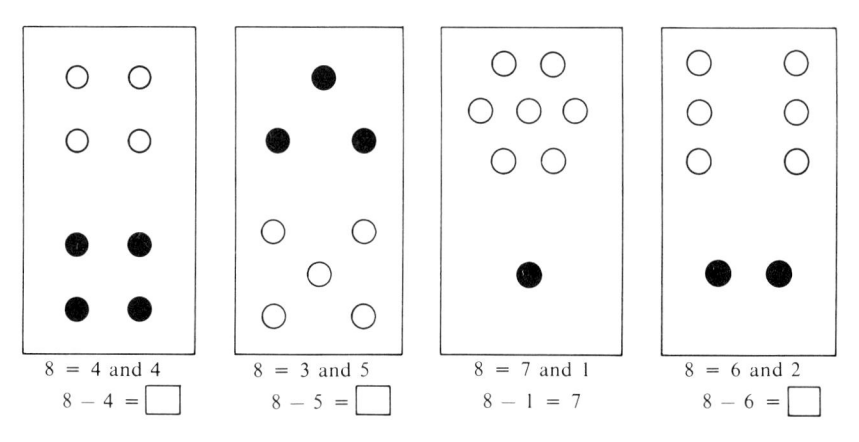

8 = 4 and 4
8 − 4 = ☐

8 = 3 and 5
8 − 5 = ☐

8 = 7 and 1
8 − 1 = 7

8 = 6 and 2
8 − 6 = ☐

FIGURE 4.103

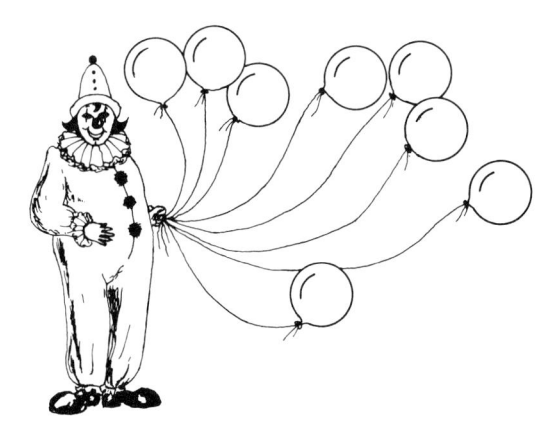

FIGURE 4.104

A clown had eight balloons. He gave three of them away. How many balloons did he have left?

Six kittens were playing together. Three of the kittens decided to play someplace else. How many kittens were left together?

Identifying the Process—Addition or Subtraction

"Listen carefully. I am going to give you a problem, but you do not have to get the answer. I just want you to tell me whether you add or subtract.

Let's do one together for practice. Jerry blew up six balloons. As he played with them, two broke. How many balloons does he have left. Do I add or subtract?"

Make certain that the children understand the illustration and then give them additional problems along the same line.

"Look at this problem: 3 __ 2 = 5. Now look at this problem: 3 __ 2 = 1. We know that 3 and 2 is 5 so we put a plus sign in the space. We know that 3 take away 2 is 1 so we put a minus sign in the space."

Once the children understand what they are to do, give them a series of problems based on the model.

Ideas for Both Addition and Subtraction and Problem Solving

Dramatization. Simple addition and subtraction problems may be dramatized in class. Here are a few examples of involving the children in the activities of these processes.

> Judy has two pencils
> Danny gives her one more.
> How many does she have now?

> Dick, will you put one dog
> on the magnet board?
> Rita, will you put one dog
> right next to it?
> How many dogs are there?

> Paul, place three blocks on
> your desk.
> Terry, take one away.
> How many blocks are left?

The Number Box. As mentioned previously, each child has a collection of objects in his number box. The teacher gives oral problems to the

Primary Mathematics for the Mentally Retarded 185

children. "Put three red paper squares on your desk. Now *add* two green paper squares. How many squares do you have?"

Bring two children to the front of the room. Instruct the others to place some counters on their desk together with a set card (5" × 7" sturdy tagboard card). The teacher may provide a variety of counters for the children including such items as cut squares of colored paper; bottle caps, plastic disks, wooden chips, and dowel rods. The teacher gives Jerome two cookies and Wanda one cookie. "How many cookies do they have all together? Show me with your counter." The children placed two counters on the card to represent Jerome's cookies, and one counter to represent Wanda's cookie. They "act out" the problem and "see" the answer. "Point with your left hand to the counters which show Jerome's cookies and with your right hand to the counters which show Wanda's cookie. How many did Jerome have? How many did Wanda have? How many were there in all? Who had more? Who had less?"

$2 + 2 = \square$	
$1 + 1 + 1 = \square$	$4 - 2 = \square$
$2 + \square = 4$	$3 - 2 = \square$
$1 + 4 = \square$	$2 - 2 = \square$
$3 + 2 = \square$	

FIGURE 4.105

Problem Chalk Boards. Paint masonite board cut to approximately 8½ × 11, with green chalk board paint. Paint problems with regular black paint as shown in Figure 4.105. A damp cloth may be used to clean the board.

The Horse Race. This game needs the figure of a horse for each player. A horse track and deck of cards may be made from poster board. The cards have various problems printed on them as shown in the illustration.

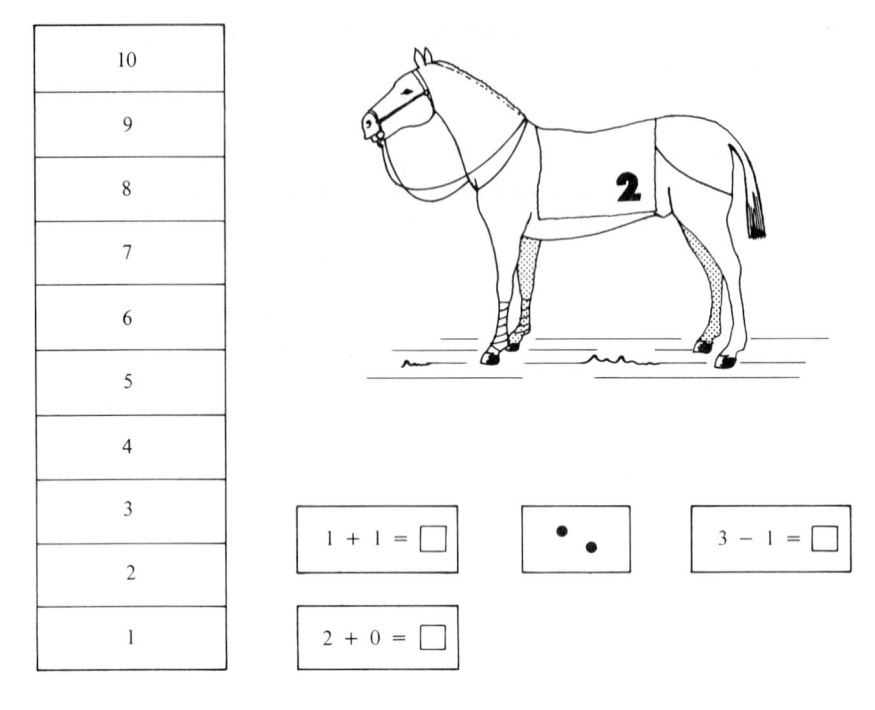

186   *Primary Mathematics for the Mentally Retarded*

FIGURE 4.106

The child draws a card and if he answers the question correctly, he moves forward one space. The first child to cross the finish line wins.

SUMMARY

It has been indicated in this chapter that children in primary educable mentally retarded classes present the special education teacher with a difficult challenge. Other children in the first through third grades are mastering a wide range of number skills including column addition, regrouping in subtraction, multiplication, division and the solution of complex word problems. On the other hand, most educable mentally retarded children at the primary level are working with much simpler concepts and many others are struggling with preschool and kindergarten skills. It has been shown that the major task of the primary level is the development of basic number ideas such as sets and numbers to ten, together with their application to measurement, money and daily problems. It was indicated that one of the major problems of instruction at the primary level is the premature introduction of the numbers ten to twenty. It was stressed that no number greater than ten should be introduced until the children have learned to handle the lower numbers with facility. The conventions of place value and positional notation should not be presented until the children have become comfortable with the lower numbers. This will avoid the embarrassing need for unlearning and reteaching with older children. Many teaching suggestions were presented to assist in the development of basic number skills.

TEACHING AIDS FOR PRIMARY LEVEL EDUCABLE MENTALLY RETARDED CHILDREN

The following list of aids for teaching mathematics to primary educable mentally retarded children was taken largely from *Suggested Basic Materials for Educable Mentally Retarded Children,* Division of Special Education, Department of Education, State of Ohio, 1968.

The list is not intended to be exhaustive, but is presented here to give examples of the types of instructional aids which may be successfully adapted to the needs of these children.

The code refers to the names and addresses of publishers given in the appendix.

PUBLISHER CODE	TITLE	DESCRIPTION
A-1	1. *I Can Count* 2. *I Can Add*	Advanced readiness materials for older primary children to use under direction.
B-2	1. One to Ten 2. Ten and More (May also be used with less mature intermediate pupils)	Materials for use under direction with those children who can demonstrate an understanding of concepts involved. Encourage activities to reinforce concepts.
C-5	1. *Measurement,* Level 1 2. *United States Money,* Level 1	Liquid duplicator sheets to be used by the children in small groups under teacher direction. This can follow actual experiences with money and measurement as small group instruction.
F-4	*Come and Count*	Another resource for the reinforcement of number concept.
H-3	1. *Let's Count* 2. *One by One*	Workbooks, not to be put into the hands of children indiscriminately, but for small group work, teacher directed.

PUB-LISHER CODE	TITLE	DESCRIPTION
H-6	*Arithmetic Foundation* Level 1	Workbook to be used for small group instruction. Supplemented with manipulative experiences.
H-7	*Learning to Use Arithmetic,* beginning book	Teacher's edition useful in securing ideas and verifying sequential development of number concepts. Has limited use with the children.
H-12	*Numbers for Beginners*	Liquid duplicator materials-may by useful, under direction, for children who have successfully completed such materials as the Contintal Press Worksheets (C-5); for the older primary children.
P-5	*Numbers for You and Me*	Workbooks, to be used under direction, on a selective basis with those children who have completed other materials.
B-3	*Add Me*	Arithmetic games, sums through ten.
P-5	*Numbers for You and Me*	Workbooks for Small Group Use.
M-2	*Training Fun with Numbers,* Books I & II	Basic concepts, value of money and understanding the clock.
C-6	Design Cubes Geometric Shapes—graded form board (circle, square, triangle) Matchmate Sets Miniature Toys—wood and plastic; wooden-by the pound, plastic—sets of eight or ten. Wooden Numbers and Math Symbols	
J-1	Flannel Board Alphabet Numbers and Geometric Shapes Judy Calendar Judy Clock Judy Numberite Judy Pegboards	
S-16	Classroom Calendar Counting Frame Counting Shapes (for use on flannel board) Cube Blocks	

PUB-LISHER CODE	TITLE	DESCRIPTION
	Jumbo Beads Kinesthetic Block Set Magnetic Board Parquetry Blocks	
T-5	Concept Clocks Configuration Cards Geometric Shapes in Color	
V-3	Match 'N Learn Number Board	
S-4	*Numbers We See*	Teacher's edition is very helpful, as it has a well defined, developmentally oriented approach. If used with children, it is suggested that pictures be covered with "windows", to reveal small groups at one time instead of cluttered pages. One copy, used with an overhead projector, is suggested. Do not use where this is basic material in primary grades.
C-9	*Cuisenare Rods*	Uses colored rods to designate number concepts.
H-10	*Structural Arithmetic* Kindergarten Kit Grade 1 Kit	Colored materials based on pupil discovery with pupil worktexts and teachers' manuals.
H-4	*Pre-Number Readiness Kit*	Manipulative materials plus unique worktext for pupils. This program contains five areas; seriation, form, logical sequence, spatial apperception and pattern.
F-5	*Number Time,* Book I	Workbook
F-5	*Arithmetic Foundation* Level L	Manipulative experiences will need to be added by the teacher.
H-9	*Sounds of Numbers*	Stories to reinforce number concepts.

PUB-LISHER CODE	TITLE	DESCRIPTION
C-11	*Stepping Stones* Plastic Peg Board and Pegs Number Learner	Manipulative items
I-4	*Pupil Number Line* *Pupil Counting Frame*	Manipulative items

REFERENCES

Cawley, John F., and Fitzmaurice, Sister Anne Marie. "The Individualization of Instruction: Illustrations from Arithmetical Programming for Handicapped Children." Report prepared with grant from the Board of Education for the Handicapped. Storrs: University of Connecticut, 1972. Mimeographed.

Cincinnati Public Schools. *The Slow Learning Program In The Elementary and Secondary Schools.* Cincinnati, Ohio: Bulletin No. 119, 1964.

Feingold, Abraham. *Teaching Arithmetic to Slow Learners and Retarded.* New York: John Day Company, 1965.

Goodstein, H. A.; Cawley, J. F.; Gordon, S.; and Helfgott, J. "Verbal Problem-Solving among Educable Mentally Retarded Children." *American Journal of Mental Deficiency* 76 (September 1971): 238-41.

Kephart, Newell. *The Slow Learner in the Classroom,* 2d ed. Columbus, Ohio: Charles E. Merrill Publishing Co., 1971.

Smith, Robert M. *Clinical Teaching: Methods of Instruction for the Retarded.* New York: McGraw-Hill Book Company.

chapter 5

Intermediate Mathematics For the Mentally Retarded

Teaching mathematics to mentally retarded children at the intermediate level can be simultaneously exhilarating and frustrating. The frustration comes from the observation that many of these children have experienced a series of devastating failure episodes over a long period of time. Some will have been exposed to a sequence of premature efforts to teach formal arithmetic skills while others will have been so delayed in learning elementary mathematics that they were retained one or more grades before placement in special education. Others will have been allowed to drift through several grade levels with the anticipation that soon they would begin to catch up with the rest of the class. These include a number of children with a mild sub-average intellectual impairment who do not exhibit severe academic retardation until the second or third grade. The older the child the more obvious mild mental retardation and slow academic progress becomes. The intermediate classroom for the mentally retarded will often include a preponderance of boys due primarily to their aggressive reaction to failure and delayed language development. In other words, the diagnosis of mental retardation will include not only the factor of general sub-average intellectual functioning and low academic achievement but also negative and hostile behavior patterns. There will be some children who have been assigned to special education for the first time who may regard their placement as a permanent consignment to the "dummy" class. These children will be more aware of their status and any stigmas attached to membership in a class for retarded children.

Other children of low intelligence who need major curriculum adaptation will remain in the regular elementary classroom. In some instances, there simply is not space for them in special classes while in other cases it may be in the best interest of the child to remain in the regular class. The special education class should be viewed only as a resource of last resort. Most slow learning and educable mentally retarded children will be able to make significant progress in regular classrooms if the curriculum is adjusted to their strengths. However, even those remaining in regular elementary classrooms become aware that they are falling further behind their classmates. In some cases, the fact that they function below grade placement results in the diminishing of their own self-esteem as well as a decline in their status among their peers.

This self-awareness of academic deficiency is due to several factors. The most important of these is that most nine year olds are reading independently and solving arithmetic problems at an abstract level. The non-reading slow learner or mental retardate in the intermediate grades is quite apparent to his classmates not only in language arts tasks but also arithmetic exercises which begin to focus on "word" and "thought" problems. Precautions should be undertaken to keep the negative effects of such perceptions to a minimum.

What makes all of this especially frustrating to the teacher is that she must not only deal with the children's intellectual impairments but also with the psycho-sociological obstacles to learning. On the other hand, the excitement of teaching mentally retarded and slow learning children comes from the challenge of overcoming these barriers. It is quite rewarding to promote the development of a child who has been unable to master even the most elementary mathematical concepts. It is exceedingly satisfying to help a child substitute feelings of self-confidence for feelings of inferiority; and attitudes of aspirations of success for hostility.

Other children will continue to experience failure due to visual-perceptual problems superimposed upon sub-average intelligence. The remediation of visual-perceptual difficulties with these children may result in maintenance in or restoration to the regular classroom while some will make otherwise unexpected progress.

In this chapter a considerable amount of attention will be given to the treatment of visual-perceptual problems at the intermediate level.

It is imperative that the intermediate teacher deal with the psycho-sociological impairments to learning as well as be alerted to the perceptual aspects of mathematics. In this sense, she must be a teacher-therapist and remedial specialist. If the psychological and perceptual aspects are dealt with effectively, the students will experience significant success in intermediate mathematics.

ABILITY LEVELS

It can be seen from Table 5.1 that educable mentally retarded children of chronological ages nine, ten, eleven, and twelve can be expected to possess mental ages ranging from four years and six months to nine years and seven months. The majority of children in special education intermediate classrooms will have mental ages of six to eight years and anticipated grade level equivalents of first and second grade.[1] In other words, these children have chronological ages similar to average children in the fourth through seventh grades. However, the mathematical skills they will learn during their intermediate school experiences will be more comparable to that which is typically taught in regular first and second grades.

It should be noted that some nine, ten, and eleven year-old children with IQ scores of 65 and below may have mental ages below six. The intermediate teacher may also have a child or two in her class with a mental age as low as four and one-half. Such children, even though few in number, comprise a significant instructional challenge. The sequence of development skills in the following discussions may not be suited to them. The prenumber and early number experiences presented in Chapters 3 and 4 should be referred to for teaching suggestions. On the other hand, a few mentally retarded children at the intermediate level will have an achievement potential somewhat above typical second grade equivalencies. The suggested activities presented in Chapter 6 may be more appropriate for them.

A useful guideline is that most educable mentally retarded children whether in the special education class or the regular elementary class will generally be capable of performing mathematical tasks typically learned by other children in the first and second grades. Some will not do this well and others will perform beyond this level. This is not to suggest that the teacher should set a ceiling on her expectations for her students. The opposite is the case. The teacher should plan for the optimum development of each child. However, it is foolish to present mentally retarded children with tasks which are too difficult for them. There is a difference between setting a ceiling of expectancy and planning sequential instruction beginning at each child's level. The instructional program described in this chapter will be appropriate for most educable mentally retarded children at the intermediate level. Some children will

---

[1] Remember that A.G.E. = MA − K and that K is five for educable mentally retarded children with chronological ages below eleven and K is six for those with chronological ages eleven and above.

need to be given material from preceding sections and other children will advance to higher levels. Considerable overlap is to be expected.

TABLE 5.1
Mental Ages of Mentally Retarded Children Chronological Ages 9, 10, 11, 12

IQ	9	10	11	12
50	4.6	5.0	5.6	6.0
55	4.11	5.6	6.1	6.6
60	5.4	6.0	6.7	7.2
65	5.10	6.6	7.2	7.9
70	6.1	7.0	7.8	8.5
75	6.9	7.6	8.3	9.0
80	7.2	8.0	8.10	9.7

OBJECTIVES

The general objective for the intermediate level is to develop basic number understandings and establish the beginnings of skills in number operations and problem solving. The mentally retarded child must be instructed through a process which places emphasis on understanding if the pitfalls summarized by Burns are to be avoided.[2] The retarded child's performances need not be characterized by careless errors, inability to identify processes and a lack of understanding. If the child understands such key ideas as base ten and place value, he will be much more able to master the techniques of problem solving. The teacher will need to guide the children in developing these essential understandings through sequential activities. More specifically, many students will:

1. correct visual-perceptual deficiencies related to mathematics and develop advanced body image and visual-perceptual skills including the ability to discriminate forms with minor differences
2. develop eye-hand motor skills such as those necessary in reproducing such geometric shapes as the triangle, rectangle, and diamond
3. begin to utilize directionality through recognition of left and right, north, south, east, and west
4. continue to develop a vocabulary associated with mathematics including terms associated with number operations, measurement, money, and problem solving

---

[2] See Chapter 2.

5. develop the ideas of place value, base ten, and positional notation
6. continue to develop counting skills
7. continue to develop the ideas of cardinal number and sets
8. comprehend the ordinal numbers at least to twelve
9. develop the measurement concepts relating to purchases, reading the calendar, telling time, the thermometer, weight, and length
10. use money up to $20.00 and make change up to $1.00
11. continue to develop skills in addition and subtraction and begin to multiply and divide

DEVELOPMENTAL SEQUENCE OF MATHEMATICAL SKILLS

The intermediate program has often been the first level introduced for the mentally retarded. By the time the educable retardate has been in school two or three years, his academic deficits have become exceedingly apparent. His teachers are frustrated because he has generally failed to learn even the simplest concepts presented to his fourth-grade counterpart. The elements of simple column addition and the subtraction of two digit numbers are often beyond him. The parents are alarmed by the discouraging school reports, and the child is depressed by his own failure. Waiting for the child to mature and "catch up" may have prolonged the decision to provide special help. The teacher of intermediate retardates, like the primary teacher, will find some youngsters who are experiencing their first special education class. Others will have been in the special education program as long as seven or eight years. In large urban school districts it may be possible to subdivide this group into two levels (generally; intermediate one and two, or lower and upper intermediate). In smaller rural school districts, there may be provisions for only one such class for all of the children. All of this means that the teacher of the intermediate retardate will be called upon to instruct a very wide range of pupil academic backgrounds.

It is imperative that the teacher survey the skills of the youngsters in her charge. Most will have satisfactory perceptual skills and adequately developed vocabulary to proceed at relatively mature levels. The concepts and skills of correspondence, sets, ordinal number, measurement, money, and problem solving will be above the elementary levels. The development of number concepts through ten should be fairly well established.

Many of the children at the intermediate level have developed some of the basic ideas of mathematics. They may be able to read and write numbers, count, combine and separate sets, tell time by the hour, read the calendar, measure by length, capacity and weight, handle money, and do simple addition and subtraction. The major thrust of the intermediate program is to further develop key mathematical ideas related to sets, place value, and positional notation. Emphasis for most children will be in the areas of measurement, money and value, and number operations. The most notable gains will probably be in the application of number facts to problem solving. The understanding of the number processes is of utmost importance. The commutative and associative laws of addition are taught to help develop this insight. The numbers beyond ten are introduced with the processes of regrouping and renaming for addition and subtraction. Multiplication and division are presented as extensions of addition and subtraction. Measurement, money and value, and the use of number in daily situations, are of major importance. It may be a considerable temptation for the intermediate teacher to avoid teaching the principles of addition and subtraction and to move into teaching the multiplication and division facts. It is easy to drill children in processes they do not understand and make some visible gain in rote skills. It requires more patience to help the children develop the comprehension and application skills needed for functional mathematics, but the teacher will be rewarded with a higher quality of learning.

Perceptual problems may not be a major learning block for all children at the intermediate level, but some may have specific visual-perceptual handicaps. This chapter will give special attention to the correction of perceptual impairments in order to emphasize its importance to mathematics.

It has been pointed out that the teacher may have children with IQ's ranging from 50 to 80. As a result, he will face children with potential achievement as low as kindergarten and as high as fourth grade.

TABLE 5.2

Checklist for Intermediate Level Mathematics for Retarded

1. *Form and Perception*
    knowledge of terms and ability to reproduce some geometric shapes such as circle, square, triangle, rectangle, sphere, cylinder, cone and cube; ability to discriminate and identify forms; ideas of left, right, north, south, east, west.

2. *Vocabulary Associated with Mathematics*

thick	next	couple	column	balance
thin	near	more	times	short
narrow	far	less	divide	shorter
wide	close	most	equals	shortest
heavy	under	least	length	higher
light	over	many	one third	highest
beside	beneath	few	one half	height

Intermediate Mathematics for the Mentally Retarded 199

largest	above	altogether	rule	weight
smallest	below	same as	yard	sign
middle	before	plus	square	divide
right	after	adding to	inch	equals
left	between	sum	distance	difference
beginning	all	minus	width	
end	some	subtract	foot	
high	each	difference	check	
low	pair	sign	sales slip	
week	clock	o'clock	tax	
year	noon	hour	admission cost	
quick	sell	postage	one fourth	
warm	coins	credit	change	
cool	per	pay	charge	

3. *Number Symbols*
    rote counting to two hundred
    order numbers one to one hundred
    reads number symbols and recognizes number names to one hundred
    reads number words to fifty
    counts by tens to one hundred
    counts by fives to one hundred
    counts by twos to fifty
    counts by threes to thirty
    knows number symbols for money values

4. *Cardinal Number*
    rationale counting fifty to one hundred
    relating number symbol to groups of objects through twenty
    recognition of groups of objects through twenty and ability to separate all possible subgroups
    recognition of pattern sets to ten
    concept of sets as readiness for simple multiplication and division
    recognition of odd and even numbers to twenty
    ability to reproduce groups as needed functionally to one hundred
    knowledge of fractions such as ½, ⅓, ¼ of a whole group
    knowledge of odd and even

5. *Ordinal Number*
    Knowledge of ordinal numbers through twelve

6. *Measurement*
    concepts of teaspoon, tablespoon, inch, foot, yard, gallon, ounce, cup, pint, quart, half dozen, pair, pound, dozen
    clock: telling time by the half hour and quarter hour; recognizing midnight, noon, AM, and PM. Telling time by five minutes and up to one minute
    calendar: knowing days of week, month of the year, seasons, the weather

record, and the date school is over; recognizing that there are fifty-two weeks in a year.
weight: reading weights on scales
concepts of sixteen ounces = 1 pound, 2 pints = one quart, four quarts = one gallon, ½ cup
thermometer: reading a simple thermometer, temperature gauge
linear: reading a foot ruler and a yardstick
concepts of twelve inches = one foot, three feet = one yard, one inch, ½ inch, how tall, how long, how wide, how high.

7. *Money and Value*
can name all of the coins and bills to $20
can utilize written money symbols
can make change up to $1.00
makes purchases up to $5.00
understands commercial and business terms (see vocabulary section)
understands basic ideas of banking and saving
understands the relative value of items

8. *Number Operations and Problem Solving*
renames and regroups in addition and subtraction
performs column addition
divides to two places
multiplies simple combinations
adds simple fractions such as ½, ⅓, ¼
understands commutative and associate properties
ability to complete simple one-step problems involving measuring, scoring, grouping, attendance, money, and calendar
picks essential facts and identifies process

FORM AND PERCEPTION

Form and perception at the intermediate level for educable mentally retarded children must give attention to the developmental skills of form discrimination and reproduction as well as the remediation of visual-perceptual problems. This section will deal with both of these facets by discussing four topics: (1) suggested activities for the intermediate special education class; (2) perceptual-motor activities correlated with music, art, and physical education; (3) the specialized perceptual-motor training programs developed by Kephart, Frostig, and Robins; and (4) the specialized instructional materials for children with perceptual deficits developed by Cheves, the Dubnoff School Program, the Pathway School Program, the Erie Program, and the Fairbanks-Robinson Program.

Classroom Activities

The main purpose of the activities suggested below is to develop visual perceptual skills which will assist the children in learning to discriminate forms and to develop eye-hand motor skills needed for form reproduction. The ideas of direction, area, and perimeter will be introduced.

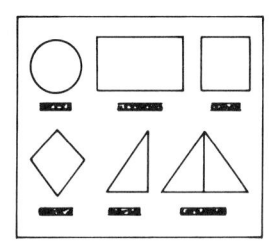

FIGURE 5.1

Form Chart. Construct a chart of common shapes using tagboard. The forms may either be drawn in outline form or colored construction paper cutouts may be used to make each shape.

Forms to Pictures. Ask the children to identify shapes in classrooms and elsewhere in the building. Charts and bulletin boards may be constructed to illustrate the general configurations of objects and the shapes they approximate. Worksheets may be devised by presenting the child with a form and asking him to list the objects in the room which are like the form.

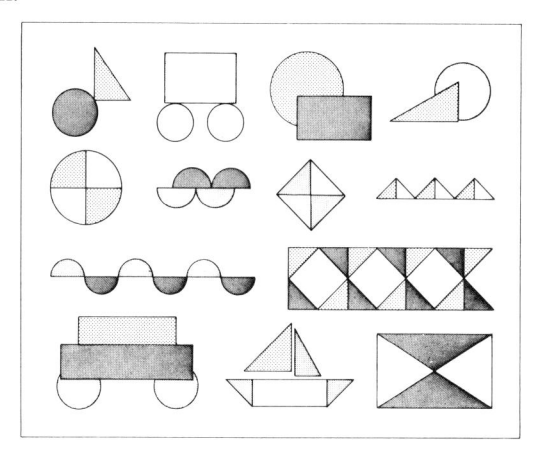

FIGURE 5.2

Designs with Geometric Shapes. Cut a variety of shapes from different colors of odds and ends of construction paper. Have the children arrange them in interesting patterns as shown in Figure 5.2.

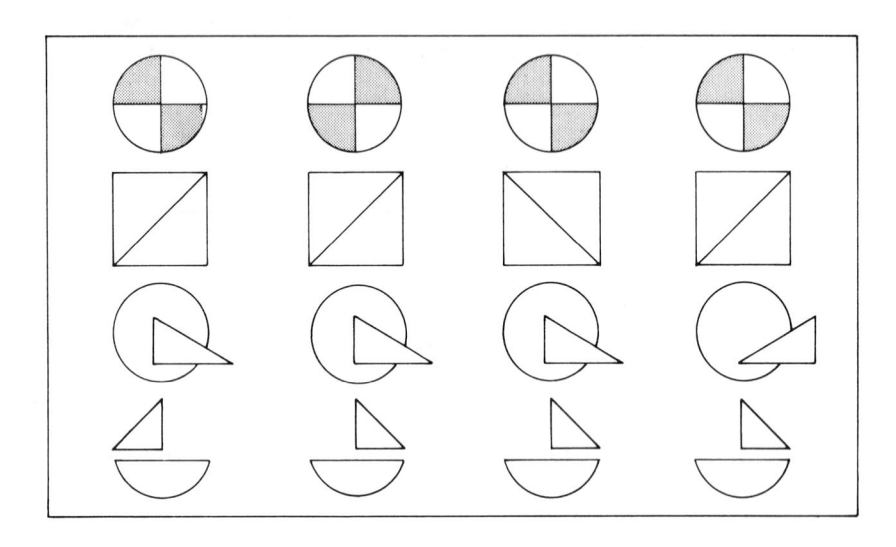

FIGURE 5.3

Discriminating Forms. Place a ring around the form that is not like the rest. Mark the one that is different.

Traffic Signs in Standard Forms. Many of the traffic signs that are important to the pedestrian can be easily recognized by their shape.

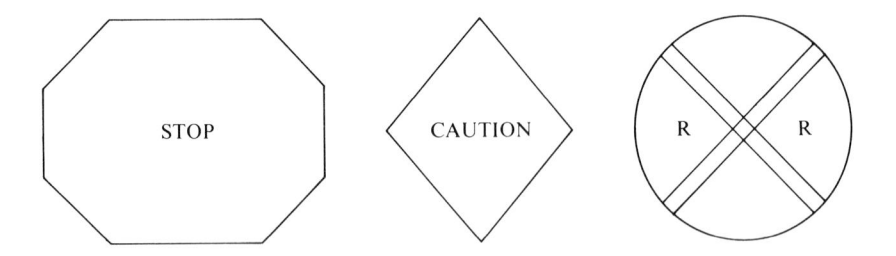

FIGURE 5.4

Match these warnings with the correct sign.

Intermediate Mathematics for the Mentally Retarded 203

Stop

Caution

Look out for trains (RR)

FIGURE 5.5

The Names of Shapes. Match the names with the correct shape.

diamond

circle

square

rectangle

triangle

FIGURE 5.6

Write the correct name below each shape.

_____   _____   _____   _____   _____

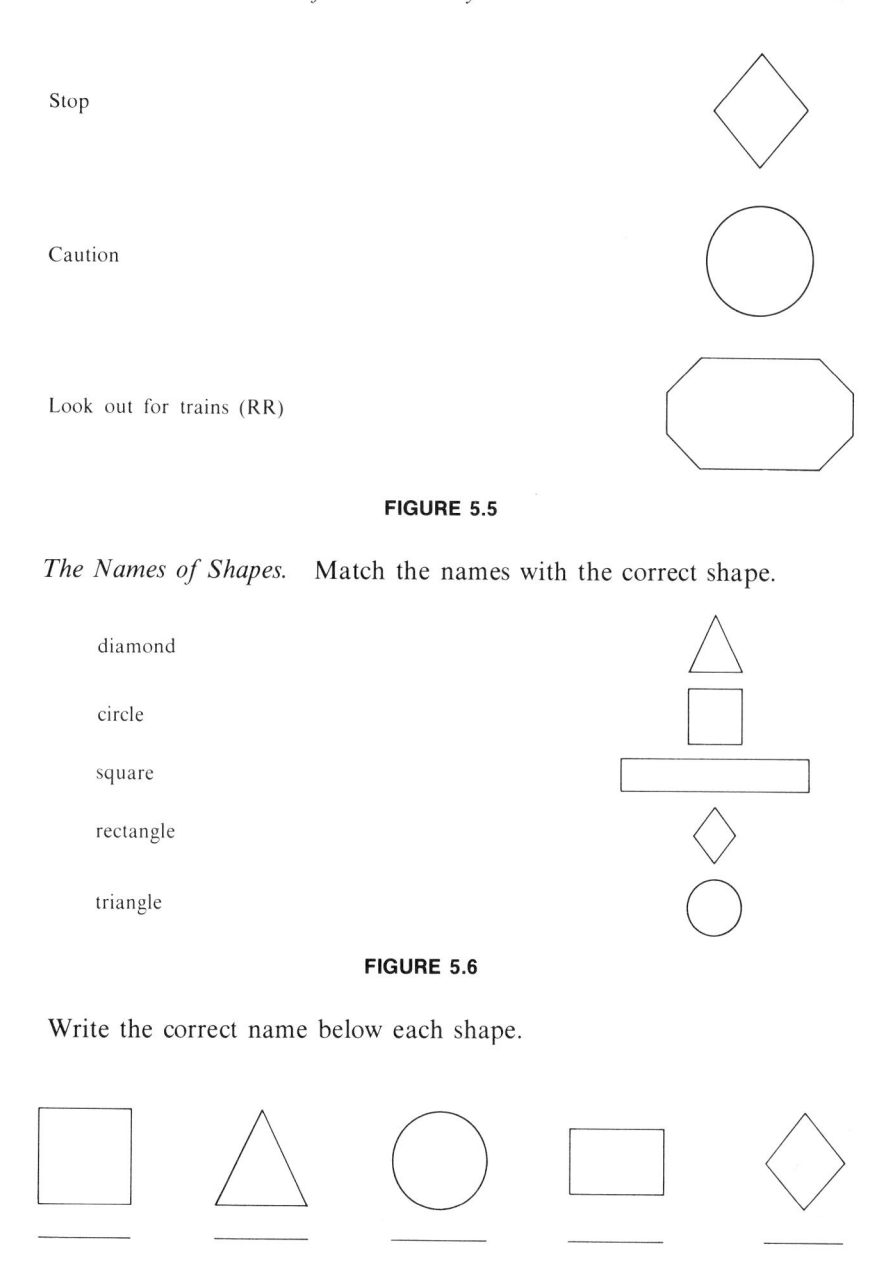

FIGURE 5.7

Draw the shapes indicated by the word.

circle   diamond   square

_____   _____   _____

FIGURE 5.8

Right and Left. The ability to use left and right as directional guidelines is one of the more difficult skills to teach retarded children. First of all, the children should come to understand the terms under a very limited set of circumstances. Tell the children that as they sit at their desk facing the front of the room that this (pointing) is their right hand and that this is their left. Place a green band on the right arm and a red band on the left arm. A tip that works with most children (southpaws disallowed) is that the hand one writes with is the right hand. Only after the children have had considerable practice in identifying their right and left sides should they be introduced to the relative idea of these references. In the beginning the teacher should face the same direction as the children when giving them practice so that her left and right sides will be the same as theirs.

North, South, East, West. The four major compass directions can be very important to children in such things as understanding maps, and following simple geographic instructions. The teacher should begin by posting signs in the room. The signs should be referred to during the day for example, "Billy go the back of the room" could be restated as "Billy go to the south end of the room." Simple games can be played that involve such directions as "Take two steps to the north, one step to the east, etc." Have the children solve such problems as "You are north and make a right hand turn. Now which direction are you going?"

Perceptual-motor Activities Correlated with Music, Art, and Physical Education

Songs and Finger Plays. Songs are more than recreational music for mentally retarded children. They not only help the child express himself but when supplemented with appropriate actions, they add to his coordination. The teacher is encouraged to utilize songs which are generally thought of as action songs as well as to add movement to songs which are not primarily considered action songs. Here are some traditional songs which lend themselves to activities which enhance the children's coordination.

IF YOU'RE HAPPY AND YOU KNOW IT

If you're happy and you know it, clap your hands.
If you're happy and you know it, clap your hands.
If you're happy and you know it, then you really ought to show it.
If you're happy and you know it, clap your hands.

Then add, stamp your feet, take a bow, turn around,
jump up high, etc.

WHERE IS THUMBKIN?

This is a delightful finger play song which is sung to the tune of "Frère Jacques." The children wiggle their fingers one at a time as described below.

Where is thumbkin?	(Hands behind back)
Where is thumbkin?	
	(Bring one hand forward in fist with
Here I am.	thumb up.)
Here I am.	(Bring other hand forward.)
How are you today, sir?	(Wiggle one thumb.)
How are you today, sir?	(Wiggle other thumb.)
Very well, I thank you.	(One hand goes behind back.)
Run away.	(Other hand goes behind back.)
Run away.	

THIS OLD MAN

This traditional folk song lends itself especially to the extension of body image since it refers to various parts of the body and locations in the room. The activities related to the song also help develop rhyming and number sequence.

This old man, he played one;
He played nick nack, on his thumb.
With a nick nack, paddy wack; give a man a dime,
He played nick nack all the time.

This old man, he played two;
He played nick nack, on his shoe.
With a nick nack, paddy wack; give a man a dime,
He played nick nack all the time.

This old man, he played three;
He played nick nack on his knee.
With a nick nack, paddy wack; give a man a dime,
He played nick nack all the time.

HANDS ON SHOULDERS

Hands on shoulders, hands on knees
Hands behind you, if you please
Touch your shoulders, now your nose
Now your hair and now your toes.

Hands up high in the air
Down at your sides and touch your hair
Hands up high as before
Now clap your hands, one two three four.

HEAD AND SHOULDERS

Head and shoulders   (touch these body parts as named)
knees and toes, knees and toes.
Head and shoulders
knees and toes, knees and toes.

Mouth and ears, and eyes and nose
Head and shoulders
Knees and toes, knees and toes.

RIGHT HAND, LEFT HAND

This is my right hand,
I'll raise it up high,

This is my left hand,
I'll touch the sky,

Right hand, left hand,
Roll them around,

Left hand, right hand,
Pound, pound, pound.

CLAP YOUR HANDS

Clap your hands, clap your hands
Clap them just like me.
Touch your shoulder
Touch your shoulder
Touch them just like me.
Tap your knees
Tap your knees
Tap them just like me.
Clap your hands, clap your hands
Clap them just like me.

Art Activities

There are many art activities which have value in the development of perceptual skills. The activities mentioned below, of course, would not be a central aspect of the mathematic curriculum. However, such activities have particular relevance for mentally retarded children with visual perceptual defects.

appliques	clay work
cutting	wet-chalk drawing
sewing	string painting
screen printing	comb painting
weaving	wash-background pictures
linoleum prints	paper-mache
crayon etching	paper folding
mural painting	

Physical Education

There are certain physical education exercises and games that assist youngsters in developing a mature body image, coordination, and visual perceptual skills. There is not sufficient space to elaborate on them here; however, the following list is presented as an indication of the interrelatedness of physical education and the perceptual-motor basis of academic instruction.

crawling	skipping	pitching
walking	rocking	passing
hiking	sliding	catching
marching	dancing	hanging
running	playing ball	kicking
jumping	tag	bowling
rope jumping	relay games	pivoting
climbing	throwing	bicycle pedaling

Specialized Visual-Perception Programs

There are a large number of specialized programs which could be used with educable mentally retarded children who have perceptual problems which may interfere with their ability to learn mathematics. Three such programs are discussed here: (1) Kephart, (2) Frostig, and (3) Robins and Robins. Each of these programs is quite extensive and there have been numerous texts and articles published about them. Only a brief presentation of each is possible here. These programs are fairly representative of the techniques available for children who have special difficulties with perceptual skills.

THE KEPHART TRAINING ACTIVITIES

The Kephart Training Activities, dealt with extensively in Dr. Kephart's book, *The Slow Learner in the Classroom*, are most effective in strengthening perceptual-motor development weaknesses in the slow-learning child. These activities are grouped under four major areas and are designed to assist the child in strengthening his (1) sensory-motor development, (2) ocular control, and (3) form perception. The chalkboard is useful in training all of these areas and thus comes under a classification of its own. In all areas the tasks begin at low-level proficiency and increase in difficulty as the child's perceptual-motor awareness and general skills become stronger.

  I. Chalkboard Training

    Through the use of the chalkboard the child can strengthen certain patterns of movement (left-right, up-down, circular, linear, etc.) which are most necessary to learning more developed motor skills such as writing and drawing. Among the activities which can be encouraged for the child are scribbling, which lets the child experiment with lines and unstructured movements which he himself can produce with chalk; finger painting, which frees movement patterns to produce free-flowing movements; chalkboard directionality movements, parallel movements, opposed movements and an imitative drawing. The child is also encouraged through chalkboard exercises to reproduce the primary shapes necessary to later writing and drawing movements.

    A. The Circle

    The child is encouraged to make circular movements through imitation and experimentation. Using templates and tactual clues the child's circular movements are more easily trained. Tracing, copying, reproduction from memory, variations of circle-making (outline figures, direction, size, speed, and solid circles) facilitate the learning of the primary shape.

    B. The Cross

    Drawing of crosses gives the child practice in vertical and horizontal line drawing, using tracings and hand guidance if necessary. The child is encouraged in avoiding diagonals, drawing straight lines, and equalizing the lengths of lines.

    C. The Square

    The child, through practice, learns to stop line length, turn corners linearly, strengthen form perception, avoid diagonals and generalize the concept of "square".

D. The Rectangle

In these exercises the child gets much practice in developing the concept of parallels, generalizing the concept of rectangles and further strengthening his form perception.

E. The Triangle, Diamond, Letters & Words

In working with the triangle and the diamond the child learns the purpose and uses of diagonal lines. He is then ready to begin forming letters and words by combining the movements of the various shapes he has mastered. From the chalkboard the child then graduates to paper and pencil. This can be approached in stages, by having the child copy from large newsprint, from large paper practice to regulation size, and from drawing large figures to small ones. The use of primary tablets and pencils is also helpful, and gives the child an opportunity to practice his gross motor movements which develop into more precise movements.

II. Sensory-Motor Training

The sensory-motor training exercises and apparatus are most helpful in teaching the child motor skills and strengthening his sensory-motor perceptions. To this end, Dunn recommends the use of the following:

A. The Walking Board

By using the walking board the child develops the skills necessary for walking forward, walking backward, walking sideways, turning, bouncing, lateral movement, and directionality.

B. The Balance Board

By using the balance board the child's balance and neuro-muscular skills can be strengthened. Through practice in balancing on the various size boards, the child gets a clearer body-image and a finer sense of balance and coordination. Other devices that are useful in balance are the trampoline, which teaches dynamic balance, coordination, body image; bouncing; and such simple exercises as making-angels-in-the-snow which strengthens bilateral movements, unilateral movements, and cross-lateral movements; altering time and position; and rhythmic exercises for figure-ground perception.

III. Training Ocular Control

Ocular exercises are useful in teaching eye control since it must be matched to general motor and kinesthetic patterns. The eye-movement patterns are trained laterally and vertically to strengthen muscular control and reinforce these patterns. Using pencils and penlights to teach eye control, the teacher is able to observe the patterns of eye movement and note uncontrolled eye movements when they occur. In later stages of ocular development, the child is asked to follow the stimulus (a light or pencil point) with his finger as well as his eyes; this develops kinesthetic and tactual perception as it is tied to eye movement and control. *Binocular* and *monocular* training is most important for eye control, so that the right eye can be moved alone. The left eye then is moved alone. (Occlusion, or the covering of the unused eyes is necessary here.)

Chalkboard aids, and play activities such as volleyball, basketball, and kickball are all helpful along with the *marsden ball*, which swings like a pendulum from the ceiling and must be touched by the child as it swings laterally by him, requiring strong ocular control.

IV. Training Form Perceptions

Training of form perceptions can be accomplished by using the following devices, which give the child a strong sense of form and shape and develop his ability to recognize and reproduce these forms.

A. Puzzles

The purpose of having the child use puzzles is to ensure that he completes the puzzle on the basis of evaluation of the total form rather than on the basis of a simple matching of some few specific elements in the form. Complex picture puzzles should be avoided, and picture puzzles should not have more than two or three main figures, none overlapping. The teacher can construct her own puzzles, and let the child do likewise, keeping the above principles in mind.

B. Stick Figures

In using stick figures, elements of the form (lines) are broken down and presented to the child separately as sticks. He must then use these elements to construct a figure like the one he has been shown. He can be asked to make squares, rectangles, triangles, diamonds, divided squares, diagonals, and trapezoids of various sizes and at different degree angles.

C. Pegboards

The pegboard consists of a square board in which rows of holes have been drilled. 12" × 12" is a good size. Pegs should be relatively large. The child is asked to imitate in his pegboard the designs that the teacher has made on hers. In one stage the child may freely consult the pegboard of the teacher in making his imitative design, but later the teacher's board should be removed and the child must use his memory to reconstruct the pattern. The child must learn not to be distracted by the other unused pegholes, to produce straight lines (horizontally, vertically, diagonally), make multiple forms and interlocking figures. These exercises aid the child in developing strong concepts of shape and their manipulations as well as strong form perceptions and recognition.

THE FROSTIG PROGRAM FOR THE DEVELOPMENT OF VISUAL PERCEPTION

The Frostig program was developed for children who exhibit a limitation or impairment in the ability to perform different visual perceptual tasks. The perceptual handicaps appear to be closely related to brain damage, emotional disturbances, mental retardation, and developmental lag. According to Frostig, what is normally referred to as visual perception actually consists of a number of different functions which are relatively independent of one another. Frostig focuses on five perceptual abilities that seem to have the greatest relevance to academic development. These five abilities are: (1) perception of position in space, (2) perception of spatial relationships, (3) perceptual constancy, (4) visual-motor coordination, and (5) figure-ground perception.

The ability to differentiate numerals which have a similar form but differ in their position—such as six and nine—and the ability to recognize the sequence of numerals in a number and the sequence of number symbols in a mathematical sentence depends upon the adequate development of perception of position in space and spatial relationships.

Adequate perception of constancy of shape and size is essential if the children are to be able to recognize numerals they know when seen in an unfamiliar context, color, size or style of print. Numerals written by the teacher on the chalkboard, placed on the flannel board, reproduced on a worksheet, or written by a child in his tablet may confuse the child and be preceived as completely distinct symbols.

Visual-motor coordination is significant since well-directed eye movements are a prerequisite to reading and writing numbers. The ability to distinguish figure from ground is necessary for such functions as the analysis of number problems, measurement tasks, and reading mathematical sentences. This skill is also indispensable for locating numbers on a page, such as in a table of contents or an index.

Mentally retarded children who are deficient in any of the foregoing abilities will most likely be hampered in their progress in reading, but will also be handicapped in other academic subjects such as mathematics. The following paragraphs present a brief outline of the training procedures for each of the five perceptual tasks.

Visual-motor Coordination. Frostig defines visual motor coordination as the ability to coordinate vision with movements of the body or with movements of a part or parts of the body. Children with such difficulties will display clumsiness in self-help skills and will be awkward in sports and games. Academic areas will be less affected but these children will certainly have difficulty in writing numbers. The training program suggested by Frostig includes such gross motor activities as catching, rolling, running, jumping, hopping, skipping, bending, climbing, and duck-walking. Fine motor activities include cutting, pasting, tracing, and finger tracing. Frostig developed a number of worksheets providing pencil-and-paper exercises for those aspects of visual-motor coordination most closely related to academic learning. She points out that the worksheets must be preceded and accompanied by training in eye movement, in gross motor coordination, fine motor coordination, in developing balance, and in the accurate perception of body image, body concept, and body schema.

Figure-ground Perception. The figure is that portion of the visual field that is the center of the viewer's attention. The ground (background) is that part of the field not focused upon which is only dimly perceived. Below is a facsimile of an illustration found in a popular arithmetic workbook. The figure is the child dressed in an Indian costume standing on a rock. The ground is the trees, grass, sky, and other children. However,

FIGURE 5.9

if the observer were to shift his attention to the two boys hiding in front of the rock or the trees behind the rock, the child dressed in the Indian costume standing on the rock would then be the ground.

Some children have poor figure-ground discrimination skills and consequently have difficulty in working with illustrations like the one in Figure 5.9. Children with this problem may appear inattentive and disorganized. They may be unable to solve familiar problems if they are presented on crowded worksheets or if they are given a cluttered set of concrete objects as aids. Frostig suggests training in figure-ground perception which should result in improved ability to shift attention appropriately, to concentrate upon relevant stimuli and ignore irrelevant stimuli, to scan adequately, and in general to solve problems in a more organized fashion. The first step she suggests is to provide the children with games and exercises involving three-dimensional objects and then to proceed to a series of pencil-and-paper activities she has designed.

Perceptual Constancy. Perceptual constancy is the skill of perceiving an object of invariant characteristics such as size, configuration, and position, as a constant in spite of the various ways it is viewed. Children with this difficulty may recognize a number in one form, color, size, or type but be unable to identify the same number when presented in another manner. Frostig presents such activities as finding objects of the same size, finding objects of different sizes, sorting by size, matching and sorting by shape.

Perception of Position in Space. Perception of position in space is defined as perception of an object in relationship with the viewer. Children with disabilities in their perception of position in space will view a distorted world and will have great difficulties in understanding what is meant by such spatial terms as *in, out, up, down,* etc. They will confuse numbers such as thirty-four and forty-three, and will have considerable difficulties in ordinal numbers. The activities suggested for the development of adequate body awareness and body image are similar to those presented in Chapters 3 and 4 under Form and Perception.

Perceptions of Spatial Relationships. The perception of spatial relationships according to Frostig is the ability of the observer to perceive the position of two or more objects in relationship to himself and to each other. Disabilities in this skill will lead to difficulties in learning mathematics. Children with this problem may be unable to properly perceive the sequence of numbers so that the number 473 may be read as 743 or written as 374. In attempting to solve mathematical problems, such children may be unable to remember the sequence of processes involved in problem solving. A host of other tasks such as map reading, understanding graphs, and learning to measure may be equally difficult for them.

Instructional Materials for Children with Perceptual Handicaps

A wide range of instructional aids have been developed over the past few years. There is not sufficient space to describe even a small portion of these materials. However, four different sets of materials are briefly described below and additional materials are listed at the end of this chapter.

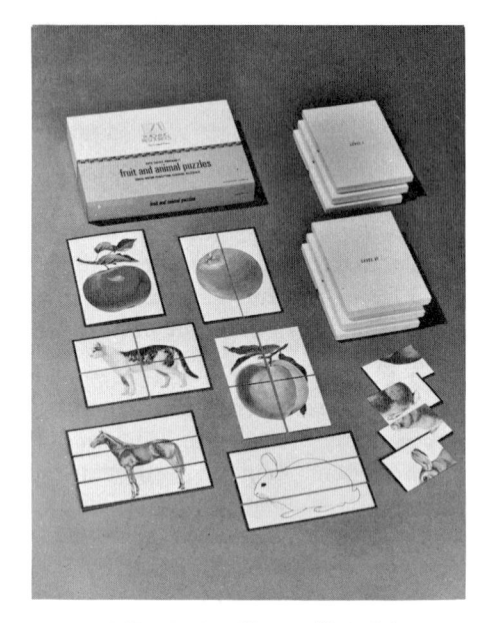

FIGURE 5.10. Cheves Materials.

Part 1 of the Cheves materials consists of a set of forty-two large puzzles which provide a medium for assisting children in developing basic patterns of learning. Concrete experiences are given in areas of spatial orientation and visual discrimination with familiar objects. Seven sets of picture puzzles depict four animals and three fruits in both horizontal and vertical formats. The set is divided into six separate levels of increasing difficulty. The early levels have a black border to limit the child's visual field. Later levels have the black borders removed in order to help condition the child to contend with an unlimited visual field.

Dubnoff Program. The Dubnoff Program consists of perceptual motor exercises related to the performance of everyday tasks. The levels can be used as a complete program progressing in sequential stages to develop proficiency in all the basic skills concepts introduced, or each level can be used individually as an independent program to develop or reinforce specific skills and deficiencies.

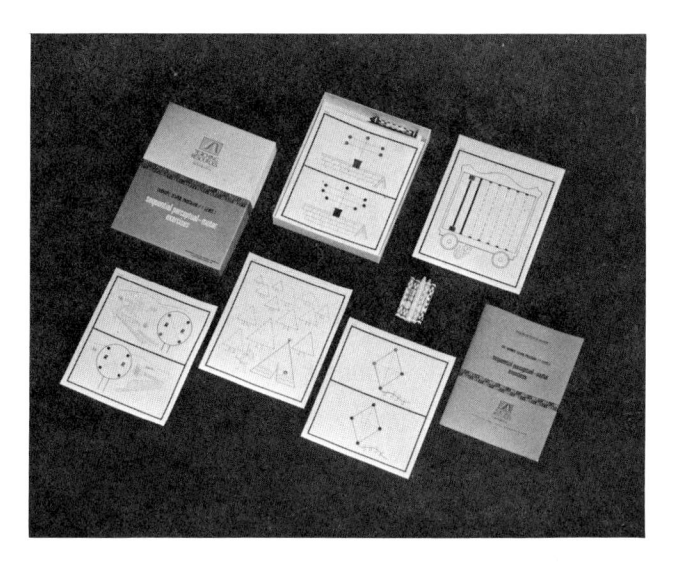

FIGURE 5.11

LEVEL 1.

Concepts of straight, circular, diagonal and intersecting lines are introduced in level 1 through four sections of tracing, copying and drawing exercises, built around themes such as flying kites and riding in cars. Visual orientation, left-right sequence, and visual-motor coordination for the reading and writing tasks are developed. Washable crayons, an acetate protector and 112 reusable exercise sheets are provided. A fifty-two page guide describes over 300 exercises and enrichment activities.

LEVEL 2.

Combinations of lines and multi-directional changes are used to develop fine motor control and perception of forms and patterns. These provide experience in integrating visual and auditory cues and patterns of response. They can be used diagnostically to discover developmental gaps and define areas for reinforcement. 120 exercise sheets, crayons,

FIGURE 5.12

and acetate protector are provided. A sixty page guide details all exercises and supplementary procedures.

Erie School Program. Four separate sets of games are provided, with boards, bingo, templates and playing cards. The games are arranged so that children of different developmental levels can play together. Each child can be challenged according to his own capabilities, yet assured of some success. The many alternate possibilities and procedures suggested with each group of materials, enable the teacher to give as much or as little practice as is necessary, for the child to attain proficiency in each area. Diagnostically the games can indicate areas where reinforcement is needed, and provide a variety of different techniques for remediation.

The exercises are so organized that they correspond to the normal maturational sequence expected to occur prior to, and at the beginning of, formal scholastic training. Each set of exercises is based on form discriminations of increasing complexity. They emphasize recognition and recall of six geometric shapes which individually or in combination, in whole or in part, are the basic forms from which alphabetical and numerical symbols are constructed.

Variations in position and orientation of the forms; incomplete forms which must be put together from dots, dashes, angles and curves; confusing or irrelevant backgrounds; changes in order and sequence; and different clustering are factors in each game. These are all simpler versions of the tasks that are required for reading.

Intermediate Mathematics for the Mentally Retarded 217

As these games progress, the individual concepts developed at a simple level are related to the child's eventual mastery of reading skills; progressing uniformly from left to right in horizontal rows; recognizing a difference between letters (or sounds) and words and combinations and groupings of letters (or sounds) which make up words; ignoring non-essential details and focusing on relevant or essential points; and understanding that basic forms (letters, sounds, or words) remain the same regardless of the style in which they are written or printed, or how they are "buried" inside a cluster of other letters or words.

A variety of visual and tactile stimuli or verbal cues and instructions are used throughout the games, to initiate a specific action or reaction from the child. Extensive practice is given in the integration of eyes and hands and fine motor control, ability to organize thought, and competence in making decisions from alternative choices and following set rules and procedures.

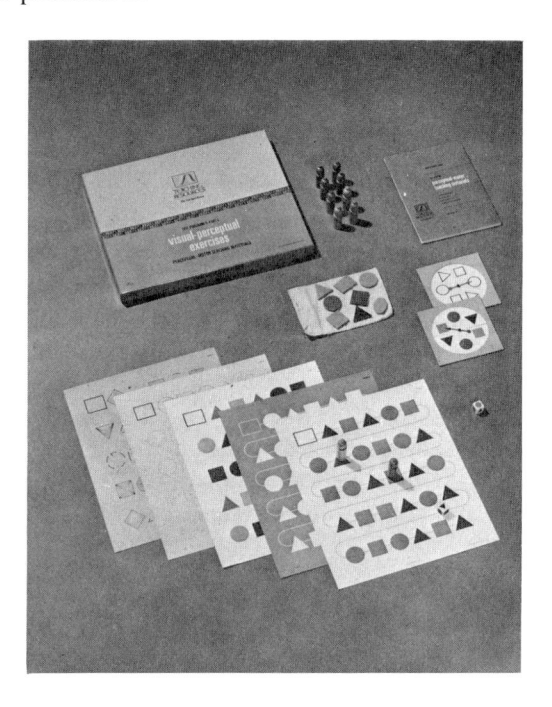

FIGURE 5.13

Part 1. *Visual Perceptual Games* provide practice in recognizing common geometric forms in different groupings under increasingly complex conditions. Five separate game-boards are of progressive difficulty, first using color as an aid, then presenting forms in various combinations of solids, broken outlines, shading, and distracting backgrounds. Ten children can play at the same time. "Stimulus" devices include dice, spinners and tactile pieces. Skills emphasized include form discrimination, position in space, left to right sequencing and fine finger and manipulative control.

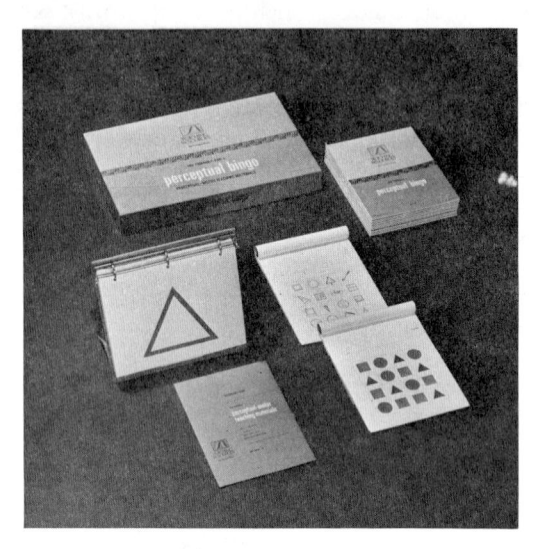

FIGURE 5.14

Part 2. Perceptual Bingo reinforces discrimination skills with the basic geometric forms either presented in different combinations of scale, position, orientation and outline, or incorporated into the design or shape of familiar objects. Padded "booklets" of bingo cards have six levels of difficulty with three exercises at each level. The instructor can control games to permit selected students to win. Sufficient materials are included for twelve students. Other skills developed include integration of visual and motor skills and response to verbal instructions.

Part 3. Visual-Motor Template Forms provide further practice in integration of perceptual skills with the motor skills which implement them. Groups of forms are presented in varying outlines, broken, and with distracting backgrounds. Drawing with wood-cased erasers on heavy textured paper gives correct "feel" for the shapes. Additional emphasis is placed on eye-hand skills for the proper execution of required movements. Books of worksheets have seven sets of exercises of increasing complexity. All materials for twelve students are provided.

Intermediate Mathematics for the Mentally Retarded 219

FIGURE 5.15

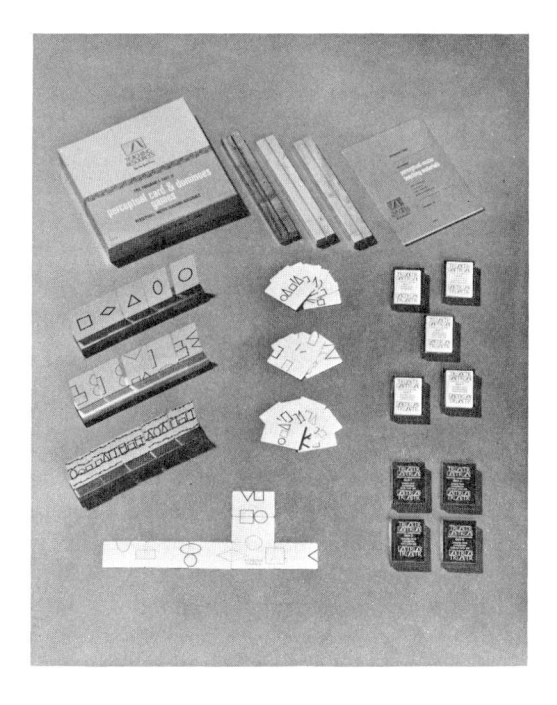

FIGURE 5.16

Part 4. Perceptual Cards and Dominoes Games includes five different decks of *Perceptual Cards* which are used to play many traditional games. They develop skills of form recognition and constancy, memory, sequencing, figure-ground discrimination, attention and concentration. Up to six children can play with each deck at different levels. *Dominoes Games* match halves of simple and complex geometric forms to make card patterns. Four decks of cards increase in difficulty, with and without color aid. Up to five children can play with each deck. Six slotted card holders are included.

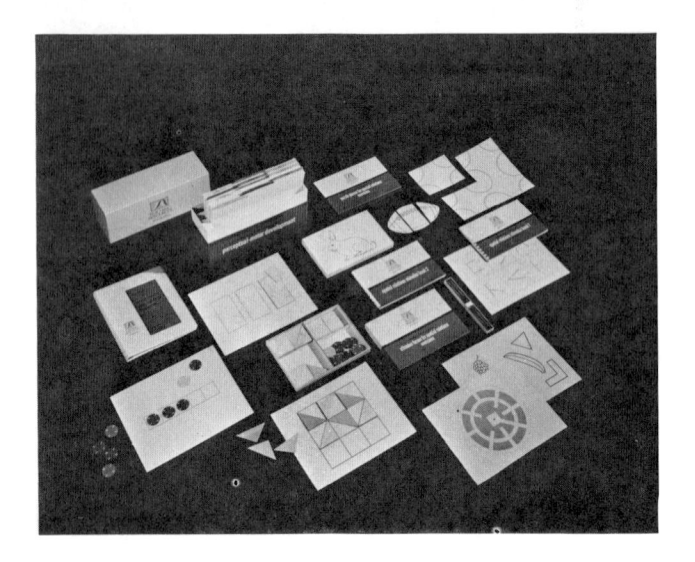

FIGURE 5.17. Fairbanks-Robinson Programs

Fairbanks-Robinson Programs. The Fairbanks-Robinson materials introduce perceptual concepts by making use of visual, manipulative and coordinative experiences. It develops a student's proficiency in the complex interrelated basic skills, necessary in order to achieve success in the classroom and learn more effectively. The skills developed are approximate to those expected of a first grade student. However the materials are suitable for students of all ages who are functioning below their age expectancy for any reason; through simple developmental lag, emotional disturbance, or specific learning disability. Content normally associated with the activities of young children has been avoided, thus maintaining the appeal of the materials to older students.

Sufficient exercise levels and materials are available to provide developmental or remedial work, on the suggested basis of twenty minutes per day for several months. The exercises may be used as a continuing program with one or two students, or by applying selected levels to a number of students individually.

Multi-sensory reinforcement is employed wherever possible, as the student experiences each concept visually, kinesthetically (tracing with the finger or copying), auditorily (by verbalization), and tactilely (by feeling the shape).

VOCABULARY ASSOCIATED WITH MATHEMATICS

A suggested vocabulary list of terms associated with intermediate mathematics is presented in Table 5.2. These vocabulary words should be developed in relationship to the other categories. The computational vocabulary should be tied to the instructor's in basic facts and processes. Teachers will stress terms related to the processes of addition and subtraction (add means plus; minus means take away). Measurement terms will be reinforced through such activities as handling thick and thin objects, showing the left and right hand, learning that we have arithmetic at 9:00 A.M., that the news program is on at 12:00 noon, that the third floor is higher than the flag pole, and the supermarket is farther than the cleaners. The use of bulletin boards and the picture file are suggestions given earlier that have applicability to the intermediate level.

NUMBER SYMBOLS

The system of numeration we use is organized around two major characteristics; (1) place value and (2) base ten. It is called the decimal or base ten system. Man having ten fingers may account for this base. If early man were counting stones, he probably counted by one-to-one correspondence (one finger to one stone) until he ran out of fingers (ten) and then began again. He needed some way to record the groups of tens. We called this technique used in the base ten system *Positional Notation*. Thus a group of ten is represented by "10" which is interpreted as one set of ten and no sets of one; a group of fifteen is represented by "15" which is interpreted as one set of ten and one set of five. Conventionally we would say "one ten and five ones." Another term used for positional notation is *place value*. It is thought that the learning of mathematical concepts among children parallels the process early man went through in an evolutionary fashion over centuries. Whether this is the case or not it does provide the teacher of mentally retarded children with some solace knowing that she is attempting to teach in a few years concepts that required the composite intelligence of mankind over centuries. The idea of the base ten system and the related concepts of place value and positional notation should receive major emphasis at the intermediate level.

The signs and symbols used in the fundamental process of addition and subtraction should be reviewed and discussed. The children should be able to name the signs and be able to explain what the sign tells them to do. Symbols introduced at the intermediate level include the signs for multiplication, division, degree, and decimal. The development of skills in reading the signs and naming and interpreting the processes are integrated into the areas of computation, mathematical reasoning and others. However, it is still advisable to consider *Number Symbols* as a separate category in order to remind the teacher that these signs are abstract and need to be introduced cautiously, practiced and reviewed systematically.

The child in the intermediate classroom for the mentally retarded will have had many exposures to number symbols. Many of these children will already be able to rote count to as high as 100, read numerals beyond twenty, and number words ten and higher. They may also be able to write many number words and symbols. The extension of these skills which may be developed at the intermediate level is indicated in Table 5.2. It can be expected that many children at this level will learn to read number names and symbols to 100 and do some counting by twos, threes, fives, and tens.

Number Line.   Cards are constructed with the numerals one to 100 printed in bold manuscript. The cards are then presented to the children in sub-sets of from ten to thirty cards. The children put the numerals in the correct order.

The Missing Number.   A number line from one to 100 is printed on a long strip of construction paper or written on the chalkboard. Cover a numeral and ask, "Which one did I cover up?"

Number Sheets.   Numerals from one to 100 are drawn on the right hand side of a paper with corresponding numerals on the left. Instruct the children to "Draw a line between the ones which are the same."

Number Builders.   The children may be taught to read number symbols with the aid of a simply constructed device called the number builder. The numerals zero through nine are printed in random order on cards of three different cuts as shown in Figure 5.19. A numeral is built each time the child turns a card. This instructional aid will allow the child to work independently or in small groups as he practices reading numerals.

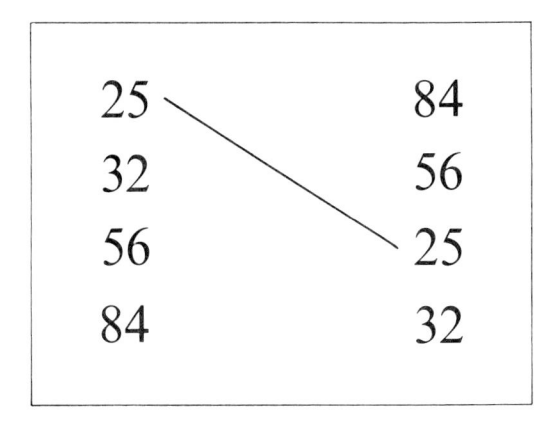

Intermediate Mathematics for the Mentally Retarded 223

FIGURE 5.18

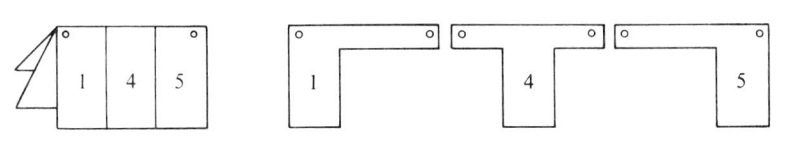

FIGURE 5.19

Place Value. This chart is a common device especially useful in helping children visualize the ideas of place value. In working with this chart the teacher asks such questions as, "How many hundreds in the numeral 321? How many tens are there in the tens place in the numeral 456?"

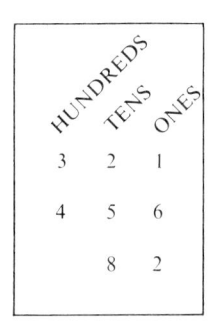

FIGURE 5.20

Intermediate Number Cards. Large cards with sets from one to one hundred are drawn on cards with the corresponding numeral printed on the bottom of the card. The sets are grouped by tens to facilitate recognition. Cards for set work may be prepared for each child matching a larger set for the teacher's use. The children follow the teacher's explanation of place value by referring to the set card which matches her card.

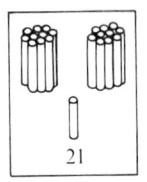

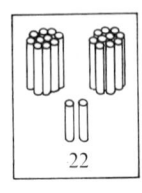

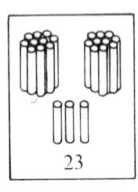

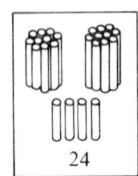

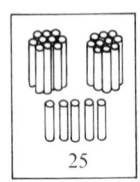

FIGURE 5.21

Matching Number Words. Prepare two sets of cards with the number words from one to fifty. Give the children a group of cards each of which has a match. Ask the children to sort them into pairs.

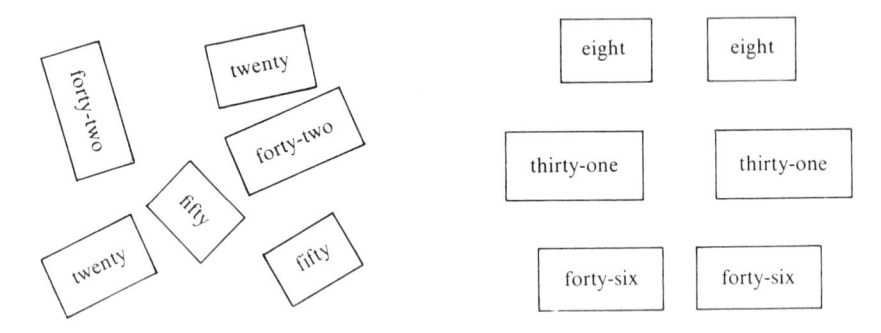

FIGURE 5.22

Number Families. This teaching aid will assist the children in reading numbers beyond twenty. Their skills in reading compound number words will be enhanced if they recognize the word patterns. Print the words, "twenty-, thirty-, and forty-," on a card and cut windows as shown in Figure 5.24. Construct an insert with the number words from one to nine printed in random order. As the insert is moved, different number words are formed.

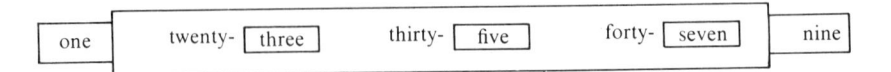

FIGURE 5.23

Intermediate Mathematics for the Mentally Retarded 225

For students who are having special problems with number words, a simplified number family could be used.

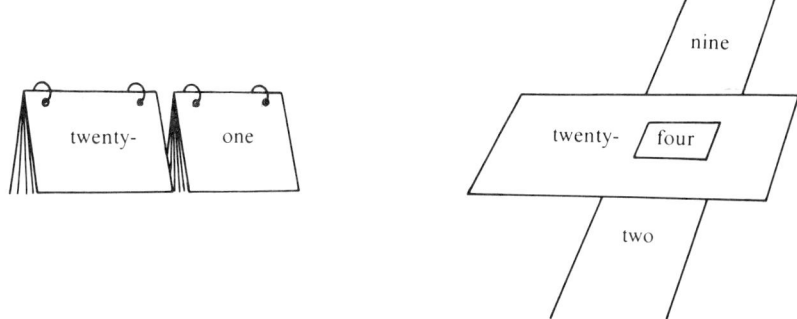

FIGURE 5.24

Matching Numerals and Number Words

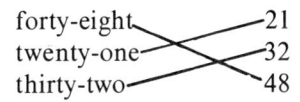

```
forty-eight        21
twenty-one         32
thirty-two         48
```

Matching exercises such as the one shown above may prove useful with children who experience difficulty in reading number words but are able to read numerals. Matching exercises may be prepared for the flannel, chalk and magnet boards or on worksheets for seatwork.

Number Symbol Chart. The teacher may find a chart such as the one shown below helpful in explaining number symbols. The standard symbols are presented with conventional interpretations. The chart should be so placed in the room as to be convenient for easy student reference.

"Here is a chart for you to use when you need help in reading the problem signs."

+	plus	add, combine, put together
−	minus	take away, separate, subtract
=	equal	is, are the same
÷	divide	goes into, (junior high)
×	multiply	times (junior high)

Action Pictures. Shown in Figure 5.25 are a number of action pictures which may be used to illustrate combining and separating. The illustration in quadrant (a) shows two blocks being combined with two additional blocks; quadrant (b) shows two birds flying away from a third bird; quadrant (c) shows two balls separated from three other balls; and quadrant (d) shows three fish being combined with a fourth fish. Pictures such as these are very useful in teaching the "process" of combining and separating and make very useful action problems since the child need not know how to read in order to solve them.

"These cards show the action of the signs."

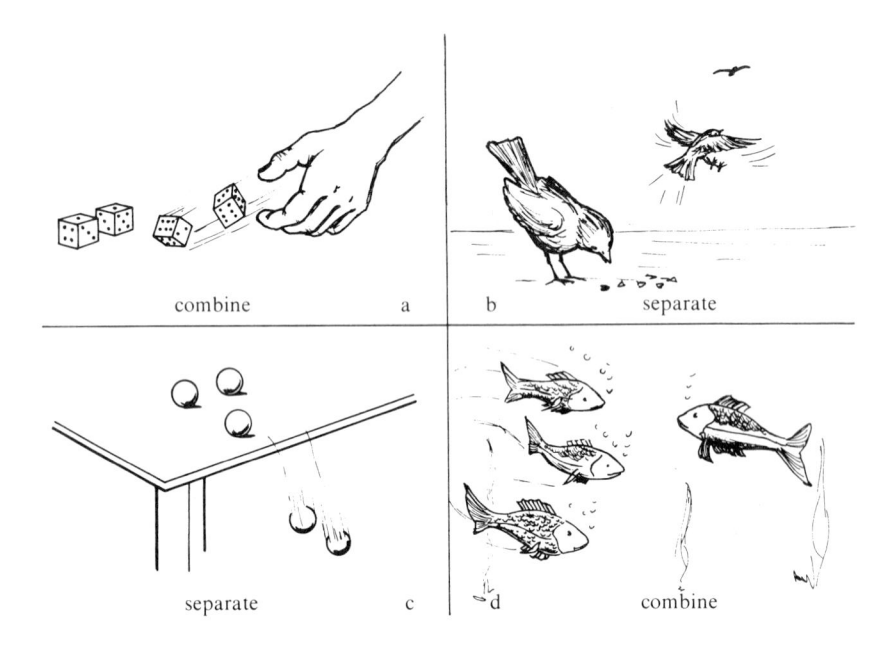

FIGURE 5.25

Counting by Twos and Threes. The exercises are designed to teach the children to count by twos and threes. Faces are used because the children understand that a face has two eyes and that the number of eyes for any group of faces may be found by counting by twos. Instruct the children to count the eyes in the first face and then add the number of eyes in the second face. They will learn that an easy way to do this is to count by twos . . . two . . . four . . . six . . . eight . . . etc.

The three leaf clover is used because the children can readily perceive that there are three leaves on each clover. Practice in counting by threes will help them learn that it is easier to count the leaves in the clovers by threes than to count them by ones.

Look at the pictures in Figures 5.26 and 5.27. Each face has two eyes. Each clover has three leaves. Count the eyes by twos and the leaves by threes.

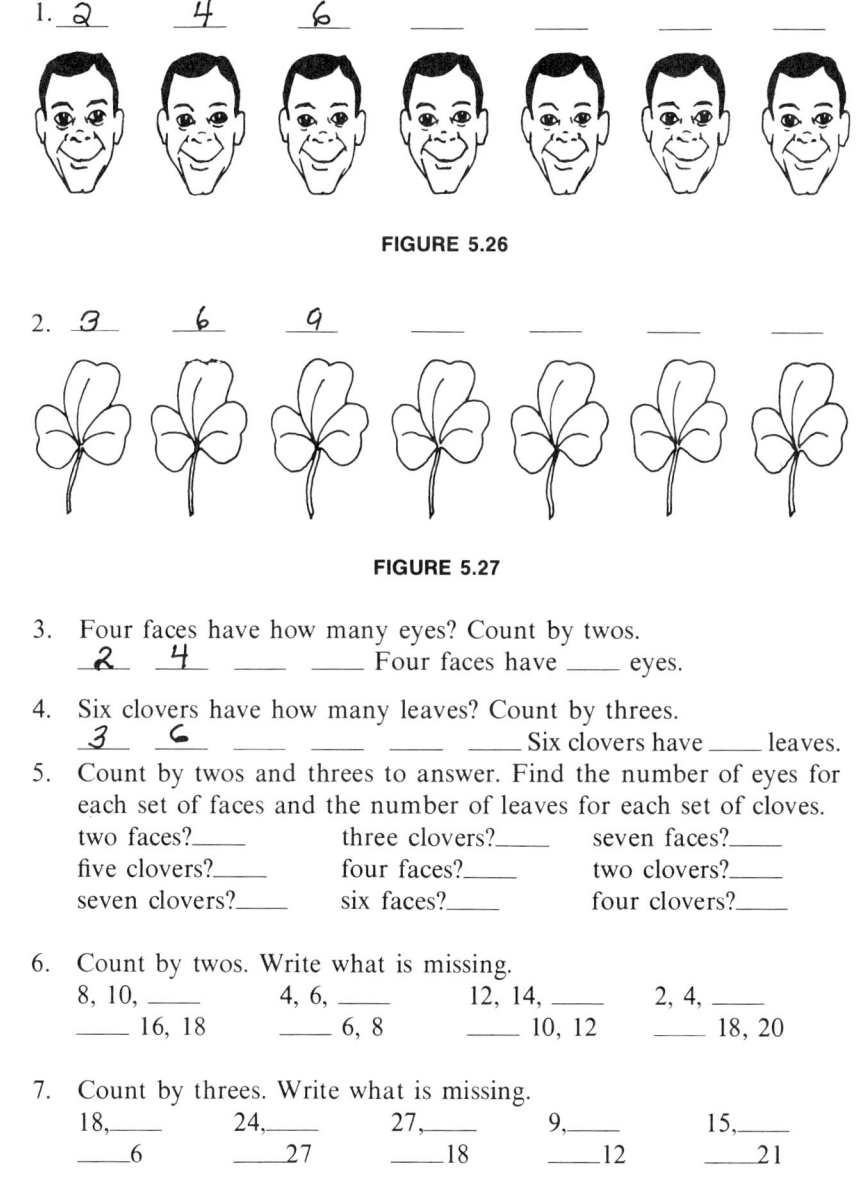

Intermediate Mathematics for the Mentally Retarded 227

1. _2_ _4_ _6_ ___ ___ ___ ___

FIGURE 5.26

2. _3_ _6_ _9_ ___ ___ ___ ___

FIGURE 5.27

3. Four faces have how many eyes? Count by twos.
   _2_ _4_ ___ ___ Four faces have ___ eyes.
4. Six clovers have how many leaves? Count by threes.
   _3_ _6_ ___ ___ ___ ___ Six clovers have ___ leaves.
5. Count by twos and threes to answer. Find the number of eyes for each set of faces and the number of leaves for each set of cloves.
   two faces?___   three clovers?___   seven faces?___
   five clovers?___ four faces?___   two clovers?___
   seven clovers?___ six faces?___   four clovers?___

6. Count by twos. Write what is missing.
   8, 10, ___   4, 6, ___   12, 14, ___   2, 4, ___
   ___ 16, 18   ___ 6, 8   ___ 10, 12   ___ 18, 20

7. Count by threes. Write what is missing.
   18,___   24,___   27,___   9,___   15,___
   ___6   ___27   ___18   ___12   ___21

Counting by Fives and Tens. The children will find it easier to count by fives and tens than it was to count by twos and threes since they have already had experience in counting with numbers higher than one. The pencils below are grouped by fives and the balls are in groups of ten. The children should be instructed to complete the blanks by counting by fives or tens. Some answers are provided to help them get started.

Look at the pictures in Figures 5.28 and 5.29. Each set of pencils has five members. Each set of balls has ten members. Count them by fives and tens.

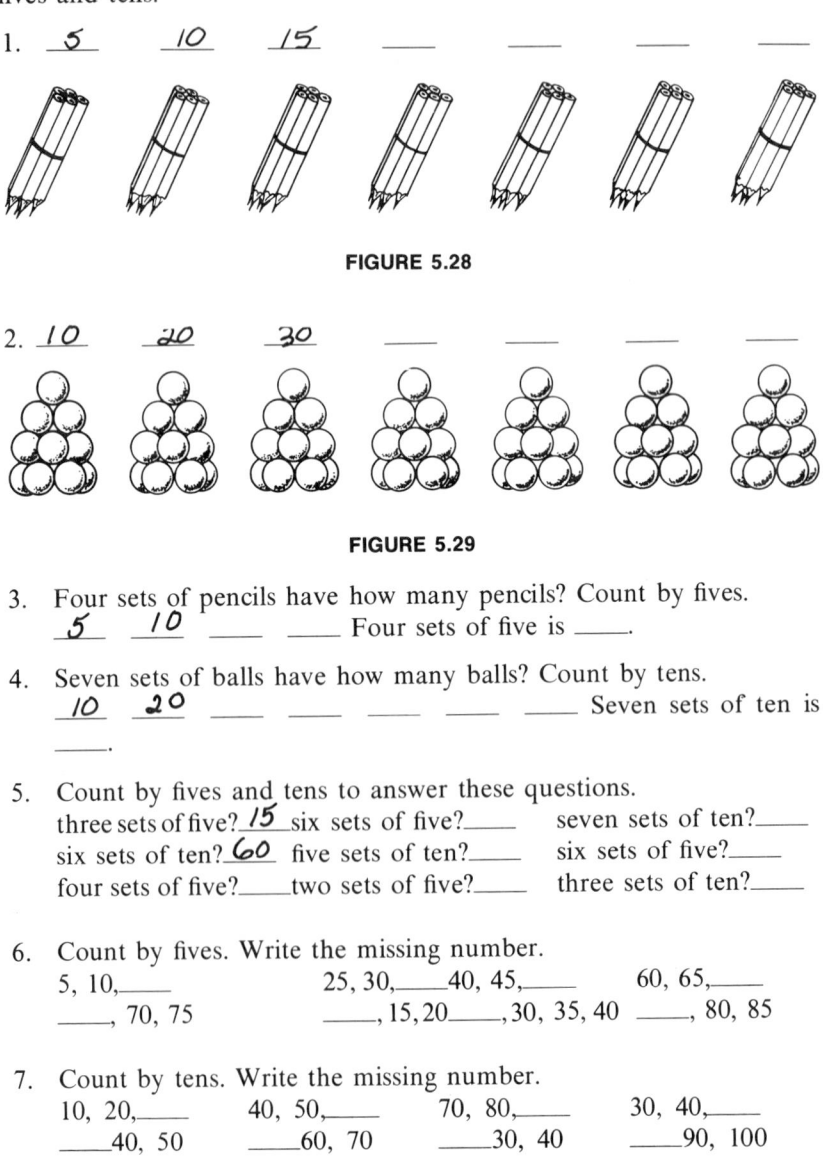

1. _5_ _10_ _15_ ___ ___ ___ ___

FIGURE 5.28

2. _10_ _20_ _30_ ___ ___ ___ ___

FIGURE 5.29

3. Four sets of pencils have how many pencils? Count by fives.
   _5_ _10_ ___ ___ Four sets of five is ___.

4. Seven sets of balls have how many balls? Count by tens.
   _10_ _20_ ___ ___ ___ ___ ___ Seven sets of ten is ___.

5. Count by fives and tens to answer these questions.
   three sets of five? _15_ six sets of five? ___ seven sets of ten? ___
   six sets of ten? _60_ five sets of ten? ___ six sets of five? ___
   four sets of five? ___ two sets of five? ___ three sets of ten? ___

6. Count by fives. Write the missing number.
   5, 10, ___   25, 30, ___ 40, 45, ___   60, 65, ___
   ___, 70, 75   ___, 15, 20 ___, 30, 35, 40   ___, 80, 85

7. Count by tens. Write the missing number.
   10, 20, ___   40, 50, ___   70, 80, ___   30, 40, ___
   ___ 40, 50   ___ 60, 70   ___ 30, 40   ___ 90, 100

Count by twos
Write the numbers that come
before and after
___ 4 ___
___ 8 ___
___ 12 ___
___ 6 ___
___ 10 ___
___ 16 ___

Count by threes
Write the numbers that come
before and after
___ 6 ___
___ 15 ___
___ 21 ___
___ 30 ___
___ 12 ___
___ 18 ___

Count by fives
Write the numbers that come
before and after
___ 10 ___
___ 25 ___
___ 50 ___
___ 90 ___
___ 45 ___
___ 15 ___

Count by tens
Write the numbers that come
before and after
___ 20 ___
___ 50 ___
___ 40 ___
___ 30 ___
___ 80 ___
___ 90 ___

CARDINAL NUMBERS

Most of the children at the intermediate level will have some concept of sets. It is the understanding which serves as the basis of the child's skills in number operations. At the primary level the children explored the concepts of sets and correspondence. The children will have had practice with equivalent sets and the concepts of greater than and less than. Picture cards, sorting decks, peg boards, dominoes, and worksheets are examples of teaching devices used at the primary level. These devices will also be appropriate for the intermediate age child. However, the pictures should be more mature. Illustrations of ducks would be replaced by racers, pictures of dolls with pictures of pre-adolescent girls and so forth.

The concept of *union of sets* ($\cup$) will be understood intuitively by most children but must be carefully reviewed for the mentally retarded. If Mary has two apples {🍎🍎} and Bill gives her one more {🍎}, she now has three apples.

$A = \{🍎🍎\}; B = \{🍎\}; A \cup B = \{🍎🍎🍎\}$

Of course the symbol $\cup$ is not presented to the children, but the concept is. Two apples joined with one apple represents a new group (set) of three apples.

The children at the intermediate level will have dealt with groups of ten and less. Now, they are introduced to the "second decade." Retarded children must have a lot of practice working with groups of eleven to twenty. The combination of seven plus six must not be taught by cumulative counting—"Seven, eight, nine, ten, eleven, twelve, thirteen." The child *must* be taught to recognize. The group should be reorganized as ten and three. To the average child and the teacher, this may be trite, however, it is anything but simple to the retarded child. He must be shown that three objects can be taken from the six and combined with the seven to make a group of ten. According to positional notation discussed earlier, the group of ten and the group of three may be seen as thirteen.

$$7 + 6 = \Box$$
$$(7 + 3) + 3 = \Box$$
$$10 + 3 = \Box$$

Practice must be given until the child understands the notation:

$$11 = 10 + 1$$
$$12 = 10 + 2$$
$$13 = 10 + 3$$
$$14 = 10 + 4$$
$$15 = 10 + 5 \text{ etc.}$$

Additional suggestions for teaching this are presented in the following.

One Greater Than

Three is one greater than two.
Five is one greater than ____.
Four is one greater than ____.
Ten is one greater than ____.
Seven is one greater than ____.

One Less Than

Four is one less than five.
Three is one less than ____.
Nine is one less than ____.
Six is one less than ____.
Two is one less than ____.

Guess the Number

I am thinking of a number two more than ten. Guess the number.
I am thinking of a number five more than ten. Guess the number.
I am thinking of a number that together with nine makes ten. Guess the number.
I am thinking of a number that together with eight makes ten. Guess the number.

Intermediate Mathematics for the Mentally Retarded 231

Grouping by Tens

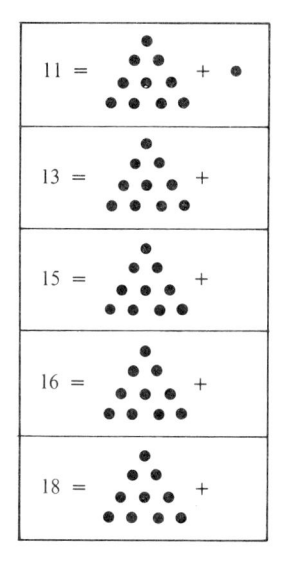

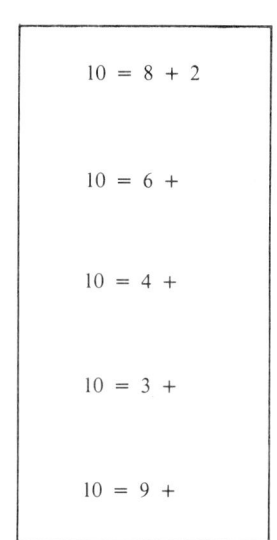

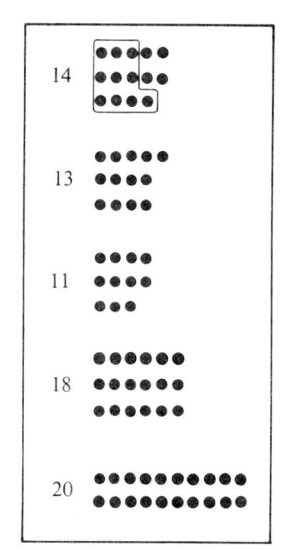

11 = △ + •	10 = 8 + 2	14 ⬚
13 = △ +	10 = 6 +	13
15 = △ +	10 = 4 +	11
16 = △ +	10 = 3 +	18
18 = △ +	10 = 9 +	20

FIGURE 5.30

Cuisenaire Materials. These are an excellent example of materials appropriate to a modern mathematics instructor. The materials consist of a set of 291 wooden rods, varying in color and length, used to show number relationships. The rods consist of five color families: red represents 2, 4, 8; blue-green represents 3, 6, 9; yellow represents 5, 10; black represents 7; and white represents 1.

The rods are not fixed with numerals, so they are useful in helping the children explore the relationships between quantities. Children can also use the rods to develop the ideas of number operations.

The four booklets which accompany the set of rods treat topics such as cardinality, ordinality, measurement, whole numbers, number properties and so on.

The teacher should be aware that merely having these materials in the classroom will not guarantee success. If the teacher becomes familiar with the Cuisenaire-Gattegno philosophy and uses the materials wisely, she should experience success with the mentally retarded children.

Stern Blocks. These materials permit the child to manipulate concrete materials that reveal the structure of our number system. Wooden blocks are used as a basis for this mathematical approach, and they include both single units and "rods." The use of this kit makes it possible for the child to examine closely the relationships between units and numbers in the first decade. A child can easily see that five yellow units equal the five-unit yellow block. The kit is especially designed for work with small groups. The Fundamath picture in Figure 5.31 can be used to teach the ideas of place value. The child is asked to solve problems similar to the one in the picture with the aid of the strings of beads. It is also fairly simple and inexpensive to construct "number pockets" using paper counting strips, counting sticks, or pencils. The idea of ten may also be taught with the aid of clear plastic bags or simple work sheets. Samples of these are shown in Figures 5.32, 5.33, and 5.34.

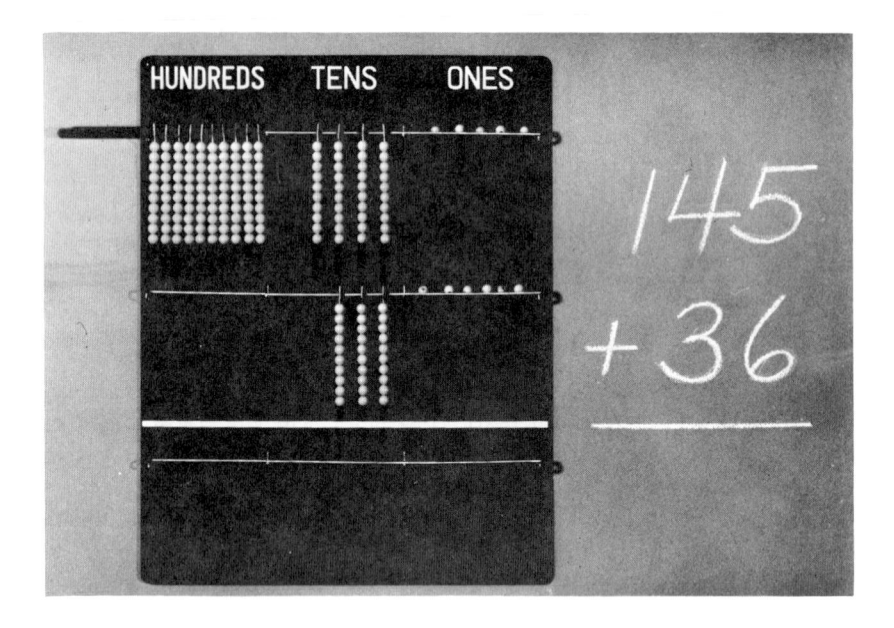

FIGURE 5.31

Number Pockets

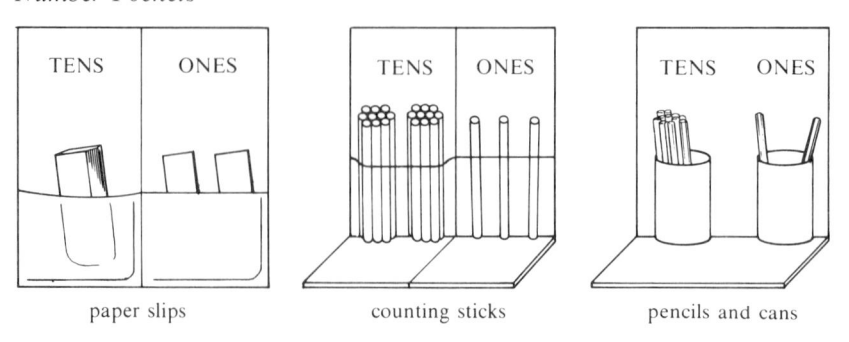

paper slips   counting sticks   pencils and cans

FIGURE 5.32

Intermediate Mathematics for the Mentally Retarded 233

Bags of Ten.

Use the bag of marbles to show me 12.

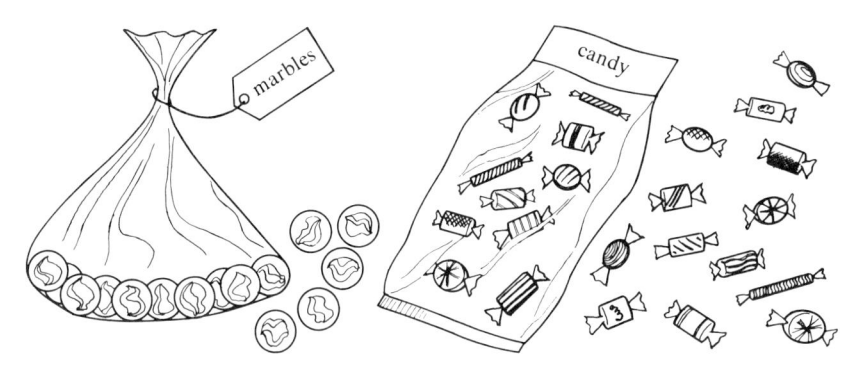

FIGURE 5.33

Use the sack of candy to show me 18.

Find the Tens and Ones

TENS	ONES	
1	11	XXXXXX XXXX XXXX
		XX XXX X X XXX X X XXXX
		XXXXXXX XXXXXX
		X XX XX X XX XX X X X X
		XX XX X XXX X X

TENS	ONES	
1	2	12
1	4	14
		16
		13
		17
		15
		11

FIGURE 5.34

What Number am I? Have a child in the room begin a game by saying, "I am three tens and two ones. What number am I?" The child who correctly answers thirty-two gives the class a new number and so the game continues, "I am five tens and four ones. What number am I?"

Which is More. Place a ring around the number which is larger.

| 6 or 9 | 2 or 1 | 1 or 0 | 10 or 20 | 18 or 12 |

Place a ring around the number which is largest.

| 18 or 17 or 15 | 18 or 12 or 2 | 20 or 15 or 13 |

Practice with Sets. Prepare cards with a variety of sets whose elements have some fairly obvious patterns. Present the cards to the children and say, "I want you to think of a way to tell me about this set."

6	2
8	4

3	9
7	5

Have the children cut pictures out of catalogs and magazines which show sets of objects.

Tell the children to draw sets (flowers, rabbits, dogs, etc.) and then to tell you about the set.

Give the children examples of sets and ask them to describe the members of the set.
1. dog, cat, horse
2. Jerry, Kenny, Michael
3. car, plane, train

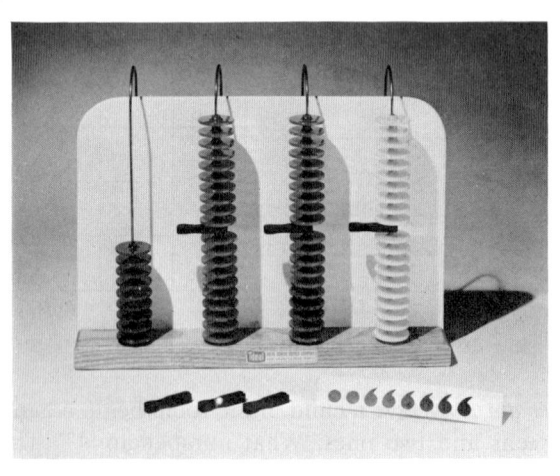

FIGURE 5.35

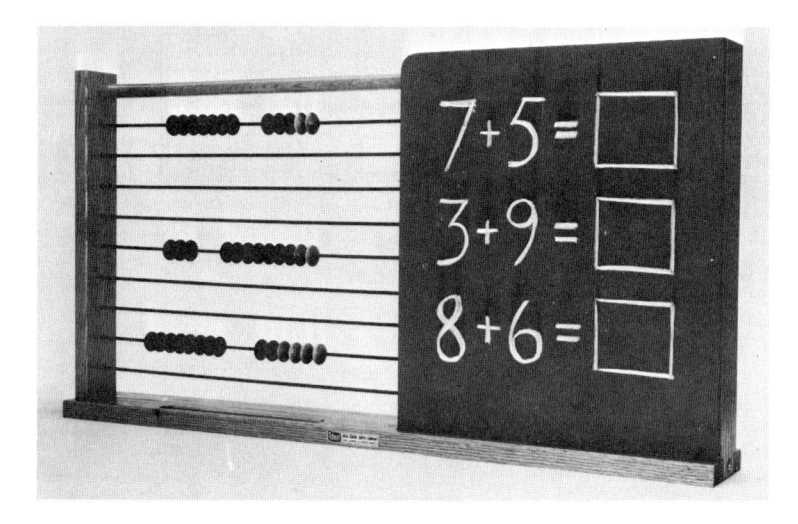

FIGURE 5.36

The Abacus. The abacus is a very popular device for teaching place value and number operations. An abacus may be purchased from commercial sources, but also may be constructed from inexpensive materials. Since the abacus is relatively simple to make, the teacher may wish to involve the children in a class project of making several of them. Two designs available commercially are pictured in Figures 5.35 and 5.36.

The diagrams in Figures 5.37 and 5.38 with the accompanying narrative describes the procedures for adding and subtracting by presenting two examples.

Addition   25
            +17

(a) To indicate the 25 to be added, count and move 5 beads down on the one's rod and 2 beads on the ten's rod.

(b) Start to bring down 7 more beads on the one's rod for the 7 ones in 17. Count 1-2-3-4-5 and remember "2" since 2 beads could not be counted.

(c) Move the 10 ones up to the top. Move 1 bead down on the ten's rod to represent the 10 ones just moved up.

(d) Bring down on the one's rod the 2 beads remembered from the second step.

(e) Move one more 10 down for the 1 ten in 17. Now read the answer: 4 tens and 2 ones.

$$25 + 17 = 42$$

(a)   (b)   (c)   (d)   (e)

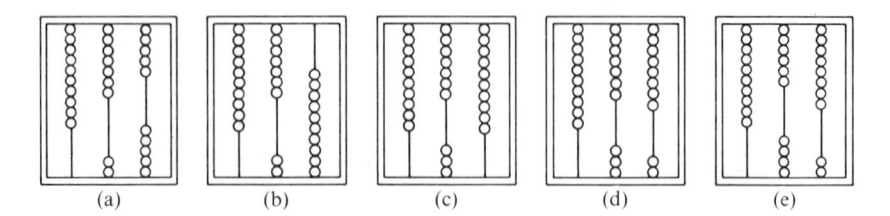

FIGURE 5.37

Subtraction   46
      − 9

(a) To show the minuend, 46, count and bring down 4 beads on the ten's rod and 6 beads on the one's rod.

(b) To subtract, begin to move the 9 beads up on the one's rod. "1-2-3-4-5-6." Since there are not 9 beads in the one's column, it will be necessary to regroup. Remember the "3" still to be counted.

(c) Move 10 ones down. Then move one bead up on the ten's rod to stand for the 10 ones just moved down.

(d) Move three more beads up on the one's rod, remember from the second step. Read the answers: 3 tens and 7 ones.

$$46 - 9 = 37$$

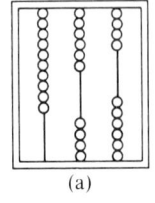

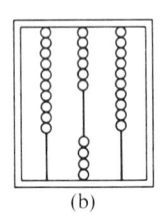

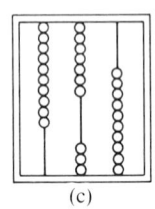

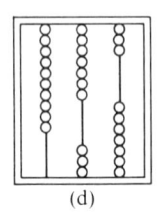

(a)   (b)   (c)   (d)

FIGURE 5.38

The Bead Line. This is a very simple and inexpensive device whether teacher constructed or commercially purchased. The bead frame in effect is a number line. Simple addition, subtraction, multiplication, and division concepts and examples can easily be demonstrated. An advantage of the bead line over the number line is that it presents number concepts at a concrete level.

Intermediate Mathematics for the Mentally Retarded 237

```
    O          OOOOOOOOO
    OO         OOOOOOOO
    OOO        OOOOOOO
    OOOO       OOOOOO
    OOOOO      OOOOO
    OOOOOO     OOOO
    OOOOOOO    OOO
    OOOOOOOO   OO
    OOOOOOOOO  O
    OOOOOOOOOO
```

Fractions. The exercises below are examples of techniques for teaching the ideas of one-half, one-fourth, and one-third.

Here are some things which are cut in two pieces. The pieces are exactly the same size so we call them *halves*. Put each pair of halves together to make a whole.

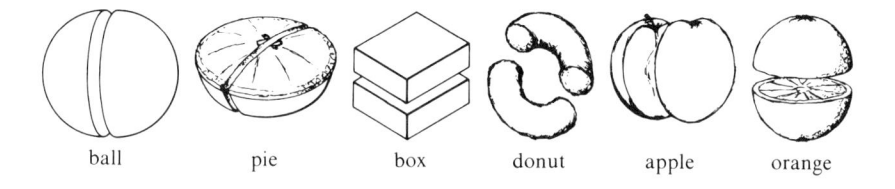

ball   pie   box   donut   apple   orange

FIGURE 5.39

Here are some things which are cut into four pieces. The pieces are exactly the same size so we call them *fourths*. Put each item together to make a whole.

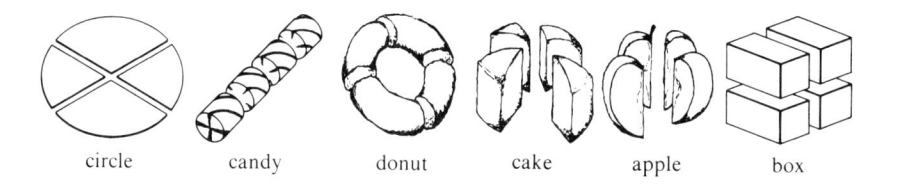

circle   candy   donut   cake   apple   box

FIGURE 5.40

Here are some things which are cut into three pieces. The pieces are exactly the same size so we call them *thirds*. Put each item together to make a whole.

pie   cake   box   banana   candle

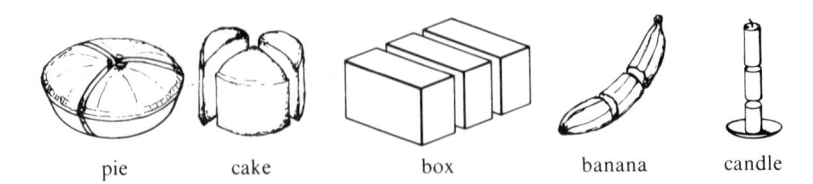

FIGURE 5.41

Which is not one cut into halves?

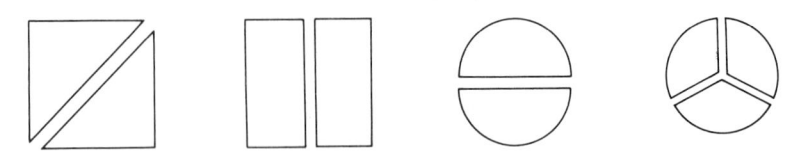

FIGURE 5.42

Which one is not cut into fourths?

FIGURE 5.43

Put a mark (X) on each half.

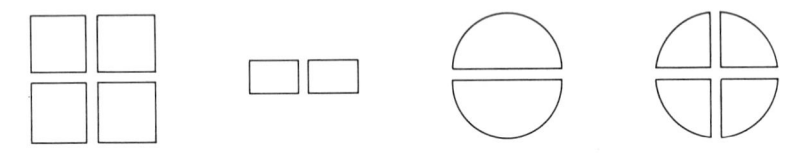

FIGURE 5.44

Put a ring around each fourth.

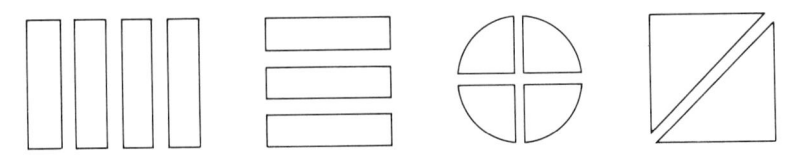

FIGURE 5.45

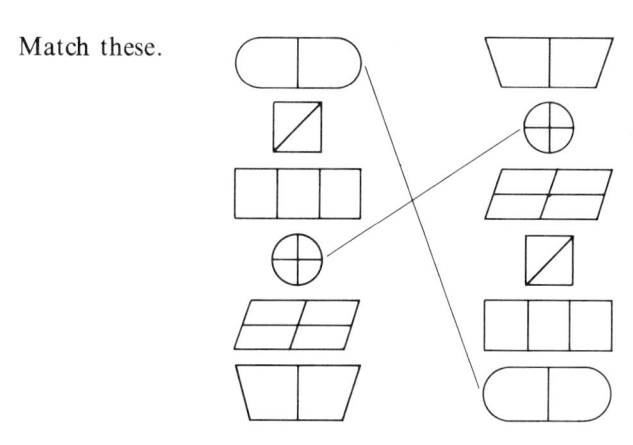

Intermediate Mathematics for the Mentally Retarded 239

Match these.

FIGURE 5.46

ORDINAL NUMBERS

Ordinal numbers are used to indicate position in an ordered sequence of objects or events. At the intermediate level the goal is to teach the ordinal numbers to twelfth, to advance the skills of seriation, and to utilize ordinal numbers in practical situations.

Ordinals to Twelve.
Place a mark on the tenth man:

FIGURE 5.47

Color the eleventh ball red:

FIGURE 5.48

Point to the ninth hat.

FIGURE 5.49

240   *Intermediate Mathematics for the Mentally Retarded*

The circle with the x is tenth. What is the position of the shaded circle?

FIGURE 5.50

Put these forms into a sequence so that the blue box is first, the red box is second, the white box is third, the orange box is fourth, the green box is fifth, the yellow box is sixth, the purple box is seventh, the gray box is eighth, the pink box is ninth and so on.

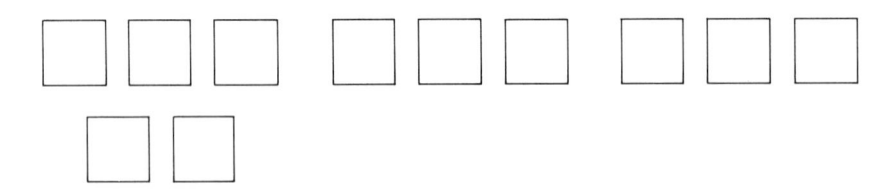

FIGURE 5.51

Seriation by Height, Length, Width, and Weight. Here are some rods of different heights. Put them in order so that the shortest one is first and the tallest one is last.

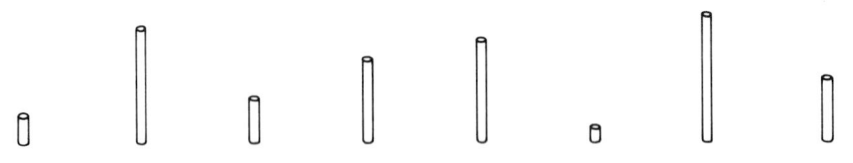

FIGURE 5.52

In Figure 5.53 are some sticks of different lengths. Put them in order so the shortest one is first and the longest one is last.

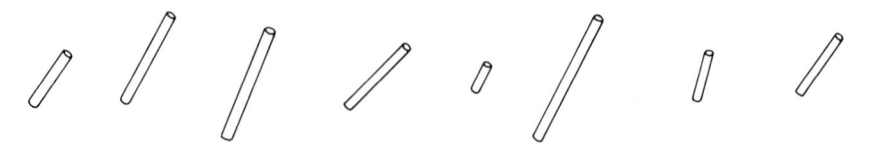

FIGURE 5.53

In Figure 5.54 are some blocks of different widths. Put them in order so the narrowest one is first and the widest one is last.

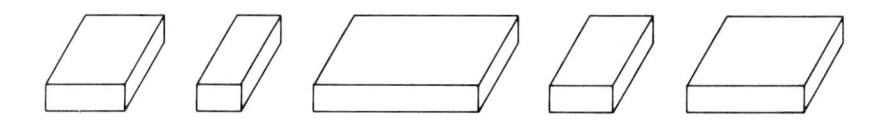

Intermediate Mathematics for the Mentally Retarded 241

FIGURE 5.54

In Figure 5.55 are some boxes of different weights. Put them in order so the lightest one is first and the heaviest one is last.

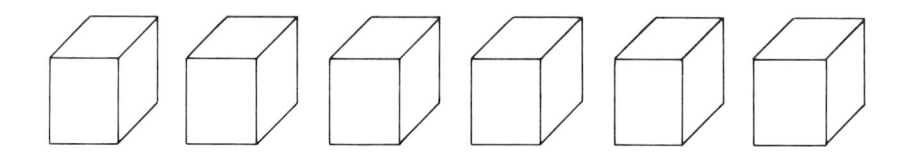

FIGURE 5.55

Book Pages. Provide the children with books, catalogs, and directories. Have them turn to different pages and locate items. If the children have different books, ask them to describe the pictures on a specific page. For example, "John, what picture do you have on page eleven? Mary, tell us about the picture on your twelfth page."

Addresses. Give the children practice with apartment numbers and street addresses. Begin with simple apartment numbers within a single building such as 1B or 2F, and proceed to more complex street addresses such as 3715 Chestnut Street or 6555 Scenic Drive.

Long Distance Game. Use a toy telephone and place it near the front of the room. Select one child to serve as the operator and another as the caller. The caller picks up the telephone and says, "I wish to call the third person in the second row." The operator calls that person's name, "Mary Anne." Mary Anne becomes the operator, the operator becomes the caller and a new call is placed. When the operator makes an incorrect call, another one is placed.

Ordinal Placement Board. The ordinal placement board is a helpful commercial teaching aid. The tabbed numerical cards are used to introduce numerical notations. The domino cards also develop language comprehension and concepts of sequential order and value.

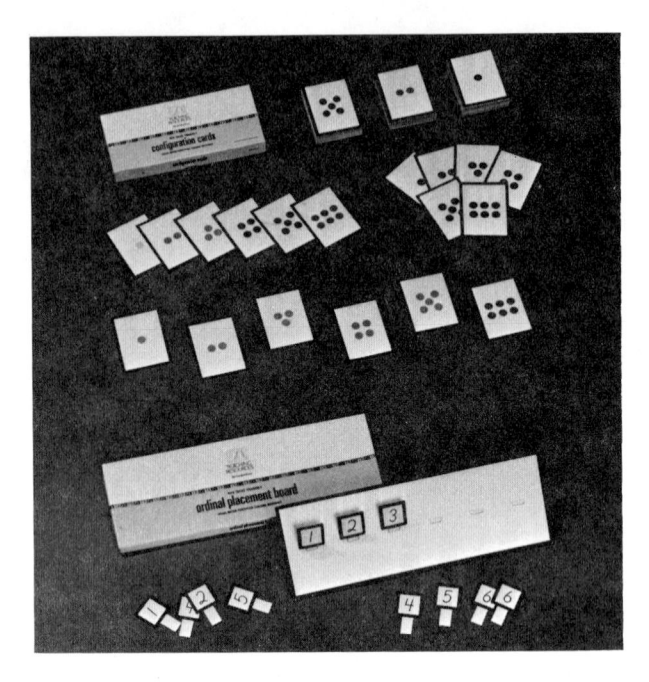

FIGURE 5.56. Ordinal Placement Board

MEASUREMENT

When a child is asked the question, "How many objects are here?" his response is given in a cardinal number. The answer to the question, "In what position is this item?" involves an ordinal number. Numbers are also used to answer such questions as "How much time? How tall? How heavy? How big?" The units used to respond to such questions are called *standard measures*. The process of selecting the appropriate number is called *measurement*.

Significant gains in the ability to utilize measurement instruments will be made at the intermediate level. The children will learn to identify pints, quarts, and gallons. They will learn to measure with a teaspoon, a tablespoon and a cup, and to use their major fractional parts. Ounce and pound will become familiar to them as well as the linear measures: inch, foot, and yard.

The ability to tell time will be extended to the quarter of an hour and they will know the days of the week, months of the year, and the seasons. Their skill in reading the thermometer will improve.

Learning about Pints and Quarts. Collect several pint and quart containers. Pictures of these items should be avoided at first but may be introduced after the children have had sufficient experience with the actual cartons. Use water colored with vegetable dye and ask the children to make a series of comparisons.

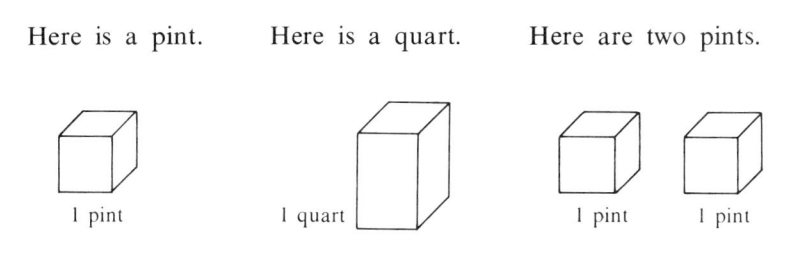

    Here is a pint.   Here is a quart.   Here are two pints.

FIGURE 5.57

    Is a pint the same as a quart? Which is more?
    Here are two pint containers. Fill them. Empty them into the quart container.
       Do two pints equal one-half quart?

Learning about Quarts and Gallons. The availability of paper milk cartons in pints, quarts, half gallons and gallons make it easy for the teacher to assemble a collection of durable, lightweight containers. A sample lesson would probably develop along the lines suggested below.
    Does one quart equal two pints? Do four pints equal one quart?
    Does one-half quart equal two pints? If you have one-half quart, how many pints do you have?
    If you have one quart, how many pints do you have?
Tell us which things are measured by quarts and pints.
    Milk? Water? Flowers? Candy? Cream? Eggs? Ice cream? Meat?
Can a baby kitten drink one quart of milk in three minutes?
Can Mary drink one pint of milk with her dinner?
Could Billy's family use two quarts of milk in one day?
Could you eat a quart of ice cream in three minutes?
Which is more, a pint of ice cream or a quart of ice cream?

Learning about Quarts and Gallons. The children will profit from learning about pints and quarts. Here is a sample lesson.
    We have learned about quarts and pints. Here is a new container that can hold more than either a quart or pint.

Here are some pints. Here are some quarts. Here is a gallon.

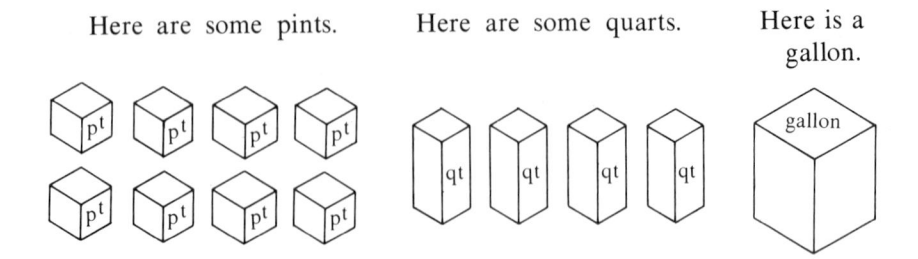

FIGURE 5.58

How many quarts are there in a gallon? How many pints are there in a gallon?

Do two quarts make one-half of a gallon? Which is more, three quarts or one gallon?

Mrs. Smith buys 2 quarts of milk. Is this the same as one-half of a gallon?

Learning to Weigh Things. The children will encounter a variety of scales used to measure different types of merchandise. Bring as many different scales as you can collect to the classroom. Explain to the children that we determine how heavy or light something is by weighing. The weight is expressed in terms of pounds. At first give the children practice in weighing items whose weight is in even pounds. Such items may be collected or made out of clay, containers of sand, and so forth. Later, half-pounds and quarter pounds may be introduced. After they have learned to weigh premeasured items ask them to do exercises such as these.

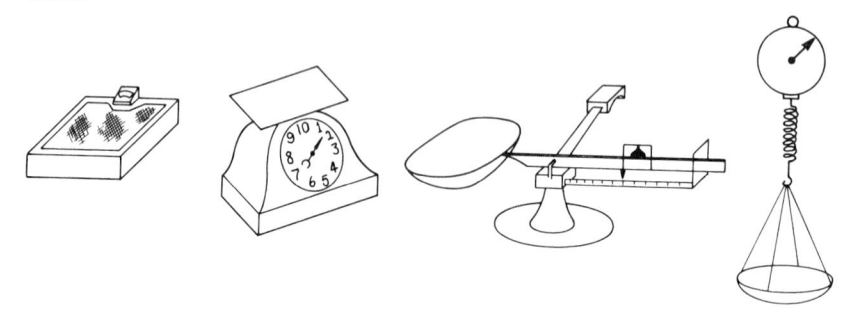

FIGURE 5.59

Weigh one pound of apples.
Give me one-half pound of clay.
Who do you think weighs more, Mary or John?

Which weighs more, this sack of rocks or this sack of feathers? Let's weigh them to see.

Let's weigh all the children the in class.

Which things do we measure by the pound? Do we weigh fish? Do we weigh milk? Do we weigh money? Do we weigh fruit? Do we weigh lumber?

Use of the Ruler. Give each child a piece of paper with a series of 12 lines an inch apart on it. Ask the children to count the number of marks on the line. Call their attention to the fact that the marks divide the line into 12 equal parts. Tell the children that the equal parts are called inches.

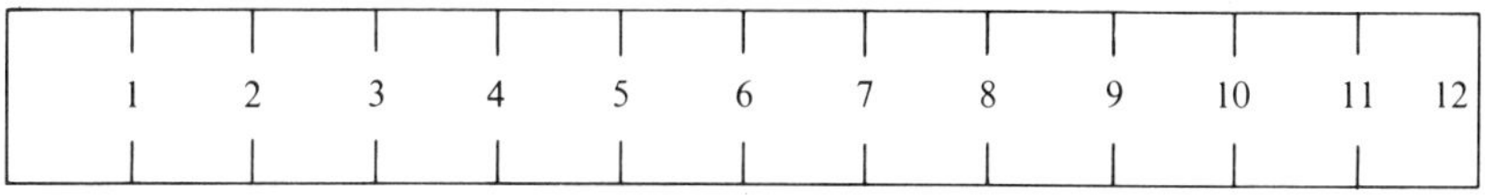

FIGURE 5.60

Write the numbers from one to twelve on your lines. With a crayon, mark off the three inches; ten inches; twelve inches; four inches.

Give each child a simplified ruler (one without fractions). This is a ruler. See, it has numbers from one to twelve just like the lines you had on your paper. The space between each number represents one inch. There are twelve inches on this ruler.

Here are some strips of cardboard. How long is the red one? Which strip is the longest? How many inches long is it?

Give the children a worksheet with a series of lines drawn on it and say, "With your ruler measure these lines. Then write how long it is in the space next to the line."

Demonstrate to the children how to measure items which may be easily measured in whole inches. Say "Here are some things to measure. Let's find out how long they are in inches."

With your ruler make a line four inches long; eight inches long; three inches long.

Give the children a group of items ten, eleven, and twelve inches long. Say, "Put all the items which are twelve inches long in one place. Find all the things which are twelve inches long. Twelve inches is one foot. So all these things are one foot long. A ruler is also one foot long."

Use of the Yard Stick. This is a yard stick. It has numbers printed on it just like the ruler. See, a yard stick is three rulers long. It is three feet long. There are some lines on the chalkboard. Find the one which is a foot long. Which is exactly one yard long? Which is two feet long?

Use Feet and Inches Together. Put two marks on the floor or chalkboard. What is the distance between these two lines? Prepare a set of sticks with a combination of lengths similar to these and use a yard stick marked with feet and inches to measure them.

1 ft. 3 in.	2 ft. 9 in.
2 ft. 6 in.	1 ft. 8 in.
3 ft. 0 in.	2 ft. 2 in.
10 in.	2 ft.

Make a mark one yard long. Make a line two feet and three inches long. Make a line two feet and five inches long. Make a line one foot and four inches long.

How tall are you in feet and inches? Have a friend measure you. How wide is this room?

Which is longer, a foot or a yard? Which is more, two feet or one yard? Which is less, one yard or one foot? Which is longest, an inch, a foot, a yard? Which is more, one yard or twelve inches?

Which things do we measure with inches, feet, and yards:

How much Mary weighs.
How tall Billy is.
How many eggs in a carton.
How much ice cream in a pint.
How wide the room is.
How long a board is.
How old your mother is.

CALENDAR

The ability to use the calendar effectively is probably not the most crucial measurement skill but it does have decided relevance to the mathematics curriculum. It was pointed out in Chapter 2 that the retarded child frequently has a poor concept of the sequence of time. This deficit may be due in part to the lack of study of the calendar and the failure to perceive time in terms of standard units of measure. The great emphasis which is placed upon learning to read the clock and to view the day in terms of hours, minutes, and seconds is not inappropriate. However, the extension of the study of time from the clock to the calendar may be easily overlooked. This may account for the reported difficulty that retarded children have in developing a concept of time sequence.

Some intermediate children may already know the days of the week, the months of the year, and the seasons of the year in sequence. These may need review and there will be others who need additional instruction. The children should also know their numbers to thirty-one. It should be mentioned that they need not know the ordinals to thirty-first but only the cardinal numbers which may be used as ordinals. For example, "It is October 27" as opposed to "It is the twenty-seventh of October."

In other words, the calendar is not a completely novel measurement device for the intermediate child. The knowledge and skill he has already gained will be extended to a more mature level.

Marking the Date, Day, and Month. Many teachers make it a practice to begin each day by indicating the month, day, and date in some fashion. One practice is simply to write the month, day of the month, and day of the week and year on the chalkboard. Another approach is to mark the day off on a calendar. There are a number of educational calendars on the market which provide for the adding of the current date daily. The purpose of each of these techniques is similar: that is, to increase the children's awareness of the ordering of time through use of the calendar. Follow-up activities usually include the writing of the name of the month, the number of the day, and the year on mathematics papers and other assignments completed during the day.

Seasons and Months. Introduce the children to the grouping of the months by the seasons. "If this is January, what is the season? etc." Of course the seasons are divided approximately two-thirds through the month so caution should be exercised so as not to confuse the youngsters.

The Days of the Week and the Months of the Year. Prior to the intermediate level the children have probably thought of the sequence of the days of week and the months of the year in a rote fashion. They should be encouraged to view these names as ordinal numbers. This can be accomplished by assigning numbers to the days of the week and the months of the year as illustrated here.

Sunday	1	January	1
Monday	2	February	2
Tuesday	3	March	3
Wednesday	4	April	4
Thursday	5	May	5
Friday	6	June	6
Saturday	7	July	7
		August	8
		September	9
		October	10
		November	11
		December	12

Some intermediate level children will even master the notation 3/15/72 for the date, March 15, 1972. However, this will more typically be delayed until the junior high school level or later. A number of games and activities will assist the children in learning the proper sequence of the days and months. For example, put the names of the days and months on cards and ask the children to place them in the proper order. Once they are in order, cover one day (or turn the card over) and ask them which day (month) is missing? Ask stimulating questions such as, "I am thinking of a day between Tuesday and Thursday. What day am I thinking of? What is the last month of the year? What is the first day of the week? What month comes before August? What day comes after Sunday? What day is tomorrow? What day was yesterday?"

Who's First Race. Place four, seven or twelve children in a row depending on whether you are practicing the days, months, or seasons. The objective of the games is to assist the children in learning the order of the days, months and seasons. Give each child the name of a day of the week, a month, or a season. Explain to them that you are going to tell them to raise and clap their hands. The catch is that they must clap their hands by the time you count to three. But you are going to call two names and only one child may respond. The child whose name is first in the sequence of months or days must clap his hands quickly, but the child whose name comes after his must *not* respond. For example, if the teacher were to say:

"Monday and Tuesday clap your hands...1...2...3!" By the time the teacher says three, Monday should have clapped his hands, but Tuesday must not have. If Tuesday does clap his hands he is out of the game. The last one standing wins. If the child who is first does not clap his hands by the count of three, he is out.

Seven Days of The Week.
Monday alone,
Tuesday together,
Wednesday we walk,
When it's fine weather,
Thursday we kiss,
Friday we cry,
Saturday's hours
Seem almost to fly.
But of all the days in the week
We will call
Sunday, the rest day,
The best day of all.

Intermediate Mathematics for the Mentally Retarded 249

The children will need a variety of practice with different types of calendars. Some calendars have a great deal of information relative to the almanac, holidays, famous events, and so forth. Others are limited to the days, month, and year.

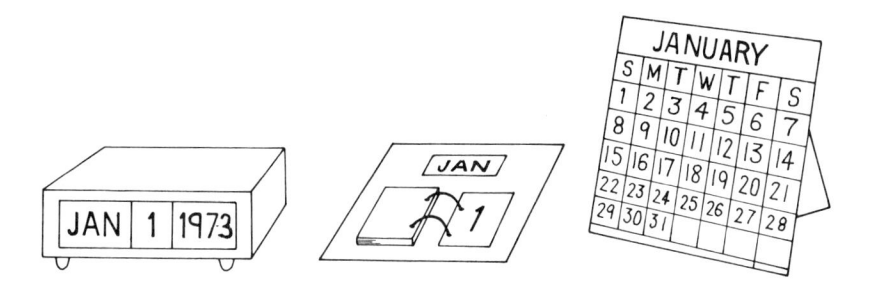

FIGURE 5.61

Keeping Records. Children will enjoy keeping their own calendars, such as the weather calendar, on a daily basis. Have the children prepare a calendar for the month and by the use of simple symbols, have them record the weather of the day. At the end of the month you may ask such questions as, "How many rainy days did we have? Count the number of sunny days, etc."

FIGURE 5.62

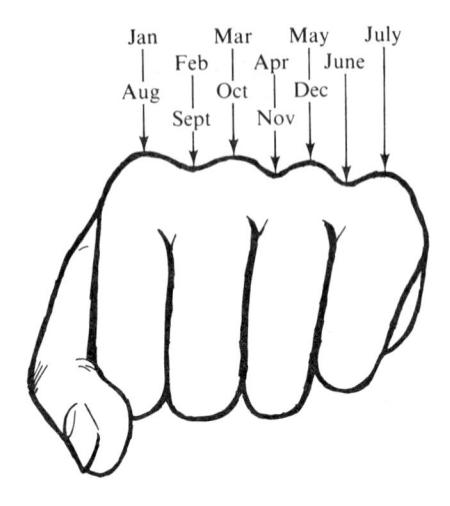

FIGURE 5.63

Knuckle-Aid. A very simple device may be used to remember how many days there are in each month. Close one hand into a fist and begin reciting the names of the months in order. Begin on the first knuckle with January (31); in the space say February (28-29); the second knuckle March (31); in the next space April (30); the third knuckle May (31); in the next space June (30); and on the last knuckle July (31). Return again to the first knuckle for August (31) since these two, August and July, are the only months in sequence which have thirty-one days each. Continue to December.

A Rhyme. The same information may be provided through this pneumonetic device:

Thirty days hath September
 April, June, and November
All the rest have thirty-one
 Except February alone
Which has twenty-eight in line
 But each leap year twenty-nine

Count Down. Probably the most common count-down game is calculating the number of days until Christmas. Close in popularity are the number of days until school is out for the summer vacation or some holiday or until one's birthday. The children will enjoy solving such problems as:

How many days until Joey's birthday?
How many days until Lincoln's birthday?
How many days until spring vacation?

LEARNING TO TELL TIME

Children at the intermediate level are familiar with the parts of the clock, are able to associate routine daily activities with specific times, and should be able to tell time by the hour. Of course, there will be some children at the intermediate level who need further practice in telling time by the hour. They should be exposed to material similar to that presented at the primary level.

The instruction at the intermediate level is geared to teach the children to tell time by the half and quarter-hours. Some of the children at this level are capable of learning to tell time by intervals of five minutes and to distinguish between such concepts as A.M., P.M., midnight, and noon.

At first glance, these may seem like uncomplicated skills below the potential of the mentally retarded children of chronological ages seven through twelve. Further inspection of the processes involved, however, reveal their true complexity.

Consider the example of telling time by the half-hour. The illustration below makes clear the confusion that can occur in distinguishing between time on the hour and time half past the hour solely through errors of visual perception. Using visual-perceptual skills, there are only two ways to distinguish between such times as 6 o'clock and 12:30 o'clock, 3:00 o'clock and 12:15 o'clock. The children must observe that the big and little hands are in opposite positions or they must see that the hour hand does not point exactly to the hour but slightly beyond it. These are subtle discriminations which must not be taken for granted. Many children have difficulty in differentiating the reversed positions of the hands and are not able to detect the difference of a hand pointing exactly at a numeral and a hand pointing between two numerals. The reader should review the suggestions presented in the previous sections on form and perception. More detailed perceptual training exercises are available in Kephart's text, *Slow Learner in the Classroom.*

Advancing the ability to tell time beyond accuracy to the hour is complicated not only by visual-perceptual skills but also by the profundity of the clock itself. Conventional usage allows the clock to be read in terms of fractions past the hour, fractions until the hour, cumulative minutes past the hour, and the total number of minutes until the hour.

6 o'clock   12:30 o'clock   3 o'clock   12:15 o'clock

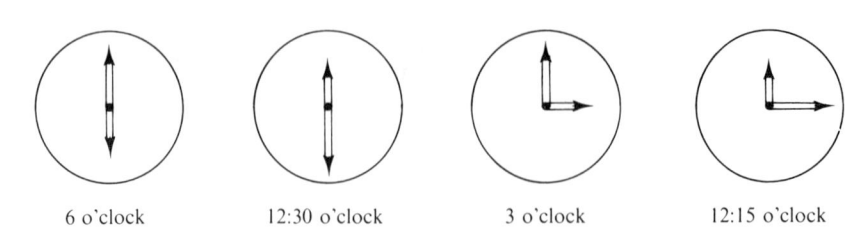

FIGURE 5.64

The technique for writing the time is not always the same as reading (saying) the time. Here is an example of the perplexities that develop. This clock can be read as:

Three quarters past three.
One quarter until four; quarter to four.
Three forty-five.
Fifteen until four.
Forty-five after three.

FIGURE 5.65

It is acceptable to write 3:45 for forty-five minutes past the hour but it is not acceptable to write 15:4 for fifteen minutes until the hour. These practices may not confuse the adult who has learned to read the clock with facility, but it should not surprise the teacher of intermediate children when the students in her class have difficulty.

The parts of the clock and telling time by the hour were introduced at the primary level. For many children at the intermediate level, this skill can be extended to telling time by the half-hour, quarter hour, and within units of five minutes. The concepts of A.M. and P.M. and such related terms as noon and midnight are also appropriate for many such children.

Teaching the Half-hour. If the children are to learn the concept of half-past the hour, they obviously must understand the idea of one-half.

Intermediate Mathematics for the Mentally Retarded 253

They have already learned that two halves of anything are equal to a whole. "If you cut an apple down the middle, you get two pieces of an apple. If you cut a pie down the middle, you get two pieces that are the same size. If you draw a line down the middle of a clockface, you divide the clock into two equal parts. Each clock is one-half of the whole clockface."

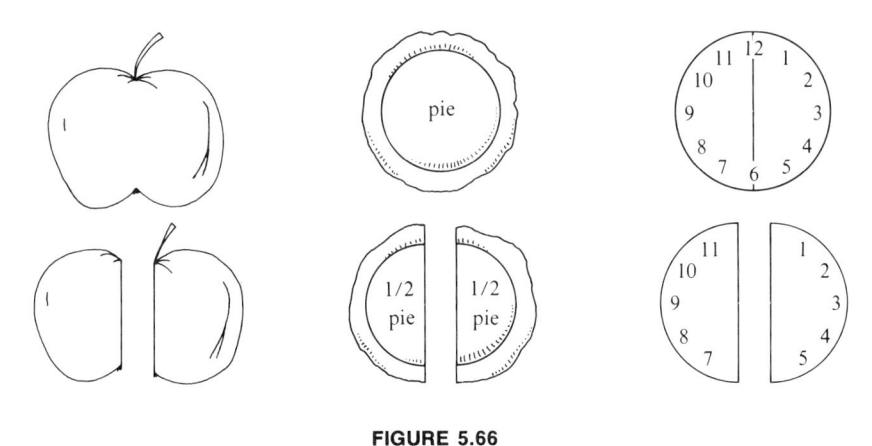

FIGURE 5.66

Have the children fold an eleven by eight paper in half the long way. Cut a half circle and unfold it. "Remember there are sixty minutes in one hour. How many minutes are there in one half-hour?"

FIGURE 5.67

The children should be given background with the half hour. There will probably be periods during the day that occupy about a half-hour, and if not they can be contrived. The lunch period, arithmetic period, story time or some other segment of the day that takes close to a half-hour should be used. Tell the children that they have about a half-hour to complete the arithmetic assignment, finish their lunch, or read their story. Present such questions as "Which is more time, an hour or a half-hour?

Which would you rather have, an hour for recess or a half-hour? Do you watch any T.V. programs which last an hour? Which ones? Which T.V. programs that you watch last a half hour? Which programs last longer than the others? What other things do you do that take an hour? What things do you do which take a half-hour?"

The discussions which follow such questioning can be supplemented by classroom activities with the alarm clock. "Here are two alarm clocks. Let's set one to ring in a half-hour and the other to ring in an hour. Which one will ring first?"

The beginning instruction with the half-hour should use a "half-hour clock." This demonstration clock should be made from a durable material with the hour hand adjustable and the minute hand either painted or glued pointing to the six. Hash marks should be spaced half-way between each pair of numerals. (' 1 ' 2 ' 3 ' 4.......12) as shown in the illustration in Figure 5.68. The hash marks are used to assist the children in accurately placing the hour hand exactly halfway between two numerals. In the illustration the clock indicates 1:30. The minute hand now points to six rather than to twelve and the hour hand points in between two numerals rather than precisely at one numeral.

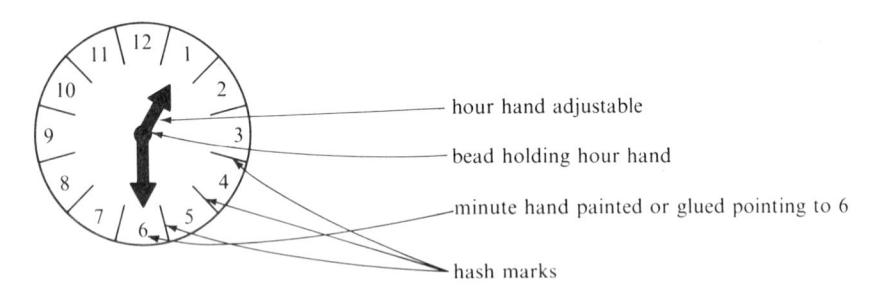

FIGURE 5.68

The children have become used to pointing the hour hand exactly at the hour and now they must become accustomed to pointing the hour hand halfway between two numerals to indicate that the time is half past the hour.

The children should be provided with individual clocks. Ask them to describe the differences between this "half-hour" clock and the "hour" clock they have been using for lessons in the past.

Call attention to the hash marks. At first it may be difficult for some children to read the hour hand when it is between two numbers. In the illustration, the hour hand is halfway between one and two. It is in front of the two and past the one. Since it is exactly between the

Intermediate Mathematics for the Mentally Retarded 255

one and the two, it can be said that it is "half-past one." Move the hour hand of the clock between the three and four. Show the children that it is not necessary to move the minute hand. "Now the clock says half-past three. Make your clocks say the same as mine. Now one of you put a time on your clock and we will match our clocks to yours."

half-past one   half-past eight

FIGURE 5.69

The left side of the clock may create some confusion, because of its circular design. When the hour hand points between the one and two its position is more easily thought of as past one since the hour hand is under the one. Beginning with six (as in half-past six) the position of the hour hand is under the seven rather than the six. It is not unusual for children to confuse such times as half-past eight and half-past nine.

Matching Clocks Which Say the Same Time. As was done with the primary level, prepare two sets of clocks so that a time indicated on a clock in one set corresponds with a time indicated on a clock in the second set. This time, use clocks which indicate the half-hour rather than the hour. Once the children have become adept at matching these, the cards with the hours on them may be mixed in with the cards with half hours on them. The cards should be mixed at first since some times are very easy to confuse.

The People Clock. Draw a large circle on the floor or playground with chalk or tempera paint. Write the numerals but omit the hands. Use lengths of ribbon to represent the hour and minute hand. Place one child in the center of the clock and select a child to represent the minute hand and the hour hand. The child in the center holds an end of both ribbons and the other two children hold their respective ends.

Give the children a time to represent. Have the minute hand stationary on twelve and ask the children to represent only hours (one o'clock, three o'clock, etc.). Later introduce appropriate times as the children are ready. Always have the hour hand move first and then the minute hand.

256 *Intermediate Mathematics for the Mentally Retarded*

Teaching Thirty Minutes Past the Hour. The children have been given practice in working with the minute and have some notion that there are sixty minutes in an hour. In order to learn such times as 1:30, they must be taught that thirty minutes past one or 1:30 is another way to say half-past one. The half-hour clock should be used just as it was in teaching the concept of half-past the hour. At first, have the children read the clock using only the new terms, but quickly begin using all terms interchangeably. For example, show a clock which indicates 5:30 and ask the children to tell you what time it says. If the answer half-past five is given, ask the children to tell you another name for half-past five; and if the answer "five-thirty" or "thirty minutes past five" is given ask the children to tell you another way to say it.

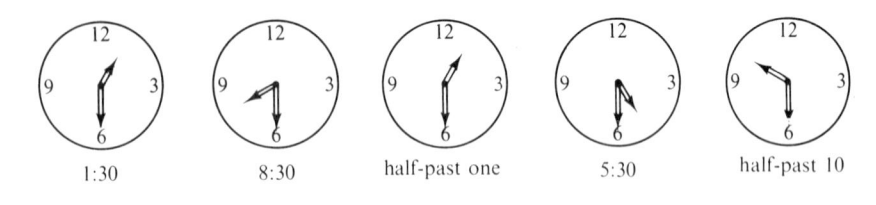

1:30   8:30   half-past one   5:30   half-past 10

FIGURE 5.70

Selecting the Correct Time. Prepare papers with clocks like the ones shown in Figure 5.71 drawn on them. "You have seen pages like this before. Look at the first clock and tell me what time it shows. Which numbers under the clock tell the correct time? Put a circle around the correct time."

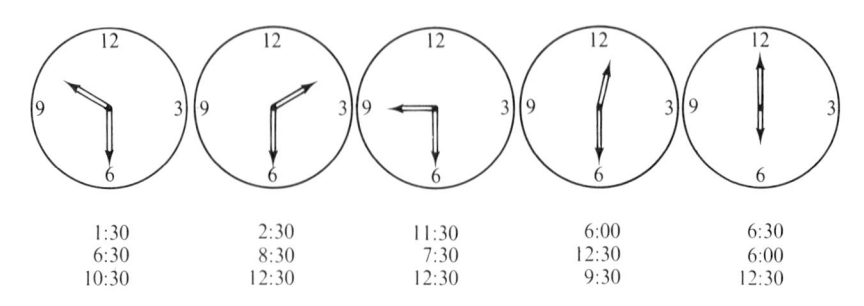

1:30	2:30	11:30	6:00	6:30
6:30	8:30	7:30	12:30	6:00
10:30	12:30	12:30	9:30	12:30

FIGURE 5.71

Which Clock is Like the First? Prepare similar papers with five clocks in a row. One or more of the clocks is like the first one. "Put a mark on the clocks which are like this one."

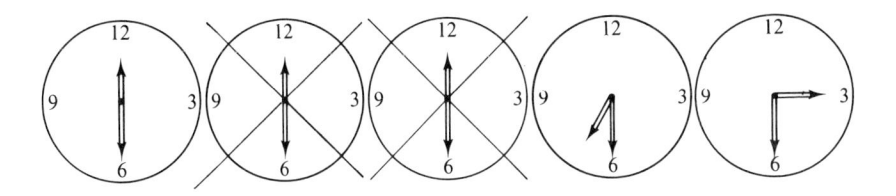

Intermediate Mathematics for the Mentally Retarded 257

FIGURE 5.72

Which Clock is Different? A variation of the previous exercise is to have all the clocks alike except one. "Put a mark on the clock which is not like the rest. Only one is different."

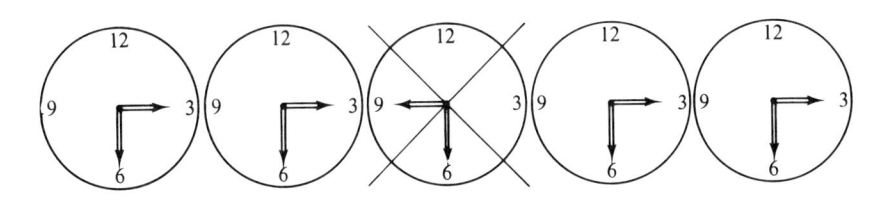

FIGURE 5.73

Making the Correct Time. Prepare a set of papers from a duplicating master with illustrated clocks complete except that one or both of the hands have been omitted. A time is written under each clock. Have the children place the hand(s) to correspond to the indicated time.

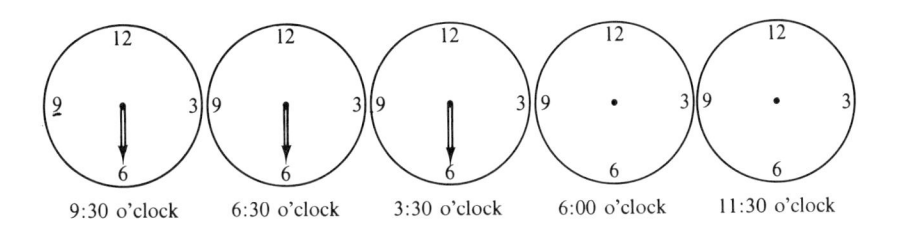

9:30 o'clock   6:30 o'clock   3:30 o'clock   6:00 o'clock   11:30 o'clock

FIGURE 5.74

Reading and Writing the Correct Time. Reverse the procedure above. Illustrate the time on the clock face and have the children write the correct time.

Teaching a Quarter Past the Hour. The idea of a quarter past the hour is related to the fraction one-fourth. Be certain that the children under-

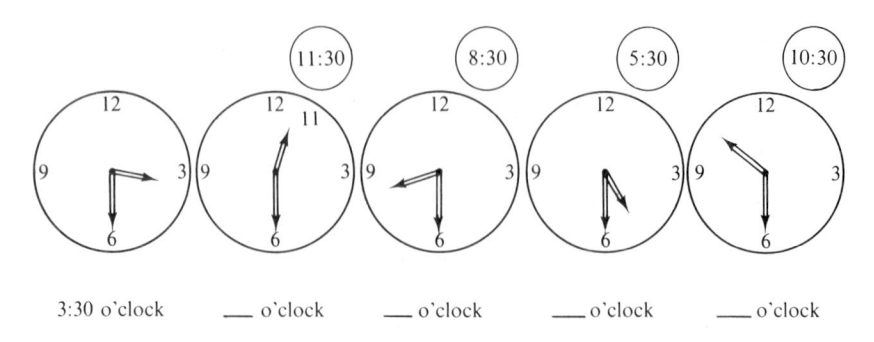

258   *Intermediate Mathematics for the Mentally Retarded*

[Clock faces showing times: 3:30, 11:30, 8:30, 5:30, 10:30]

3:30 o'clock   ___ o'clock   ___ o'clock   ___ o'clock   ___ o'clock

FIGURE 5.75

stand such concepts as four quarters of anything are equal to a whole; one-half is more than one-fourth; one-fourth is less than one-half; and so forth. "If you cut an apple down the middle, you get two pieces of an apple and if you cut these two pieces down the middle you get four pieces of an apple. The same thing happens with a pie. First cut the pie in half and then cut it in half again like this.

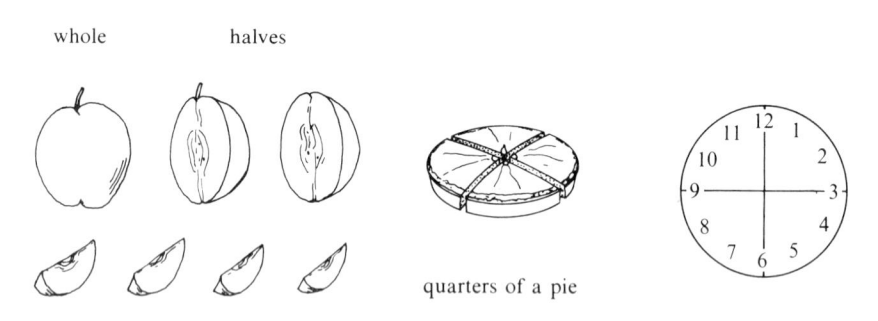

whole   halves

[Illustrations of whole apple, halved apple, quartered apple pieces; a pie cut in quarters; a clockface divided into quarters]

quarters of a pie

quarters of an apple   quarters of a clockface

FIGURE 5.76

Now we have four equal parts that we call quarters. If you do the same thing to the clockface, you divide the clock into four equal parts. The first quarter is marked at the three. This is all we are interested in for the moment."

Teaching quarter past the hour should not be attempted until the children can read the clock by the half-hour and have some concept of the quarter-hour. There may be activities during the day that require about a quarter of an hour. For example, the children may be allowed a quarter of an hour after lunch for free play. Other situations may

Intermediate Mathematics for the Mentally Retarded

be planned. Tell the children that they have about a quarter of an hour to finish their mathematics assignment; that it is about a quarter of an hour until lunch; that they have been reading their library books for about a quarter of an hour, etc.

The alarm clock can again prove useful. Set two of them for different intervals of a half hour and quarter hour respectively. The children will make observations similar to those made about other time comparisons. It can be illustrated that there are two quarter-hours in a half-hour; two half-hours in an hour; and so on.

The children have become familiar with instructional clocks, so the "Quarter Past Clock" will be understood quickly. The procedure and the materials are similar to previous instructional clocks. The minute hand is fixed at the three to indicate a quarter past; hash marks are placed one-fourth of the distance between each pair of numerals; and the hour hand is adjustable. By now the children are accustomed to pointing the hour hand either directly at the hour or half-way between the hour and the next numeral. They will learn this third position easily. Again, each of the children should be provided with his own clock. Time should be spent discussing the differences among the hour clock, the half-hour clock, and the quarter-past clock. Demonstrate this clock like the others. Be certain to avoid confusing the children when presenting times on the left-hand face of the clock. The hash mark will appear to some youngsters as before the hour on the left-hand face of the clock since its relative position moves from below to above the numeral (see the discussion related to this problem on page 255: half-hour clock).

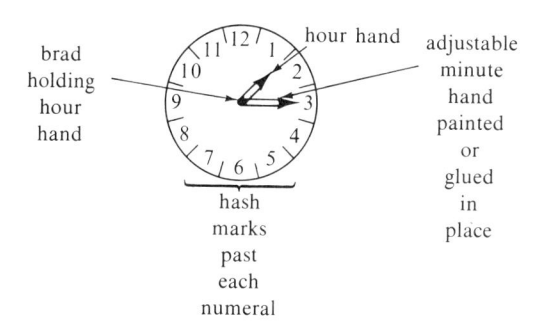

FIGURE 5.77

Again present the exercises of matching cards with the same time indicated on clockfaces. At first use only the clockfaces which indicate a quarter past the hour but then mix in cards with times on the hour and half past.

Teaching Fifteen Minutes Past the Hour. The instruction presented on sixty minutes in an hour and thirty minutes in a half hour will help the children understand that another way to say a quarter past the hour is fifteen minutes past the hour, or one-fifteen. Use the quarter past clock to teach that all three terms are interchangeable.

Using Worksheets and Clocks. The children can now be provided with individual instructional clocks with both hands adjustable. Through worksheets like those used in teaching other times, give them plenty of opportunities to apply their skills of telling, selecting, and writing time.

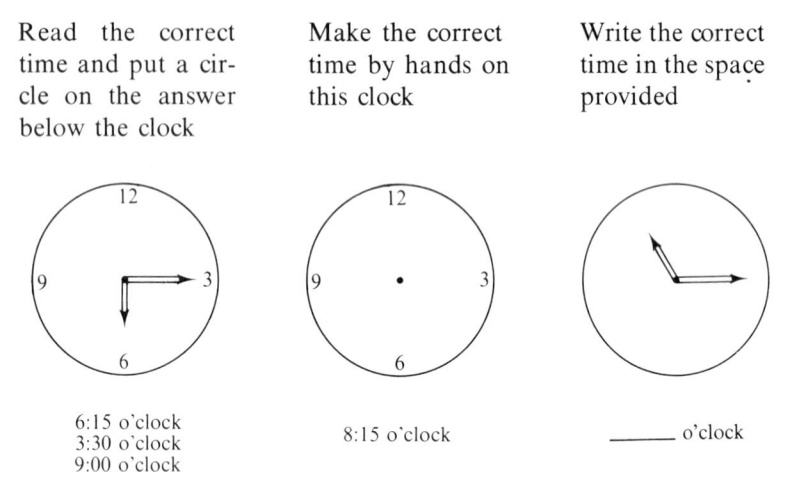

Read the correct time and put a circle on the answer below the clock

Make the correct time by hands on this clock

Write the correct time in the space provided

6:15 o'clock
3:30 o'clock
9:00 o'clock

8:15 o'clock

_____ o'clock

FIGURE 5.78

Teaching Three Quarters Past the Hour. The clock indicating 1:45 may be thought of as:

1. three quarters past the hour of one
2. one quarter until the hour of two
3. forty-five minutes past one o'clock
4. fifteen minutes until two o'clock

FIGURE 5.79

The children should be given a "three quarters past the hour clock" similar to the other instructional clocks. The minute hand should be fixed on the nine; there should be hash marks three quarters the distance

Intermediate Mathematics for the Mentally Retarded 261

past each pair of numerals and the hour hand should be movable. In the beginning use the clock in the same fashion as the others; first presenting the fractional concepts, the duration of time concepts; and the idea of three-quarters and forty-five minutes past the hour.

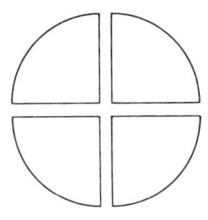

FIGURE 5.80

For example, have the children cut a circle into four quarters. "We call each of these parts a quarter. Show me one quarter. Show me three quarters."

After the children have achieved facility with these concepts and terms, the idea of a quarter until the hour may be introduced. Fifteen minutes until the hour will be presented as another name for a quarter until the hour. The idea of before the hour will be very important as the skills of telling time are improved.

The exercises given the children should parallel those illustrated earlier in this section. Again, they should also be provided with a clock with both hands adjustable.

Reading Clock by Five Minutes. In order to teach reading the clock within five minutes, it is necessary that the children learn to count to sixty by fives. Start with a number line.

5   10   15   20   25   30   35   40   45   50   55   60

FIGURE 5.81

Practice which number comes before and after a given number. For example, "Which number comes before forty? After fifty?" Then use a card to cover a number and ask "Which number did I hide?"

Once the children have mastered the linear number line, place the numbers around a circle used to represent a clock. Follow the same

262 *Intermediate Mathematics for the Mentally Retarded*

procedure as above. The next step is to present an unnumbered clock with the intervals of five minutes indicated by marks.

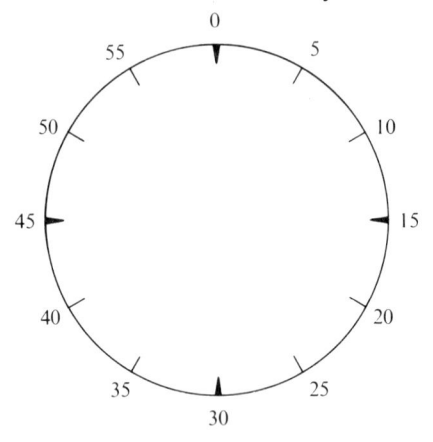

FIGURE 5.82

Give the children practice in locating the position indicating fifteen minutes, thirty minutes, forty-five minutes, etc.

unnumbered clockface

unnumbered clockface with minute hand

unnumbered clockface with minute and hour hand

FIGURE 5.83

As the children gain confidence, add the minute and hour hand. Only after such practice will the child be ready to read the marked clock.

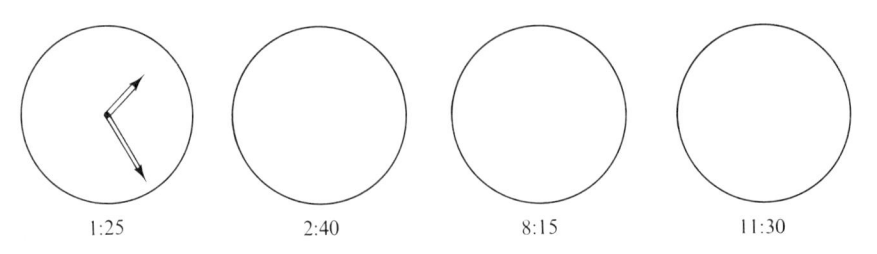

1:25   2:40   8:15   11:30

FIGURE 5.84

Teach the child to read the hour position first and the minute hand second. Time is written with the hour first, but is spoken with minutes first. That is, it is twenty after two or ten minutes to five.
Give the children such problems as:

1. Time of T.V. show, how long to wait
2. Time of school bus departure
3. Time to bake a cake, etc.

A.M. *and* P.M. The day has been divided into twenty-four hours. That means that the hour hand goes all the way around the face of the clock two times every day. When it goes around the first time, from twelve midnight to twelve noon, we call it A.M. because it is before noon. When it goes around the second time, we call it P.M. because it is afternoon.

Have the children construct a chart showing twenty-four hours. Fill in the chart to show how their hours are generally spent.

"When is morning? A.M. or P.M.?"
"When is evening? A.M. or P.M.?"
"When is afternoon? A.M. or P.M.?"

Which is later?	Which is earlier?
1:00 P.M. or 8:00 A.M.	10:45 P.M. or 10:45 A.M.
9:45 A.M. or 9:55 P.M.	1:15 A.M. or 1:15 P.M.
6:30 A.M. or 6:30 P.M.	5:15 A.M. or 5:45 P.M.
10:55 A.M. or 1:15 P.M.	7:30 P.M. or 8:45 A.M.

MONEY AND VALUE

The instructional program with money and value should not exceed the children's understanding of numbers and their skills in basic number operations. The children will already have learned the names of the coins and should know all the equivalent values to ten cents. Since at the primary level great emphasis is placed on numbers to ten, many of the children will be able to handle problems involving the reproduction of sets of money and making change for amounts to ten cents. Some children will have learned to count pennies beyond ten and rationally count to amounts up to twenty-five cents. The intermediate level program builds upon this background in teaching concepts related to a quarter, half-dollar, and dollar, as well as the skill of making change for amounts up to fifty cents to a dollar. Many children will not progress to this level, but most will be able to make change accurately for twenty-five cents. The following material provides suggestions for teaching these skills.

COIN AND CURRENCY RECOGNITION

The children at the intermediate level have learned to recognize the penny, nickel, dime, quarter, and half dollar. Exercises involving these coins should be presented for review and the silver dollar and dollar bill should be introduced. Of course, the ability to name the coins and currency accurately does not guarantee an understanding of their value. However, just as children must learn the number names before they can deal maturely with the number ideas, they must also learn the money names before they can accurately handle money. The teacher can easily construct a money picture by attaching the coins and a dollar bill to a frame and covering it with glass. The money picture may be used by the children to respond to the teacher's questions such as, "Where is the silver dollar? Show me the dollar bill. Find the quarter."

Other activities which parallel those discussed at the primary level may be expanded by simply including the half-dollar, silver dollar, and dollar bill. These exercises include:

Finding the circle which is the same
Finding the circle which is different
Matching circles and coins
Identifying coins by size
Finding the coin which is the same
Finding the coin which is different

EXTENDING MONEY COUNTING SKILLS

The children have received instruction in counting money up to twenty-five cents using (1) twenty-five pennies, (2) one nickel and twenty pennies, and (3) one dime and fifteen pennies. At the intermediate level, real money should be used to give the children practice in reproducing all the sets valued at twenty-five cents. The reader may be surprised to note that there are thirteen different combinations of coins equal to twenty-five cents.

    1 quarter
    1 dime, 3 nickels
    2 dimes, 1 nickel
    5 nickels
    25 pennies
    20 pennies, 1 nickel
    15 pennies, 1 dime
    15 pennies, 2 nickels
    10 pennies, 3 nickels
    10 pennies, 1 dime, 1 nickel

Intermediate Mathematics for the Mentally Retarded

        5 pennies, 2 dimes
        5 pennies, 1 dime, 2 nickels
        5 pennies, 4 nickels

In order for the children to produce these combinations, they must be provided with twenty-five pennies, five nickels, two dimes and one quarter. Continue the instruction by having the children rename amounts of money by use of equivalent values. The teacher should continue to develop the notion that coin values can be renamed in many ways.

What is another name for one dime and three nickels?
Are five nickels and twenty-five pennies the same value?
Is a set of twenty-five pennies the same value as twenty pennies and one nickel?

Which Does Not Belong? Put a mark (X) through the set of coins which does not belong with the other sets.

4 quarters	2 half dollars	15 nickels	10 dimes
1 half dollar	3 quarters	10 nickels	5 dimes
2 dimes	25 pennies	1 quarter	5 nickels

Match These Sets of Coins

1 dollar	5 dimes
2 dimes	1 quarter
1 half dollar	15 nickels
3 quarters	2 half dollars
5 nickels	4 nickels

Decimal Notation in Writing Money Values. Introduce the decimal notation by a chart similar to the one shown below:

                1¢ $ .01
                5¢ $ .05
                10¢ $ .10
                25¢ $ .25
                50¢ $ .50

The teacher may develop worksheets such as the ones illustrated below.

Rewrite these values as shown.
15¢ $.15
10¢   _____
14¢   _____
5¢   _____
23¢   _____

Match these.	
12¢	$ .47
50¢	$ .30
30¢	$ .23
23¢	$ .50
47¢	$ .12

Rewrite these values as shown.	Match these.	
$ .32 32¢	Twenty cents	$.75
$ .54 _____	1 dime	$ .50
$ .74 _____	thirty-three cents	$ .20
$ .05 _____	3 quarters	10¢
$1.00 _____	1 half dollar	33¢

THE CLASSROOM STORE

The children are now ready to extend their ability to use money as a medium of exchange. There is a great deal of difference between selecting the exact coins for a small purchase and making change. Some intermediate children may not be able to make change for amounts greater than twenty-five cents but they should be able to count the correct amount of money for purchases up to $1.00. Here are two problems which illustrate the comparative difficulty of the tasks.

Bill wants to buy eighteen cents worth of candy.
He gives the store keeper a quarter.
How much change does he receive?

FIGURE 5.85

In this case the children must be able to think, "Twenty-five cents is another name for a quarter." Then they will probably solve the problem by either writing or thinking . . . .

$$18¢ + \square = 25¢ \qquad \begin{array}{r} 25¢ \\ -18¢ \\ \hline \square \end{array} \qquad 25¢ - 18¢ = \square$$

Bill wants to buy a toy which costs eighteen cents.
He has a dime, two nickels, and five pennies.
Which coins will he give the store keeper?

In this instance, the children need only to be able to count the coins up to eighteen cents. That is one dime (ten cents); one nickel (five cents) and three pennies (three cents).

The children should be provided with opportunities to count real money in the classroom. This may be accomplished through taking lunch orders each morning, planning the purchases of school supplies, or figuring the money spent at the candy counter. Bulletin boards displaying the relative values of various foods and school supplies are helpful in teaching computation with money. Children at the intermediate level will continue to enjoy "playing store" although a few of the older youngsters may find this immature. Almost all of the youngsters will enjoy trips to the grocery store or neighborhood novelty shop. Dramatization of eating in a restaurant or shopping from the advertisements in the newspapers will appeal to most children of this age. The following examples indicate how the teacher might present money skills through the lunch menu, the candy store, and the school supply center.

Lunch Menu. Have the children view the school cafeteria menu and determine the total cost of various orders.

EAST SCHOOL

Lunch Menu	Sept. 10
Meatballs	15¢
Macaroni	14¢
Cheese Sandwich	15¢
Peanutbutter Sandwich	10¢
Hamburger	20¢
Corn	7¢
Peas	6¢

Carrots	8¢
Green Salad	10¢
Jello Salad	15¢
White Milk	4¢
Chocolate Milk	8¢
Orange Drink	9¢
Cake	10¢
Cookies	5¢

Mary's Lunch   Paul's Lunch
Peanut butter sandwich ____   Meatballs   ____
Jello salad   ____   Green salad   ____
Carrots   ____   Peas   ____
White milk   ____   Chocolate milk   ____
Cake   Cookies   ____
           Total   ____   Total   ____

John has fifty cents for lunch. Order a lunch for him and determine his change.

Kathy has thirty-five cents for lunch. Order her a lunch and find out how much change she would get.

Frank has forty-five cents for lunch. He only wants to spend forty cents because he wants to save five cents a day from his lunch money. Order a good lunch for him so that he will have at least five cents left.

Buying School Supplies. Pictures in Figure 5.86 are some common items children may have to buy for school. Answer the questions about the purchases.

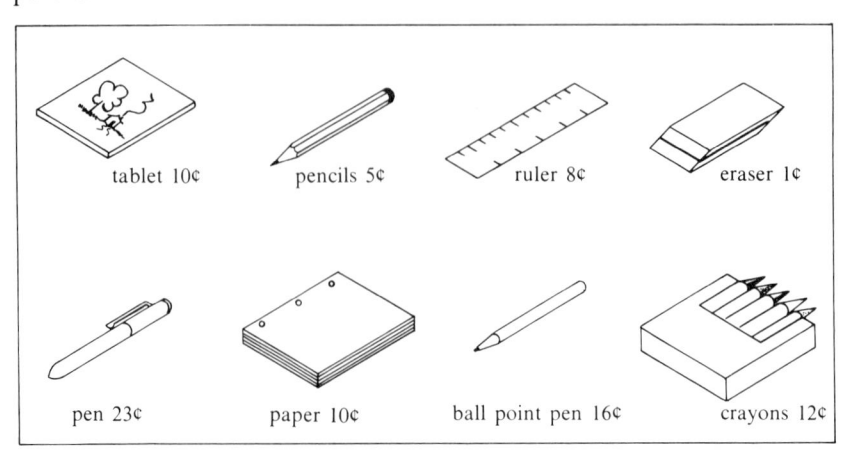

tablet 10¢   pencils 5¢   ruler 8¢   eraser 1¢

pen 23¢   paper 10¢   ball point pen 16¢   crayons 12¢

FIGURE 5.86

Intermediate Mathematics for the Mentally Retarded 269

Jack bought these items. How much did he spend?
one tablet   _____
two pencils   _____
one eraser   _____
Total   _____

Jill bought these items for school. How much did she spend?

one pack of paper   _____
one box of crayons _____
one ruler   _____
Total   _____

Henry asked the clerk for one pencil and two erasers. He gave the man one dime. How much change did he receive?

Susan wants to buy a box of crayons, a tablet and a pencil. She has twenty-five cents. How much more money does she need?

The Candy Store. Here are the prices at the candy store (Figure 5.87). See if you can solve these problems.

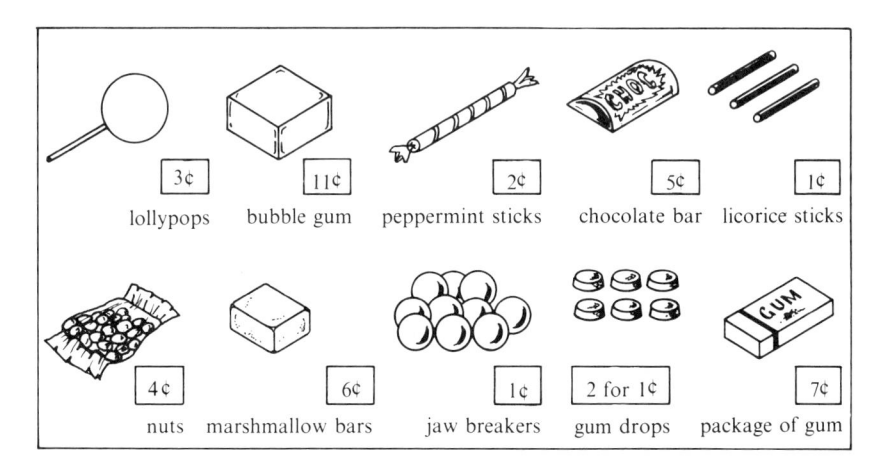

lollypops 3¢	bubble gum 11¢	peppermint sticks 2¢	chocolate bar 5¢	licorice sticks 1¢
nuts 4¢	marshmallow bars 6¢	jaw breakers 1¢	gum drops 2 for 1¢	package of gum 7¢

FIGURE 5.87

Frank bought these items. How much did he spend?

two lollipops   _____
one jawbreaker   _____
three bubble gums _____

Anne purchased some candy. How much did it cost?

one pack of gum   ____
two gum drops   ____
four licorice sticks ____

Betty asked the clerk for one package of nuts, and three peppermint sticks. How much change will she get from a dime?

Kenny wanted to buy all three of his brothers a chocolate bar and one for himself. He had one dime and one nickel. How much more money will he need?

BUDGETING AND SAVINGS

It is not too early to present some of the basic ideas of budgeting and savings. The children will enjoy preparing for a classroom Halloween and Christmas party or spring picnics. Budgeting should be introduced as the concept of not wasting one's money or property. The children will be able to develop some notion of the value of saving for special occasions or prized toys. The teacher may want to organize a class bank as a way of helping the children save for special things they want. The children should also be taught that any property or money borrowed must be returned. This idea will help build the background necessary for an understanding of banking.

NUMBER OPERATIONS

There are a number of ideas which are basic to the structure of mathematics. Several of these properties were introduced at the primary level and they shall be expanded here. The idea of sets, the concepts of the commutative and associative properties of addition, the inverse process of subtraction, the mathematical sentence, and place value continue to occupy key positions at the intermediate level. Multiplication, division and their respective properties, the ideas of regrouping from the tens place and expanded notation are given attention at this level.

It has been stated on several occasions that the basis of number operations is the concepts of sets. An insight into sets is gained through the manipulation of sets of real objects. This concept of number is expanded by moving gradually from the concrete to abstract ideas. The children at the primary level were given some experience with this but it shall be extended at the intermediate level. The reader will recall that we began with a set of real objects, proceed to the cardinal number of sets, and then consider numbers in relation to one another. These ideas of sets are essential to the teaching of number operations which receive paramount emphasis at the intermediate level.

Intermediate Mathematics for the Mentally Retarded

ADDITION

At the primary level, we introduced the properties of numbers and the addition and subtraction of whole numbers. In this section, those ideas are elaborated.

The technique for developing sixty-four basic addition facts was shown in Chapter 4 on page 171. Once these basic addition facts have been developed, the children are ready for further instruction. The other thirty-six addition facts in the table can be discovered by combining the understanding of place value with the associative property of addition. Here is an example of the process. It was indicated in the study of sets that we can give five a number of different names. For our example let's rename five as (2 + 3).

8 + 5 =
8 + 5 = 8 + (2 + 3)   Renaming
      = (8 + 2) + 3   Associative property
      = (10) + 3   We already discovered that 8 + 2 = 10
      = 13   Knowledge of place value

Consider another example to clarify the point.

6 + 6 =
6 + 6 = 6 + (4 + 2)   Rename 6 as 4 + 2
      = (6 + 4) + 2   Associative property
      = (10) + 2   We discovered previously 6 + 4 = 10
      = 12   Knowledge of place value

TABLE 5.3

Addition Table developed through associative property and place value.

+	0	1	2	3	4	5	6	7	8	9
0	0	1	2	3	4	5	6	7	8	9
1	1	2	3	4	5	6	7	8	9	10
2	2	3	4	5	6	7	8	9	10	11
3	3	4	5	6	7	8	9	10	11	12
4	4	5	6	7	8	9	10	11	12	13
5	5	6	7	8	9	10	11	12	13	14
6	6	7	8	9	10	11	⑫	13	14	15
7	7	8	9	10	11	12	13	14	15	16
8	8	9	10	11	12	⑬	14	15	16	17
9	9	10	11	12	13	14	15	16	17	18

The teacher can assist the children in completing the remainder of the addition table by using this approach. The circled numerals represent facts discovered in the two examples given above and the diagonal separates the facts less than eleven previously illustrated.

Expand the examples presented in the primary level. Use examples like that in Figure 5.88. Write number sentences telling about these sets.

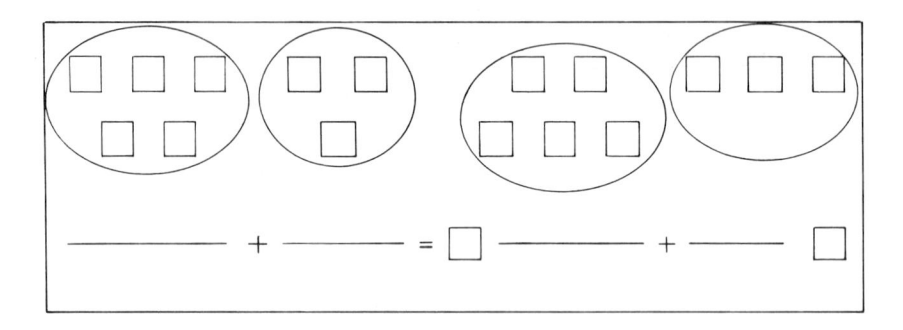

FIGURE 5.88

When place value and the basic addition facts are developed through the use of sets and the properties of addition, it is possible to develop a number of other combinations readily. Since we know that 4 + 2 = 6 and that 2 + 4 = 6, then

$$\begin{array}{r} 40 \\ +20 \\ \hline 60 \end{array}$$

The set of four tens and the set of two tens is another name for the set of six tens; i.e.,

$$40 + 20 = 60$$

Adding without Regrouping. As soon as the children know the set facts having sums of nine and less, they can use these facts in adding two or more digit numbers. No regrouping is involved since the new ideas used in dealing with these examples have to do with the addition of numbers named in like places in numerals. The teacher should introduce addition of two-place numbers without regrouping by having the children solve mathematical sentences similar to 32 + 24 = ☐. The place value chart was introduced in the section on cardinal numbers and it should be utilized here. Have the children write each digit with its place value and then find the sum. Also use expanded notation.

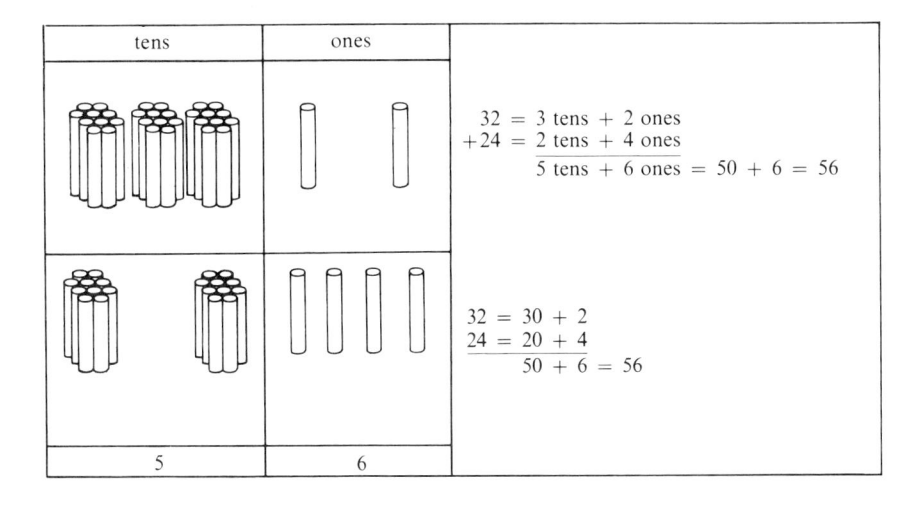

Intermediate Mathematics for the Mentally Retarded 273

tens	ones	
(3 bundles of tens)	(2 ones)	32 = 3 tens + 2 ones +24 = 2 tens + 4 ones 5 tens + 6 ones = 50 + 6 = 56
(2 bundles of tens)	(4 ones)	32 = 30 + 2 24 = 20 + 4 50 + 6 = 56
5	6	

FIGURE 5.89

The next step is to show the standard form of the addition algorism.

$$\begin{array}{r} 32 \\ +24 \\ \hline 56 \end{array}$$

Then show that

$$\begin{array}{r} 32 \\ 24 \\ \hline 56 \end{array} \quad \begin{array}{r} 24 \\ 32 \\ \hline 56 \end{array}$$

Also show examples such as

$$\begin{array}{r} 23 \\ +5 \\ \hline 28 \end{array} \quad \begin{array}{r} 23 \\ +10 \\ \hline 33 \end{array}$$

Adding with Regrouping. The children will first encounter the need to regroup in addition when the sum of the numbers named in the ones column is ten or more. We say that the ones place is overloaded and must be regrouped. In traditional mathematics, regrouping is called *carrying*. It is more desirable to use the phrase *regrouping*. The following example will indicate how to deal with a sum when the sum in the ones place is ten or more.

274   Intermediate Mathematics for the Mentally Retarded

$$25 = 20 + 5$$
$$+46 = 40 + 6$$
$$60 + 11 = 60 + (10 + 1)$$
$$= (60 + 10) + 1 = 71$$

The place value chart introduced previously will help solve the problem.

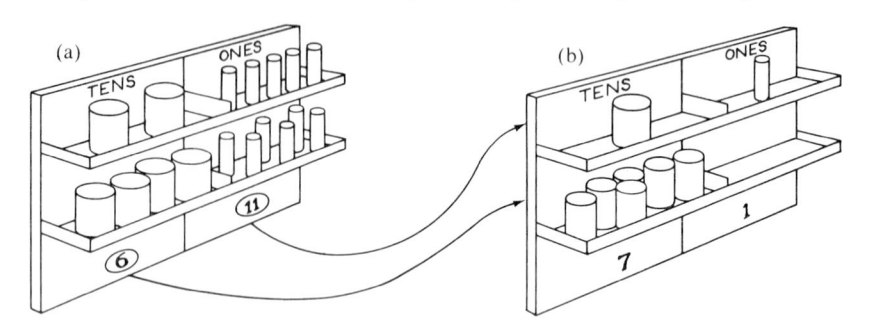

FIGURE 5.90

The illustration in Figure 5.90 shows how the children may place sticks (singles for the ones place and packaged in sets of ten for the tens place) in their proper pockets as they describe the process of adding 25 and 46. It should be demonstrated that they can add the tens and then the ones as shown in (a). There are six tens but the ones place is *overloaded,* since there are eleven ones. Ask the children, "How do we regroup the sticks in the ones place?" By this time, they should be able to indicate that eleven may be regrouped as 10 + 1. To eliminate the overloading, the extra ten is moved to the tens place leaving the one in the ones place. The problem then appears as shown in (b). The children should see readily that seven tens and one one is 70 + 1 = 71. The number strips, the abacus, and the number line may also be used.

Addition Algorithm. These techniques stress place value. Once the children demonstrate understanding of what has taken place, they are ready for the addition algorithm. It can be presented something like this.

```
              tens   ones
    25         2      5               25
   +46        +4      6              +46
                     11 = 1 ten 1 one  71
```

The sum in the ones place is eleven which is too many because the ones place can only hold nine ones. But we know that another name for eleven is ten and one. In order to avoid overloading the ones place,

Intermediate Mathematics for the Mentally Retarded 275

write the one in the ones place and move the extra ten to the tens place. The sum in the tens place is seven and our answer is seventy-one.

$$\begin{array}{r} 25 \\ +46 \\ \hline 11 \\ 60 \\ \hline 71 \end{array}$$ The method of partial sums

Number Line. The number line may also be used to solve the problem 25 + 46 = ☐. First, have the children count 25 spaces for the first addend. Second, the children should continue counting 46 addition spaces across the number line. Third, they have now counted to the number 71 on the number line which is the correct sum.

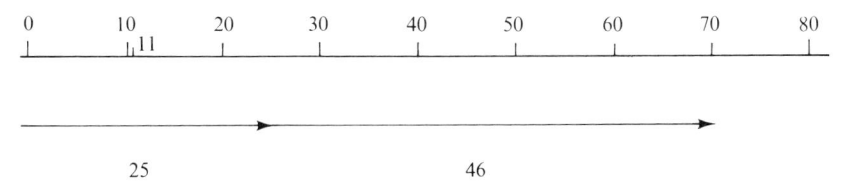

FIGURE 5.91

Using Counting Strips. The problem may also be solved with counting strips. The children should be provided with a box of strips representing

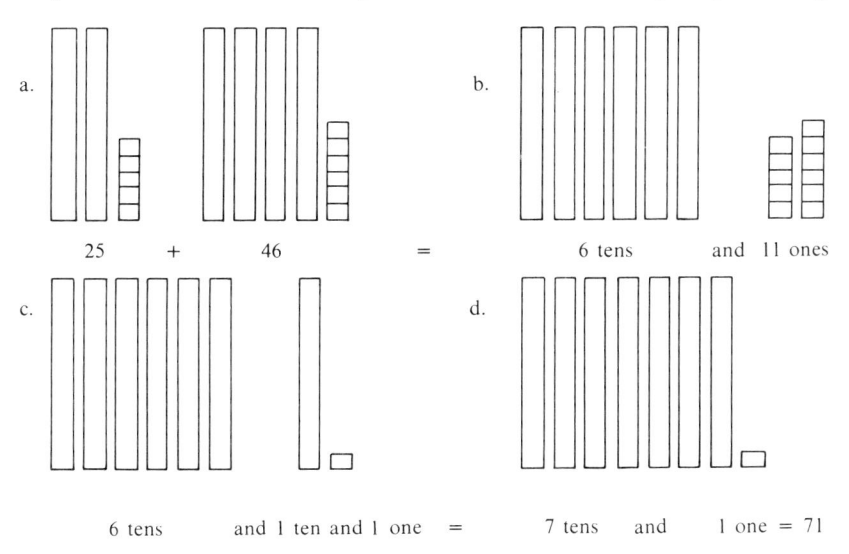

FIGURE 5.92

numbers one and ten. The first step is to represent the problem with counting strips as shown in Figure 5.92(a). The second step is to combine the tens and ones as indicated in Figure 5.92(b) showing six tens and eleven ones. The third step is to rename the eleven ones as one ten and one one as illustrated in 5.92(c). The final step is to regroup the tens so that the correct sum 71 (seven tens and one one) may be easily counted.

Column Addition. The children will be ready to deal with column addition once they have mastered the basic facts of addition and the idea of place value as shown in the example below. The children will use the associative principle in working with both the vertical and horizontal forms of the addition algorism.

$$2 + 3 + 4 = (2 + 3) + 4 = 5 + 4 = 9$$
$$2 + 3 + 4 = 2 + (3 + 4) = 2 + 7 = 9$$
$$12 + 13 + 14 = 12 + (13 + 14) = 12 + 27 = 39$$

				Tens	Ones
2 }		2	2	2 { ①2	5
3 }	5	3 }		{ ①3	
+4	+4	+4 }	+7	1 { ①4	4
	9		9	3	9

The children will find multiple digit addition more complex when solving problems involving regrouping. Complex multiple digit problems are those which require the children to regroup the ones and form sets of tens. The place-value chart or abacus should be used to illustrate the process of regrouping. This should make it clear to the children that the regrouping process is simply renaming a number. The children should learn that the commutative and associative principles are convenient tools and that it is frequently more comfortable to use groups of ten with column addition. Note that the tens column uses circles to indicate place value.*

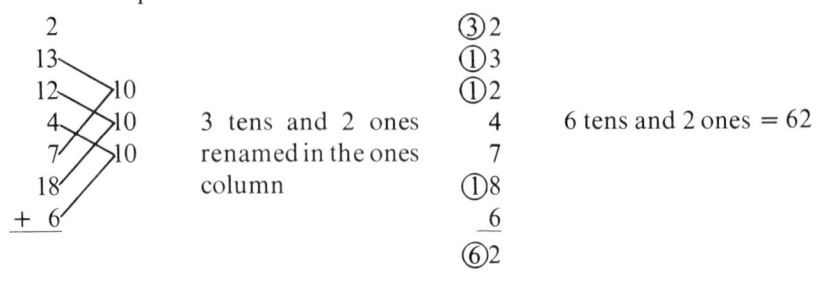

```
   2                              ③2
  13                              ①3
  12   10                         ①2
   4   10    3 tens and 2 ones     4      6 tens and 2 ones = 62
   7   10    renamed in the ones   7
  18         column               ①8
 + 6                               6
                                  ⑥2
```

---

*This suggestion came from Robert Underhill, Ohio University.

Intermediate Mathematics for the Mentally Retarded 277

SUBTRACTION

The children should learn that the addition tables can be used for subtraction facts also. This will help them learn the inverse nature of subtraction.

As soon as the children understand subtraction as the inverse operation of addition, place value, the number line, and the basic addition facts, they should be ready to learn how to subtract numbers with two digits without renaming. Here is an example.

$$43 = 40 + 3$$
$$\underline{-21} = \underline{-(20 + 1)}$$
$$ 20 + 2 = 22$$

$$66 = 60 + 6$$
$$\underline{-42} = \underline{-(40 + 2)}$$
$$ 20 + 4 = 24$$

The children have been exposed to the process of "another name for fourteen is 10 + 4." This is actually the process of expanded notation. The idea that a number can be named in many ways has been stressed repeatedly. This patient instruction will begin to pay high dividends when teaching the process of renaming (regrouping for borrowing) in subtraction. The number 463, for example, can be written as

$$400 + 60 + 3$$
$$200 + 160 + 3$$
$$200 + 150 + 10 + 3$$
$$200 + 140 + 20 + 3$$
$$200 + 130 + 30 + 3 \text{ etc.}$$

Subtraction with Regrouping. As soon as the children have gained skill in subtraction without regrouping, they should be introduced to problems which require regrouping. (The teaching of the subtraction algorithm parallels closely the steps followed in the teaching of the addition algorithm.) The teacher should present the children with a problem which requires regrouping. The children need to learn that in subtraction in the set of whole numbers every column must have a sum greater than the addend to be subtracted. An example using expanded notation will help.

$$31 = (30 + 1) \quad \text{Sums} \quad 31$$
$$\underline{-14} = \underline{-(10 + 4)} \quad \text{Known addends} \quad \underline{-14}$$
$$\square = \square + \square \quad \text{Missing addends} \quad 17$$

The children will be unable to solve this problem without regrouping since the sum in the ones column is not greater than the addend in that column (1 ≯ 4). Therefore, the sum must be regrouped.

278　*Intermediate Mathematics for the Mentally Retarded*

$$\begin{array}{rcccc}
31 & = & (30 + 1) & = & (20 + 11) \\
-14 & = & -(10 + 4) & = & -(10 + 4) \\
\square & & 10 + 4 & & 10 + 7 = 17
\end{array}$$

The place value chart (Figure 5.93) again will prove helpful in demonstrating the process.

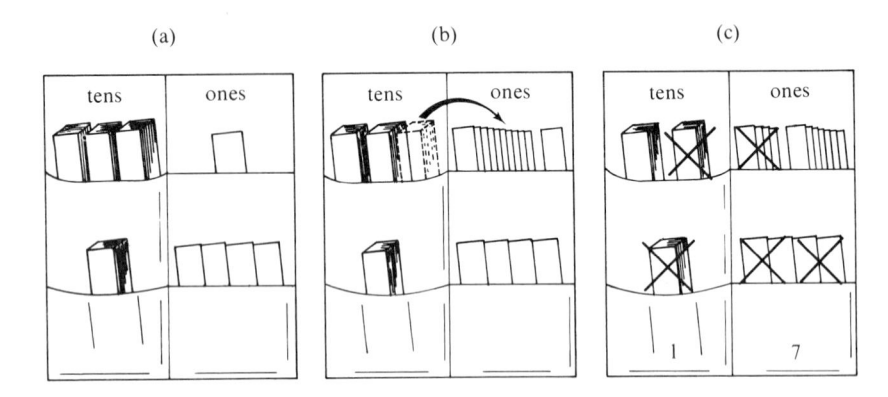

FIGURE 5.93

In this example, Figure 5.93(a) represents thirty-one in the expanded notational form three tens and one one; and fourteen in the expanded notational form one ten and four ones; 5.93(b) indicates the regrouping in the sum to two tens and eleven ones; and 5.93(c) shows the difference after removing one ten and four ones. It will be clear to the children that one ten and seven ones are seventeen. Counting sticks, number strips and other aids such as the number line may also be used.

Use Counting Sticks. Provide the children with three bundles of ten and one stick to represent thirty-one. Instruct them to subtract (take away) fourteen. The children will remove one ten and then four ones. However, there is only one stick so a bundle of tens will be undone so that there are two sets of ten and eleven ones. The children remove one set of ten and four ones leaving one set of ten and seven ones indicating that $31 - 14 = 17$.

Bundle together so they can be easily separated with rubber bands, sticks in groups of ten. The sticks should be rectangular or flat on one side so they will not roll off the children's desks. Use problems and procedures similar to those used with the place value chart.

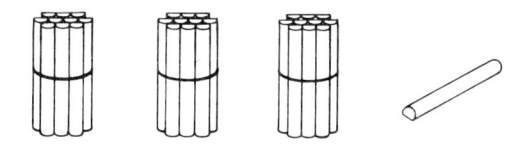

FIGURE 5.94

Use Number Strips. Another approach to solving the problem is to use number strips. In this instance, the process is somewhat more complicated than using counting sticks. Counting sticks need only have a rubber band removed to convert one set of ten into ten ones, while there must be an exchange of one strip of ten for ten ones squares if counting strips are used. Otherwise, the procedure is identical. First, the children attempt to remove 14 from 31. This is not possible because there are too few ones. A strip of ten is exchanged for ten ones. The children then remove one set of ten and four ones leaving one strip of ten and seven ones square indicating that 31 − 14 = 17.

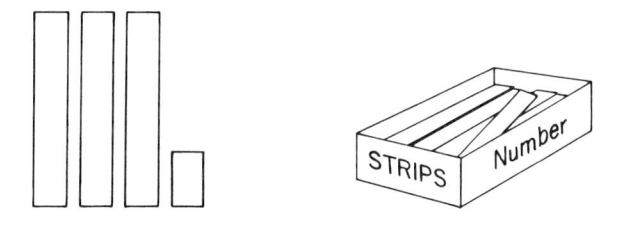

FIGURE 5.95

Use the Number Line. The children will also profit by using the number line to solve subtraction problems. First, the children locate the number 31 on the number line and then count fourteen spaces to the left which represents the problem 31 − 14 = ☐. They have now counted to the number 17 on the number line which is the correct solution.

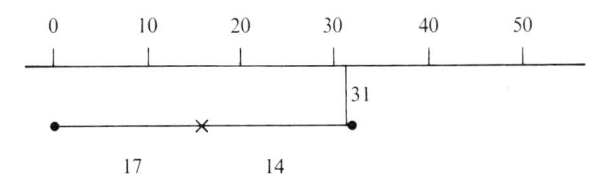

FIGURE 5.96

Subtraction Algorithm. The children must understand what they are doing in the regrouping through numerous experiences with place value charts, counting sticks, number lines, and number strips. Once they grasp the process, the subtraction algorism may be introduced.

The reader will recall that subtraction was introduced as the opposite of addition. It is simple for retarded children to understand this if they are not confused with such terms as minuend and subtrahend. In teaching the subtraction algorism continue to use the terms "sum" and "addend" while reviewing the inverse property of subtraction.

$$\begin{array}{rl} 14 & \text{addend} \\ +17 & \text{addend} \\ \hline 31 & \text{sum} \end{array} \qquad \begin{array}{rl} 31 & \text{sum} \\ -14 & \text{addend} \\ \hline 17 & \text{addend} \end{array}$$

Not
$$\begin{array}{rl} 31 & \text{minuend} \\ -14 & \text{subtrahend} \\ \hline 17 & \text{remainder} \end{array}$$

Teach the subtraction algorithm with reference to expanded notation. This way the algorism will not appear as a mysterious complex new task but simply as a short cut for keeping track of the regrouping necessary in some subtraction problems.

$$\begin{array}{rl} 31 = & 3 \text{ tens } 1 \text{ one} \\ -14 = & 1 \text{ ten } 4 \text{ ones} \\ \hline \square = & \square \qquad \square \end{array} \begin{array}{l} = 2 \text{ tens } 11 \text{ ones} \\ = 1 \text{ ten } \quad 4 \text{ ones} \\ = 1 \text{ ten } \quad 7 \text{ ones } = 17 \end{array}$$

or

$$\begin{array}{rl} 31 = & (30 + 1) = & (20 + 11) \\ -14 = & -(10 + 4) = & -(10 + 4) \\ \hline \square = & \square + \square = & 10 + 7 = 17 \end{array}$$

The three in the addends ten place is thought of as three tens while the one in the ones place is thought of as one one, and likewise for the known addend. The children discover that four can not be subtracted from one since $4 \not> 1$. Therefore, we deliberately overload the ones place as is shown in expanded notation. However, we use a shorter method of indicating this. We write the appropriate digit in each regrouped place in the numeral.

$$\begin{array}{r} 31 \\ -14 \\ \hline \end{array} \qquad \begin{array}{r} 31 \\ -14 \\ \hline \end{array} \qquad \begin{array}{r} 2\;\;\overset{\textcircled{\scriptsize 11}}{} \\ \cancel{3}\cancel{1} \\ -14 \\ \hline 17 \end{array}$$

Intermediate Mathematics for the Mentally Retarded

rather than

$$\begin{array}{r}(20 + 11)\\-(10 + 4)\\\hline 10 + 7 = 17\end{array}$$

The three tens are changed to two tens and the one one is changed to eleven ones. Use a circle to show that the ones place has been deliberately overloaded. In the ones place we may now subtract four from eleven and in the tens place one from two. Our answer is seventeen.*

---

*There is another method of subtraction which may be used as a last resort. Some retarded children seem unable to learn this algorism in spite of their background with sets and place value. With these children, the equal-additions method may help them. The teacher should be aware that although the mechanisms may be simpler, this process involves little understanding and may result in many of the pitfalls present in teaching subtraction through the tradition rote algorism method.

The equal-additions approach may be shown with the same example previously used in the more conventional method. In the conventional technique, the thought process goes like this: "four from eleven is seven and one from two is one." In the equal-additions method, the reasoning pattern proceeds like this. "Four from eleven is seven and two from three is one." The difference, of course, is that instead of regrouping in the tens and ones places, ten is added to the ones place in the sum and ten is added to the tens place in the known addend.

This may be done because adding the same number to the sum and to the known addend does not change the value of the missing addend. In other words, adding ten to a number named by a digit in the sum is equivalent to adding one to the number named by the digit one place to the left in the known addend.

This method is not recommended for children who are able to learn the conventional approach because the principles involved are hard to grasp and difficult for the teacher to demonstrate.

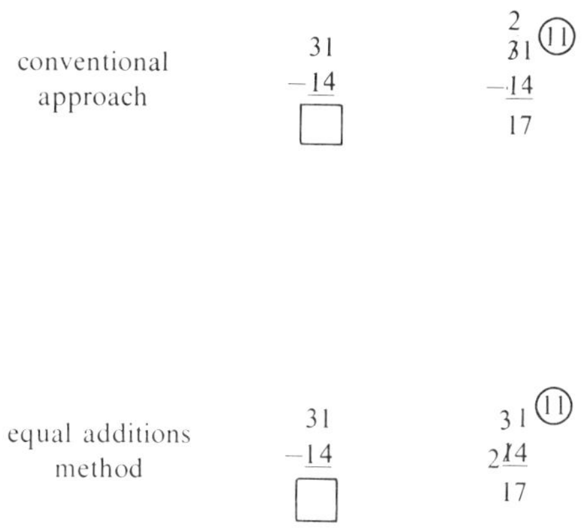

conventional approach

$$\begin{array}{r}31\\-14\\\hline\square\end{array}\qquad\begin{array}{r}\overset{2}{\cancel{3}}1\,\circled{11}\\-14\\\hline 17\end{array}$$

equal additions method

$$\begin{array}{r}31\\-14\\\hline\square\end{array}\qquad\begin{array}{r}3\,1\,\circled{11}\\2\,\underline{1}4\\\hline 17\end{array}$$

FIGURE 5.97

MULTIPLICATION

Background

Multiplication, like the three other basic number operations, is a binary operation. Only two numbers at a time are considered.

The set approach was used in teaching addition and a similar method will be employed for the introduction of multiplication. Here is an example using three disjoint sets.

$$A = (a, b, c)$$
$$B = (d, e, f)$$
$$C = (g, h, i)$$

Remember, these are disjoint sets with no members in common. The union of the three sets is simply illustrated.

$$A \cup B \cup C = (a, b, c, d, e, f, g, h, i)$$

Therefore $n(A) + n(B) + n(C) = 3 + 3 + 3$

It is easy to see that

$$n(A) + n(B) + n(C) = 3 + 3 + 3$$
$$n(A + B + C) = 9$$
$$3 + 3 + 3 = 9$$
$$3 \times 3 = 9$$

The flannel board can be used to clarify the operation of multiplication.

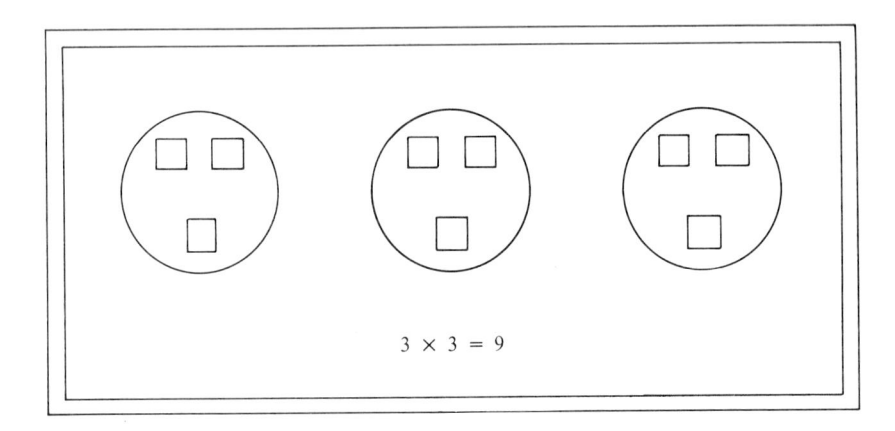

FIGURE 5.98

Intermediate Mathematics for the Mentally Retarded 283

This mathematical sentence is read, "Three times three is nine." The threes are called factors and the nine is called the product. The × symbol is the sign for the relationship we call multiplication. The major point here is that in terms of sets multiplication is viewed as repeated addition. When multiplication is introduced through the set approach and is viewed as repeated addition, it is seen by the children more of as an extension of previously learned material than as a frighteningly strange new process.

add four ones	add four twos	add four threes	add four fours
1	2	3	4
1	2	3	4
1	2	3	4
+1	+2	+3	+4
4	8	12	16

1 × 4 = 4   2 × 4 = 8   3 × 4 = 12   4 × 4 = 16

It is just as important that children have pre-multiplication experiences as it was for them to have had such opportunities with addition. The teacher should use the flannel board, collection of objects, the number line and similar materials to prepare the children for experiences with multiplication.

The Flannel Board

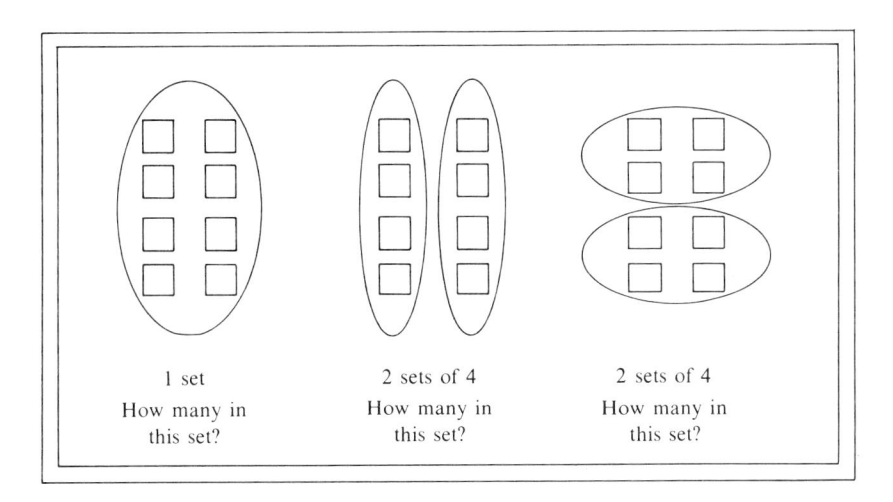

1 set
How many in this set?

2 sets of 4
How many in this set?

2 sets of 4
How many in this set?

FIGURE 5.99

Use a collection of disks (any group of objects will do):

Make two sets of four. Make four sets of two. Make three sets of two.

2 × 4 =   4 × 2 =   3 × 2 =
4 + 4 =   2 + 2 + 2 + 2 =   2 + 2 + 2 =

FIGURE 5.100

Make use of the number line to solve number sentences.

3 + 3 + 3   = ☐   2 + 2 + 2   = ☐
2 + 2 + 2 + 2 = ☐   3 + 3 + 3 + 3 = ☐
              4 + 4 + 4   = ☐
              4 + 4 + 4 + 4 = ☐

1 2 3 4 5 6 7 8 9 10 11 12 13 14 15 16 17 18

FIGURE 5.101

Use counting sticks to show multiplication.

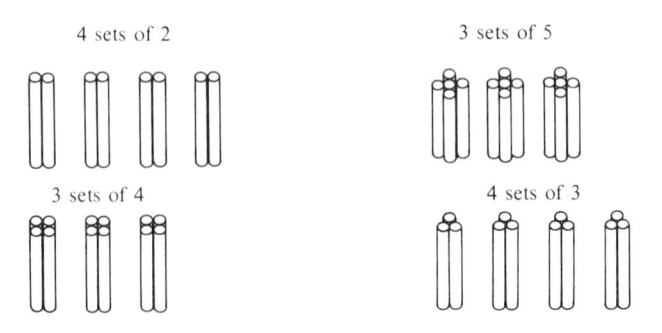

4 sets of 2   3 sets of 5

3 sets of 4   4 sets of 3

FIGURE 5.102

Complete these number patterns by using the number line:
2, 4, 6, ___, ___, ___, ___, ___, ___
5, 10, ___
4, 8, ___, ___
6, 12, ___

Intermediate Mathematics for the Mentally Retarded 285

Use the number line to solve these:
3 × 3 =   2 × 3 =   4 × 3 =
2 × 4 =   3 × 4 =   4 × 4 =

After the children have worked with these ideas, they will understand that multiplication is a short cut for repeated addition. The process of combining sets is not new to them. Multiplication is an extension of the idea of combining sets to the special circumstance of combining a series of equivalent sets into a single set. The children will eventually be able to relate the new symbol for multiplication (3 × 4) to the more familiar symbol for addition, (4 + 4 + 4).

Introducing Multiplication

It is recommended that the teacher begin instruction with the two's (2 × 1, 2 × 2, etc). The two's are related to doubles in addition (2 + 2, 3 + 3, 4 + 4) and are the simplest set of facts to teach. It will be shown later that one is the identity element for multiplication and that zero has special properties in multiplication. Considerable concentration will be placed on the two's so that the children will learn the basic facts involving two's. Emphasis should be given to renaming as in these examples: 2 × 1 = 1 × 2; 2 × 3 = 3 × 2. With the application of this commutative property, the children will be able to make significant discoveries about the two's table. Once the child has discovered that 2 × 3 = 6, he will be able to find that 2 × 4 = 8. The procedure is shown below.

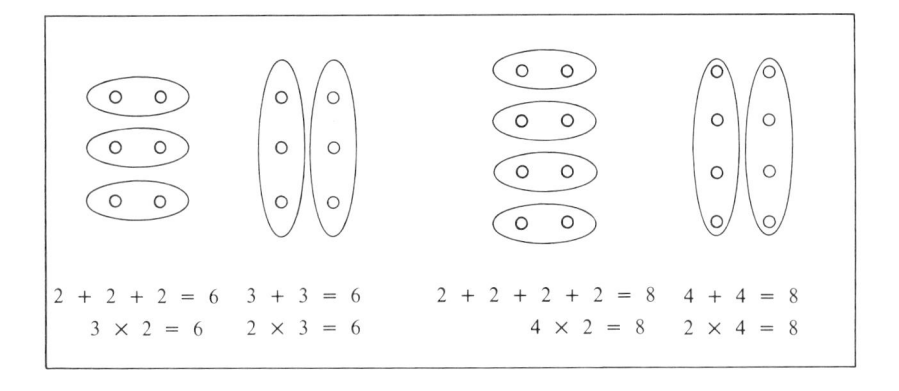

2 × 3 = 3 × 2 = 2 + 2 + 2   = 6
2 × 4 = 4 × 2 = 2 + 2 + 2 + 2   = 8
2 × 5 = 5 × 2 = 2 + 2 + 2 + 2 + 2 = 10

2 + 2 + 2 = 6   3 + 3 = 6   2 + 2 + 2 + 2 = 8   4 + 4 = 8
3 × 2 = 6   2 × 3 = 6   4 × 2 = 8   2 × 4 = 8

FIGURE 5.103

In other words, the children discover that each new fact in the table of two's is two more than the preceding fact.

X	2	3	4	5
2	4	6	8	10

Illustrations which emphasize the relationship between repetitive addition and multiplication make it much easier for the children to see why each new fact in the table of two's is two more than the previous fact. The children will have a greater understanding of why 2 × 3 is more than 2 × 2; why 2 × 4 is less than 2 × 5.

The use of the multiplication table is very helpful in teaching the relationship among the multiplication facts. Caution should be exercised to be certain that the children understand the construction of the table and how to use it. A few activities like the ones suggested here will give some insurance in that regard.

The Horizontal Table. The horizontal table can be used to show the facts of the 2 × *n* type. At first have the children write only the multiplication; in later exercises include product. Once the children indicate under-

×	2	3	4	5
2	2 × 2	2 × 3	2 × 4	2 × 5

×	2	3	4	5
2	2 × 2 4	2 × 3 6	2 × 4 8	2 × 5 10

standing of tables constructed in this manner, the indicated multiplication can be dropped and only the products shown.

×	2	3	4	5
2	4	6	8	10

The Vertical Table. The horizontal table is used to show only the 2 × *n* type facts. In order to show the *n* × 2 facts a vertical table needs

	2
2	2 × 2
3	3 × 2
4	4 × 2
5	5 × 2

	2
2	2 × 2 4
3	3 × 2 6
4	4 × 2 8
5	5 × 2 10

	2	3	4	5
2	2 × 2 4	2 × 3 6	2 × 4 8	2 × 5 10
3	3 × 2 6			
4	4 × 2 8			
5	5 × 2 10			

Intermediate Mathematics for the Mentally Retarded 287

to be constructed. Always instruct the children to read the number in the left column first, the number in the top row second, and the number in the body at their point of intersection third. The procedure for teaching the vertical tables should parallel that use with the horizontal. Have the children write only the multiplication first. Then proceed to include both the indicated multiplication and the product. Later, the indicated multiplication can be dropped and the body of the table need only show the products.

With this background, the children are ready to use a more complete multiplication table. Only products of eighteen and less have been included. The method for discovering the new facts was indicated with the two's (2), and the reader should also note that the facts for zero and one have been excluded for the moment. The products of eighteen and below are sufficient for the intermediate level. It is true that many children may be able to memorize multiplication facts beyond this number; but we are striving for understanding.

TABLE 5.4

×	2	3	4	5	6	7	8	9
2	4	6	8	10	12	14	16	18
3	6	9	12	15	18			
4	8	12	16					
5	10	15						
6	12	18						
7	14							
8	16							
9	18							

The beginning work with the two's purposely ignored such facts as 2×0 and 2×1. After the children have had extensive practice with multiplication, they will quickly recognize such relationships as $2 \times 0 = 0 + 0$; and that $2 \times 1 = 1 + 1$. By using the commutative property which applies to multiplication as well as addition, it can be shown that

$3 \times 0 = 0$ $3 \times 1 = 3$ $4 \times 1 = 4$
$0 \times 3 = 0$ $1 \times 3 = 3$ $1 \times 4 = 4$

The generalizations that $n \times 0 = 0$; $0 \times n = 0$; $n \times 1 = n$; $1 \times n = n$ (the number one is the identity element for multiplication) enables children to quickly discover thirty-six elements on the multiplication table. These are shown in Table 5.5.

TABLE 5.5

×	0	1	2	3	4	5	6	7	8	9
0	0	0	0	0	0	0	0	0	0	0
1	0	1	2	3	4	5	6	7	8	9
2	0	2								
3	0	3								
4	0	4								
5	0	5								
6	0	6								
7	0	7								
8	0	8								
9	0	9								

By this time the children should have no problem handling number sentences related to these basic multiplication facts.

$2 \times 4 = \square \quad 3 \times 6 = \square \quad 4 + 4 + 4 = 3 \times \square = \triangle$
$4 \times 2 = \square \quad 6 \times 3 = \square \quad 2 + 2 + 2 + 2 = \square \times 2 = \triangle$

Properties of Multiplication at the Intermediate Level.

Multiplication is commutative: the order of the factors does not affect the product.

Identity element for multiplication:

$4 \times 1 = 4 \qquad 2 \times 1 = 2 \qquad n \times 1 = n$
$1 \times 5 = 5 \qquad 1 \times 6 = 6 \qquad 1 \times n = n$

DIVISION

Background

The children have had a great deal of experience with subtraction as the inverse process of addition and have come to understand multiplication as an extension of addition. The next step is to teach them that the operation of division has the same inverse relation to multiplication that subtraction has to addition. As subtraction "undoes" addition, division "undoes" multiplication. The method for teaching division will parallel the teaching of multiplication. Therefore, division is introduced as the process of repeated subtraction. The answer to the number sentence $8 \div 2 =$ can be obtained by repeated subtraction. It can be shown that two can be subtracted from eight four times. There are four twos in eight.

Intermediate Mathematics for the Mentally Retarded 289

```
  8                          8
 -2  (1)                    -4  (1)
  6                          4
 -2  (1)   8 ÷ 2 = 4        -4  (1)
  4                             (2)      8 ÷ 4 = 2
 -2  (1)                       4)̄8̄
  2
 -2  (1)   2)̄8̄
     (4)
```

It can also be demonstrated that four may be subtracted from eight two times. Hence there are two fours in eight. The mathematical sentence for this process is read "eight divided by two equals four" and "eight divided by four equals two." The division sign ( )̄) is used for computation and should be reserved until the children are able to solve problems by writing correct number sentences. The reader will recall that multiplication was defined in terms of two factors and a product. Just as we thought of subtraction as looking for the missing addend; division can be thought of as finding the missing factor. In the traditional program, division was defined in terms of dividend, divisor, and quotient. A dividend is divided by a divisor to obtain a quotient. These terms have no special value and we want the children to understand the relationship between multiplication and division. Hence, division is defined as the process of finding the missing factor. In determining the missing factor in the example $2 \times \square = 8$, the sentence can be rewritten as

$$8 \div 2 = \square$$

$4 \times \square = 8$ can be rewritten as

$$8 \div 4 = \square$$

1 set of 8   How many sets of 2 in 8?   How many sets of 4 in 8?

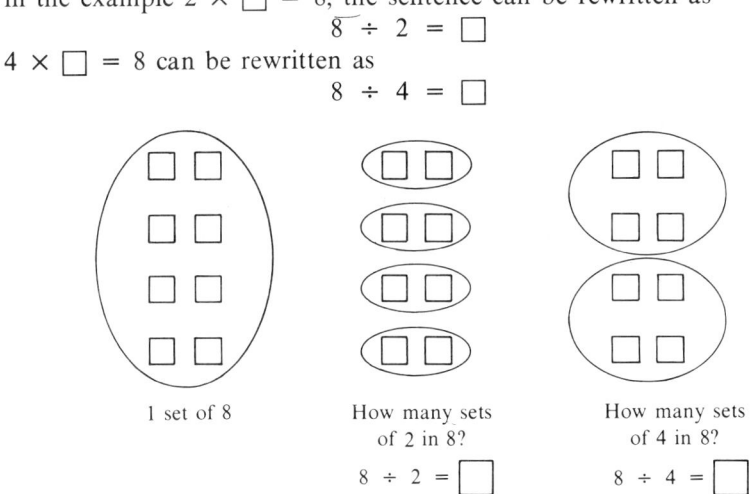

$8 \div 2 = \square$ $8 \div 4 = \square$

FIGURE 5.104

A collection of objects such as counting disks can be used. Count twelve disks for each child. How many sets of three are there in twelve? Use repeated subtraction. Show the children that multiplication is combining (putting together).

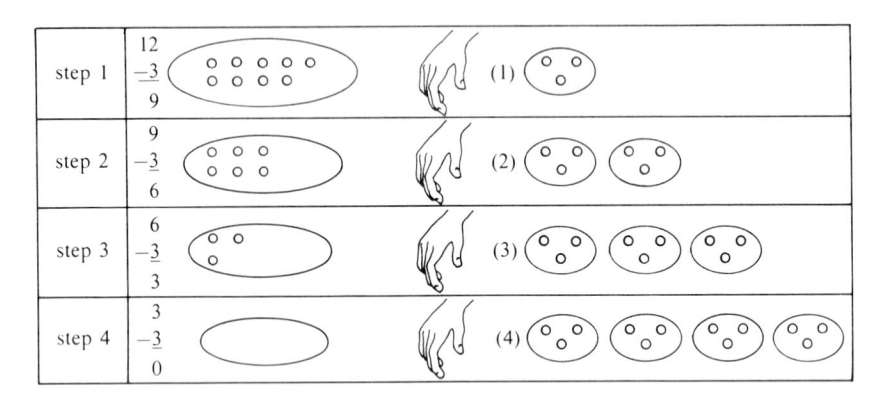

FIGURE 5.105

Present four groups of two.   Combine them into one group

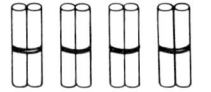

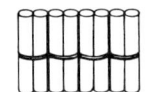

FIGURE 5.106

How many are there altogether?
$$4 \times 2 = 8$$

so there are eight altogether. Show the children that division "undoes" (takes apart) multiplication. How many groups of two are there in eight? Separate the group into four groups of two.

Present the group of   Separate the group of 8
8 just combined   into four groups of 2.

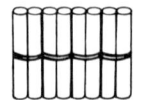

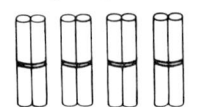

FIGURE 5.107

Intermediate Mathematics for the Mentally Retarded 291

$$8 \div 2 = 4$$

so there are four groups of two in eight. Illustrations such as this will help the children visualize the relationship between multiplication and division.

Use Counting Sticks. Here are eighteen sticks. Group them in bundles of two. How many bundles do you get? Group them in bundles of three. How many bundles do you get? Group them into three equal bundles. How many are there in each bundle? Use rubber bands to group the counting sticks.

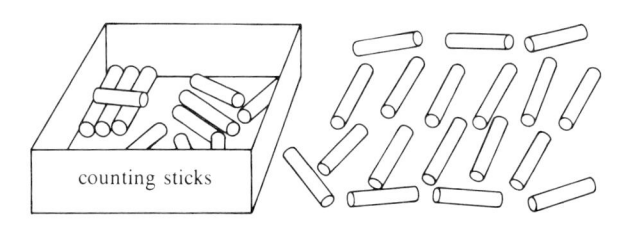

FIGURE 5.108

Make use of the number line:
How many threes in twelve?

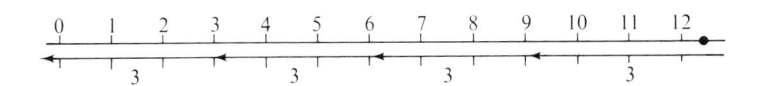

$$12 \div 3 = \square$$

FIGURE 5.109

Properties of Division

It was shown that both addition and multiplication were commutative and have the identity elements zero and one respectively. There are parallels between subtraction as contrasted to addition and division as contrasted to multiplication. Just as $8 - 4 \neq 4 - 8$; $8 \div 4 \neq 4 \div 8$. Further illustrations confirm the observation that division is not commutative. It can also be shown that division does not have an identity element.

$$1 \div 3 \neq 3 \div 1 \text{ and } 1/3 \neq 3/1$$

SUMMARY

This chapter has described the complexities of teaching educable mentally retarded children during their intermediate school years. It has been pointed out that many of these children have experienced years of sustained failure and have developed intricate compensatory defense mechanisms. The teacher must, therefore, address herself not only to the level of the children's understanding of arithmetic but also to their sophisticated avoidance techniques. Special attention has been given in this chapter to visual-perceptual problems which may complicate learning for mentally retarded children. A major goal of the curriculum at this level was shown to center around such ideas as sets, place value, and positional notation. Considerable emphasis was placed on the understanding of number processes and the principles of number operations. Another key focus was on the practical use of measurement and money skills in daily situations.

TEACHING AIDS FOR INTERMEDIATE LEVEL EDUCABLE MENTALLY RETARDED CHILDREN

The following list of aids for teaching mathematics to intermediate educable mentally retarded children was taken largely from *Suggested Basic Materials for Educable Mentally Retarded Children*, Division of Special Education, Department of Education, State of Ohio, 1968.[*]

The list is not intended to be exhaustive, but is presented here to give examples of the types of instructional aids which may be successfully adapted to the needs of these children.

The code refers to the names and addresses of publishers given in the appendix.

PUB-LISHER CODE	TITLE	DESCRIPTION
H-10	*Structural Arithmetic Program*, Grades II and III	Kit and work texts with teacher's manuals.
C-9	*Cuisenaire Rods*	Size and color coded to aid in development of concepts.
K-1	*Flash Cards,* Addition and Subtraction	

[*]Developed by Amy Allen and Jaque Cross.

Intermediate Mathematics for the Mentally Retarded

PUBLISHER CODE	TITLE	DESCRIPTION
S-16	Measuring sets, Bead Abacus, Classroom Calendar	Manipulative devices
C-11	Clock, Thermometers—Rulers marked with one-half and one-quarter inches	Manipulative devices.
C-5	*Measurement, Time, Money* (use with actual money)	Liquid duplicator sets, teacher must add manipulative items.
F-5	*Arithmetic Foundation* Level II, III	Workbook used with small groups
S-1	*Self Teaching Arithmetic* Books 1, 2, and 3	Supplementary practice books with teacher's manuals.
J-1	Count-to-ten Boards Flannel boards—1 large size, several of desk size Geometric forms Number matchettes Number punch Place value peg holders Place value tab racks Stick-o-mats (to use on flannel board; make others) Work boards—#10 #20 #100	
C-3	1. *Mystery of the Farmer's Three Fives* 2. *The True Book on Money*	These and similar stories can be used to interest children in uses of arithmetic as well as to reinforce number meanings and processes. Room library shelf.
K-1	*Addo Arithmetic Game*	Practice of 100 addition combinations
M-2	*Training Fun with Numbers* Books II and III	Work text; Sequential program will need to be supplemented
T-5	Flip-and-Build cards Form puzzles Ordinal placement board	

PUBLISHER CODE	TITLE	DESCRIPTION
Unspecified Source	Audio-visual and kinesthetic aids to concept development	
	Magazine pictures	
	Mounted pictures which show groupings	
	Matching kits	Made by more mature pupils (or pupils in junior-senior high school units) for all to share.
	Slides	Commercial or teacher-pupil made.
S-4	Arithmetic readiness cards—with teacher's guidebooks 　Set 1—Grouping 　Set 2—Numeration System 　Set 3—Addition Basic Facts 　Set 4—Subtraction Basic Facts	These two are also used in primary classes. Use under teacher direction or for extra practice.
S-11	The Green-Eyed Monster	A game to reinforce the skill of telling time as timetables and the business community use it.
C-6	Design Cubes Geometric shapes—graded form board Matchmates Mozaic Number sorter Sum stick Time learning kit	
C-9	*Holiday Storybook*	Another book for the room library which relates to arithmetic.
G-4	*How to Tell Time*	Reference book for classroom library—good to reinforce concepts.
H-3	*Growth in Arithmetic,* Book II	Teacher's edition is helpful in developing skills in sequence. Material should be carefully selected and adapted for pupils—not used directly. *One copy only.*

PUB-LISHER CODE	TITLE	DESCRIPTION
H-6	*Arithmetic Foundation,* Level II, Level III	Workbooks used with teacher direction and supplemented with activities.
H-7	*Learning to Use Arithmetic,* Book I, Book II	Teacher's edition can provide guides to the development of a sequential skills program. Because of the unfortunate tendency to note "The second grade boys and girls had . . ." "The children in the second grade were getting ready to . . ." material should be *adapted,* rather than used directly with the pupils.
L-3	*Telling Time*—first half (Last half usable in Jr. High)	This workbook, planned for slow learners, has good supplementary work pages for the children who have learned to tell time by the clock and calendar. The intermediate child should *not* be expected to comprehend problems of time in relation to distance (m.p.h.) or dealing with geographical time zones
S-4	1. *Numbers in Action* 2. *Seeing Through Arithmetic*	Teacher's editions helpful for developmental sequence. If used with overhead projector, pictures can be covered with windows to avoid clutter. Do not use where these are basic materials in primary grades.
S-18	*The Thanksgiving Story*	Another book for the classroom library that relates to arithmetic (as well as to social studies.)

REFERENCES

Callahan, John J. and Jacobson, Ruth S. "An Experiment with Retarded Children and Cuisenaire Rods." *The Arithmetic Teacher* 14 (January, 1967): 10-14.

Cincinnati Public Schools. *The Slow Learning Program in the Elementary and Secondary Schools.* Cincinnati, Ohio: Bulletin No. 119, 1964.

Feingold, Abraham. *Teaching Arithmetic to Slow Learners and Retarded.* New York: John Day Company, 1965.

Frostig, Marianne. *Developmental Test of Visual Perception.* Palo Alto, California: Consulting Psychologists Press, 1966.

Kephart, Newell C. *The Slow Learner in the Classroom.* 2d ed. Columbus, Ohio: Charles E. Merrill Publishing Co., 1971.

Stern, Catherine. "Concrete Devices of Structural Arithmetic for the Slow Learner." *Arithmetic Teacher,* 5, (April, 1958): 257-69.

Vigilante, Nicholas J. *Mathematics in Elementary Education.* London: MacMillan Company, 1969.

chapter 6

Pre-Adultation Junior High Mathematics

A modern approach to mathematics for the mentally retarded provides systematic instruction at the preprimary and primary levels. Much of what is taught at these levels still tends to be thought of by many teachers as "readiness" levels, or as topics which "fit" better with other topics. By the latter part of the intermediate level, the situation changes as these teachers sense that now at last they are teaching "real arithmetic." The children have some understanding of the base ten system of numeration and the role of place value. They have some skill in working with sets. Their ability to deal with real life problems, to perform calculations independently, and to check their own results, attest to this comprehension. Such should be the background of the child who comes to the junior high school.

It is true that by junior high level most mentally retarded youngsters have considerable concepts and abilities in mathematics. The work of this level, however, will involve inevitably intensive reteaching of concepts introduced in the three preceding levels in addition to a substantial block of new material.

ABILITY LEVELS

It is indicated in Table 6.1 that educable mentally retarded youngsters of chronological ages thirteen and fourteen can be expected to demonstrate mental ages ranging from six and one-half years to eleven years.

The mental age range has increased quite dramatically since the pre-primary level. A chronological five-year-old with an IQ of 50 would have a mental age of two years and six months while a child of the same chronological age with an IQ of 80 would have a mental age of four years; a range of one year and six months. However, a chronological fourteen-year-old with an IQ of 50 would have a mental age of seven years while another child of the same chronological age with an IQ of 80 would have an MA of eleven years and two months; a range of four years and two months. The range of differences in mental age has at no level been greater than in the junior high school program. The junior high teacher of the mentally retarded can anticipate, all other things equal, that all of her students will have some mathematical skills and number concepts. However, the range indicated above should serve as a cautionary note. A number of these youngsters will be performing at the primary and intermediate levels. A very few in some areas of mathematics may be able to accomplish tasks which are generally allotted to the regular fifth and sixth grades. As a rule of thumb, however, it is safe to estimate that most junior high level retardates will be doing work equivalent to regular third and fourth grade levels.

TABLE 6.1
Mental Ages of Mentally Retarded Children Chronological Ages 13 and 14*

IQ	13	14
50	6.6	7.0
55	7.2	7.8
60	7.9	8.4
65	8.5	9.1
70	9.1	9.9
75	9.9	10.6
80	10.5	11.2

* Mental ages are stated in years and months.

OBJECTIVES

The junior high age educable retardates will learn to count, read, and write numbers, and solve problems at a third and fourth grade level of achievement. In other words, they will learn: to read simple maps, graphs; to use a more mature mathematics vocabulary; to deal with number symbols to the thousands place; to tell time to the minute;

to read thermometers to degrees; to use the calendars to plan; to use liquid and dry measures; and calculate with simple fractions. They will learn to solve to a more advanced extent basic problems through the processes of addition, subtraction, multiplication and division. The use of money and knowledge of relative values will become quite functional. Most significantly, these children will learn to meet persisting life problems of quantification on a semi-independent level with a minimum of assistance. More specifically, many junior high age educable retardates will:

1. Improve in the ability to sort, match, classify and otherwise deal with geometric figures.
2. Continue to develop a meaningful vocabulary associated with mathematics including location, other measurements, terms of business, dimensions, computation and problem solving.
3. Master new mathematical symbols such as Roman Numerals and number symbols and words to one hundred. Place value becomes established to 9999.
4. Learn the ordinals through thirty-first or beyond.
5. Improve in the use of measuring instruments to include 60 seconds; 32 degrees; clock to minutes; scales to ounces; temperature to degrees.
6. Extend the skills with money and value to include the purchasing power of money, names to twenty dollar bills, decimal point placehold, budgets, time and rate.
7. Continue to develop number operations skills including all addition and subtraction facts, column addition, carrying, borrowing, multiplication facts and division facts through 5, skills in dividing two and three digits by one digit.
8. Use the correct processes to solve two-step problems and deliniate and identify processes. Problems will involve measuring, scheduling, counting, computing, as well as the social security numbers, and identification numbers on such items as purchase orders.

DEVELOPMENTAL SEQUENCE OF MATHEMATICAL SKILLS

At the intermediate level, the children will have made significant progress toward systematic mathematical methods of problem solving. These skills will be substantially extended at the junior high level. This will incorporate recognizing and interpreting the nature of a problematic situation, expressing the quantitative relationships in symbolic form, and solving the problem through computation. Emphasis throughout the mathematics program has been on understanding. The mentally retarded child will have as much difficulty with mathematics as his non-handicapped counterpart when instruction is primarily drills and rote. The temptation for the teacher of the retarded to use meaningless drill is at no time greater than at the junior high level. Too often the approach to problem solving can become superficial and unstructured. The pitfall of emphasizing computational skills at the junior high level must be avoided. A healthy balance between the problem solving abilities and computational skills is crucial. Therefore, one of the major approaches of the junior high program is to study carefully the fundamental methods of attacking mathematical problems.

By the time mentally retarded children enter junior high they should have learned all of the addition and subtraction facts well enough so that each fact may be spontaneously and automatically retrieved. Many of the youngsters will have made a solid start on the mastery of multiplication and division facts. The scope of the base ten numeration system will have developed as far as the hundreds place. These learnings will be expanded at the junior high level and emphasis should be placed on understanding. The associative and commutative principles of addition are reviewed. Subtraction has been taught as the inverse of addition. The processes of multiplication have been introduced at the intermediate level and the application of associative and commutative principles should be made clear at the junior high level.

TABLE 6.2

Checklist for Junior High Level Mathematics for Retardates

1. Form and Perception
    experience with the following:
        vertical vs. horizontal
        different sizes, shapes, and parts
        end points
        angles

2. Vocabulary Associated with Mathematics

average	air mail	height
check	lay-away	full
balance	past due	depth
account	due bill	minutes
endorse	earn	seconds
installment	rent	luxury
signature	expense	necessity

Pre-Adultation Junior High Mathematics 303

    checking   charge
    savings   salary
    budget   fare
    debt   length

3. Number Symbols
   rote counting as needed
   reading number symbols to 1000
   reading number words to one hundred
   writing numbers through hundreds
   counting by 2's to 100
   counting by 3's to 99
   counting by 4's to 48
   reading dollars and cents numbers and symbols
   reading Roman Numerals to XII
   reading decimal points
   knowing symbols for inch (") and foot (')
   knowing odd and even numbers

4. Cardinal Numbers
   counting groups through hundreds
   relating number symbols to groups of objects to 100
   recognition of groups of objects through 50 and ability to separate all possible subgroups
   knowledge of fractions such as 1/2, 1/8, 2/3, 3/4
   concept of sets to interpret division
   grouping as: 14 into 2 equal groups; 15 into 3 equal groups; 18 into 6 equal groups

5. Ordinal Numbers
   knowledge of ordinals through 31, or as needed
   use in addresses

6. Measurement
   concepts of AM, PM, 24 hours in a day, 4 seasons, 52 weeks, A.D., B.C., century, 1 hour, 60 minutes
   clock telling time by the hour and minute hands; reading and writing time; associating time with schedules; common equivalents
   calendar: reading all dates; knowing relationship of days, weeks, months, years, and seasons; knowing birth dates and holidays
   weight: understanding ounces, pounds, and fractions—and abbreviations for same
   thermometer: using a household thermometer; reading freezing point (above and below)
   linear: understanding inches, feet, and yards
       concept of 36 inches = 1 yard
       reading graphs and charts

volume: understanding cups, pints, quarts, gallons and their relationships; using fractions of the above terms; knowing the various types of containers; utilizing concepts of teaspoon and tablespoon.

7. Money and Value
   concept of coins and their relationships
   using decimal point in money problems
   ability to make change for $1.00 (with extension to $10.00)
   equivalents to $1.00 (25¢ = quarter, 2 dimes + nickel etc.)
   cost of stamps; movie, lunch etc.

8. Number Operations and Usage
   one column

$$5 + 7 + 8 + 9 = 38$$

```
  5      4     3¢
  1      8     9¢
  2      1     1¢
```

addition: two and three column without carrying

```
  21    32    24    142
   6     4    51    221
              12    433
```

two column with carrying from first column

```
$0.68   29   26   45¢   45   11  Check by adding in reverse
 0.29    2    5    6¢   24   26  Fraction 1/4 + 1/4 · 1/3 + 2/3
                        13   37
```

subtraction: Higher decade subtraction combinations; one, two and three place numbers from up to a three-place number; borrowing from units and tens columns.

```
25   35   50   10   $0.94   739   821   535   692
15   20   16    8    0.64    26    12    54   193
```

simple fractions: 2/4 − 1/4, 2/3 − 1/3, 1/2 − 1/4
multiplication: 2's through 9's and reverses
```
  2  2  3  8  9  9
  2  3  2  9  8  9
```

two and three digit by one digit:
```
   7   32   73   $2.98
 124    4    3       2
```

division: 2's through 5's

2)4   3)27   3)$1.29   5)$2.05   8 ÷ 2

FORM AND PERCEPTION

The concepts and skills related to form and perception are most important at the preprimary through intermediate levels. There are specific abilities which are definite prerequisites to the learning of mathematics. These skills should be very well established by the junior high level for most youngsters, but there will be a few students who continue to experience considerable difficulty with the spatial tasks related to number usage. These individuals should be given a thorough diagnostic survey to determine the extent and nature of their difficulties and a corrective program based on the results of that evaluation should be prescribed. The reader is referred to the specific evaluation instruments discussed in Chapter 9 and the sample remedial programs outlined in each of the preceding chapters.

There are some visual-perceptual skills which should be a part of the curriculum for most junior high educable mentally retarded youngsters. Many students will need to recognize more complex pedestrian and vehicle traffic signs; use tools with wood and metal in industrial arts classes; and deal with such skills as map reading, measuring angles, and calculating area. Some suggestions for working with these abilities are presented below.

Matching Shapes and Names. In Figure 6.1 examine the shapes on the left and match them with the correct words on the right. Put the appropriate letter on the line.

a.

b.

c.

d.

e.

_____ curved line

_____ parallel lines

_____ perpendicular lines

_____ square

_____ diamond

f. ☐   _____ circle

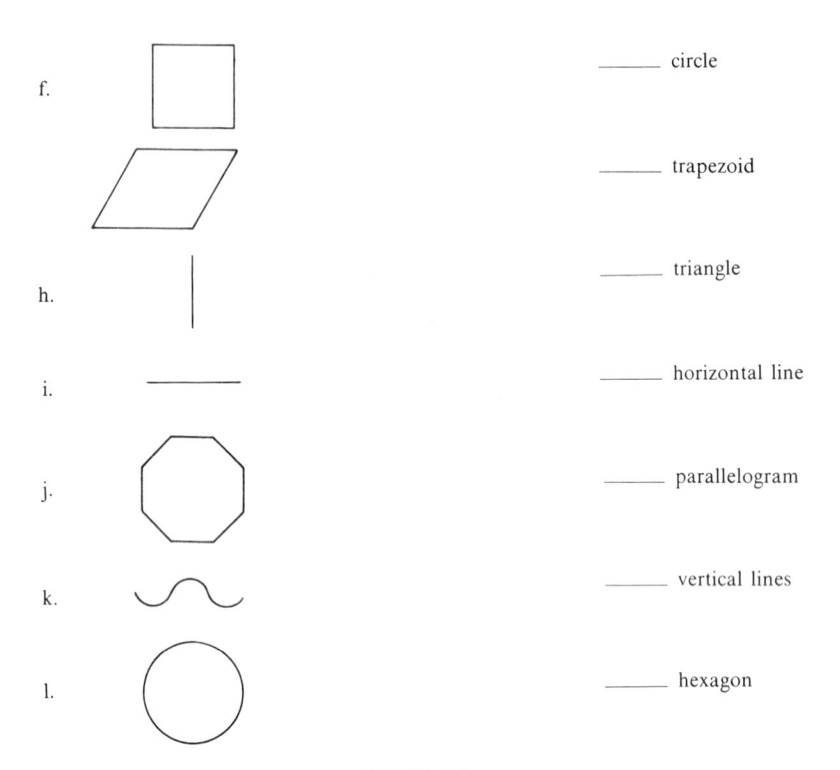

                         _____ trapezoid

h. | _____ triangle

i. —   _____ horizontal line

j. ⬡   _____ parallelogram

k. ⌢   _____ vertical lines

l. ○   _____ hexagon

FIGURE 6.1

Building With Shapes (Playpax). Skills in the perception of space may be enhanced through a variety of colorful and entertaining construction materials. The set pictured in Figure 6.2 consists of multi-colored rings

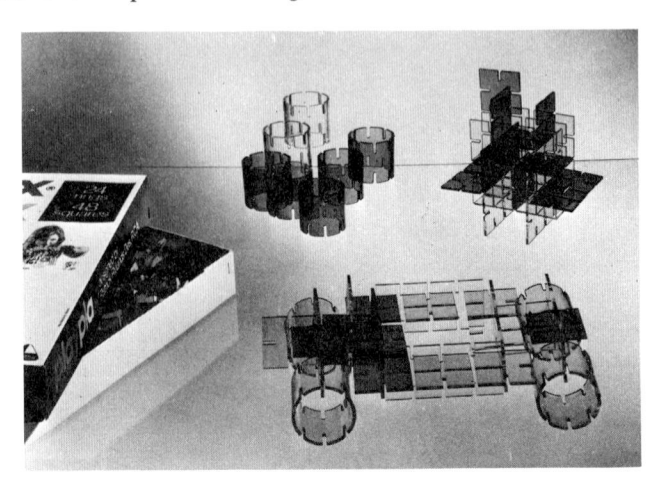

FIGURE 6.2

Pre-Adultation Junior High Mathematics 307

and squares made of durable polystyrene. Materials of this type appeal to teenagers simply because of the creative challenge they present both in design and color.

Discriminating Shapes. Examine the shapes in Figure 6.3 and put a mark on the one that is different from the others.

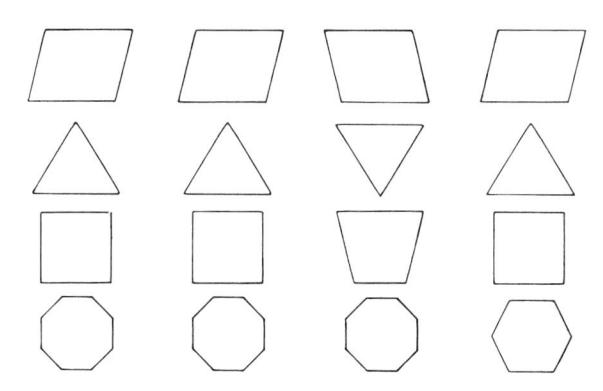

FIGURE 6.3

Block Design. For this exercise use a set of nine blocks with each side divided into a right triangle and painted different colors. These are similar to the blocks used in the WISC and also available in toy departments. Begin by having the students match a design which you have formed with a set of your own blocks. After they have developed skill in copying a design from a set of blocks, have them reproduce the designs from a drawing.

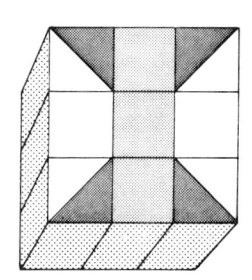

Use your blocks to make a design like the one I have made with my block.

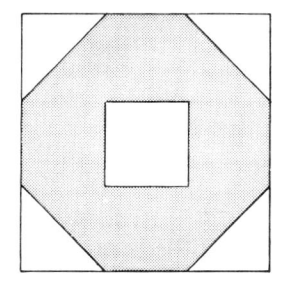

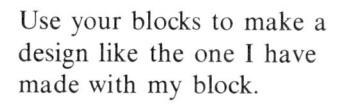

Use your block to make a design like the one you see on this card.

FIGURE 6.4

The Cheves Program

The Ruth Cheves program (Teaching Resources, 100 Boylston Street, Boston, Massachusetts 02111), consisting of six groups of cards, puzzles, and games, was introduced at the intermediate level. Some youngsters at the junior high level may be able to profit from this program. Parts of this aid are described below.

Form Puzzles

The visual discrimination of forms is a necessary beginning skill for arithmetic. These puzzles assist the child in areas of visual perception, spatial organization, relationships of parts to the whole, concepts of number. The basic geometric forms and left to right sequencing are other important skills developed in these puzzles.

FIGURE 6.5

Twelve puzzles are provided. Six are six inches square and six are four inches square. Each puzzle is cut into quarters with each quarter divided diagonally being half colored and half white. Six solid primary and secondary colors are used.

Pre-Adultation Junior High Mathematics 309

An almost unlimited variety of designs can be made with the quarters of the puzzle forms. A series of procedures are described in the instructions, with the teacher preparing a model which the child copies. Memory and recall are enhanced as each progression becomes more difficult. From simple two-piece designs to complex multi-pieced patterns in rows, the concepts of order, sequence, and organization are introduced. Questions in each procedure elicit both verbal and motor responses. Examples are given in the instructions for each step of the presentation.

FIGURE 6.6

Geometric Shapes and Association Cards

An understanding of shapes and forms is the basis of learning letters and words. Experience in the abstractions of associating from the known to the unknown provides further integrative skills necessary for learning.

Geometric Shapes. This consists of 36 cards—six each of three shapes (circle, square, and triangle) and three forms (rectangle, diamond, and hexagon) in the primary and secondary colors. The cards are used to teach the names of colors and perception of color, as well as the specific concepts of shapes and forms and the differences between them. The procedures suggested in the instructions develop, in a series of exercises, the concepts of spatial orientation, visual differentiation, position (up/down, etc.) left to right sequence, order and quantity.

Association Cards. These stabilize and reinforce the structural concept and shape and assist in developing the abstract associations important later in reading and language comprehension. For example, the word "boy" is the same whether printed lower case, or written in script or cursive. Six sets of five cards are provided. Each set has one of the six shapes shown in outline, solid color, and three associated common objects in color.

Using Tools. Here (Figure 6.7) are several tools and a number of pieces of hardware which are used with each tool. Match them.

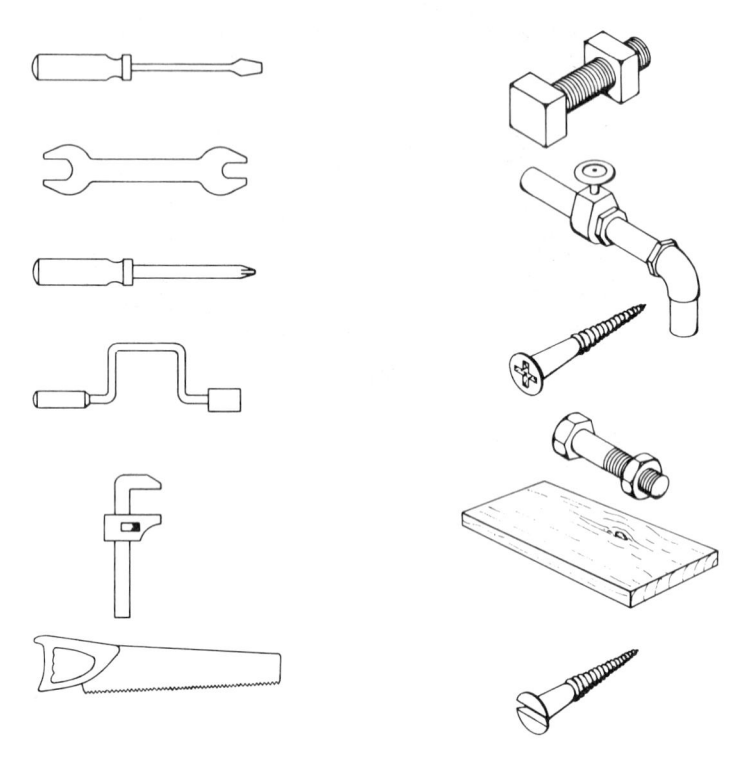

FIGURE 6.7

Reading Traffic Signs. Here (Figure 6.8) are some traffic signs which are important to the driver and the pedestrian. Look at each sign carefully and then explain what the sign means and tell where it would be located. Do you encounter signs like these on your way home?

Pre-Adultation Junior High Mathematics

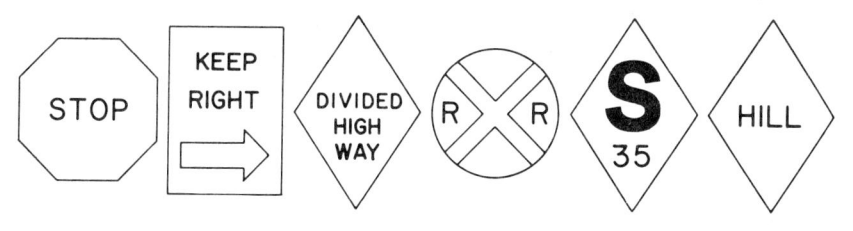

FIGURE 6.8

Comparing Angles. There are some angles drawn in Figure 6.9. The first angle in the right hand column is a right angle (90°). Find another angle in the same row that is the same.

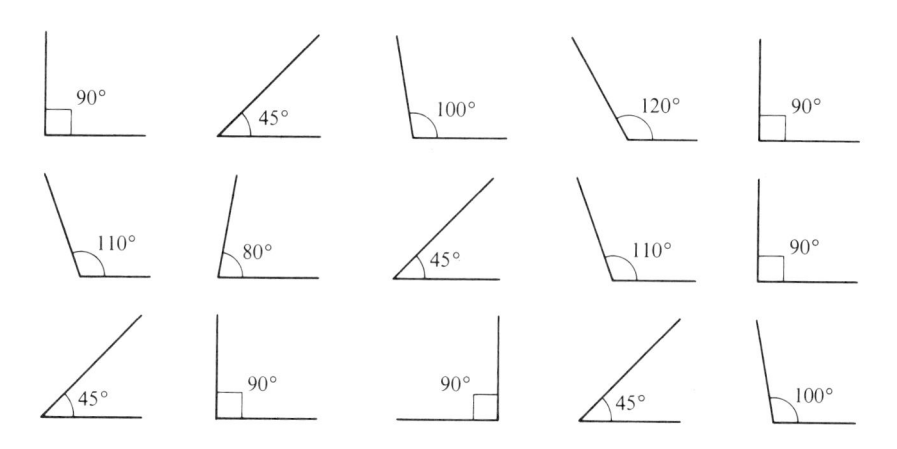

FIGURE 6.9

Examine the angles in Figure 6.10 and find the one in each row that is not the same as the others.

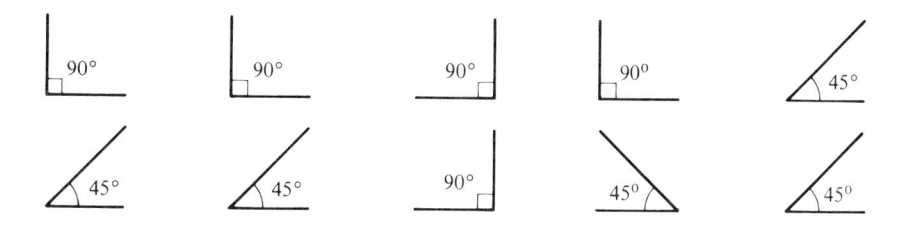

FIGURE 6.10

Measuring Areas. It will not be appropriate to teach most retarded students such concepts as calculating area or converting inches to feet or feet to yards. It will generally be sufficient to know that a certain floor is nine feet × twelve feet, or that a given one-half inch board is six feet × two feet. That is, it is just as legitimate to refer to a room which is nine feet × twelve feet as it is to say that a room has a 108 square feet or 12 square yards. However, some students will be capable of figuring area (A = 1 × w) and making conversions involving inches, feet, and yards.

Give the students opportunities to measure a variety of surfaces such as book covers, desk tops, window casings, floor areas and so forth. Encourage the more advanced students to determine the area of these surfaces in terms of square measures. Deal with approximations when figuring square measures to avoid such complex problems as multiplying inches by feet, etc.

MAP READING

A road map presents a very complex set of perceptual and cognitive problems. The typical map available at service stations presents so much coded information that it would require a book to explain the same facts in narrative form. There are certain conventions utilized in map making that require considerable exploration and practice. For example, the top of the map is North. The bottom is South. Most maps are color coded and are drawn to scale. Special symbols are used to designate airports, divided highways, toll roads, bridges, and so on. Extensive instruction will be required to teach the students the basic skills of map reading.

The teacher should write one of the major oil companies in her city and ask for a quantity of maps of her state. It is important that each student has a map of his own and that this map is of familiar territory. The teacher should use transparencies, the chalkboard, and other visual aids to emphasize specific details of the map. For example, show the students how cities are indicated and let them discover the distance from one point to another by reading the mileage and by using the mileage scale. They will enjoy these activities because of the association with travel and the automobile.

VOCABULARY ASSOCIATED WITH MATHEMATICS

The vocabulary developed at the junior high school level for educable mentally retarded youngsters centers mostly on measurement and money terms. It is especially important that these students understand the language of work, banking, and budgeting. The problems of earning a living and managing an income are difficult enough without complicating the matter with what may appear to the retarded youth as a strange new language of economics. Terms such as *lay-away, installment, interest rate, double time, endorsement,* and *money order* represent complex financial ideas. If these young adults are to learn to live independently in our sophisticated business and consumer society, they must be given extensive assistance. Special attention should be given to the development of a basic vocabulary associated with handling one's financial affairs. Of course, the vocabulary may not be developed in isolation from the concepts. Therefore, the suggestions for improving vocabulary at this level are found within the discussions in other sections. However, it is important to remember that it is just as important to stress the new and review vocabulary in a mathematics lesson as it is in reading, social studies, and science. A few suggestions follow.

1. Bring newspapers and magazines to class. Have the youngsters examine them for new words and phrases.
2. Department store catalogs represent the whole range of advertising vocabulary. Spend time using these catalogs in class giving special attention to vocabulary.
3. Encourage the youngsters in the construction of a bulletin board emphasizing new vocabulary.
4. Play games similar to Concentration with financial terms.
5. Have the youngsters keep a file box with a business term and its definition on each card.
6. Assign some students to make a list of the advertising vocabulary found in a department store window.
7. Use large flash cards with terms on one side and explanations on the other. Allow the children to work in teams checking on their own understanding.

NUMBER SYMBOLS

The reading and writing of numerals and number words should be fairly well established by this level. The children should be given assistance in reading number symbols to 1000 and number words to one hundred. They should also learn to write their numbers through the hundreds. Some attention should also be given to reading the decimal form of writing dollars and cents. The teacher may wish to give the children practice in reading additional Roman numerals.

Number Word Wheel. This wheel is a simple variation of the devices introduced at the intermediate level. The wheel is easily constructed and provides an opportunity for seat work. As the lower wheel is rotated, different number combinations appear.

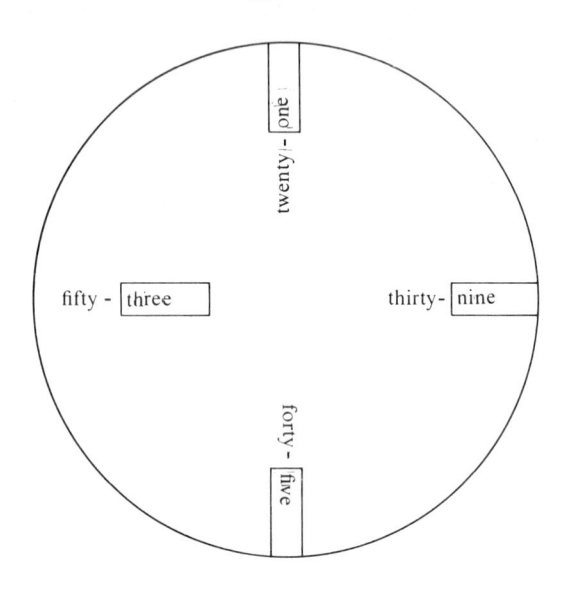

FIGURE 6.11

Match these Money Symbols

25¢	$.32
18¢	$.60
60¢	$.25
32¢	$.18

Roman Numerals

1	II
12	XI
2	IV
10	VI
11	I
9	X
3	V
8	XII
5	III
6	IX
4	VII
7	VIII

Write the Roman Numerals for these Numbers

one	I
five	V
eight	_____
three	_____
twelve	_____
four	_____

Use of the Comma with Numerals. A comma is sometimes used to make large numbers easier to read. The numerals 10 and 100 need no comma, but numerals 1,000 and above use commas to help identify them. Put commas in the appropriate numbers below.

10	1335	1005
100	345	6987
1000	4678	9287
998	9207	8345

Match these Numerals and Number Words

1000	Three hundred and forty-five
345	One thousand three hundred and thirty-five
4675	One thousand
1335	Six thousand nine hundred and eighty-seven
6987	Four thousand six hundred and seventy-five

CARDINAL AND ORDINAL NUMBERS

The ideas of place value and positional notation are the major cardinal number concepts emphasized at the junior high school level. The use of ordinal numbers to thirty-one are reviewed in connection with some practical applications.

The students should be given ample experience in rational counting through the hundreds with accuracy. Place value charts should be used to teach the reading and understanding of numbers in the thousands. A number of activities which emphasize these concepts should be developed. The teacher should also show how numbers are used to keep score in such major sports as baseball, football, and bowling. They should be given some practice in reading a variety of illustrations including pie charts, line graphs, bar graphs and tables. More advanced fractions should be introduced including eighths and sixths. A number of examples which may be appropriate at the junior high school level are given below.

Place Value Chart

thousands	hundreds	tens	ones
1	0	0	0
3	0	0	0
4	8	0	0
3	2	5	0
5	7	9	2

Have the students read numbers such as the ones given in the chart above. Ask questions such as these:
How many ones in the first number?
How many hundreds in the second number?
What is the first number?
Read the second number.
How many tens in the last number?
How many hundreds in the next to last number?
Read the last number.
What is the fourth number?

Reading for Hundreds, Tens, and Ones. Read these numbers and indicate how many thousands, hundreds, tens, and ones in each number.

	thousands	hundreds	tens	ones
268	0	2	6	8
1485	___	___	___	___
584	___	___	___	___
1087	___	___	___	___
57	___	___	___	___
3359	___	___	___	___

Thinking Of Numbers in Different Ways
467 means:
    (1)   4 hundreds   6 tens   7 ones
    (2)   400   60   7
    (3)   46 tens   7 ones

Write the different ways to think of these numbers:
358 means:

Pre-Adultation Junior High Mathematics 317

```
                  (1)   _____   _____   _____
                  (2)   _____   _____   _____
                  (3)   _____   _____   _____
935 means:
                  (1)   _____   _____   _____
                  (2)   _____   _____   _____
                  (3)   _____   _____   _____
```

Write the Numbers
  Write in figures the numbers which mean:
    52 tens and 4 ones _____524_____
    2 hundreds and 3 ones_____
    1 thousand, 3 hundreds, 1 ten, and 1 one _____
    2 hundreds, 3 tens, and 4 ones_____

Keeping Score. Sports and games are very popular among teenagers as major social occasions and provide a key motivational device for the mathematics teacher. The weekly football game, for example, provides a splendid opportunity for junior high school youngsters to meet with friends and make new acquaintances. In order to derive these social benefits it is not necessary that the young spectators understand the game or for that matter even watch it. However, the youngsters' peer prestige may rise and their own enjoyment increase if they know how this and other games are scored. The understanding of scoring in major sports is central to the sports page which is an especially popular piece of reading among teenage boys (second only to the comic section).

Most games are fairly easy to learn to score and do not involve complex skills. The teacher should begin with the more popular sports: baseball, football, and basketball. The ideas of rankings and boxes scores should be included. Other games such as volleyball, bowling and tennis may also be presented. The youngsters may also enjoy learning simple card games.

Reading Charts, Graphs, and Tables. The youngsters will encounter many charts and graphs in their reading material. Their understanding should improve with some first-hand practice in the construction of simple charts such as the ones shown in Figure 6.12.

The charts may begin with such simple concepts as variations in temperature and weight. Charts may also be used to compare sales in a school magazine sales contest or to record individual scores on spelling tests. The pie chart is a very frequent visual aid. The youngsters will probably be familiar with it through their study of fractions, but it should be reviewed in connection with charts and graphs.

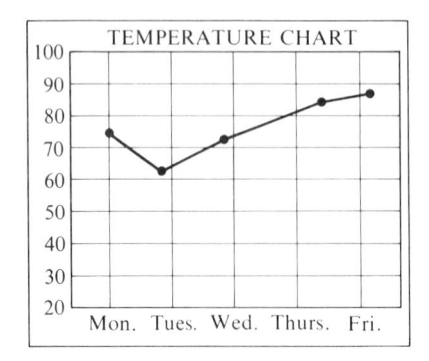

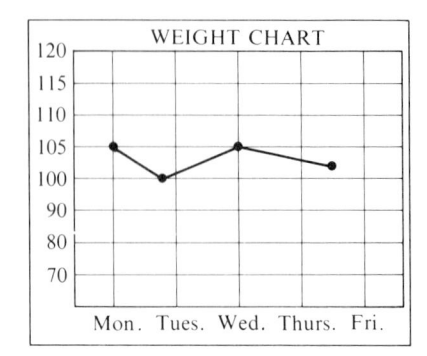

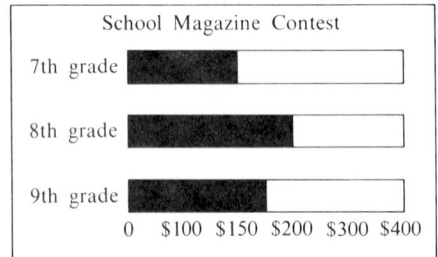

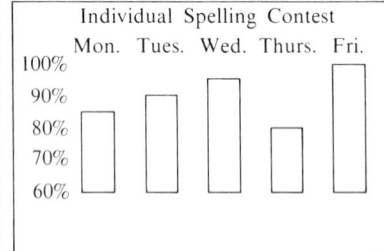

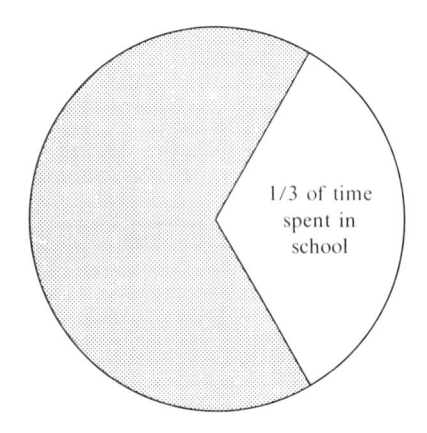

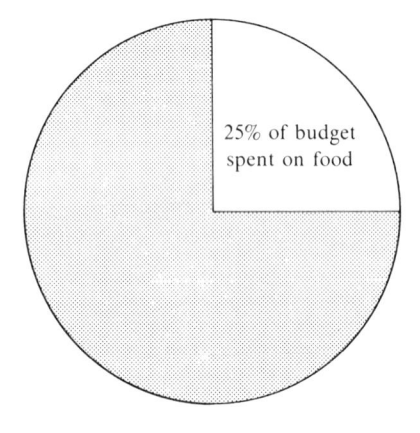

FIGURE 6.12

Many youngsters may learn to read tables such as Table 6.3. This table gives the times of high and low tide. Another table frequently found in newspapers gives the times of sunrise and sunset. The youngsters will enjoy learning to read and interpret these tables which are not nearly as complex as they first appear.

Pre-Adultation Junior High Mathematics

TABLE 6.3
Hilton Head Island Table

	Port Royal Sound		Hilton Head Harbor Marina	
Date	High	Low	High	Low
August 14	5:54 a.m.	11:56 a.m.	6:33 a.m.	12:20 a.m.
	6:32 p.m.	12:02 p.m.	7:21 p.m.	12:26 p.m.
August 15	6:54 a.m.	12:50 a.m.	7:33 a.m.	1:20 a.m.
	7:26 p.m.	1:02 p.m.	8:15 p.m.	1:26 p.m.
August 16	7:54 a.m.	1:50 a.m.	8:33 a.m.	2:14 a.m.
	8:30 p.m.	1:56 p.m.	9:09 p.m.	9:09 p.m.
August 17	8:42 a.m.	2:38 a.m.	9:21 a.m.	3:02 a.m.
	9:18 p.m.	2:50 p.m.	9:57 p.m.	3:14 p.m.
August 18	9:36 a.m.	3:26 a.m.	10:15 a.m.	3:50 a.m.
	10:06 p.m.	3:44 p.m.	10:45 p.m.	4:08 p.m.
August 19	10:24 a.m.	4:14 a.m.	11:03 a.m.	4:38 a.m.
	10:48 p.m.	4:32 p.m.	11:27 p.m.	4:56 p.m.
August 20	11:12 a.m.	5:02 a.m.	11:51 a.m.	5:26 a.m.
	11:42 p.m.	5:26 p.m.	12:21 p.m.	5:50 p.m.

Fractions. The youngsters should be given additional practice with fractions. The study of fractions will typically include thirds, fourths, eighths, and sixths. The fraction should be shown as a part of a whole. Here is an example.

Sue baked a cake for her father's birthday. Their are six members of her family and she wants each one to have a piece of cake. She wants each to have the same size so each piece of cake is one-sixth.

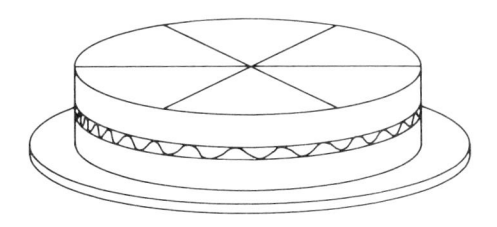

FIGURE 6.13

Match These. The circles and squares in the right hand column of Figure 6.14 represent fractions. The first circle is ⅓ because it is divided into

320   *Pre-Adultation Junior High Mathematics*

three parts and one part is shaded. A line should be drawn connecting this circle and ⅓. Now match the others.

$\frac{1}{8}$

$\frac{2}{3}$

$\frac{1}{3}$

$\frac{3}{4}$

$\frac{2}{8}$

$\frac{1}{6}$

FIGURE 6.14

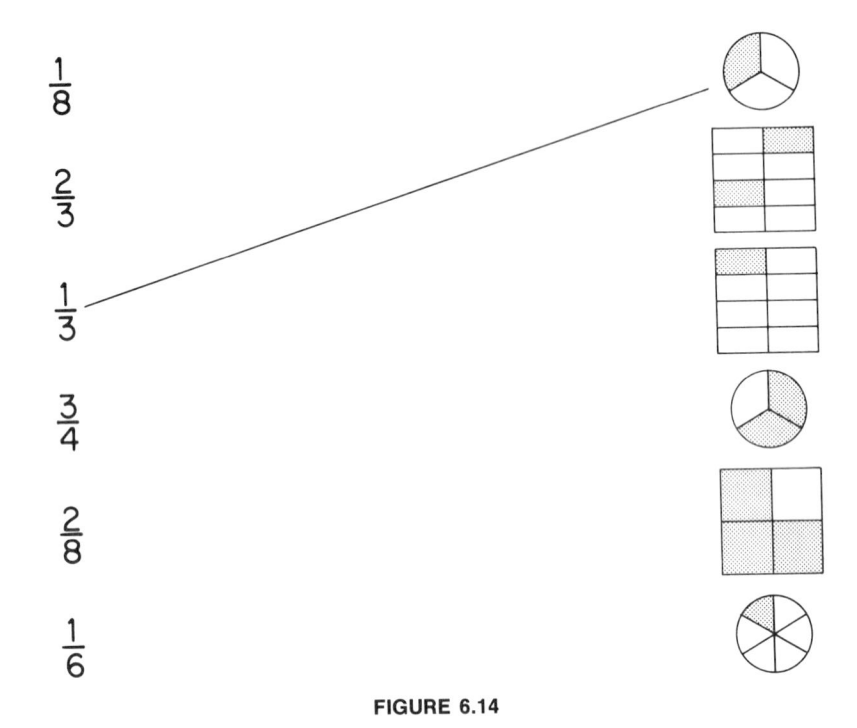

FIGURE 6.15

Fraction Line Set. A number of youngsters at the pre-vocational level will learn to work with fractions to a limited degree. However, one should be especially cautious in teaching the addition and subtraction of mixed fractions, and there is probably little justification for introducing the multiplication and division of fractions. The major goal is simply to make the youngsters aware of the relative value of fractions. The materials pictured above should prove to be valuable instructional devices for those youngsters who are capable of learning simple skills.

Comparing Fractions. Due to terminology, there may be some confusion in comparing fractions. The students have learned that three is more than two, eight is greater than six and so on. Now they learn that ⅓ is less than ½ and that ⅛ is less than 1/6 and so forth. Abundant use of visual aids and ample practice will minimize this obstacle. One simple example is seen in Figure 6.16.

Find the one in this line which is largest. Use flannel cut-outs so the pieces can be compared.

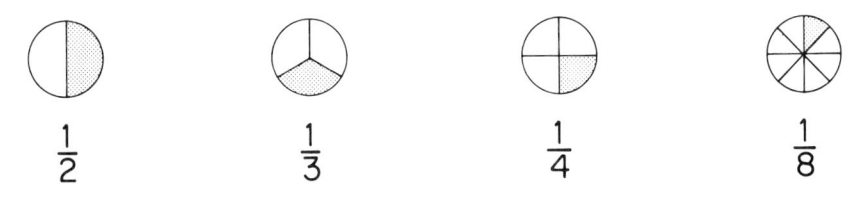

$$\frac{1}{2} \quad \frac{1}{3} \quad \frac{1}{4} \quad \frac{1}{8}$$

FIGURE 6.16

Grouping. The ideas of multiplication and division are closely related to grouping. Give the youngsters many experiences in dividing and combining sets. Give the youngsters sets of objects and have them divide them into equal subsets.

> Separate these 14 disks into 2 equal groups. How many in each set?
> Place these 15 counters into 3 equal groups. How many in each group?
> Here are 18 pennies which you should put into 6 equal groups. How many in each group?
> Here are 24 disks. Separate them into groups of 2. How many groups of 2 are there?

ORDINAL NUMBERS

There will probably not be much need to place major emphasis on ordinal numbers at the junior high school level, but the key ideas should be reviewed. The use of ordinal numbers in reading the calendar should be given special attention. Some time might be well spent on the second order use of ordinal numbers. For example, have a student indicate who is seated in the third desk of the fifth row.

MEASUREMENT

The youngsters at the junior high school level have been introduced to the basic concepts of measurements during their intermediate school years. They have been exposed to the idea that measures are used to help answer such questions as "How much?" "How far?" "How heavy?" "How long?" "What day?" "What time?" They have been shown how to measure capacity by pints, quarts, and gallon; to measure weight by pounds, one-half pounds and one-quarter pounds; and to measure length by inches, feet, and feet and inches together. They have also engaged in activities involving the days of the week, months of the year, and the practical uses of the calendar. They may also have learned to read the clock by one-half hour, one-quarter hour, three-quarter hour, and by five minutes. The first step at the junior high level is to determine precisely where each youngster is functioning in these measurement skills. Most of them will be able to deal with the measurement skills of length, weight, capacity, and time with a considerable degree of success. These youngsters will further their development by learning such skills as weighing by ounces, using the ruler to fractions of an inch, improving their use of the calendar and learning to read the clock by minutes.

Reviewing Pints, Quarts, and Gallons. The skills of measuring capacity by pints, quarts and gallons is sometimes impeded by a lack of practice with real containers.

Containers may be used to illustrate the relative sizes of pints, quarts, pecks, and bushels. Those pictured in Figure 6.17 are available through a commercial company (Ideal School Supplies) but peck and bushel baskets are easily obtained from supermarkets or produce stands.

A study of these units of measure through pictorial devices may be satisfactory for students of average intelligence, but mentally retarded youngsters need concrete experiences. It is important that the teacher keep in mind that the ideas of measurement by capacity are much more difficult than those associated with length. Two containers may vary in shape but hold the same amount while on the other hand two other containers may be identical in height but hold different amounts. Thus the youngsters are frequently called upon to overrule their visual perception through accurate measurement.

The ideas presented at the junior high level do not extend appreciably beyond those introduced at the intermediate level. However, the teacher

Pre-Adultation Junior High Mathematics 323

FIGURE 6.17

should provide the youngsters with a sufficient number of experiences with the standard measures of capacity to insure mastery. This review should be conducted with a wide variety of pint, quart, and gallon containers and a number of non-standard measures for comparison. This review should include the following:
pints in a quart
quarts in a gallon
quarts in a half gallon
pints in a gallon
pints in a half gallon.

Measuring Weight by Ounces. The youngsters will have already learned to weigh by the pound. They should now be introduced to the ounce, and the relationship of pounds to ounces.

Provide the youngsters with a kitchen scale which weighs by ounces. If a scale is not available in your school, there are several inexpensive varieties at hardware stores. Assemble a quantity of light-weight items such as letters, small packages, produce, and other confectionary items. For example, the youngsters might be given a set of six small envelopes which weigh from one to six ounces. The envelopes should be designed so that the size does not give a clue to weight.

Measuring by Fractions of a Pound. Some scales do not weigh by ounces, so the youngsters should be taught to read the weight to the nearest pound or estimate by fractions. The latter skill is probably best taught by estimating by the one-half or one-fourth pound. The teacher should prepare a number of items which do not weigh an even number of pounds. The first articles should have weight of fourths and halves.

Measuring by Pounds and Ounces. The scales which weigh by ounces generally also indicate pounds and ounces. Prepare a set of items which weigh more than one pound but do not weigh an even number of pounds. After practice, both the teacher and student may be amazed at the accuracy with which the mentally retarded student can weigh items. There is probably no useful purpose served in teaching these youngsters to convert pounds to ounces and fractions of pounds to ounces.

The youngsters should be given practice in reading and writing the abbreviations for pounds and ounces. They should have ample opportunities to read weights listed in pounds and ounces on packaged meat and grocery items.

Reading the Thermometer. The youngsters have had many opportunities to read the temperature on a variety of thermometers. At the junior high school level, the teacher should be certain that the students are able to read the thermometer and that they have some general understanding of the meaning of temperatures. They should learn something about such ideas as room temperature, cooling temperature, the freezing and boiling temperatures, and body temperature.

The best approach is to give the youngsters experience in working with actual temperature measuring instruments in realistic situations. An outdoor and indoor thermometer should be available to them. A clinical thermometer is inexpensive and should be used by the youngsters. It is important for the teacher to remember that perceptual problems may interfere with taking accurate readings.

Measuring Length. The youngsters have learned to use the ruler to determine the lengths of objects. They have been introduced to the inch and the foot as standard units of measure. They will need continued practice in measuring objects by these units. Some students will learn to determine length by inches, feet and inches, inches and fractions of inches.

The youngsters should be provided with some items to measure. Begin with items which may be measured exactly by inches and then introduce objects which do not measure in even inches. This will create the need to measure by fractions of an inch. The fractions of an inch to include are halves, fourths, and eighths. Once the youngsters have mastered the skills of measuring small items, they will experience the need to measure greater lengths. The youngsters will then need to measure by feet and

Pre-Adultation Junior High Mathematics 325

yards. The exercises which follow are examples which are representative of the types of learning experiences which may be helpful.

Measuring by Inches. The youngsters have been introduced to measurement by inches, but they should be given a systematic review. The teacher should have available a variety of objects to measure. They need not be measurable in even standard units.

FIGURE 6.18

Measuring by Fractions of an Inch. The purpose of this exercise is to teach the youngsters to measure by fractions of an inch. A valuable instructional aid is a set of simple fraction rulers made from white poster board. One includes inches only; a second is marked by inches and halves; a third is marked by inches and fourths; a fourth is marked by inches and eighths; and a fifth combines all of these fractions.

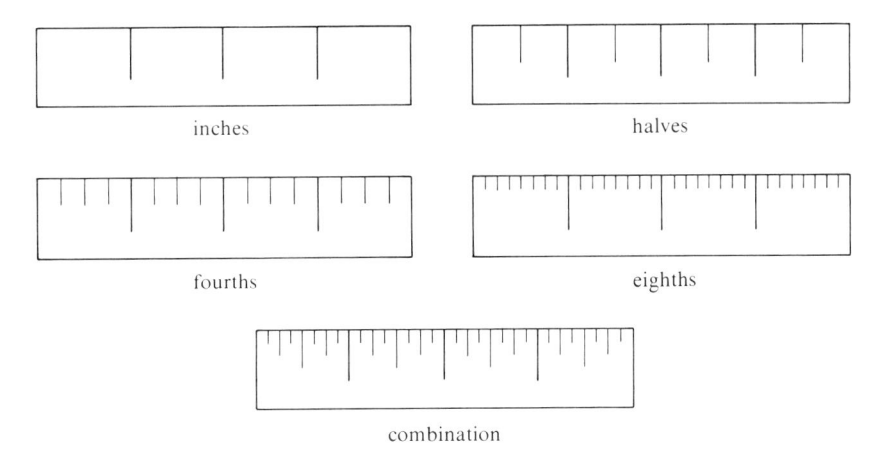

inches

halves

fourths

eighths

combination

FIGURE 6.19

The youngsters should be given sets of objects, strips of paper, lengths of string; and lines to measure with each of these until they become efficient with the standard ruler.

Measuring by Yards and Feet. The youngsters have been introduced to the yard stick. They should be taught to measure lengths by yards and feet. Begin by having them measure lines on the chalkboard since these can be drawn to exact lengths. Then have them measure the lengths and widths of pieces of tagboard, bulletin boards, windows and other surfaces within the classroom. Some youngsters may need the assistance of a simplified yardstick which is marked only by feet and inches. Others will be able to work with a standard yard stick immediately.

Measuring Length with the Tape Measure. A carpenter's tape measure is actually easier to use in determining lengths beyond three feet than the yardstick. The boys will delight in measuring heights of walls, widths of halls and so on. The girls will enjoy measuring lengths of cloth with a fabric measuring tape.

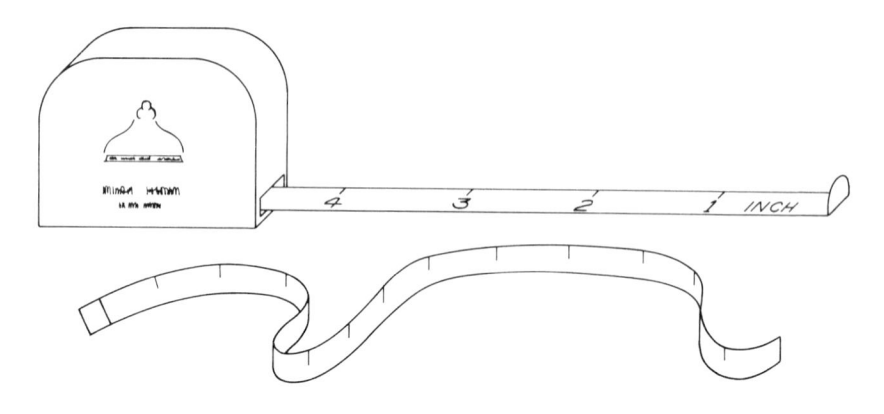

FIGURE 6.20

Reviewing the Calendar. The junior high school youngsters should have considerable facility in utilizing the calendar. They should be able to read the dates on the calendar, and understand the relationship of days, weeks, months, seasons and years. The use of significant birthdates and holidays will help make instruction more meaningful. The sequence of the days of the week and months of the year should be reviewed. Special attention should be given to the concepts of A.D. and B.C., the number of weeks in a year and the number of years in a century.

Reading the Clock. The youngsters at the junior high school level have given a great deal of time to learning to tell time. However, some will still have very minimal skills and will need further instruction if they are to learn to tell time. Much of the instruction suggested at the earlier levels will be appropriate for youngsters who have not yet progressed very far. The teacher should avoid teacher-made and commercially prepared instructional aids which are designed for younger children. Dancing bears, paper plate clock faces and first-grade clock puzzles have no place in junior high school even for the mentally retarded. However, there are many commercially prepared materials and teacher constructed aids which are not immature in design. With this caution, then, the teacher is referred to the suggestions in preceding chapters for youngsters who have not yet learned to tell time within an accuracy of five minutes.

Other youngsters are ready for instruction in learning to read time with accuracy to one minute. This is the major objective of the junior high school instruction with the clock. The junior high program, then, should survey previously introduced time telling skills, and teach the youngster to tell time by the minute.

Reviewing Reading Time. The ability to tell time is so vital for vocational and social adequacy that it is necessary to distinguish among those youngsters who have already developed the skills of telling time by the intervals of hour, half-hour, quarter-hour, and those who have not. A survey of these skills should be made early in the academic year and may include some new observations about the clock. The teacher should have a clock or two that are in working condition and several discarded clocks on which the hands may be turned. Realistic teacher-made or commercial clocks should also be at hand. Use these materials in conjunction with a series of clocks pictured on posterboard. The survey of time telling skills should be conducted with questions and activities such as those below.

> This clock indicates 1:00. Where does the short hand point? Where does the long hand point?
>
> The art class will begin at 2:00. At that time where will the short hand point? Where will the long hand point? Whenever the time is exactly on the hour, where does the long hand point? What do we know about the position of the hour hand?

Let the youngsters experiment with the discarded clocks.

> We know that the clock always moves in the same direction. We call that clockwise. Move the hands in a clockwise direction. Am I moving this hand in a clockwise direction? Now I will change the direction in which I move the hand. It is not clockwise now. We call that counter-clockwise because the hands are moving in the opposite direction.
>
> The short hand of the clock is the hour hand. In one hour it moves from one numeral to the next. It takes the short hand (hour hand) one hour to move from one number to the next number. It takes twelve hours for the hour hand to go completely around the face

328   *Pre-Adultation Junior High Mathematics*

of the clock. The hour hand is pointing to the twelve. At one o'clock where will the hour hand point? How far has it moved?

The long hand of a clock is the minute hand. In one hour it moves all the way around the clockface. How far does the minute hand move in a half hour? In a quarter of an hour? In three quarters of an hour? Where does the minute hand always point when it is quarter til the hour? At fifteen minutes after the hour? At half past the hour? What is another way to say quarter to three o'clock? How do you write the time when the clock says half-past five?

The minute hand moves from one numeral to the next in five minutes. It takes the long hand five minutes to move from the three to the four. How long does it take the minute hand to move from the six to the seven? How much time does it take for the minute hand to go from the three to the six?

Have the children complete worksheets by following the directions printed by the clocks pictured.

Put hands on these clocks to make the clock faces agree with the times written on the clocks in Figure 6.21.

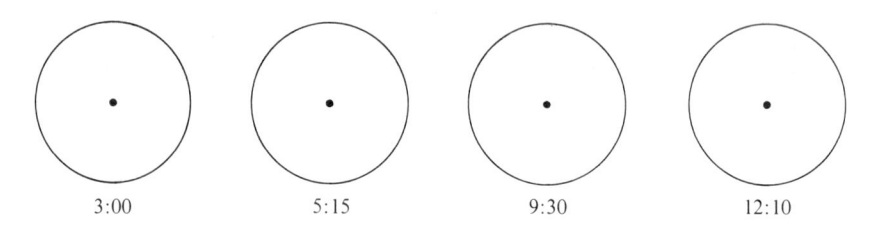

3:00   5:15   9:30   12:10

FIGURE 6.21

In the space provided beneath each clock, write the time shown on the clock face (Figure 6.22).

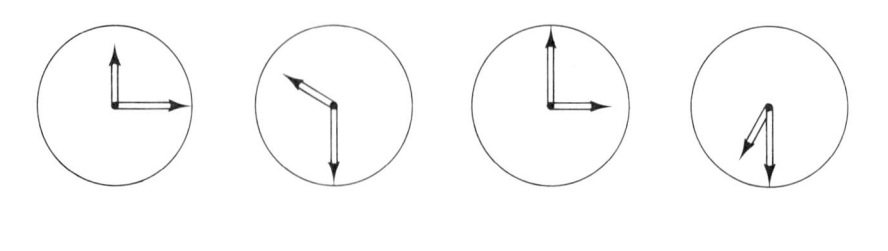

FIGURE 6.22

Pre-Adultation Junior High Mathematics 329

Put hands on the clocks outlined in Figure 6.23 to make the clock faces agree with the times shown below the clock.

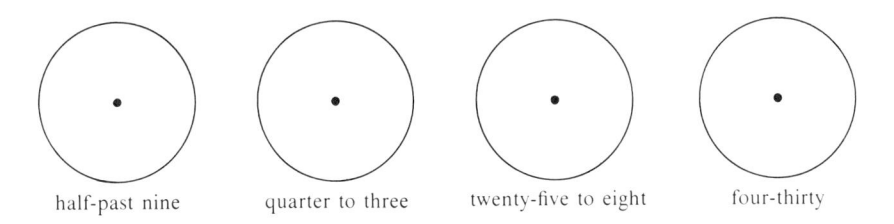

half-past nine   quarter to three   twenty-five to eight   four-thirty

FIGURE 6.23

Telling Time by the Minutes. Review with the youngsters the concepts presented in teaching about the minute hand. "The long hand is called the minute hand. Since there are sixty minutes in an hour, it moves all the way around the clockface in one hour. In five minutes it moves from one numeral (showing the hour) to the next numeral. In ten minutes it moves the distance of two numerals and in fifteen minutes it moves the distance of three numerals."

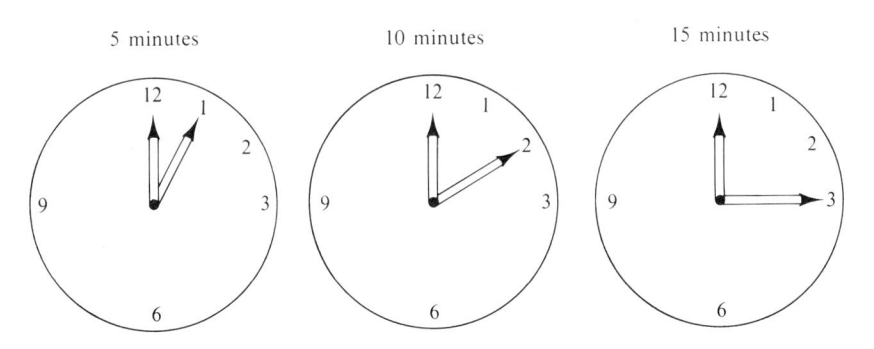

5 minutes   10 minutes   15 minutes

FIGURE 6.24

Design a pasteboard clock which has dots to indicate the minutes. Have a large one for the teacher to demonstrate with and smaller ones for each child. Explain that the dots around the clock are minute marks. "Count the number of marks on the clock. How many are there? How many minute marks in a half hour? How many minute marks in a quarter of an hour?" Since there are sixty minutes in an hour, there are sixty minute marks on the clock. Have the children practice with their clocks. Read a time, and have them set their clocks to that time. Ask a youngster to name a time and instruct the rest of the group to set their clocks to that time.

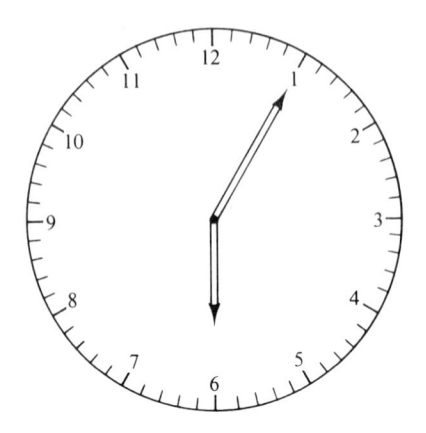

FIGURE 6.25

Activities can now be timed quite accurately. Use the classroom wall clock to keep track of the time it takes to do certain tasks. "I want you to keep record of how long it takes you to do your social studies assignment. How long did it take Bill to erase the chalkboard? How many minutes did it take Mary to take the absence list to the principal's office?"

Give each youngster a card with a direction and a time written on it. For example, "Water the flowers at 1:32." Give all of the youngsters an assignment similar to this each day. "Did Bill complete his assignment on time? Did he start too early or too late?"

Have the youngsters keep a time record of the weather on a rainy or snowy day. "Bill, each time it begins to snow, write the time on the board. When it stops snowing, write the time on the board. Let's put a cup on the outside of the window and catch the snow that falls today. Then we will be able to tell how many minutes snow fell to accumulate the snow in the cup."

Many incidental opportunities will arise during the day. Ask different children during the day to tell you what time it is. For those able to tell the time only by the hour, wait until it is exactly the hour and so forth. That way everyone will get a chance.

Ask the youngsters to help you remember the time. "Bill, remind me when it is 1:25. I want to have at least five minutes to explain the assignment before the 1:30 bell rings."

Give the youngsters practice with the Roman numeral clock. Review the numerals. Of course they will be helped since they know the relative positions of the numerals on the clock and thus they will not need to rely completely upon their knowledge of the Roman numerals. The position will be a clue to the meaning of the numerals.

Pre-Adultation Junior High Mathematics 331

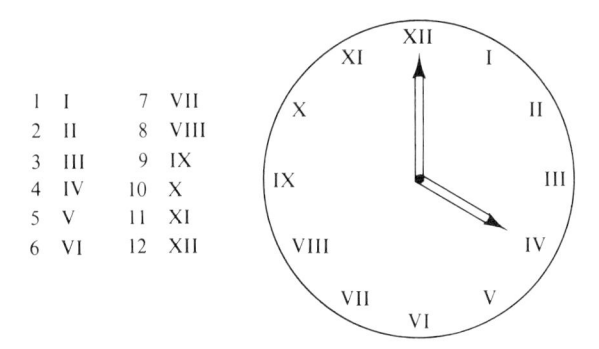

1	I	7	VII
2	II	8	VIII
3	III	9	IX
4	IV	10	X
5	V	11	XI
6	VI	12	XII

FIGURE 6.26

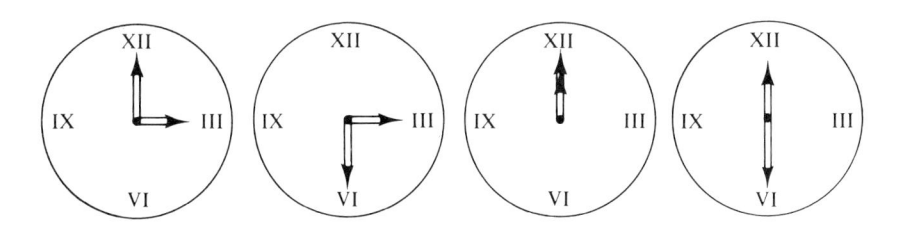

FIGURE 6.27

Here are two clocks with minimal markings. Can you read them?

FIGURE 6.28

Teaching A.M. and P.M. with the 24 Hour Clock. One of the more confusing aspects of telling time by the conventional clock is distinguishing between A.M. and P.M. Some of the youngsters may benefit from the introduction of the twenty-four hour clock which is used in aviation. With this clock, or system of telling time, 1 P.M. is thirteen o'clock; 6 P.M. is eighteen o'clock and so forth. A twenty-four hour clock can easily be constructed our of tag board and used for study. The function of the minute hand remains the same on the twenty-four hour clock.

332 Pre-Adultation Junior High Mathematics

The use of this clock will generally motivate the students and if carefully introduced will clarify the idea of A.M. and P.M.

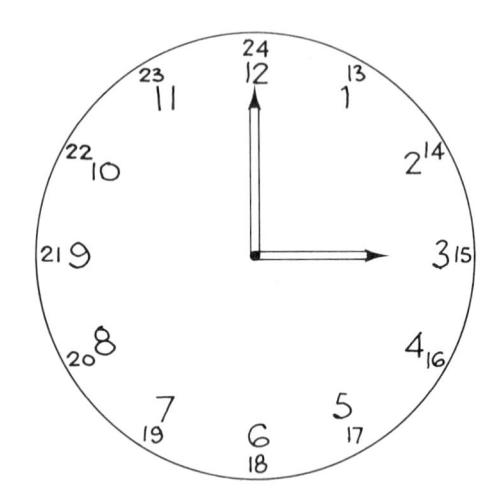

FIGURE 6.29

MONEY AND VALUE

The major emphasis with money and value at the junior high school level should be placed on making change and using money in commercial transactions. Attention should also be given to the ideas of budgeting and savings. The teacher is reminded that teenagers are especially sensitive and that the teaching of money skills should be housed in very mature terms. Specifically, the teacher should avoid the use of play money and other facsimile teaching aids which are regarded by teenagers as childish.

The exercises which follow emphasize checking and making change and problems related to such activities as operating a refreshment stand to pay for a picnic and finance classroom projects. A number of other ideas should be introduced regarding saving, earning, and spending money. However, these concepts and the ideas of consumer and earner mathematics are given major attention in the following chapter. Youngsters who are capable should move forward with these activities.

Making Change for Vending Machines and the Telephone. Here is a half dollar (Figure 6.30). In the space below draw four different ways of giving a person change for a half dollar for a vending machine.

Pre-Adultation Junior High Mathematics 333

FIGURE 6.30

FIGURE 6.31

Here is a dollar bill (Figure 6.31). Indicate four ways to make change for a dollar for someone who wants to use the telephone.

Which Would You Rather Have? Using real coins or writing the amounts on the chalkboard present problems similar to those shown below. Ask the students to select the coins they would rather have.

	these coins	or	these coins
1.	quarter, nickel, dime		quarter, quarter
2.	quarter, penny		dime, nickel, nickel, penny
3.	half dollar		quarter, dime, dime
4.	dollar		quarter, half dollar, dime, nickel, nickel
5.	seven half dollars		five dollars

Selecting the Correct Change. Prepare a list of merchandise with total costs from $.50 to $9.99. Make two possible change combinations; one correct and one incorrect. Have the youngsters select the correct change.

For example, Mary bought items in the drug store totaling $.94. She gave the clerk $1.00. Look at these two amounts of change. Which one is correct?

Cost of the Merchandise	Money Given to Clerk
$.94	$1.00
$4.59	$5.00

Point to the correct amount of change

FIGURE 6.32

Checking the Change. Prepare a cost list with various combinations of coins given to the clerk. Have the youngsters indicate if the correct amount of change was given. If not, what change should have been given?

For example, Henry bought items in the grocery store costing 38¢. He gave the clerk two quarters. Look at the amount of change he received. Is it correct?

Cost of the Merchandise	Money Given to Clerk	Change Received
38¢		12¢

Pre-Adultation Junior High Mathematics 335

64¢   1¢

FIGURE 6.33

Checking the Change. Here are a list of problems. Check to see if the amount of change received was correct. Write "OK" if it is correct and "NO" if it is incorrect.

1. 69¢ from $1.00   leaves 41¢   _____
2. 74¢ from $1.00   leaves 26¢   _____
3. 42¢ from $ .50   leaves 7¢   _____
4. 83¢ from $1.00   leaves 17¢   _____
5. $1.25 from $2.00   leaves 75¢   _____
6. $2.24 from $5.00   leaves $2.66   _____
7. $6.92 from $10.00   leaves $3.08   _____
8. $3.36 from $3.50   leaves $.14   _____

Giving Correct Change. Look at the chart below. In the first column you will see the cost of items purchased at the store. In the second column is the amount of money given to the clerk. Pretend that you are the clerk and indicate in the spaces provided, the number and kind of coins and bills necessary to give the correct change.

Change Returned

Price	Money Received	pennies	nickels	dimes	quarters	½ dollars	dollars
$ .75	$ 1.00				1		
$7.83	$ 8.00	2	1	1			
$5.20	$10.00						
$ .34	$ 5.00						
$3.61	$10.00						

Figuring the Correct Change. The price of a number of items is shown under the column below marked "cost." The amount of money given to the clerk is shown under the column marked "money given." Write the correct amount of change one would receive in each problem in the space provided under column marked "change."

Cost	Money Given	Change Received
46¢	50¢	_____
23¢	25¢	_____
77¢	85¢	_____
16¢	50¢	_____
69¢	75¢	_____

Selecting the Correct Cost. Below are some prices for items several students want to buy. The coins indicate the money each student has. Put a ring around the amount of money each will give to the clerk.

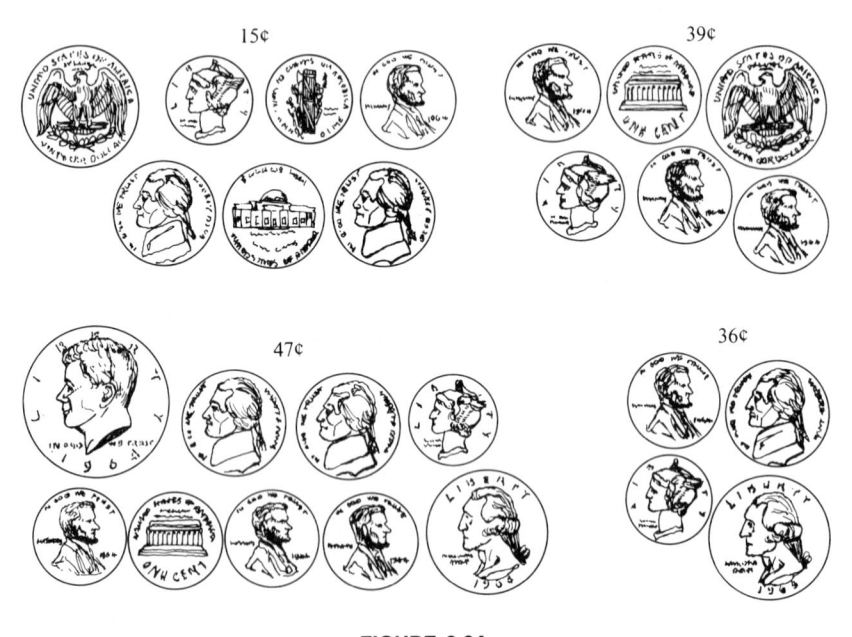

FIGURE 6.34

How Clerks Give Change. Bob buys an ice cream bar which costs 10¢. He gives the clerk a quarter. As the clerk gives Bob his change he counts, "10¢ for the ice cream bar, and 5¢ makes 15¢ and 10¢ makes 25¢."

The clerk could have figured the change another way. He would still makes 25¢."

The clerk could have figured the change another way. He would still give Bob a dime and a nickel as change.

Pre-Adultation Junior High Mathematics

$$\begin{array}{r}25¢\\-10¢\\\hline 15¢\end{array}$$

Many clerks give change by counting it out to you so that the money you gave and the amount he counts back to you (including the cost of the purchase) are the same. Here is another example. Susan bought a notebook for 29¢ and gave the clerk $1.00. The clerk gives her change as he says "29¢ for the notebook and 1 penny makes 30¢, 2 dimes makes 50¢, and one half dollar makes $1.00."

Have the youngsters count change as the clerk does with these combinations.

Cost	Paid With	
78¢	$1.00	Count out the change by
63¢	75¢	taking the cost of the item
33¢	50¢	bought and adding enough
19¢	20¢	coins to bring the amount
$2.37	$5.00	up to the money given the
$5.98	$10.00	clerk.

Checking Cash Register Tapes. The store clerk generally uses a cash register to add up the cost of purchases. There is not much of a chance that the machine will make a mistake so you should watch the clerk ring up your purchases to make certain he puts the right amount into the machine. Another way to avoid overpaying is to add the total yourself and then figure your own change.

Here are some problems to give you practice.

Sept. 1
$.18 The clerk is given $1.00.
 .22 What will the change be?
 .31
 .19
$

Sept. 2
$.17 The clerk is given $1.50.
 .24 What will the change be?
 .75
 .26
$

Sept. 3
$.14 The clerk is given $2.00.
 .42 What will the change be?
 .37
 .51
 .17
$

Sept. 4
$.42 The clerk is given $2.00.
 .17 What will the change be?
 .65
 .24
 .13
$

The Refreshment Stand. The eighth grade runs the refreshment stand at the football games in order to make money for the class dance. Their expenses and income are listed below. Answer the questions.

EXPENSES
Popcorn   7¢ box
Soft Drinks   6¢ bottle
Candy Bars   4¢ bar
Gum   4¢ package
Ice Cream Bars   7¢ each
Candy Apples   5¢ each

PRICE LIST
Popcorn   10¢ box
Soft Drinks   10¢ bottle
Candy Bars   10¢ bar
Gum   5¢ package
Ice Cream Bars   10¢ each
Candy Apples   8¢ each

They sold 200 boxes of popcorn.
They sold 354 bottles of pop.
They sold 75 candy bars.
They sold 62 packages of gum.
They sold 132 ice cream bars.
They sold 42 candy apples.

1. How much did they pay for the popcorn?
2. How much profit did they make on each box?
3. How much did they make altogether on the popcorn?
4. How much did they pay for the soft drinks?
5. How much money did they take in for the soft drinks?
6. How much profit did they make on the soft drinks?
7. How much did they pay for the candy bars?
8. How much money did they take in for the candy bars?
9. How much profit did they make on the candy bars?
10. How much did they pay for the gum?
11. How much did they take in for the gum?
12. How much profit did they make on the gum?
13. How much did they pay for the ice cream bars?
14. How much money did they take in for the ice cream bars?
15. How much profit did they make on the ice cream bars?
16. How much did they pay for the candy apples?
17. How much money did they take in for the candy apples?

18. How much profit did they make on the candy apples?
19. Which item earned the most profit for each one sold?
20. Which item was most profitable for the total sold?
21. How much profit did they make altogether?

Paying for a Picnic. Some of the kids decided to go on a picnic. Four boys each invite a girlfriend. The boys will pay for the food and the girls will cook it. Each boy will share an equal amount of the cost. Here is a list of the groceries they bought.

>   4 lbs. of hamburger @ 69¢/lb.
>   2 dozen hamburger buns @ 32¢ a dozen
>   1 bottle catsup for 18¢
>   1 jar mustard for 15¢
>   12 bottles of pop @ 10¢ each
>   2 bags of potato chips @ 49¢ a bag
>   3 onions @ 60¢ a dozen
>   3 cans of beans and bacon @ 23¢ a can
>   12 cupcakes @ 59¢ a dozen
>   1 jar of pickles for 43¢
>   1 package of paper plates @ 25¢
>   1 package of cold cups for 18¢

1. How much did they pay for the hamburger?
2. How much did they pay for the hamburger buns?
3. How much did the catsup, mustard, and pickles cost?
4. How much did they pay for the potato chips?
5. How much did they pay for the pop?
6. How much did they pay for the beans?
7. How much did the onions cost?
8. How much did they pay for the cups and plates?
9. How much did they spend altogether?
10. What was each boys share of the cost?

Making Valentines. The junior high class decided to make their own valentines. Read the story and then answer the questions.

> They spend three dollars on red and gold paper. From one large sheet of red paper they cut 12 hearts. They used 5 sheets of paper. They cut out 120 arrows, 6 each from each sheet of gold paper. They bought 5 dozen envelopes at 20¢ a dozen. They bought 1 stamp for each envelope.

> How many valentines did they make?
> How many sheets of gold paper did they use?
> How much did the envelopes cost?
> How much did they spend altogether?

Other Ideas for Working with Money

1. Have the students operate their own school supply store. Stock such items as pencils, ball point pens, ink, tablets, scissors, erasers, rulers, paper clips, notebook paper. Have the students take turns in serving as clerk. The store can be used to teach the idea of profit and loss.
2. Give the students a large quantity of change to count. Show them that they can count faster by arranging the coins this way:

Pennies in sets of 10	Nickels in sets of 5	Dimes in sets of 10	Quarters in sets of 4	Half dollars in sets of 2

   Give the youngsters equal amounts to count and see who can count their change the fastest. It will help if the sets above are regrouped in amounts of one dollar.
3. Plan picnics, trips to the zoo, parties, and dances. Have the students plan the financial aspects of the project including estimating costs, collecting money, and budgeting expenditures.
4. Introduce the idea of cost of living. Make a chart showing the cost of living for a teenager for a year. Include food, clothing, housing, and entertainment. Take field trips to clothing stores, and food markets in order to stimulate interest and get better estimates. Have the students make individual charts showing the amounts of money they spend over a given period of time.
5. Present the students with hypothetical budgets and discuss the need for a plan in spending. Construct examples of wise and foolish spending. Show the students how to make a budget.
6. Show how an average family's income is spent. Indicate the relative amounts of money spent on housing, food, clothing, utilities, recreation, and savings. Point out the need to budget for family as well as individual expenses.
7. Develop the ideas of savings. The need for saving should be developed through concepts such as saving for a rainy day, saving for an expensive item, and saving for a camping trip or vacation. Introduce the idea of the savings account, encourage saving a percentage of one's income or allowance. Introduce U.S. Savings Bonds. Present such problems as:

   In order to save $50 a year, how much would you have to save each month?
   If Mary saved 5¢ out of her lunch money for two weeks, how much money did she save?

NUMBER OPERATIONS

The basic structure of mathematics is formed by the properties of numbers. The idea of the properties of numbers will continue to be developed at the junior high school level for educable mentally retarded youngsters. Many of the properties of numbers have been previously developed in sections on the four basic operations of addition, subtraction, multiplication, and division. These ideas will be expanded with the introduction of the associative property of multiplication. The multiplication and division algorithms are presented. The ideas of regrouping, the number facts and number sentences are extended.

Addition

The children have been exposed repeatedly to the ideas of place value and by this time they have a fair command of the addition facts. The youngsters have learned that $4 + 2 = 6$ and that $2 + 4 = 6$. From this it has been shown that

$$\begin{array}{r} 40 \\ +20 \\ \hline 60 \end{array}$$ The set of 4 tens and the set of 2 tens is another name for the set of 6 tens, i.e., $40 + 20 = 60$.

It is not difficult to illustrate the further application of these ideas

$$\begin{array}{r} 400 \\ +200 \\ \hline 600 \end{array}$$ The set of 4 hundreds and the set of 2 hundreds is another name for the set of 6 hundreds, i.e., $400 + 200 = 600$

$$\begin{array}{r} 200 \\ +400 \\ \hline 600 \end{array}$$ The set of 2 hundreds and the set of 4 hundreds is another name for the set of 6 hundreds, i.e., $200 + 400 = 600$.

$$\begin{array}{r} 4000 \\ +2000 \\ \hline 6000 \end{array}$$ The set of 4 thousands and the set of 2 thousands is another name for the set of 6 thousands, i.e., $4000 + 2000 = 6000$.

$$\begin{array}{r} 2000 \\ +4000 \\ \hline 6000 \end{array}$$ The set of 2 thousands and the set of 4 thousands is another name for the set of 6 thousands, i.e., $2000 + 4000 = 6000$.

A parallel procedure may be followed to expand all the basic facts which were presented in Chapter 5.

Adding without Regrouping. Since the youngsters now know the basic facts and understand positional notation at least to the tens place, it will be easy to show that the principles which apply to addition of numbers involving two digits also apply to addition involving three or more digits.

$$
\begin{array}{rl}
132 = & 100 + 30 + 2 \\
+213 = & 200 + 10 + 3 \\
\hline
& 300 + 40 + 5 = 345
\end{array}
$$

$$
\begin{array}{rl}
1324 = & 1000 + 300 + 20 + 4 \\
+2131 = & 2000 + 100 + 30 + 1 \\
\hline
& 3000 + 400 + 50 + 5 = 3455
\end{array}
$$

The place value chart should be utilized in a fashion similar to that shown at the intermediate level.

$$
\begin{array}{rl}
123 = & 1 \text{ hundred } + 2 \text{ tens } + 3 \text{ ones} \\
+132 = & 1 \text{ hundred } + 3 \text{ tens } + 2 \text{ ones} \\
\hline
& 2 \text{ hundreds } + 5 \text{ tens } + 5 \text{ ones}
\end{array}
$$

$$
\begin{array}{rl}
123 = & 100 + 20 + 3 \\
+132 = & 100 + 30 + 2 \\
\hline
& 200 + 50 + 5 = 255
\end{array}
$$

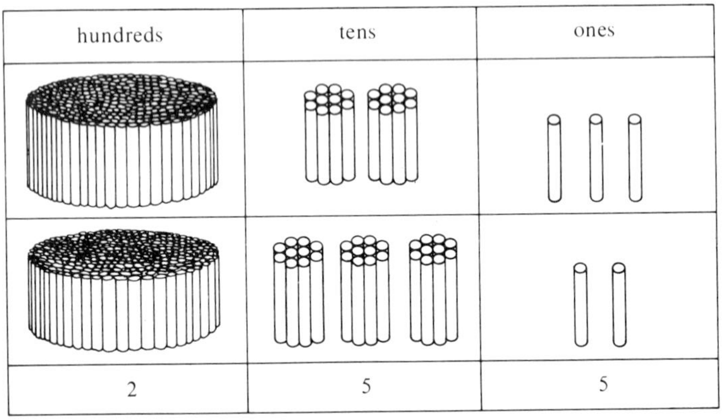

hundreds	tens	ones
2	5	5

FIGURE 6.35

The place value chart can be used to show the thousands place also (Figure 6.36).

Pre-Adultation Junior High Mathematics 343

thousands	hundreds	tens	ones

FIGURE 6.36

Give the youngsters more practice with the addition algorithm using the hundreds and thousands place

```
  432     132     123     241    1343    3431    1432
+ 132   + 432   +  15   +   7   +4321   + 213   +  56
  564     564     138     248    5664    3644    1488
```

adding with zero:

```
  402    1201
+ 210   +3010
  612    4211
```

Adding with Regrouping. The youngsters have already learned to regroup when the sum of numbers in the ones column is ten or more. The idea will be extended to the tens and hundreds columns. Just as the youngsters learned that the ones column can be overloaded, they will now learn that the tens and hundreds place can be overloaded. Whenever overloading occurs in addition, we must regroup. The following example will indicate the process to follow when the sum in the tens place is ten or more.

$$
\begin{array}{rl}
252 = & 200 + 50 + 2 \\
+461 = & 400 + 60 + 1 \\
\hline
& 600 + 110 + 3 = 600 + (100 + 10 + 3) \\
& = (600 + 100) + 10 + 3 \\
& = 700 + 13 = 713
\end{array}
$$

The place value chart will help visualize the regrouping.

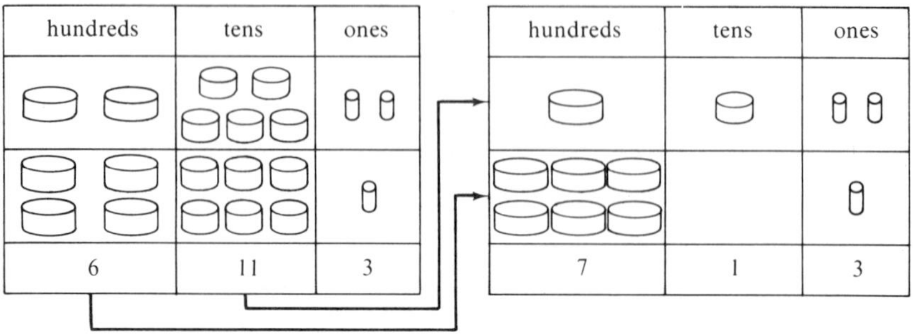

FIGURE 6.37

By this time the children have had enough experience with the place value chart, abacus and counting sticks so that, instead of the wrapped bundles used previously, different colored strips of paper may be utilized to represent ones, tens, and hundreds. This will reduce the bulkiness of dealing with higher decade numbers. Illustrate that they can add the hundreds, tens, and then the ones as shown in Figure 6.37 part (a). There are 6 hundreds and 3 ones, but the tens place is overloaded, since there are 11 tens. They know that 110 may be regrouped as 100 + 10. To eliminate the overloading, the extra 100 is moved to the hundreds place leaving the 1 in the tens place. The problem then appears as shown in part (b). The youngsters will readily see that 7 hundreds, 1 ten, and 3 ones is 700 + 10 + 3 = 713.

The same process should be replicated to indicate overloading in the hundreds place. Use the chart outline given on page 343.

Give the youngsters practice with problems such as the ones given below. At first overloading should be restricted to one place at a time necessitating only limited regrouping. Then practice should be given in multiple regrouping: ones and tens place; ones and hundreds place; tens and hundreds place; ones, tens, and hundreds place. Once the youngsters have demonstrated the ability to regroup one, ten, and one hundred, they should be taught to regroup greater numbers.

```
   Overloading in the tens place      Overloading in the hundreds place
     1           121        1           1         1          1
      145         152      1341          351      1390       2431
     +271        +163     +1282         +927     + 801      +1825
      436         336      2623         1278     2191        4256
```

Pre-Adultation Junior High Mathematics

Overloading in the ones and tens place			Overloading in the hundreds and tens place		
11	11	11	1	1	11
146	143	3272	4526	1461	1342
+275	231	213	443	72	223
421	+147	+ 126	+ 321	+ 703	681
	521	3611	5326	2236	+ 152
					2398

Overloading in the ones place by more than 1 ten	Overloading in the tens place by more than 1 hundred	Overloading in the hundreds place by more than 1 thousand
2	2	2
18	182	1632
9	51	821
+ 5	+ 83	+ 913
32	316	3366

The possibilities of regrouping becomes infinite. Once the youngsters grasp the idea of regrouping, they will have a firm foundation from which to proceed to each succeeding level of difficulty. If the youngsters do not understand the processes of regrouping they are apt to become confused and may be accused of carelessness and lack of insight whenever they make errors.

Checking in Addition. The most commonly used procedure in checking the accuracy of addition is to re-add the problem in the opposite direction. The probability of repeating the same error is reduced by adding the same set of numbers twice in opposite directions. In the example (a)

	(a)	(b)	(c)	
	4	2	4	(10)
	3	1	3	(6)
	1	3	1	(3)
	2	4	2	
	10	10	10	

the thought goes (4 + 3 = 7; 7 + 1 = 8; 8 + 2 = 10); and in (b) the thought goes (2 + 1 = 3; 3 + 3 = 6; 6 + 4 = 10). Since addition is a binary operation, adding a column of figures in reverse order changes the subsets that are actually added. This can be done, because addition is commutative, and the order of the addition does not affect the sum. Of course, in actually checking, the numerals are not reordered as shown in (b) but simply by adding upward rather than downward as shown in (c).

Subtraction

The youngsters bring a broad background to the continued study of subtraction. They have learned that subtraction is an inverse operation since it "undoes" (separates) what addition "does" (combines). Their practice with expanded notation and regrouping in addition forms the base for further instruction in subtraction. The perspective for the teaching of subtraction continues as an operation related to addition rather than as a new process. The properties of subtraction as contrasted to addition are reviewed here.

Addition	Subtraction

1. Is commutative:
  8 + 6 = 6 + 8
  14 = 14
	1. Is not commutative
	  8 − 4 ≠ 4 − 8
	  + 4 ≠ − 4

2. Is associative:
  (4 + 6) + 3 = 4 + (6 + 3)
  10 + 3 = 4 + 9
  13 = 13
	2. Is not associative:
	  (8 − 4) − 2 ≠ 8 − (4 − 2)
	  4 − 2 ≠ 8 − 2
	  2 ≠ 6

3. Has 0 as an identity element:
  (0 + 3 = 3   3 + 0 = 3)
  0 + 3 = 3 + 0
	3. Has no identity element:
	  0 − 3 ≠ 3 − 0

The youngsters should know the basic subtraction facts and understand positional notation to the thousands place. They have learned to use expanded notation to solve subtraction problems without regrouping to the tens place and it is a simple matter to show that the principles which apply to the subtraction of numbers involving two digits also apply to the subtraction of numbers involving three or more digits.

$$\begin{array}{rl} 324 = & (300 + 20 + 4) \\ -112 = & (100 + 10 + 2) \\ & \overline{200 + 10 + 2} = 212 \end{array}$$

$$\begin{array}{rl} 4324 = & (4000 + 300 + 20 + 4) \\ -2112 = & (2000 + 100 + 10 + 2) \\ & \overline{2000 + 200 + 10 + 2} = 2212 \end{array}$$

Pre-Adultation Junior High Mathematics 347

The place value chart can be utilized to show the process. Using the illustration from above:

THOUSANDS	HUNDREDS	TENS	ONES
4	3	2	1
2	1	1	2
2 (thousands)	2 (hundreds)	1 (tens)	2 (ones)
2000 +	200 +	10 +	2 = 2212

FIGURE 6.38

Give the youngsters more practice with the subtraction algorithm using the hundreds and thousands places.

$$\begin{array}{cccccc} 432 & 123 & 248 & 4674 & 5436 & 1478 \\ -132 & -22 & -7 & -1352 & -213 & -56 \end{array}$$

Subtracting with zero in the known addend.

$$\begin{array}{cccc} 230 & 432 & 5436 & 1478 \\ -100 & -130 & -2010 & -302 \end{array}$$

Subtraction with Regrouping. At the intermediate level, problems were presented that required the deliberate overloading of the ones place (regrouping) in order to get a sum in the ones column which was greater than the known addend in that column. Using expanded notation in the problem, it can be seen that six ones can not be separated from two ones but that six ones may be separated from twelve ones. The subtraction algorithm for this was also discussed at the intermediate level. After much practice, the children should be able to extend their understanding of subtraction to problems in which regrouping is needed in the tens' place and the hundreds place. The youngsters should discover that the pattern for regrouping in these problems is identical to the process of regrouping in the ones place.

$$42 = (40 + 2) = (30 + 12) \qquad \overset{3\ 12}{\cancel{4}\cancel{2}}$$
$$-16 = -(10 + 6) = \underline{(10 + 6)} \qquad \underline{-16}$$
$$ 20 + 6 = 26 \qquad 26$$

Regrouping in the tens place:

$$529 = (500 + 20 + 9) = (400 + 120 + 9)$$
$$-274 = -(200 + 70 + 4) = \underline{-(200 + 70 + 4)}$$
$$ 200 + 50 + 5 = 255$$

Regrouping in the hundreds place:

$$6358 = (6000 + 300 + 50 + 8) =$$
$$-2645 = \underline{-(2000 + 600 + 40 + 5)} =$$

$$(5000 + 1300 + 50 + 8)$$
$$\underline{-(2000 + 600 + 40 + 5)}$$
$$3000 + 700 + 10 + 3 = 3713$$

1. Algorithms for 10's   2. Algorithms for 100's

$$\overset{4\ 12}{\cancel{5}\cancel{2}9} \qquad\qquad \overset{5\ 13}{\cancel{6}\cancel{3}58}$$
$$\underline{-274} \qquad\qquad \underline{-2645}$$
$$255 \qquad\qquad 3713$$

$$6368$$
$$\underline{-2645}$$

THOUSANDS	HUNDREDS	TENS	ONES
6 🯅🯅🯅🯅🯅🯅	3 🯅 🯅 🯅	5 🯅🯅🯅🯅🯅	8 🯅🯅🯅🯅 🯅🯅🯅🯅
2 🯅 🯅	6 🯅🯅🯅🯅🯅🯅	4 🯅🯅🯅🯅	5 🯅🯅🯅🯅🯅
(thousands)	(hundreds)	(tens)	(ones)

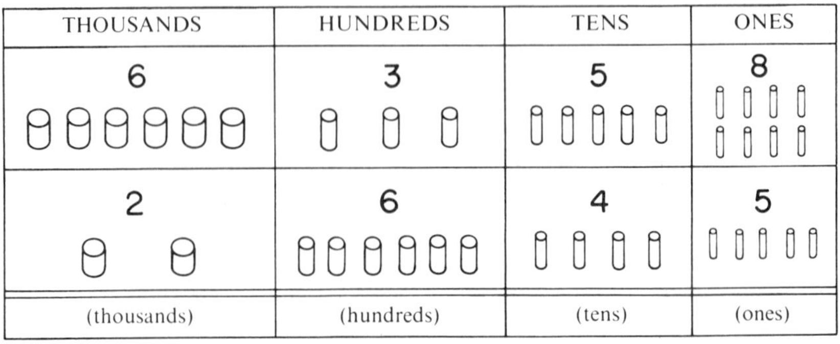

FIGURE 6.39

Pre-Adultation Junior High Mathematics 349

$$\begin{array}{r} 6358 \\ -2645 \\ \hline \end{array}$$

THOUSANDS	HUNDREDS	TENS	ONES
6̸ 5	(10 + 3) = 13	5	8
2	6	4	5
3 (thousands)	7 (hundreds)	1 (tens)	(ones)

FIGURE 6.40

1. Identify the columns to be regrouped. One needs to regroup in the hundreds place, since 3 ≯ 6.

2. Rename 6 thousands as 5 thousands and 10 hundreds, leaving 5 in the thousands column.

3. Move the 10 hundreds to hundreds column to make 10 + 3 hundreds.

4. Proceed with subtraction.

Multiple Regrouping in Subtraction. Once the youngsters have learned to regroup in the ones, tens, and hundreds places, they should learn how to regroup in two or more places. This should present no special difficulty since the same sequence applies. The example used for regrouping in the hundreds place has been modified slightly to illustrate multiple regrouping. The expanded notation and place value chart are not shown because both processes follow exactly the same method which has been shown repeatedly.

$$\begin{array}{r} 6358 \\ -2675 \\ \hline 3 \end{array} \qquad \begin{array}{r} 2\,\text{⑩} \\ 6\,3\,5\,8 \\ -2675 \\ \hline 3 \end{array} \qquad \begin{array}{r} 2\,\text{⑮} \\ 6\,3\,5\,8 \\ -2675 \\ \hline 83 \end{array}$$

1. No need to regroup in the ones place

2. The sum in the tens column must be regrouped since 7 ≯ 5.

3. Subtract 7 tens from 15 (10 + 5) tens

$$\begin{array}{r}\overset{(12)}{\cancel{2}}\overset{(15)}{\cancel{5}}\\ 6\cancel{3}\cancel{5}8\\ -2675\\ \hline 83\end{array}$$

$$\begin{array}{r}\overset{(12)}{\cancel{2}}\overset{(15)}{\cancel{5}}\\ 5\,\cancel{2}\,\cancel{5}\\ \cancel{6}\cancel{3}\cancel{5}8\\ -2675\\ \hline 683\end{array}$$

$$\begin{array}{r}\overset{(12)}{\cancel{2}}\overset{(15)}{\cancel{5}}\\ 5\,\cancel{2}\,\cancel{5}\\ \cancel{6}\cancel{3}\cancel{5}8\\ -2675\\ \hline 3683\end{array}$$

4. Again we find that the hundreds column must be regrouped since 6 $\not> $ 2.

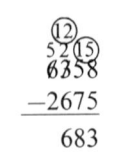

5. Subtract 6 hundreds from 12 (10 + 2) hundreds

6. No need to regroup in the thousands place

The children should have no difficulty in regrouping in the tens place since they have had much practice with this. Regrouping in the hundreds place may prove an obstacle since they have not encountered multiple regrouping before. The hundreds column has been renamed
(3 hundreds = 2 hundreds + 1 hundred = 2 hundreds + 10 tens) and the group of tens transferred to the tens position. Now it is discovered that six hundreds can not be subtracted from two hundreds. The thousands column, then, must be renamed
(6 thousands = 5 thousands + 1 thousand = 5 thousands + 10 hundreds) and the group of ten hundreds transferred to the hundreds position. The notations in the algorithm becomes somewhat cumbersome as the regrouping process is repeated for the second time. If caution is exercised to be certain the youngsters understand the process of multiple grouping, notational difficulties should eventually be surmounted.

Checking in Subtraction. The most prevalent check used in subtraction is to add the found difference, or unknown addend, to the known addend. This check is based upon the inverse nature of subtraction and as such should be nothing startlingly new to the youngsters. If there are no errors in the subtraction the known addend (421) and the unknown addend (111) will equal the sum. When this occurs the problem is said to have been checked and the found difference is assumed to be correct. Of course, it is possible to make an error in addition while performing the check. This possibility should be guarded against. Again, the whole value of this check is that it not only confirms the correctness of the subtraction but also reinforces the idea that addition and subtraction are opposite.

```
         sum      532            421  known addend
known addend     -421           +111  difference (unknown addend)
unknown addend    111            532  sum
```

Pre-Adultation Junior High Mathematics

Give the youngsters more practice with regrouping in the subtraction algorithm. It is not unusual to find a student who has special difficulty with zeros in subtraction. Even though proper experience with expanded notation should reduce the frequency of such problems, provision should be made for sufficient practice with zero as a placeholder in the problems presented for practice.

$$\begin{array}{cccc} 423 & 403 & 4634 & 5400 \\ -132 & -132 & -1355 & -\ 560 \end{array}$$

Have the youngsters check their answers.

$$\begin{array}{cccccccc} 3\,\fbox{12} & & 3\,\fbox{10} & & 5\,\overset{\fbox{12}}{\cancel{2}}\fbox{14} & & 4\,3\,\overset{\fbox{13}}{\fbox{10}} & \\ \cancel{4}23 & 132 & \cancel{4}03 & 132 & \cancel{46}\cancel{3}4 & 1355 & \cancel{3}40\cancel{0} & 560 \\ -132 & +291 & -132 & +271 & -1355 & +3279 & -\ 560 & +4840 \\ \hline 291 & 423 & 271 & 403 & 3279 & 4634 & 4840 & 5400 \end{array}$$

Multiplication

Multiplication will continue to be viewed as an extension of addition. The youngsters are able to understand this if they are frequently reminded of the renaming concept which has been mentioned so often. The number sentence 2 × 3 can be renamed 3 × 2; and 2 × 3 × 1. Renaming in this fashion effectively reviews the ideas about multiplication which were introduced at earlier levels, namely:

1. Multiplication combines sets.
2. Multiplication is a short method for repetitive addition of identical sets.
3. Multiplication is commutative.
4. The identity element for multiplication is 1.
5. The product $0 \times n = n \times 0 = 0$.

There are three major aspects of multiplication treated at the junior high level:

1. Developing the multiplication tables.
2. The multiplication algorithm.
3. The associative property of multiplication.

In the paragraphs which follow the remainder of the multiplication facts will be developed. Throughout the discussions it will be shown that multiplication is both associative and commutative. Considerable attention will also be given to the multiplication algorithm.

Developing the Remainder of the Multiplication Table. The multiplication table has been developed for products up through 18 at the intermediate level (see page 282 in Chapter 5). The youngsters can complete the table by applying the distributive property. We know that 6 × 2 = 12 and that another name for 2 is (1 + 1). With this knowledge, the distributive property of multiplication over addition can be denmonstrated.

6 × 2 = 12 = 6 × (1 + 1) = (6 × 1) + (6 × 1) = 6 + 6 = 12 = 6 × 2	(1 + 1) is another name for 2. This is another distribution property of multiplication over addition

We can now use the distributive property to show that 6 × 3 = 18.

6 × 3 = 6 × 3 = 6 × (2 + 1) = (6 × 2) + (6 × 1) = 12 + 6 = 18	(2 + 1) is another name for 3 which applies the distributive property of multiplication over addition

Other facts for the multiplication table can be developed using this principle.

$$\begin{aligned} 6 \times 4 &= \\ &= 6 \times (3 + 1) \\ &= (6 \times 3) + (6 \times 1) \\ &= 18 + 6 \\ &= 24 \end{aligned}$$

Application of the commutative property shows that 4 × 6 = 24. Recall that it has already been demonstrated that 2 × 3 = 3 × 2; 2 × 4 = 4 × 2, and so on.

These approaches permit the youngsters to complete the remainder of the table. Inspection of the table will indicate that once the students have learned one half of the basic facts, they will already know the other half. It is important, then, that the youngsters understand the commutative property of multiplication since it cuts in half the number of facts they need to learn. The parallel lines enclose the complementary

Pre-Adultation Junior High Mathematics

facts indicated only once and the facts on either side of the parallel lines show the symmetry resulting from the commutative property of multiplication.

TABLE 6.4

×	0	1	2	3	4	5	6	7	8	9
0	0	0	0	0	0	0	0	0	0	0
1	0	1	2	3	4	5	6	7	8	9
2	0	2	4	6	8	10	12	14	16	18
3	0	3	6	9	12	15	18	21	24	27
4	0	4	8	12	16	20	24	28	32	36
5	0	5	10	15	20	25	30	35	40	45
6	0	6	12	18	24	30	36	42	48	54
7	0	7	14	21	28	35	42	49	56	63
8	0	8	16	24	32	40	48	56	64	72
9	0	9	18	27	36	45	54	63	72	81

The knowledge of place value will allow the students to extend their mastery of the basic multiplication facts to a whole series of related problems.

```
2 × 4   = 8      4 × 4   = 16     7 × 1   = 7
2 × 40  = 80     4 × 40  = 160    7 × 10  = 70
2 × 400 = 800    4 × 400 = 1600   7 × 100 = 700
```

The Multiplication Algorithm. The horizontal form of the multiplication mathematical sentence has been used up to this point. Once the youngsters have learned the basic facts and a number of related problems such as 3 × 2 = 60, the vertical form should be presented.*

---

* It is acceptable to introduce the vertical form at earlier levels.

$$\begin{array}{cc} 3 & 30 \\ \times 2 & \times\ 2 \\ \hline 6 & 60 \end{array}$$

Expanded notation should be used in teaching the multiplication algorithm just as it was used to teach addition and subtraction. The youngsters will have learned the multiplication facts for two quite well by now, so expanded notation in multiplication will be understood readily using these facts in early examples. They have been introduced to the distributive property of multiplication and this concept can be utilized to teach the multiplication algorithm.

$2 \times 12 =$
$2 \times 12 = 2 \times (10 + 2)$ (10 + 2) is another name for 12
            $= (2 \times 10) + (2 \times 2)$ Distributive property
            $= 20 + 4$
            $= 24$

The process is illustrated in the example $2 \times 12 = \square$. The next step is to introduce the form for the algorism still making use of expanded notation. The same example, $2 \times 12 = \square$ is continued.

$$\begin{array}{ccc} 12 = & 10 + 1 & 12 \\ \times\ 2 = & \times\ \ \ \ \ 2 & \times\ 2 \\ \hline & 20 + 4 = 24 & 24 \end{array}$$

Associative Property of Multiplication and the Algorithm. The associative property of multiplication can also be put to effective use in teaching the algorithm. The youngsters have had background with the associative property of multiplication. Examples of this type should be employed.

Does $(2 \times 3) \times 4 = 2 \times (3 \times 4)$

Let's find out. $(2 \times 3) \times 4 = 2 \times (3 \times 4)$
                    $6 \times 4 = 2 \times 12$
                        $24 = 24$

Therefore the statement is true and multiplication is associative.

The knowledge the youngsters have of renaming and of the associative property of multiplication can be combined to enhance their understanding. Consider this example:

$2 \times 30 =$
2×30 Factors

Pre-Adultation Junior High Mathematics

$$\begin{aligned} &2 \times (3 \times 10) & &\text{Renaming 30} \\ &(2 \times 3) \times 10 & &\text{Associative property} \\ &6 \times 10 & &\text{Renaming } (2 \times 3) \\ &60 & &\text{Renaming } (6 \times 10) \end{aligned}$$

Further insights may be gained by using both knowledges: (1) renaming and (2) associative property of addition. This example illustrates the point.

$$\begin{aligned} 2 \times 36 &= 2 \times (30 + 6) & &\text{Renaming} \\ &= 60 + 12 & &\text{Renaming } (2 \times 30) \text{ and } (2 \times 4) \\ &= 60 + (10 + 2) & &\text{Renaming 12} \\ &= (60 + 10) + 2 & &\text{Associative Property of addition} \\ &= 70 + 2 & &\text{Renaming} \\ &= 72 \end{aligned}$$

Algorithm

$$\begin{array}{r} 36 = 30 + 6 \\ \times\ 2 \times\ 2 \\ \hline 60 + 12 = 60 + (10 + 2) \\ = (60 + 10) + 2 \\ = 70 + 2 = 72 \end{array} \qquad \begin{array}{r} 36 \\ \times\ 2 \\ \hline 72 \end{array}$$

Expanded notation can be used to show the multiplication of a three place number by a one place number. The youngsters should also solve the problem by repeated addition in order to comprehend the work saving value of the multiplication algorithm.

$$\begin{array}{r} 123 \\ 123 \\ 123 \\ + 123 \\ \hline 492 \end{array}$$

$$\begin{aligned} 4 \times 123 &= 4 \times (100 + 20 + 3) & &\text{Renaming} \\ &= (4 \times 100) + (4 \times 20) + (4 \times 3) & &\text{Distributive property} \\ &= 400 + 80 + 12 & &\text{Renaming} \\ &= 400 + (80 + 10) + 2 & &\text{Renaming} \\ &= 400 + 90 + 2 \\ &= 492 \end{aligned}$$

The multiplication can be simplified after the youngsters have a thorough understanding of expanded notation.

```
      123
    ×   4
       12    (3 × 4)   =  12
       80    (4 × 20)  =  80
      400    (4 × 100) = 400
      492
```

As soon as the youngsters understand the meaning of the multiplication operation, they should be able to use the familiar short algorithms.

```
      123
    ×   4
      492
```

The shortened notation and conventional algorithm shown above can be illustrated to two digit multiplication which will meet the need of most mentally retarded youngsters.

```
       34                        34
     × 12                      × 12
        8   (2 ×  4)             68
       60   (2 × 30)             34
       40   (10 ×  4)           408
      300   (10 × 30)
      408
```

The youngsters will discover that the need to regroup occurs in the steps of some multiplication problems just as it does with addition.

```
                   34
      34         × 12
    × 12   or      68           60 + 8
       8           34       300 + 40
      60          408       300 + 100 + 8 = (300 + 100) +
      40                                     8 = 408
     300
     408
```

Consider another example of regrouping in multiplication:

```
 178 =   100 +  70 +   8                       178              178
×  2  =   ×            2                     ×   2            ×   2
          200 + 140 +  16                      16 (2 × 8)       356
      =   200 + (100 + 40) + (10 + 6)         140 (2 × 70)
      =   (200 + 100) + (40 + 10) + 6         200 (2 × 100)
      =   300 + 50 + 6                        356
      =   356
```

The ten in the ones column is moved to the tens column, and the hundred in the tens column is moved to the hundreds column.

Here is one final example of the multiplication algorism.

```
         345
      ×   12
           10  (2  × 5)
           80  (2  × 40)
          600  (2  × 300)
           50  (10 × 5)
          400  (10 × 40)
         3000  (10 × 300)
         4140
```

Division

Division is the most difficult of the four fundamental operations for mentally retarded youngsters. It is not unusual for junior and senior high retardates to be completely mystified by the operation. Even the youngsters who are able to use the conventional algorithm may often become easily confused, making careless but critical errors which might have been avoided if there had been a greater insight into the processes. The instruction at the junior high level should continue to emphasize the relationships among the four fundamental operations. In the preceding section multiplication was presented as an extension of addition and here division should be presented as the inverse of multiplication. This approach does not guarantee that retarded youngsters will find division a simple skill and that they will not make careless errors. It is suggested that the errors will be more readily discerned if the youngsters are able to *see* why their errors are silly. If it is understood why something is wrong, the remedy is more easily effected.

It has been previously shown that division undoes multiplication. Division "takes apart" through repeated subtraction what multiplication "puts together" through repeated addition. The major aspects of the division operation which have already been discussed but which are given further attention are:

1. Division separates sets.
2. Division is a short cut method for repetitive subtraction of identical sets.
3. Division is not communtative (6 ÷ 2 ≠ 2 ÷ 6)
4. There is no identity element for division (1 ÷ 2 ≠ 2 ÷ 1)
   ½ ≠ 2

The major facets of division treated at the junior high level are:

1. Division is not associative.
2. Division by 0 is not possible.
3. The division algorithm.

Division is a binary operation because it combined two numbers to produce a third unique number. Multiplication is also a binary operation, and their relationship can be illustrated in a simple paradigm. Division is commonly defined in terms of dividend, divisor, and quotient. The dividend is the number divided, the divisor is the number that does

$$2 \times 4 = 8 \qquad 8 \div 2 = 4$$

$$\text{factor} \times \text{factor} = \text{product} \qquad \text{product} \div \text{vector} = \text{missing factor}$$

the dividing, and the quotient is the result obtained. However, in order to remain consistent and exploit the relationship of division to multiplication, division should be thought of as the process of finding the missing factor.

In discovering the missing factor in the problem, 2 x ☐ = 8, we rewrite the sentence as 8 ÷ 2 = ☐.

The inverse relationship between multiplication and division should be illustrated through a variety of mathematical statements similar to these:

Pre-Adultation Junior High Mathematics 359

$$2 \times 4 = 8 \qquad 8 \div 2 = 4$$
$$4 \times 2 = 8 \qquad 8 \div 4 = 2$$
$$3 \times 6 = 18 \qquad 18 \div 3 = 6$$
$$6 \times 3 = 18 \qquad 18 \div 6 = 3$$

The youngsters have made extensive use of the multiplication table and should be at ease with it. The close relationship between multiplication and division can be further demonstrated by teaching the children to use the multiplication table as a division table. Let's consider one of the examples used above. To find the solution to the sentence 2 × 4 = ☐, the 2 is located in the column of factors and the 4 is located in the row of factors. The product 8 is found in the body of the table where the horizontal extension from the 2 to the right intersects with the vertical extension downward from the 4. In division the product and one factor are known and the task is to find the missing factor 8 ÷ 2 = ☐. To make use of the table for division, the known factor 2 is located in the column of factors and the product 8 is located along the horizontal extension from the 2. A vertical extension upward from the 8 intersects with the unknown factor 4 in the row of factors. Therefore 8 ÷ 2 = 4.

TABLE 6.5

X	0	1	2	3	④	5	6
0	0	0	0	0	0	0	0
1	0	1	2	3	4	5	6
②	0	2	4	6	8	10	12
3	0	3	6	9	12	15	18
4	0	4	8	12	16	20	24
5	0	5	10	15	20	25	30
6	0	6	12	18	24	30	36

```
       Multiplication                    Division
   × |          4   (2nd)          ÷ |          4   (3rd)
     |          ↓                    |          ↑
(1st) 2 ───────→ 8  (3rd)      (1st) 2 ───────→ 8  (2nd)

        2 × 4 = ☐                        8 ÷ 2 = ☐
```

This illustration indicates the two different procedures with the table present in abbreviated form. In multiplication the factors are located and then the product is found, while in division the given factor and the product are located and then the missing factor is found.

The relationship between division and subtraction should be extended at the junior high level. Any missing factor (quotient) may be obtained by repeated subtraction. The products up to and including eighteen were presented at the intermediate level so the example 18 ÷ 6 = ☐ should have relevance. The youngsters are asked, "How many sixes are there in eighteen?" or told to "Separate eighteen into six equal sets." In both directives, repeated subtraction will achieve the correct response. When we subtract six from eighteen we get twelve; six from twelve is six; six from six is zero. We discontinue subtracting when a difference of zero is obtained.

$$18 \div 6 = 3 \begin{cases} \begin{array}{r} 18 \\ -\ 6 \\ \hline 12 \end{array} & (1) \\ \begin{array}{r} -\ 6 \\ \hline 6 \end{array} & (1) \\ \begin{array}{r} -\ 6 \\ \hline 0 \end{array} & (1) \end{cases}$$

3 sixes in 18.

The number line again proves itself as a useful device. The division of whole numbers such as 18 ÷ 6 = ☐ can be indicated on the number line by using this same repeated-subtraction method.

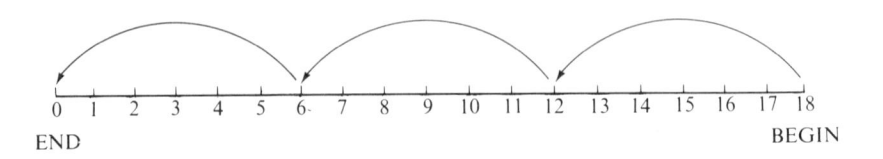

FIGURE 6.41

In this example of division on the number line in Figure 6.41 we begin at the right at eighteen (rather than beginning at zero as in multiplication) and count off groups six. Therefore, there are three sixes in eighteen.

Make use of the number line to solve these number sentences:

Pre-Adultation Junior High Mathematics 361

$3 \times 6 = \square$ $2 \times 9 = \square$ $6 \times 3 = \square$
$18 \div 3 = \square$ $18 \div 9 = \square$ $18 \div 6 = \square$

Complete these number patterns using the number line:

3, 6, 9, ___, ___, ___, ___, ___.

2, 4, 6, ___, ___, ___, ___, ___, ___.

6, 12, ___.

18, 16, 14, ___, ___, ___, ___, ___, ___, ___.

The junior high youngsters will probably prefer to use the magnet board instead of the flannel board. Many chalkboards in the junior and senior high schools are magnetized and this aid will seem more mature to them. Again consider the set of eighteen. How many columns of six are there? How many rows of six are there?

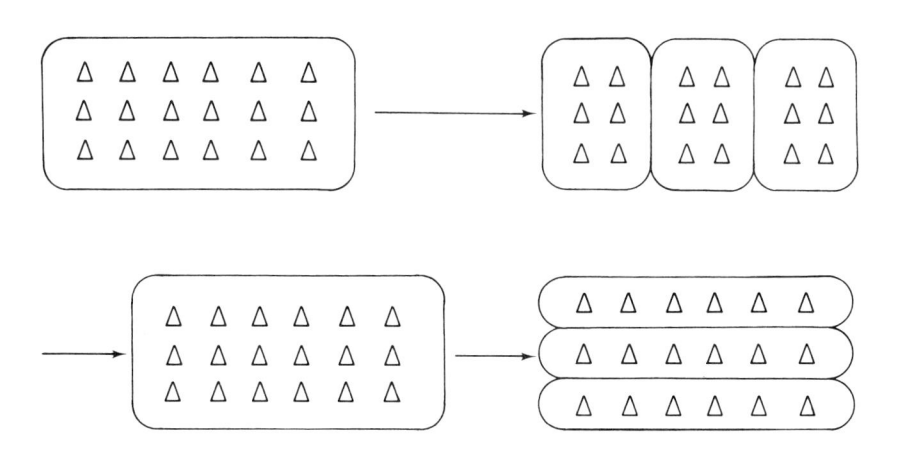

FIGURE 6.42

Here is another opportunity to reinforce the relationship between division and multiplication. It can be seen that there are several different ways we could express the relationship.

$$3 \times \square = 18 \qquad 18 \div 3 = \square \qquad 18 \div \square = 3$$

After the youngsters have experimented with these ideas, they will understand that division is a short cut for repeated subtraction. The process of separating sets is a familiar one. Division is an extension of the idea of separating sets in the special circumstance of separating a series of equivalent sets from a single set. The youngsters will not find it difficult to relate the new symbol for division ($\div$) to the symbol for subtraction ($-$).

The Properties of Division. It has been shown that division is not commutative.

$$8 \div 4 \neq 4 \div 8$$
$$2 \neq \tfrac{1}{2}$$

It is not possible to group in division as it is in multiplication. Since division is the undoing of multiplication, the youngsters should not be confused by this idea. A familiar example will make the point that division is not associative.

$$(8 \div 4) \div 2 \neq 8 \div (4 \div 2)$$
$$2 \div 2 \neq 8 \div 2$$
$$1 \neq 4$$

Since division is neither associative nor commutative, is division distributive with respect to addition? Consider the example of distribution to the right of the division sign.

$$18 \div 9 \neq 18 \div (6 + 3)$$
$$2 \neq (18 \div 6) \div (18 \div 3)$$
$$2 \neq 3 + 6$$
$$2 \neq 9$$

Therefore

$$18 \div 9 \neq 18 (6 + 3)$$

We discover that division is not distributive to the right of the division sign. But now consider the example of distribution to the left of the division sign.

Pre-Adultation Junior High Mathematics 363

$$18 \div 9 \stackrel{?}{=} (9 + 9) \div 9$$
$$2 \stackrel{?}{=} 18 \div 9$$
$$2 = 2$$

Therefore, we now discover that division is distributed to the left of the division sign.

$$18 \square 9 = (9 + 9) \div 9$$

The use of zero continues to be an obstacle for some youngsters in division just as it has been a problem in the other three basic number operations. Keep in mind that in the sentence $3 \times n = 0$, n is always zero. This statement may be rewritten for division as $0 \div 3 = n$. Since the answer for n in the first statement is zero it must also be zero the second statement. We can then say that zero divided by any number is always zero. But now consider the statement $0 \times n = 3$. There is no solution to this statement since zero multiplied by any number is zero. The statement $0 \times n = 3$ may be rewritten as $3 \div 0 = n$. Since zero times any number is always zero, there is no solution to the problem $3 \div 0 = n$. Therefore, we find that it is impossible to divide by zero.

The Division Algorithm. The mathematical sentence for division has been utilized primarily up to this point. The youngsters can now be shown that another way to write $8 \div 2 = \square$ is $2\overline{)8}$.* The use of this form for division should be grasped quickly since the youngsters have been given many opportunities to understand that division is the inverse of multiplication and a short cut for repetitive subtraction. Allow ample practice with this way of writing division statements. Since the youngsters have learned the multiplication facts to a product of eighty-one, these problems present nothing new other than the rewriting of the number sentence.

$$2\overline{)8} \qquad 4\overline{)8} \qquad 3\overline{)18} \qquad 6\overline{)18}$$
$$8\overline{)64} \qquad 6\overline{)68} \qquad 5\overline{)45} \qquad 9\overline{)81}$$

Dividing Without Regrouping. Teaching division by a one-digit number without regrouping is the next logical step. The importance of incorporating place value and expanded notation can be demonstrated through this example which makes use of the distributive property of division.

$$\begin{array}{r} 40 + 3 = 43 \\ 2\overline{)86} = 2\overline{)80 + 6} \end{array}$$

---

* It was indicated at the intermediate level that it was acceptable to use the $\overline{)}$ symbol. The advantage of delaying the introduction of the $\overline{)}$ symbol is that it protects against the rote teaching of the algorithm.

Another way to show the same example applying the distributive property is

$$\frac{86}{2} = \frac{80 + 6}{2} = \frac{80}{2} + \frac{6}{2} = 40 + 3 = 43$$

The traditional algorithm for division in examples of this type is shown below. This form should not be used until the youngsters have had ample opportunities to apply their knowledge of place value and their skill

$$\begin{array}{r} 34 \\ 2\overline{)86} \end{array}$$

in expanded notation. They should also be at ease with the mathematical sentence form and repeated subtraction for finding the missing factor (quotient) when no regrouping is necessary. In other words, the youngsters should be able to expand the example $2 \times 43 = \Box$

$$2 \times 43 = 2 \times (40 + 3) = 80 + 6 = 86$$

In a similar manner they should be able to express the example $86 \div 2 = \Box$ as

$$86 \div 2 = 2\overline{)86} = \frac{80 + 6}{2} = \frac{80}{2} + \frac{6}{2} = 40 + 3 = 43$$

Dividing with Regrouping. The previous experience the youngsters have had with expanded notation and regrouping will be invaluable in solving problems such as $2\overline{)76}$. Of course, they know that such a problem may be solved by repeated subtraction, but subtracting two from seventy-six thirty-eight consecutive times would be quite cumbersome. A shorter technique is shown below with two methods of notation.

$$
\begin{array}{r}
2\overline{)76} \\
\underline{20} \\
56 \\
\underline{20} \\
36 \\
\underline{20} \\
16 \\
\underline{16} \\
0
\end{array}
\qquad
\left.\begin{array}{r}
10 \\
10 \\
10 \\
8
\end{array}\right\} 38
\qquad
\left.\begin{array}{r}
8 \\
10 \\
10 \\
10
\end{array}\right\} 38
\quad
\begin{array}{r}
2\overline{)76} \\
\underline{20} \\
56 \\
\underline{20} \\
36 \\
\underline{20} \\
16 \\
\underline{16} \\
0
\end{array}
$$

Pre-Adultation Junior High Mathematics 365

The method illustrated on the right showing the quotient above the dividend is called the pyramid technique.

In order to find the solution to the problem $2\overline{)76}$ using the mature algorithm the youngsters must:

1. Select the largest multiple of the divisor in the tens place of the dividend. Two ones times three tens equals six tens equals sixty.

$$\begin{array}{r} 30 \\ 2\overline{)76} \\ \underline{60} \end{array}$$

2. Find the difference between the largest multiple of the divisor in the tens place and the number in the tens place of the dividend.

$$\begin{array}{r} 30 \\ 2\overline{)70 + 6} \\ \underline{60} \\ 10 \end{array}$$

3. Express the difference between the largest multiple of the divisor in the tens place and the number in the tens place of the dividend as part of the number named in the ones place.

$$\begin{array}{r} 2\overline{)70 + 6} \\ \underline{60} \\ 10 + 6 = 16 \end{array}$$

4. Select the largest multiple of the divisor (2) in the ones place of the dividend. After regrouping there are 16 ones in the ones place and 2 ones times 8 ones equal 16.

$$2\overline{)60 + 10 + 6} = 2\overline{)60 + (10 + 6)}$$
$$30 + 8 = 38$$
$$= 2\overline{)60 + 16}$$

5. Therefore

$$\begin{array}{r} 38 \\ 2\overline{)76} \end{array}$$

6. The knowledge that division is the reverse of multiplication provides the method for checking.

$76 \div 2 =$
$76 \div 2 = 38$ (as found in the algorithm above)
If $76 \div 2 = 38$ then $38 \times 2 \stackrel{?}{=} 76$. Is this a true statement?

$$\begin{array}{r} 1 \\ 38 \\ \times\ 2 \\ \hline 76 \end{array}$$

so
$$76 \div 2 = 38$$

As more examples of this type are presented the teacher should provide the youngsters with concrete materials such as counting sticks (bound in groups of tens as well as loose); and the number line. If the proper foundation has been laid and the use of concrete materials are supplemented with relevant questioning, the youngsters should be able to discover the necessity and procedure of regrouping.

The same procedure can be used to indicate more advanced forms of the division algorithm. So far the illustrations have used numbers in which the dividend is a multiple of the divisor. Consider an example in which this is not the case but which has been modified only slightly from the preceding illustration. The same algorithms apply regardless of whether or not the dividend is a multiple of the divisor. The procedure is the same as in the example $2\overline{)76}$ until the last step. It can be seen that $17 - 16 \neq 0$ but that $17 - 16 = 1$. Yet two can not be subtracted from one nor can two be divided into one. There is a remainder of one which is written next to the quotient with the designation (r 1). The algorithms are shown in three forms (a) pyramid technique, (b) modified conventional method, and (c) conventional approach.

The algorism when the dividend is not a multiple of the divisor.

```
    38              38              38
     8           2)77            2)77
    30              60   30          60
  2)77              17              17
    60  (2 × 30)    16    8         16
    17               1   38          1
    16  (2 × 8)
     1
```

A few retarded youngsters may be able to proceed to dividing by a two-digit number. This is perhaps the most difficult topic in all of computational arithmetic. The scope of the possible problems and the range of their difficulty make this a topic of questionable value for educable mentally retarded youngsters. If the topic is spaced through the primary and intermediate levels by separation of sets, repetitive subtraction, and the pyramid techniques youngsters may be able to solve such problems as $20\overline{)80}$. If the adult algorithm is presented abruptly, there will certainly be no possibility of such attainment.

Pre-Adultation Junior High Mathematics

The problem presented below will not be suitable for any but the most capable students with the richest backgrounds. It is shown here more as an example of the upper level of achievement than as a realistic goal.

```
      34              52 )1768                  34
       4                 1560   30         52 )1768
      30                  208                 1560
 52 )1768                 208    4             208
    1560  (52 × 30)         0   34             208
     208                                         0
     208  (52 × 4)
       0
```

SUMMARY

The youngsters in the junior high school have developed independent mathematical abilities. This chapter has discussed in detail how these mathematical skills can be advanced and applied to major problems of daily living. Comparatively little attention was given to perceptual skills, vocabulary, number symbols, cardinal and ordinal number. The major emphasis was on measurement, money, and number operations.

TEACHING AIDS FOR JUNIOR HIGH LEVEL EDUCABLE MENTALLY RETARDED CHILDREN

The following list of aids for teaching mathematics to junior high level educable mentally retarded children was taken largely from *Suggested Basic Materials for Educable Mentally Retarded Children*, Division of Special Education, Department of Education, State of Ohio, 1968.

The list is not intended to be exhaustive, but is presented here to give examples of the types of instructional aids which may be successfully adapted to the needs of these children.

The code refers to the names and addresses of publishers given in the appendix.

PUB-LISHER CODE	TITLE	DESCRIPTION
E-4	Fractional Wheel	
H-10	*Structural Arithmetic* Grade 3	Manipulative items and work text and teacher manuals.

PUBLISHER CODE	TITLE	DESCRIPTION
K-1	*Flash Cards*, Addition, Subtraction, Multiplication, Division	
T-4	*Arithmetic Handy Pack*	Pad which includes calendar blanks, practice check blanks, table of measures.
R-5	*Arithmetic That We Need*	Work text—emphasis on measuring, money, time and temperature.
F-1	*Money Makes Sense Using Dollars and Sense.*	Use real money!
C-6	*Quizmo* Addition and Subtraction Multiplication and Division	Lotto game using number combinations.
C-6	*Rubber Fraction Pies*	Color coded to indicate parts of whole.
S-1	*Self Teaching Arithmetic Books*, Books 4-5	Practice books.
M-10	*Tell Time Quizzo*	Played like lotto.
R-5	*Useful Arithmetic*	Arithmetic related to adult needs.
T-1	*Individual Mathematics Maintenance Problems*, Level one	Cards with problem solving situations for individual use.
M-2	*Training Fun with Numbers*, III, IV	Concepts of arithmetic are introduced and reinforced with practical work problems.
C-3	*The True Book of Money*	One copy should be on the room library shelf for reference. (Can also relate to social studies.)
C-5	*Measurement*, Level 3 *Time*, Levels 2 and 3 *United States Money*, Level 3	Liquid duplicator sheets. Good to review and refine basic ideas relevant to time, money, measurement. Basic information needed

Pre-Adultation Junior High Mathematics

PUB-LISHER CODE	TITLE	DESCRIPTION
		for successful participation in shop and home ec. classes.
D-6	*It Happened on a Holiday*	Recreational library reading that can be used to alert pupils to social uses of arithmetic. One copy.
H-3	*Growth in Arithmetic,* Book 3	Teacher's edition for guidelines in developing sequence. Some pages can be used for review of computation; most should not be used directly. Lends itself to adaptation. One copy sufficient.
H-7	*Learning to Use Arithmetic,* Book 3	Teacher's copy gives clear sequential guidelines. Care must be taken to *adapt* materials, since too many times phrases such as "The third grade planned . . . ." are used. One copy sufficient.
S-16	Cube blocks Fraction inlay boards Measure set (pint, quart, gallon) Permanent number line Parquetry blocks	
Unspecified sources	Audio-visual aids, kinesthetic aids, other resources for developing and extending arithmetic concepts and skills	
	Mounted pictures which show arithmetical situations	
	Matching kits (may be pupil made)	
	Slides	Commercial or teacher-pupil made.
	Pupil's pictures and models	Built or drawn to demonstrate arithmetical situations.

PUB-LISHER CODE	TITLE	DESCRIPTION
	U.S. coins and currency (NOT toy money!)	
	Newspapers	For food and clothing ads and for developing awareness of arithmetic in sports, theatre, and TV news.
	Thermometers	Outside; inside; cooking thermometers—candy, meat; oven thermometers.
	Calendars	
	Clocks	With and without second hand.
	Empty containers of various kinds, shapes, sizes	Including cans and packages, liquid measures.
	Measuring cups and spoons	Both aluminum and plastic.
	Yardstick Tape Measures	Steel, cloth
	Rulers Tri-squares	Marked for ½, ¼, ⅛.
	Maps—	City, county, state road maps (also used in social studies).
M-6	*At the Bank*	One copy should be on the room library reference shelf. (Also related to social studies.)
O-2	*How to be a Wise Consumer*	One of the Oxford Adult Education series, this book is designed to help develop awareness of good purchasing habits.
O-3	*Around the Year*	One copy should be on the room library shelf for reference. Relates time and seasons. (May also be useful in science.)
W-5	*Money, Then and Now*	Good for use with a more advanced group within the class. (Relates to social studies, also.) Develops concepts which are relatively abstract.

Pre-Adultation Junior High Mathematics 371

PUBLISHER CODE	TITLE	DESCRIPTION
W-11	*Understanding Time*	Single copy for library reference shelf. Good to extend concepts for the few who are ready to move beyond general class presentations.
C-9	Cuisenaire Rods and other arithmetical devices	with teacher's manual
S-4	Arithmetic readiness cards Set 3—Addition Basic Facts Set 4—Subtraction Basic Facts Set 5—Multiplication Basic Facts Set 6—Division Basic Facts	with teacher's guidebooks In addition, the pupils should be encouraged to make their own sets to work with. Two pupils can work with each other to reinforce skills.
S-11	*The Green-Eyed Monster*	A game for reinforcing telling time—can be related to school schedules and social uses in the community.
J-1	Fraction Inlay Boards Fraction Simplifier Number Lines Number Punch	
S-4	*Seeing Through Arithmetic* Special Book A	Several copies—with teacher's guide—would be useful in working with groups within the class on developing number concepts, computational skills, problem solving skills, that others in the class may already know.
V-2	*The Story of Our Calendar*	One copy for library reference shelf, for individual pupils who are anxious to get more information than is presented in class.

REFERENCES

Cincinnati Public Schools. *The Slow Learning Program in the Elementary and Secondary Schools.* Cincinnati, Ohio: Bulletin No. 119, 1965.

Kolstoe, Oliver P. and Frey, Roger M. *A High School Work-Study Program for Mentally Retarded Students.* Carbondale: Southern Illinois University Press, 1965.

Sniff, William F., *A Curriculum for the Mentally Retarded Young Adult.* Springfield, Illinois: Charles C. Thomas, 1967.

chapter 7

Mathematics for Adultation

SENIOR HIGH CONSUMER-VOCATIONAL MATHEMATICS

The criterion of functional mathematics makes its most dramatic impact in the senior high school. At no other level is the progress towards mathematical objectives more realistically evaluated. The youth's readiness for his place in competitive society comes finally to the question, "Is this young adult able to take his place vocationally in society, and does he have the skills to function as a wise consumer?"

The major thrust of the high school program is to complete the final steps to social-vocational independence. Most special education programs have associated vocational training, occupational education, work-study programs, or some comparable avenue as the major aspect of the senior high programs for the mentally retarded.

Typically, the three or four years the youngsters spend in high school become progressively more devoted to this aspect of their training. The Ohio program (1967) provides a good example of the relative time allotments to vocational and academic instruction.

During the freshman year the student is given a brief introduction to the formalized work situation through a work assignment of fifteen to thirty minutes daily. The student usually works in food, custodial services, the school office or library. By the sophomore year, many of these students will have expanded their work time to two hours. At the junior level the work-study experiences consist of a half-day in the special class setting and a half-day of on-the-job training in the community. The students spend at least a portion of their senior year in full-time work in the community with only one or two weekly late afternoon or evening seminars at school.

Of course, not all vocational preparation programs cut so heavily into the adolescent's school time. The Ohio program does illustrate the need to present instruction quite economically since the student will have relatively little time for the study of mathematics. Consequently, it is important that the curriculum relate to the immediate social and work situations which directly confront the youngster.

ABILITY LEVELS

The youngster in the senior high school will range in chronological ages from fifteen to nineteen years. The reader will note that the Table 7.1 is limited to chronological ages sixteen and below. The upper limit of the developmental period is generally accepted as sixteen years. In other words, the concept of mental age is not a relevant predictor of learning potential for youngsters above age sixteen. This is not to say that they will not continue to learn more mathematics. Mental age simply ceases to be the best predictor of that potential. The most reliable predictor of future success in mathematics becomes previous achievement. The teacher should build the curriculum upon each youngster's present level of functioning. The current status of a youngster's knowledge gives the best single guide to the next instructional step.

It can be seen from Table 7.1 that educable mentally retarded youngsters of chronological ages fifteen, sixteen and above can be expected to have mental ages ranging from seven years and six months to twelve years and nine months. The majority of these students in the senior high special education classroom will have mental ages from ten to twelve years and anticipated grade potential of fourth to sixth grade. That is to say, these youngsters will have chronological ages similar to other high school students, but will function in mathematical skills at a fourth- to sixth-grade level.

Inspection of Table 7.1 also indicates that some youngsters at this level may perform at a first or second grade level AGP = MA − K = 7.6 − 6 = 1.6. These students will be few in number, but the teacher should be alerted to their needs. The instructional suggestions presented in Chapters 4 and 5 may be helpful when planning the curriculum for these students.

In summary, it is estimated that many educable mentally retarded high school students are capable of learning mathematics at a fourth- to sixth-grade level. However, it will become apparent in subsequent paragraphs that many of the ideas important in consumer education for the retarded are well within the difficulty level of third and fourth grade.

TABLE 7.1

Mental Ages of Mentally Retarded Children Chronological Ages 15 and 16

IQ	C.A. 15	16 and up
50	7.6	8.0
55	8.3	8.9
60	8.11	9.7
65	9.8	10.4
70	10.5	11.2
75	11.3	12.0
80	12.0	12.9

OBJECTIVES

The major objectives for the senior high level are the development of social-vocational mathematics and consumer education. Relatively minor attention will be given to form and perception, vocabulary, number symbols, cardinal numbers, and ordinal numbers. The main focus of the senior high school program will be on measurement, money and value, and problem solving. More specifically, many students will:

1. Culminate the basic skills in visual motor coordination and the ability to work with geometric properties such as sphere, square, cube, and other forms.
2. Continue to develop vocabulary associated with mathematics, especially business and money terms.
3. Develop the use of number symbols to a level of automatic facility.
4. Develop cardinal and ordinal numbers to a functional level including all the common fractions and ordinals.
5. Develop skills in use of all common measuring instruments including using schedules and budgeting time with the clock, understanding the relationship of salaries, rents, taxes and budgets to the calendar, and utilization of the thermometer.
6. Understand the use of dry and liquid linear measure, especially related to cooking, sewing, and vocational usages.
7. Develop skill in one, two, and three dimensional measuring, particularly the comparative usages of such measurements.

8. Develop ability to read maps and draw to scale.
9. Use ratio in such problems as mileage and time.
10. Understand and use financial concepts at an independent level as demonstrated by the ability to make change, set up a budget, maintain money records, grasp the value of insurance, compare various systems of credit and the mechanics of financing, compute a range of taxes, and utilize banking services.
11. Develop the skills of number operations and usage including column addition, higher decade subtraction, multiplication facts through twelve and simple division.

DEVELOPMENTAL SEQUENCE OF MATHEMATICS

Most retarded youngsters at the senior high school level will understand the basic ideas of mathematics and will be able to engage in simple problem solving tasks utilizing the four fundamental number operations. In other words, they will be able to add, subtract, multiply, and divide with some degree of proficiency. The major thrust of the senior high school program is vocational and consumer education. Therefore, the categories which receive the most attention are measurement, money and value, and problem solving.

In this chapter, the same form of the mathematics checklist that appears at the lower levels is utilized. The teacher will find this particularly helpful in identifying areas of remediation for less developed students and areas of enrichment for more advanced pupils. It should be pointed out again that all the students will not accomplish all that is listed on the checklist. The teacher should place much emphasis for all students in the areas of money and value, measurement, and the problem-solving skills related to these topics. It may be necessary to return to the study of form and perception, number symbols, cardinal numbers, ordinal numbers, and number operations for students who have difficulty with those aspects of the curriculum. Naturally, the difficulty of the problems presented must reflect the computational abilities of the pupils. More advanced students may be presented with more complex problems while others will need to have their problems kept very simple.

TABLE 7.2

Checklist for Senior High Level Mathematics for Retardates

1. Form and Perception
   experience with the following:
   sphere   surface

length   area
square   perpendicular
cube   perimeter
angle

2. Vocabulary Associated with Mathematics

profit	time payment	billions
loss	social security	millions
expire	revolving charge	cancelled
insurance	time clock	twice
utilities	wheel tax	endorse
increase	job rating	perimeter
decrease	credit rating	perpendicular
deduction	deposit slip	volume
loan	bill of sale	surface
receipt	sales tax	angle
withdrawal	time tables	capacity
economical	property tax	stamps
employment	parcel post	value
payment	special delivery	lease
refund	state	annual
city	federal	installment
C.O.D.	F.O.B.	bills

3. Number Symbols
   reading numbers to five places
   reading number words into thousands
   writing numbers through 1000
   reading Roman numerals to X, L, and C

4. Cardinal Numbers
   relating numbers and groups
   knowing all common fractions
   comparing fractions

5. Ordinal numbers
   knowing all common ordinals

6. Measurement
   clock: using schedules and time tables; computing time, telling time by the second, understanding the relationship of time and distance, knowing how to set a clock.
   calendar: understanding concepts of 1/2 year, 1/4 year, century, knowing calendar relationship to salaries, rents, taxes, budgets
   weight: understanding concepts of 100 pounds and ton
   thermometer: understanding concepts of boiling point and freezing point, reading degrees on thermometer
   linear: reading maps and drawing to scale, using concepts of dimensions, perimeters, and miles, reading speedometers

dry: understanding concepts of quart, peck, and bushel weighing such things as water and sand

7. Money and Value
ability to make change to $100.
understanding concepts of per, bills, banking, installment, account, down payment, mortgage, and loans, wise buying
ability to make purchases and obtain correct change (groceries, lunches, bus fares, gasoline, etc.)
cost of recreation and maintenance, etc.

8. Number Operations and Usage
(The reader should see Chapter 6 and the sections on the unit approach)
addition: straight and irregular column addition with carrying to 3 and 4 places

$$310 + 376 + 139 =$$

```
 746      756
 513    4,320
 189    3,679
```

subtraction: higher decade subtraction up to four-place numbers

```
9,282    5,413    $90.10
3,973    4,186     62.96
```

multiplication: 10's through 12's and reverses

```
10   11   11   11   12   12
 9   11   12    8    6   12
```

two and three digits by two digits

```
87   76   197   $2.08
36   35    48     .12
```

division: one and two-place divisors

$$8\overline{)5{,}984} \quad 4\overline{)4{,}011} \quad 12\overline{)1248}$$

fractions: reducing to lowest terms
2/4   4/8   2/6   4/6

percentage: simple percentages as needed in budgeting, banking, borrowing, etc.

FORM AND PERCEPTION

It is not necessary to spend a great deal of time on the problems related to form and perception at this level. However, experiences with geometric terms and concepts will have some functional utility for certain vocational-occupational tasks. The concepts of surface, area, length, angle, perpendicular and perimeter are important to some of the skills mentioned in the measurement section of this chapter. The teacher is cautioned that some children at this level will continue to have difficulty with elementary visual-perceptual skills. When these appear, the suggestions presented in preceding chapters concerning the development of adequate spatial perceptions should be reviewed.

Most of the youngsters in special education will be very interested in learning to drive a car. Of course, automobile driving demands many perceptual-motor skills which are beyond the scope of this text. However, the teacher may wish to present some activities with a variety of road signs such as those shown in Figure 7.1. Traffic signs are standardized by geometric configuration and the students will generally need little motivation to work with these symbols.

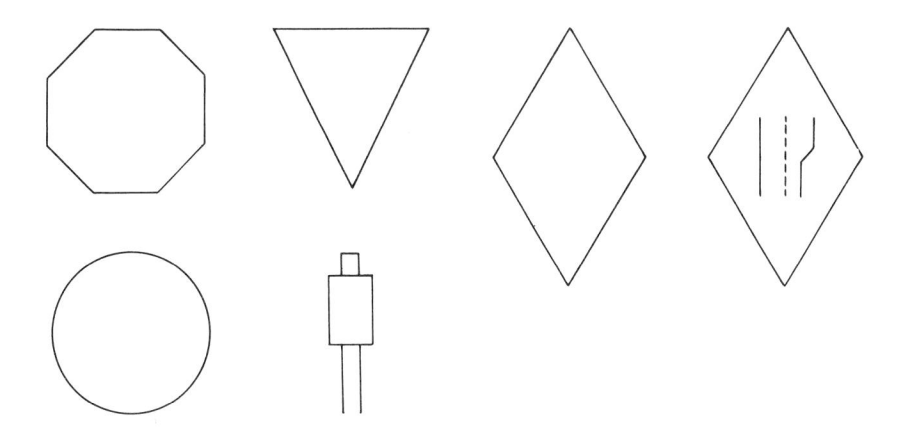

FIGURE 7.1

There are a number of other ideas related to geometry which are discussed in the section on measurement. Among the skills related to geometry which are presented in the discussion of measurement are map reading and measuring distance and area.

VOCABULARY ASSOCIATED WITH MATHEMATICS

The vocabulary associated with mathematics at the senior high school level is so well integrated with the other categories that there is little need for a separate consideration of vocabulary as a distinct category. In addition, a list of terms is presented in the senior high level checklist. The words listed are especially pertinent to the categories of measurement and money and value. The following suggestions should prove helpful in reviewing and expanding the youngsters' vocabulary.

Do not assume that high school youngsters have mastered simple vocabulary merely because they are common terms.

Determine precisely which words are essential for any given problem-solving tasks.

Measure the youngsters' comprehension of these words. Distinguish among oral comprehension, reading comprehension, oral usage, and written usage.

Systematically review terms previously learned and present new terms in a sequential, continuous manner.

Identify problem terms and give the youngsters special practice with them.

Present new words in a meaningful context.

NUMBER SYMBOLS

The major objective of this category is to teach the reading and writing of higher numbers and number words. More specifically, many senior high level educable mentally retarded youngsters will learn to read and write numbers to 10,000. An understanding of place value will serve them well in developing this ability. Some activities are listed below including the use of Roman Numerals.

Reading numbers to thousands

ten thousands	thousands	hundreds	tens	ones
1	0	0	0	0
3	0	0	0	0
4	8	0	0	0
3	2	5	0	6
5	0	7	9	2

Using the Comma. A comma is used to help make large numbers easier to read. For example: 10 and 100 have no commas. 1,000 and 10,000

Mathematics for Adultation

frequently make use of the comma. Put the commas in the numbers below. (Hint: count three places to the left starting at the ones place.)

100	87000
1000	100000
10000	343600
60000	937000
56000	870000
100.00	207065
$1000.00	$789857
$10000.00	329074
	698762

Matching Numerals and Number Words. Match these numerals and number words.

1,000	one hundred
10,000	one thousand
7,000	ten thousand
32,000	seventy-four thousand
100	seven thousand
74,000	thirty-two thousand

Matching Roman Numerals and Number Names. Here are some more Roman Numerals. Match them.

X	hundred
L	ten
C	fifty

Writing Roman Numerals. Write the Roman Numerals for these numbers

twenty-two	XXII
fifty-one	LI
38	XXXVIII
sixty-eight	

CARDINAL AND ORDINAL NUMBERS

The basic ideas of cardinal and ordinal numbers should be reviewed to be certain that the youngster understands the key concepts.

The youngster will probably need further instruction with fractions. A few activities are given below.

384   *Mathematics for Adultation*

Write the correct numeral for the shaded portion of each circle in Figure 7.2.

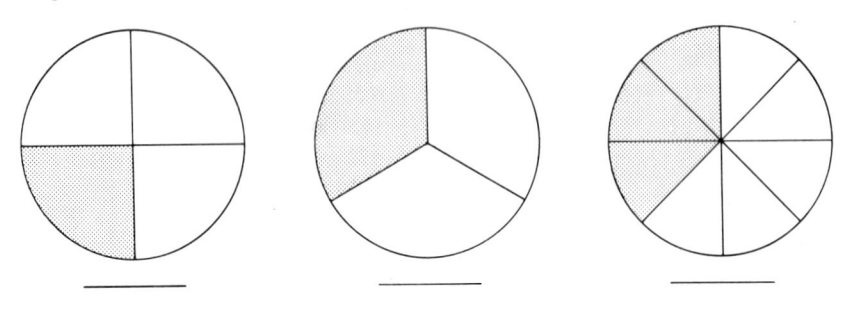

FIGURE 7.2

Shade the portion of each circle indicated by the fraction in Figure 7.3.

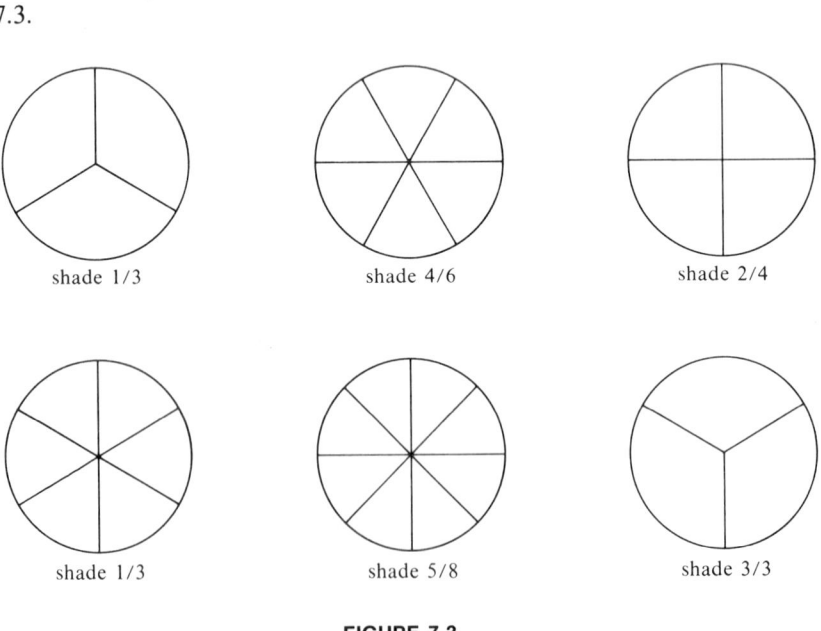

shade 1/3   shade 4/6   shade 2/4

shade 1/3   shade 5/8   shade 3/3

FIGURE 7.3

Complete these sequences

½ 1 1½ 2 2½ ___ ___ ___ ___
¼ ½ ¾ 1 1¼ ___ ___ ___ ___

Put a mark on the fraction that does not belong in the set.

¼   ¾   ½
½   ²/₄   ⅓

Put a mark (X) on the larger of each pair.

½   ⅝   ⅓   ⅔   ½   ¼
⅔   ¼   ⅛   ¼   ½   ⅜
⅝   ½   ⅓   ½   ¼   ⅓

Complete these:

$$\frac{1}{2} = \frac{}{4} \; \frac{}{6} \; \frac{}{8} \; \frac{}{16}$$

$$1 = \frac{2}{2} \; \frac{}{3} \; \frac{}{4} \; \frac{}{5}$$

The youngsters should know all common ordinals and be able to use numbers to seriate. This is especially important in working with ideas of time, such as months, seasons, days, and hours. The reader should refer to previous chapters for detailed suggestions on ordinal numbers, and consider the implications of ordinal numbers to the development of time concepts as discussed in the section on measurement.

MEASUREMENT

Young adults need a host of measurement skills in order to function independently. They will be faced with problems whose solutions depend upon the understanding and ability to work effectively with measurement in clothing and cooking, in comparisons, costs, measurement and mileage. The concepts and skills related to time are among the most crucial to be mastered by the fledgling adult. The young employee must be able to utilize the clock to plan his morning routine and travel so that he arrives at work on time. If he uses public transportation, he must understand and be able to interpret the time schedules of the city transit system. The ability to budget time can make one's social and vocational life much smoother and make it possible to avoid many conflicts. The frantic Dagwood bursting out the front door, racing down the street just in time to jump aboard a departing bus is a comic example of the confusion and frustration that may be avoided by simple planning. Just as foolish is the young lady who stands in the rain to wait thirteen minutes for a bus that passes that stop every fifteen minutes. Many young ladies shy away from very rewarding experiences in cooking and sewing simply because they are not comfortable with a few basic measurement units. The following exercises are examples of the types of activities which may be carried out to ensure the orderly development of minimal measurement skills.

Building a Recreation Room. Bob wanted to convert part of his basement into a recreation room. He decided that he would place a linoleum on the floor, paint the walls in one end and build a small room divider. The end of the basement was fourteen feet wide and he decided to come out from the back wall about twelve feet. The basement has an eight foot ceiling.

Draw a diagram of Bob's basement which is fourteen feet by twenty-five feet. Mark off the area to be used for a recreation space.

The floor covering and paint store has linoleums in rolls. The rolls are marked nine feet, ten feet, twelve feet, fourteen feet, sixteen feet. Which rolls will Bob select from? How many running feet should he tell the man he needs?

Bob selects the color of paint he wants to buy. One small can says it will cover 100 square feet and a larger can says it will cover 500 square feet. Which size should he buy?

Visualizing Cubic Measure. Some of the youngsters will be able to develop some understanding of cubic measures if appropriate visual aids are used. The instructional aids pictured in Figures 7.4 and 7.5 should serve that purpose well. (Ideal School Supplies, Inc.)

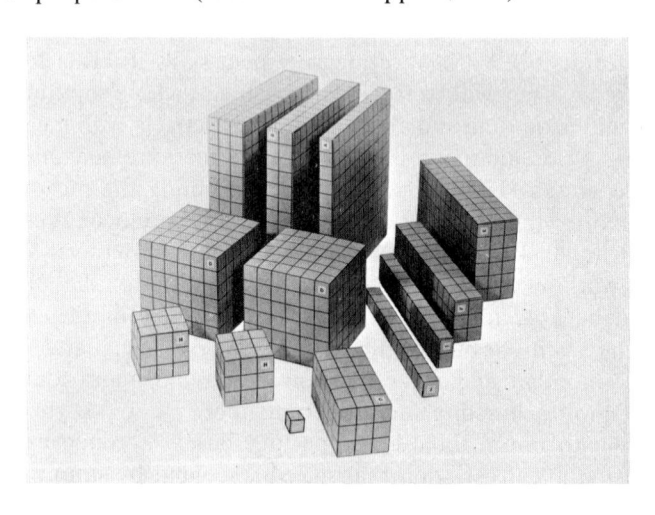

FIGURE 7.4

Mathematics for Adultation

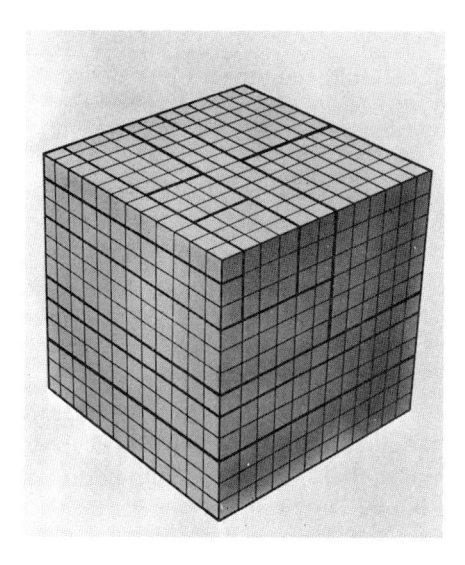

FIGURE 7.5

Conversions. Allen has a box which is one foot long. How many inches is that? Mary has a box which is one and one-half feet long. How many inches is that? How many inches longer is Mary's box?

Sue had some cloth that was two yards long. How many feet is that? How many inches?

Noon Temperatures

Week	Sun	Mon	Tues	Wed	Thur	Fri	Sat
1	30°	41°	28°	21°	33°	34°	27°
2	90°	105°	101°	98°	92°	96°	94°
3	70°	68°	72°	69°	74°	73°	69°

What time of the year do you think it was for each of the above temperatures?

Using a Room Thermostat. Most houses have a thermostat that controls the temperature for the house or the room in which it is located. Match the temperatures with the appropriate descriptive statement of thermostatic setting.

a little cool	80
about right	65
slightly warm	50
too hot	74
too cold	90

Betty feels cold so she decides to adjust the room thermostat. The thermostat reads 72. Should she turn it up or down? Which temperature should she try: 68, 70, 74, 76?

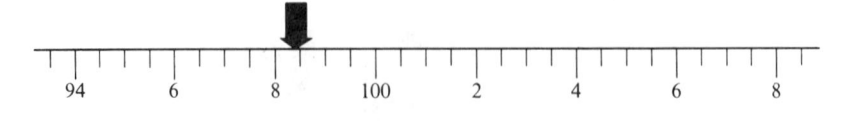

```
    ↓
|''''|''''|''''|''''|''''|''''|''''|''''|
94    6    8   100   2    4    6    8
```

FIGURE 7.6

The illustration in Figure 7.6 shows the scale on a fever (clinical) thermometer. The labels on the scale are spaced at two degree intervals and the scale is graduated decimal parts of a degree.

Why does the clinical thermometer need to be so much more accurate than the ordinary indoor thermometer?

The arrow above the scale points to the average normal temperature for an adult. What temperature is that?

When Billy had the flu, his temperature was 102.3°. Find that temperature on the scale above.

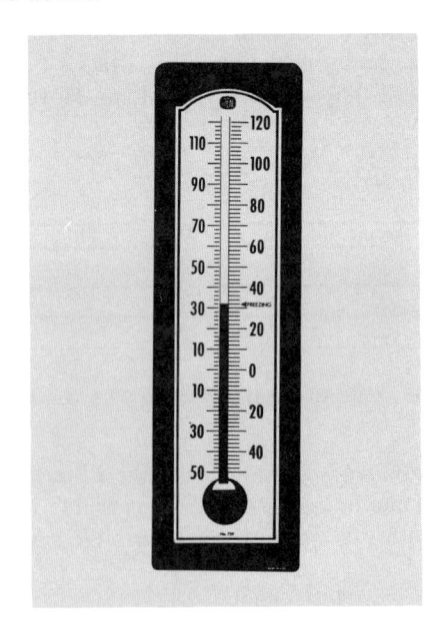

FIGURE 7.7

Mathematics for Adultation 389

Using the Outside Thermometer. Julia notices that the outside thermometer reads 85°. Will she need to wear a coat today? Match the articles of clothing listed on the right to the temperature on the left.

          90   light coat
          50   bathing suit
          60   warm coat, gloves, ear muffs
          20   sweater

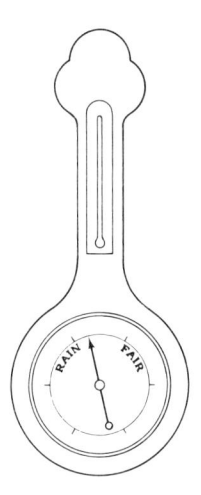

FIGURE 7.8

Reading the Barometer. Figure 7.8 is a picture of a barometer. It measures the pressure or weight of the air (atmosphere) in which we live. The average barometric pressure is 29.95. A falling barometer usually means that bad weather is coming; a rising barometer generally means fair weather is on the way.

Write the barometric pressure in the space provided.

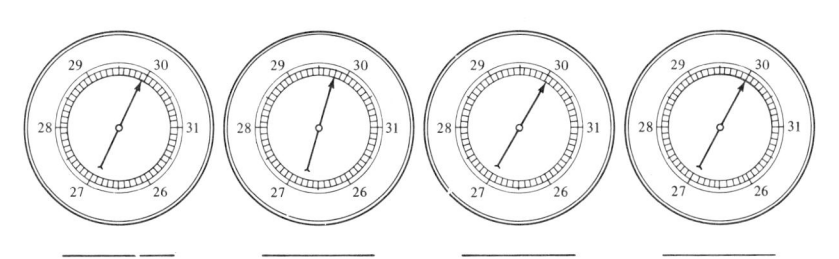

FIGURE 7.9

If an hour ago the barometric pressure was 30.00, indicate in the space provided what change you would expect in the weather. If you expect the weather to be fair (rising barometer) write the word *fair,* and if you expect the weather to be bad, write the word *bad.*

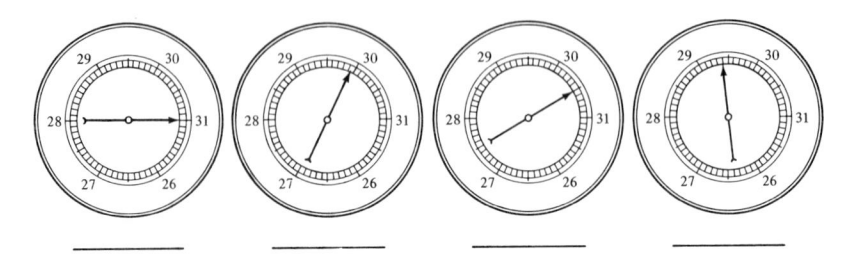

FIGURE 7.10

MATHEMATICS AND CARS

Problems Associated with the Automobile.

One problem encountered at the senior high level is providing mathematics materials which interest the youngsters. Most teenagers are fascinated by the automobile and want to learn to drive. This significant interest and motivation can be utilized to the youngsters' benefit. The problems given below serve two purposes. First, they familiarize the youngsters with some of the mathematical concepts very important to mature driving practices, and, secondly, they help the youngster overcome the deficit he might encounter when taking driver's education. The students will enjoy solving problems related to tire pressure, gasoline mileage, oil pressure, the odometer, miles per gallon, the speedometer, safe driving and stopping speeds.

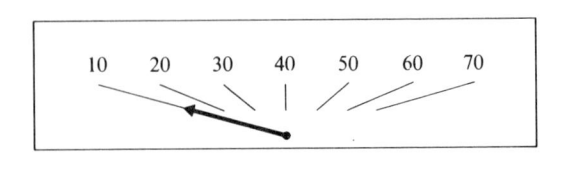

FIGURE 7.11

Speedometer. The speedometer in an automobile is presented in various ways. Figure 7.11 shows two designs. Read the speedometer on the left.

Mathematics for Adultation 391

Read the speedometer on the right. Which car is going faster? Problems on minimum and maximum speed may be used. Which car is going too slow? Too fast?

The Driver's Manual. The students will enjoy working with the state driver's manual. These booklets have a wide range of fairly simple problems related to speed, stopping distances, road signs and so on. The teacher should relate the mathematics curriculum to such problems.

Gas Gauge. The tank in Figure 7.12 holds twenty gallons. Read the gauge and indicate the approximate amount of gasoline in each tank. For example, the needle of the first gauge points to one-half. One-half of twenty gallons is ten gallons. Now you do the others.

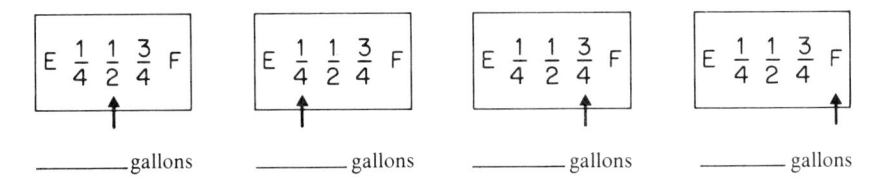

E $\frac{1}{4}$ $\frac{1}{2}$ $\frac{3}{4}$ F	E $\frac{1}{4}$ $\frac{1}{2}$ $\frac{3}{4}$ F	E $\frac{1}{4}$ $\frac{1}{2}$ $\frac{3}{4}$ F	E $\frac{1}{4}$ $\frac{1}{2}$ $\frac{3}{4}$ F
_____ gallons	_____ gallons	_____ gallons	_____ gallons

FIGURE 7.12

Odometer. On the dash of every car is a device that indicates how many miles the car has traveled. If it has not been tampered with, this device (called an odometer) keeps an accurate record of the total miles the car has traveled. It can also be used to figure the mileage for any given trip. For example, the odometer in Jack's car read 10266.5 miles this morning. He drove the car to work and noted that his odometer now read 10300.5 miles. How many miles did he have to drive to work? Now complete the exercise.

First Reading	Second Reading	Miles Traveled
10266.5	10300.5	34
24561.3	24649.0	_____
68393.0	68420.7	_____
09000.0	09005.5	_____
00538.9	00548.9	_____

The Odometer (Mileage Indicator). Frank is going to take a trip from Greensville to Mount Hope. The trip is 78 miles long. He plans to stop about half way to eat lunch. His odometer indicates 11542.8. What will it register when he reaches Mount Hope? What will it read when he stops for lunch?

Frank's car averages about fourteen miles per gallon. He has the gas tank filled (twenty gallons). How far will he be able to travel on that amount of gas? How much gas will he use to travel to Mount Hope? What will the total mileage be? How much gas will be used for the entire trip? How much gas will be left in the car when he returns to Greensville?

At the service station Frank checks his tire pressure. One tire reads twenty-two pounds. The tires should hold twenty-eight pounds of pressure. How much air pressure should he add?

Map Reading. The youngsters will find it helpful to have some skill in map reading. They should be able to use a map to the extent that they understand map legends, can find cities by using the location chart, and read the mileage chart. The local unit of the American Automobile Association, the Chamber of Commerce or a service station may be willing to provide road maps. The youngsters should begin with a map of their home town if one is available. The next step is to use a state map and then move on to a national map.

Reading the Map Legend. Many youngsters will have difficulty in reading the symbols found on road maps. It would require many volumes of printed narrative to describe the information which is coded in the typical highway map. Therefore, the teacher must give the youngsters extensive experiences in reading symbols. The size of print used to indicate the name of a city may indicate its population; the color of a highway may indicate whether it is a toll expressway or a secondary route; the outline of a pine tree may represent a national park. Most maps include an index of cities and towns which not only indicates their location on the map, but also indicates their population. It is also common for maps to provide information about state parks and other recreational facilities. The city index shown below is taken from the Rand McNally 1971 map of Ohio. State maps can generally be obtained free from service stations, travel agencies, or petroleum companies.

City Index

City-Population	Code
Adrian, 100	D-6
Athens, 23,310	K-9
Bainbridge, 1057	K-6
Chillicothe, 24,842	K-7
Dayton, 243,601	I-3
Gallipolis, 7490	M-9
Glouster, 2121	J-9

Park Legend

Ohio State Parks

	Camping	Boating	Fishing	Swimming
Adams Lake			X	X
A. W. Marion		X	X	X
Barkcamp		X		X
Beaver Creek		X	X	X	X
Blue Rock	X	X	X	X

The legend above indicates which parks have various recreational facilities. Ask the youngsters such questions as, "Which parks have fishing? Which parks have camping? Which park has boating, fishing and swimming, but no camping?"

Reading a Mileage Chart. Provide the youngsters with a mileage chart similar to the one on page 394. Have them read the distances between two points. For example ask, "What is the distance between Columbus, Ohio, and Indianapolis, Indiana? Which trip is the greater distance, Columbus, Ohio, to Detroit, Michigan, or from Columbus, Ohio, to Louisville, Kentucky?"

Have the youngsters plan a trip of their own choosing and compute mileage and time. They may be able to learn to improve their concept of mileage by relating the distance between familiar points.

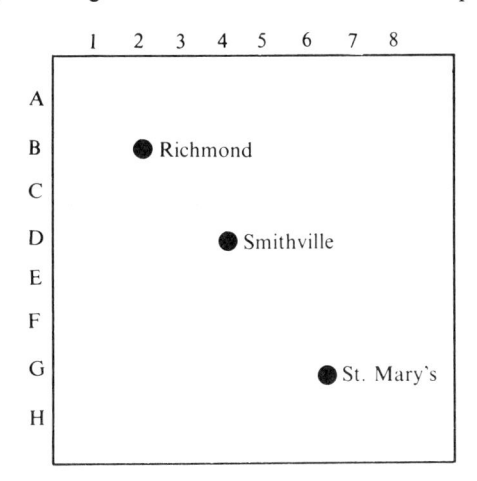

FIGURE 7.13

394 Mathematics for Adulation

	Akron, Ohio	Atlanta, Ga.	Baltimore, Md.	Birmingham, Ala.	Boston, Mass.	Buffalo, N.Y.	Chicago, Ill.	Cincinnati, Ohio	Cleveland, Ohio	Columbus, Ohio	Detroit, Mich.	Indianapolis, Ind.	Jacksonville, Fla.	Louisville, Ky.	Memphis, Tenn.	Milwaukee, Wis.	Montreal, Que.	New Orleans, La.
Akron, Ohio		668	321	698	651	207	346	226	32	119	177	288	919	336	705	435	588	1045
Albany, N.Y.	491	986	317	1080	167	286	811	707	470	605	538	761	1110	817	1186	893	231	1435
Atlanta, Ga.	668		671	154	1072	877	692	461	691	549	718	508	314	394	366	781	1212	501
Baltimore, Md.	321	671		787	399	345	667	494	351	579	498	564	795	604	949	756	547	1144
Birmingham, Ala.	698	154	787		1190	907	652	474	715	750	731	480	421	366	247	740	1288	347
Boston, Mass.	651	1072	399	1190		447	967	852	629	750	699	922	1191	962	1326	1056	316	1540
Buffalo, N.Y.	207	877	345	907	447		527	430	191	328	269	484	1067	545	909	1418	618	1250
Chicago, Ill.	346	692	667	652	967	527		292	341	306	271	186	1006	298	538	89	748	927
Cincinnati, Ohio	226	461	494	474	852	430	292		241	109	256	107	775	113	479	381	810	820
Cleveland, Ohio	32	691	351	715	629	191	341	241		139	167	295	944	351	538	427	850	1250
Columbia, S. Car.	625	215	510	367	911	770	785	517	655		733	601	297	499	720	874	1054	709
Columbus, Ohio	119	549	392	579	750	328	306	109	139	172		171	807	127	436	354	585	926
Detroit, Mich.	177	392	498	731	699	269	271	256	167	544	189	277	996	366	668	380	1029	1076
Evansville, Ind.	450	415	718	364	1076	651	292	224	462	189	444	436	1173	546	941	729	862	642
Harrisburg, Pa.	294	719	79	812	385	294	640	469	316	331	471	1173	1095	369	369	273	1340	1167
Indianapolis, Ind.	288	508	564	480	922	484	186	107	295	172	277		862	112	1011	1095	920	805
Jacksonville, Fla.	919	314	795	247	1326	1067	1006	775	944	807	996	822		708	619	387	1287	570
Louisville, Ky.	336	394	604	366	1542	909	298	109	351	127	366	112	708		1011	619	1691	710
Memphis, Tenn.	705	366	949	247	1239	1418	538	381	944	172	713	173	369	369	394	1446	939	394
Miami, Fla.	1270	665	1146	765	1542	1418	1357	1126	1295	1158	1347	173	369	1059	1287	836	939	328
Milwaukee, Wis.	435	781	843	94	1239	984	748	563	427	395	354	273	348	387	200	939	1098	1628
Montgomery, Ala.	775	173	547	1288	316	385	850	810	795	656	819	576	1340	462	334	619	1360	534
Montreal, Que.	588	1212	727	187	1123	720	447	290	567	709	585	862	351	920	1287	1446		1098
Nashville, Tenn.	515	256	1144	347	1540	1250	927	820	531	396	546	294	1340	180	200	535	1098	1628
New Orleans, La.	1045	501	1144	347	1540	1250	927	820	1061	926	1076	805	570	710	394	1008	1628	

Mileage Chart

FIGURE 7.14

* Adapted from "Eastern United States Mileage Chart" from Sohio Road Map of Ohio. Courtesy of Rand McNally, 1971.

Using the Coordinates to Locate Points on a Map

In Figure 7.13 put a mark at F,4. Put another mark at B,8. How would you indicate St. Mary's? Smithville? Richmond?

MEASUREMENT IN COOKING

Most retarded female adolescents have an opportunity to enroll in a home economics or domestic arts program. Rarely is the teacher of home economics trained in special education, and the child's ability to perform in her classroom may be improperly assessed. The teacher may have difficulty in determining the retarded child's readiness for work in cooking and sewing. These tasks demand considerable measurement knowledge and skills which the typical high school youngster has mastered. Retarded girls will need special assistance if they are to overcome the obstacles imposed by this absence of measurement skill.

In some instances the retarded girls will be grouped together, while in other programs they will be sprinkled among regular home economics classes. Regardless of the organization of the home economics program for the retarded, it is important that valuable instruction time in the home economics room not be expended on remedial arithmetic. If the youngster has been inadequately instructed before, the home economics teacher can easily become discouraged and underestimate the retardate's potential. In such cases, another failure experience will be added to the long list that the retardate has already encountered. The responsibility of instruction in measurement rests primarily with the special education teacher. The success of the retarded girl in the home economics program can largely be credited to the preparation she has received in the special education classroom.

More Measures

```
1 cup      = 1/2 pint
2 cups     = 1 pint
4 cups     = 1 quart
4 quarts   = 1 gallon
8 quarts   = 1 peck
4 pecks    = 1 bushel
bushels of apples
peck of tomatoes
quarts and gallons of ice cream
```

The student therefore will need to use common measures and fractions with facility. Especially crucial are cup, teaspoon, tablespoon, ounces, pounds, liquid and dry measures. The student must be able to read and operate thermostatic controls and properly set a timer and other common oven and range dials. In order to increase or decrease a recipe, the student must be able to multiply and divide.

Reviewing Cooking Measures. In order to be a good cook, you will have to use many cooking measures. The three most common aids are the measuring spoons, the measuring cup for wet measures, and the measuring scoops for dry measures.

measuring spoons   measuring cup

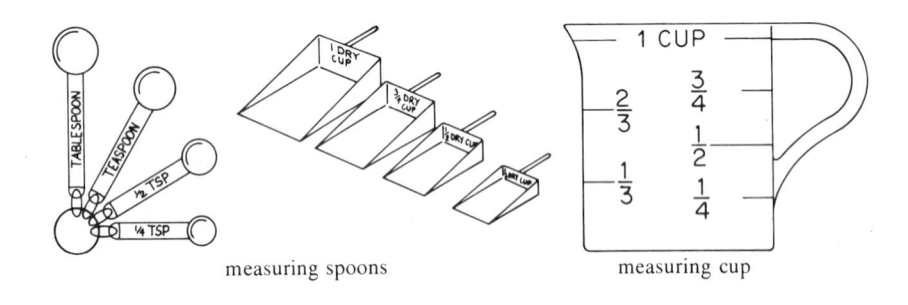

FIGURE 7.15

Good cooks use many fractions, and this table will help you answer the questions. After you learn to work well with these devices, you will find cooking much easier and more fun.

$$\begin{aligned} 3 \text{ teaspoons (tsp)} &= 1 \text{ tablespoon (tbsp)} \\ 16 \text{ tablespoons} &= 1 \text{ cup (c.)} \\ 2 \text{ cups} &= 1 \text{ pint (pt.)} \\ 2 \text{ pints} &= 1 \text{ quart (qt.)} \\ 1 \text{ cup} &= 8 \text{ ounces} \end{aligned}$$

How many tablespoons are there in one cup?
Four tablespoons is the same as 1/2 cup, 1/4 cup, or 1/3 cup?
How many cups are there in 1 pint?
How many cups are there in 1 quart?

Notice that the measuring cups are marked to indicate both thirds and fourths of a cup. Change the tablespoons and teaspoons to fractions of a cup then shade the correct portion of the cup in Figure 7.16.

Mathematics for Adultation 397

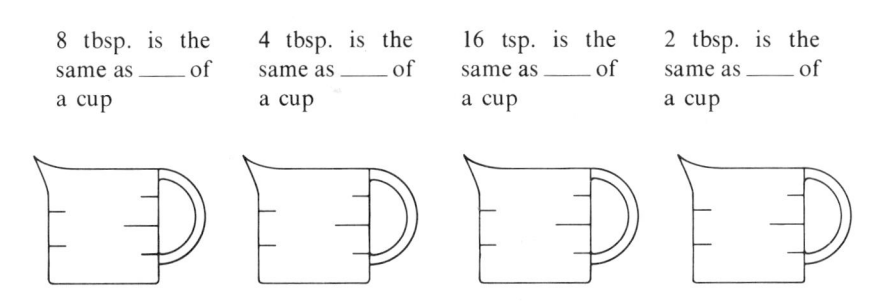

| 8 tbsp. is the same as ___ of a cup | 4 tbsp. is the same as ___ of a cup | 16 tsp. is the same as ___ of a cup | 2 tbsp. is the same as ___ of a cup |

FIGURE 7.16

The need for the use of fractions in cooking becomes quite apparent after a brief review of popular cook books. If at all practical, the students should be given opportunities to practice simple recipes. Even if the classroom is not equipped with a cooking range, the recipes may be prepared in classroom and cooked in a separate room.

Using an Oven Chart. Most recipes will indicate the temperature to which the oven should be set. However, it is helpful to have some practice in selecting a good oven temperature for cooking various foods. Use the oven chart below to fill in the blanks.

OVEN CHART	
Very slow oven	250-275
Slow oven	300-325
Moderate oven	350-375
Hot oven	400-425
Very hot oven	450-475
Extremely hot oven	500-525

Angel food cake should be baked in a _____ oven at about 375.
Custards are generally baked in a slow oven at about _____ to _____.
Biscuits should be baked in a _____ oven at about 450.
Fruit cake should generally be baked in a very slow oven at about _____ to _____.

The charts below are used in determining how long beef must be cooked in order to have it properly cooked for one's taste. The problems of the type indicated give youngsters practice in interpreting such tables.

Timing beef for rare, medium, and well done

Roasting	Temp.	Minutes per pound
Rare	325	18-20
Medium	325	22-25
Well done	325	35

Broiling Beef Steaks	Total time in minutes
1 inch	15-20
1½ inch	20-25
2 inch	30-35

Rare and medium should be 3-5 inches from heat and well done should be 5.

Thermometer Readings. If you do not wish to time your meat, but wish to know when it is ready, you can use a meat thermometer. One is pictured in Figure 7.17.

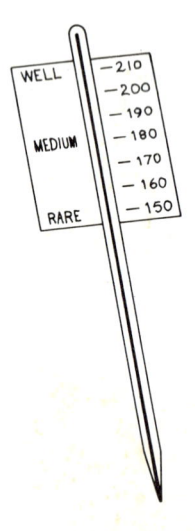

FIGURE 7.17

Beef	Temperature of the meat
Rare	140
Medium	160
Well	170

Frank likes his beef well done. Patty prepares a three pound roast for dinner. How long should she cook it and at what temperature?

Mathematics for Adultation 399

Jerry likes his steaks broiled rare. Wanda is preparing a 2 inch steak for dinner. How long should she broil it and at what distance from the heat?

Anna is fixing a nice roast for dinner for the whole family and decides to cook it medium well done. She uses a meat thermometer. What will the thermometer read when the roast is ready?

Can Sizes
   No. 1 flat = 1 cup or 8-9 ounces
   No. 300 = 1 1/3 cups or 1 pound
   No. 303 = 2 cups or 16-17 ounces
   No. 2 vacuum = 1 3/4 cups or 12 ounces
   No. 2 = 2 1/2 cups or 20 ounces
   No. 2 1/2 = 3 1/2 cups or 28 ounces
   No. 3 cylinder = 5 3/4 cups or 46 ounces
   No. 10 = 13 cups or 6 pounds 10 ounces

You can see from the illustrations above that a can is not always a can. The youngsters should not be expected to know all of the can sizes but they should have enough experience in working with them that they can use the above table.

Which holds more?
No. 1 flat	No. 10
No. 2 vacuum	No. 2
No. 10	No. 300
No. 2	No. 2 1/2
No. 3 cylinder	No. 303

The Calorie. Many adolescents are concerned about their weight, but do little about it because in part they do not really understand why they gain weight. Of course, even the retarded child knows that if she eats less she would probably lose weight. But she may become confused by the terminology and mathematics involved. Phrases such as grams of protein, milligrams of iron, calcium sources, vitamin A and B can cause the retarded girl to shy away from any plan of nutrition. A simple explanation of the calorie as a unit of measure can simplify the whole issue.

It may be explained to the youngsters in this way:

When you eat more than your body requires, it is stored as fat. When you eat less than your body requires, your fat will be changed to energy and you will lose weight.

How do I know how much my body needs?
How do I know which foods are fattening?

In order to answer the first question, the teacher can use a weight chart to determine the ideal weight for her students. These charts are generally based on the average person and large-boned youngsters may top this average by ten to twenty per cent. Slender-boned youngsters fall under it. Three simple steps may be followed to determine the amount that should be eaten at the three meals in order to lose or gain weight.

Calories for Desired Weight. First, multiply your desired weight by 15 since your body needs 15 to 20 calories per pound a day. (Mary wants to weigh 100 pounds. 15 × 100 = 1,500. So Mary should eat about 1,500 calories a day to maintain a weight of 100.)

Calories to Lose or Gain Weight. Second, in order to lose weight, reduce this amount by one-third. That is, multiply your answer in step one by .33 and subtract this amount from the calories for your desired weight.

Mary actually weighs 110 pounds and she would like to lose 5 pounds. In order to do that she needs to eat less than 1500 calories per day. 1/3 of 1500 is 1000. If she were to reduce her calories to 1000 per day she would lose weight. She wants a good breakfast, so she plans to have 200 calories for breakfast, 300 calories for lunch, and 500 calories for dinner. She should begin to lose weight soon and once she has reduced to 105 pounds, she may return to eating 1500 calories a day.

Measurement for Clothing

Most adults know their basic clothes sizes, but even in cases of uncertainty it creates no problem since it is easy to have one's measurements taken. Actually, measurements are more accurate when taken by someone else such as an experienced clothes sales clerk. When ordering from a mail-order house, it may be necessary to take one's own measurements. The guidelines are available in department stores such as Sears and Wards.

Shoe Sizes. The youngsters should also learn something about shoe sizes. The teacher will probably be able to recruit a salesman from a local shoe store to visit the class to discuss shoes and their fitting. If this is not possible, the teacher should borrow a shoe measuring device, and conduct related activities with her students. This will help develop their self-concept and improve their ability to handle their own affairs independently.

Sewing

The objective of the mathematics instructor is not to teach her students how to sew, but rather to make certain that they have the measurement skills to handle the task. The mathematical skills necessary include use of the tape measure, following directions in sequence, measuring by an inch and fraction of an inch (fourths, eighths, halves).

The teacher should avoid teaching beginning sewing with doll clothes but should begin with such simple activities as making aprons and towels. Once the students have the mechanics, they should proceed to sewing simple patterns.

Calendar

The ideas of the calendar should be reviewed and integrated with regularly occurring activities such as paying taxes, monthly bills, savings, and budgeting.

Telling Time—Senior High Level, EMR

The senior high school youngsters will already be able to read the clock with a fairly high degree of accuracy. Many will be able to tell time to one minute but others will not have progressed to this level. The techniques for teaching the telling of time to within one minute are described in previous chapters. The steps discussed in the preceding sections apply to youngsters at this level who have not yet learned to tell time by the minute and hour. However, the teacher should be aware of the pitfalls involved in using teacher aids intended for younger children.

The new skills which should be introduced to the youngsters who have mastered the telling of time to within the minute include:

1. Telling time by seconds
2. Understanding time zones
3. Using the clock to budget time for
   study and recreation
   household chores
   work
   travel
4. Using the clock to figure the time card
5. A.M. or P.M.

Telling Time by the Second. The concepts presented in teaching about the hour and minute hand should be reviewed with the youngsters. The knowledge that there are sixty minutes in an hour will help the youngsters understand that there are sixty seconds in a minute. It is somewhat less complex to teach the time elapse of a second since it is so brief. Give the children sample practice in estimating seconds. "I am going to count the seconds you can hold your breath. How many circles can you draw in thirty seconds? How many seconds can you stand on one foot?"

Show the children several clocks with a second hand.

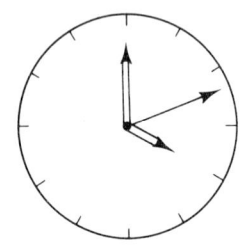

FIGURE 7.18

"What do you notice that is different about this clock? That's correct. It has three hands. You have already learned to read the minute and hour hand. The third hand is the *second hand.* You know how long a second is; this third hand tells exactly what second it is. See the second hand goes all the way around the face of the clock every minute."

There are ____ minutes in each hour.
There are ____ seconds in each minute.
There are ____ seconds in two minutes.

Which hand moves the fastest: the minute, hour, or second hand?

All of these clocks in Figure 7.19 say one o'clock. The first clock indicates one o'clock and no seconds. The second clock indicates that it is fifteen seconds after one o'clock. Write the times of the other clocks.

0 seconds after one   15 seconds after one   ___ seconds after one   ___ seconds after one   ___ seconds after one

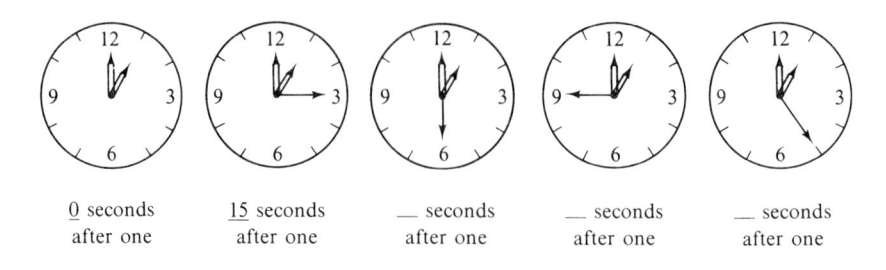

FIGURE 7.19

Mathematics for Adultation 403

The youngsters will probably have been exposed to the concepts of parallels of latitude and meridians of longitude in their study of geography. The meridians are used to designate time belts. A day is the time which elapses while the earth makes one complete revolution of 360°. Since the day is divided into 24 hours, in one hour the earth revolves 15°. Noon is the time when the sun lies directly above a meridian. The standard practice is to establish a time belt for each 15° of longitude which accounts for a difference of exactly one hour between each belt. In the United States there are five such belts important in telling time. In general, all the places within a given time zone have the same standard time. The time from one zone to the next varies by one hour.

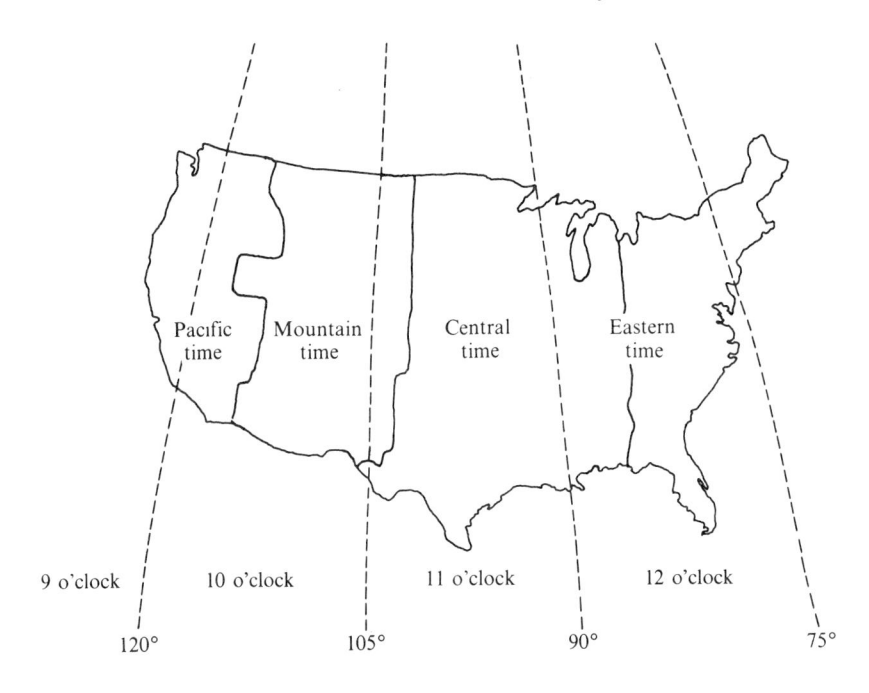

FIGURE 7.20

The dividing lines are somewhat irregular since many communities near borders of the zones find it convenient to use the time designations of neighboring communities and commercial centers. The illustration above shows the time zones in the United States and the meridians of longitude which approximate the zones. When it is 11 A.M. Central Standard time, it is 10 A.M. Mountain Standard time, 9 A.M. Pacific Standard time and 12 P.M. Eastern Standard time. The youngsters will encounter such terms as "Eastern Standard time" and Mountain Standard time" while listening to announcements of radio program scheduling, viewing the weather reports on television, figuring airline or bus schedules, and reading about national events in the newspaper.

Here is a problem which will help them understand the idea of time zones.

Billy lives in California. His clock indicates that it is 6 P.M. What time is it in New York, where his Aunt Mary lives?

The earth's surface has been divided into standard time zones by international agreement. In general, all the places within a given time zone have the same standard time. The time from one zone to the next varies by one hour.

Mark the clockfaces in Figure 7.21 to show the standard time in each of the time zones shown when it is three P.M. Central Standard time.

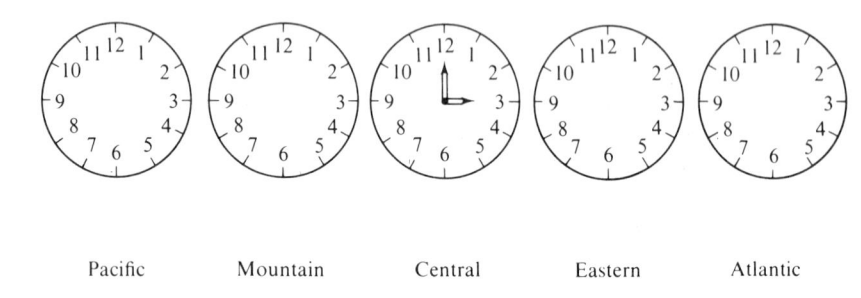

Pacific   Mountain   Central   Eastern   Atlantic

FIGURE 7.21

An idea closely associated with time zones is standard and daylight savings time. With the national trend towards uniform time practices, it is important that the youngsters have a firm grasp of the daylight savings time practice.

When do we go on daylight savings time?
Why do we have daylight savings time?
On what date do we change from standard time to daylight savings time?
On what date do we change from daylight savings time to standard time?

Mathematics for Adultation 405

It is essential that the senior high school youngsters learn to relate their understanding of time concepts and devices to everyday problems. They should be able to plan the amount of time spent on their job, with their studies, in recreation, and with household chores. Further, they should be able to compute the amount of time they spend in such activities as travel, eating, and sleeping. (This will aid them in learning to budget their time wisely.) The time related concepts and skills the youngsters have learned should be applied to such vocational problems as figuring out a time card, figuring out overtime pay, and social tasks such as planning train and bus travels.

Some illustrative problems are given below.

Bob has maintained a complete time record of his activities yesterday. He went to bed at 10:00 P.M. and he got out of bed at 6:30 A.M. He brushed his teeth, washed and dressed and ate breakfast at 7:00. He walked to the corner to meet the school bus at 7:15. The bus arrived at 7:30. He arrived at school at 8:00 . . . . . and so on. How much time did he spend sleeping? How much time did he spend traveling? How much time did he spend in school? and so on.

Tom lives eight blocks from school. It takes him two minutes to walk one block. How long does it take him to walk to school?

Judy is going to bake some cookies. She spends ten minutes mixing the ingredients and warming the oven. The recipe says to bake the cookies for twenty minutes. She wants to take the cookies with her to school for the bake sale. She is going to bake them in the morning so they will be nice and fresh. How much earlier than usual will she have to get up in order to have enough time to bake the cookies and still meet the school bus on time?

Jerry decides that he needs to spend more time studying. Since he has a part time job, plays on the football team, and has a number of household chores, he must budget this time wisely. Let's look at how he spends his time and help him plan his time for the additional half hour of study.

John wishes to travel from Kansas City to St. Louis to visit a friend. He decides to go by train. He wishes to leave for St. Louis as soon after work as he can. He gets off work at 4:00 and is 45 minutes from the train depot. He wants to come home as late as he can on Sunday, but still be back in Kansas City in time for the 8:30 P.M. bus. Use the table.

Friday, Saturday, Sunday

Leaves Kansas City	Arrives St. Louis	Leaves St. Louis	Arrives Kansas City
4:00	8:00	4:00	8:00
5:00	9:00	5:00	9:00
6:00	10:00	6:00	10:00
7:00	11:00	7:00	11:00
8:00	12:00	8:00	12:00
9:00	1:00	9:00	1:00

1. What time will he leave Kansas City?
2. What time will he arrive in St. Louis?
3. What time will he leave St. Louis?
4. What time will he return to Kansas City?

Here is Tom's time card. Tom is paid $2.50 an hour. Let's use the time card to figure his pay for the week.

Name _____ Payroll # _____

Week Ending _____ 19___
              month   day   year

	A.M. (Morning) IN	OUT	P.M. (Afternoon) IN	OUT	Hours
S					
M	8:00	12:00	12:30	4:30	8
T	8:00	12:00	12:30	4:30	8
W	8:00	12:00	12:30	4:30	8
T	8:00	12:00	12:30	4:30	8
F	8:00	12:00	12:30	4:30	8
S					

Hours	Rate	Earnings
40	$2.50	$90.00

Here is another card. Bill's card shows overtime. He earns $2.50 per hour for the first 40 hours. He earns time and a half ($3.75) for each hour beyond 40. Let's figure his pay for the week.

Name _____ Payroll # _____

Week Ending _____ 19___
              month   day   year

	A.M. IN	OUT	P.M. IN	OUT	Hours
S					
M	8:00	12:00	1:00	5:00	
T	8:00	12:00	1:00	5:30	
W	8:00	12:00	1:00	6:00	

T	8:00	12:00	1:00	5:30				
F	8:00	12:00	1:00	5:00				
S								
	Regular hours		40	Hourly rate		$2.50	Earnings	$90.00
	Overtime hours		2	Hourly rate		$3.75	Earnings	7.50
	Total hours		42				Total	$97.50

MONEY AND VALUE

Money skills are probably the most important part of the mathematics curriculum at the senior-high level. The youngsters must be capable of handling money in everyday transactions and in general manage their financial affairs. Most of the functional problems of daily living are closely tied to mathematical concepts. They must master the problems associated with earning a living such as filing the application, determining salary and wages, and understanding the concepts of overtime, docking, release time, and deductions. The student should be aware of the services of banks such as checking and savings accounts, safe deposit boxes, Christmas and vacation savings clubs, travelers checks, cashier checks, loans, and so forth. It is imperative that they develop skills in budgeting in order to avoid a severe financial crisis. Adolescents should develop the capacityfor making intelligent major purchases such as a car, furniture, and appliances. They should become skilled in wise buying at special sales, auctions, used stores and garage sales, as well as develop the capacity for prudent use of sales catalogs and coupons. Understanding the judicial use of credit is perhaps the single most important concept to be taught at this level. Taxes are a part of the American way of life. The retarded youth must have some elemental understanding of sales tax, property tax, and intangible tax. In short, he must be able to manage money and his financial affairs sensibly. The following topics will be discussed in this section highlighting suggestions for developing money management skills:

Money and Banking
Budgeting
Saving
Credit
Taxes
Insurance

Money and the Job
Making Purchases
    and Paying Bills
Wise Buying
Transportation

MONEY AND BANKING

Making Change. The first prerequisites for effective handling of money are that the youngsters understand the value of money, learn how to count money, and master the skills of making change. It has been stated in previous chapters that real money should be used to teach the child real value and to provide a strong incentive for counting money and making change. The temptation to use play money must be resisted if the teacher is to avoid undue damage to the child's self-esteem. It is simply inappropriate to teach an adolescent the value of money through the use of instructional aids which insult his social maturity. At the senior high level one objective is to learn to deal with money in amounts up to $100.00. It is recommended that the teacher secure a cash drawer with approximately $25.00 per youngster. The local PTA, Association for Retarded Children, Council for Exceptional Children could be approached if the school system itself is reluctant to supply the funds. The use of real money is highly motivating and should provide no particular problems as long as the proper precautions are taken. The presence of real currency inspires trust and the inconvenience it causes is far outweighed by the benefits. The counting and change-making problems used should be similar to those presented later in the section under figuring and paying bills.

Banking—Using Checks. The scope of banking services were introduced at the pre-vocational level. At the senior high level the concern is basically with savings, loans, and checking accounts. Savings and loans will be discussed in a subsequent section, so the topic here will be limited to the checking account. The objective is to teach the youngsters the skills necessary for the proper use of a checking account. First they must develop some understanding of the purposes of a checking account. The teacher can illustrate the value of a checking account in terms of safety and convenience.

> A check is not filled out until you need to pay for something while money can be lost or stolen.
> If a check is lost, you can let the bank know so payment on the check can be stopped.
> A cancelled check serves as a record of bills you have paid.
> A check may be written for any amount of money on deposit in your checking account.
> A check can be cashed only when properly endorsed or signed by the named payee.
> It is easier to mail a check than to take cash directly to a person.

Mathematics for Adultation 409

The next step is to assist the youngsters in learning how to open and maintain a checking account. Specifically, they will need to learn to:

1. Complete an application including a signature card.
2. Complete a deposit slip.
3. Write the check.
4. Complete the check stub or the check record.
5. Maintain the cumulative balance by adding deposits and subtracting checks and service charges.
6. Check the monthly bank statement.

There are a wide variety of signature cards, deposit slips, check forms and records. One procedure is to give the youngsters in class practice through the use of genuine forms secured from local banks. A wise precaution is to stamp the forms as samples. There are a number of workbooks that provide ample practice through the use of facsimile checks and records.

A number of sample exercises are given below.

Depositing

	Dollars	Cents	CHECKING DEPOSIT
Currency and Coin			Date _____
Checks			for credit to account of
			Name _____
			Address_____
Total			Bloomville Bank

FIGURE 7.22

Fill out the form in Figure 7.22 when you have $59.32 in cash to deposit. Complete the deposit slip when you have a check for $10.15. If you were going to deposit a check for $14.85, a check for $35.05 and $21.10 in cash, how would you complete the form?

410   *Mathematics for Adultation*

Check Writing. In Figure 7.23 is a check. Write a check to Kenneth Smith for $6.86.

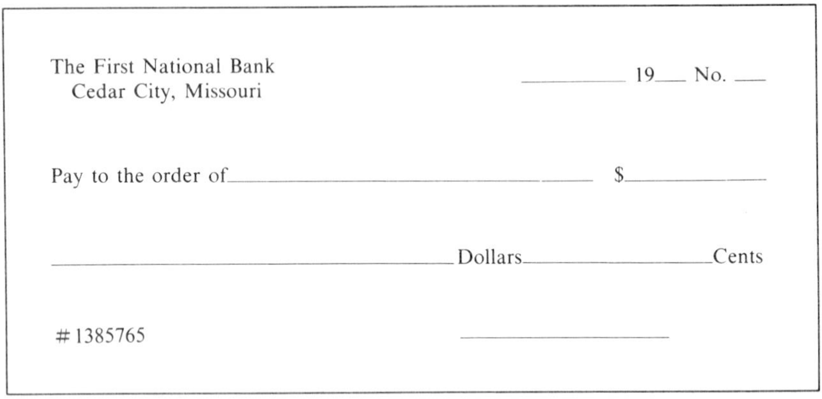

```
┌─────────────────────────────────────────────────────────────────┐
│                                                                 │
│    The First National Bank                   _____ 19__ No.__ │
│       Cedar City, Missouri                                      │
│                                                                 │
│                                                                 │
│    Pay to the order of_____  $_____   │
│                                                                 │
│                                                                 │
│    _____ Dollars_____Cents     │
│                                                                 │
│                                                                 │
│    # 1385765                                 _____    │
│                                                                 │
└─────────────────────────────────────────────────────────────────┘
```

FIGURE 7.23

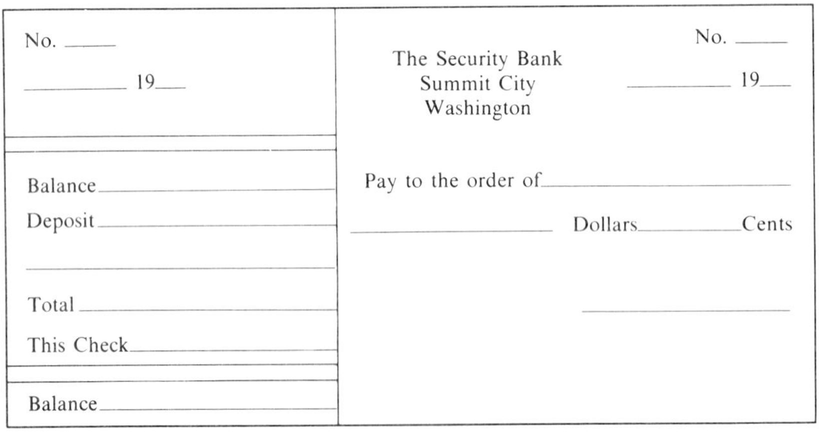

```
┌─────────────────────────┬───────────────────────────────────────┐
│  No. ____               │                              No. ____ │
│                         │       The Security Bank               │
│         _____ 19__     │          Summit City         _____ 19_│
│                         │          Washington                   │
│                         │                                       │
│                         │                                       │
│  Balance_____   │   Pay to the order of_____  │
│  Deposit_____   │                                       │
│                         │   _____ Dollars_____Cents  │
│                         │                                       │
│  Total_____   │                                       │
│  This Check_____   │                    _____  │
│                         │                                       │
│  Balance_____   │                                       │
└─────────────────────────┴───────────────────────────────────────┘
```

FIGURE 7.24

Record Keeping. Indicate a balance of $65.00. Show a deposit of $20.00. What is the total? Write a check to Jerry Jones for $5.00. What is the new balance?

Mathematics for Adultation 411

```
┌─────────────────────────────────────────────────────────┐
│     Webster Groves Bank              No. 34             │
│     Webster, Arkansas                                   │
│                                                         │
│     Pay to the Order of _____   $_____      │
│                                                         │
│     _____ Dollars_____ Cents  │
│                                                         │
│     732154                          _____       │
└─────────────────────────────────────────────────────────┘
```

Number	Date		Deposit	Check	Balance
					$80.00
33	7/6	Frank Smith		$ 5.00	75.00
34	7/10	Flying Gasoline		10.00	65.00
35					
36					
37					

FIGURE 7.25

Write check number 35 to Henry Jones for $15.00. Make a deposit of $10.00.

Checking the Bank Record

David J. Foster
10 Rose Lane   in account with
Pike City, Oklahoma   CITY NATIONAL BANK

Checks	Deposits	Date	Balance
	Forwarded Balance		$ 35.15
$10.00-		4/1/69	$ 25.15
8.00-		4/2/69	17.15
2.00-		4/8/69	15.15
	$55.00+	4/15/69	70.15
2.40		4/16/69	67.75
13.00-		4/25/69	54.75
Unlisted	Unlisted		
Checks	Deposits		

The teacher introduces the bank statement and has the youth check his records against the banks. The form will have a provision for balancing the check book by listing additional checks and deposits and comparing the balance of the check book with that of the bank statement.

As a means of assessing the understanding of opening and maintaining a checking account, the following terms should be reviewed.

Account	Check Stub
Account number	Deposit
Check	Endorsement
Balance	Joint Checking Account
Currency	Payee
Cash	Signature Card

Problems such as the ones shown below will give the students the appropriate kind of practice.

Add:

$23.04	$18.00	$ 42.00
7.90	66.94	110.00
	14.28	30.00

Lloyd deposited a $21.00 check, three $1.00 bills, and 35¢ in coin into his checking account. How much was his deposit?

Mary deposited one check for $40.00, four $1.00 bills, three half dollars, two nickels, one dime, and two quarters. What was her deposit?

Subtract:

| $16.24 | $554.14 | $1,298.64 |
| 8.08 | 13.19 | 801.19 |

Kenny's bank balance is $350.00. He writes a check for $40.19. What is his new bank balance?

Judy's bank balance is $698.35. She writes a check for $97.14. What is her bank balance now?

BUDGETING

For all young adults money management is of major concern to independent living. It presents a particularly critical problem for young mentally retarded persons since their computational and problem solving abilities are less well developed. The retarded adult will need special assistance in learning how to get the most for his money since he is probably less able to profit from negative economic experiences. In most cases, the retarded youth will have less margin for error since his limited ability to compete in the job market will result in employment in lower-paying, unskilled and semi-skilled positions. A higher percentage of his wages will have to be expended on the necessities of life and less for luxuries. It can not be assumed that these youngsters will manage efficiently the money they earn. They must be taught to budget wisely and avoid accumulating needless debts. They must be taught to utilize planned as opposed to impulsive spending. One approach is to use a budget.

The Budget

A budget is simply a technique for dividing in advance one's income among the many necessary and desirable expenditures which arise during a given period of time. It is a pre-conceived plan for spending. One's income can only be spent once. The purpose of the budget is to assist in achieving the greatest possible satisfaction from that income. A person is going to dispose of his income either with or without the aid of some plan. Whimsical expenditures almost always result in realizing less value from income and may sometimes result in economic disaster. A person generally follows some pattern in his spending even if it could be characterized by such phrases as "money burns a hole in my pocket" or "there is no electricity to operate the color television set." Since each of us tends to follow some spending pattern it is better to have some conscious control of that pattern. The rhetorical question, "Where does all the money go?" should be answered so that in the future it will go where it can do the most good.

Advantages of Budgeting

The general advantage of the budget is that it assists people in getting more of what they need and want for their money. It does this by:
1. Making it possible to purchase more priority items.
2. Avoiding wasteful spending.
3. Avoiding spending too fast.
4. Avoiding the need to borrow and overextend credit.
5. Improving the accumulation of savings.
6. Avoiding financial crisis.
7. Developing a sense of pride in managing one's own financial affairs.

How to Construct a Budget and Stick To It. It requires a high degree of social maturity to manage one's financial affairs wisely. The teacher may not be able to stem the impulsive buying habits of her students, but she can make certain that any thoughtless spending on their part was not due to a lack of knowledge. If the retarded youngster spends himself into financial chaos let it be the result of his own immaturity rather than the lack of understanding which should have been learned while he was still in school. The teacher, of course, may be able to shape attitudes about money management as well as teach specific skills in budgeting.

How the Youngster Follows these Steps

1. "Know what you have to spend." The fact that a youngster earns a given weekly salary does not mean that he will have that amount of money to spend each week. He must be alerted to and taught to understand the deductions which shrink every paycheck. The difference between gross salary and take-home pay can be significant. He should also have an understanding of such concepts as lay-offs, seasonal employment, piece work, and strikes. A failure to grasp their significance can spell disaster.

2. "Know your expenses." There are certain costs which are termed "fixed" since they are relatively stable over a period of time. Examples of fixed charges are rent, insurance, and car payments. Of course, these expenses can be indirectly controlled by moving to a less expensive apartment, reducing the amount of insurance, or buying a less expensive car. They are referred to as fixed because they do not tend to vary much unless some new factors come into play. Certain other costs are termed "flexible" because they are relatively unstable and vary considerably over a period of time. Examples of flexible expenses are food, clothing, and medical costs. The fixed costs are relatively easy to determine in advance while the flexible costs are more difficult to predict.

3. "Keep a record." A method of estimating future costs is to keep a record of both flexible and fixed costs which can be studied at a later date. This will enable the youngsters to determine three salient elements of budgeting: (1) determine monthly fixed costs; (2) determine average monthly flexible costs; and (3) determine monthly discretionary income. A knowledge of these three factors can become the basis of a guide to future expenditures. This record will not only indicate how the income was spent but will also reveal a pattern of spending. This pattern will point to strengths and weaknesses which will help shape more careful planning for the future.

One major factor revealed by such a record which deserves special mention is the limited amount of discretionary income. After all fixed and flexible costs are paid, there is typically only a small percentage of one's income remaining. Pay of $100.00 per week may sound like a lot of money until it begins to shrink through payroll deductions. The take-home pay from gross salary of $100.00 is apt to be less than $80.00. By the time the essential fixed and flexible bills are paid, it is unlikely that as much as $20.00 would be remaining. The young adult may really have less than 20% of his gross pay to make judgments about. The rest is accounted for before the check is ever cashed.

4. "Determine Priorities." Each person has only so much money to spend and it can only be spent once. Each time a given amount of money is spent on one item it precludes another expenditure. If a decision is made to buy a new car, one might have to forego remodeling the basement. If a family elects to go on a vacation, they may not be able to afford a new color television set. The youngsters must come to understand that each time a purchase is made that they not only have to consider the price of the item but also the other things they might have to give up as a result of that purchase. Life is one series of choices so when something is bought it is important to consider the other things which might have been purchased instead. It is not unusual for a person to look back with regret on a previous purchase. The rent payment may be paid late because new seat covers were bought for the car earlier in the month. The new television should not have been purchased until the clothes dryer had been paid for. It is important that the youngsters be given experiences in determining priorities.

EXPENSE RECORD

Month and Date	Food	Rent	Expenditures Utilities	Car	Ins.	Clothes	Others
September 1							
2							
3							
4							
5							
6							
7							
8							
9							
10							
11							
12							
13							
14							

Month and Date	Food	Rent	Expenditures Utilities	Car	Ins.	Clothes	Others
15							
16							
17							
18							
19							
20							
21							
22							
23							
24							
25							
26							
27							
28							
29							
30							
TOTALS							
PERCENTAGES							

FIGURE 7.26

There are guidelines which should help in determining priorities.

1. Essentials should come first.
2. Savings should be a priority.
3. Discretionary income should be expended by design.

There are certain essentials which must come first, namely: food, clothing, home, and health care. After these necessities have been cared for and some regular saving has been put aside, decisions need to be made regarding the balance of the income. The money remaining after expenditures for basic needs and savings is called discretionary income. There is no one way this money should be spent. One person may wish to spend this income on recreation while another would want to enhance his overall style of living. Another individual might want to add to his savings for a future purchase. The important guideline is that people should plan how to spend their money, that they spend for necessary items first, that they set something aside for savings, and that they avoid buying anything they hadn't planned to buy unless they are willing to take from unneeded savings or give up something else they had previously budgeted.

5. "Make a Written Budget." The budget should be constructed with a full knowledge of one's income, expenses, pattern of spending, and priorities. The purpose of the budget is to assist in the development of wise spending habits in order to realize more from one's resources. The budget, then, should take into consideration not only one's present pattern of spending, but also the development of a more desirable pattern. The first step is to develop a plan of spending for several months in advance, based primarily upon essentials and priorities for discretionary income. At this point, it will prove valuable to compare the record of past expenditures with some type of standard. Since there is no average family budget, percentages may be used as a guide. The percentage of income spent for various purposes for a low-income family of four would probably look something like that in Figure 7.27.

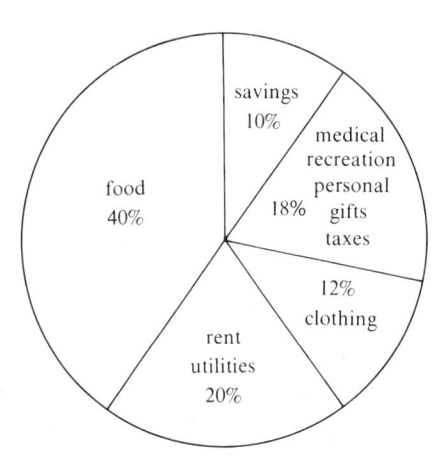

FIGURE 7.27

The largest single category of purchase for most families is food, including such items as drinks and cigarettes. The actual percentage expended will vary according to the size of the family and income, but for most low income families an estimate of 40% would be close. Housing, including utilities, will typically account for about 20% of family income while approximately 12% will be expended on clothing. This leaves only 28% for most families to provide all other expenses such as medical expenses, furnishings, personal needs, charity, savings, and recreation. The youngsters should be given a variety of budgets to study. They should have the opportunity to determine the approximate percentage of spending in different categories in order to judge the wisdom of the budgets.

BUDGET PLAN SHEET

FIXED EXPENSES	Planned Expenditure	Actual Expenditure
Taxes		
Housing and Utilities		
Insurance		
Car		
Other Payments		
FLEXIBLE EXPENSES		
Food		
Clothes		
Furniture		
Appliances		
Medical		
Recreation		
Other		

FIGURE 7.28

6. "Stick to the Budget." The ability to abide by a predetermined budget plan requires a great deal of maturity. Many adults find themselves in severe financial difficulties because they were not able to budget their money wisely. The teacher of mentally retarded children will not be able to magically wish her youngsters to a sufficient level of maturity to handle the tremendous financial temptations to which they will be exposed. However, she can provide them with some wise counsel.

Think first and spend later rather than spend first and think later.
Anticipate emergencies.
Think before you borrow or use credit.
The only ways to increase the goods you buy are (1) increase your income; (2) spend more wisely; (3) go into debt; (4) budget.
A budget will not always get you more, but it will get you more of what you really want and need.
Think of how you will feel about a purchase in a week, month, and year before you make it.
Keep records so you know where your money goes.
Each time you buy, think of the other things you might rather spend your money on.
Give the budget a fair trial.
Don't be impulsive.
Take the whole family and all expenses into account.

The Teenage Budget

The teenage mentally retarded youngster may not find the family budget relevant to him. The teacher may find that problems associated with his immediate economic life will have more appeal. Here are some samples:

Harry decided that he should find out how he spent the money he earned on his part time job. He made a record for one week.

DAY	ITEM	COST
Monday	Candy bar	$ .10
	Ice cream sundae	.35
Tuesday	Coke	.10
	Magazine	.50
Wednesday	Potato chips	.15
	Coke	.10
Thursday	Notebook	.20
	Milk shake	.35
Friday	Gasoline	2.00
	2 football tickets	1.50
	2 popcorn	.30
	2 cokes	.20
Saturday	Movie	1.25
	Snack	.80
Sunday	Church collection	.50
	Total	

How much did Harry spend on cokes?
How much did he spend on food?
How much did Harry spend on his Friday date?
How much did he spend altogether?
Use the chart below and make an expense account like Harry's.

DAY	ITEM	COST
Monday		
Tuesday		
Wednesday		
Thursday		
Friday		
Saturday		
Sunday		
Total		

Mary has earned $10.50 babysitting. She wants to save $2.00 towards a new dress. She can spend the rest on weekly expenses. If you were Mary, how would you budget the remaining money?

DAY	ITEM	COST
Monday		
Tuesday		
Wednesday		
Thursday		
Friday		
Saturday		
Sunday		
	TOTAL	

Other Activities

Make a chart indicating the approximate cost of supporting a high school student for one month.

Make a chart showing the earnings of students in the class. Plan realistic budgets for them.

Discuss the advantages of using budgets.

Have the pupils keep a record of their weekly expenses. Discuss the factors which affect their spending.

MAKING PURCHASES AND PAYING BILLS

The retarded youth needs to have sufficient money management skills to be able to deal with the problems which will confront him in shopping and paying bills. He should understand the process of billing at least to the extent that he is able to estimate the accuracy of the statements he receives. In this section, the problems of making purchases and paying bills are discussed including shopping at the grocery store, eating out, taking a vacation, having a party, going bowling, buying tickets. The figuring of household costs includes the following bills: telephone, gas, electricity, rent, installment payments, labor, medical bills, and laundry.

soup 18¢

bread 38¢

pickles 32¢

mustard 15¢

Mathematics for Adultation

tuna 37¢
milk 29¢
coffee 78¢ lb.
cheese 59¢ lb.
orange 10¢ each
bacon 79¢ lb.
meat 89¢ lb.
salt 17¢ box
soda pop 15¢ bottle
light 36¢ each
sugar 89¢ lb.

FIGURE 7.29. Grocery Shopping

Using the prices in Figure 7.29, indicate how much you would have to pay for the following purchases:

1. 3 oranges
   1 quart of milk
   2 cans of soup

2. 2 pounds of meat
   1 box of salt
   6 bottles of pop

3. 2 cans of tuna
   1 jar of mustard
   1 can of coffee

4. 3 light bulbs
   2 pounds of cheese
   1 jar of pickles

Figuring Household Bills

Below are some sample problems which are appropriate for most senior high school mentally retarded youth.

Telephone Bills. The monthly charge for the telephone is $7.00. This month Mrs. Jones made three long distance telephone calls. One to New York for $1.90; one to Kansas City for $.95; and one to Chicago for

$1.50. She also charged a telegram which cost $1.89. What will the telephone bill be for the entire month?

Mr. Smith looked at his telephone bills over the past six months. The basic charge is $7.00.

February	$10.69
March	11.45
April	18.32
May	7.00
June	9.00
July	15.91

How much more did he pay in April than February?
Which month cost the most and which cost the least?
How much less did he pay in March than July?
Why do you think April was so high and May so low?

Gas Bills. A family rented an apartment and each month had to pay the gas bill. They used gas for cooking, the water heater, the washer, and for the furnace.

January	$16.35
March	11.62
August	3.29

How much more did he pay in January than August?
How much more did he pay in March than August?
Why do you think his bill was so low in August?

Electric Bills. A family uses electricity for such things as lights, toasters, refrigerators, radios, televisions, stove, irons, power tools, washers, dryers. Here are the bills for one year.

January	$13.50	July	$ 8.14
February	9.40	August	7.56
March	11.54	September	8.91
April	9.62	October	9.15
May	9.20	November	11.71
June	8.36	December	12.20

Which month was the bill the highest?
During which month was the electric bill the least?
How much was the average bill?

Mathematics for Adultation

Water Bills. A family uses water to do dishes, wash clothes, take baths, wash the car, water the lawn and so forth. Here are some bills from last year.

January	$6.24	July	$7.24
February	6.24	August	8.53
March	6.24	September	7.50
April	6.24	October	6.48
May	6.54	November	6.24
June	6.70	December	6.24

What was the largest bill?
What was the smallest bill?
How many bills were $6.24?
Why were so many bills of the same amount?
How much was the water bill for the entire year?
What was the average water bill per month?

Rent. The payment made to a landlord for the privilege to live in his house or apartment is called rent. Harry is charged $100 a month for the apartment he rents. He earns $100 a week.

Harry is paid once a week, but pays his rent only once a month. What percentage of his earnings are spent on rent?

Harry read an ad for a smaller apartment for $80 a month. How much would he save each month if he moved to the smaller apartment? How much money would he need to put aside each week from this $100 a week if he moved to this smaller apartment?

Installment Payments. The Robinson family could not afford to pay for their new davenport and chair with cash. They needed the new furniture, so they decided to pay for it over a twelve-month period. They also have a loan on their car and two small charge accounts in local stores. Here are their bills for last month.

Store	Payment	Balance
Sam's Furniture Store	$24.50	$122.50
Acme Car Loan Company	54.25	651.00
Altman's Department Store	10.60	53.00
Mary's Dry Goods	5.75	17.25

What is the largest monthly payment?
What is the smallest monthly payment?
Which account has the largest due balance?
What is the total amount of all monthly payments?

How long will it take to pay for the furniture?
How many months will it take to pay for the car?
What is the total amount owed?

The davenport and chair cost $330 including service and carrying charges. The Robinsons paid $36 down. This left a balance of $294 to be paid off over twelve months. Complete the payment card below.

Name: Mr. John Robinson
Address: 123 Maple Avenue, Rocky Falls, Missouri

Item: Davenport and chair

Cost: $330.00   *Down Payment:* $36.00   *Balance:* $294.00

Monthly Payment: $24.50

Month	Payment	Balance
December	$24.50	$122.50
January		
February		
March		
April		

Medical Bills. The Smiths want to keep a record of their medical bills for tax purposes. Here is a record of their expenses for last year.

January	dentist	$12.00	July	medicine	$ 2.83
	medicine	5.00			
February	doctor	15.00			
	medicine	3.25	August	medicine	.98
March	medicine	2.24	September	doctor	22.96
April	dentist	8.00	October	medicine	.25
May	medicine	1.81	November	medicine	.72
June	medicine	.76	December	medicine	9.48

What was the largest single medical bill?
How much was spent for dental work during the year?
How much was spent on doctor bills for the entire year?
How much was spent on medicine for the entire year?
What was the total amount spent on medical expenses for the year?

Laundry Bills. Ton's Cleaners will wash and iron white shirts for 30¢ each or 4 for $1.00. Mrs. Harrington brings three shirts to be washed and ironed. How much will the laundry bill be? How much would 4 shirts cost? Would she have been wiser to bring 4 shirts?

Mathematics for Adultation

Mrs. Mills has her clothes done at the laundry. She is charged 15¢ per pound for washing and drying and 25¢ for each pressed white shirt.

June	Laundry	Shirts
Week One	26 lbs. × 15¢ = $_____	5 shirts × 25¢ = $_____
Week Two	23 lbs. × 15¢ = $_____	7 shirts × 25¢ = $_____
Week Three	19 lbs. × 15¢ = $_____	4 shirts × 25¢ = $_____
Week Four	22 lbs. × 15¢ = $_____	6 shirts × 25¢ = $_____

During which week did she spend the most for laundry?
During which week did she spend the least for laundry?
How much did she spend during the month for shirts?
How much did she spend during the month for washing?
How much did she spend during the month for both washing and shirts?

Eating at a Restaurant. Mr. Jones and his wife were going to a local restaurant for dinner. Mr. Jones did not want to spend more than $10.00 but he wanted to get as good a meal as possible for his money.

Soups
Vegetable........ $ .30
Bean .... .30
Tomato........... .15
Onion .... .10

Salads
Tossed Green .... $ .50
Jello .... .40
Cottage cheese .... .40
Lettuce-tomato .... .45

Dinners
Fried Chicken .... $ 1.75
Baked Ham 2.25
Round Steak 1.95
Sirloin Steak 3.50
Shrimp 5.75
Lobster 6.70
Fresh Fish 2.75

Desserts
Sherbert .... $ .30
Ice cream .... .30
Cake .... .30
Pie .... .25

Beverages
Milk .... $ .20
Ice Tea .... .15
Coffee .... .10
Coke .... .10

Select two nice meals for a total bill which will be more than $8.00 but less than $9.25. Save $.75 for the tip. Use the menu above.

Eating at a Drive-In Restaurant. Sally eats at Doln's Drive-In because it is close to where she works and it is inexpensive. She and a friend order 2 hamburgers, 2 cokes, and one order of french fries.

Mathematics for Adultation

CHECK

#81	DATE	WAITRESS	#
2	Hamburgers		
2	Cokes		
1	French fry		
		Tax (4%)	
		Total	

Doln's	
Hamburger	$ .30
Deluxe Hamburger	.50
Hot Dog	.20
French Fries	.25
Coke	.10
Coffee	.10
Milk	.15

FIGURE 7.30

Complete the cost of each line.
How much were the hamburgers?
How much were the cokes?
What was the total amount before the tax?
What was the amount of the tax (4%)?
The girls decided to split the bill evenly. How much did each girl pay knowing that they left a 20¢ tip?

Fountain Snacks. Using the menu below, work the following problems.

Sandwiches		Fountain		
Regular Hamburger	25¢	Coke	10¢	20¢
Cheeseburger	35¢	Ice tea	10¢	
Hamburger Deluxe	55¢	Milk shake	30¢	
Hot Dog	25¢	Soda	35¢	
Coney Dog	35¢	Ice Cream Cone	10¢	20¢
Fishburger	40¢	Sundae	30¢	
Beefburger	69¢	Lime Freeze	25¢	
Steakwich	80¢	Banana Split	45¢	

French Fries 25¢   Potato Chips 10¢   Pie 30¢

1. 1 Hot Dog   _____   2 Cokes   _____
   1 Coney Dog   _____   Change from $5.00 _____

Mathematics for Adultation

2. 1 Hamburger _____
   1 Cheeseburger _____
   2 Fries _____
   2 Cokes _____
   2 Sundaes _____
   Change from $5.00 _____
3. 3 Sodas _____
   3 Cokes _____
   Change from $2.00 _____
4. 2 Lime Freezes _____
   1 Fishburger _____
   1 Hamburger Deluxe_____
   2 Chips _____
   Change from $5.00 _____
5. 1 Steakwich _____
   1 Ice Tea _____
   1 Fry _____
   Change from $10.00 _____
6. 1 Banana Split _____
   3 Cones (small) _____
   1 Cone (large) _____
   5 Cokes (large) _____
   Change from $5.00 _____
7. 4 Hot Dogs _____
   2 Lime Freezes _____
   Change from $2.00 _____
8. 2 Hamburgers _____
   2 Cokes _____
   1 Milk Shake _____
   1 Piece of pie _____
   Change from $5.00 _____

Bowling. Jerry and Wanda decide to go bowling on each Thursday evening. They generally play three games each night at the cost of 50¢ per person per game. Sometimes they play an extra game or practice on other nights.

June	Games	Cost
First Thursday		
Jerry	3	_____
Wanda	3	_____
Second Thursday		
Jerry	3	_____
Wanda	3	_____
Third Wednesday		
Wanda	2	_____
Third Thursday		
Jerry	4	_____
Wanda	3	_____
Fourth Thursday		
Jerry	4	_____
Wanda	3	_____

How much did Jerry spend bowling?
How much did Wanda spend bowling?
How much did they spend bowling together?

Buying Tickets. Wayne and Sue enjoy going to the movies, the theatre, the circus, and dances. Here is a list of his expenditures for last year.

January	Movie _____	July	Theatre _____
February	Theatre _____	August	Circus _____ Movie _____ Theatre _____
March	Movie _____	September	Movie _____
April	Spring Dance _____	October	Movie _____
May	Movie _____	November	Theatre _____
June	Movie _____ Theatre _____	December	Movie _____

Movie $1.25   Theatre $2.50   Circus $1.50   Dance $3.00/couple

Using the prices shown above, answer these questions.
How much was spent each month on admission tickets?
During which month did they spend the most?
How much did they spend on movies?
How much did they spend on plays at the theatre?
How much did they spend on tickets for the year?

Neighborhood Barbecue. The Johnsons and Smiths decided to have a cookout. There would be four adults and five children. Here is their grocery list.

18 hot dogs	$ .94
18 hot dog buns	.64
1 jar relish	.54
1 jar mustard	.18
1 bottle catsup	.23
9 bottles of pop	.90
1 jar pickles	.69
1 bag potato chips	.89
9 cup cakes	.90
2 cans baked beans	.60
potato salad	.79
Total	____

How much did they spend on food?
What was each family's share of the costs?
What were the two most expensive items?
Would $10.00 be enough to pay the grocery bill?
If so, how much change would they get?
If not, how much more money is needed?

Mathematics for Adultation

WISE BUYING

One of the most valuable concepts retarded youngsters can learn is the monetary benefits of planned versus impulsive buying. The young adults who anticipate their needs and plan for them will get much more for their dollars. One way to receive more value for one's dollars is to buy at sales and to hunt for bargains. In this section, some basic principles for wise buying at sales will be discussed and specific attention will be given to bargain hunting at the grocery store (approximately 40% of the family budget); good buys at private sales; savings at stores which specialize in used and slightly damaged materials; and wise buying through catalogs.

Buying Items on Sale

Merchandise on sale is presented to the consumer in a variety of ways. The advertising of both consumable and durable goods make use of such terms as

factory sale	discount
clearance sale	unclaimed freight
overstocked	truck sale
going out of business	warehouse sale
inventory sale	weekend special
bargain	one cent sale
10% off	repossessed
sidewalk sale	reduced by 1/3
marked down	save 25%
two for one sale	end of season sale

There needs to be an exploration of what these terms mean and how they can help guide the purchasing of the consumer. Not all sales are bargains, and any item purchased unnecessarily is no bargain even if the price reduction is 75 percent.

It is sometimes difficult to know whether the price of the sale item is a true savings. An item marked "30% off" at a neighborhood drug store may actually be more expensive than the same item at the regular price of a shopping center discount store. On the other hand, some purchases may appear considerably discounted when it is simply an inferior product.

Sales Calendar. A merchant uses sales to bring more customers into his store and the consumer may use sales to save money if he finds things on sale that he really needs. For example, the wise buyer may be able to save money by waiting to buy a winter coat until after

Christmas or delay purchasing a new swimming suit until after Labor Day. The "good time" to buy any item will vary from region to region. Below is a calendar of sales which may be used as a guideline of what one might anticipate.

Sales: Calendar

January	linen, after Christmas inventory, used car buys improved for next several months.
February	Washington's birthday sales, furniture sales
March	Housewares, garden supplies
April	Easter clothing sales
May	pre-season airconditioners, spring clean-up sales
June	outdoor equipment, sporting goods
July	floor coverings
August	swimming suits, summer suits, camping equipment
September	glassware and china
October	spring flower bulbs, car model changes
November	Thanksgiving and pre-Christmas sales
December	clearance sales immediately after Christmas

Here are some tips on watching for sales:

1. Maintain a record of the sales in your town. This will help you anticipate bargains.
2. Don't buy things on sale unless you need them.
3. Compare the before sale price with the sale price.
4. Even though an item is on sale in one store, it may still be even less expensive at another store. One store's bargain is another store's regular price.
5. Check the quality of the merchandise because some stores buy special items for sales which are not the same high quality of their regular stock.
6. Sales often do not allow returns if the material is defective or the wrong size.
7. Watch especially for sales which come only once or twice a year since merchants use these to dispose of the surplus goods.

Wise Buying at the Grocery Store. Food will account for approximately 40% of the budget of the average size family of modest income. Therefore it is important that the money spent on food be expended wisely. Here are some guidelines well within the understanding of young mentally retarded persons.

1. Food "specials" often allow the consumer to save considerable amounts of money.
2. Meat accounts for about 25% of the grocery budget. "Store" and "Private" brands are often as good as "name" brands and are less expensive, especially ham, bacon, and prepared meats.
3. Whole chickens are less expensive than cut up chickens.
4. Food sales are the retailers' way of getting customers in the store.
5. Compare national, store, and private brands.
6. Watch for fat and bone when you compare meat prices.
7. Compare canned, frozen, and fresh foods.
8. Prices are generally lower at large supermarkets than at small local groceries.
9. Vegetable and fruit stands often have very cheap prices, especially when located in farming country.
10. When buying fresh foods on sale be certain they have not started to spoil and that you can use them before they spoil.
11. Good buys can be made at "one day old" bread stores.
12. The bakery will usually have higher quality goods than the supermarket, but in some cases will also charge more.
13. Dairy products comprise about 20% of the food budget. Non-fat powdered milk for cooking and baking can reduce milk costs. Also, large families can save by buying in quantity since milk is cheaper in half-gallon or gallon containers.
14. Bargains are costly when you buy things you don't need simply because they are cheaper.
15. Eat out only when you can afford it.
16. Snacks from vending machines in airports, depots, and service stations frequently cost more than at the supermarket.
17. Buying more than one of an item can often save money.
18. Consider using a deep freeze to help save on meat prices. Frequently you can save considerably by buying a whole, side, or quarter of a beef.
19. Buy what is in season when prices are down.
20. Compare the regular and sale price.

Trading Stamps. Many stores give trading stamps. Before you decide to buy something at a store that gives you trading stamps rather than a store that does not offer trading stamps, think of the cost of stamps. One buys them; they are not really free.

On a dollar's worth of groceries you get stamps worth between two and three cents. If the difference between the store which gives stamps and the one which does not is more than two or three cents, you are paying too much for the stamps.

Don't buy just to fill a stamp book. You might have to spend as much as $40.00 to get $1.00 worth of stamps.

Problems such as these will help develop the concepts of wise buying.

Mary is grocery shopping. Her family eats a lot of soup. She has soup on her grocery list. Her favorite soup is 17¢ a can. She sees a sign which says

17¢ each/4 cans for 60¢

If she bought 4 cans one at a time at the regular price how much would the soup cost?
How much would she save if she bought all 4 cans now?
Do you think she should buy 1 or 4 cans?

Mary also wants to buy some milk. Milk is 27¢ a quart and 50¢ a half gallon. How much would she save by buying the half-gallon rather than 2 quarts? What things should she think about before deciding to buy a quart or a half gallon?

Here are some other items on Mary's list. Subtract the sale price of the item from the regular price to find how much she could save by buying more than one. Write the answer in the space provided.

ITEM	COST	QUANTITY PRICE	SAVINGS
Gum	7¢ each	5 for 25¢	_____
Beans	15¢ a can	3 for 40¢	_____
Bread	20¢ a loaf	2 for 37¢	_____
Toothpaste	45¢ each	2 for 89¢	_____

A large can of green beans is 32¢. It is a national brand. Another can of beans the same size is sold under the store label for 30¢. How much would be saved by buying 4 cans of the store label? How would one decide which to buy?

Mary wants to buy corn for dinner. She wants to serve three people. A can of corn is 33¢. A box of frozen corn is 36¢. Fresh corn is 10¢ an ear or 6 ears for 50¢. What would need to be considered to determine the best buy? If you were Mary, what would you buy?

Mary sees that grapefruit juice is on sale, but that orange juice is the regular price. She decides to buy the grapefruit juice because it is a bargain even though no one in her family likes grapefruit juice. Do you think she was foolish?

Mary is shopping during the month of August. Which items are more likely to be bargains?

watermelon	oranges
strawberries	gum
grapefruit	candy bars
lettuce	canned beef
hamburger	bread
bacon	milk
grapes	crackers
turkey	chicken

Used Stores, Damaged Freight Outlets, etc. Any town or city of consequence will have a used furniture store and antique shop. Good Will and Salvation Army Stores are examples of outlets which have prices on used items from nicknacks through clothes and appliances. However, it is just as easy to make a poor purchase in the used market as it is in the new market. The condition of the item and its duration of usefulness should be evaluated against the cost of the item new.

Auctions, Garage Sales and Rummage Sales. Auctions, garage sales and rummage sales offer many bargains. However, the author has visited such sales and witnessed customers buying items at an auction at a price greater than the cost of the identical item at a department store. In one such case a woman purchased a set of salt shakers for 35¢ which were available at the local dime store for 25¢ a pair. On the other hand, couples have been known to furnish an apartment for less than $150.00 with auction bargains. In an actual incident, a young married couple bought the following items—used but in good condition—at several auctions and through classified advertising.

Dining Room Table, Buffet, six chairs	$ 60.00
Davenport and Matching Chair	20.00
Rocker	10.00
Refrigerator	10.00
Gas Range	8.00
Kitchen Table and Four Chairs	6.00
Coffee Table and End Tables	7.00
Bed and Mattress	10.00
Dressing Table	2.50
Three Lamps	4.00
Lamp Table	2.50
Radio	3.00
Book Case	2.00
Kitchen Metal Cabinet	1.00
	$146.00

Used clothing, linens, and other goods may likewise be acquired at reasonable prices.

Catalogs. In order to provide some frame of reference, it is suggested that the youngsters be given practice in using Department Store catalogs. Sears and Roebuck and Montgomery-Wards are representative examples. These catalogs typically present three levels of quality, and their prices are generally in line with the economy. Mail order purchasing is an economical practice with name brands and reputable companies.

The objective of this section is to teach the students how to use catalogs and how to complete order forms. Students need to become aware of both the advantages and disadvantages of buying by mail.

The youngsters will need experience in buying from the catalog and their major problems will include proper use of the index, payment decisions, and costs of shipping. An ancillary benefit of the catalog is that it provides a frame of reference for price comparisons. When there is a doubt regarding the true savings on a "bargain item" found on sale, the consumer should compare the price with that found in the catalog. This will help determine whether the item is really a bargain.

Here are some suggested activities:
Bring to class several catalogs from mail order houses. Provide such activities as:
    locating items through the index
    comparing quality and price of given items
    comparing newspaper ads with catalog prices
    comparing catalog prices with prices in local stores
Give each student a hypothetical amount of money to spend on gifts for his family. Have him use the catalog. Have him select the gifts, and figure costs including weight charges.

TRANSPORTATION

Our society is a mobile one. One usually needs some form of transportation to get to his job, his church, his school or his favorite place of recreation. In addition to everyday transportation, there is an upward swing in the amount of travel away from home on business and pleasure. The retardate must know how to ride the city and suburban bus lines and be able to select the most economical means of payment. He must understand bus routes and transfer systems. When going to a location beyond the bus route, he must decide whether a taxi, a bus, or a combination of the two would be the most economical. When traveling beyond the city, he must be able to compare expenses and timetables of buses, trains, and air lines. There will even be some circumstances when knowledge of car rental will be valuable. Here are some problems.

Mathematics for Adultation 435

Mary Anne has a job at Tom's Cleaners in the city. She works five days a week. To get to work she takes the downtown bus, and then transfers to the South Side bus. The fare is 25¢ plus 5¢ for each transfer. However, the bus company sells 5 tickets for one dollar.
1. How many bus trips will she make each day?
2. How many transfers must she buy each day?
3. How many regular tickets will she need each week?
4. How many transfers will she need each week?
5. How much will the tickets cost?
6. How much will she pay each week for transfers?
7. How much will the bus cost each week?

John doesn't know his way around St. Louis and his friend does not have a car. John decides to take a taxi. His friend lives 3¼ miles from the train depot. John learns that the taxi costs $.50 for the first ⅛ mile and $.25 for each additional mile.
1. How much will the taxi cost?
2. How much should John give as a tip?
3. How much will he have to pay altogether?

Transportation by Car

Buying a Car. It has become accepted phenomena for teenagers to learn to drive the family car. The purchase of one's own car generally follows graduation from high school. This pattern is as typical of the graduate of a special education program as it is of any other graduate. The high school curriculum must provide for this contingency.

Adults are well aware of the hazards of automobile buying. The financial questions associated with a loan, insurance, tax, and license are but a few of the problems with which the young retarded adult must cope. Some representative problems associated with an automobile purchase are given below.

The Cost of a Car. Frank wants to buy a used car. He looks at a five-year-old Ford at Joe's Used Car Lot. The price is $800. Frank has saved $500 from his pay. He will leave $100 and use the remainder of his savings for a down payment on the Ford.
1. How much money will Frank pay down on the car?
2. How much money will he still owe on the car?
3. How much money will he have to borrow?

Borrowing Money for a Car. Sam buys a car for $1000. He makes a down payment of $500. He takes a loan of $500. The interest on the loan is $40.00 for one year.
1. How much will Sam pay to the loan company altogether?
2. How much will he have to pay each month?

Title and License. Andy has bought a car. He goes to the court house to buy a title and a state license and city sticker. The title costs $6.00. The state license is $10.00 and the city sticker is $5.00.

How much does he pay for the title and licenses?

Insurance. Hank is 19 years old. He buys a car. He knows that the law requires him to carry insurance in case he damages someone else's car or property. He also wants to have protection in case something happens to his own car. This insurance is $300 a year.

How much will he have to pay on his insurance each month?

Repairs. John dented his front fender when he accidentally hit the garage door. He takes the car to the Smith Repair Shop. They gave him an estimate of $75.00. The Ford Garage made an estimate of $68.00 and Joe's Body Shop gave an estimate of $70.00.
1. Who made the lowest estimate?
2. How much was the lowest estimate?

Cost of Car Transportation. Mike bought a used car to drive to work. He paid cash for it. How much does it cost to run the car for one year?

Price of car	$500.00
License Plates	10.00
City Sticker	3.00
Driver's License	5.00
Gas and Oil	180.00
Repairs	27.00
Insurance	200.00

Ed bought a brand new car. He learned that it took a lot of money to run a car. He borrowed money to pay for it. Here are his monthly costs.

Monthly car payment	$45.00
Gas and oil	32.00
Repairs	15.00
Insurance	35.00

1. How much are his costs for one month?
2. How much will it cost him to run the car for one year?

Mathematics for Adultation 437

SAVING

Banking-Savings. During the junior high and high school levels, the students are encouraged to save ten percent of any earnings. The most common method is a savings account with a local bank or other lending institution. However, the students should be made aware of other types of savings such as Christmas and vacation clubs, Saving Bonds, Credit Union Savings Deductions and so forth. The importance of regular savings and some understanding of interest should be a part of the mathematics program. Below are some representative examples of appropriate activities.

Percentage Savings. The teacher should review converting percents to decimals. For example, 10% may be converted to .10, 5% to .05; 3% to .03; and 6% to .06. The class should then be ready for such problems as: "Bill plans to save 10% of his pay each week. He earns $40.00 per week. How much will he save?"

Savings Account Deposit. The youth will have completed the necessary application forms and signature card. A decision of how much to save each payday will have been decided.

```
┌─────────────────────────────────────────────────────────────┐
│                                                             │
│      For Credit with                Dollars        Cents    │
│                                                             │
│      Amesville City Bank       Currency                     │
│                                                             │
│      SAVINGS DEPOSIT           Coins                        │
│                                                             │
│      for credit to the account of  Checks                   │
│                                                             │
│                                                             │
│                                                             │
│      ..........................    Total                    │
│            (signature)                                      │
│                                     Less Cash               │
│      Date.............. 19...       Returned                │
│                                                             │
│      Account Number ...........     Total                   │
│                                     Deposit                 │
│      #387542920                                             │
│                                                             │
└─────────────────────────────────────────────────────────────┘
```

FIGURE 7.31

"Show a deposit of one check for $51.03 and cash of $8.47. Ask for $10.00 in cash. What is the total deposit?"

Vacation and Christmas Savings. A key factor in budget and sound money usage is prior planning. The students should be shown the advantages of anticipating their needs. Frequently, families commit much of their future earnings in over-spending for Christmas gifts and summer vacations. Just about the time the family has repaid the money (paid the account off) for one item, it is time for the other. Savings clubs provide a convenient way to prepare for these two common expenditures. The saver deposits a certain amount of money to the account each pay period for about fifty weeks. It should be mentioned that many of these clubs do not give interest on the savings, although this is not universally true.

If I join a vacation club for $5.00 a week for 50 weeks, how much will I have for my vacation? If I save $10.00 a week for Christmas and winter expenses, for 50 weeks, how much will I have saved?

Savings Bonds. A popular form of deduction savings is the bond-a-month plan. A regular amount is deducted each payday until enough is withheld to purchase a bond. The savings bonds are an excellent investment in securities. They pay a moderate rate of interest and have a fixed redemption value which includes an interest rate which increases to a limited degree the longer the bond is held. The bonds are available in low denominations (a $25 bond costs $18.75) so one does not have to accumulate a lot of money to buy one. The teacher should check with a local bank to ascertain the current purchase price of bonds.

To save a bond a month, how much will be deducted from your check each week?

The Credit Union. It is a fairly common practice for unions and businesses to operate credit unions to receive the savings of workers and to make loans to them. In addition, many of the credit unions provide life insurance plans that provide protection for members at minimum costs. The worker can request that a certain amount of his salary be withheld from his check for deposit in his credit union savings account. Usually these deposits are in the form of shares and are in multiples of five.

How much would you save in ten weeks if you have $10.00 a week deducted from your check? If you wanted to save $20.00 a month through credit union deductions, how much should you have deducted each week?

Interest on Savings. Banks and savings and loans vary their interest on savings just as they do on loans. Some institutions pay an interest rate on certain accounts around the 5% level. Indications are that the fluctuations over the long run will be upward. Assuming a deposit of $100.00 have the students calculate interest at 3%, 4½%, 4¾%, 5%, and 5¾%.

```
   $100.00        $100.00        $100.00        $100.00
       .03           .04½           .0475            .05
   $  3.00        4.0000          50000          $5.00
                  5000            70000
                  $4.50           40000
                                  $4.75
```

CREDIT

One can purchase almost any item on credit ranging from life's necessities through the luxuries of an opulent society. Gasoline, suits, colored televisions, and mobile homes are among the common credit purchases. It is even possible to borrow money to repay money borrowed for the purchase of merchandise! If properly utilized, credit can be of immeasurable assistance to the young adult striving to establish an independent life. It is possible to allow debts to get so out of control that within a few months the young adult can stumble into a financial crisis that perpetuates itself for years.

The young retarded adult must have a functional understanding of credit and the pitfalls it presents. He must understand that credit is not an easy road to the accumulation of otherwise unattainable frills. It is much more prudent to view credit as an agreement to allocate a certain amount of future income to the seller. In other words, the buyer agrees to an automatic reduction of his income for the period during which the debt is being repaid. The greater the debt, the greater the amount of the income which goes to debt reduction and the less the purchasing power. (The purchaser bets that the money now going to creditors for the next six months or year won't be needed.) As the effective purchasing power becomes reduced through debt obligations, it becomes more tempting to buy even more items on credit.

The financial crisis typically develops along lines like these. Bill is a graduating senior from a special education work-study program. His eye has been taken by a stereo record player-radio combination displayed in a downtown department store. There are signs advertising the item which look something like those in Figure 7.32.

Of course, Bill does not have $320 and it would be quite difficult to save that much money. But he does have $16.00 in his billfold, that he could use as a down payment. "Surely" he reasons, "I can afford $8.00 per week, and I would be saving $80.00!" The salesman encourages

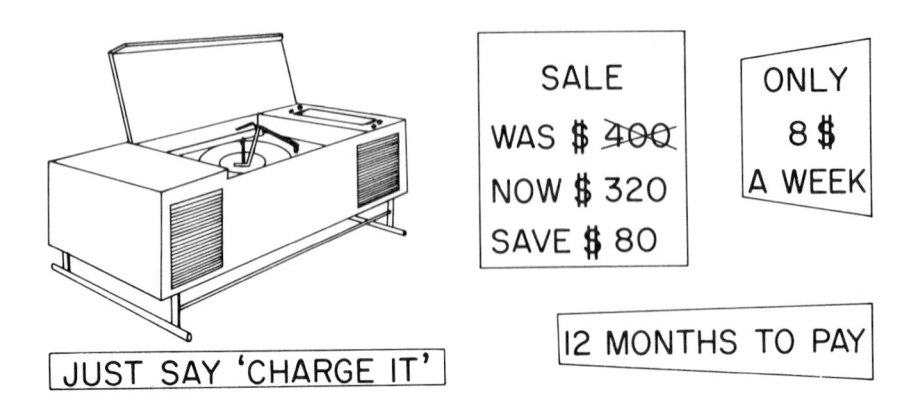

FIGURE 7.32

his spurious logic. "Only $8.00 a week and this beautiful instrument is all yours. You would hardly miss that little amount of money." If Bill were to make this purchase, he would in effect agree to reduce his monthly take home pay by $32.00 a month or about $400 for the year. The salesman may not have made it clear that the originally quoted price did not include sales tax, interest and carrying charges and it probably will not occur to Bill that rather than getting a $400 stereo-record player for $320 he has agreed to pay $416. He did not save $80 but rather paid $16 more than the cash price.

Now that Bill has full-time employment he needs some new clothes. He quickly runs up a $150 debt in his revolving charge account which he is paying off at the rate of ten percent a month. He borrowed a few hundred dollars to purchase a used car. All in all, bill payments are draining $100 a month from his take home pay of $300. That leaves $200 to pay his rent, buy his food, maintain his car, pay his insurance, and take care of recreational and miscellaneous expenses. This leaves him so short of cash that as fast as he reduces his revolving charges, he has to add new purchases to the balance. Within a few months he has to borrow $200 from a small loan company to pay for repairs on his car and clear up some dental bills. No sooner than this debt is about paid off than he has to borrow again to pay off accumulated past due bills.

Examples such as the one above should be presented to the children so they understand the pitfalls of credit. They should also understand that overspending is frequently encouraged because credit is at times erroneously regarded as "savings in reverse." For example, the 1½ percent service charge on the usual revolving charge account amounts to 18-per-cent-a-year interest. A 7½-percent bank loan repaid in installments works out to approximately 15-percent a year. Increased borrowing results in a corresponding reduction of effective purchasing power. A person can become tied down to long term debts that embroil him in an economic trap that can lead to financial disaster. It is especially critical for the young retarded adult with a marginal subsistence income, for the over use of credit increases the vulnerability to emergencies (and unexpected expenses).

Fortunately, it is unnecessary for the retardate to wander aimlessly into debt. If the retarded adult foolishly flounders into the credit trap, let it be the result of immaturity and not the failure of his school program properly to forewarn him. Much time and effort must be given to problems such as the ones presented below in order to insure proper understanding on the student's part. Armed with such knowledge he will be much more apt to avoid financial difficulties due to the misuse of credit.

Check your credit.
No more than 25% of your take-home pay should go into debt payments.
New debts should not be assumed unnecessarily until old debts are paid.
Do not borrow unless you must.
Do not borrow for luxuries.
Do not stretch payments beyond twelve months—pay off debts as quickly as possible.
Shop around for credit—don't be careless and take the first deal that comes along.
Use free credit. 30 days same as cash.
Do not use long-term credit for short-term luxuries—Christmas, vacations.
Save!

Sample Problems. Mary buys a new coat for $64.00. She puts it on her charge account. The carrying charges are $4.50. How much will she pay for the coat altogether?

Julie paid for her hair dryer in ten months. She paid $5.00 down and $5.00 a month. The cash price was $50.00. How much did it cost to buy the hair dryer on credit?

One of the most important understandings for these youth is that credit commits money not yet earned and reduces the amount of the take-home pay remaining after the bills are paid. The amount left after the bills are paid is the cash from which one saves, meets unforeseen contingencies, and pays for simple recreation and other pleasures. Overextended payments can result in a personal or family income which is expended before the check comes home. The worker can develop the feeling, "I am always broke the day after payday" and "Where does all my money go?"

Sample Problem. Mr. Harrison has a take-home paycheck of $60.00. His car payment is $40.00 a month so he must put $10.00 aside each week for that. Groceries and lunch will cost about $20.00 if he is careful. His room is $9.00 a week. Automobile insurance is $24.00 a month. Gas and oil cost about $6.00 a week. How much does he have left each week for spending money? Can he afford to make any purchases on credit and make monthly payments?

Charge Account Statement

Dick's Department Store
Box 123
Kensas City, Missouri 48836

DATE ....

NAME ....
ADDRESS..
CITY .... STATE ....

AMOUNT PAID ....

Detach and return with payment

DATE	PREVIOUS BALANCE	CURRENT PURCHASES	RETURNS	PAYMENTS	PRESENT BALANCE
TOTAL					

FIGURE 7.33

Mathematics for Adultation 443

Charge Account. There are certainly legitimate times to use a charge account and most young adults will have some charge account of their own shortly after their graduation. It should be explained to the student that not every customer is permitted to open a charge account and that he might not be allowed to add items to an existing charge account unless he has *good credit.*

The teacher should have the students complete sample applications for credit. Present the students with some examples of good credit risks and poor credit risks.

The student should understand the terms of his credit card. Here is an example of terms of credit.

> no charge if he pays for purchase within 10 days of receipt of bill.
>
> 1½ cents on each dollar or $1.50 on each $100 of the previous month's balance. A service charge on $50 would be $.75 for the month, if he paid off $10 then it would be $.60 for the next month, $.45 for the next, etc.

Sample Problem. Place these transactions on the charge account statement form. Figure the totals for each column. Figure the balance owed by the customer at the end of the month.

TAXES

The youngsters will need to concern themselves with two types of taxes immediately. The first is sales tax. They need not master the calculation of sales taxes but they should learn to read a sales tax chart like the one shown on page 444. It is also important that they become familiar with procedures involved with federal income tax. Some youngsters will profit from experiences with property taxes, intangible taxes, as well as state and local income taxes, depending upon their local situation.

"Sales Tax"

One problem in teaching youth to solve sales tax problems is that the rate varies from state to state. The teacher should use the tax rate of the state in which the children reside, but should also include some practice with other rates.

It should be pointed out to the students that we pay sales tax on most purchased merchandise. The taxes collected are used for highway construction, public buildings, and other government projects.

Sales taxes may vary from none at all to as high as 7%.

In Ohio, the sales tax is 4%. A sales tax chart is on page 444.

What would be the sales tax on purchases of the following amounts?

$ .13	$ 1.63	$12.12
$2.50	$ .95	$21.25
$ .34	$26.90	$ 8.00

The sales tax may also be computed by multiplying the price of the item by the sales tax rates. For example, the sales tax on a dress costing $6.00 in Ohio would be

$$\begin{array}{r} \$6.00 \\ \underline{.04} \\ .24 \text{ or } 24¢ \end{array}$$

Compute the sales tax for the following items at a 4% rate.

$3.00 $10.00 $21.00

SALES TAX CHART—4%

Price Range	Tax	Price Range	Tax	Price Range	Tax
.13- .31	.01	9.13- 9.37	.37	18.13-18.37	.73
.32- .54	.02	9.38- 9.62	.38	18.38-18.62	.74
.55- .81	.03	9.63- 9.87	.39	18.63-18.77	.75
.82-1.08	.04	9.88-10.12	.40	18.88-19.12	.76
1.09-1.35	.05	10.13-10.37	.41	19.13-19.37	.77
1.36-1.62	.06	10.38-10.62	.42	19.38-19.62	.78
1.63-1.87	.07	10.63-10.87	.43	19.63-19.87	.79
1.88-2.12	.08	10.88-11.12	.44	19.88-20.12	.80
2.13-2.37	.09	11.13-11.37	.45	20.13-20.37	.81
2.38-2.62	.10	11.38-11.62	.46	20.38-20.62	.82
2.63-2.87	.11	11.63-11.87	.47	20.63-20.87	.83
2.88-3.12	.12	11.88-12.12	.48	20.88-21.12	.84
3.13-3.37	.13	12.13-12.37	.49	21.13-21.37	.85
3.38-3.62	.14	12.38-12.62	.50	21.38-21.62	.86
3.63-3.87	.15	12.63-12.87	.51	21.63-21.82	.87
3.88-4.12	.16	12.88-13.12	.52	21.88-22.12	.88
4.13-4.37	.17	13.13-13.37	.53	22.13-22.37	.89
4.38-4.62	.18	13.38-13.62	.54	22.38-22.62	.90
4.63-4.87	.19	13.63-13.87	.55	22.63-22.87	.91
4.88-5.12	.20	13.88-14.12	.56	22.88-23.12	.92
5.13-5.37	.21	14.13-14.37	.57	23.13-23.37	.93
5.38-5.62	.22	14.38-14.62	.58	23.38-23.62	.94
5.63-5.87	.23	14.63-14.87	.59	23.63-23.87	.95
5.88-6.12	.24	14.88-15.12	.60	23.88-24.12	.96

Mathematics for Adultation 445

Price Range	Tax	Price Range	Tax	Price Range	Tax
6.13-6.37	.25	15.13-15.37	.61	24.13-24.37	.97
6.38-6.62	.26	15.38-15.62	.62	24.38-24.62	.98
6.63-6.87	.27	15.63-15.87	.63	24.63-24.87	.99
6.88-7.12	.28	15.88-16.12	.64	24.88-25.12	1.00
7.13-7.37	.29	16.13-16.37	.65	25.13-25.37	1.01
7.38-7.62	.30	16.38-16.62	.66	25.38-25.62	1.02
7.63-7.87	.31	16.63-16.87	.67	25.63-25.87	1.03
7.88-8.12	.32	16.88-17.12	.68	25.88-26.12	1.04
8.13-8.37	.33	17.13-17.37	.69	26.13-26.37	1.05
8.38-8.62	.34	17.38-17.62	.70	26.38-26.62	1.06
8.63-8.87	.35	17.63-17.87	.71	26.63-26.87	1.07
8.88-9.12	.36	17.88-18.12	.72	26.88-27.12	1.08

FIGURE 7.34

If you bought several items in a grocery store, you would find the tax by first adding the cost of the items and then finding the sales tax. The cost of the merchandise and tax are added to find the total cost. A grocery bill would look like Figure 7.35. The total before tax is added is called sub-total.

```
$  .10
   1.05
    .20
    .17
    .33
   2.04
    .11
  $4.00 sub total
    .16 tax
  $4.16 total
```

```
$  .19
    .41
    .22
    .69
   sub total
   tax
   total
```

FIGURE 7.35

1. Find the subtotal for this purchase made in Ohio.
2. What is the sales tax?
3. What is the total cost of the merchandise?

Form **1040** US Department of the Treasury / Internal Revenue Service **Individual Income Tax Return** 1970

For the year January 1–December 31, 1970, or other taxable year beginning ...., 1970, ending ...., 19....

Please print or type

Mary Smith
1176 Liberty Avenue
Elm City, N. Y. 11953

Your social security number
Spouse's social security number
Occupation: Yours / Spouse's

Filing Status—check only one:

1 ☐ Single; 2 ☐ Married filing jointly (even if only one had income)
3 ☐ Married filing separately and spouse is also filing. If this item checked give spouse's social security number in space above and enter first name here ▶
4 ☐ Unmarried Head of Household
5 ☐ Surviving widow(er) with dependent child
6 ☐ Married filing separately and spouse is not filing

Exemptions Regular / 65 or over / Blind — Enter number of boxes checked ▶
7 Yourself ☐ ☐ ☐
8 Spouse (applies only if item 2 or 6 is checked) ☐ ☐ ☐
9 First names of your dependent children who lived with you .... Enter number ▶
10 Number of other dependents (from line 34) ▶
11 Total exemptions claimed ▶

Please attach Copy B of Form W–2 to back

Income

12 Wages, salaries, tips, etc. (Attach Forms W–2 to back. If unavailable, attach explanation) . 12
13a Dividends (see pages 5 and 9 of instr.) $.......... 13b Less exclusion $.......... Balance ▶ 13c
(Also list in Part I of Schedule B, if gross dividends and other distributions are over $100)
14 Interest. Enter total here (also list in Part II of Schedule B, if total is over $100) 14
15 Income other than wages, dividends, and interest (from line 40) 15
16 Total (add lines 12, 13c, 14 and 15) 16
17 Adjustments to income (such as "sick pay," moving expense, etc. from line 45) 17
18 Adjusted gross income (subtract line 17 from line 16) 18

- *See page 2 of instructions for rules under which the IRS will figure your tax and surcharge.*
- *If you do not itemize deductions and line 18 is under $10,000, find tax in Tables. Enter tax on line 19.*
- *If you itemize deductions or line 18 is $10,000 or more, go to line 46 to figure tax.*

Tax and Surcharge

19 Tax (Check if from: Tax Tables 1–15 ☐, Tax Rate Schedule X, Y, or Z ☐, Schedule D ☐, or Schedule G ☐) 19
20 Tax surcharge. See Tax Surcharge Tables A, B and C in instructions. (If you claim retirement income credit, use Schedule R to figure surcharge.) 20
21 Total (add lines 19 and 20) 21

Please attach Check or Money Order here

Payments and Credits

22 Total credits (from line 55) 22
23 Income tax (subtract line 22 from line 21) 23
24 Other taxes (from line 61) 24
25 Total (add lines 23 and 24) 25
26 Total Federal income tax withheld (attach Forms W–2 to back) 26
27 1970 Estimated tax payments (include 1969 overpayment allowed as a credit) 27
28 Other payments (from line 65) 28
Make check or money order payable to Internal Revenue Service.
29 Total (add lines 26, 27, and 28) 29

Bal. Due or Refund

30 If line 25 is larger than line 29, enter BALANCE DUE. Pay in full with return ▶ 30
31 If line 29 is larger than line 25, enter OVERPAYMENT ▶ 31
32 Line 31 to be: (a) Credited on 1971 estimated tax ▶ $; (b) Refunded ▶ $

Under penalties of perjury, I declare that I have examined this return, including accompanying schedules and statements, and to the best of my knowledge and belief it is true, correct, and complete.

Sign here

▶ Your signature
▶ Spouse's signature (If filing jointly, BOTH must sign even if only one had income)
▶ Signature of preparer other than taxpayer, based on all information of which he has any knowledge. Date
Address

FIGURE 7.36

Mathematics for Adultation

Federal Income Tax

The regional office of the Bureau of Internal Revenue should be contacted. They will be able to supply the teacher with a resource unit on federal taxes which includes facsimile forms, charts, a variety of teaching aids and suggestions for instruction. The teacher should be certain that these basic ideas are covered.

 Who must file a federal income tax form?
 When must the form be filed?
 What are payroll deductions?
 What is a W-4 form and how is it filled out?
 Where can I obtain information about federal taxes as well as assistance in completing the form?
 What is a dependent and how many can I claim?
 What is taxable income?
 What do these terms have to do with income taxes?
  W-4
  1040 A
  Social Security Number
  Signature
  joint return
  gross income
  withholding statement
  total income
  District Director
  Internal Revenue

FIGURE 7.37

W-4 Forms. The company you work for will take some money out of your paycheck each week for federal taxes. For yourself and each person you support, you can claim one exemption. Your boss will take out less money for taxes if you claim yourself and your dependents.

Mr. Jones has a wife and three children. Fill out his W-4 form.

Mrs. Shoemaker is a widow. How many exemptions can she claim? Mark her W-4 form.

INSURANCE

All young adults should become acquainted with the basic purposes and functions of insurance. Mentally retarded youngsters should be exposed to auto insurance, life insurance, property insurance and health insurance. Many employers provide fringe benefits which include partial or full payment of premiums on life and health insurance. However, many of the youngsters will be required to pay for their own insurance programs.

High school youngsters are quite interested in automobiles, so the study of insurance may seem more relevant to them if it begins with automobile insurance. They will need to learn to differentiate between these types of insurance: bodily injury, property damage, comprehensive, and collision. A local agent will be able to provide the youngsters with vital information regarding costs and average. They should become aware of the factors which determine the cost of insurance and the problems which can occur if adequate insurance policies are not owned.

A second type of insurance which should be presented is home-owners insurance. It is easy for the youngsters to understand that a family would be in severe difficulty if their house were to burn down and they had no place to go nor money to buy another house.

Hospitalization, medical, or health insurance is a third type of protection the youngsters should study. Sickness and accidents can result in financial ruin if no provisions for insurance have been made.

Life insurance is perhaps the most difficult to understand. The provisions of term, straight life, and endowment insurance policies can be quite confusing. The advantages and disadvantages should be made clear to the youngsters so that they might plan a projected insurance program to fit their needs.

Here are some questions the youngsters may explore.

How is insurance a form of savings?
How is life insurance like a wager or bet?
What does it mean to be "insurance poor"?

When is insurance regarded as an employee fringe benefit?
What insurance benefits are provided by the government?

Social Security

Social Security is one of the principal types of savings and insurance affecting almost all workers in our society. The Social Security Act of 1935 was one of the New Deal Laws and has been amended frequently as a vehicle for providing immediate and long-range assistance. The act provides for a wide range of health, welfare, retirement, and survivors benefits. The frequency of amendments to this legislation precludes a description here; however, the teacher is encouraged to keep informed regarding new provisions and to expose the youngsters to the basic ideas of Social Security. The teachers should also beware that with this law there are specific provisions for mentally retarded children and adults.*

THE JOB

Money and the Job

Weekly Wages. Jerry Smith works in a grocery store. He is paid $1.65 for each hour he works. Jerry works in the store each Monday, Tuesday, Wednesday, Friday and Saturday, from 8:00 to 5:00.

1. How many hours does he work each day?
2. How many hours does he work each week?
3. How much will he earn each day?
4. How much will he earn each week?

Hank Peterson got a job in a glass factory. His boss told him that he would earn $2.00 an hour. He will work eight hours every week day.

1. How many hours will he work each week?
2. How much money will he earn each week?

Paul Nelson is the janitor at the Downtown Office Building for $2.25 an hour. He must work Monday through Friday from 8:00 until 4:30. He has one-half hour off for lunch.

---

* *Social Security and What It Means for the Parents of a Mentally Retarded Child.* HEW, Social Security Administration, March, 1968.

1. How many hours does he work each day?
2. How much does he earn a day?
3. How many hours does he work each week?
4. How much money does he earn each week?

Overtime. Mike Gross works 40 hours every week @ $1.50. Some weeks he works a few extra hours. For the time he works over the usual number of hours he gets $2.25 an hour. Last week Mike worked 44 hours.

1. How much did he earn for the 40 hours?
2. How much did he earn for the 4 overtime hours?
3. How much did he earn altogether last week?

Docking. Kenny Tracy was one hour late for work today. He earns $1.70 an hour and works 40 hours each week. He will not be paid for the hour he missed.

1. How much does he usually earn?
2. What will his paycheck be this week?

Release Time. Tuesday was election day. Bill left work 2 hours early in order to vote. His boss told him it would be alright to leave early because the company had a "release time" policy on election days. Bill works forty hours a week at $2.50 an hour.

1. How much does he earn a day?
2. How much does he usually earn each week?
3. How much will he earn this week?
4. How many hours does he usually work each week?
5. How many hours does he work this week?

Holiday Pay. Frank and Tim work for the Gasoline Station. Memorial Day was a holiday with pay. If you work on a holiday you earn your regular pay plus the holiday pay. Frank took Memorial Day off. Tim worked. They both earn $1.80 an hour. For this week:

1. How much will Frank earn?
2. How much will Tim earn?

The Paycheck. Bob Jones has a job working in a repair shop. He earns $75.00 per week. However, some money is taken out (deducted) from his check.

a.	Union check off	$ 1.00
b.	Social Security	2.25
c.	Federal Income Tax	13.40

d. City Tax .... .75
  e. Health Insurance 1.75
1. How much was deducted from Bob's pay?
2. What is his net (take-home) pay?

Mary Roberts works for the Lucky Dime Store. Here is her pay stub:

GROSS PAY	DEDUCTIONS	NET PAY
$65.45	$9.34	$56.11

FIGURE 7.38

1. How much is Mary's gross pay?
2. How much was deducted?
3. What is her net (take-home) pay?

NUMBER OPERATIONS

The senior high student will continue to need assistance in number operations. The teacher will need to refer to the ideas presented in preceding chapters for many of the youngsters. However, emphasis should be placed on vocational mathematics and the applications of number skills to practical situations. Many such settings have been presented throughout this chapter especially in the sections of measurement and money. The following vocational mathematics units give further examples of this practical approach.

THE UNIT APPROACH TO VOCATIONAL MATHEMATICS INSTRUCTION

The primary purpose of the senior high school special education mathematics program is to equip mentally retarded youth with the skills for independent living. In order to accomplish this, it is necessary to focus on the number skills required for vocational success. The unit method to instruction has more feasibility in the senior high school than at any other level. At this phase of instruction, the relevance of mathematics to the task of earning a living may be shown. The two units of instruction which follow were developed under the direction of the author by three graduate students at Ohio University. They were edited by the author for this text in order to demonstrate the application of academic instruction to the world of work. The first unit "Mathematics and the Service Station Attendant" was developed by Lynne Hungerford and Patricia McHugh and the unit on "Mathematics and the Waitress" was developed by Patricia Chase.

MATHEMATICS AND THE SERVICE STATION ATTENDANT*

This unit should be especially appealing to young men interested in the care and maintenance of automobiles. This unit was developed in outline form to indicate the scope of the activities that would be carried out as the students prepared to work in a service station.

General Objectives

To develop the mathematical skills essential to success in the role of a service station attendant.

To apply these skills in a practical situation for success in this occupational role.

Upon completion of this unit, the student will be observed in his performance of this role and will be required to complete satisfactorily a mathematical competency examination covering this unit.

Topics

1. The Work Week and Pay
2. Reading and Operating the Gasoline Pump
3. Oil Supply
4. Working with Lubrication and Maintenance of Fluid
5. Tire Maintenance
6. Maintaining Windshield and Lights
7. Distinguishing between free service and that for which a person pays
8. Payment by Cash
9. Payment by Credit
10. How to Operate a Cash Register and Make Change
11. Operation of the Stamp Machine
12. Maintaining Stocks
13. Other Responsibilities
14. Unit Examination

1. THE WORK WEEK AND FIGURING YOUR PAY
    A. Begin with questions about the hours the station is open and the work schedule of the service attendant.

---

*Used with the permission of the authors, Lynne Hungerford and Patricia McHugh.

Mathematics for Adultation 453

Which days of the week is the station open for business?
What hours is the station open each day?
What time should an attendant arrive for work?
Are attendants allowed coffee or coke breaks?
When should they be taken and for how long?
How much time is allowed for lunch and when is it scheduled?

B. Give the youngsters practice in figuring their own pay. The depth of study and the complexities of the calculations should of course, be geared to the capacities of the students. Here are some problems which many youngsters will be able to solve.

Find the number of hours worked by Bill Shephard for the week of November 12-17. Bill is not paid during his lunch hour.

November 12	8 A.M.–12 noon	1 P.M.–5 P.M.
November 13	7 A.M.–12 noon	1 P.M.–4:30 P.M.
November 14	8 A.M.–11 A.M.	
November 15	8 A.M.–12 noon	1 P.M.–5 P.M.
November 16	9 A.M.–12 noon	2 P.M.–4 P.M.
November 17	8 A.M.–12 noon	

If Joe worked 2 hours Monday, 6 hours Tuesday, and 5 hours Thursday, how many hours did he work?

Forty hours comprises a standard work week. If James worked 54 hours last week, how many hours did he work over 40?

Compute the following hours for Greg. Omit lunch periods.
12 noon– 5 P.M.   5:30–8:00 P.M.
11 A.M.– 4 P.M.   5:00–8:00 P.M.
8 A.M.–12 noon   2:30–4:30 P.M.

What is the time and a half rate if the regular pay is $1.80 per hour?

Does 40 hours at $2.00 per hour total $75.00?

Add $12.28; $37.45; $89.36; and $12.49. Total?

If John worked 38 hours at $2.75 per hour and 5 hours at time and a half, what was his pay?

Jerry's regular pay is $80 for a 5-day work week. He misses 1 day. How much money is deducted from his salary?

2. READING AND OPERATING THE GASOLINE PUMP

The outline below directs the student's attention to three specific knowledges and skills: (1) the pump dials, (2) grades of gasoline, and (3) quantity of gasoline by gallons or dollars.

   A. Pump Dials
      1. Attendant must know the three dial indicators and relate their meanings to the customer.
         a. Total sale dial
         b. Gallons dial
         c. Price per gallon dial

| $4.35 |
| total sale dial |
| 13 9/10 |
| gallons |
| 37 9/10 |
| cost per gallon |

FIGURE 7.39

      2. Adjust Gasoline Lever for New Customer
         a. Rotate handle on right side of pump clockwise
         b. Dials in sales and gallons window should register zero
         c. Use automatic shut-off lever for fill-ups.
   B. Grades of Gasoline—Various Brand Names
      1. Low-Priced Grades
         a. Economy
         b. 160
      2. Medium-Priced Grades
         a. Regular
         b. 180-200
         c. Extron
      3. High-Priced Grades
         a. High test
         b. Premium
         c. Boron

Mathematics for Adultation 455

        d. Ethyl
        e. 240
  C. Quantity of Gasoline Desired
     1. In terms of gallons
        a. Small purchase such as one gallon for use in lawn mower.
        b. Large purchase such as a full tank in a Chrysler.
        c. Specific purchases such as, "I'll have 10 gallons, please."
     2. In terms of money
        a. Small purchases as for utility gasoline can or motorcycle.
        b. Specific purchase such as, "Five dollars of regular, please."
        c. Indefinite large purchases such as "Fill it up, please."
  D. Here are some questions which many of the youngsters will find challenging.

Using the pump dials in example A of Figure 7.40, what is the amount of change returned to the customer if he gives you a $10 bill?

A
$3.50
total sale
11%
gallons
29 9/10
cost per gallon

B
$5.00
total sale
14%
gallons
35 9/10
cost per gallon

FIGURE 7.40

Using example B of Figure 7.40, what is the change to be returned to the customer from a $20 bill?

If Ted asked for two gallons of regular gasoline for his motorcycle and the price per gallon is 38¢, what is the total Ted must pay? What is the change Ted would receive from a $1 bill?

Mr. Blair requests 20 gallons of gasoline at 39¢ per gallon. What is the total charge? What change will Mr. Blair receive from a $10 bill?

3. OIL SUPPLY

The youngsters should learn the differences in the qualities and prices of oil, how to determine the amount of oil in the engine, and how to add more oil when it is needed.

  A. Differences in oil
    1. Grades
      a. SAE 10 or 20 is light weight and used in cold weather
      b. SAE 30 or 40 is heavy weight and used in warm weather
      c. 10-W-30 Standard ⎫
                                     ⎬ Year-round
      d. 10-W-30 Premium Plus ⎭
    2. Quality
      a. Detergency determines the quality
      b. Different qualities are better for different makes of cars
  B. Make-up Oil
    1. Oil should be added when dipstick indicates one quart low (see Figure 7.41)
    2. Do not fill past the "full" indicator
    3. If oil level is between the one quart and two quart line, one quart of oil should be added
    4. If the oil is below the two quart line on the dipstick, two quarts of oil should be added

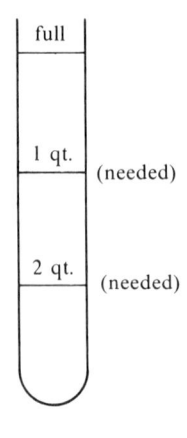

FIGURE 7.41

4. WORKING WITH SELECTED LUBRICATION AND FLUID MAINTENANCE

The youngsters should be exposed to the routine maintenance of the radiator, battery, master cylinder, and the automatic transmission. The outline below should prove helpful.

   A. Radiator
      1. Spring Season
         a. Drain radiator thoroughly
         b. Flush antifreeze if nonpermanent
         c. Refill with clean, fresh water
      2. Summer Season
         a. Water level should be *full* at all times
         b. Overheating occurs from lack of sufficient water
         c. Do not loosen water cap if car is excessively warm—will blow up in face
      3. Fall Season
         a. Drain radiator and engine block
         b. Standard capacity is twenty quarts or five gallons
         c. Close valves and add one and one-half gallons of anti-freeze for protection of approximately twenty degrees below zero
         d. To maintain "full" level, add water
         e. Station should have antifreeze chart available indicating the various measurements necessary for different temperatures desired.
   B. Battery
      1. Six-Volt System
         a. Found in foreign cars, tractors, and trucks
         b. Consists of 3 cells
         c. Cells should be filled to *full* indicator *at all times*
      2. Twelve-Volt System
         a. Found in most automobiles today
         b. Consists of 6 cells
         c. Cells should be filled to *full* indicator *at all times*
   C. Master Cylinder
      1. Brake Fluid needed
      2. Location is against fire wall on driver's side
      3. Brake fluid should *always* be at the *full* indicator at the top of the cylinder
      4. If you are losing brake fluid, you should have your brake system checked
      5. Someone low a few "squirts" would not be charged for the fluid

D. Power Steering
  1. Automatic transmission fluid is needed
  2. Indicator is located next to the fan belt
  3. Fluid should be filled to the *full* level
  4. Engine should be turned on while checking
     a. Place transmission in park
  5. Do not add fluid until one quart low
E. Here is a brief exercise which will measure understanding of lubrication and fluid maintenance.

Directions: In the space to the left of the question, mark a plus (+) for TRUE and a zero (0) for FALSE. An example is:

    <u> + </u>   1) Grass is green.

____ 1) Twenty quarts equal five gallons.
____ 2) Always drain the antifreeze from an automobile in the spring.
____ 3) A 6-volt battery has 4 cells, which must be filled with water.
____ 4) The brake fluid should never be low or something is wrong and a thorough check is in order.
____ 5) Usually when automatic steering fluid is low, a person can wait until it is as low as one quart before adding more.
____ 6) The engine should be turned off while adding automatic transmission fluid.
____ 7) In the summer, you should not check the water when a car is excessively warm or overheated.
____ 8) A 6-volt battery is found on Cadillacs.
____ 9) It is very important in the care of an automobile to make certain that antifreeze, water, brake fluid, and automatic transmission fluid is at the appropriate mark on the particular level indicator.
____ 10) If you check these items, you will be on your way to becoming a successful and competent employee: antifreeze, water, brake fluid, and power steering fluid.

5. TIRE MAINTENANCE
  A. Necessary Air Pressure for Maximum Safety Standards
    1. Twenty-eight to thirty-two pounds of air is the range in the majority of automobiles for air pressure (American manufactured)

2. First, remove cap from air valve on tire when checking air pressure
3. Then press tire gauge onto the valve; gauge will trigger a lever indicating the present amount of air pressure in the tire
4. Follow your particular manufacturer's suggested air pressure for your tire size
5. Using the Air Pump
   a. Turn dials to desired level of air pressure
   b. Bell rings once for every pound of air entering tire
   c. Add air to tire by pressing air hose
   d. When dials and air pressure match—pump stops
6. Replace cap on air valve

B. Lug Nuts
   1. Purpose of lug nuts is to hold the tire onto the wheel armature
   2. Lug nuts are concealed under each of the four hubcaps
   3. Number of lug nuts depends on the type of automobile
      a. Majority of American cars have 5 on each wheel
      b. Small economy cars and foreign models have 4 lug nuts on each wheel
   4. Tightening the Lug nuts
      a. Skip every other one as you circle the tire
      b. Count to yourself -1-3-5-7-9
      c. This helps balance the wheel

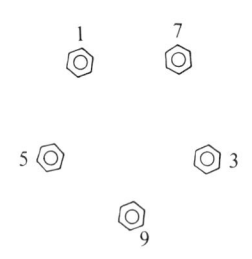

FIGURE 7.42

6. MAINTAINING WINDSHIELD AND LIGHTS
   A. Windshield
      1. Using a spray bottle filled with clean water, moisten the windshield
      2. With a paper towel, starting on the driver's side of the automobile, wipe in a circular motion toward the center of the glass

3. Repeat Number (2) on the passenger's side
4. The rear window is cleaned in the same manner
5. The rear-view mirror should also be cleaned
   B. Lights
      1. Clean both headlights with a circular motion
      2. Clean tail lights with a back and forth motion

7. DISTINGUISHING BETWEEN FREE SERVICES AND THOSE FOR WHICH THE PATRON PAYS
   A. Free Services Available at *all* Stations
      1. Wiping the windshield and headlights
      2. Checking the air pressure in the tires and replacing lost air if needed
      3. Checking the water in the radiator and filling it if necessary
      4. Checking the oil
      5. Checking the battery and putting water in the cells if necessary
      6. Filling the gasoline tank
      7. Furnishing road maps
      8. Giving directions
      9. Furnishing rest rooms
      10. Checking antifreeze
   B. Services and products available at stations for which a person pays
      1. Gasoline
      2. Oil
      3. Windshield solvent
      4. Tires
      5. Food items
      6. Antifreeze
      7. Transmission fluid
      8. Fixing flat tires
      9. Car wash
      10. Brake fluid
      11. Batteries
      12. Part replacements
   C. This brief exercise will give the youngsters practice in distinguishing between free and cost services.

   Directions: In the space provided at the left, indicate your answer with a (C) for charge items, or a (NC) for a noncharge item.

Mathematics for Adultation 461

    ____ 1) Filling the gas tank
    ____ 2) Gum
    ____ 3) Car wash
    ____ 4) Fan belt
    ____ 5) Towing
    ____ 6) Drink of water
    ____ 7) Wiping the windshield
    ____ 8) Oil
    ____ 9) Furnishing road maps
    ____ 10) Checking the oil
    ____ 11) Filling a tire with air
    ____ 12) Water for the battery
    ____ 13) Windshield wipers
    ____ 14) Checking the antifreeze
    ____ 15) Tune-up

8. PAYMENT BY CASH
   A. Cash—Total Purchase
      1. Gasoline Purchase
         a. Read total sale dial on pump
         b. Tax is included in this price
      2. Oil Purchase
         a. Know prices of various grades of oil
         b. Use chart
      3. Miscellaneous Items Purchased
         a. Windshield solvent
         b. Car wash
         c. Other chargeable services
   B. Using the Sales Slip (see page 462)
      1. When any type of work is done on an automobile, a sales slip is issued in duplicate. The original is given to the customer and the station manager keeps the copy for his files
      2. Recording Service Charges on the Sales Slip
         a. Check the item ordered and place the amount charged in the proper column
         b. Other services may be added to the sales slip in the blank space provided at the bottom, e.g., food items
         c. Total amount of purchases
         d. Figure the sales tax (see page 463) on all amounts except gasoline
         e. Ohio tax is 4 cents on a dollar (2/70)

f. Add gasoline purchased
g. Arrive at total

C. Paying for Purchases in Cash
1. Attendant states total charge: $3.72. Amounts may be itemized such as $3 for gasoline and 72¢ for oil
2. Customer hands attendant a $5 bill
3. Change is made at the cash register in the station
4. Attendant makes proper change, inserts amount rendered into cash register compartment and returns proper change to the customer—being certain to count it back properly
5. Manager (in approximately 5% of situations) may make all change transactions connected with the station; therefore, the attendant would give the bill rendered for pay-

WORK ORDER
AND
SALES SLIP

	NAME		
	ADDRESS		
✓	CHECK ITEM ORDERED		CHARGES
	REGULAR 1000 MILE LUBE SERVICE		
	MOTOR OIL ☐ DRAIN ☐ ADD QTS. GRADE		
	OIL FILTER		
	AIR CLEANER		
	TRANS. ☐ ADD ☐ DRAIN QTS. PTS.		
	DIFF. ☐ ADD ☐ DRAIN PTS.		
	WHEEL BEARINGS ☐ INSPECT ☐ REPACK		
	BRAKE FLUID		
	TOTAL		
	SALES TAX		
	_____ GALS.		
☐ PREMIUM ☐ REGULAR	TOTAL CHARGES		
99840 B			

FIGURE 7.43

Mathematics for Adultation 463

ment to the manager and only return proper change to the customer, being certain to count it back properly
D. Payment made by Check
   1. Checks may be accepted for amount of purchases in many stations
   2. Check cashing requirements might be:
      a. A driver's license for identification
      b. A charge-a-plate
      c. The license-plate number on the car being driven.

STATE OF OHIO
DEPARTMENT ON TAXATION
68 East Gay Street, Columbus, Ohio 43215

NEW OHIO SALES TAX RATES

LESS THAN 16¢ .... NO TAX

$ .16 to	.31	inclusive	1¢ Tax
.32 to	.51	"	2¢ Tax
.52 to	.71	"	3¢ Tax
.72 to	1.08	"	4¢ Tax
1.09 to	1.31	"	5¢ Tax
1.32 to	1.51	"	6¢ Tax
1.52 to	1.71	"	7¢ Tax
1.72 to	2.08	"	8¢ Tax
2.09 to	2.31	"	9¢ Tax
2.32 to	2.51	"	10¢ Tax
2.52 to	2.71	"	11¢ Tax
2.72 to	3.08	"	12¢ Tax
3.09 to	3.31	"	13¢ Tax
3.32 to	3.51	"	14¢ Tax
3.52 to	3.71	"	15¢ Tax
3.72 to	4.08	"	16¢ Tax
4.09 to	4.31	"	17¢ Tax
4.32 to	4.51	"	18¢ Tax
4.52 to	4.71	"	19¢ Tax
4.72 to	5.08	"	20¢ Tax
5.09 to	5.31	"	21¢ Tax
5.32 to	5.51	"	22¢ Tax
5.52 to	5.71	"	23¢ Tax
5.72 to	6.08	"	24¢ Tax
6.09 to	6.31	"	25¢ Tax
6.32 to	6.51	"	26¢ Tax
6.52 to	6.71	"	27¢ Tax
6.72 to	7.08	"	28¢ Tax

7.09 to	7.31	"	....	29¢ Tax
7.32 to	7.51	"	....	30¢ Tax
7.52 to	7.71	"	....	31¢ Tax
7.72 to	8.08	"	....	32¢ Tax
8.09 to	8.31	"	....	33¢ Tax
8.32 to	8.51	"	....	34¢ Tax
8.52 to	8.71	"	....	35¢ Tax
8.72 to	9.08	"	....	36¢ Tax
9.09 to	9.31	"	....	37¢ Tax
9.32 to	9.51	"	....	38¢ Tax
9.52 to	9.71	"	....	39¢ Tax
9.72 to	10.08	"	....	40¢ Tax

FIGURE 7.44

3. All checks should be approved by station manager. The attendant is under no obligation or risk in case of a bad check
4. Attendant should know the proper form in which personal checks are written (see page 465)

E. Here are some additional exercises.

Find the total sale amount. One quart of oil at 65¢, one air cleaner at $3.20, and $4 worth of super gasoline. What is the customer's change from $20?

Regular gasoline is priced at 39¢ per gallon. Fred purchases 3 gallons for his tractor and buys two 10¢ candy bars. He hands the attendant $5. What is the amount of change returned to Fred?

Jim and Sally purchase a bag of potato chips for 15¢, three-15¢ candy bars and a pack of gum for 5¢. What is the total?

Mr. Jackson purchased 4 new tires at $24.39 each. A) What is the total of the tires? B) What is the sales tax charged on the 4 tires? C) What is Mr. Jackson's change from $100?

A customer asked for $2 worth of gasoline. What is his change from a $20 bill?

Total the following:

1	oil filter	@	$ 4.12	
½	pint brake fluid	@	.50	
1	tune-up	@	24.00	
	gasoline	@	7.50	(tax included)
	Sub total		$ _____	

Mathematics for Adultation 465

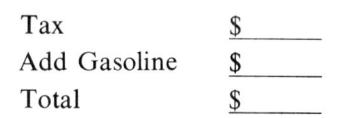

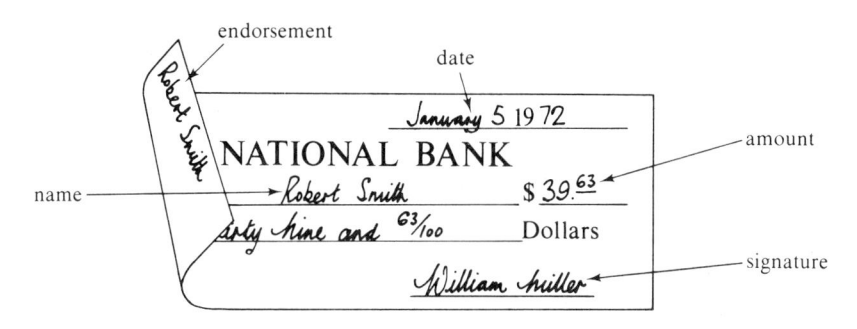

Tax	$ _____
Add Gasoline	$ _____
Total	$ _____

FIGURE 7.45

Sam purchased eight quarts of oil. Two quarts cost $.65 each, three were $.70 each, and three were $.85 each. A) What is the total cost of the oil? B) What is the sales tax charge? C) What is the change from $8?

The purchase price for parts and labor totaled $8.22. What is the sales tax charge?

George bought two bottles of windshield cleaner at $.89 per bottle. What is the total purchase including tax?

Gordon purchased $3.55 worth of gasoline and had five pounds of air put in his left tire. What is the change he received from a $5 bill?

9. PAYMENT BY CREDIT
   A. Preliminary Information
      1. Place credit card and blank in machine and make impression
      2. Put in the appropriate spaces your initials, the license number, and date
   B. Purchases: Record quantity, price, and amount of each purchase.
      1. Gasoline: record number of gallons and dollars from pump reading
      2. Oil: record number of quarts and multiply number by price of one quart for total. Tax should be added

$ .65 per quart
× 3 quarts
$1.95
+.08 state sales tax
$2.03 total

3. Miscellaneous purchases: record price of the following food, gas, bug spray, etc.
4. Parts: it may be necessary to use a separate blank for the purchase on parts

C. Example of Credit Blank (Figure 7.46)

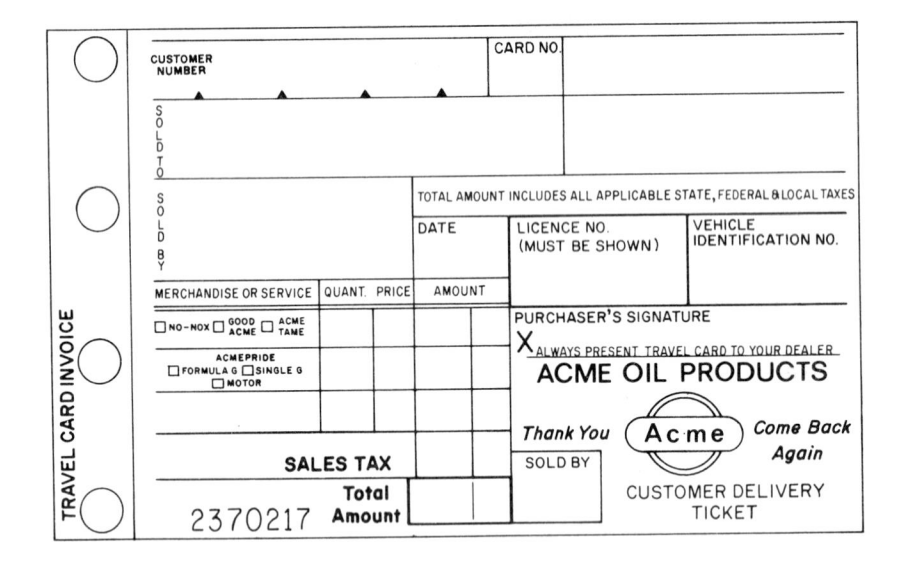

FIGURE 7.46

10. HOW TO OPERATE A CASH REGISTER AND MAKE CHANGE
    A. Identification of various parts on the cash register pertinent to proper operation
        1. Attendant should know how to operate the various levers and buttons pointed out on page 467
        2. A cash register may be obtained from a service station or a retail store so that students may personally operate the register
        3. If a cash register is unavailable, use a box and make compartments for the various bills and coins

Mathematics for Adultation 467

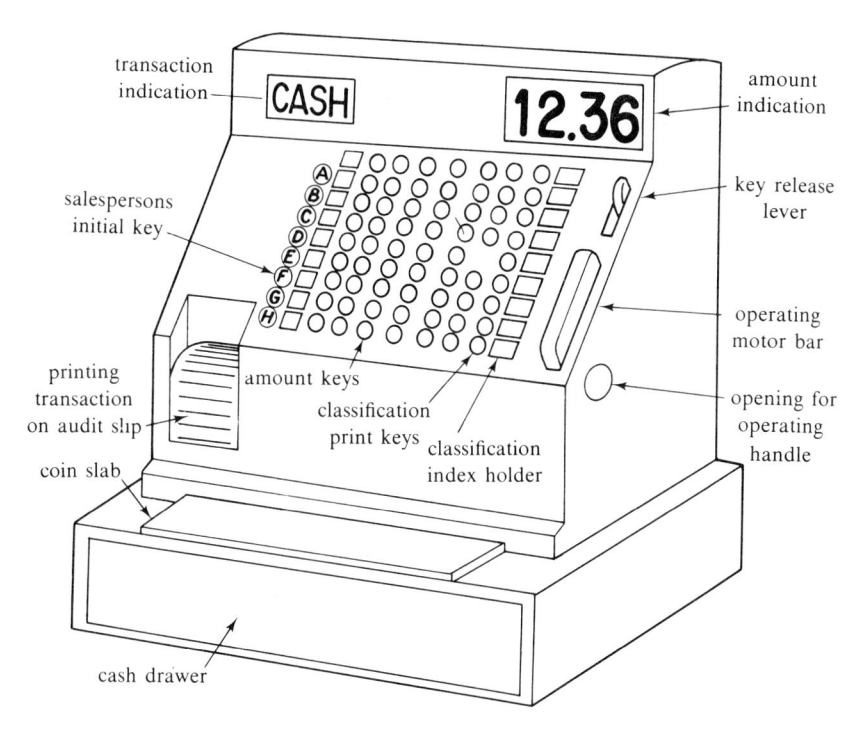

FIGURE 7.47

FIGURE 7.48

B. Demonstration of the Cash Register and Role Playing
   1. The teacher or manager should demonstrate to the attendant how to operate properly the register
   2. In classroom situations, the teacher can be the customer, a student the attendant, and role-play making change
C. Making Change (See below.)
   1. Mention total of sale and amount received from customer
   2. Place the customer's money on the register change plate
   3. Record the sale on the cash register
   4. Count change carefully
   5. Deliver change receipt or sales slip and (if any) merchandise to customer
   6. Thank the customer
      If the purchase is $3.25, the customer gives the attendant $4.00. The $4 is placed on the change plate. The attendant counts to himself—$3.25 and 25 is $3.50 plus two more quarters are $4.00. This is the proper way to count the change back to the customer. He places the $4.00 in the one's compartment and shuts the register drawer
D. Here is a Change Chart

	Amount of Sale	Amount Tendered	1¢	5¢	10¢	25¢	50¢	$1	$5	$10	$20
1.	$ .82	$ 1.00	3	1	1						
2.	$ 4.02	5.00									
3.	$ 1.25	2.00									
4.	$ 1.43	5.00									
5.	$ 3.75	10.00									
6.	$ 2.98	5.00									
7.	$ 6.37	10.00									
8.	$ 11.31	12.50									
9.	$ 7.42	10.02									
10.	$ 23.50	50.00									
11.	$ 7.94	20.00									
12.	$ 3.04	5.04									
13.	$121.32	150.00									
14.	$ 6.98	7.00									
15.	$ 15.95	21.00									

FIGURE 7.49

11. OPERATION OF THE STAMP MACHINE
    A. Trading Stamps
    Many stores give trading stamps with certain purchases. The example given here is for a service station which gives one one

Mathematics for Adultation 469

stamp for each ten cent purchase, one ten stamp for each dollar purchase, one fifty stamp for each five dollar purchase, and so on. The process for calculating the number of stamps to be given with a purchase is shown below.
1. Using the total price of customer's purchases, cover the numeral in the one's column and the remaining number indicates how many stamps should be given to the customer
2. If stamps are available in denominations of ones and tens, look in the tens column of the new number of tens stamps and in the ones column for the number of ones stamps
3. If a machine is used for stamps, depress the buttons corresponding with the total amount of purchase and the correct number of stamps will be dispensed.
4. An example is:
Total Sale $3.99
Stamps: 3 ten stamps
              9 one stamps

B. Problems Using Trading Stamps
Problem: How many stamps would you give the customer for the following purchase totals?
a. $15.89
b. $ 4.17
c. $ 6.66
d. $11.98

12. MAINTAINING STOCKS
A. Shelves: maintain a 1 to 1 correspondence of empty spaces and items to fill them such as the following:
1. Oil
2. Credit card blanks
3. Items on display rack
4. Automobile parts
5. Antifreeze
6. Food items
7. Paper towels for cleaning rest rooms
8. Wax, polish, bug spray, etc.
B. Containers—maintain a level of the item that is near or completely equivalent to the area of the container. The following items should be considered:
1. Paper towels in dispenser
2. Solvent for washing windshields
3. Water for batteries
4. Water for radiators

C. Records
  1. Keep record of items that need to be reordered
  2. Record items by number and call letter found on box or container
  3. Record low stock items on a Reorder Stock sheet

13. OTHER RESPONSIBILITIES
  A. Use of the Telephone
    1. Take the receiver off the holder
    2. Deposit one dime or two nickels for local calls
    3. Turn dial clockwise for each digit in the telephone number
    4. Replace receiver when call is completed
  B. Giving Directions to Customers
    1. Refer to streets and roads by proper number and name
    2. Use terms left and right for turns
    3. Indicate directions in terms of east, west, north, and south
    4. Try to estimate as accurately as possible distances in fractions of a mile or city blocks
  C. Keep Station and Surrounding Area Clean
    1. Read and follow directions for measurement of cleaning solution
    2. Know measurement terms: teaspoon, tablespoon, cup, pint, quart, gallon
    3. Start cleaning flat surfaces at one side and progress to opposite side until area is completed. Example: Station window—start on the left side and finish on right
    4. Dilute with water any spilled gasoline in the service station area

14. UNIT EXAMINATION
  1. If Bob worked 60 hours last week, how many hours overtime did he work?
     Ans._____
  2. If George worked the following hours, what is the total hours he worked for the week?

     12 noon-5 P.M.   5:00-8:00 P.M.
     5:30-8:00 P.M.   8 A.M.-12 noon
     11 A.M.-4 P.M.   2:30-4:30 P.M.

     Ans._____
  3. If William gets paid $1.60 per hour, what is his overtime rate per hour if he receives time and a half for hours worked over 40 hours?
     Ans._____

Mathematics for Adultation 471

4. If Jim worked 40 hours at $1.50 per hour, and 6 hours at time and a half, what is his total pay for the week?

   Ans._____

5. If a customer purchases 12 gallons of gasoline and drives 200 miles before needing a refill, how many miles per gallon is he getting?

   Ans._____

6. If gasoline costs 35¢ per gallon, what is the charge for 12 gallons?

   Ans._____

7. If a car is overheated should you remove the radiator cap immediately?

   Ans._____

8. What should the water level in the radiator be?

   Ans._____

9. Foreign cars, tractors, and trucks have a battery consisting of how many cells?

   Ans._____

10. Most American cars have a system consisting of how many volts?

    Ans._____

11. Fluid for brakes and power steering should be at what level?

    Ans._____

12. If the dipstick shows oil up to the 2 quart mark, how many quarts are needed?

    Ans._____

13. American cars require how many pounds of air pressure?

    Ans._____

14. Number the lug nuts in Figure 7.50 in the proper order for tightening.

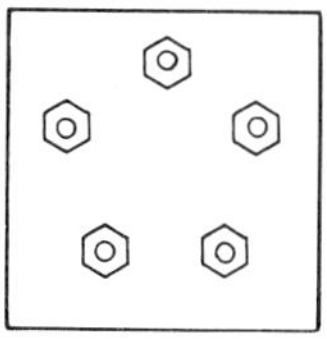

FIGURE 7.50

15. Should the customer be charged for road maps?

    Ans._____

16. Mr. Walters purchased gasoline totaling $4.25 and 2 quarts of oil at 69¢ each plus tax. What is the total on his sales slip?

Ans._____

17. Total the following:

	gasoline	@	$3.25
1	oil filter	@	$4.12
½	pint brake fluid	@	$ .50
1	tune-up	@	$9.99

Sub total _____
Tax _____
add gasoline _____
Total _____

18. Mrs. Hart purchased a total of $7.34. What would her change be from a $10.00 bill?
19. What would the change from a $20.00 bill be for a purchase of $3.70?
20. What should you use to dilute gasoline that has been spilled in the service station area?

Ans._____

MATHEMATICS AND THE WAITRESS*

This unit should be especially appealing to young women interested in restaurant work. It was designed to prepare high school educable mentally retarded students for positions as waitresses. This unit utilizes a narrative form and indicates the number skills related to the job of a waitress.

Introduction

It is assumed that the language skills of the students are well developed and that social skills have been adequately mastered for vocational placement. In preparing for such a work experience as waitress, then, the senior high level educable mentally retarded student will be primarily concerned with mathematical skills which are specifically related to the duties of a waitress and to work experience in general. All eight categories of mathematical skills from perceptual skills to money management and problem solving are important.

---

*Used with the permission of the author, Patricia Wheeler Chase.

In terms of specific objectives, at the completion of the work-study unit the student will have a working proficiency in the following specific skills.

A. Perceptual Skills   The student will have good eye-hand coordination needed for balance, body coordination, and manipulative skills such as setting a table, carrying trays, placing items in their correct places on tables without spilling them or disturbing patrons, filling glasses carefully and so on.

B. Money and Value Skills
  1. Ability to recognize various currency and coinage and a working knowledge of its value.
  2. Knowledge of tax tables and how to interpret and use them.
  3. Ability to use a cash register correctly.
  4. Understanding of how to cash checks and process credit cards.
  5. Ability to count money and give change for amounts up to $50.00.

C. Measurement and Time Skills
  1. Ability to tell time to the minute.
  2. Ability to read and use timetables and use transportation schedules for busses, trains, etc.
  3. Ability to understand and use a timeclock on the job.
  4. Ability to use measuring devices such as quarts, pints, half-gallons, gallons, ounces, and pounds.

D. Problem Solving Skills
  1. Ability to collect amounts due and give correct change.
  2. Ability to add, total and understand customer's checks.
  3. Ability to compute checks singly or figure the correct amount for each member of a party, if they wish to pay separately.
  4. Ability to compute percentages to figure tax to be added to subtotaled checks and to determine tips.

E. Reinforcement of Social Skills Previously Learned
  1. Understanding responsibility to employer to be on time, dependable, industrious, and courteous.
  2. Ability to get along with and work effectively with others.
  3. Learning to make decisions for independent living.
  4. Development of self-image and self-confidence through effort and success.

It is assumed that our hypothetical students will have been previously involved in a level of pre-adultation vocational training, and will have already had some experience in the general aspects of work, responsibility, economic independence, and, to a degree, money management.

Social skills such as courtesy, knowledge of a service position, responsibility to employers, hygiene, safety, and willingness to work have been previously taught. These same social skills should be expanded and reinforced, but our main concern in this unit is to teach the specific mathematical skills necessary to the job of being a waitress. The focus on social skills should and must be encouraged by the teacher with various motivating activities such as mock interviews, role-playing, posters and class-made bulletin boards. The teacher should structure mock interviews with members of the class taking the roles of employers and prospective employees. Include practice in filling out applications, creating a good impression, and accepting the job. The teacher might let the rest of the class observe and critique the "interviews" and on the basis of their grooming, manners, poise and bearing, decide what "interviewees" merit the job. Role-playing is an especially appropriate technique for shy, uncooperative, or overly boisterous students. The class may strive to build personality strengths in order to work with others more pleasantly and effectively.

Motivating Activity. A field trip to a restaurant can be a significant motivating and learning experience. For those students who cannot afford the luxury of eating out, funds can probably be obtained from school funds or from class sponsored money-making projects. By visiting a restaurant, the students can see a waitress or waiter at work and observe the many duties involved in such a job. It would be wise to prepare students in advance to watch the duties performed by the waitress while serving them. Upon returning to the classroom have students list and discuss what duties the waitress performed. They might begin by discussing the social aspects. Was the waitress friendly and courteous? Did she seem eager to be of service? Was she careful not to keep them waiting? Did she seem to enjoy her work? Students might then list what specific tasks the waitress performed while waiting on them. The list would probably look somewhat like the one given here:
1. Gave menues
2. Filled water glasses for everyone
3. Took orders and wrote them down
4. Brought food and placed correct order at each person's place
5. Was able to balance and carry a heavy tray
6. Refilled water glasses and coffee cups
7. Checked to see if food was good and if anything else was wanted
8. Cleaned table of dirty dishes
9. Took dessert orders
10. Brought dessert and placed it correctly
11. Figured each check (or one total check), added tax

Mathematics for Adultation 475

12. Reset the table correctly for the next patrons
13. Rang the bills on the cash register and gave correct change to each person

This simple experience will show students the many mathematical skills needed to be a waitress. It will at the same time give them an idea of what kind of a job it is and what they must master in order to be a successful waitress.

At the level of vocational training we are concerned with here, the majority of time spent in the classroom should be spent on specific mathematics skills and practices which will be of prime importance to those training presumably for waitress positions. Much of the prospective work situation can be simulated in the classroom and practiced there.

Form and Perception

There are two essential skills related to form and perception that must be mastered by the waitress. The first of these is the table arrangement and serving. The waitress must master the place setting and table arrangement quite early in her training. The second is the skill of delivering heavy trays. Both of these skills are discussed below.

How to Set the Table. Set each place twenty-four inches from the next one—this is the minimum distance for comfort. Line silverware up evenly one inch from the edge of the table. Knives and spoons go on the right of the plate, forks on the left. Always place the pieces to be used first on the outside. The soup spoon goes to the right of other spoons. Turn the sharp edge of the knife toward the plate in readiness for cutting. Put the cocktail fork at the extreme right of the spoons or on the plate holding the cocktail service. Salad fork goes to the right of the dinner fork unless the salad is an appetizer or a third course.

You have three choices of where to place the butter spreader on the bread-and-butter plate: across the top, parallel to the edge of the table; across the right side, straight up and down like the rest of the silver; or across the right side at a slant.

Your table will look lovelier if not more than three pieces of silver are on each side of the plate at one time. Generally, dessert silver is brought in with the course as it's served. Any serving silver in the center of the table should be at right angles or parallel to the sides of the table. If the service plate has a design with a top and bottom to it, be sure it's turned straight to the eyes of the individual in front of it.

How to Serve. Serve all dishes from the left, except beverages: serve them from the right. Never lift a glass from the table to refill it except at very informal meals when the water service is on the table. Take hold of goblets by the stem and tumblers close to the bottom.

In passing dishes of food, offer them from the left, low enough so that guests can serve themselves easily.

If the salad is served with the main course, place it at the left or directly above the dinner plates. Hot beverages go on the right, just below the water glass. Bread-and-butter plates may be omitted at informal meals and buttered rolls served instead. Always fold hot breads in a napkin or piece of linen to keep them warm.

When the dessert course is served, clear the table of everything but the centerpiece. Start with the service dishes, then remove the dishes from each setting. Don't stack them—remove one at a time with your left hand, transfer it to the right, and then pick up a second in your left hand.

Never leave the space in front of a person empty. As soon as one plate is removed, replace it with another for the next course.

If you need any additional silver for the dessert course, put it in place at the right of the dessert plate, or serve it directly on the dessert plate.

Serve the coffee last. Have it at the table with dessert if you wish.

Carrying Food Trays. A major problem of the novice waitress is that she must carry trays of food without dropping them. This requires a fine sense of balance. A short demonstration of the principles of balance, using scales would be useful to this end. Set up the scales where students will be able to gather around and participate actively in the experiment. Using weights or heavy objects on one side of the scale, have students try to put equal weight in smaller objects or weights on the other side. Ask the students to guess how many smaller weights or objects will be needed to make the scales balance and let them test their theory. By doing this several times, with different objects (a hardback book on one side, paperback books on the other, etc.) students will grasp that in order to balance, the weight must be evenly distributed. Let them perform the same balancing exercise with a large tray, so that it too will balance according to the weight distribution. After they have mastered this, have them practice loading a tray with plates, glasses of water, etc., and carrying it. They will soon learn that in order to balance the tray they must re-distribute their *own* weight, being sure to put the pressure high on the shoulder. It is necessary that the tray be carried in this position, so that food will not be spilled or splashed onto customers. Have them practice walking with trays and placing them on tray holders. This will take much practice, but as any waitress will testify, it is a learned skill and comes only with practice. At first, it might be prudent to use unbreakable dishes, which may be found in the home economics department.

Mathematics for Adultation 477

Money and Value Skills

Money skills are among the most important used by the waitress trainee. Not only will the student have to understand and manage her own earnings with a knowledge of budgeting and saving, but will be called upon in her work to figure checks, use tax tables, give change, work a cash register, cash checks and process credit cards, and possibly compute a total night's profits from her tables. She may also need to compute tips. If tips are put into a kitty and divided, (which is a common practice among waitresses) she will need to have skill in percentages to figure what her share should be.

In a waitress position the employee will be expected to deal in money transactions frequently and must have a thorough understanding of money and value in order to be an effective worker. It might be wise to teach money and value concepts in two phases. First, the teacher must teach the students in vocational training as thoroughly as possible the concepts of salary, hourly wage, budgeting, saving, credit, and banking. This has been covered in early sections of this chapter and suggestions made there can be used extensively. Students must be able to budget and save their money with care. As is suggested earlier in this chapter, this can be taught in the classroom using practice budgets, sample salary checks, tax forms, sample credit purchasing, and checking and saving account principles. Sample forms for all these exercises can be obtained from department stores, banks, loan companies and the tax bureaus. For further suggestions, refer to the money and value section of this chapter. Secondly, the student must learn the specific money and value skills relevant to a waitress position. Among these would be the following

1. Recognition of the value of all currency up to $50.00 and ability to make change for $5.00, $10.00, and $20.00 bills. This can and should be practiced extensively in class using funds from the school budget.

Using available funds in $5.00, $10.00, and $20.00 denominations and all change, have students practice making change quickly and accurately. Pair students in twos. One student should play the role of the hypothetical customer, and the other the clerk or waitress. The teacher might give out slips of paper as "checks" or "bills" with varying amounts written upon them, such as $.54 due, or $15.61 due, etc. The "customer" should give the clerk a twenty-dollar bill from which he will receive correct change. Then have two students in each pair decide together if the amount given in change is correct. Students might also work with worksheets giving hypothetical problems such as the ones below.

a. Mr. Jones has had a steak dinner which costs $4.50. The state tax is $.18. What is the total cost of his meal? If he gives the waitress a $10.00 bill, how much change will he receive?
b. Sarah buys a quart of ice cream at $.69 per quart. The tax is $.02. What is the total of her purchase? If she gives you a $5.00 bill what change will she receive?
2. Ability to understand and read tax tables in order to add the necessary tax to a customer's checks. If a tax table is not available the student will have to depend on problem solving techniques in order to figure the correct percentage of the total purchase, depending on the state.

Students will have had some practice in percentages but added practice will help them in calculating tax amounts quickly and accurately. Sales tax in Ohio at the present time is 4%. Students learn that in reaching a solution to a percentage problem they must write this as .04 and multiply it by the amount of the purchase. If they buy an item for $5.75, they learn that they must multiply that by .04 to get a total amount of purchase. Therefore, the total purchase would be $5.98. (However, it will be sufficient to teach most students to use the tax table.) A few sample problems that would help students master percentages are given below.

a. If a man buys a quart of ice cream at $.69 and a pint of cream at $.39, what will his total purchase be without tax? At 4%, what will the tax on that amount be? What is the total cost of his purchase with tax included? Exactly how much money has he spent?
b. What is the tax, at 4%, on a $50.00 purchase?
c. What is the tax, at 4%, on a $5.00 purchase?
d. If a man charges a meal that costs $12.00, what will his total bill be, including tax at 4%?

3. Ability to cash checks and process credit cards such as Diner's Club, Bankamericard, and Master Charge. Sample credit slips and necessary processing devices can be obtained by simply writing to the companies who, under the circumstances, are usually glad to comply. In this way, students can compute credited meals in class as well as learn how to process credit cards and cash checks. EMR students also must learn that, unlike cash, checks and credit slips must be signed by the customer in order to be valid. They should have adequate practice in filling out sample forms like the one in Figure 7.51 in order to remember this important aspect.

Mathematics for Adultation 479

FIGURE 7.51

With sample credit slips such as the one in Figure 7.51, students can gain adequate practice in adding sums, tax and percentages, filling out forms correctly, and the principles of credit purchasing. By having the students fill them out, step by step, they will be able to develop automatic skills in processing credit cards. Again, adequate understanding of these principles and processes will help educable mentally retarded students develop more self-confidence as well as a mastery of skills required for such jobs. The same kind of exercises can be done with sample checks such as the one in Figure 7.52.

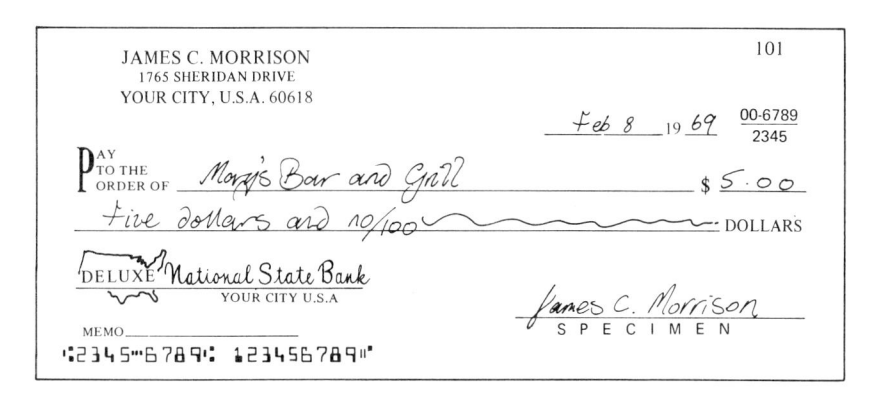

FIGURE 7.52

4. Ability to use a cash register, recognize all the keys, and ring up items separately, subtotal them, add tax, and then total the sale. By using either the school cafeteria cash register or a donated one, students can practice using the keys and learn that each

vertical row of keys denotes either dollars or cents, with the highest denominations on the left and progressively lower ones to the right. They must learn to recognize and use subtotal keys, total keys, tax keys, void keys, and be able to change the tape in a cash register. After all the students have become familiar with the registers, and each has had practice in punching the keys, it would be a good idea to have students separately, or in pairs, ring up sales based on hypothetical problems such as the one below.

   a. Mr. Jones has had a steak dinner priced at $5.50. He had dessert at $.45 and ice tea at $.15. Ring each item separately. What is the subtotal? How do you find the subtotal, using the cash register? What tax, at 4% will there be on the subtotal? Ring it. What is the total of the sale rung on the cash register?
   b. Miss Myers purchases a dinner for $4.25. She has ice tea at $.15. What is the subtotal of her meal? What is the tax, at 4%? How much is the total cost of her meal? Ring each item separately. Ring the amount of the tax. Now ring the tax key. Now total. What is the total amount rung on the cash register? Is it the same as the amount you figured yourself?

Students must now learn that customers charge meals or write checks to pay for them. In this case, the credit slip and the check are *always* inserted into the lefthand slot of the cash register just before the total key is rung. In this way, only the total is registered in ink on the check or credit slip. Students must remember with checks and credit slips that they must insert them just before ringing the totaling key. Therefore they will have two tasks. First, they must figure the sub-total of the purchase, add tax, total it, and transfer the amount to the credit slip. The sale is rung on the cash register, which will add the amounts again for them. Before giving one copy to the customer and placing the others in the cash register, they must insert the slip and ring the final total with the slip in the register. Since this is a multi-step process, students must have a adequate understanding of totaling purchases by adding, figuring tax, filling out credit slips, using a cash register, etc. This will require considerable practice for most students, and the teacher must allow time for grasping these processes and developing them into automatic skills. Teachers can evaluate at intervals how well students are doing by having them work out problems with both credit slips, cash registers, and sample checks.

   a. Tom Smith, a customer, has a meal which costs $5.65. He also orders a cup of tea at $.10, and a piece of pie at $.30. What is the subtotal of his meal? How much tax will be added to

Mathematics for Adultation 481

his bill? What is the total cost of his meal that you will have written on the sales check in Figure 7.53?

17	2/17/69 SAMPLE	203
1	Chicken dinner	5.65
1	tea	.10
1	apple Pie	.30
		6.05
	tax	.24
	total	6.29

FIGURE 7.53

b. Suppose Tom wishes to charge his meal on his Bankamericard? Fill out the form in Figure 7.54 as it should look. Ring the sale on the cash register. Where does the credit slip go on the cash register? What should come out on the credit slip after you have rung the sale?

		Date	Sales No.	Initials	Take	X
		2/17/64	4	P.C.	Send	
	1	dinner			5	.65
	1	tea				.10
Tom Smith	1	dessert				.30
452, Jackson St						
Marietta, Ohio.						
Bob's Restaurant						
Marietta, Ohio					6	.05
				Tax		.24
Tom Smith				Total	6	.29
Purchase Acceptor						

FIGURE 7.54

Filling Out Checks and Problem Solving

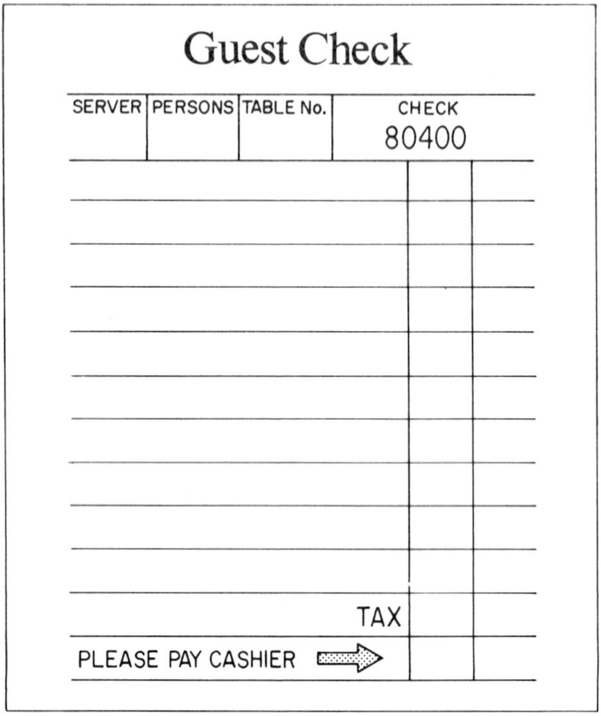

```
┌─────────────────────────────────────┐
│           Guest Check               │
│  ┌──────┬───────┬────────┬────────┐ │
│  │SERVER│PERSONS│TABLE No│ CHECK  │ │
│  │      │       │        │ 80400  │ │
│  ├──────┴───────┴────────┤        │ │
│  │                       │        │ │
│  │                       │        │ │
│  │                       │        │ │
│  │                       │        │ │
│  │                       │        │ │
│  │                       │        │ │
│  │                       │        │ │
│  │                       │        │ │
│  │                   TAX │        │ │
│  │ PLEASE PAY CASHIER ⇨  │        │ │
│  └───────────────────────┴────────┘ │
└─────────────────────────────────────┘
```

FIGURE 7.55

Obtain a menu from a local restaurant and present a problem similar to this one.

1. Tom orders his lunch at a restaurant. From the menu he selects an egg roll, a large order of fried rice, a small bowl of rice pudding, and a cup of tea. Fill out the check as it should look. Use the menu to find the prices of the items that Tom ordered. What is the price of each item? What is the subtotal? How much tax, at 4%, will there be? What is the total to be paid for the whole meal plus tax?

2. Mary Jones wishes to buy three gallons of ice cream at $1.10 per gallon. What will three gallons cost? How much tax, at 4%, is then due? Suppose she wishes to write a check for that amount? What things must you be sure to look for on the check? Now ring the sale on the cash register. What is the total sale? If Mary wants to write her check for $10.00, what change will you give her?

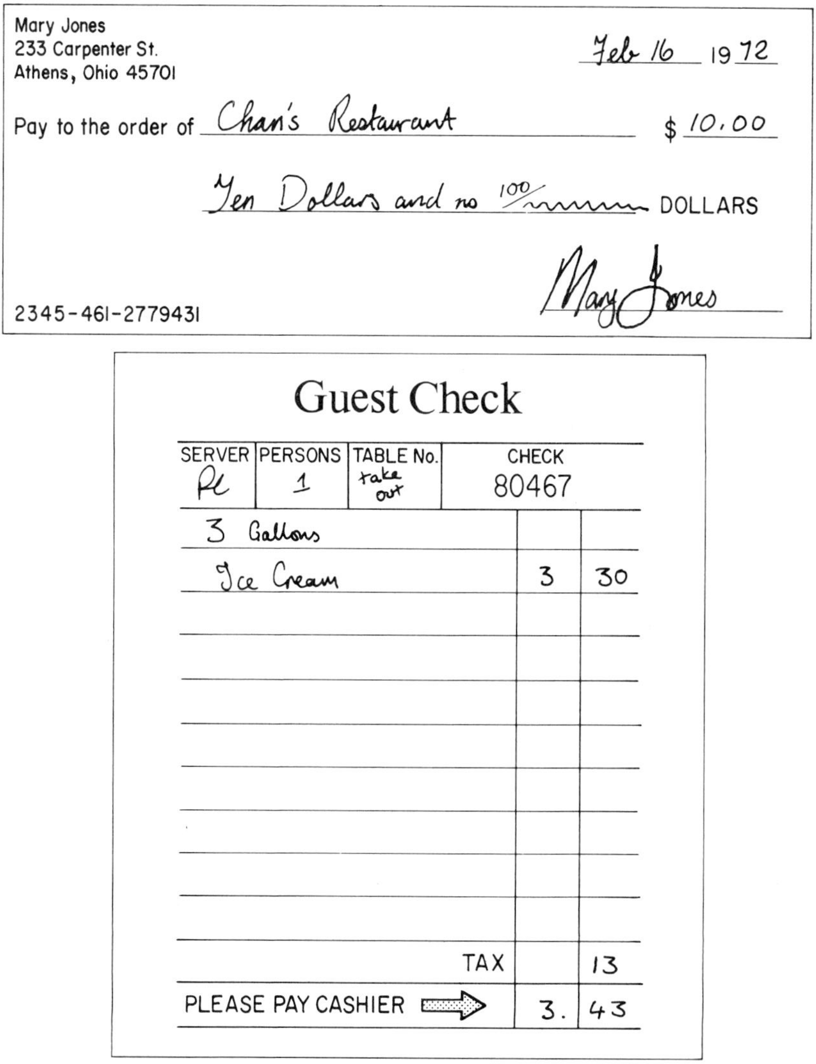

Mathematics for Adultation 483

```
Mary Jones
233 Carpenter St.                    Feb 16   19 72
Athens, Ohio 45701

Pay to the order of  Chan's Restaurant        $ 10.00

            Ten Dollars and no 100/_____ DOLLARS

                                    Mary Jones
2345-461-2779431
```

```
              Guest Check

SERVER | PERSONS | TABLE No. |    CHECK
  PL   |    1    |   take    |    80467
       |         |    out    |
  3 Gallons
    Ice Cream                     3 | 30




                           TAX      | 13
   PLEASE PAY CASHIER ⇨     3.| 43
```

FIGURE 7.56

Measurement Skills

The mathematical concepts of measurement are of particular importance in training a girl for a waitress position. For her own use in independent living, the educable mentally retarded student must have adequate knowledge of time in order (1) to clock in and out on time cards (this can be practiced in class by having students punch in and out on time cards when they arrive at school, leave for lunch, and leave at the end of the day), (2) to use timetables and bus schedules, and (3) to use in computing number of hours worked at the end of the pay period. By senior high level, as indicated earlier in this chapter, the student should be able to tell time by the minute. Earlier in the chapter appropriate exercises and work sheets are suggested for those students who do not have this time-telling skill.

Waitresses must have a "feel" for time since they must be able to estimate when an order is ready, how long since they have replaced water or coffee at a particular restaurant table, and how soon to check with customers to see if they wish to order anything more. Since a waitress is usually assigned by number a specific group of tables, she should be able to gauge which customers are ready for their dessert, which ones are ready to leave and want their checks, and which tables must be waited on. This usually will come with practice and experience, but the teacher can be of aid here, if students are accustomed to estimated blocks of time for specific activities. Simple exercises can be devised which encourage students to estimate amounts of time necessary for given activities such as completing a work sheet, making a measurement, filling out a form, etc. Students then should match their estimated times with the actual time elapsed.

Measuring devices, particularly scales, must be understood and used by trainees since a waitress must have a working knowledge of quarts, pints, half gallons, gallons, ounces, and pounds. This is necessary for their own use in cooking and independent living, but will be even more important in a waitress position, since in many restaurants they will be called upon to sell such items as ice cream or liquids in those units.

It should be a relatively easy matter to obtain paper containers in quart, gallon, half gallon, pint, and half pint sizes as well as a simple scale. Using these items, students can practice measuring these quantities using water, crushed ice or some other readily available substance. Using a few pounds of inexpensive hard candy, they can also learn to weigh ounces and pounds, while at the same time getting more practice with fractions. After adequate class practice in measuring, students will be able to solve problems with a minimum of assistance. Some sample problems to evaluate their skills in measurement and at the same time problem solving are given below.

1. If Tom wishes to buy 2 quarts of ice cream, at $.60 per quart, what will the total cost be? Measure this amount in one of the containers (using ice cream, etc.) If he gives you a $5.00 bill, how much change will he receive? (Check to see that students have added tax to the total, before subtracting the amount due from $5.00.) Ring the sale.

Mathematics for Adultation 485

2. Candy is $.36 per pound. If Ellen wants to buy one half a pound of candy, what will the total cost of her purchase be? If she gives you a $20.00 bill, what will her change be? Ring the sale.

3. Punch is $.89 per gallon. Joan and Tom wish to buy a gallon and a half. Measure out that much liquid. What will the cost of their punch be? What is the tax? How much do they owe? If they wish to write a check for $3.00, what must you do? How much change do they receive? Ring the sale.

In these exercises the student must be able to measure, use fractions, understand money and value, compute tax, give change, use a cash register, understand check cashing techniques, and be skilled in many kinds of problem solving. Therefore these exercises are meant to test many of the skills needed for a waitress position and can give accurate guidelines to the teacher for preparing students for on-the-job experience.

Culminating Activity

Throughout this unit, students have been involved in the mathematical aspects of a waitress position. It is further assumed that along with their classroom training the students will have spent some time working part-time in either a restaurant or the school cafeteria.

Since students will soon be placed in full-time waitress or waiter positions, a culminating experience that simulates a real restaurant with the various coordination, problem-solving, and money and value skills inherent in that particular job would be most appropriate. The Home Economics laboratory would be most practical for this, since students can actually cook food to be served. The menu might include hamburgers, sandwiches, soup, salad, pastries, and beverages which students themselves can easily prepare. Tables in the Home Economics laboratory can be set up with a restaurant atmosphere and the dishes and eating utensils of the laboratory can be used. A cash register, menus, checks, credit slips, and customer checks can be made by the students or borrowed for the activity. Each student would have a specific "role" as either customer or waitress. The teacher might fill out slips of paper with the word "customer" or "waitress" on each slip and let students select them randomly. Each student, according to his or her role, would receive an instruction sheet that might read somewhat like this: "You are a customer. You order a meal from the waitress. You will pay for your meal with a credit card."

The waitress will then have to set the tables, fill out the order, serve the food, clear the table, total the check, collect the money owed, credit card, or check, ring the sale on the cash register, and make change.

The customer will then grade the waitress on her master of the skills using a checklist such as the one which follows:

Checklist of Waitress Skills

1. Was the waitress quick and courteous? yes____ no____
2. Did the waitress take the correct order? yes____ no____
3. Did the waitress set the table correctly? yes____ no____
4. Did the waitress bring the food quickly? yes____ no____
5. Did the waitress balance and serve the food without spilling anything? yes____ no____
6. Was the check correctly added up? yes____ no____
7. Did the waitress remember to add the tax? yes____ no____
8. Was the table cleaned off properly? yes____ no____
9. After paying, did the waitress give you the right change? yes____ no____
10. If you wished to pay by making out the check over the amount did the waitress give you the correct change? Did she check to see that you had signed the credit slip or check? Did the number symbol (i.e., $5.00) on the check match the written out words? (i.e., five dollars and no/100). yes____ no____ not applicable____
11. If you wished to charge your meal, did she correctly process your credit card? yes____ no____ not applicable____
12. Did the waitress insert your credit slip into the cash register before ringing the total sale? yes____ no____ not applicable____
13. Did the waitress use the cash register correctly? yes____ no____
14. Did the waitress thank you for your patronage and encourage you to come again? yes____ no____

What grade would you give your waitress?   Circle one: A   B   C   D
Waitress name _____ Customer name _____

By rotating, each student can take a turn at being a waitress and each student will have a chance to be a customer-critic. This activity will give students reinforcing practice in the many skills they have learned and from the results the vocational trainer or math teacher can see what mathematical strengths and weaknesses each student has. This will help in evaluative techniques and planned further instruction for those who need it.

SUMMARY

This chapter has focused upon measurement, consumer education, and vocational mathematics. Major sections of this chapter have been devoted to the handling of money and the management of one's financial affairs. Two examples of the unit approach to instruction at the senior high school level were presented.

TEACHING AIDS FOR SENIOR HIGH LEVEL EDUCABLE MENTALLY RETARDED YOUTH

The following list of aids for teaching mathematics to senior high educable mentally retarded youth was taken largely from *Suggested Basic Materials for Educable Mentally Retarded Children,* Division of Special Education, Department of Education, State of Ohio, 1968.

The list is not intended to be exhaustive, but is presented here to give examples of the types of instructional aids which may be successfully adapted to the needs of these young people.

The code refers to the names and addresses of publishers given in the appendix.

PUBLISHER CODE	TITLE	DESCRIPTION

Newspapers		Ads related to
		  Food
		  Clothing
		  Furniture-care
		  Cars
		  Rental property

Checks, deposit slips		Used for all phases of banking services Savings accounts—including interest due Checking accounts Club accounts—Christmas, vacation, tax, etc. Loans—including interest paid Loan companies
Calendars		Figuring—days, dates, holidays, vacation, etc.—date books
Clocks		And watches of many kinds, makes, sizes
Phone books		Alphabetizing, uses of yellow pages
Catalogues		Mail order buying
Schedules Transportation		Public transportation
T.V.		Entertainment—T.V., Theatre Sports, meetings

PUB-LISHER CODE	TITLE	DESCRIPTION
		School hours
		Working hours
		Time allowances in travel
	U.S. Monies	Coins and currency—as used in true life situations. (Play money is not a realistic teaching aid.)
	Tickets	Cost of tickets—athletic events, dinner, concerts, plays, admittance or hourly fee for skating rink, swimming pool, golf course, etc.
	Application blanks	Practice in filling out forms.
	Measures	
	Liquid	Pint, quart, half gallon, gallon, etc.
	Dry	Cup, 1/2, 1/4, 1/3, cups, Tbsp., Tsp., (oz., lb., doz., box, etc.)
	Linear	Ruler, yardstick, carpenter's square, gauges of various types.
	Heat—Cold	Thermometers of various kinds, hydrometer
	Schedules	Public transportation Entertainment—T.V., theatre, Sports, meetings School hours Working hours Time allowances in travel
A-2	Math Practice Slate	Five volume soft-cover semi-programmed text series with magic slates. Teacher's manual. Introductory to intermediate reading level. Traditional approach to arithmetic. Childish format. Difficult for use in independent study.
A-3	*Adult Adventures in Arithmetic*	Five volume soft cover graded series. Write-in workbooks. Mostly figure

PUBLISHER CODE	TITLE	DESCRIPTION
		problems. Few word problems. Useful for adults with low reading skills, but of limited use as the problems are without a practical context.
B-1	*Consumer Mathematics Series*	Seven volume soft-cover programmed text series, plus teacher's manual and test booklet for each volume. Includes: *Vocational Opportunities & Lifetime Earning, The Pay Check, The Household Budget, The Wise Buyer, Income Tax, Insurance, Investments.* Advanced reading level. Programmed format makes books too tedious. This material is extremely well suited for adults in terms of subject matter and practical application. In order to be of use to the ABE student, the material needs to be subdivided into smaller volumes that are not so extensive.
C-1	*Tests of Adult Basic Education*	Three volume soft-cover series of test booklets. Tests are at three levels. Tests include: E (easy)—Reading, Arithmetic M (medium)—Reading, Arithmetic, Language D (difficult)—Reading, Arithmetic Accompanied by Examiner's Manual for each level and Catalog 1970-71. For use when diagnostic tests are

490   *Mathematics for Adultation*

PUB-LISHER CODE	TITLE	DESCRIPTION
		necessary or desirable. Not instructional material. For testing purposes only.
E-5	*Math Workshop*	Six volume soft-cover programmed text series. Levels A, B, C, D, E, F. New Math drills and exercises in application of concepts. Useful only for RFD member with special interest in math.
	Whole Numbers & Numerals	Two volume soft-cover programmed text series. Developmental reading level. Uses new math concepts and approach. Not suitable for RFD.
F-4	*Accent/Jobs Series*	Single Unit soft-cover workbook. Intermediate reading level. Each chapter is a short reading followed by questions and exercises. Adult oriented. Easy to follow. Could be used as instructional unit or supplementary instructional material relating to *About Me & My Money* content center.
	Accent/The World of Work	Four volume soft-cover workbook-text series, plus teacher's manual for each volume. Series includes: *Getting that Job; Keeping that Job; You and Your Occupation; You and Your Pay.* Intermediate reading level. Youth oriented. Too closely connected to a classroom learning situation for RFD use. Coverage of the relevant coping skills is sketchy.

PUB-LISHER CODE	TITLE	DESCRIPTION
	Figure it Out	Two volume soft-cover semi-programmed workbook series, plus instructor's book for each volume. Intermediate level. Takes up arithmetical skills in simple, direct workbook format. Covers addition through decimals. Problem oriented. Does not apply to practical situations. Can be used with adults and in independent study if student is highly motivated.
	Turner Career Guidance Series	Six volume soft-cover workbook-text series, plus comprehensive teacher's guide. Series includes: *Wanting a Job, Training for a Job, Starting a Job, Looking for a Job, Holding a Job, Changing a Job*. Intermediate reading level. Urban youth-oriented. Useful only as a resource for RFD. Short readings followed by questions and exercises. Readings form a connected story throughout the six volumes.
G-2	*New Mathematics*	Two volume soft-cover programmed write-in text series. Developmental level. Useful for those who need and want it, but RFD members not likely to be interested. Subject matter theoretical and abstract. Not useful for completely independent

PUB-LISHER CODE	TITLE	DESCRIPTION
		study for those not familiar with New Math concepts.
H-9	*Trouble-Shooting Mathematics Skills*	Single unit hard-bound text. Intermediate reading level. Expert review and survey treatment of basic math operations. Good back-up.
R-5	*Arithmetic That We Need*	One volume workbook with teacher's manual. Contains story problems and figure problems. Story problems child-oriented. Not suitable for RFD audience.
	Getting Along Series of Skills	Five volume soft-cover semi-programmed text series. Includes: *After School is Out; Al Looks for a Job; A Job at Last; Money in the Pocket; From Tires to Teeth.* Intermediate reading level. An integrated program of reading and math.
W-4	*Programmed Math*	Eight volume soft-cover programmed text series. Includes: *Basic Addition; Advanced Addition; Subtraction, Multiplication; Division; Fractions; Decimals; Measurements.* Accompanied by Work Problem Book for each volume, teacher's manual and placement examination book for the series. Very good program. Designed for completely independent study. Student needs help getting started, but continues alone.
U-1	*Farm People & Social Security*	28-page pamphlet. Developmental reading level. Rural adult oriented.

Mathematics for Adultation 493

PUB-LISHER CODE	TITLE	DESCRIPTION
		Gives information on how social security works for farmers. Too advanced for independent study.
	Social Security: What it Means for the Parents of a Mentally Retarded Child	This leaflet describes the special protection social security provides for the child who is disabled by mental retardation.
	Social Security Benefits	Single unit pamphlet written at the developmental reading level. Includes such topics as how to estimate the amount of social security one will get, when the maximum benefits are payable, and medicare. Language is sophisticated and compact. Not for independent study
	Your Social Security	Single unit soft cover. Teacher resource or supplementary reading for the highly advanced ABE student. Publication includes graphs and charts. Language in this booklet is very sophisticated, dealing with payments receivable, work covered under the Social Security Act and provisions for working after payment.
B-1	*Buying a Used Car Isn't Easy*	Eight-page pamphlet. Introductory reading level. Comic book format. Tips on buying a used car. What to watch out for. Very well done, practical. Independent use.

PUB-LISHER CODE	TITLE	DESCRIPTION
	Consumer Counseling Series	Four-page pamphlet series. Titles include: "Save When You Buy"; "Appliance Repairs"; "Retail Credit"; "Cosmetics"; "Fabrics"; "Life & Health Insurance"; "A Television"; "Drugs and Medicine"; "A Used Car"; "Rugs & Carpets"; "Furniture"; "Clothing"; "Food"; "Appliances"; "A safer car can save your life"; "Where oh Where does your Money Go?"
	Creditors and Collection Agencies	Four-page pamphlet. Comic-book format. Introductory reading level. Contains information about what the individual can do about garnishment of his wages. Well done, interesting, readable.
	Money for Rent	Four-page pamphlet. Comic-book format. Concept of borrowing money is portrayed very well. On last page is a chart of what 3/4% a month on unpaid balance really means. Adult orientation. Designed for new readers.
	12 Secrets of Smart Food Buying	Four-page pamphlet. Introductory reading level. Includes tips not usually found in pamphlets. Very useful for every shopper. Independent use.
	What's So Good About a Credit Union	Four-page pamphlet. Introductory reading level. Comic-book format explains what a credit union is, how it works, why it

Mathematics for Adultation 495

PUB-LISHER CODE	TITLE	DESCRIPTION
		is good. PR for a particular credit union in San Francisco. Factual information good. Format allows for independent use by beginners.
B-2	*How Money and Credit Help Us*	Hard bound text. Developmental reading level. Written for children but information is valuable for adults too. Explains theory of money and credit. Good information on how money actually works.
B-4	*The ABC's of Credit*	Fifteen page pamphlet. Intermediate reading level. Supplementary reading. Review Format. Concise information on credit.
	The ABC's of Life Insurance	Fifteen page pamphlet. Developmental reading level. Review format. Useful, concise information on life insurance. Teacher resource or supplementary reading for good readers.
	How to Buy a Home	Fifteen page pamphlet. Intermediate reading level. Coverage of problem and organization of the discussion are quite good. Could be used directly by anyone who is interested or able to buy a home.
	How to Save Money	Fifteen page pamphlet. Intermediate reading level. Review format. Useful information on this subject. Can be used independently.
F-2	*Food Shopping Tips That Make Cents*	Pamphlet. Developmental reading level. Deals

PUB-LISHER CODE	TITLE	DESCRIPTION
		with reading ads in newspapers. Budget saving hints, reading labels and selecting different kinds of food.
F-1	Getting a Job	Soft cover text. Intermediate reading level. Excellent terse presentation but distinctly urban black in its frame of reference. Could not be adapted to a rural white or mixed audience.
F-4	Accent/Family Finances	Five volume soft cover text series plus teacher's manual. Includes: *Family of Five; On Your Own; Just Married; Head of Household; Containers.*
	Accent/The World of Work	Four volume soft cover text series includes: *Getting that Job; Keeping that Job; You and your Occupation; You and your Pay;* plus exercise book and instructor's book for each volume. Intermediate reading level. Too closely connected to a classroom learning setting. Coverage of coping skills is inadequate.
	The Money You Spend	Soft cover text with charts. Workbook format. Intermediate reading level. Contains stories followed by exercises with some math built in. Emphasis on money predicaments of a family. Somewhat middle class oriented. Also directed toward high

Mathematics for Adultation 497

PUB-LISHER CODE	TITLE	DESCRIPTION
		school youth. Useful for some young adults.
	Paycheck	Soft cover workbook plus teacher's manual. Intermediate reading level. Somewhat urban orientation, but not predominant enough to preclude its use. Can be used with or without a teacher. Has information on interpreting a paycheck, understanding and computing payroll deductions. Ideal for use as instructional material.
	You and Your Pay	Soft cover semi-programmed text. Introductory reading level. Instructional material useful only with a teacher. Contains information on getting, spending, and increasing pay. Stresses writing and reading skills.
H-2	*Mind Your Money . . . When You Shop*	Sixteen-page pamphlet. Developmental reading level. Suggests looking around and planning before buying to get the best deal.
	Mind Your Money . . . When You Use Credit	Sixteen page pamphlet. Developmental reading level. Useful as a teacher resource, instructional material or supplementary reading for good readers. Lists things to consider before using credit. Contains a glossary of useful terms. Informational content helpful.
I-2	*Making the Most of Your Money*	Soft cover booklet. Intermediate reading level. In-

PUB-LISHER CODE	TITLE	DESCRIPTION
		formation on buying used cars, stretching dollars at the supermarket, credit. Story form. Questions and word review at end of each unit. Good for independent use by adults.
M-4	Consumer Economics	Hard bound semi-programmed text. Contains graphs and charts. Intermediate reading level. Contains information on budgeting and financial planning, saving investment, credit, installment buying, insurance, etc. Very good as a teacher resource or supplementary reading for interested students. Straightforward presentation. Simple, step-by-step explanation.
R-5	Using Money Series	Four volume soft cover semi-programmed text series. Titles include: *Counting My Money; Making My Money Count; Buying Power; Earning, Spending and Saving.*
U-1	Social Security Information Brochures	Informational packet includes: Two pamphlets—*Social Security Information for Young Families. Your Social Security;* plus four informational charts and posters. Advanced reading level. Background information on QASI benefits and programs and methods of presentation. Information good but complex. Most useful as teacher resource.
	Budgets	In terms of size of family and amount of income; priority listing of individual or family ex-

Mathematics for Adultation 499

PUB-LISHER CODE	TITLE	DESCRIPTION
		penses. Relates to work-study program.
Math problems related to work		Gross and net earnings, withholding, holiday and vacation pay, sick leave, overtime pay (time-and-half and double-time), piece work rate, computing pay on basis of hours and pay, salary vs. hourly wage scales, etc.
U.S. Money —coin and currency		Amounts up to $30, which may be borrowed, short term (for the day or period), through appropriate channels. Needed to develop facility and accuracy in making change. (Actual money is needed to teach this. It cannot be left entirely to discussion and paper and pencil work. Play money is not a teaching aid.)
N-5	*The Money you Spend*	Related to work-study.
P-2	*Everyday Business Mathematics in Living*	Workbooks developed by special class teacher.
R-5	*Getting Ready for Pay day* *Checking Accounts* *Savings Accounts* *Planning Ahead*	Workbooks to develop practice in money matters.
R-5	*Useful Arithmetic*	Good review for some senior high pupils.
C-7	*The Arithmetic Workbook*	Designed for adult illiterates, this provides material for working with the occasional high school pupil whose arithmetic skills are almost non-existent. Should *not* be used with any who can score above 2.5 on a standardized arithmetic test.
O-2	*How to be a Wise Consumer* (is also used in 9th grade	Good to reinforce and review information from junior high program or for use with those

PUB-LISHER CODE	TITLE	DESCRIPTION
	when this grade is included in junior high)	who were not ready to assimilate this information at an earlier age level.
S-4	*Seeing Through Arithmetic* Special Book B	In a senior high class there may be one or more pupils whose skills are weak—not to the point where they need *initial* instruction, but where *remedial* instruction is indicated. Because the format is juvenile, although the content is basic to adult needs, teachers may prefer to have one copy, with the guidebook, and adapt material for their students.
S-14	*Modern Practice Book in Arithmetic* (Working with Numbers)	Devised as a review for adults who have limited literary skills, this provides a good review at ninth- or tenth-grade level.
P-5	*Everyday Consumer Business*	This provides information from which the teacher can expand and build depth into instruction for groups using P-2, above. A single copy should suffice, since it is *not* recommended as a book to put into the hands of the students. (On rare occasions an individual pupil may be permitted to use this for a specific assignment.)

REFERENCES

Better Homes and Gardens New Cook Book. New York: Meredith Publishing Company, 1953.

Brueckuer, Leo J. "Use of Units in Arithmetic Teaching," In *Improving Mathematics Programs.* Columbus, Ohio: Charles E. Merrill, Inc., 1961. p. 41.

Crawford, William L. *Work-Study Programs for Slow Learning Children in Ohio.* Columbus, Ohio: Ohio Department of Education, 1967.

Johnson, G. Orville. *Education for the Slow Learner.* Englewood Cliffs, New Jersey: Prentice-Hall, Inc., 1963.

Kolstoe, Oliver P. *Teaching Educable Mentally Retarded Children.* New York: Holt, Rinehart and Winston, Inc., 1970.

——— and Frey, Roger M. *A High School Work-Study Program for Mentally Subnormal Students.* Carbondale: Southern Illinois University Press, 1965.

Miller, Donald Y. and Danielson, Richard H. *Work-Study for Slow Learners in Ohio.* Columbus, Ohio: Ohio Department of Education, 1965.

Sniff, William F. *A Curriculum for the Mentally Retarded Young Adult.* Springfield, Illinois: Charles C. Thomas, 1967.

chapter 8

Mathematics for the Trainable Mentally Retarded

The educational programs for the trainable mentally retarded are of comparatively recent origin and have been experiencing unprecedented growth throughout the last decade. In the early phases of their development, more energy was directed towards the establishment of the programs than towards their content.

This is understandable for a number of reasons. The majority of early programs were sponsored by parental associations and often the parents and other volunteers staffed the programs. For the most part there were not adequate funds to hire professional personnel, and if there had been sufficient financial resources, universities had not yet accepted the responsibility of preparing teachers of the trainable mentally retarded. There was no model for curriculum development and the only agreement was that these children could not benefit from the traditional offerings of public schools. There were complex administrative problems and questions concerning eligibility, groupings of children for classes, transportation, facilities, instructional materials, and in-service training of personnel that remained largely unresolved. Much progress has been made in recent years, but there continues to be confusion about the potential of the trainable mentally retarded child. This confusion leads to vague and uncertain educational goals. Thus, it should not be surprising that, in the realm of academics especially, there is still no general agreement on what should be taught to the mentally retarded and how it should be taught.

The educational objectives for trainable mentally retarded children usually include some combinations of the following:

1. Self-help Skills—feeding, dressing, hygiene
2. Social Skills—relating to people
3. Communication Skills—speech, conversation, listening
4. Perceptual Motor Skills—coordination, visual discrimination
5. Emotional Behavior—dealing with anger, frustration, pleasure, compassion, affection
6. Creative Expression—painting, dancing, singing, rhyming
7. Safety—awareness of hazards, safety around tools, machines, etc.
8. Academics—number concepts, handling money, limited writing, reading
9. Physical Fitness and Recreation
10. Vocational and Occupational Adequacy

Academic skills usually occupy a less significant status in the hierarchy of objectives and generally include those reading, writing, and number skills usually acquired by a child of age five or six in the formal public school setting.

Little emphasis is given to academic goals for the trainable mentally retarded in contrast to the educational programs for the educable mentally retarded. Our concern is with the instruction of mathematics, and in this regard it is appropriate to mention Hudson's observation (see page 15) that time allotted to the trainable for the study of arithmetic is quite small. In addition to this, it is well to recall that on the basis of the mental age criteria explained in Chapter 2, the most generous prediction of academic success would indicate a ceiling level comparable to a third-grade level. The research reviewed in Chapter 1 suggests that it is probably more realistic to expect a first-grade level of achievement. In other words, these youngsters will accomplish at best only marginal independent mathematical skills and more typically will perform at a very beginning and minimal level. Why, then, should any consideration be given to the teaching of mathematics for the trainable mentally retarded child?

The author takes the position that mathematics should be a part of their curriculum for several different reasons. First, since the entire educational program for trainable mentally retarded children is relatively new, there is too little research to justify categorical rejection of mathematic instruction. It is true that research has indicated that trainable mentally retarded children have achieved only minimal number skills. But it is also true that many instructional efforts have been sporadic and haphazard. A well-designed, continuous, sequential approach to arithmetic might have produced remarkably different results. What is, is not necessarily what could be.

Secondly, ours is a quantitative world which requires some limited mathematical knowledge for even semi-independent living. Even simple productive tasks in a closely supervised sheltered workshop require some quantitative skills. Some understanding of numbers is also demanded by everyday encounters with such things as the telephone, house numbers, and admission prices. The experiences children have with numbers will determine to some degree the efficiency with which they lead their daily lives. It has been shown that most trainable children are capable of learning some mathematics. Even the limited potential of the trainable child may be enhanced by expanding the perspective base from which he views his world and by developing concepts which help him qualify and quantify his environment.

But equally important, some of these trainable mentally retarded children may well be reassigned to educable programs on the basis of their academic achievement. If opportunities to learn academic skills are not provided, an important diagnostic criteria is eliminated.

The position has been taken, then, that mathematics should be part of the curriculum for the trainable mentally retarded. The next step is the determination of just what should be included in such mathematics programs. This is difficult to do since there is not general agreement on what should be taught. This lack of consensus is illustrated by an example related to what should be taught about money. According to Perry (1960, p. 154), advanced trainable retardates will find these money activities suitable:

> select from pictures or real store items things that can be bought for nickel, penny, dime.
>
> select correct amount for bus money; count it.
>
> select correct amount of money for small purchases.
>
> from a variety of small change, select correct amount for specific small purchases.
>
> learn quarter, dollar and half-dollar.

Rosenzweig and Long (1960, p. 114) indicate that the trainable child will learn

> to recognize coins and their values; to identify by name: penny, nickel, dime, quarter; to make change up to a dollar.

Kolburne (1965, p. 133) is less optimistic as he advocates:

> Teach the recognition and value of a quarter. Very few of these children can learn to count change that includes a quarter, plus

dimes, nickels, and pennies. It seems too complicated for most of them.

Perry (1960, p. 154) seems to suggest that advanced students could learn to master money values to some extent to five dollars; the second writers suggested that this ability would be limited to making change up to a dollar; while the third author says that "many trainable children can be taught to add a dime, a nickel and several pennies together," but that skills beyond this are too complex for them.

SPECIFIC OBJECTIVES FOR THE TRAINABLE MENTALLY RETARDED

There is such a wide range of abilities among the trainable mentally retarded that it is difficult to formulate specific objectives for them. Assuming an IQ spread of 25 to 50 among a group of sixteen-year-olds, for example, one could expect to find a mental age range of four to eight years. On this basis, the prediction of academic achievement in mathematics would range from nursery school up to a third-grade level. Some education programs for the trainable admit children who have intelligence scores that are slightly above fifty. Other children in the trainable program demonstrate an unusual ability to deal with numbers. By contrast, the more intellectually impaired children will be unable to gain even modest number skills. The author does not suggest that the goals indicated in this chapter are attainable by all trainable mentally retarded children, but they are within the reach of the more capable. Yet since the study of mathematics proceeds along a sequential continuum, even the less talented of these youngsters should be encouraged towards these goals.

The more capable young adult in this program is able to learn to count rationally, to develop a fairly accurate body image, to master basic visual-perceptual skills, to handle money in a limited fashion, to utilize the clock and calendar, and to do simple problem solving. Of course, the less capable will not achieve even this amount of mathematical knowledge. Their achievement may be restricted to such limited skills as one-to-one correspondence and rote counting. But even these limited skills equip students for numerous tasks in sheltered workshops. Those who do not learn to use the clock or calendar can learn such concepts as "the time to go to school" and "the day to go to church". Some will not learn to add or subtract even simple numbers but they can learn their age, house number, and the use of the telephone. Abilities such as these help prepare the children for vocational placement in a selected workshop and will assist them in adjusting to the many demands of daily living. The following objectives are presented in this chapter to indicate a program for progressing towards these goals. Some youngsters will progress to the most advanced level while others will not move beyond the first level. However, in this regard, it is relevant to mention again that all children are ready to learn something. The division of mathematics presented in this chapter should assist in the identification of the child's present level of functioning, and in planning the next step forward. The objectives suggested here will give direction to the formulation of reasonable expectancies.

Trainable mentally retarded children are capable of developing number awareness and can learn to use numbers in a variety of ways. More specifically, many such children will:

1. Learn to recognize basic geometric shapes, develop skills in visual-motor coordination, and develop a fairly accurate body image.
2. Develop a meaningful vocabulary related to mathematics.
3. Make limited use of rational numbers.
4. Gain an understanding of the use of measurement instruments such as the clock, calendar, and the thermometer; develop limited skills in the use of measures relating to cooking.
5. Learn to recognize coins, and their equivalencies, and to use money in simple transactions.
6. To understand and use simple number facts in problem solving situations.

The following sections elaborate the program content which promotes progress towards the achievement of these objectives.

In previous chapters, the material for the educable mentally retarded was organized on a chronological basis. This is the way children are grouped in school and it seemed wise to present the material most consistent with the actual situation confronting the teacher. However, there is a major problem in organizing the material for instruction for the trainable mentally retarded. The major objectives for the trainable retarded do not center on academic achievement, but rather on self-help, social and occupational skills. Therefore, the children in this program are grouped according to chronological rather than mental age. Each level has a very wide range of potential for academic instruction. The difference in the ability to achieve academically range from infancy up to a third-grade level. For example, a child with an IQ of 25 at age sixteen will have a mental age of four years while a child of the same chronological age with an IQ of 50 will have a mental age of eight years. Such youngsters may be housed in the same classroom but there will be a great disparity in the academics such youngsters are able to perform. The lower IQ child will not perform in a true academic sense while the higher IQ child may be capable of second or third grade work. The range in achievement is greatest at the sixteen-year-old level but similar wide ranges could be demonstrated at other levels. Thus this material is organized in a mental age level, although classrooms will be organized primarily on a chronological basis. The teacher will have to provide instruction on several mental age levels at the same time. The complexity of doing this may be one of the reasons that it has been tempting in the past to avoid academic instruction.

PRE-PRIMARY MATHEMATICS PROGRAM FOR THE TRAINABLE RETARDED

There is a new focus on the early childhood education programs for the economically disadvantaged, the sensory, physically, emotionally, and intellectually handicapped. The trainable mentally retarded child has been included in this trend. Educational programs for young trainable mentally retarded children have value not only for the growth and development they foster, but also for their diagnostic value. It was demonstrated in Chapter 3 that trainable and educable children function fairly closely together at the pre-primary level. It is often difficult to predict where a given child (especially the moderately retarded youngster) will eventually function. Further, there are some primary syndromes which have mental retardation (sometimes referred to as pseudo-mental retardation) as a secondary and perhaps resultant handicap. Examples of this are depressed intelligence as a result of emotional disturbance and social maladjustment. Some young aphasic and autistic children have been confused with the mentally retarded. For this reason, the author does not advocate early childhood education programs which are exclusive to any given type of intellectually handicapping condition. Children who have been mistakenly diagnosed as trainable mentally retarded or who are functioning in this level for a typical reason may be housed or grouped together. Their response to intense enrichment experiences often serve to differentiate their disabilities. That is to say, the early childhood education program for these children should be diagnostic in nature and should not automatically consign children selected for such programs to lifetime placement in programs for the trainable retarded.

The trainable children will grow intellectually at the rate of one-quarter to one-half of a year in any given calendar year. Therefore, at the age of three, they will be able to solve problems similar to those solved by typical children nine months up to eighteen months. At the age of six they will be able to solve problems similar to those solved by typical children of one and one-half years to three years. The pre-primary program is designed for children with mental ages of three years and younger. The chronological ages of such children will usually range from four to six. Some three-year-olds at the lower age range and some seven-year-olds at the higher range may also be included. An examination of the mental age chart shown in Table 8.1 indicates that some of the less capable trainable mentally retarded children will not reach a mental age of three until they are eight, nine, or even ten or eleven. However, these will have a lower level IQ of 30 and below. Most others will perform on a higher level. Those who perform at a lower level will be able to profit from much of the suggested material in this chapter, but it would not be wise to group them with the younger children because of the great differences in sheer physical size and social-personal needs. The teacher will need to provide instruction for such children in groups formed more along chronological age lines. In larger systems, there may be sufficient numbers to separate the high IQ trainable and the lower IQ trainable into two or more separate groups. In smaller systems this will not be possible. In either case, as has already been noted, the teacher is confronted with the formidable task of providing instruction suited to the individual needs of the children.

TABLE 8.1
Pre-Primary Level
Trainable Mentally Retarded Children with Mental Ages 1 and 2*

Intelligence Quotients	\multicolumn{9}{c}{Chronological Ages}
	2	4	5	6	7	8	9	10	11
25	.9	1.0	1.3	1.6	1.8	2.0	2.2	2.6	2.10
30	1.0	1.2	1.6	1.10	2.1		2.5	2.8	3.0
40	1.2	1.7	2.0	2.5	2.10				
50	1.6	2.0	2.6	3.0					

* Mental ages are given in years and months

OBJECTIVES FOR PRE-PRIMARY LEVEL, TRAINABLE MENTALLY RETARDED

The major thrust of the preprimary program is the development of adequate body image, motor coordination and vocabulary. These are the skills from which an understanding of numbers will eventually develop. The rationale for the inclusion of body image and motor coordination in the mathematics curriculum is presented in detail in Chapter 3. The position was taken there that the development of an adequate understanding of the coordinates of space and other mathematically related perceptual skills is fundamental to solving problems related to the questions, "How many" and "What order?" The children will be introduced to some notion of number symbols, the idea of indefinite cardinal number, the use of measurement in size and weight, and the value of money as a medium of exchange. More specifically, many children will:

1. Develop body image and perceptions related to size and position.
2. Develop vocabulary associated with mathematics including terms of position, time, money, and other quantitative characteristics.
3. Begin to do some rote counting and develop some concept of indefinite cardinal number.
4. Begin to distinguish gross differences in size, shape, position and weight.
5. Begin to recognize money as an item of value for exchange.

TABLE 8.2

Checklist of Mathematics for the Trainable Mentally Retarded Child

Pre-primary Level

1. Form and Perception
   body image program including laterality and directionality, motor coordination, identification of body parts, imitating movements

2. Vocabulary Associated with Mathematics
   up-down, in-out, inside-outside, big-little, hot-cold, wet-dry, all gone, empty, on-off, high-low, top-bottom, front-back, heavy, penny, money, night, tomorrow

3. Number Symbols
   rote use of numbers 1,2,3

4. Indefinite Concepts of Cardinal Number

5. Measurement
   distinguish gross difference in size (big-little) and weight (heavy-light)

6. Money and Value
   recognize money as an item of value and use penny in vending machine

FORM AND PERCEPTION

A wide variety of activities for the development of form and perception have been discussed in detail in Chapters 2, 3, 4. This section is meant only to furnish examples of the typical skills and activities which are appropriate at this level.

Skill to be developed	*Suggested Activities*
Walking and running	Use walking board; walk a straight path between two lines eighteen inches apart; play competitive walking games, march to music.
Running	Play games involving running, such as tag.
Climbing	Walk up and down stairs; go up and down slides; climb ladder to slide.
Hopping and skipping	Hop on both feet like a rabbit; twirl like a top.
Imitation of body movements	Watch me raise my hands; now you do it. Stomp my feet, spread my legs, etc.
Playing ball	Have one child throw the ball and another chase it; play catch; throw the ball at a target; also throw the bean bag.
Crawling	Crawl through tunnels, under and around furniture and other obstacles.
Eye-hand coordination	Scribble on paper and chalk board; build with blocks, use form boards, puzzles. Use peg boards; string beads; turn door knobs, light switches; play with clay; use pounding toys.
Identifying body parts	Eye, mouth, hands, fingers, feet, nose, hair, elbows, etc.
Spatial relation terms	Understanding concepts of in-out, inside-outside, on-off, top-bottom, front-back, high-low.

FIGURE 8.1

Spool Stringing. Stringing empty spools of thread on a string helps the child develop eye-hand motor coordination.

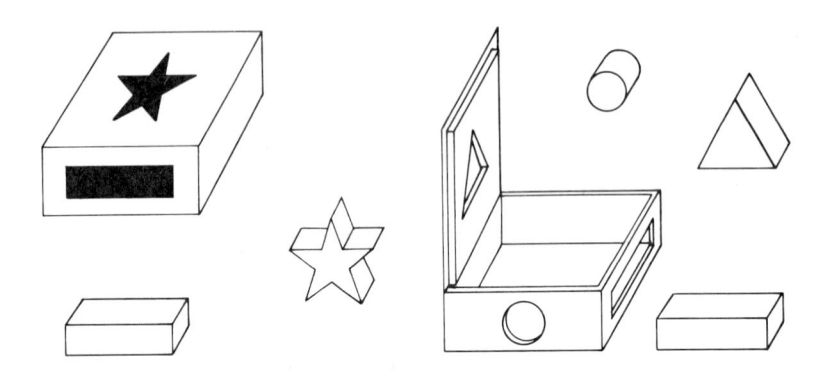

FIGURE 8.2

Form Boxes. Children can learn to discriminate different shapes by placing shapes into boxes which are so constructed that each space will admit only one form. The boxes should have removable sides.

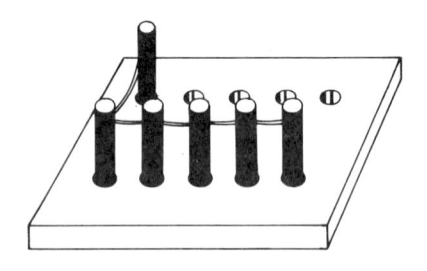

FIGURE 8.3

Fence Building. Pole rods are cut into equal lengths to serve as the fence posts and holes are drilled in the rods. A board is cut and drilled so that the rods fit securely. The string is strung through the rods to make a fence. This actually improves fine motor skills and also helps develop perception of space.

Puzzles. A large number of appropriate puzzles are available from commercial sources. The teacher should begin with the wooden, single piece puzzle and proceed to the more complex multi-piece interlocking puzzles. Perceptual motor skills will be enhanced through the use of a sequence of increasingly difficult puzzles.

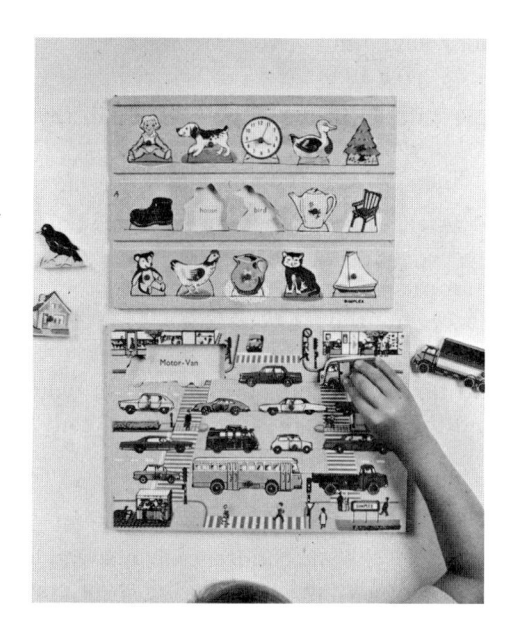

Mathematics for the Trainable Mentally Retarded

FIGURE 8.4

NUMBER SYMBOLS

The children will learn the oral numerals one, two and three, but they probably will not learn to recognize the symbols 1,2,3. The teacher will provide the children with ample opportunities to hear the words one, two, three and to echo them. Their learnings at this point will be rote and will not have positional or quantitative meaning. That is to say that the number concepts of definite cardinal and ordinal value will not be introduced.

Count slowly such items as cups and crackers, and give them to the children. "Here is one cup; now here are two crackers."

Use the phrase "One, two, three, go!" to initiate activities. "I want you to stand up. Ready? One, two, three, stand up! I want you to clap your hands like this (demonstration). Ready? One, two, three . . . clap!"

March in cadence around the room to music. "Children, we are going to march to the music. You say what I say, One, two, three, march; One, two, three, march, etc."

Use rhymes to reinforce the rote use of the oral numeral words. March, sing or clap to such rhymes as:

Hey, one, let's have fun
Hey, one, let's have fun.

Point to different children in the circle and say in rhyme:
One, two, I know you.
One, two, I know you.

On the numeral three, jump as if stung by a bee and say:
One, two, three, stung by a bee
O-U-C-H (jump)
One, two, three, stung by a bee
O-U-C-H (jump)

"I am going to toss you into the air (push you on the swing, chase you around the room, etc.) Here I come. Ready? One, two, three . . .".

CARDINAL AND ORDINAL NUMBER

At the pre-primary level some children may respond to such directives as "give me one pencil; give me a whole bunch of crayons; that is too many cookies; put some back. Mary, go first". However, it is quite doubtful that there is any true understanding of cardinal and ordinal number. Number words should be used in ordinary conversation on a planned basis, but little is expected of the child other than that he respond to the total meaning of the sentence or directive. For example, when a child is asked to give each child one cookie, he is performing at a primitive level of one-to-one correspondence. The teacher will need to assist him so that every child does in fact get one cookie. He will tend to overlook some children and supply too many cookies to others. With help, he can succeed. At the primary level, he will be capable of carrying out such tasks independently. He will understand more fully the concepts: "Do you want *one* M & M or *several?* Do you want some *more?* Will the child select *two* M & M's or *many?* The M & M's are *all gone.* The packages are *empty*".

MEASUREMENT

Very little will be accomplished in the area of measurement with the pre-primary trainable youngster. However, the child will learn some indefinite measurement terms such as "big-little" (size), "heavy-light" (weight), "up-down" (direction), "night-tomorrow" (time), "hot-cold" (temperature).

MONEY AND VALUE

Some children will be able to learn the name "penny" and to select pennies from among a set of foils such as buttons, chips and checkers.

Many trainable mentally retarded children of this chronological age learn the use of the penny in vending machines quite early. Which serves to show the value of using positive reinforcement for learning behavior, since the child learns to associate the penny with the acquisition of a desired object, such as a piece of candy or gum.

THE PRIMARY MATHEMATICS PROGRAM FOR THE TRAINABLE MENTALLY RETARDED

The primary program for trainable mentally retarded children includes those youngsters with mental ages above three years and below five years. The chronological ages of such children will usually range from seven to nine years. The mental age table (Table 8.3) indicates that the teacher of the lower IQ trainable children (below IQ 30) will find the material presented within this chapter at the upper limit of their capability. The content presented within the intermediate level will exceed their maximal anticipated performance. As with other classifications of trainable children, it is not prudent to group solely on the basis of mental age. If mental age were used as the grouping factor, one would place children with chronological ages of seven with those chronologically aged sixteen. It is true that mental age is the best single predictor of academic performance, but it is also true that the major objective of the program for the trainable is not academic performance. The teacher of the older trainable (intermediate and adultation levels) will find much of the content presented at this level appropriate for them.

TABLE 8.3
Primary Level
Trainable Mentally Retarded Children with Mental Ages 3 and 4

Intelligence Quotients	6	7	8	9	10	11	12	13	14	15	16
25								3.2	3.6	3.8	4.0
30						3.3	3.7	3.11	4.2	4.5	4.10
40				3.2	3.7	4.0	4.5	4.10			
50			3.6	4.0	4.6						

(Chronological Ages)

OBJECTIVES FOR THE PRIMARY LEVEL, TRAINABLE MENTALLY RETARDED

The primary level program for trainable mentally retarded children continues to be concerned with perceptual skills, vocabulary and number symbols. However, children at this level are able to learn to work with rational numbers, enumerate sets, successfully perform one-to-one correspondences, use some ordinal numbers, comprehend gross measures, use money, and use additive and subtractive action. More specifically, many children at this level will:

1. Continue to develop body image and work with geometric shapes.
2. Develop a wider vocabulary.
3. Successfully rote count to ten, perform limited rational counting and make limited use of ordinal numbers.
4. Recognize common measurement instruments and apply gross measures to daily situations.
5. Use money in simple transactions and add and subtract up to five.

TABLE 8.4

Checklist of Mathematics for the Trainable Mentally Retarded Child

Primary Level

1. Form and Perception
   basic manipulative experiences with geometric forms such as rectangles, squares, circles and triangles; continue the development of body image, reproduction of lines and circles, further identification of body parts, and imitation of movement.

2. Vocabulary Associated with Mathematics
   long, short, tall, thick, wide, bunch, narrow, middle, top, bottom, on, off, in, out of, next to, outside, inside, all.

3. Number Symbols
   rote count to 10; write numerals 1 and 2; repeat three sequential digits.

4. Cardinal Number
   indefinite cardinal number such as most and few, more, less; one-to-one correspondence; one-to-two and one-to-many correspondence; reproducing sets of 1,2,3, and 4,5; set recognition of 2,3,4; answer question "how many?"

5. Ordinal Number
   first, last, middle.
6. Measurement
   recognition of common measurement instruments, scales, ruler, calendar; simple concepts of time, such as today, tomorrow, day, night, time to go to bed, time to go to school, time to get up, time for lunch, time for recess, time to go home; simple concepts of calendar such as the names of the days of the week and their location on the calendar; knowledge of their own age, birthdays; experiences with non-standard measurements of capacity, volume, length.
7. Money and Value
   recognition of comparative values, identification of penny and nickel, discrimination of money, knowledge of money usage.
8. Number Operations
   addition and subtraction with combination to five.

FORM AND PERCEPTION

There has been considerable emphasis on the development of perceptual motor skills for trainable mentally retarded children over the past several years. It has been observed that trainable mentally retarded children are markedly clumsy, poorly coordinated and grossly deficient in perceptual skills when compared to other children. These characteristics have implications not only for the development of self-help, locomotion, communication, recreational and vocational skills but also for the mastery of simple number concepts. The rationale for the inclusion of form and perceptual skills in the arithmetic curriculum is based on the observation that number ideas are inherently related to the conceptualization of space. For example, a child who has not developed basic body awareness will be unable to judge height, distance, shape, position, and motion. Any attempt to teach such a child even the most elementary qualitative and number ideas will be very apt to meet with failure.*

The types of activities suggested for the trainable mentally retarded children functioning at this level are designed to assist in the development of body image, gross coordination, fine coordination, and eye-hand motor coordination. Many of the typical experiences presented to children in regular three-and four-year kindergarten are suited for these youngsters. A number of these activities are shown below.

*For a more detailed discussion see Form and Perception. Chapter 2 Chapter 3.

Gross Motor Areas	Activities
Crawling	Have the children crawl through paste-board cartons, around obstacles, up planes, down stairs, through tunnels under tables, etc.
Walking	Have the children walk in rhythm to the count, one-two, up and down stairs, through simple obstacle course, on balance boards.
Running	Play simple running games; some children will be able to race each other; some will be able to play such games as tag, ring-around-the-rosey, and London Bridge is Falling Down. The less mature children may be limited to such simple activities as being chased by or chasing another child.
Swinging	Even very young children enjoy being pushed in a swing, or bouncing in a seat. More capable children will develop the ability to swing themselves. The skill required to swing not only develops coordination but also rhythm and motion.
Throwing	Play with large balls, balloon, etc.

Fine Motor Areas

Dressing	Have the children play dress-up in old clothes. Some children will be able to dress dolls.
Bead Play	Use a variety of plastic and wooden beads. Have the children string the wooden beads with plastic "pop heads."
Puzzles	The children may now be able to complete more complex, two and three piece puzzles like the ones shown in Figure 8.5.
Forms	Present the children with many opportunities to work with a variety of forms and shapes of different colors, size and texture.

FIGURE 8.5

Mathematics for the Trainable Mentally Retarded 519

△ ○ ♧ ☆ ☾
◇ ⌣ ∞ ▭

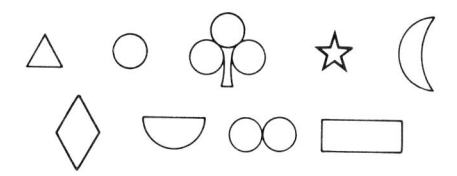

FIGURE 8.6

Peg Boards   Many of the children will be capable of using peg boards. These come in a wide range of complexity. All of the children will be able to remove the pegs, some will be able to replace the pegs and a few will be able to place the pegs in some simple pattern.

FIGURE 8.7

Building Blocks—
(Multiway Rollaway)   Here is a game which will motivate most children. Children design their own lay outs and race marbles along the tracks.

Triangle Games   Cut a number of triangles out of stiff colored paper. Make each triangle large enough so the children can handle them with ease. Figure 8.8 shows some samples of the patterns which can be made.

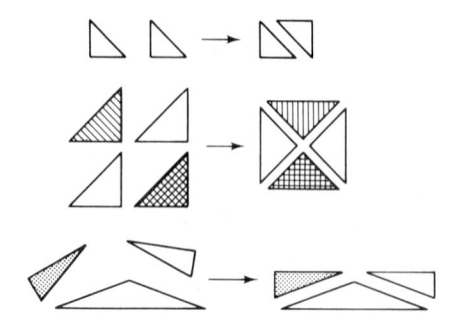

FIGURE 8.8

Marking Paper	Have the children scribble on large pieces of paper with kindergarten crayons. Also use finger paints. Some children will be able to mark pictures such as putting an X on the picture of a cat.
Drawing	Circles, lines.
Tracing	Squares, rectangles.
Books	Turning pages.

VOCABULARY ASSOCIATED WITH MATHEMATICS

The vocabulary associated with mathematics will develop within the context of general vocabulary acquisition. There are some specific quantitative terms which can be taught to trainable children of this age. The

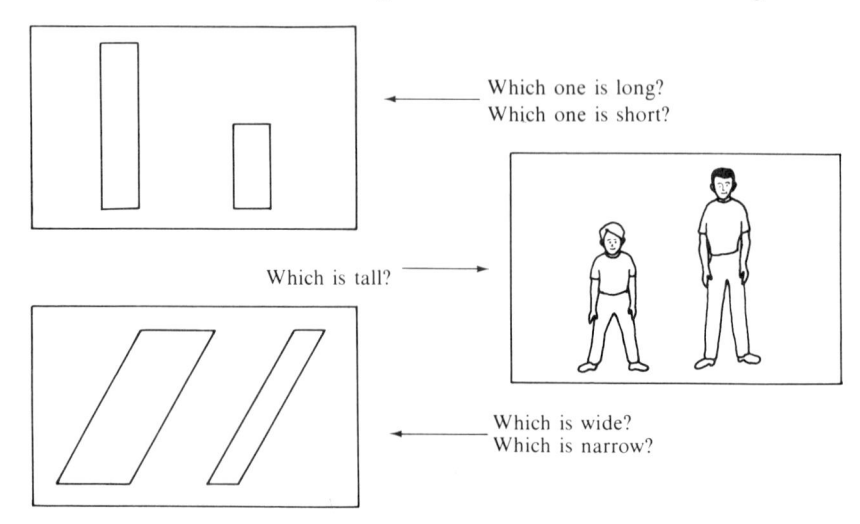

Which one is long?
Which one is short?

Which is tall?

Which is wide?
Which is narrow?

FIGURE 8.9

vocabulary associated with mathematics is taught in conjunction with the number concepts. Some examples are: The number words, *one, two, three, ... ten;* indefinite cardinal terms, *few, many, more, less;* ordinal numbers *first, last, middle;* and measurement terms, *early, late, heavy, long, short;* money terms, *penny, nickel, pay, cost;* and number operation terms, *add* and *equal.* Suggestions for teaching terms such as these are discussed in later sections. The use of pictures and toys are a valuable aid to teaching quantitative words. The pictures should be of simple uncluttered design and the toys should be attractive and colorful.

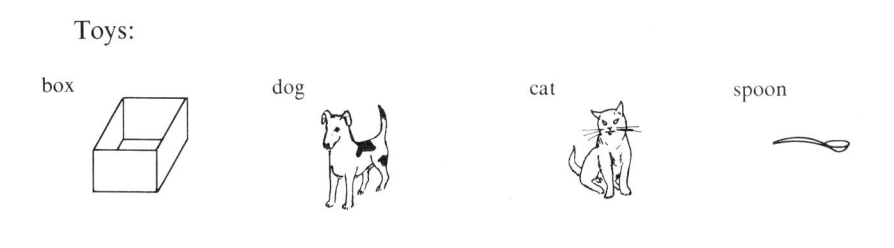

Toys:

box   dog   cat   spoon

FIGURE 8.10

Give these directions: "Put the (cat, dog, etc.) *in* the box."
"Take the (cat, dog, etc.) *out* of the box."
"Put the dog *next* to the box."
"Give me all the dogs, cats, and spoons."

NUMBER SYMBOLS

Studies have shown that a majority of children entering first grade can count by rote. They have memorized at least a few of the number words in sequence through incidental experiences in the family and neighborhood. The teacher of the typical first grader need not concern herself with this skill other than to check up on each child's ability to count by rote. The special education teacher can make no assumptions with the trainable mentally retarded children in her charge. This is a very difficult task for the trainable mentally retarded child because there is no logic in the number names from one to twelve. There are no keys within the words which clue the child and help him to unlock their meaning. No amount of reasoning can enable the child to discover that "three" is the correct word for a collection of three objects. Other than for etymological (history of words) reasons, the name might just as well have been "mod" or "nigik" or "due." The names assigned to the number ideas from one to twelve are merely conventional labels which the child must commit to memory. Furthermore, there is no reason other than convention for the order of the words from one to twelve. Why does the name three come before four and after two? Just because. Simple skills which have been learned very early are so automatic that it is difficult to realize that they were ever learned at all. There seem to be things that we have just always known. This can cause us to become impatient with children of low IQ when they fail to learn simple things like rote counting even after extensive practice. A couple of simple exercises might serve to make the teacher more appreciative of the problems that the learner encounters in learning to recite a list of meaningless words in an exact order. Try counting to ten with this bogus series of number names:

1	veri
2	misso
3	dule
4	fam
5	depe
6	hun
7	funk
8	happ
9	roce
10	cong

See how long it takes you to learn to count to ten if the number names remain unchanged but are assigned to different number concepts. For example, if three were called "seven" and so forth.

one	nine
two	five
three	seven
four	one
five	six
six	two
seven	four
eight	three
nine	ten
ten	eight

If you paused for a few moments to attempt these two exercises you have some appreciation of the formidable obstacles which the trainable mentally retarded child must overcome. This is one instance in the study of mathematics during which the child must rely totally upon his memory. The teacher should begin by concentrating on the series to five, and when that has been mastered, expand it to ten.

Mathematics for the Trainable Mentally Retarded 523

The use of rhymes such as those used here are not intended to teach the children to count but rather to give him experience in hearing and saying the number words in order. The child's ability to recite the rhyme "One, two, buckle my shoe" should not be confused with the ability to rote count apart from the poem or the understanding of number. They do offer a method of practice which could otherwise be quite distasteful.

The child will be taught to make the numerals one and two. A step-by-step approach to accomplishing this is given in the outline below.

Writing the Numerals One and Two Through Kinesthetic and Tactic Experiences. Use trace patterns, sandpaper and cardboard cut out in numerals. Let the children get the "feel" of the numbers. Or, give the children cards with the numerals one and two printed on them. Play sort and match games.

Making one

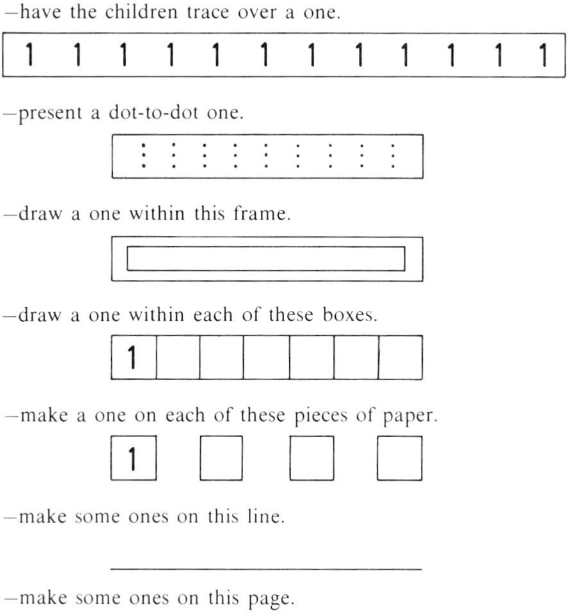

—have the children trace over a one.

| 1 | 1 | 1 | 1 | 1 | 1 | 1 | 1 | 1 | 1 | 1 | 1 |

—present a dot-to-dot one.

—draw a one within this frame.

—draw a one within each of these boxes.

—make a one on each of these pieces of paper.

—make some ones on this line.

—make some ones on this page.

FIGURE 8.11

When the children have mastered one's, do the same exercises with two's. Give the children practice in repeating digits: "Say after me, one, two, three. Now say, three, two, one. Now say, four, five, six. Now say, six, five, four, etc."

Examples of rhymes and songs: Ten Little Indians—dramatize as the children sing. Bring ten children into a group. As the song proceeds, one child, then two, and then a third, step forward until all ten are forward.

Clap your hands only once and no more; one, two, three, four (clap). Stomp your feet, only once and no more: "one, two, three, four stomp!"

"One, two, three, four, five, heavens sake, took a bribe

Six, seven, eight, nine, ten, got locked up in the pen."

The teacher should give the children many opportunities to hear the counting words. She should count as she hands out materials. For instance, "Here are three for you, one, two, three."

CARDINAL NUMBER

Basic concepts to be taught at the primary level would include the understanding of indefinite cardinal numbers, such as many, most, few, more, less, etc. Also at this level, the child can understand the concept of one-to-one correspondence which increases his ability to understand specific number concepts, one-to-two and one-to-many correspondence, reproducing sets of one, two, and three and set recognition of three, four, and five so that the child is able to answer the question "how many?" with some degree of understanding. The child must be able to differentiate between few and many. He must be made to understand that one or two is few, while five and six are many. This can be demonstrated by using containers. The teacher puts certain items in the box and the child imitates. The child imitates putting "few" objects such as marbles, clips, etc. as the teacher does so. Then the teacher puts "many" objects in the box. This way the child can readily see that there is a difference between few and many. The teacher is in a position to reinforce throughout the day the indefinite concepts such as many and few and most by simple oral observance. For instance, "Today *most* of you have sweaters on." "*Few* of us brought our umbrellas today." "There are only a *few* of you who remembered your overshoes" etc.

In teaching definite numbers, and one-to-one correspondence, the children must have an understanding of how many is one, how many is two, etc. For instance, the teacher might use an egg carton to teach one-to-one and one-to-many correspondence. Have the children put one marble in each space in the carton, then two marbles in each space, then three and so on. This is effective also in teaching sets of numbers such as two's, three's, etc. On the following pages are some suggestions for specific learning activities which teach cardinal number concepts.

Mathematics for the Trainable Mentally Retarded 525

Skill to be developed	*Suggested Activities*
Indefinite cardinal number few, more, less, most...	Look at this card, which has more?

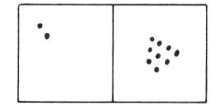

FIGURE 8.12

Which boy has fewer?

FIGURE 8.13

Bill has three, John has one. Which one has more?

FIGURE 8.14

One-to-one correspondence   Demonstrate one-to-one correspondence using flannel and magnet boards.

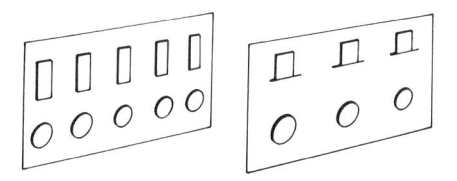

FIGURE 8.15

Use egg cartons, muffin tins, and other partitioned containers. Put one (marble, disk, etc.) in each place.

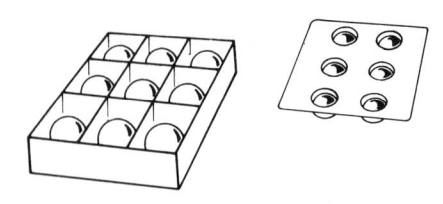

526 *Mathematics for the Trainable Mentally Retarded*

FIGURE 8.16

See this egg carton. Which place needs an egg? Which place has too many eggs?

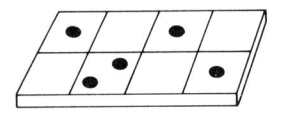

FIGURE 8.17

One-to-two correspondence	Put two beans in each place. Give each child two cookies.
Reproducing sets	Find two like this. Hold them up.
	Make five marks here.
	Give me three beans, marbles, blocks, etc. Put three, etc. on your square.
Work sets	Mark three faces.

FIGURE 8.18

Set recognition	Use domino patterns, then others. Sort, match, identify.
	Use standard patterns.
Bead Frame	The bead frames shown in Figure 8.19 are constructed of a clothes hanger, clothes pin, and string beads. The illustration shows three ways of talking about three.
	Another approach is to use colored counting cubes to illustrate the ways to talk about the number three.

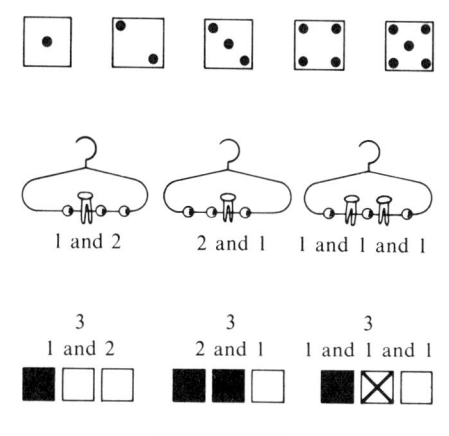

Mathematics for the Trainable Mentally Retarded 527

FIGURE 8.19

Counting activities

Have the children count slowly with you the children in the classroom. Count the juice glasses, the cookies.

Count the beads on a clothes hanger abacus.

Use counting incidentally throughout the day. Count the number who brought an apple for lunch, the number of valentines, the fingers on one hand, the eyes and ears on a doll.

Count the number of items on picture cards.

Give the children small sacks with a number of objects in them and ask them to discover how many things are in their sack.

Counting objects with pictures

How many cups? Sandwiches? Chairs? Tables?

FIGURE 8.20

How many books? Pencils?

FIGURE 8.21

ORDINAL NUMBER

Skill to be Developed	Suggested Activities
First	It is time to go play. Jerry, you be first, go stand by the door. The rest of you line up behind Jerry.
	Listen. First, I want you to put your pencils in your desks. Now put away the rest of your things.
Last	I want the *last* one out to turn off the lights.
Middle	Which one is in the middle?
	Put this one first (cat), this one last (rabbit) and this one in the middle (dog).

MEASUREMENT

Children at the primary level are able to develop some skills of measurement. Specifically, they may be able to comprehend simple ideas related to the clock and the calendar. Some children will learn to recognize measuring instruments and develop ideas of comparative weight, length, volume and capacity.

Skills to be Developed	Suggested Activities
A Familiarity with clock	Ability to recognize the parts of a clock, face, hands, numerals.

Mathematics for the Trainable Mentally Retarded

	Refer to the clock at various times: It is time to____(eat)____. etc. Discuss time concepts incidentally during the day. Early, late, after school, before lunch, after recess. Ask questions involving time: What do you do before bedtime? What do you do before dinner?
Familiarity with calendar	Prepare a birthday calendar for the month. Put the picture (or name) of the child whose birthday is on a given date on the calendar.
	How old are you? Who is seven? Who is nine? What day is it today? Is it Monday? Who is older, Jerry or Wanda?
	See the days of the week. Let's read them. Monday, Tuesday, Wednesday, etc. Just let the children hear them and practice saying them without being able to recite them in order.
	When is your birthday?
	See. This is a calendar. It will tell us many things.
	Write the day, month, ordinal number of the month and year on the board.
Measurement Instruments	If I want to know how old I am what do I use? If I want to know how much I weigh, which do I use? I want to know how tall I am, which do I use?
Simulated weight boxes	Weigh a set of boxes. Identify the graduated weights. Introduce the heaviest and lightest first.
Non-standard measures of length, capacity, volume and weight	Cut up pieces of paper. Which is longer? Show me the one which is shorter.
	Here are some boxes. Which one is heaviest?
	Here are some glasses. Which hold more? Let's practice and see.
Long and short	Have the child put the boards in the proper spaces. Use the terms long and short.

MONEY AND VALUE

The money skills taught at this level are limited to the identification of coins and the understanding that coins have value. The children will not be able to differentiate the relative value of coins although they may be able to name the penny and the nickel. Some children may be able to count five pennies. Their use of money will be limited to using pennies, nickels and dimes in vending machines and mechanical rides like those found in supermarkets (ride the horse for a dime).

Skill to be Developed	*Suggested Activities*
Discrimination of coins	The purpose of this exercise is to help the children differentiate between coins and other objects. Attach a coin to a placard among several other items such as buttons, bottle caps, and so forth. Say to the children, "Look at these things. Point to the money".
Sorting coins and objects	Give the children a set of objects similar to those listed above. Have the children put the coins (pennies, nickels, dimes) in one box and the trinkets (buttons, bottle caps, etc.,) into another box.
Counting Pennies	Provide each child with some pennies. Depending on their counting skills have them reproduce sets of one, two, three, four, or five pennies.
Using coins	Give the children opportunities to use coins in vending machines and to buy penny candy.
Equivalents	A few of the more capable children may learn that five pennies are equal to a nickel. However, this skill will typically not be introduced until the intermediate level.

NUMBER OPERATIONS

Children at this level are not ready for formal additive and subtractive action. However, the extensive attention given to the idea of grouping cardinal number provides the background for number operations. The children have learned that a group of three is one more than a group of two. They have compared a group of four objects with a group of five; a group of two with a group of one and so forth. The understanding

Mathematics for the Trainable Mentally Retarded 531

that there are several ways to "see four" is the prelude to beginning computational skills. These will be introduced at the intermediate level.

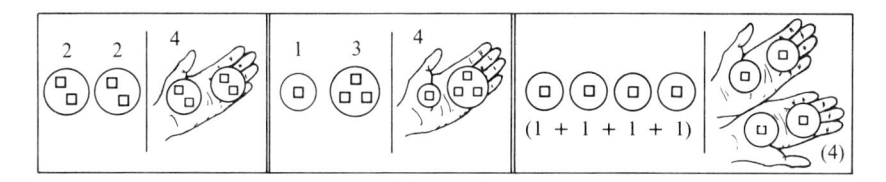

FIGURE 8.22

INTERMEDIATE PROGRAM FOR THE TRAINABLE MENTALLY RETARDED

The intermediate program for trainable mentally retarded children includes those youngsters with mental ages of five and six years. The chronological ages of such children are ten and above. Youngsters with IQ's below 40 cannot be expected to accomplish the objectives for this level. Teachers of youngsters with chronological ages ten and above will have some in their classes capable of performing at the intermediate level. Table 8.5 below indicates the chronological age span and the IQ levels for trainable children with mental ages of five and six.

TABLE 8.5

**Intermediate Level
Trainable Mentally Retarded Children
with Mental Ages 5 and 6**

Intelligence Quotients	Chronological Ages						
	10	11	12	13	14	15	16+
40	m a below 5			5.2	5.7	6.0	6.5
50	5.0	5.6	6.0	6.6	m a 7 and above		

The material presented in the previous two sections of this chapter is comparable to the pre-number and early number experiences which non-intellectually impaired children discover through experiences with their family and friends and through nursery school. Some educators would not regard it as really academic arithmetic. By contrast, the content at the intermediate level is quite similar to the items presented to children in the kindergarten and first grade. There is one major difference, of course. The children being taught this material are not chronologically five and six, but ten and older. Nonetheless, many intermediate level children are ready for academic instruction.

OBJECTIVES FOR INTERMEDIATE LEVEL, TRAINABLE MENTALLY RETARDED

The major focus of the mathematics program for the trainable mentally retarded at the intermediate level is on number usage. Many children will learn their number facts through ten and will be able to apply these skills to problems involving money and measurements. The teacher will continue to work with number symbols, cardinal and ordinal number. Relatively less attention will be given to form and perception and vocabulary. More specifically, many children will:

1. Continue to develop visual-perceptual skills including reproducing shapes.
2. Continue to develop vocabulary associated with mathematics with emphasis on terms of measurement, time, position, shape, and money.
3. Continue to develop rote and rational counting skills to as high as 31.
4. Continue to develop ordinal number skills as applied to particular situations such as house numbers and the telephone.
5. Improve measurement skills including use of the calendar, reading the clock by the hour, and gross measurement of weight and length.
6. Develop money skills to making simple transactions.
7. Learn the number facts of addition and subtraction up to 10.

TABLE 8.6

Checklist for the Mathematics for the Trainable Mentally Retarded Child

Intermediate Level

1. Form and Perception
   recognition of common geometric shapes; drawing lines, circles and squares; using stencils to reproduce shapes

2. Vocabulary Associated with Mathematics
   a variety of terms related to mathematics including measured time, position, shape, money and numbers

3. Number Symbols
   rote counting possibly as high as fifty; reading number symbols as high as thirty-one; reading number words to ten; introduction of counting by two's.

4. Cardinal Number
   rational counting to twenty-five; concept of more than, less than, equal to; matching number symbol to groups of objects through ten; sub sets of ten; reproducing sets to twenty

5. Ordinal Number
   first, second, third, last, house numbers, apartment numbers

6. Measurement
   concepts of time for breakfast, lunch, play, and so forth, time by the hour; use of terms related to the thermometer such as hot, cold, warm; recognition of the basic parts of the clock, face, hands, numerals for hours; recognizing ruler and yardstick as measuring instruments and the concept of longer and shorter; concept of body weight and weights of gross differences; understanding of the calendar to thirty-one days

7. Money and Value
   knowledge of the function of money; ability to name nickel, dime, quarter; use of money for simple transactions such as vending machines, carnival rides, theatre admissions, etc.

8. Number Operations
   knowledge of addition and subtraction facts through ten

FORM AND PERCEPTION

The importance of developing an adequate concept of the physical self in order to structure space has been emphasized repeatedly throughout this text. At the intermediate level, this clear body image can best be realized through the tactual manipulations so vital to the development of spatial relationships. The further broadening of mathematical ideas cannot be continued without the ordering of the spatial environment. Previous discussions have elaborated upon a variety of sensory training to aid the child in the perception of space. The use of educational toys and games and equipment should continue as the child becomes more aware of form, space and configuration.. This will improve his ability to deal with the quantitative ordering of his environment.

534   *Mathematics for the Trainable Mentally Retarded*

Skill to be developed	*Suggested Activities*
Recognition of geometric shapes **FIGURE 8.23**	Use pictures, felt cut-outs, for the flannel board, three dimensional wooden forms, etc. Have the children match, sort, and name the shapes including circles, squares and triangles.
Reproducing various patterns of interlocking circles, lines and squares **FIGURE 8.24**	Give the children pieces of felt or construction paper cut into different shapes. Give them such directions as "See these two shapes. You put yours together just like mine."
Bead String in a pattern **FIGURE 8.25**	Make yours just like mine.
Drawing a square	Use a stencil or cardboard cut out like this one to help you draw a square. **FIGURE 8.25A**

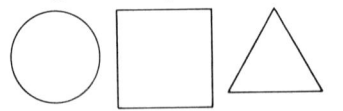

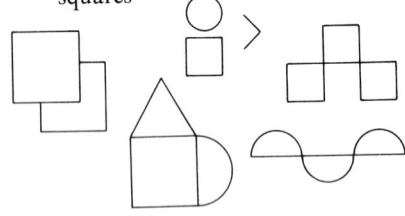

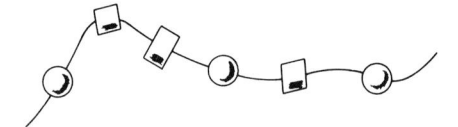

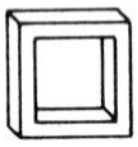

Finish these squares.

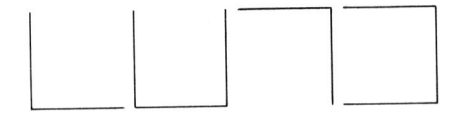

FIGURE 8.26

Make one just like this one:

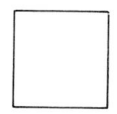

Mathematics for the Trainable Mentally Retarded 535

FIGURE 8.27

Trace a diamond and triangle   Use stencil and cardboard cut outs. "Use this to make a diamond like mine."

FIGURE 8.28

Copying designs   Make your square look like mine.

FIGURE 8.29

Matching and sorting   Make two sets of duplicated cards with geometric shapes and ask the children to match and sort.

FIGURE 8.30

Identifying shapes   Find one that looks like this. Use a series of shapes with only one matching the stimulus.

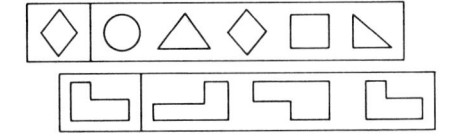

FIGURE 8.31

536　　　　　　　　　　*Mathematics for the Trainable Mentally Retarded*

Discrimination of shapes　　Make a series of cards with a number of shapes on each card with one different from the rest. "Find the one which is not the same as the others."

FIGURE 8.32

Walking boards (three to ten piece interlocking puzzles)　　Use more complex walking boards. Have the children go forward and backwards.

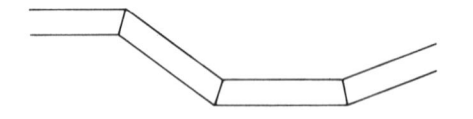

FIGURE 8.33

VOCABULARY ASSOCIATED WITH MATHEMATICS

Check these words out on your list; they are from the Ginn primer.

as much as	cold	late	over	temperature
above	coin	last	penny	whole
add	cost	least	price	
after	count	less	ring	
ahead	down	little	round	
around	early	low	save	
back	enough	many	sell	
before	far	money	small	
behind	fast	more	some	
below	few	more than	slow	
between	figure	most	spend	
beside	front	much	squares	
big	group	near	together	
bottom	how many	next	top	
buy	high	nickel	take away	
change	hot	number	triangles	
cup	half	off	under	
circle	large	on	up	

NUMBER SYMBOLS

It was indicated in the preceding section on the primary level that the number symbols and their order from one to twelve had to be learned completely by rote. Beyond twelve, however, it is possible to gain some insight into the meanings of the number words by thinking about the parts of the word. For example, in the words *thirteen* (three-ten), *fourteen* (four-ten), *fifteen* (five-ten) and so forth, the syllable *teen* indicates the presence of ten. From the number word *twenty* on, some logic can be used to detect the sense in the repetition in the number plan. The number words correspond to the place value of the number concepts they represent. For instance, twenty-one is two tens and one one; thirty-four is three tens and four ones, and so forth. In a real sense, then, the learning of the number names should not be totally rote, but reasoning should enable the child to discover the meaning of the number beyond twelve. The words for indicating the decades have been abbreviated, on course, but if the *ty* is thought as "ten" and the *twen, thir, for, fif* are seen as substitutes for *two, three, four,* and *five,* then within the decade the child can learn to repeat the basic numerals from *one* to *nine* as in *forty-one, forty-two,* etc.

In teaching the number words from *thirteen* to *nineteen,* the *teen* should be stressed in pronunciation. The children should be able to learn that teen really means "ten" and that *thirteen* means "three and ten."

Skills to be developed	*Suggested Activities*
Writing the numerals three through ten	Utilize the pattern illustrated in Figure 8.34.

1. Trace over lightly printed numeral.
2. Trace through dot-to-dot numeral.
3. Complete these numerals:

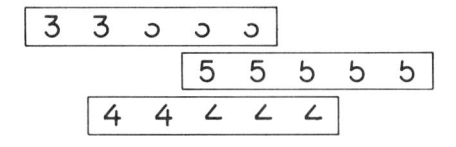

3	3	ɔ	ɔ	ɔ

		5	5	ꝋ	ꝋ	ꝋ

4	4	ㄥ	ㄥ	ㄥ

FIGURE 8.34

4. Tactual numerals: sand paper and poster board numerals. Have the child feel the numeral.

Tracing numerals in a cookie sheet.

Purchase a rimmed cookie sheet and line the bottom with colored paper. Cover the cookie sheet with a thin layer of "malta meal," fine sawdust, or other grain. Present the child with a numeral and have him trace it on his tray. This provides a new type of kinesthetic experience in a novel setting.

FIGURE 8.35

Rote counting to fifty (many children will not progress this high)

A number of simple games can be played to help the children extend their rote counting skills. Have the children see if they can stand on one foot until the count of fifty. Have two children see which one can count to fifty the quickest.

Reading number symbols

Matching numerals:
```
12    15
15    13
11    14
14    11
13    12
```

Finding the one which is different:
```
12  12  14  12
21  12  21  21
28  26  28  28
```

Find the one which is the same:
```
18  31  27  18
27  18  27  31
31  31  27  18
```

Use these patterns in writing the numerals. Suggestions for teaching the writing of these numerals is given in Figure 8.36.

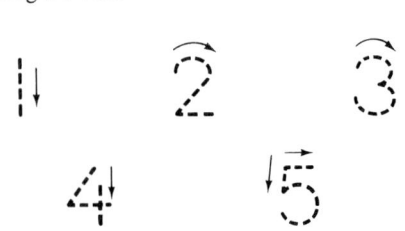

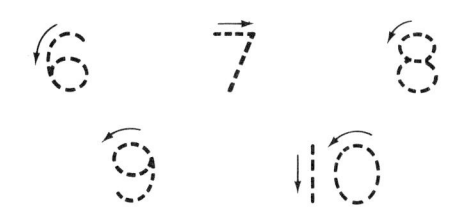

Mathematics for the Trainable Mentally Retarded

FIGURE 8.36

Reading number words

| ONE | TWO | THREE | FOUR | FIVE |

| SIX | SEVEN | EIGHT | NINE | TEN |

Use a set of flash cards to introduce the words. Then provide a series on matching, sorting, and differentiating activities similar to these.

FIGURE 8.37

Match these words

one	three
two	five
five	one
three	two

one   five
three two
five   six
two   seven
six   four
seven three
four   one

FIGURE 8.38

Find the word that is different

one	one	two	one
ten	ten	ten	three
three	three	three	six

one   one   two   one
ten   two   ten   ten
three three three four

FIGURE 8.39

Find the word that is the same

one   two   three one
three two   three one

540   *Mathematics for the Trainable Mentally Retarded*

one	six	one	three
ten	five	three	ten
three	three	six	seven
eight	four	eight	two

two   three   two   four
eight five   seven eight
ten   ten   two   five

FIGURE 8.40

Writing numerals to 20

| 11 | | 15 | | 18 | | 20 |

FIGURE 8.41

The children now have the skills of writing the numerals. The task of writing numerals beyond them is merely a matter of copying the numerals in correct sequence. Have the children copy the numerals.

CARDINAL AND ORDINAL NUMBER

It is important that the youngsters understand the distinction between cardinal and ordinal numbers. The teacher will not have to use the terms *cardinal* and *ordinal* but sufficient practice should be provided so the differences are clear. The teacher will have some children who can recite the number words "one, two, three ... ten" as they successively raise the fingers on both hands, but are unable to answer correctly the question, "How many fingers do you have?" For example, the "ten" refers to the last finger they touched (i.e., the ordinal). To these children, the question "how many" does not make sense. Every natural classroom situation should be taken advantage of to make this distinction clear. Teaching situations should be devised to further make the point.

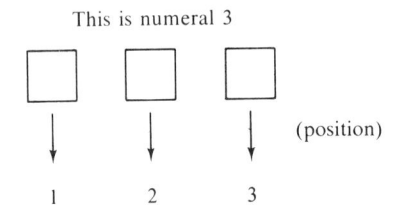

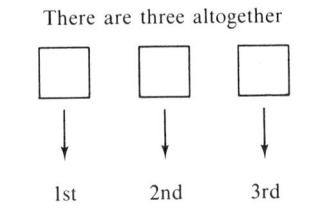

This is numeral 3   There are three altogether

  □   □   □   (position)   □   □   □
  ↓   ↓   ↓   ↓   ↓   ↓
  1   2   3   1st   2nd   3rd

FIGURE 8.42

The next step in the intermediate program for the trainable mentally retarded is to develop the understanding of sets from five through ten. Each of these groups should be introduced by indicating some of the less complex subsets associated with the set. Experiences will help the child learn the difference between odd and even sets.

Each even numbered set can be represented by combining subsets of two. It is easy to demonstrate that eight may be represented by two, two, two, two. Each set of six, eight and ten may be separated into an array of two equal subsets. A set of six may be separated into two three's or can be formed by the combination of two sets of three. The ability to visualize these subsets assists the child in grasping the meaning of the concepts of the numbers six, eight, ten and of course, contributes to the child's progress toward learning some of the basic facts of addition and subtraction. The understanding of number concepts can be further developed by elaborating all the possible subsets. The set of the number eight may be arranged into three sets of component subsets: four, four; five, three; six, two; and seven, one. The intermediate program will complete the introduction of all sets through ten.

In contrast to even-numbered sets, odd-number sets cannot be separated into two groups of equal size. The child will discover, for example, that a group of seven consists of three groups of two *plus* one, four and one as groups of five, and two and three as component subgroups of five.

Skill to be developed	*Suggested Activities*
Counting	Use paste sticks, tongue depressors, popsicle and craft sticks for counting.
Matching numerals to sets	Poster board cut into 5" x 8" cards may be illustrated with objects like these shown in Figure 8.43

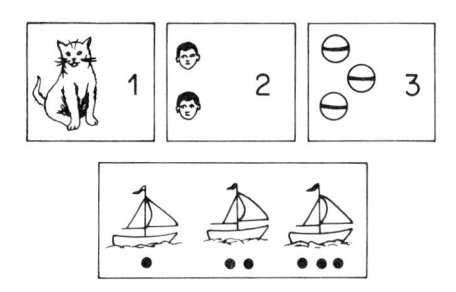

FIGURE 8.43

| Concepts of subsets | Use different colored blocks; miniature toys in polyethylene bags and so on to teach the component subsets |

542   *Mathematics for the Trainable Mentally Retarded*

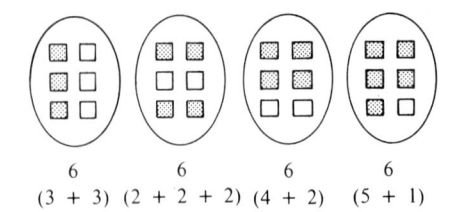

```
   6        6        6        6
(3 + 3) (2 + 2 + 2) (4 + 2) (5 + 1)
```

FIGURE 8.44

Use two different colored beads in a polyethelene bag to illustrate some subsets. Give the children practice in counting. How many beads in this bag? How many are red? How many are white? How many are there altogether?

FIGURE 8.45

Here are three bags of blocks. How many in this bag? How many in this bag? How many in this bag? Now, how many are there altogether?

FIGURE 8.46

The domino cards in Figure 8.47 may be used as flash cards to teach instantaneous set recognition. Two or three cards together may be used to illustrate subsets. For example, another name for three:

Mathematics for the Trainable Mentally Retarded 543

domino cards

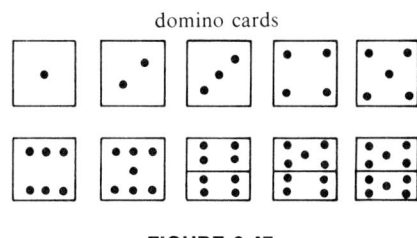

FIGURE 8.47

Abacus

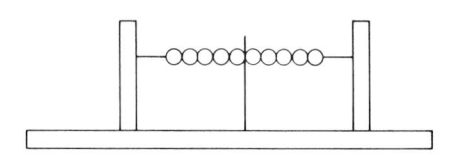

FIGURE 8.48

Non-equivalent sets

Which do you have more of: How many cups? How many saucers?

FIGURE 8.49

How many more cups do you need to make ten?

Which kites do not have tails? Put tails on all the kites. How many tails did you add?

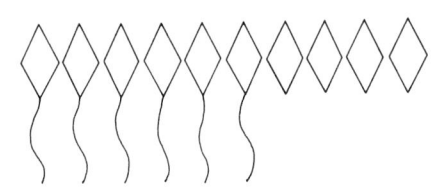

FIGURE 8.50

Count the balls. Count the bats.

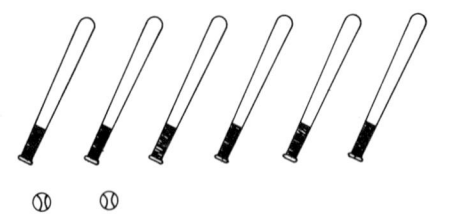

FIGURE 8.51

Make enough balls so that there is a ball for each bat.

FIGURE 8.52

Matching numerals to sets.

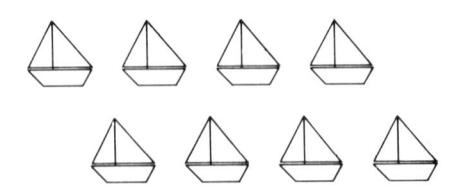

FIGURE 8.53

Circle the right number: 3 10 8

3   10   ⓼

FIGURE 8.54

The muffin tin

Mathematics for the Trainable Mentally Retarded 545

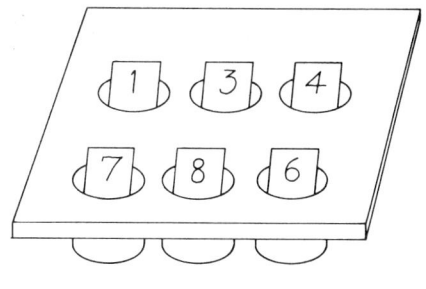

FIGURE 8.55

MEASUREMENT

Trainable mentally retarded children with mental ages of six will learn to tell time by the hour, use a calendar, and thermometer as well as develop a more advanced idea of length and weight.

Skill to be developed

Telling time by the hour

Suggested Activities

Review basic parts of the clock and the numerals which represent the hour. Make or purchase individual clocks. The minute hand may be stationary but the hour hand should be adjustable. What time does this clock say? Have the children match their clocks to yours.

Give the children papers prepared with illustrative clocks. Make your clock say three o'clock, nine o'clock, etc.

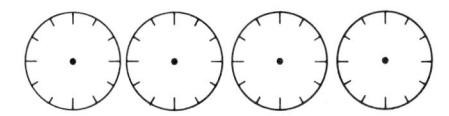

FIGURE 8.56

Tell what time these clocks show.

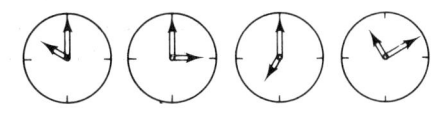

FIGURE 8.57

Understanding time during the day	What time do you have breakfast? What time do we eat lunch?
The Calendar	Some children will be able to learn only the days of the week and months of the year in order. However, many intermediate level children will be able to read the numerals representing the date of the month. Prepare a classroom calendar, refer to the date each day, maintain calendars relating to birthdays. Discuss the children's age. Keep track of holidays. Make calendars which reflect the weather for the month and talk about the number of raining and sunshine days.
The Thermometer	Construct a ribbon thermometer which is adjustable. Give the children experience in seeing that the higher the red mark is, the warmer it is.
Weight	Weigh the children and teach them their weight. Give them practice in differentiating gross weights. Which weighs more, a car or a tricycle? Which weighs less, a man or a baby?
Length	Introduce a twelve-inch ruler and have the children measure various items. Give them pieces of paper which are cut in lengths from one to twelve inches. Have them sort the pieces by length. Introduce the word "inch."

MONEY AND VALUE

There will be considerable variation in the understanding of intermediate children regarding their knowledge of money. Some of the children will recognize and name coins and be able to do some coin counting. However, most of the children will need further help in learning to identify coins and their equivalents. The teacher will also emphasize making simple purchases and change. At this level it is still important to use real money.

Skill to be developed	*Suggested Activities*
Identifying coins	Give each child a set of coins including pennies, nickels, dimes and quarters.

Mathematics for the Trainable Mentally Retarded

	Hold up a penny and say, "Find one like mine." Repeat the directions with the other coins.
Find the one that is different	Paste a series of coins on cardboard. Have all the coins the same except one. Have the children point to the one that is different.
Find the one that is the same	Paste a series of coins on cardboard with the first coin in each line matching one of the other coins in the line.
Sorting coins	Give the children a set on coins. Have them sort the coins into piles of pennies, nickels, dimes, and quarters.
Matching coins	Attach two vertical sets of coins in columns on tagboard. Ask the children to match the coins using yarn.

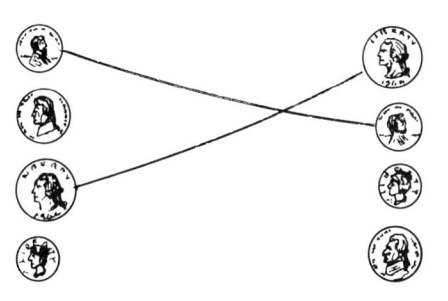

FIGURE 8.58

Equivalent values—a nickel and five cents	Explain to the child that five pennies will buy the same things as one nickel. It will help to teach the children that five cents is another name for a nickel. Give the children five nickels and twenty-five pennies. Have the children count out five pennies for each nickel and place them side by side.
	Make a chart with five nickels in a vertical column on the left with a corresponding row of pennies to the right of each nickel. Have the children indicate how many more pennies are needed in each row of pennies to make it equal to the nickel.

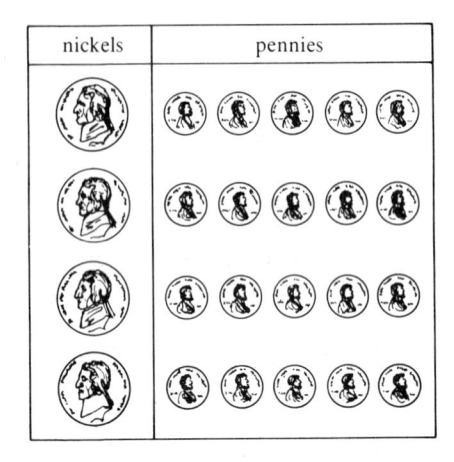

548 *Mathematics for the Trainable Mentally Retarded*

FIGURE 8.59

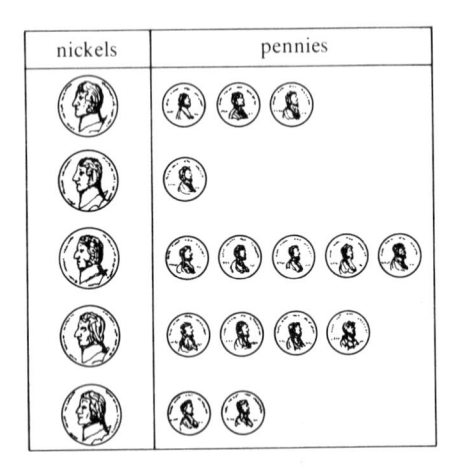

FIGURE 8.60

Have the children stack a group of fifty pennies into sets of five each.

FIGURE 8.61

A dime and ten cents

Explain to the children that ten pennies will buy the same things as one dime. Just as five cents is another name for

Mathematics for the Trainable Mentally Retarded 549

a nickel, ten cents is another name for a dime. Give the children ten dimes and fifty pennies. Proceed in the same manner as with the nickels and pennies.

Counting by nickels and pennies — Teach the children to count with a combination of a nickel and pennies. When counting, the nickel must be referred to as "five cents" and a penny as "one cent." If these terms are used automatically by the children, counting coins will be very much simplified. Always start with the nickel. Count in this fashion. Five cents . . . six cents . . . seven cents

nickel   penny   penny

FIGURE 8.62

Continue this procedure until the children can count a nickel and five pennies.

Counting by dimes and pennies — Teach the children to count with a combination of a dime and pennies using the above technique.

Two nickels and a dime — The next step is to teach the children that two nickels is worth the same as one dime. Illustrate these equivalencies to the children.

2 nickels   10 pennies   1 dime

ten cents   ten cents   ten cents

FIGURE 8.63

Matching coins to costs — Present the children with a number of items. Give them a number of coins to work with. Have the children select the correct amount of coins for each purchase.

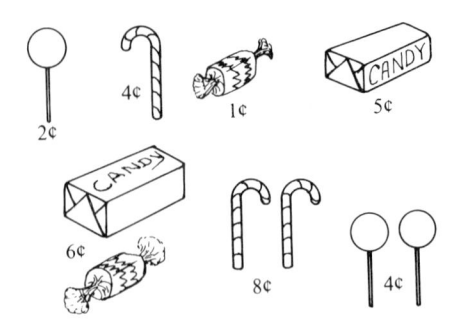

550   *Mathematics for the Trainable Mentally Retarded*

FIGURE 8.64

Making change for nickels

Give the children a variety of exercises like the one illustrated in Figure 8.65. Assume that the clerk is given a nickel for each purchase. Have the children determine the change in pennies (cents).

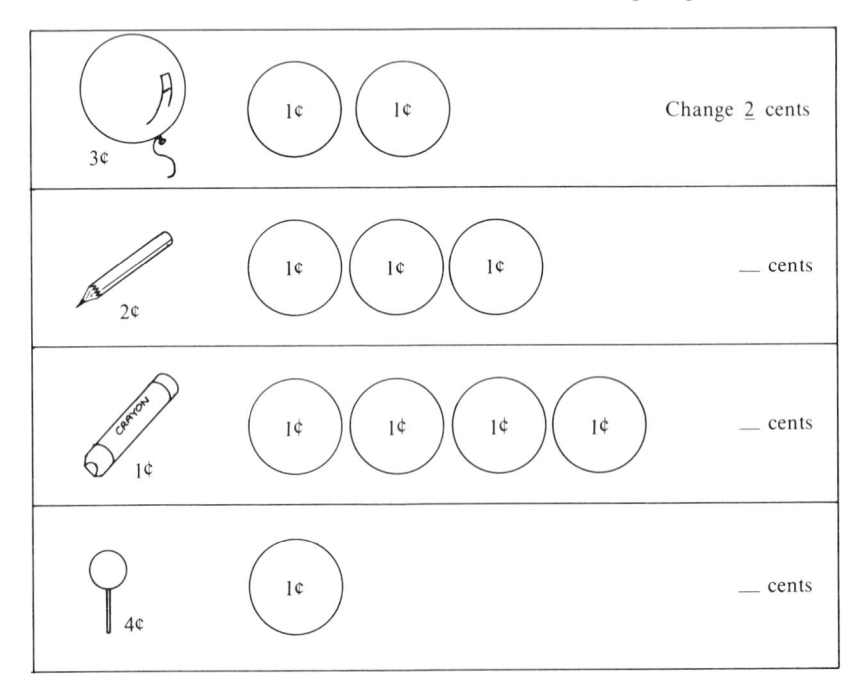

FIGURE 8.65

Making change for a dime using pennies only

Present the children with activities which require the making of change with pennies only.

Item		Change	
6¢	candy	4	pennies
7¢	pencil	3	pennies
8¢	gum	2	pennies

Play store — To afford opportunities for working with money in varying amounts, collect a group of objects which may be found in local stores: i.e., empty boxes of cereal, detergents, sugar, and cans of soup, beans, corn, etc. (Open the cans on the bottom side so the labels will be right side up.) Include spools of thread, a few toys and tools. Pictures may be substituted for the actual articles if necessary. The cost may be shown by a price tag or, in the case of pictures, with a price indicated below the article. All of the items should be priced for less than a dime. The children may select and count the coins required for each purchase. The play store may be used for the children who have only minimal understanding of money (one cent for one piece of candy) while more capable students can buy more than one thing, add the amount, and figure the change.

Play cafeteria — This is an activity similar to the play store except that the picture of food is pasted on to cardboard. The pictures are marked with a price and the children pass through a line and select food and place it on a paperplate.

NUMBER OPERATIONS

During the intermediate years, many children will gain an understanding of addition with sums to ten, and subtraction with minuends to ten. The concepts of addition and subtraction need to be taught carefully. The abstract forms using numbers alone need not be introduced until the basic ideas are learned. The children should learn to understand and work with concrete and semi-concrete materials prior to engaging in written activities. Some trainable mentally retarded children never develop sufficient skills to warrant instruction in addition and subtraction.

So it is important to know which children are ready to learn simple addition and subtraction. First, the children must understand the vocabulary words *group* (set), *add, how many, subtract* and *take away*. The children have studied varied arrangements of subgroups until they have learned the concept of two groups making a whole. They must be able to think of two or more objects as a whole as discussed in the section on cardinal number. If a child has to rely on enumeration to tell that three apples are three, he is not ready to learn to use addition to determine that two apples and three apples are five apples. As with all early number work, ideas are first developed through classroom activities with manipulative materials. Be certain that the children are familiar with subgroups composing the numbers to ten and that they have learned to handle these combinations when working with concrete materials. The beginning written work should be limited to the smaller sums of two, three, four, and five.

In the following paragraph the discussion of addition and subtraction will be separated. However, it is somewhat misleading to treat addition and subtraction as separate processes because they are actually very closely related. Subtraction is the opposite of addition and the idea of subtraction stems from the same basic idea: the concept of set. The idea of set was discussed under cardinal number, and now its relation to additive and subtractive action will be shown. An example will make the case. The idea of the number five may be presented to the children in these ways: When the child understands that one and four, two and three, three and two, and four and one are all ways of naming five, he has within his grasp the subtraction and addition facts related to five. If the child understands that one and four is another name for five, it is a simple step to one plus four is five, four plus one is five, five minus one is four, five minus four is one. The same process may be used with the other combinations of five. With this in mind, the steps for teaching formal addition and subtraction are presented in the following paragraphs.

FIVE STEPS IN TEACHING ADDITION

The beginning written work should be limited to the smaller sums of two, three, four, and five. The children should not be moved beyond this level until they can handle these combinations easily.

ADD	0	1	2	3
0	0	1	2	3
1	1	2	3	4
2	2	3	4	5
3	3	4	5	

The steps to be used in developing these ideas will typically follow the sequence outlined below.

Step 1 Dramatization and Demonstration. Use simple problems that are easily dramatized. Here are a few samples which permit the children to perform actions suggested and to see the sums of the objects.

Bill has two sticks.
Joe gives him one more.
How many does he have altogether?

Sue places one kitty on the flannel board.
Mary puts two more kitties beside it.
How many kitties are there altogether?

There are three pencils on the desk.
Bob places no more pencils on the desk.
How many pencils are there on the desk?

These problems are presented orally using the names of the children in the classroom so that the action may be carried out as the problem is given.

Step 2 Concrete Materials and Counters. The teacher should collect a variety of counters such as sticks, blocks, buttons, small toys, lima beans, straws, and cut cardboard. The teacher recites the problems orally and each child carries out the action. The children also use counters to solve problems similar to this one letting the counters represent the balls.

Jack has one ball (one counter)
Sally had two balls (two counters)
How many balls do they have in all?

Step 3 Action Pictures. The teacher may collect or draw a set of pictures depicting addition action. The picture in Figure 8.66 shows two balls on the ground and a little boy throwing another one.

$3 - 1 = \square$

FIGURE 8.66

Figure 8.67 shows more pictures which illustrate more additive action.

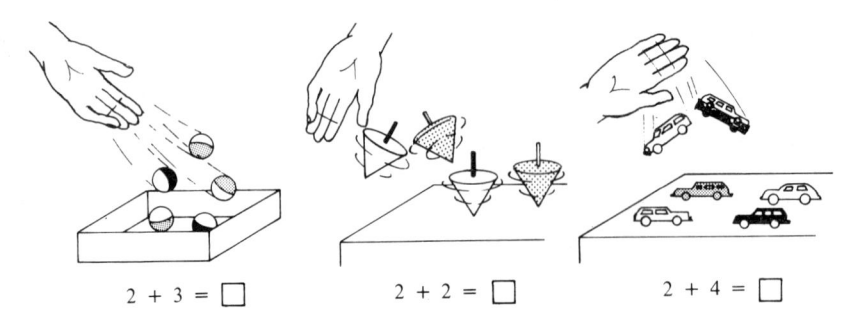

2 + 3 = ☐   2 + 2 = ☐   2 + 4 = ☐

FIGURE 8.67

Step 4 Vertical Form. After the child has a firm understanding of the addition of two groups arranged horizontally, the vertical form is introduced. Use shelves and number numerals on cards. Three boxes arranged on top of each other with the open ends toward the students will work well. After the children have gained facility in using the vertical addition box, the teacher may turn to flannel board illustrations and then to chalkboard problems.

After the children have learned to think of problems in the vertical arrangement, the outline of the shelves may be omitted. Both the horizontal and vertical arrangement of *known* addition facts may be combined on worksheets for the purpose of *review*.

$$\begin{array}{ccc} 5 & 1 & 2 \\ \underline{2} & \underline{3} & \underline{3} \end{array}$$

Step 5 Sign for Addition. The next step is to introduce the sign for addition and the abstract form. The children know that sign gives directions and the sign for addition tells us to *combine* or *put together*. Sometimes it is called the "plus" sign. After the children have become accustomed to using the addition sign, the abstract form may be presented. Sums taught will generally be limited to ten.

$$\begin{array}{ccccccc} 2 & 1 & 3 & 5 & 4 & 3 & 4 \\ \underline{+1} & \underline{+3} & \underline{+3} & \underline{+2} & \underline{+3} & \underline{+2} & \underline{+6} \end{array}$$

FIVE STEPS IN TEACHING SUBTRACTION

The steps in teaching the idea of subtraction and the number facts related to it parallel those for the teaching of addition. Subtraction is often viewed as a much more difficult skill than addition. However, if the children are taught the basic idea of number as in the example

Mathematics for the Trainable Mentally Retarded 555

of five, and are shown the relationship of subtraction to addition, the complexity of subtraction should be minimized. As with addition, the beginning work should be limited to two, three, four, and five. The children should not go beyond this level until they can work with these combinations with ease.

Subtract	1	2	3	4	5
1	0	1	2	3	4
2		0	1	2	3
3				1	2
4				0	1

Step 1 Teaching Related Facts. Give the children a number of red and white counters. Have them show various ways to make three. The teacher will guide the children so that the following related facts are illustrated.

$$\begin{array}{cccc} 2 & 1 & 3 & 3 \\ +1 & +2 & -2 & -1 \\ \hline 3 & 3 & 1 & 2 \end{array}$$

The children will come to realize that if you know that two and one is three, they also know that one and two is three, that three take away two is one, and that three take away one is two.

Step 2 Dramatization and Demonstration. Understanding the process of subtraction is somewhat more difficult than simple addition, especially for trainable mentally retarded children. The only concept to be presented in addition is the combining of two groups into a total. This is not the case with subtraction. The children must distinguish between the number to be subtracted and the number to be subtracted from. The children will learn that they can take two from three, but cannot take three from two. The question to be asked in subtraction is not always the same. One may want to know how many are left, how many are gone, how many more are needed, which group is larger. At this level, the only subtraction problems which are presented are those which ask how many are left.

Bill has three marbles.
He gave one away.
How many are left?

Susan's cat had four kittens.
She gave two away. (Use flannel board)
Now how many does she have?

There are five pencils on the teacher's desk.
Bob and Sue each took one.

How many are on the desk now?

Step 3 Concrete Materials and Counters. The teacher may use commercial counters or collect disks, buttons, etc. to use as counters. Some problems may be given in this fashion:

Put five buttons on your desk.
Put two of them in the box.
How many do you have left?

The children will then learn to use disks or other items as counters. The disks represent the elephants.

There are three elephants in the circus.
One became ill.
How many are now in the circus?

Step 4 Action Pictures. The teacher should utilize pictures similar to the one shown in Figure 8.68.

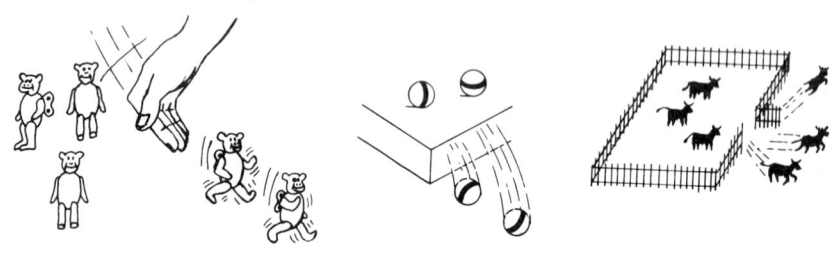

FIGURE 8.68

(5 take away 2)   (4 take away 2)   (6 take away 3)

FIGURE 8.69

(2 take away 1)   (6 take away 4)   (9 take away 3)

Step 5 Sign for Subtraction. The final step is to introduce the sign for subtraction and the vertical form for writing the problems. The children already know the sign for addition and understand the phrase "take away". Be certain that the abstract form is presented only after there is full understanding of the process. For example:

$$\begin{array}{cccccccccc} 2 & 5 & 8 & 4 & 7 & 3 & 6 & 9 & 10 & 10 \\ \underline{-1} & \underline{-4} & \underline{-7} & \underline{-3} & \underline{-6} & \underline{-2} & \underline{-5} & \underline{-2} & \underline{-1} & \underline{-9} \end{array}$$

Do not move beyond ten until the child has demonstrated he is ready.

THE ADVANCED PROGRAM FOR THE TRAINABLE MENTALLY RETARDED

The advanced program for the trainable mentally retarded includes those youngsters with mental ages of seven years. The chronological ages of such children range from fourteen, fifteen, sixteen and above. Youngsters with IQ scores below 44 may not be able to achieve the skills presented at this level. Teachers with fourteen-, fifteen-, and sixteen year-olds in their classes will find that many of them are able to learn the ideas found at this level. The material included in this section is somewhat similar in difficulty to that taught in the regular second grade in the public school. It should not be assumed that because a given child has a mental age of seven that he will automatically be able to achieve the material presented in this section. The teacher should be certain that he has satisfactorily mastered the ideas outlined in the intermediate program.

The table below indicates the IQ's and chronological ages of children with mental ages of seven to eight.

TABLE 8.7

Advanced Level

Trainable Mentally Retarded Children with Mental Ages 7 to 8*

Intelligence Quotients	Chronological Ages		
	14	15	16
44			7.0
45			7.2
46			7.4
47		7.0	7.6
48		7.2	7.8
49		7.4	7.10
50	7.0	7.6	8.0

* Mental age is expressed in terms of years and months

OBJECTIVES FOR ADVANCED LEVEL, TRAINABLE MENTALLY RETARDED

The general objective for this level is to assist the youngster in using numbers to solve practical problems. Mathematics is taught to the trainable mentally retarded youngster primarily for social reasons. Our society is a highly quantitative one, and the degree to which these youngsters are able to participate effectively in it depends on their competency in dealing confidently with the many quantitative situations of daily living. The youngsters at this level will be given more experience with visual perception and vocabulary associated with mathematics. The idea of numbers will be expanded and number operations will go on to simple problem solving including the areas of measurement and money usage. More specifically, many children at this level will:

1. Continue the development of body image and increase their ability to recognize, manipulate, and reproduce forms.
2. Increase the vocabulary associated with mathematics especially terms related to number awareness, operations, money and measurement.
3. Extend the ability to count rationally beyond twenty-five and develop an understanding of place value and fractions.
4. Develop the idea of ordinal number especially as related to practical ideas such as house numbers and the telephone.
5. Learn to tell time by the half hour, quarter hour and by minute for some. The ability to use common measures related to cooking and sewing will be developed. The use of the calendar will expand to days of the week, months and season of the year.
6. Develop the ability to make change up to a dollar.
7. Continue to develop their knowledge of the addition and subtraction facts beyond 10.

TABLE 8.8

Checklist for Mathematics for the Trainable Mentally Retarded Child

Adultation Level

1. Form and Perception
   continue to develop body image and form recognition and reproduction

2. Vocabulary Associated with Mathematics

right	next	close	all	same is	hour
left	week	under	some	plus	postage

beginning	year	over	each	minus	credit
stop	quick	beneath	couple	subtract	pay
end	warm	above	more	difference	inch
high	cool	below	least	sign	foot
low	near	between	altogether	o'clock	

3. Number Symbols
   rote counting to one hundred
   reading and writing number symbols as high as one hundred
   count by five's to twenty-five
   count by ten's to one hundred

4. Cardinal Numbers
   rational counting beyond twenty-five
   place value for tens place
   one to one correspondence to one hundred
   recognition of set patterns to ten
   fractions of one-half, one-fourth
   reproducing sets beyond twenty

5. Ordinal Numbers
   use of number names to indicate position (i.e., this is number five, etc.)
   possibly ordinal numbers beyond third

6. Measurement
   telling time by the hour and by the minute for some
   cup and common fractions thereof which relate to cooking
   days of week, months, and seasons of the year
   read simple thermometer
   reading ruler to the inch and yardstick to the foot

7. Money and Value
   making change for amounts up to fifty cents and one dollar
   counting money (counting dimes to fifty cents)

8. Number Operations
   knowledge of addition and subtraction facts beyond ten

FORM AND PERCEPTION

The importance of form and perception does not diminish for the trainable mentally retarded at the advanced level but it does become more integrated with activities more commonly associated with such areas as physical education, dance, and music. There may be some youngsters at this level who have specific problems in this area which directly interfere with their ability to learn simple number skills. For such youngsters, the reader is referred to the *Purdue Perceptual Motor Survey* (Roach,

1966) and the *Slow Learner in the Classroom* (Kephart, 1971) details of diagnosis and perception of special disabilities in this area. The suggestions given below will be sufficient for most students at this level.

Gross Motor Areas	*Suggested Activities*
Climbing	Give opportunities to climb stairs, ladders, jungle gyms, and ropes.
Running	Relay and tag games continue to be popular among youngsters of this age.
Jumping	Encourage the youngsters to improve their skills by jumping over boxes, high jumps; some youngsters will learn to jump rope.
Ball play	A number of games; catch, throwing a ball into bushel basket, hitting a beach ball with lightweight plastic bat, throwing softball for distance.
Trampoline	Play on the trampoline is a popular activity for all teenagers including the retarded.
Balancing	Use more complex walking boards, also introduce balancing on tires.
Dancing	Present simple rhythm and dance. More capable youngsters can learn to square dance.
Fine Motor Areas	
Easel Painting	Use a variety of colors on a large easel with tempra paints.
Peg boards and marble boards	Use patterns similar to the ones shown in Figure 8.70.

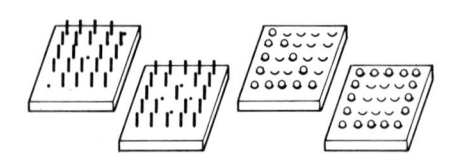

FIGURE 8.70

Block designs — One inch blocks may be used to construct designs similar to those in Figure 8.71. Use nine blocks such as this.

Mathematics for the Trainable Mentally Retarded 561

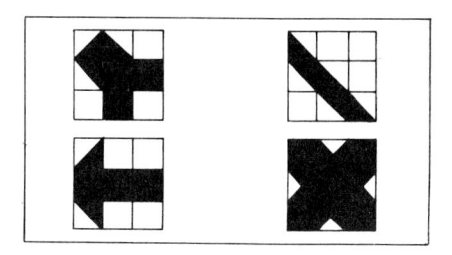

FIGURE 8.71

Stick patterns

Use counting sticks or tooth picks and have the youngsters reproduce such configurations as those in Figure 8.72.

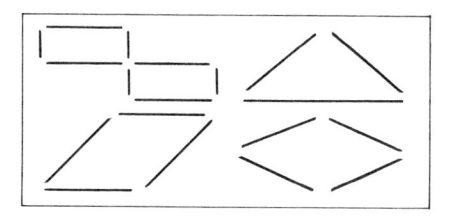

FIGURE 8.72

Reproduce shapes

The youngsters will have had practice in copying circles, squares and rectangles. Many of them will now be able to copy a diamond.

Discrimination
Distinguishing difference

Give the youngsters practice in finding the forms which are different.

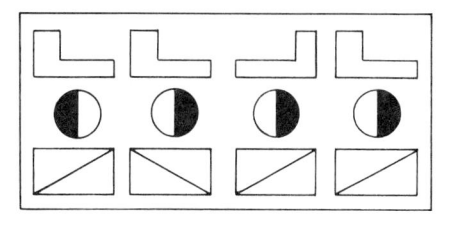

FIGURE 8.73

Identifying similarities

Have the youngsters find the one which is identical to the one on the left as in Figure 8.74.

FIGURE 8.74

Have the children match forms such as those in Figure 8.75.

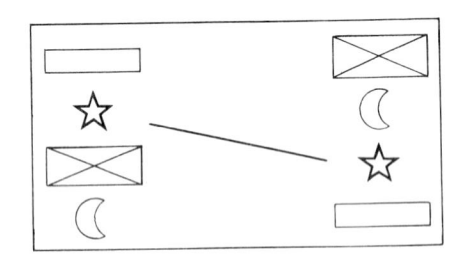

FIGURE 8.75

Name geometric forms   Ask the youngsters to name these forms.
    square
    rectangle
    triangle
    circle

VOCABULARY ASSOCIATED WITH MATHEMATICS

The terms to be taught at this level are listed on the checklist above. The techniques for teaching these words are reviewed briefly below. For further elaboration and additional suggestions the reader is referred to the appropriate sections in Chapters 4 and 5.

Skills to be Developed

Understanding of terms related to size, position, shape, quantity, measurement, money, and number operations. Also problem solving. For a specific list, see page 558.

Suggested Activities

Picture file. Number terms dictionary. Use objects and have the children manipulate them to help them learn such terms as *right, left, next to,* etc. Dramatize directives such as "Give Julie *all* the blocks. Put the red blocks *between* the green blocks, etc." Construct bulletin boards to illustrate terms.

NUMBER SYMBOLS—ADVANCED LEVEL, TRAINABLE MENTALLY RETARDED

The ability to rote count to 100 and to read number symbols as high as 100 are among the most significant objectives for the advanced level. Counting by 5's and 10's is also important in skills related to handling money and reading the clock. The reading and writing of number symbols need not be totally rote. An understanding of place value will assist in determining the meaning of number symbols.

Skills to be Developed	Suggested Activities
Rote counting to one hundred	Have children listen to each other count. Have one child start counting as fast as he can from one. Let another child take over where he left off as soon as he makes an error.

CARDINAL NUMBER

Young trainable children who have progressed to this level have had many opportunities to deal with groups up to ten. The introduction of numbers beyond ten must include the presentation of place value. If the youngster does not have some understanding of this concept and the collary of positional notation, he may be able to deal modestly with numbers beyond ten. However, the absence of understanding will limit his effectiveness since he will have to rely solely on rote memory. Furthermore, a lack of understanding restricts the possibility of developing the skills of solving problems through simplified algorithms to almost nil. The reader is referred to the cardinal number intermediate level for the EMR in Chapter 5 for additional ideas such as those listed below.

Skills to be Developed	Suggested Activities
Adding to ten	Present the youngsters with problems related to positional notation. 10 and 7 more = 10 + 7 = 17 10 and 9 more = 10 + 9 = 19 Practice with the same idea of positional notation can be given through exercises such as: 13 = 1 ten and 3 ones 34 = 3 tens and 4 ones 17 = ____ tens and ____ ones 45 = ____ tens and ____ ones Finish these problems: 10 + 7 = ____ 30 + 2 = ____ 40 + 4 = ____ 20 + 6 = ____

Identifying a ten group

Draw a line to make a group of tens and a group of ones:

```
11  XXXXXXXXXX  X
12  XXXXXXXXXX  X X
13  XXXXXXXXXX  X X X
    XXXXXXXXXX  X X X X
17  XXXXXXXXXX  X X X X X X
18  XXXXXXXXXX  X X X X X X X
```

ORDINAL NUMBER

By this level, the youngsters should be able to make a distinction between ordinal and cardinal number. They should be able to use the words *first, second,* and *third* orally. The ability to seriate to indicate position by use on the number names will be expanded at this level.

Skills to be Developed	*Suggested Activities*
Use of ordinals beyond third	Use pictures, objects, and games to teach position.
	Use the words fourth, fifth, etc. to incidentally teach these concepts through the day.
Seriate objects	Give the children items graded by heights, width, length, weight and have them arrange them in order. For example, a series of sticks from shortest to tallest.

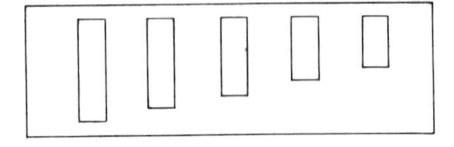

FIGURE 8.76

Use some items which vary by two qualities simultaneously, for example, by length and width.

MEASUREMENT

Learning to tell time is not only very functional socially but it is also a prestigious skill. Young adult retardates who are able to learn to tell time by the quarter hour, five minutes, or minute are quite proud of their skill. Their feeling of self-worth in wearing a watch that they can actually read makes the effort of teaching the skill very rewarding. The calendar need not be a mysterious instrument to most of the youngsters at this level for they can learn the order of the days of the week, months and seasons of the year. An equally important skill is the ability to measure by cups, teaspoons, tablespoons and their common fractions, ½, ¼, ¾. This simple knowledge will enable the youngsters to follow simple recipes and do some of their own cooking. The skills of linear measurement especially the inch, the foot, and their fractions make it possible for them to do some simple sewing. The thermometer is helpful in understanding the weather, in doing some cooking, in setting a comfortable room, and in taking body temperature. The skill of utilizing the thermometer, then, will be expanded at this level.

FIGURE 8.77

Suggestions for teaching these skills are presented below. Additional suggestions may be found in the chapters on the EMR.

Skills to be Developed	Suggested Activities
Measurement in cooking	Familiarize students with the cup, the one-half cup and the one-third cup, one-fourth cup, three-fourths cup and two-thirds cup, which is marked on the

	measuring cup. Introduce the measuring spoons, tablespoon, teaspoon, one-half teaspoon, pint, quart, gallon. Have children make a cake or a casserole by following a recipe. Make sure students understand the meaning of "preheat" and "blend," "fold" and other cooking terms.
Measurement in sewing	Familiarize child with concept of inch, one-half inch and five-eighths inch, foot, yard. Have children work with measuring tape and measure their bodies: ankle, wrist, height, neck, chest, waist, hip, arm and leg length. Then have students select patterns according to their measurements. Have them work with simple patterns and material to make a garment that will fit them.
Use of the thermometer	Explain the concept of body heat, introduce the concept of normal body temperature of 98.6 degrees. Have children take each other's temperature. Teach them how to set and read the thermostat and have children practice setting the thermostat for comfort in the home and at school.
Telling time by half hour and quarter hour	Teach the concept of the twelve hour day. Divide the clock of sixty minutes into quarters and show children the idea of quarter of, quarter after, half past. Make sure they understand that nine forty-five means quarter to ten. Initiate various practice sessions throughout the day.
Telling time by five minutes and one minute	Discuss the significance of pointing and have the children understand the nature of pointing. Then construct a number line: 12 1 2 3 4 5 6 7 8 9 10 11 12 Cover numbers and have child guess which is covered. Then take the line (paper or string) and make it into a circle, or a round clock. Explain that each number is not only an hour on the small pointer, but five, four, three, two or one minute on the big pointer. Ex-

Mathematics for the Trainable Mentally Retarded 567

	plain that between each of the numbers are five minute periods. Have children make their own clocks this way and practice on them in telling time.
Using time in daily situations	Ask frequently "What time is it? What time do we go to lunch? What time do we go home?" Make appropriate pictures (children going home, eating lunch, coming to school) with clocks showing the time beneath the pictures.
Use of calendar days of the week months of the year seasons of the year	Explain the concept that there are thirty days in one month. Have children make a large calendar and mark off each day until a whole month has passed. Have them mark it off by weeks. Explain that some months have thirty days and some more or less. You can teach the simple "Thirty days has September . . ." to help the children understand.
	Explain that there are four seasons of the year and we tell them apart by the weather. Using pictures (children in the snow, at the beach, the leaves falling, etc.) and ask "What season of the year is this?" In a simpler way, ask "What time of the year do we swim? When do we make snowmen? When do the leaves come back on the trees? When do the leaves turn color and fall?"

MONEY AND VALUE

The monetary system used in this country is actually quite complex. It is unlikely that the trainable mentally retarded child can develop an understanding of this system beyond the level of identifying coins and bills, doing some simple counting with coins and currency, making simple purchases, making change, paying simple bills, and doing simple banking. Only a few of the youngsters will be able to master all of the material outlined here. However, many of the fifteen-and sixteen-year-olds with IQ scores in the high 40's will find this content appropriate.

Skills to be Developed	*Suggested Activities*
Currency and coin recognition	Give the child a set of coins and currency including dimes, quarters, half dollars,

	and dollar bills (ones, fives, ten). Hold up a coin or bill and say "Find one like mine. Tell me the name of this."
Find the one that is different	Paste a series of dimes, quarters, and half dollars in a set of lines. For example, three dimes and one quarter, three half dollars and one quarter, and so forth. Have the student point to the one which is different.
Naming coins and currency	Give the students practice in naming the coins and currency to ten dollars.
Equivalent coins	Teach the common coin equivalents, namely:

1 nickel	5 pennies
1 dime	10 pennies
1 dime	2 nickels
1 quarter	5 nickels
1 quarter	1 nickel, 2 dimes
1 half dollar	2 quarters
1 half dollar	5 dimes
1 dollar	2 half dollars
1 dollar	4 quarters
1 dollar	1 half dollar, and 2 quarters

Counting money	Provide the students with coin boxes. Have them count to a predetermined amount. 8¢ 13¢ 25¢ 34¢ 46¢ 52¢ 65¢
Simple purchase—exact amount	Give the children a number of store items and have them select the current coins from their coin boxes.
Simple purchase—sufficient coins	The idea of this exercise is to teach the youngsters to select a coin large enough to cover a purchase even though they may be unable to count the correct change. For example, Billy buys candy costing ten cents. He will give the clerk one coin. Pick a coin that requires the least amount of change. Which one would Billy select? The penny, nickel, dime or quarter? From the coins below which *one* coin would be best for each of these purchases?

Mathematics for the Trainable Mentally Retarded   569

		Coins		
nickel	dime	penny		quarter
		half dollar		
3¢	47¢	22¢	32¢	9¢
24¢	11¢	5¢	7¢	26¢
6¢	19¢	29¢	2¢	38¢

Making change up to one dollar   The teacher should continue to use real money. Present the youngsters with an item or number of items totaling between six cents and ninety-nine cents. Remember that most trainable chillren will not progress to the highest level. Be certain to proceed in the sequence given below:

making change for dime using:
pennies only
nickel and pennies

making change for quarter using:
nickels only
nickels—dimes
nickel—pennies
dimes—pennies
pennies—nickels—dimes

making change for half-dollar using:
dimes only
quarter only
quarter—dimes—nickel
quarter—nickels
quarters—dimes—pennies—nickels

making change for dollar using:
half dollar—dimes
half dollar—quarters
half dollar—quarter—dimes—nickels
half dollar—quarter—nickels
half dollar — quarter — dimes — nickels—pennies

Understanding bills   Practice reading simple bills. Place emphasis on the amounts due. Bill the youngsters small amounts for classroom supplies, field trips to the theatre and so on. The skills developed in this area will be limited.

Banking   The two banking services to be taught are savings and check cashing. Familiarize them with different types of payroll checks. Teach them how to endorse and deposit the checks. Help them to develop the idea of regular savings through classroom accounts. The youngsters who are employed on a full or part-time basis should be encouraged to open their own savings account with a local bank. They should also learn about the payroll savings plan to buy bonds, Christmas clubs, and other ways of saving.

NUMBER OPERATIONS—ADVANCED LEVEL, TRAINABLE MENTALLY RETARDED

Many trainable mentally retarded youngsters will find the material taught at this level too difficult. However, a number of the more capable youngsters will learn simple column addition, more addition facts, adding of 10's, addition of two place numbers, several types of subtraction problems, more subtraction facts, subtraction of tens, and subtraction of two place numbers.

Teaching Column Addition

Column addition of three figures with sums of less than 10 may be presented at this level. Column addition is fairly complex because adding three groups is like doing two problems in one. It requires that the answer to the first problem be held in mind and that a second number be added to it. For example, the youngsters might place five apples in groups:

$$\begin{array}{r} 2 \text{ apples} \\ 2 \text{ apples} \\ \underline{1 \text{ apple}} \\ 5 \text{ apples} \end{array}$$

First add the two and two, keeping the four in mind, and make another problem of four and one which tells how many apples there are in all. As skills improve, the youngsters may use counters and then move to tallies to illustrate the problems.

In time, only number symbols will need to be written. Story situations like the above could be dramatized with the numbers written on the chalkboard or placed on a magnetic or flannel board. The playstore or play cafeteria described in this chapter may provide a ready source of interesting problems.

Addition Facts to Eighteen

When the children have attained proficiency in working with the combinations through ten, the number facts through eighteen should be presented. The combinations using five and six are usually presented first.

$$\begin{array}{r} 5 \\ +\ 6 \\ \hline 11 \end{array} \qquad \begin{array}{r} 6 \\ +\ 5 \\ \hline 11 \end{array} \qquad \begin{array}{r} 6 \\ +\ 6 \\ \hline 12 \end{array}$$

The teacher gives the students counters with instructions to arrange them on his desk to represent the numbers five and six. Use stick counters that can easily be assembled into bundles of ten. As the problems are solved, have the counters separated into sets of ten and ones.

Borrowing with Subtraction

The process of regrouping in subtraction is even more difficult to do than in addition.

$$\begin{array}{r} 22 \\ -\ 3 \\ \hline \end{array} \qquad \begin{array}{r} ^{1\,1}\!2\!\!\!/2 \\ -\ 3 \\ \hline 19 \end{array}$$

The youngsters have already learned that a larger number cannot be subtracted from a smaller one. They also know the subtraction facts through twenty. These skills should be illustrated with the place-value charts and the chalkboard. Have one of the students indicate the number twenty-two on the place-value chart. Write the number twenty-two on the board putting a ring around the two indicating the two tens. Ask the student to remove three sticks from the number twenty-two. This cannot be done without unwrapping one of the tens bundles. When it is necessary to unwrap a bundle, the sticks must be moved to the ones side. This is shown on the chalkboard by

$$\begin{array}{r} ^{1\,1}\!2\!\!\!/2 \\ -\ 3 \\ \hline \end{array}$$

The problem may now be solved both on the place-value chart and the chalkboard. The same procedure is used to present other problems. Some youngsters may learn the process without the aids.

Follow this pattern for all the addition facts through eighteen. Do not move to succeedingly difficult levels until the previous level has been mastered.

Addition Tower 1–18

		5	6	6		
		6	5	6		
		11	11	12		

4	7	5	7	6	7	7
7	4	7	5	7	6	7
11	11	12	12	13	13	14

3	8	4	8	5	8	6	8	7	8	8
8	3	8	4	8	5	8	6	8	7	8
11	11	12	12	13	13	14	14	15	15	16

2	9	3	9	4	9	5	9	6	9	7	9	8	9	9
9	2	9	3	9	4	9	5	9	6	9	7	9	8	9
11	11	12	12	13	13	14	14	15	15	16	16	17	17	18

Adding Tens

The youngsters must first learn to count by tens so that they recognize that twenty is two tens, thirty is three tens and so on. The use of bundles of ten sticks each or piles of ten counters each is the typical way to present the idea of ten. Prepare sets of ten bound together with rubber bands so they may be easily separated. Then have the children count:

    1   ten
    2   tens
    3   tens
    4   tens
    5   tens
    6   tens
    7   tens
    8   tens
    9   tens

Give the youngsters varying numbers of bundles so that, for example, Mary has two tens, Bill has three tens, Sue has four tens. The youngsters discover that two tens are twenty ones, that three tens are thirty ones, that four tens are forty ones and so on. Instead of writing two tens, we write twenty, for three tens we write thirty, for four tens we write forty. The zero tells us that we have no ones.

The idea of position notation and zero as a place holder will need to be given considerable attention. Many hours of work will have to be spent using the place value chart. Only after the youngsters have demonstrated facility with the place value chart should they be asked to work similar problems on work sheets.

Addition of Two Place Numbers

After the youngsters have gained skill in adding tens, some will be able to advance to adding two-place numbers with values other than zero in the ones place. The total for the ones column should always be less than ten, since the students are not ready for the idea of regrouping. The problems presented here should relate to concrete activities in the beginning. The teacher might start with a problem such as:

> Henry has thirteen collectors stamps. He bought twelve more at the store. How many does he have altogether?

The student places the sticks in the top row of the place value chart to show how many stamps Henry has, and in the next row to show how many he bought at the store. After the two numbers are shown properly in the chart, the ones are counted together, and then the tens, to find the answer twenty-five. Emphasize that large numbers are added the same way as smaller ones. Use a procedure similar to this by asking such questions as "What number is in the ones place in thirteen? In twelve? Three ones and two ones are how many ones? Write five under the ones. Now add the tens. How many tens are one ten and one ten? Write two under the tens. Now read the number for how many stamps Henry had altogether." Give many examples like this one. When the youngsters have demonstrated their ability to solve problems in this manner, they may work on their place value chart.

Teaching Subtraction.

The youngsters have learned to work with problems which ask, "How many are left?" In concretely demonstrated problems, it may be illustrated by removing a specified number of objects. At the advanced level, other types of subtraction problems may be introduced.

At this point, the youngsters are able to find remainders, but in some problems we know how many were in the total group before some were taken away and we need to find how many were removed. For example:

> John had five candy whistles.
> He now has three left.
> How many did he eat?

This is much more complex than the more familiar problem:

> John had five candy whistles.
> He ate two.
> How many does he have left?

In the last example the student represents the whistles with counters, takes away two, and sees that he has three left. In the first problem, the teacher must instruct the students carefully to be certain that the proper sequence is followed. The instructions should follow this pattern. "With your counters show the number of whistles John had at first. Now place your hand over some of the counters so that only three are left. The number you have covered up are the numbers which he ate. The problem is written

$$\begin{array}{r} 5 \\ -3 \\ \hline 2 \end{array}$$

Many problems of the same type should be similarly presented. A series of problems using all four of the related addition and subtraction facts will help develop the idea. For example, construct a series of problems which correspond to this set of facts.

$$\begin{array}{cccc} 6 & 1 & 7 & 7 \\ +1 & +6 & -1 & -6 \\ \hline 7 & 7 & 6 & 1 \end{array}$$

Subtraction is also used to determine how many more or how many fewer there are in one group than in another. The problem may be phrased, "How much more?" or "How much less?" These problems are all solved through the idea of one-to-one correspondence developed earlier in the program. These concepts should be reviewed along with the vocabulary such as *more, fewer,* and *less.* The students should be given many activities with comparison of concrete materials before any work sheet activities are introduced. The blocks, counters, pictures, and illustrations are divided into two groups. Have the students indicate how many are in each group in order to discover which group has more and which group has less. For specified examples, see the section on cardinal numbers in this chapter.

Subtraction Facts to Eighteen.

After the youngsters have attained skill in dealing with the subtraction facts to ten, the number facts through eighteen should be presented. The problems are selected from this chart.

Subtraction Tower 1–18

$$\begin{array}{ccc} 11 & 11 & 12 \\ -5 & -6 & -6 \\ \hline 6 & 5 & 6 \end{array}$$

$$\begin{array}{cccccc} 11 & 11 & 12 & 12 & 13 & 13 & 14 \\ -4 & -7 & -5 & -7 & -6 & -7 & -7 \\ \hline 7 & 4 & 7 & 5 & 7 & 6 & 7 \end{array}$$

Mathematics for the Trainable Mentally Retarded 575

```
 11  11  12  12  13  13  14  14  15  15  16
  3   8   4   8   5   8   6   8   7   8   8
  8   3   8   4   8   5   8   6   8   7   8

 11  11  12  12  13  13  14  14  15  15  16  16  17  17  18
  2   9   3   9   4   9   5   9   6   9   7   9   8   9   9
  9   2   9   3   9   4   9   5   9   6   9   7   9   8   9
```

The problems using 11, 5, and 6 might be given first.

```
   11        11
 -  5      -  6
    6         5
```

The teacher has the students use counters with instructions to arrange a set of sticks to represent 11. As the problems are solved, have the bundles of ten separated into ones.

Subtracting Tens

The youngsters have already learned to count by tens and to add by tens. Bundles of ten are used and the notation is reviewed. Remember zero means no ones.

```
 2 tens    20       3 tens    30
-1 ten    -10      -2 tens   -20
 1 ten     10       1 ten     10
```

Some of the students will be able to work with this idea using dimes. "If I have two dimes and spend one for candy, how many do I have left?" Here are two ways to write this.

```
 2 dimes      20 cents
-1 dime      -10 cents
 1 dime       10 cents
```

Since the youngsters have been taught that one dime is ten cents, it should not be too difficult to prepare them for such problems as:

```
  50    40    60    70
 -20   -30   -30   -20
```

Subtraction for Two Place Numbers

After practice with the subtracting of tens, some youngsters are ready to subtract two place numbers with values other than zero in the ones place. Problems requiring regrouping should not be used. The place value chart may be used to illustrate the process. The teacher would put a number, say thirty-five, on the chalkboard and ask one of the students to show it on the chart. "Now let's subtract twelve from thirty-five," writing twelve on the board below thirty-five. "Now find the answer by using the chart. How many ones do we take away? How many tens?"

A student is asked to perform this step by removing the correct number of tens and ones. "How many are left?" The teacher illustrates the process on the chalkboard. Give more practice with problems such as these:

$$\begin{array}{cccc} 36 & 24 & 56 & 42 \\ -13 & -12 & -15 & -11 \\ \hline \end{array}$$

Regrouping in Addition and Subtraction

Not many trainable children can master this aspect of mathematics; however, since some do, it is included here as a possible goal. The youngsters who reach this phase of development will generally be fifteen-years-old and older with IQ scores in the high 40's or low 50's.

Carrying with Addition

Begin the process by reviewing problems similar to these. Have the children place the ones in the box □ and the tens in ring ○.

$$\begin{array}{cccc} 6 & 8 & 4 & 9 \\ +5 & +7 & +6 & +3 \\ \hline \bigcirc\square & \bigcirc\square & \bigcirc\square & \bigcirc\square \end{array}$$

As an immediate step have the boxes and rings placed to the side. The box represents ones and the ring represents tens.

$$\begin{array}{ccc} 16 & 16 & 16 \\ +\ 7 \quad ①\ \boxed{3} & \underline{\ \ 7}\quad ①\ \boxed{3} & \underline{\ \ 7}\quad ① \\ & 3 & 3 \end{array}$$

It may help some youngsters to circle the tens in the problems.

$$\begin{array}{cccc} ⓖ \\ +\ 7 \end{array}\Big\}\ ①\ \boxed{3} \quad \begin{array}{c} ⓖ \\ +\ 7 \\ \hline 3 \end{array}\ 1\ \boxed{3} \quad \begin{array}{c} ⓖ \\ +\ 7 \\ \hline 3 \end{array}\ ① \quad \begin{array}{c} 16 \\ +\ 7 \\ \hline 23 \end{array}$$

SUMMARY

The capacities of trainable mentally retarded children for learning basic number concepts was explored in this chapter. It was indicated that there is limited agreement on exactly what content is appropriate for these youngsters. The suggestions presented in this chapter were intended to give the teacher some guidelines organized into levels of instruction based upon mental age abilities. Emphasis was placed upon perceptual skills and simple number usage. These suggestions should prove helpful in improving the children's abilities to deal with their physical world in a more quantitative fashion.

Mathematics for the Trainable Mentally Retarded

TEACHING AIDS FOR TRAINABLE MENTALLY RETARDED CHILDREN

The following list of suggested aids for the trainable mentally retarded is presented here to give examples of the types of instructional aids which may be adapted to these children. It is not intended to be exhaustive. The code refers to the names and addresses of publishers given in the appendix.

PUBLISHER CODE	TITLE	DESCRIPTION
C-6	Miscellaneous aids	Design cubes, form boards puzzles, miniature toys, wooden numbers, climbing devices.
P-5	Parquetry Blocks Training Kit	Assists individuals with perceptual problems to improve visual awareness and develop kinesthetic or motor skills. Consists of plastic blocks, templates, designs and patterns.
P-5	Ruth Cheves' Visual-Motor Perceptual materials	Consists of six groups of cards, puzzles and games. The materials have broad application both developmentally and remedially. A game or puzzle approach is used throughout and each component part includes a guide providing procedures.
J-1	Miscellaneous aids for teaching number and measurement	Flannel board, numbers and geometric shapes, calendars, clocks, pegboards.
S-16	Miscellaneous school supplies	Calendars, counting frames, blocks, magnetic boards, flannel boards with counting shapes, measurement devices.
D-7	Numero-Cubes Set I	A set of ten different dice presenting both the figure and configuration in developmental sequence.

PUB-LISHER CODE	TITLE	DESCRIPTION
D-7	Shapes, Puzzles	Intended to build form concept through twelve puzzles using triangles, circles, squares, diamonds, etc.
D-7	Dyna-Balance Series	A series of devices for motor training and for spatial orientation development. This integrated group of materials is designed for physical activities involving the dynamic balance of a child's body. Units of the series available are the walking board and the rocking platform.
M-2	Training Fun with Numbers	A series of workbooks providing practice with number concepts, counting, and number operations.
D-1	Performance Goal Record (PGR)	An evaluation instrument developed at the Julia Malloy Learning Center specifically for trainable mentally retarded children. The desired student outcomes are stated in behavioral terms with specific criteria for evaluation of progress. Many items relate to mathematics.
D-1	Performance Goal Record	This instrument is designed to measure behavior goals for trainable mentally retarded children. There are many items which related to mathematics instruction. It was developed at the Julia Malloy Learning Center

REFERENCES

Barsch, Ray H. *Enriching Perception and Cognition.* Seattle, Washington: Special Child Publications, 1968.

———. *Achieving Perceptual-Motor Efficiency.* Seattle, Washington: Special Child Publications, 1968.

Baumgartner, Bernice B. *A Curriculum Guide for Teachers of Trainable Mentally Handicapped Children.* Springfield, Illinois: Department of Public Instruction, Circular Series B-2, 1955.

———. *Helping the Trainable Mentally Retarded Child.* New York: Bureau of Publications, Teachers College, Columbia University, 1960.

———. *Guiding the Retarded Child.* New York: The John Day Company, 1965.

———, and Lynch, Katherine D., *Administering Classes for the Retarded.* New York: The John Day Company, 1967.

Cain, L. F., and Levine, S. A. *A Study of the Effects of Community and Institutional School Classes for Trainable Mentally Retarded Children.* Washington: U.S. Office of Education, 1961.

Conner, Frances, and Talbot, Mabel. *Curriculum for Young Mentally Retarded Children.* New York: Bureau of Publications, Teachers College, Columbia University, 1964.

Frankel, Max G., Happ, F. William, and Smith, Maurice P. *Functional Teaching of the Mentally Retarded.* Springfield, Illinois: Charles C. Thomas, Publisher, 1966.

Guenther, R. J. *Final Report of the Michigan Demonstration Research Project for Severely Retarded.* Lansing, Michigan: State Department of Public Instruction, 1965.

Hottel, J. V. *An Evaluation of Tennessee's Day Class Program for Severely Mentally Retarded Children.* Nashville: Peabody College Press, 1958.

Johnson, G. Orville. *Training Program for Severely Mentally Retarded Children.* Albany: New York State Inter-Department Health Resources Board, 1958.

Kephart, Newell C., *Slow Learner in the Classroom,* 2d ed. Columbus, Ohio: Charles E. Merrill Publishing Co., 1971.

Kolburne, Luma Louis. *Effective Education for the Mentally Retarded Children.* New York: Vantage Press, 1965.

Malloy, Julia. *Trainable Children.* New York: John Day, 1963.

Montgomery County, Maryland, Public Schools. *Guide For Teachers of Trainable Retarded Children.* Bulletin No. 140. Montgomery County, Maryland: The Public Schools, 1955.

Perry, Natalie. *Teaching the Mentally Retarded Child.* New York: Columbia University Press, 1960.

Peterson, Daniel L., ed. *Curriculum for the Trainable Mentally Retarded.* Athens: Ohio University Press, 1971.

———. *Mathematical Knowledge of Young Retardates.* Ph.D. dissertation, University of Missouri, 1967.

Reynolds, M. C. and Kiland, J. R. *A Study of Public School Children with Severe Mental Retardation.* (St. Paul, Minnesota: State Department of Education) reported in Lloyd M. Dunn (ed.) *Exceptional Children in the Schools.* New York: Holt, Rinehart and Winston, Inc., 1963.

Roach, Eugene G., *The Purdue Perceptual Motor Survey.* Columbus: Charles E. Merrill Books, 1966.

Rosenzweig, Louis E. and Long, Julia. *Understanding and Teaching the Dependent Retarded Child.* Darien, Connecticut: The Educational Publishing Corporation, 1960.

Williams, Harold M. *Education of the Severely Retarded.* Washington, D.C.: United States Government Printing Office, 1961.

chapter 9

The Evaluation of Pupil Progress In Mathematics

The classroom teacher is continually making educational judgments and decisions involving the progress of students. Was the mathematics unit successful in helping Julie master the skills of telling time by the hour? Is Lloyd now ready for instruction in multiplication? When the intermediate teacher gives a test at the end of a unit on telling time, the purpose is to determine how well the children have met the objectives of that unit. The analysis of their performance will also assist in judgments concerning the appropriateness of the unit, of the methods of instruction, and of the equipment and materials used. This evaluation will guide the teacher in planning the next steps in the instructional process. The purpose of achievement testing then, is to provide information to the teacher so she can make intelligent educational decisions. The most important decision is the determination of the next steps to pursue in the curriculum. Of course, the information gleaned from tests can be utilized in research, help the children evaluate their own performance, and guide the teacher in reporting to parents. But the most significant impact of test results is on the formation of curriculum objectives, teaching methods and the selection of materials and equipment.

Parenthetically, it is important to point out here that the purpose of evaluation is not to determine what letter grade to assign a child on his eighth-week report card. It is the contention of the writer that letter grades for mentally retarded children are justified only to the degree that they promote self-esteem and learning. The grades A, B, C, D, and F should be assigned to homework papers, classroom assignments or a test performance only if it helps the child learn. Using grades to measure mentally retarded children against the standards established for average children or to compare retarded children to each other is absurd. The teacher must evaluate pupil progress in order to determine if the child has made satisfactory progress. If the child has not achieved adequately, the reasons should be determined and the appropriate alterations made in the curriculum. When a mentally retarded child does not progress according to reasonable predictions, there must be an explanation. Marking the child's report card with a D or an F serves only to discourage the child and confirm his own feelings of self-depreciation. In many instances, the F should be assigned to inadequate materials, faulty methodology, haphazard curriculum, improper motivation, and sloppy assessment. Every child, including the mentally retarded child, wants to think well of himself and be regarded positively by others. The child who has confidence in himself and has the esteem of others will work harder for self-worth and to advance his esteem among his peers. It is also doubtful that letter grades for mentally retarded children can be meaningfully interpreted by parents. Parents should be, and typically are, most interested in how their handicapped children are faring in comparison to their potential. The writer would like to discourage the use of letter grades; but if they must be used, let the criteria be the usefulness to the child. A discussion of how to report to parents the pupil's progress in mathematics will be presented later in the chapter.

It is not possible for the teacher to judge how much growth a child has made in mathematics unless he knows the level of the child's skill prior to instruction. It is equally obvious that he has to know where the child is functioning before he can introduce new material. It is not enough, however, merely to know the child's present level of competency in order to introduce properly new ideas and later to measure the mastery of those ideas. The teacher must also have some idea of the child's capacity for learning before he can determine whether the measured improvement is "good."

INTERPRETING THE PSYCHOMETRIC REPORT

The teacher should already know a great deal about each of the students before he attempts to determine pupil progress in mathematics. The child would not be in special education unless he had sub-average intelligence and was impaired in adaptive behavior. That is, the child would not have been assigned to the class in the first place unless he had a low IQ as measured by an individually administered intelligence test and had performed below grade level in academic areas.

The Evaluation of Pupil Progress in Mathematics

The psychometric report can be a very valuable aid to the teacher. The psychologist will not only report the IQ score but also will provide relevant background information and relate pertinent data about the child's performance on specific subtests. The report should also indicate any behaviors which are thought to have implications for educational planning. The two most widely used individual intelligence tests are the *Stanford-Binet* and the *Wechsler Intelligence Scale for Children*. There are a number of mathematical items on both of these tests which can provide the teacher with very useful information. A number of such examples from the Stanford-Binet and the WISC are shown in Tables 9.1 and 9.2 respectively.

It can be seen that the WISC has a specific subtest on arithmetic while the Stanford-Binet has a considerable number of items related to mathematics. The teacher should be aware of the scope of the arithmetic items on the WISC and the related items on the Stanford-Binet so that he might make intelligent inquiries of the school psychologist.

The questions which the special education teacher might ask the school psychologist regarding the capacity of a mentally retarded child for mathematics include:

1. Did you observe any behavior which might suggest a negative attitude toward mathematics?
2. Did the performance of the child indicate any deficiencies in the psychomotor or visual-perceptual domains which might contribute to poor achievement in mathematics?
3. Did you detect any signs of self-depreciation which might account for poor performance in mathematics?
4. Were there any patterns uncovered in the child's responses which might indicate specific cognitive strengths or weaknesses relevant to the mastery of mathematics?
5. Was there anything in the child's responses to specific subtests which would suggest the advisability of one modality over another?
6. Did you obtain any background information which might be helpful in assessing the child's potential for mastery of mathematics?
7. What is your estimate of the child's potential for independent living at adultation?
8. Did you find any characteristic verbal patterns which might influence the child's performance in mathematics?
9. What is your estimate of this child's present capacity for learning mathematics?

10. What is the child's present IQ and mental age and at what grade level would you reasonably expect the child to function in light of all the information you have at hand? Did you see any signs of sensory deficits?
11. Is there anything additional that you can tell me which would guide me in structuring the educational experiences for this child?

TABLE 9.1

Selected items from the Stanford-Binet (Termon & Merrill, 1960) which relate to Mathematics

LEVEL:	ITEM:	ABBREVIATED DIRECTIONS:
II-6	Repeating 2 Digits	"Listen; say 2." "Now, say 4-7, etc."
III	Copying a Circle	"Make one just like this. Make it right here."
V	Number Concepts	Use twelve 1-inch cubes. "Give me three blocks. Put them here." (Also 10, 6, 9, 7)
VI	Opposite Analogies II	"An inch is short, a night is. . . .?"
VII	Copying a Diamond	"Make one like this. Make it right here."
VIII	Naming the Days of the Week	"Name the days of the week for me." "What day comes before Tuesday? . . Thursday, Friday?"
X	Block Counting	"How many blocks are here? Now count them and tell me how many there are in each square beginning here . . ."
XIV	Reasoning	"My house was burglarized last Saturday. I was at home all of the morning but out during the afternoon until 5 o'clock. My father left the house at 3 o'clock and my brother was there until 4. At what time did the burglary take place?"

For further information, the teacher is referred to *A Profile for the Stanford Binet (L-M)* which classifies the SB test items in six categories: (1) general information, (2) visual-motor ability, (3) arithmetic reasoning, (4) memory and concentration, (5) vocabulary and verbal fluency, (6) judgment and reasoning*

* Robert E. Valett, *A Profile for the Stanford-Binet (L-M)* (Palo Alto, California: Consulting Psychologists Press, 1965).

TABLE 9.2**

How many nickels make a dime?

What is the advantage of keeping money in a bank?

Sam had three pieces of candy and Joe gave him four more. How many pieces of candy did Sam have altogether?

Three men divided eighteen golf balls equally among themselves. How many golf balls did each man receive?

If two apples cost 15¢, what will be the cost of a dozen apples?

In what ways are a circle and triangle alike?

** Selected Paraphrased Items Related to Arithmetic from the Wechsler Intelligence Scale for Children (Wechsler, 1949) reprinted by permission of Psychological Corporation, New York, New York.

The special education teacher should be familiar enough with the standard individual intelligence tests that he is able to ask pertinent questions and to interpret replies in an intelligent and informed manner. The results of the individual intelligence test are of minimal value if they fail to assist in the development of sound instructional plans for the child.

GATHERING BACKGROUND INFORMATION

The above questions indicated that a prediction of a child's capacity to learn includes not only information about intellectual functioning, but also information concerning health and physical factors, sensory deficits, perceptual problems, family background, interpersonal relationships, and other social-psychological factors.

Among the difficulties the teacher might expect to find in the typical class of mentally retarded children are:

1. Poor attitude due to repeated defeats
2. Tension due to frequent frustrations
3. Reading deficiencies
4. Perceptual-motor deficits
5. Problems of concentration due to mild emotional stress
6. Disruptive family life
7. Poor vision
8. Hearing loss

9. Brain damage
10. Experiential deprivation
11. Prolonged illnesses
12. Social immaturity
13. Poor self-esteem
14. Peer rejection
15. Social isolation

This is not an exhaustive list by any means but it does serve to indicate the variety of problems which can unduly affect academic performance. The experienced teacher knows that these problems are likely to emerge in various combinations rather than as isolated traits. It is perfectly obvious that these difficulties can adversely affect the child's performance in mathematics. The sensitive teacher will be on the alert for symptoms of problems such as these and be prepared to make the proper adjustments in methodology and curriculum.

The question then becomes: How, other than through the psychometric report, does the teacher discover the variables which affect mathematics achievement?

It has already been indicated that the mentally retarded child would not have come to the attention of the school officials unless he has a poor academic record compared to his peers. The details of this record, and factors contributing to it, can assist the special education teacher in planning the curriculum. He is generally able to secure additional information about the child from these sources:

1. A study of the child's cumulative record
2. Conferences with past and current teachers
3. Visits to the child's home and parent conferences at school
4. Conferences with the school psychologist, guidance counselor, school nurse and other specialists
5. Observation of the child in the classroom, playground, and other areas around the school
6. Informal conversations with the child outside of the classroom

ASSESSING MATHEMATICS ACHIEVEMENT

The teacher should gather. as much information from these sources as feasible. However, her main, initial task is to discover the child's status of mathematical knowledge and subsequently to determine how much mathematics has been learned since the last evaluation period. There are many ways of measuring this achievement, but we shall discuss here the five most common techniques.

1. Anecdotal records
2. Analysis of performance
3. Questionnaires
4. Standardized tests
5. Teacher-made inventories

Anecdotal Records

Sample Anecdotal Note

Billy Martin

Date

November 8   Today during the arithmetic lesson, Billy was working a word problem. He raised his hand and asked in a shaky voice, "Why do we always have to do these dumb thought problems?"

November 12   Billy brought his paper up to my desk today with a big smile on his face. He asked me to grade his paper which included a number of subtraction problems involving regrouping. He had them all correct. Yesterday, he made a number of careless mistakes on similar problems.

Each remark should be dated and include other information such as the place and situation. The anecdotal note itself should describe the actual behavior rather than interpret the incidents. For example, the observations recorded for Billy Martin on November 8 would be inappropriately interpretative if it had been written: "Billy became very nervous and angry when doing the word problems in today's assignment. He really hates thought problems."

Over a period of time, anecdotal or progress notes will gradually accumulate. Special problems or small amounts of progress may be revealed that would not have been evident on unit tests. As the notes are reread the teacher may detect patterns of behavior which would have otherwise gone unnoticed or have been forgotten. Of course, it is very important that the teacher record those behaviors which are relevant to learning mathematics. Teachers are too busy to maintain a running record of the child's behavior.

The characteristics of a good anecdote were discussed succinctly by Prescott (1957, pp. 153-154):

> In order to help teachers learn to discipline their perceptions, we have developed a description of the characteristics of a good anecdote. Observing behavior with the idea of writing an anecdote about it changes the teacher's mental set, alters the way he views the

behavior of a child and thereby alters his perceptions. Discriminating the essential components of the anecdote he will write enables the teacher to be objective and to forget his feelings of being helped or hindered by the child.

The characteristics of a good anecdote are:
1. It gives the date, the place, and the situation in which the action occurred. We call this setting.
2. It describes the actions of the child, the reactions of other people involved, and the response of the child to these reactions.
3. It quotes what is said by the child during the session.
4. It supplies "mood cues"—postures, gestures, voice qualities, and facial expressions that give cues to how a child felt. It does not provide interpretation of his feelings, but only the cues by which a reader may judge what they were.
5. The description is extensive enough to cover the episode. The action or conversation is not left incomplete and unfinished but is followed through to the point where a little vignette of behavioral moment in the life of the child is supplied.

Analysis of Performance

The analysis of the child's performance in mathematics must be made against a background of broader information. The teacher must have some knowledge of the factors which affect growth and condition behavior. As mentioned earlier, such information is generally available to the teacher through school and social records. The teacher will then proceed to inspect the child's worksheets and other written assignments and to analyze oral responses and problem solving in functional situations. He may discover faulty work habits and inefficient methods of study. Some children perform poorly because they do not have a mastery of the basic number facts or because they do not really understand the number operations. Others will have difficulty with word problems, utilize immature processes, or make careless and technical errors. An examination of written and oral work will reveal these faults and improper procedures. The teacher should also be on the lookout for poor attitudes and other symptomatic behavior. The teacher should maintain copies of the child's written work and record illustrations of boardwork and oral responses. This provides another cummulative record of performance. If a weakness is identified, the teacher should construct informal test items which will uncover the seriousness of the problem.

The list below gives some of the types of errors or immature habits the teacher may observe in the arithmetic performances of mentally retarded children.* It simply represents the errors made by one group

---

* Errors made by mentally retarded children in an ESEA Title VI Program, Pike County, Ohio, 1969.

of retarded children and is not intended to exhaust all possible errors made by such children.

Addition	Subtraction
Add same number twice	Add instead of subtract
Subtract instead of add	Fail to borrow
Skip a number	Borrow improperly
Fail to carry	Confuse subtraction facts
Carry improperly	
Count on fingers	
Count with fingers	
Confuse addition facts	

Multiplication	Division
Confuse multiplication facts	Confuse division facts
Add instead of multiply	Multiply instead of divide
Errors with zero	Errors with zero
Mistakes in addition	Errors with remainder
Problems with horizontal form	Mistakes in subtraction

Questionnaires

Questionnaires are generally used to measure attitudes and interests. Children are asked to respond to a set of attitude statements similar to these:

I think arithmetic is more fun than another subject in school.

I never do very well in arithmetic.

Arithmetic is just as important as reading.

I wish we spent more time on arithmetic and not so much on other things.

I don't like arithmetic.

It is very simple to have the children rank mathematics among all their school subjects. When mathematics does not fare very well it is time to look for the reasons. A pupil's distaste for mathematics is often related to the series of defeats he has experienced. However, there may be physical, emotional, or social factors which are interferring with the development of a healthy attitude. Whatever the reason, a poor attitude can contribute to low achievement and should be modified if possible. If the child begins to experience success in mathematics, is aware of that success, and receives the recognition of his teacher, the chances are that his attitude will be positive towards the subject.

Standardized Tests

Though there are large numbers of mathematics achievement tests available commercially, the teacher of mentally retarded children is confronted with testing problems not typically encountered by other teachers. In this section, we will discuss these problems and how they may be overcome.

The most obvious testing problem for the teacher of the mentally retarded is the inappropriateness of most standardized tests. Most standardized achievement tests sample the content of regular elementary and secondary school programs and the norms developed are based on the performance of large numbers of typical children. Their norms are based on the average results of children in regular school programs taught by typical teachers with conventional materials. Of course, mentally retarded children are not average. They are assigned to classes for exceptional children and are taught by special education teachers using different sets of goals, methods, and materials. Most standardized achievement tests are too difficult for mentally retarded children since much more material is covered by the test than is taught in special education classrooms for such children. It is difficult to evaluate and interpret the scores of mentally retarded children on these tests since there are few items at the lower achievement levels. Consequently, we learn from the administration of standardized mathematics achievement tests that an individual mentally retarded child is performing at the fifth-percentile level. We probably knew that before the test was ever given. We might also learn that an intermediate aged retarded child was functioning at the first-grade level, but this information is of little value since such an interpretation of his score is based on a comparison with average children. To say that an intermediate aged mentally retarded child functions at a first-grade level when compared to chronological peers simply means that he is performing well below the average of typical intermediate children on the particular test. It does not tell the teacher how well the child is doing in comparison to other retardates nor how his performance measures up to stated objectives. There is no real guarantee that the child could compete with actual first graders. He may be better or worse than that. Actually the grade equivalent score is relatively meaningless for mentally retarded children since they are so low in the range that the grade equivalent score is usually an extrapolation. There is even the possibility that the grade equivalent scores of the retarded occur below the level of chance. The purpose of standardized achievement tests is to form criteria for judging the effectiveness of the mathematics curriculum as indicated by the degree that individual children or groups of children make progress toward the achievement of stated objectives. Since most standardized tests are based on goals accepted for average children, they are of little value to the teacher of the mentally retarded. The curriculum for the mentally retarded is quite different from that of the average child; therefore, the same tests generally should not be used with both groups. The solution, of course, is to use standardized instruments which are based on the curriculum for the mentally retarded with the norms based on the performance of large numbers of mentally retarded children. Although at this writing there are no tests of this specific design, there are a limited number of instruments which are suitable for use with mentally retarded students. A brief description of five such tests is presented below.

Wide Range Achievement Test.* The Wide Range Achievement Test measures pupil progress for children from five years of age to adulthood. There are subtests in reading, spelling, and arithmetic. The entire test may be administered in twenty to thirty minutes. The arithmetic subtest is divided into two levels and is composed of an oral and a written part. The oral part is always administered individually while the written part may be administered in groups. The arithmetic areas covered are counting, reading, number symbols, solving oral problems, and performing written computations. Three types of scores are used in reporting the WRAT results: (1) grade ratings, (2) percentile, and (3) standard scores or deviation quotient on grade ratings.

KeyMath Diagnostic Arithmetic Test. This test is especially useful with slow learners and educable mentally retarded children because it is diagnostic in structure, functional in content, and individually administered. The range of the test is from preschool through seventh grade although there is no upper limit for individual remedial use. The test requires about thirty minutes to administer and consists of fourteen subtests organized into three major categories: *content* (numeration, fractions, geometry and symbols); *operations* (addition, subtraction, multiplication, division, mental computation, numerical reasoning); and *applications* (word problems, missing elements, money, measurement, time). *KeyMath* yields a grade equivalent score based on the total test performance, a diagnostic profile depicting the child's relative performance in the fourteen areas, and a description of each item's content and an indication of whether the child has or has not mastered it.

---

* J. F. Jastak, S. W. Bijou, S. R. Jastak, Guidance Associates, 1526 Gilpin Avenue, Wilmington, Delaware.

Y.E.M.R. Performance Profile.** This is an evaluative scale of individual performance based upon teacher observation. It is designed for use with young moderately and mildly retarded children. There are ten major subtests including such topics as social behavior, communication, academics, perceptual and intellectual development. The academic area consists of items used for rating performance in concepts of size, shape, and number; numeral identification; and skills in telling time, addition, subtraction, handling money, writing, and spelling. A score is derived from the test results which indicates the child's progress towards measurable objectives in arithmetic.

Fundamental Processes in Arithmetic.† This instrument is used to determine errors in addition, subtraction, multiplication, and division. It is not a standardized test, but rather a diagnostic instrument. The test results provide the teacher with a diagnostic chart illustrating just how the pupil performs his work with suggested remedial procedures.

Peabody Individual Achievement Test.†† The purpose of the test is to provide a wide-range screening measure of achievement in mathematics, reading, spelling, and general information. The PIAT is an untimed power test. The mathematics subtest consists of eighty-four multiple-choice items, each with four options, which range from testing such early skills as matching, discriminating, and recognizing numerals; to measuring advanced concepts in geometry and trigonometry. PIAT raw scores may be converted into four types of derived scores: (1) grade equivalents, (2) age equivalents, (3) percentile scores, and (4) standard scores.

There are many other survey tests which assess factors of arithmetic achievement. Some of the more widely used tests of this type are listed below with an indication of the factors tested in the arithmetic subtests.

Name of Test	Factors Tested
California Achievement Tests	Fundamentals
	Reasoning
SRA Achievement Series	Concepts
	Reasoning
	Computation
Stanford Achievement Tests	Computation
	Reasoning
Metropolitan Achievement Tests	Computation
	Problem Solving

** Alfred J. DiNola, Bernard P. Kominsky, Allan E. Sternfeld, Reporting Services for Children, 563 Westview Avenue, Ridgefield, New Jersey.
† G. T. Bushwell, Lenor John, Bobbs-Merrill Company, Inc., 4300 West 62nd Street, Indianapolis, Indiana.
†† Lloyd M. Dunn, Frederick C. Maskwardt, American Guidance Service, Inc., Circle Pines, Minnesota.

It is acceptable to use these tests with the mentally retarded if the teacher avoids the numerous pitfalls described in the preceding pages. One approach is to administer the battery at a lower level than called for in the standardization. For example, an intermediate group of children might be given a primary level achievement test. The interpretation of the test results would have to be on a clinical basis rather than utilizing the standardized scales and tables found in the test manual. Inspection of the test results and item analysis could provide useful information if cautiously interpreted.

A more acceptable approach is the development of mathematics inventories.

Most of the remainder of this chapter will be devoted to the steps involved in constructing a mathematics inventory. The general procedure will be discussed first and then a sample of a classroom inventory and several samples of individual inventories presented.

CONSTRUCTING AN INVENTORY

REVIEW THE OBJECTIVES

It has been emphasized frequently in this text that the careful formation of educational objectives for the mentally retarded is the key to effective curriculum planning and instruction. Pupil progress must be evaluated with respect to clearly stated goals. One cannot determine progress toward a goal if a goal is unspecified any more than a pilot can estimate the distance to his destination if he has not decided upon an airport. Throughout this text, objectives for each level of instruction have been presented. The teacher can use these broad objectives to determine the specific goals for each child. These goals should be specified early in the academic year as an initial guide to instruction and continually revised as the child makes progress and the teacher comes to know him better. These revised goals and the instruction flowing from them generate the test items. Reference to the outline of objectives will reveal certain concepts which have not been adequately covered and other skills which have been given considerable attention. The test items must coincide with the emphasis of instruction if they are to be of value in assessing the children's responses and the effectiveness of teaching. The teacher needs to review the objectives frequently to insure sufficient coverage of the material and to compose test items proportionate to the emphasis of instruction. Any given test probably will not be comprehensive. One should not attempt to test too broad an area of instruction at one time.

CONSTRUCT THE ITEMS

The way to evaluate pupil growth is to sample behavior which will indicate the extent of the child's progress towards each of the goals selected for testing. In most cases, the teacher will not have satisfactory commercial tests available and therefore will need to construct her own instruments. A good instrument must be planned in advance and should not emerge from last minute, haphazard desperation. The major task of constructing a test is accomplished when the outline of objectives is completed. In this section, we are concerned with the individual items within a teacher-made mathematics achievement test.

The major obstacle to proper evaluation of pupil progress through teacher-made tests is the inability of many teachers to compose good items and to assemble a representative set of items. Too often the items selected do not proportionately represent the important content of a unit. There is a great temptation to select items which assess computation skills rather than problem-solving abilities and to use items which measure rote learnings rather than understandings of mathematical principles. The items should not be slanted toward one category of mathematical skills and knowledge but rather broadly reflect the entire area to be tested.

The teacher of mentally retarded children has many demands placed upon her time. She is asked to build many of her own teaching aids and to chart the curriculum for each child on an individual basis. Consequently, even with reduced classroom enrollment, it is unreasonable to expect her to devote weeks to the preparation of sophisticated measurement devices. However, a few simple suggestions will assist the development of adequate tests.

1. Test items should proportionately reflect the outline of content.
2. There should be a division of each major category into a series of subsections.
3. A number of items should be composed for each subsection and arranged in their order of estimated difficulty.
4. There should be a sufficient number of each type of problem to insure reliability.
5. Test items should avoid trivial information and skills. They should be simple to administer and require only essential skills.
6. The test should be relatively simple to score, interpret, and report.
7. The test should not require reading unless the skill to be measured is reading or the teacher is certain that reading the directions or problems presents no obstacle.
8. The test should be administered individually to help insure that the child understands what he is to do. This also provides the

teacher with an opportunity to observe behavior and detect faulty work habits.

There are a great variety of objective items which may be used in the construction of a teacher-made mathematics test. The most common may be classified into four major types: (1) true and false items; (2) fill-in items; (3) matching items; and (4) multiple-choice items. Each of these is discussed below.

True-False Items

The true-false item is used more widely in areas other than mathematics; however, it does have its place in measuring quantitative skills. The teacher should be alerted to its strengths and weaknesses. The most obvious advantages to the true-false is the ease of construction and the quick response. The most glaring fault is the affect of guessing. Even if a student were completely without knowledge regarding a set of concepts and skills, he could get about half of the T-F items correct simply by guessing. Another serious shortcoming is the difficulty of writing statements that are absolutely true or false.

T.F. It is better to pay for a purchase by check than with cash.

T.F. An advantage of paying for a purchase by check is that it provides a receipt.

Space does not permit an exhaustive treatment of the advantages and disadvantages of the other types of items listed below. The reader is referred to *Making the Classroom Test, A Guide for Teachers* available free from Evaluation and Advisory Service, Educational Testing Service, 1947 Center Street, Berkeley, California 94704.

Fill-In Items

The fill-in question asks the student to provide the number or word which completes a statement.

One part of 9 is 5. The other part is _____.
2 + 5 = _____.   8 + 2 = _____.
78 = _____ tens and _____ ones.
The clock in Figure 9.1 says half past _____.

FIGURE 9.1

The question should be limited generally to one blank and at the most no more than two blanks. Here is a poor example using excessive blanks. Can you improve it?

There are ____ balls in row ____ than in row ____.
A x x x x x x x
B x x x

The statement should have only one term which would reasonably complete it. Here is an example of a poor fill-in statement:

Another way to write 23 is ____ + ____.

In addition to the intended answer of 20 + 3, equally correct would be 15 + 8; 19 + 4 and so forth. How would you improve upon this item?

Matching

In this item, the student is presented with two lists of facts or terms which they are to match. Here is an example:

40	Thirty
50	Ten
10	Twenty
30	Forty
20	
60	

In this example, the students are asked to draw a line connecting the numeral and the corresponding number word for that numeral. One of the lists should be considerably longer than the other to avoid guessing. The shorter of the two lists should have only four or five items to avoid mistakes due to misdrawing lines when the students actually know the correct response.

Multiple-Choice Items

The multiple-choice item is one of the most popular of objective items. It requires the student to select one alternative response to a problem. Here is a sample:

Draw a ring around the picture in Figure 9.2 that shows halves.

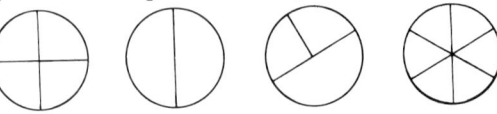

FIGURE 9.2

Mark the number one:
2   1   4   3

Which number is the same as 2 and 3?   4   6   5   8

The items in the inventories used for illustrations attempt to follow the principle of sound item construction. It can be seen that only a minimum of testing supplies are needed, that the procedure is kept simple, and that the directions for recording and scoring the responses are clear. Reading is not a factor in the performance on the items.

ADMINISTRATION OF THE INVENTORY

Teachers have been made aware of many factors which may affect classroom performance. All children have their "good" and "bad" days. A restless night of sleep, a missed breakfast, an argument with a sibling are examples of incidents outside the classroom which can severely impede test performance and result in a misinterpretation of the child's achievement status. Conditions within the classroom can have an equally negative result. For example, it would be unwise to administer an arithmetic test after a child has been sent to the principal's office because of an emotionally disruptive incident. The testing conditions themselves can have an influence on the child's test performance. A test which is given as a surprise or is presented in a hurried, disorganized fashion or introduced by fuzzy directions can give rise to tension which interferes with performance. Even seemingly minor facets of the testing situation can significantly alter the children's achievement. A crowded desk top, a dirty eraser, and poor lighting are examples of minor aspects which may have a decided effect on test scores. Even when all of these conditions are optimal, some children will have such a high degree of test anxiety that they need constant reassurance and praise to build their self-confidence and insure representative performance.

Here are a series of questions which should help the teacher evaluate the testing setting:

1. Did I properly prepare myself to administer this test by becoming familiar with all the materials and directions?
2. Did I make certain that the physical conditions were conducive to test taking?
3. Did I properly motivate the children so that I can be certain that they are doing their best?
4. Did I take steps to reduce test-anxiety by the way I announced and presented the test?

5. Was I sufficiently friendly and cheerful during the administration of the test so that discouragement was kept to a minimum?
6. Did I avoid giving the children answers but encourage them to do their best?

AN EXAMPLE OF A CLASSROOM INVENTORY

The teacher cannot be expected to recall the exact level of each child's number achievements without the help of some system or device for recording results. She may elect an inventory chart for the entire class in order to more rapidly check the progress of each child and to detect those who need special help in a given category.

It is fairly simple to construct such a chart for classroom use which is generated from the outcomes for students over a given interval of time. The first step is to state the objectives as briefly and clearly as possible. Each objective should be reduced to its simplest form and a heading written for each column. The space in the columns is to be used to indicate the date and progress toward the objective. The sample inventory shown below is based on the suggested content for primary trainable mentally retarded children as detailed in Chapter 8. The checklist is also reproduced for the convenience of the reader.

A classroom inventory such as the one illustrated in Figure 9.3 will help the teacher visualize the term's work in a single glance and help in selecting children who might be worked with together and those who need individual assistance.

TABLE 9.3
Checklist for Primary Level
Trainable Mentally Retarded Children

1. Form and Perception
   A. puzzle—can complete simple two- to five-piece inlay puzzles.
   B. line—can reproduce a line.
   C. body image—can identify major body parts: eyes, nose, arms, etc.
2. Vocabulary
   A. identification of terms—can properly use such terms as long, short, tall, thick, wide, bunch, narrow, middle, top, bottom, on, off, in, out of, next to, outside, inside, all.
3. Number Symbols
   A. rote counting—knows number names in correct order to ten.
   B. writing numerals—can correctly copy the numerals one and two.
   C. repeats digits—can correctly repeat two or three digits.

4. Cardinal Number
   A. indefinite number—can properly use indefinite number concepts on "more, less, most," and "few."
   B. correspondence—can successfully solve problems involving one-to-one correspondence
   C. reproduce sets—can correctly produce a set for any number one through five.
   D. recognize sets—can name correctly any set one through five.
5. Ordinal Number
   A. first and last—can identify the first and last in a line.
6. Measurement
   A. time—has simple concepts of time such as time to go to school, bedtime, lunch time, day, night, today, tomorrow.
   B. calendar—knows names of days, own age.
   C. instruments—recognizes common instruments: scales, ruler, calendar.
7. Money
   A. identification of coins—can properly identify a penny and nickel.
8. Number Operations
   A. addition—has mastery of number combinations with sums to five.
   B. subtraction—has mastery of number combinations with no missing addend greater than five.

EXAMPLES OF INDIVIDUAL NUMBER INVENTORIES

The individual mathematics inventory has the same purpose as the classroom inventory. It has the added advantage of detailed observation and recording. However, it is more time consuming and does not allow as well for the comparison of children to each other.

For the convenience of the teacher, a sample inventory has been developed for each of five levels for the educable mentally retarded. A sample record blank and a set of directions has been prepared for each of these levels. Of course, the items are based upon the objectives and activities as detailed in Chapters 3-7. These inventories are presented as examples for each of the five instructional levels for educable mentally retarded children. The inventories actually used by the classroom teacher would probably be balanced much differently. If a major portion of instructional time in mathematics had been given to measurement concepts, then the items sampled in the inventory would reflect that emphasis. The items presented are but a few of the wide range of possibilities. The inventories require a few simple and inexpensive materials, including a pencil and paper, a number of 8½″ × 11″ cards made on posterboard on which illustrations are drawn, money, counting cubes, and parquetry

		Pupil's Name									
Opera-tions		sub 1-5									
		add 1-5									
Measure-ment	Money	nickel									
		penny									
		instruments									
		calendar									
		time									
		first last									
Number Ideas		recognize sets 1-5									
		reproduce sets 1-5									
		one to one correspondence									
		most few									
		more less									
Vocabu-lary	Number Symbol	repeat 2-3 digits									
		rote 1-10									
		write 1 & 2									
Form and Perception		forms									
		body parts									
		line									
		puzzle									

FIGURE 9.3. Classroom Number Inventory Chart for Primary Level Trainable Mentally Retarded Children

blocks. The responses generally call for pointing to the card, and writing and reading are held to a minimum.

NUMBER INVENTORY FOR EDUCABLE MENTALLY RETARDED CHILDREN

Preprimary Level

Record Blank

Name _____ Date _____
I.Q. and Name of Test_____ _____
Chronological Age _____ Estimated Mental Age _____

1. Form and Perception
    1. identification of body parts: eyes, feet, hands, ears, nose, hair
    2. match geometric forms: square, circle, rectangle, triangle
    3. make a mark: scribble, line, circle

2. Vocabulary Associated with Mathematics
    4. big____
    5. next to____
    6. tall____
    7. narrow____

3. Number Symbols
    8. rote count (4)   1 2 3 4 5 6 7 8 9 10
    9. match numerals   1 2 3 4 5 6 7 8 9 10
    10. name numerals 1, 2, 3, 4, 5, 6, 7, 8, 9, 10
    11. repeat three digits: 1,2,3____1,3,2____2,1,3____

4. Cardinal Number
    12. indefinite cardinal number: most ____, few ____
    13. separating a set of 4: ____
    14. set of recognition of 3____ 2____

5. Ordinal Number
    15. first____
    16. last____

6. Measurement
    17. identify the clock____ weight scale____
    18. identify the heavy one: 1st trial____ 2nd trial____

7. Money
    19. identify the penny_____ nickel_____
    20. discriminate money
8. Number Operations
    21. 1 + 1_____
    22. one apple and one more_____

NUMBER INVENTORY FOR EDUCABLE MENTALLY RETARDED CHILDREN

Preprimary Level

DIRECTIONS FOR ADMINISTRATION:

This number inventory is designed for educable mentally retarded children of chronological ages three, four, and five years with mental ages from nine months to four years. All such children have some skills associated with number. This inventory attempts to identify these abilities in order to furnish a definite basis upon which to construct the mathematics curriculum.

The items in this inventory reflect the mathematical categories, objectives, content, and activities discussed at length in the earlier chapters. A checklist of the mathematics content for the preprimary level is shown in Chapter 3.

This inventory should be administered individually and should be presented as a "number game" rather than as a test. The administration of the items will typically require approximately ten minutes, but should more time be necessary a second session should be scheduled to avoid fatigue and the other problems associated with short attention span.

The inventory is divided into eight categories each of which has from two to four items. The materials required for each item, and the procedure to follow in presenting the question and recording the response are given below.

1. Form and Perception
    1. *Identification of body parts*
        Materials   A large flat picture of a doll clearly illustrating the body parts.
        Procedure   "Here is a picture of a doll. Show me. . . . Point to . . . etc. the dolly's eyes, feet, hands, ears, nose, hair."

The Evaluation of Pupil Progress in Mathematics

    Record   Circle the correct responses and place a line through the items missed.

2. *Match Geometric Forms*
   Materials   Four small stimulus cards and one larger response card with line drawings of a square, circle, rectangle, and triangle.

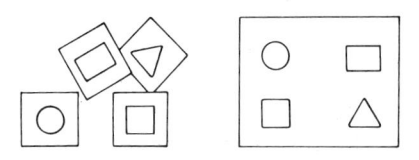

   FIGURE 9.4

   Procedure   Present the response card and say, "See all of these" (pointing to forms). Hold up one stimulus card and say, "Find one that looks just like this one. Point to it with your finger." Repeat the directions for the remaining three stimulus cards.
   Record   Circle the correct responses on the record blank and place a line through the items missed.

3. *Make a Mark*
   Materials   8½" × 11" piece of paper with a circle the size of a half dollar drawn in the lower left hand corner. A pencil or a crayon.
   Procedure   Place the paper in front of the child. Say, "Watch me" (making a scribble in the upper left hand corner). Hand the child the pencil and say, "Now you do it" (pointing to the space to the right of the demonstration scribble).

   Say, "Watch me" (making a line on the left hand side of the paper under the scribble). Hand the child the pencil and say, "Now you make one like mine." Point to the space to the right of the demonstration line.

   Say, "See this circle. You make one just like it."
   Record   Circle the correct responses on the record blank and place a line through the items missed.

2. Vocabulary Associated with Mathematics
   4. *Vocabulary "big"*

Materials Response card with two line drawings of balls.
Procedure Say, "Show me the big ball . . . Point to the big one."

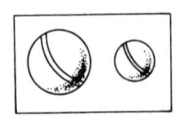

FIGURE 9.5

Record Place a plus in the space on the record blank if the response is correct and a minus sign if it is incorrect.

5. *Vocabulary* "next to"
   Materials Response card with line drawings showing a bird next to a cage.
   Procedure "Show me the bird next to the cage."
   Record Place a plus in the space on the record blank if the response is correct and a minus sign if it is incorrect.

FIGURE 9.6

6. *Vocabulary* "tall"
   Materials Response card with a tall and short person pictured in line drawings.

FIGURE 9.7

Procedure "Which one is tall?"
Record Place a plus in the space on the record blank if the response is correct and a minus sign if it is incorrect.

The Evaluation of Pupil Progress in Mathematics   607

   7. *Vocabulary "narrow"*
      Materials   Response card with a wide and narrow line.

      FIGURE 9.8

      Procedure   "Show me the one that is narrow."
      Record   Place a plus in the space on the record blank if the response is correct and a minus sign if it is incorrect.

3. Number Symbols
   8. *Rote Counting*
      Materials   none
      Procedure   Say, "I want you to count. Ready? 1 . . . ." The child should pick up the counting and continue 2 . . . 3 . . . 4 (and perhaps higher). If the child fails to continue the counting you may count to 3 for him, but then start over again saying, "Now I want you to count. Ready? 1 . . . ."
      Record   Circle the highest number given in the correct sequence.

   9. *Match Numerals*
      Materials   A response card with numbers to 10 and individual stimulus cards with one number on each.

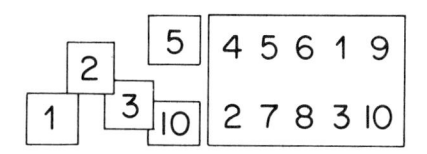

      FIGURE 9.9

      Procedure   Present a stimulus card and the response card and say, "Find the one which looks just like this one . . . Put your finger on the one (number) which is the same as this one."
      Record   Circle the number(s) correctly matched.

10. *Name the Numerals*
    Materials   Use the stimulus cards from item 9.
    Procedure   Hold up one card at a time and ask, "What number is this?"
    Record   Circle the number(s) correctly named.
11. *Repeating Three Digits*
    Materials   none
    Procedure   "Listen to me carefully. Then I want you to say exactly what I say. Ready? 1 . . . 2 . . . 3" (count slowly). ("Now you say it"—if necessary). Repeat the procedure for 1,3,2 and 2,1,3.
    Record   Check the sequence correctly repeated.

4. Cardinal number
    12. *Indefinite Cardinal Number*
        Materials   Response card with four flower vases, with different numbers of flowers in each.

FIGURE 9.10

        Procedure   "See all of these. Which one has the most? Which one has just a few?"
        Record   Place a plus in the space on the record blank if the response is correct and a minus sign if it is incorrect.
    13. *Separating a Set of 4*
        Materials   Ten cubes.
        Procedure   Place the cubes before the child and say, "Put four blocks here. Give me four."
        Record   Place a plus in the space on the record blank if the response is correct and a minus sign if it is incorrect.
    14. *Set Recognition*
        Materials   Cubes
        Procedure   Place three (then two) cubes in front of the child. Say, "How many blocks are here?"

The Evaluation of Pupil Progress in Mathematics 609

        Record   Place a plus in the space on the record blank if the response is correct and a minus sign if it is incorrect.

5. Ordinal Number
   15- *Ordinal Number*
   16. Materials   A response card with a group of children or cars pictured in a line.
       Procedure   For item number 15 ask, "Which is first?" For Item number 16 ask, "Which one is last?"
       Record   Place a plus in the space on the record blank if the response is correct and a minus sign if it is incorrect.

6. Measurement
   17. *Clock*
       Materials   A response card with a clock, scale, ruler, cup pictured.

FIGURE 9.11

        Procedure   "Show me the clock. Which one tells us how much we weigh?"
        Record   Place a plus in the space on the record blank if the response is correct and a minus sign if it is incorrect.

   18. *Heavy*
       Materials   Two boxes of identical size and shape (jewelry size) filled with material of grossly different weights ... clay and cotton.

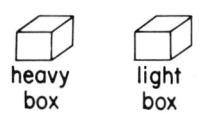

FIGURE 9.12

610 *The Evaluation of Pupil Progress in Mathematics*

Procedure   "Here are two boxes. Which one is heavy? Give me the heavy one."
Record   Place a plus in the space on the record blank if the response is correct and a minus sign if it is incorrect.

7. Money
   19. *Identifying Coins*
       Materials   A card with five different coins pasted firmly in place.

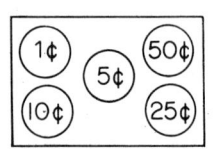

```
┌─────────────────┐
│  (1¢)      (50¢)│
│       (5¢)      │
│ (10¢)     (25¢) │
└─────────────────┘
```

FIGURE 9.13

Procedure   "Point to the penny. Point to the nickel."
Record   Place a plus in the space on the record blank if the response is correct and a minus sign if it is incorrect.

   20. *Money Discrimination*
       Materials   A response card with a picture of a penny and three foils.
       Procedure   "Point to the money."

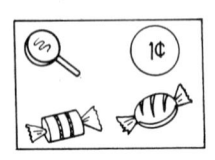

FIGURE 9.14

Record   Place a plus in the space on the record blank if the response is correct and a minus sign if it is incorrect.

8. Number Operations
   21- *Number Operations*
   22. Materials   none
       Procedure   For item number 21, say, "How much is one plus one?" For item number 22, say, "Mary had one

apple and her mother gave her one more. How many apples does Mary have altogether?"

Record   Place a plus in the space on the record blank if the response is correct and a minus sign if it is incorrect.

NUMBER INVENTORY FOR EDUCABLE MENTALLY RETARDED CHILDREN

Primary Level

Record Blank

Name _____ Date _____
I.Q. and Name of Test_____ _____
Chronological Age _____ Estimated Mental Age_____

1. Form and Perception
    1. match forms: star, rectangle, diamond, circle
    2. copy a square____
    3. imitation of arm positions

FIGURE 9.15

2. Vocabulary Associated with Mathematics
    4. day____ night____
    5. stamp____
    6. price tag____
    7. whole____ half____

3. Number Symbols
    8. rote count: 5   10   15   20+
    9. reading numerals 6   8   12   22   45
    10. reading number names: one, three, five, ten
    11. writing numerals: 4   2   8   15   47
    12. reading symbols: +   =   ¢   —

4. Cardinal Number
   13. separating sets: 5 8 12
   14. instantaneous set recognition: 2 3 4 5
   15. less than____ more than____

5. Ordinal Number
   16. second____
   17. fifth____

6. Measurement
   18. identify hour hand ____
   19. lunch time ____
   20. calendar—location of month
   21. birthday ____
   22. reading clock by hour ____

7. Money and Value
   23. identify coins: penny, nickel, dime, quarter
   24. pennies equivalent to nickel
   25. how many nickels are in a dime?
   26. count pennies: 3, 5, 10, 15

8. Number Operations and Problem Solving
   27. $2 + 1 =$ $2 - 1 =$
       $3 + 3 =$ $4 - 2 =$
       $5 + 1 =$ $5 - 1 =$
       $4 + 2 =$ $6 - 2 =$
   28. here are six chips; remove three ____
   29. age on next birthday ____

NUMBER INVENTORY FOR EDUCABLE MENTALLY RETARDED

Primary Level

DIRECTIONS FOR ADMINISTRATION

This number inventory is designed for educable mentally retarded children of chronological ages six, seven, and eight years with mental ages from three years to six years and three months. The typical child in such a program will achieve skills and concepts in mathematics at a level comparable to that reached by non-handicapped children in kindergarten and first grade. This inventory attempts to identify these abilities in order to furnish the teacher with a definite basis upon which to construct the mathematics curriculum.

The items in this inventory reflect the mathematical categories, content, and activities outlined in the "Checklist of Mathematics—Primary Level." This checklist is shown in Chapter 4.

This inventory should be administered individually and should be presented as a number game rather than as a test. The administration of the items will typically require approximately fifteen to twenty minutes.

No score is yielded by this inventory and no attempt to quantify the results should be made. The items in the inventory reflect the curriculum to such an extent that children who have progressed through the primary curriculum for the educable mentally retarded should respond to eighty or ninety percent of the questions correctly. In this sense, the inventory is a mastery test. Those who perform less well than this should be given the preprimary level inventory or another form of the primary level should be constructed from the checklist. There are relatively few items in each category and the responses to these should not cause the teacher to conclude that the child in question has a particular deficit or strength. Further observations should be made. However, the overall performance on the inventory will indicate fairly well whether the child has mastered the primary level mathematics curriculum.

The inventory is divided into eight categories each of which has from two to five items. The materials required, the procedure to follow in presenting the questions, and the method of recording the responses are described below.

1. Form and Perception
    1. *Match Forms*
        Materials   8½" × 11" card with star, rectangle, diamond, and circle.
        Four smaller cards with identical forms.

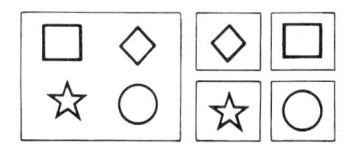

FIGURE 9.16

        Procedure   "Here is a card with some forms on it. Show me the one like this." Present all four forms.

Record   Circle the forms correctly matched on the record blank and draw a line through the forms not properly matched.

2. *Copy a Square*
Materials   3" card with a 2" square; 8½" × 11" paper.

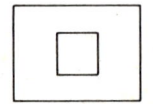

FIGURE 9.17

Procedure   "See this (showing the square). You draw one just like it right here" (pointing to the piece of paper).
Record   Circle the (+) sign if the child reproduces the square so that the corners are close to 90° (75°-90°) and the sides are roughly equal. Circle the (−) sign if the square is not correctly reproduced.

3. *Imitation of Arm Positions*
Materials   None
Procedure   "Watch me. You do just as I do. Put your arms just the way mine are." Do this for the four positions shown in Figure 9.18.

FIGURE 9.18

Record   Circle on the record blank the position correctly imitated and draw a line through the positions incorrectly imitated.

2. Vocabulary Associated with Mathematics
    4. *Day and Night*
    Materials   8½" × 11" card with a picture of day and one of night.

FIGURE 9.19

The Evaluation of Pupil Progress in Mathematics 615

    Procedure   "See these? Which is a picture of day? Which is a picture of night?"
    Record   Place a plus sign in the blank on the record sheet if the response is correct and a minus sign if the response is incorrect.

5. *Stamp*
    Materials   8½" × 11" card with an illustration of a stamp and three foils.

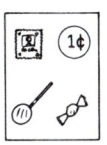

FIGURE 9.20

    Procedure   "See these? Which is the stamp? Point with your finger to the stamp."
    Record   Place a plus sign in the blank on the record form if the response is correct and a minus sign if the response is incorrect.

6. *Price Tag*
    Materials   8½" × 11" card with an illustration of a price tag and three foils.

FIGURE 9.21

    Procedure   "See these? Show me the one with a price tag."
    Record   Place a plus sign in the blank on the record form if the response is correct and a minus sign if the response is incorrect.

7. *Whole and Half*
    Materials   8½" × 11" card with an illustration of a whole apple, a half an apple and two foils.

FIGURE 9.22

616   *The Evaluation of Pupil Progress in Mathematics*

        Procedure   "See these? Show me a whole apple. Now point to half of an apple."
        Record   Place a plus sign in the blank on the record form if the response is correct and a minus sign if the response is incorrect.

3. Number Symbols
   8. *Rote Counting by Fives*
      Materials   None
      Procedure   "I want you to count by fives. Ready? five. . . ." The child should pick up the counting and continue ten . . . fifteen . . . twenty (and perhaps higher.) If the child fails to continue the counting you may begin again saying, "Now I want you to count by five's. Listen to me then you do it. five . . . ten . . . You try it. Ready? five . . ."
      Record   Circle the highest number in the sequence.

   9. *Reading Numerals*
      Materials   8½" × 11" card with the numbers six, eight, twelve, twenty-two, and forty-five printed as shown in Figure 9.23.

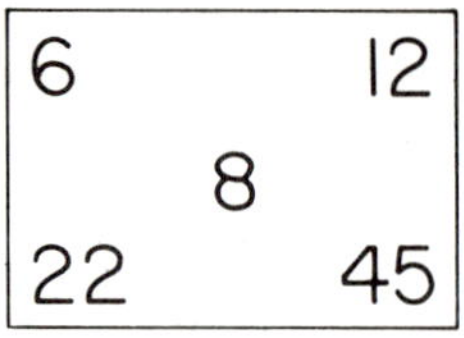

```
┌─────────────────┐
│  6          12  │
│       8         │
│  22         45  │
└─────────────────┘
```

FIGURE 9.23

       Procedure   "See these numerals. Find six. Point to twenty-two . . . eight . . . forty-five . . . twelve."
       Record   Circle the numerals that were correctly identified and place a line through those incorrectly identified.

   10. *Reading Number Names*
       Materials   8½" × 11" card with the words one, three, five, and ten printed as shown in Figure 9.24.

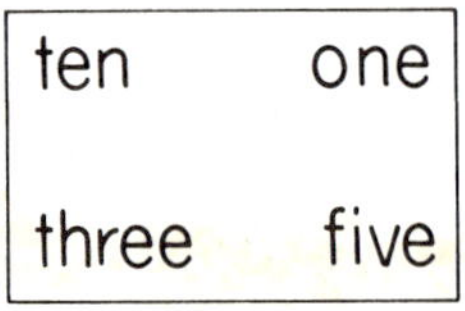

```
┌─────────────────┐
│  ten      one   │
│                 │
│  three    five  │
└─────────────────┘
```

FIGURE 9.24

Procedure "See these words. Which one is three? Find ten. Where is five? Show me one."
Record Circle the words that were correctly identified and place a line through those incorrectly identified.

11. *Writing Numerals*
    Materials 8½" × 11" piece of primary ruled paper.
    Procedure "I want you to write some numbers on this piece of paper. I'll read the number and then you write it. Four. Write the number four." (then two, eight, fifteen, thirty-six)
    Record Circle the numerals on the record blank which were correctly written and place a line through those incorrectly written.

12. *Reading Number Symbols*
    Materials 8½" × 11" card with symbols =, +, ¢, — as shown in Figure 9.25.

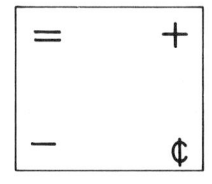

FIGURE 9.25

Procedure "See this card. Which one means plus? Show me the minus sign . . . cents sign . . . equals sign."

4. Cardinal Numbers
   13. *Separating Sets*
       Materials One set of sixteen one-inch cubes of the same color.
       Procedure Place the blocks in front of the child. "Give me five blocks. Put them right here." Same for eight and twelve.
       Record Circle the numbers on the record blank which were correctly reproduced and place a line through those incorrectly reproduced.
   14. *Instantaneous Set Recognition*
       Materials Five smaller cards made from an 8½" × 11" card with four sets of objects (two, three, four, five) illustrated as shown in Figure 9.26. One card with one item.

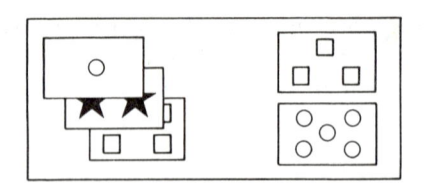

FIGURE 9.26

Procedure   "I am going to show you a card with a picture of some things on it. I want you to tell me how many things are on the card. I am going to show it very fast so pay attention." Practice with the card with one apple on it. Then show the other cards one at a time. As you hold the card in plain view of the child say to yourself "one thousand one . . . one thousand two" and turn the card over.

Record   Circle the numbers on the record blank corresponding with the sets properly named and place a line through those sets improperly named.

15. *Less Than and More Than*
    Materials   8½" × 11" card with the numerals four, eight, twelve, sixteen, and two arranged as shown in Figure 9.27.

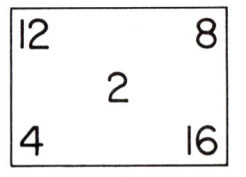

FIGURE 9.27

Procedure   "Point to the number which is more than three. Which number comes after fifteen? Show me the number which is one less than thirteen. Which number comes before nine?"

Record   Place a plus sign in the blank by "less than" if both responses for "less than" are correct and a minus sign if one or both responses are incorrect. Do the same for "more than."

5. Ordinal Number
   16. *Second*

The Evaluation of Pupil Progress in Mathematics 619

Materials 8½″ × 11″ card showing children lined up at a water fountain.

FIGURE 9.28

Procedure "See the children line up to get a drink of water. Point to the child who is second in line to get a drink."

Record Place a plus sign in the space on the record blank if the correct response is given and a minus sign if the response is incorrect.

17. *Fifth*

    Materials 8½″ × 11″ card showing children lined up at a water fountain. Same as number 16.

    Procedure "See the children lined up to get a drink of water. Point to the child who is fifth in line."

    Record Same as 16.

6. Measurement

    18. *Identify Hour Hand*

        Materials 8½″ × 11″ card with an illustration of three clocks as shown in Figure 9.29.

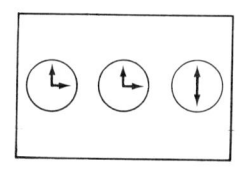

        FIGURE 9.29

        Procedure "Here is a picture of a clock. See the hands of the clock? Show me the hour hand." Repeat for two other clocks.

        Record Mark the space on the record blank with a plus if the child identifies the hour hand two out of three times correctly. Use the minus sign to indicate less than two out of three identified correctly.

    19. *Lunch Time*

Materials   None
Procedure   "What meal do children usually eat at school around noon time?"
Record   Mark the space on the record plan with a plus if the response is "lunch" and a minus sign if the response is incorrect.

20. *Calendar*
    Materials   8½" × 11" card with an illustration of a calendar as shown in Figure 9.30.

	1973	MAY		1973
M	—	7	14	21	28
T	1	8	15	22	29
W	2	9	16	23	30
Th	3	10	17	24	31
F	4	11	18	25	—
S	5	12	19	26	—
Su	6	13	20	27	—

FIGURE 9.30

    Procedure   "Here is a picture of a calendar. Show me where it says the name of the month. Point to the month with your finger."
    Record   Mark the space on the record blank with a plus if the response is correct and a minus if incorrect.

21. *Birthday*
    Materials   None
    Procedure   "When is your birthday?" If the child gives only the month or only the date of the month say, "Yes, and what (month, day, date of month?)"
    Record   Mark the space on the record blank with a plus if the child gives both the month and date of month correctly (e.g., February 13) and a minus sign if only one or neither is given correctly.

22. *Reading Clock by Hour*
    Materials   8½" × 11" card with four clocks showing the hours of three, six, ten, twelve o'clock.

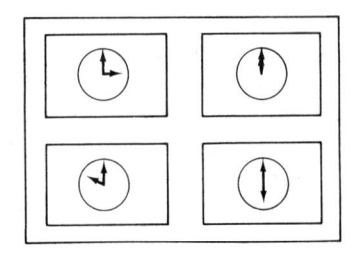

FIGURE 9.31

The Evaluation of Pupil Progress in Mathematics 621

    Procedure   "Here are some pictures of clocks. Show me the clock which says three o'clock (ten, six, twelve).
    Record   Mark the space on the record blank with a plus sign if three out of four are identified correctly and with a minus sign if less than three out of four are identified correctly.

7. Money and Value
    23. *Identifying Coins*
        Materials   8½" × 11" card with coins attached as shown in Figure 9.32 including penny, nickel, dime, quarter and half dollar.

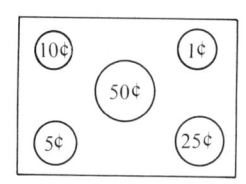

FIGURE 9.32

        Procedure   "See these coins. Point to the nickel. Where is the penny? Find the quarter. Show me the dime."
        Record   Circle the words on the record blank corresponding to the coins properly identified and place a line through those incorrectly identified.

    24. *Pennies Equivalent to a Nickel*
        Materials   8½" × 11" card with four sets of pennies attached in the patterns shown in Figure 9.33.

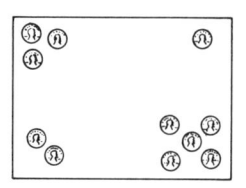

FIGURE 9.33

        Procedure   "See these groups of pennies. Show me the group of pennies that is the same as one nickel. How many pennies are there in a nickel?"
        Record   Place a plus in the space on the record blank if the response is correct and a minus sign if it is incorrect.

25. *Nickels in a Dime*
    Materials   None
    Procedure   "How many nickels are in a dime? How many nickels are the same as one dime?"
    Record   Place a plus in the space on the record blank if the response is correct and a minus sign if it is incorrect.

26. *Counting Pennies*
    Materials   Twenty pennies
    Procedure   "Here are some pennies. Give me three . . . five . . . ten . . . fifteen."
    Record   Circle the numbers on the record blank corresponding to the coins properly counted and a line through the numbers incorrectly counted.

8. Number Operations and Problem Solving
    27. *Computations*
        Materials   8½" × 11" piece of paper with the problems as shown in Figure 9.34.

$$\begin{array}{cccc} 2 & 3 & 5 & 4 \\ +1 & +3 & +1 & +2 \end{array}$$

$$\begin{array}{cccc} 2 & 4 & 6 & 5 \\ -1 & -2 & -1 & -2 \end{array}$$

FIGURE 9.34

        Procedure   "Here are some problems. Write the answers as quickly as you can but do not make careless mistakes."
        Record   Circle the numbers on the record blank corresponding to the problems answered correctly and place a line through those answered incorrectly.

    28. *Separating a Subset*
        Materials   Six disks.

FIGURE 9.35

Procedure "Here are six chips. Give me three. How many do you have left."
Record Place a plus sign in the space if the response is correct and a minus sign if it is incorrect.

29. *Age on Next Birthday*
Materials None
Procedure "How old will you be on your next birthday?"
Record Use a plus mark if the answer is correct and a minus sign if it is incorrect.

NUMBER INVENTORY FOR EDUCABLE MENTALLY RETARDED CHILDREN

Intermediate Level

Record Blank

Name _____ Date _____
I.Q. and Name of Test_____ _____
Chronological Age _____ Estimated Mental Age_____

1. Form and Perception
   1. name forms: circle, square, rectangle, triangle
   2. advanced form discrimination ____

2. Vocabulary Associated with Mathematics
   3. largest
   4. highest
   5. what is a check?
   6. what is a sales slip?

3. Number Symbols
   7. fifteen . . . twenty . . . thirty-one
   8. count by 2's . . . 2,4,6 to 20 _____
   9. place value to two places: (a) tens and ones place, (b) how many tens are there in 20? 30? 45? _____

4. Cardinal Number
   10. If there are ten sticks in each group, how many are on this card? . . . (50) On this card? . . . (100)
   11. From these 20 blocks, give me 15; then 19.
   12. Which is ⅓, ¼ (of a pie?)

5. Ordinal Numbers
   13. Which is 10th (in a row of 12)?

6. Measurements
    14. Which holds more, a quart or a gallon? +−
    15. Which is more, a teaspoon or a tablespoon? +−
    16. Read this clock (2:30. . . . .9:30)
    17. Read this thermometer . . . (show two different thermometers)
    18. How many inches in a foot? +−
    19. Which is longer, a foot or a yard? +−
    20. How tall are you? +−

7. Money and Value
    21. If you bought an ice cream cone for a dime and gave the clerk a quarter, how much change would you get? +−
    22. How many quarters are there in a dollar? +−

8. Number Operations and Problem Solving
    23. $10 - 4 =$ $12 - 9 =$ $8 - 3 =$ $16 - 7 =$
        $128 - 53 =$ $65 - 6 =$ $46¢ - 33¢ =$
    24. $2 \times 4 =$ $3 \times 2 =$
    25. 2 divided into 8 =   3 divided into 9 =
    26. $9 + 4 =$ $2 + 8 =$ $1 + 4 + 3 =$
        $65 + 2 + 2 =$ $37 + 4 =$
    27. There are five boys and three girls getting on a school bus. How many children get on the bus? +−
    28. At the first stop of the bus two boys and one girl get off the bus. How do you find out how many children are left on the bus? Do you add, subtract, or divide? +−

NUMBER INVENTORY FOR EDUCABLE MENTALLY RETARDED CHILDREN

Intermediate Level

DIRECTIONS FOR ADMINISTRATION

This number inventory is designed for educable mentally retarded children of chronological ages nine, ten, eleven, and twelve with mental ages from six years up to eight years. The typical child in such a program will achieve skills and concepts in mathematics at a level comparable to that reached by non-handicapped children in the first and second grades. This inventory attempts to identify these abilities in order to furnish a definite basis upon which to construct the mathematics curriculum.

The Evaluation of Pupil Progress in Mathematics

The items in this inventory reflect the mathematical categories, objectives, content, and activities outlined in the "Checklist of Mathematics—Intermediate Level." This checklist is shown in Chapter 5.

This inventory should be administered individually and should be presented as a *number game* rather than as a test. The administration of the items will typically require approximately fifteen to twenty minutes.

No score is yielded by this inventory and no attempt to quantify the results should be made. The items in the inventory reflect the curriculum to such an extent that children who have progressed through the intermediate curriculum should respond to eighty or ninety percent of the questions correctly. In this sense, the inventory is a "mastery" test. Those children who perform less well than this should be given the Primary Level or another form of the Intermediate Level. There are relatively few items in each category and the responses to these should not cause the teacher to conclude that the child in question has a particular deficiency or strength. Further observations should be made. However, the overall performance on the inventory will indicate fairly well whether the child has mastered the intermediate level mathematics curriculum.

The inventory is divided into eight categories each of which has from two to four items. The materials required and the procedures to follow in presenting the questions are presented below.

1. Form and Perception
    1. *Name Forms*
        Materials   8½" × 11" card with circle, rectangle, square, and triangle.

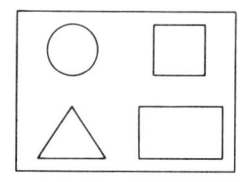

        FIGURE 9.36

        Procedure   "Here is a card with some forms on it. Show me the circle . . . Where is the square . . . triangle, rectangle?"

        Record   Circle the correct responses and draw a line through the items missed.
    2. *Advance Form Discrimination*
        Materials   8½" × 11" card with forms as shown in Figure 9.37. A stimulus card for each of the forms.

626   *The Evaluation of Pupil Progress in Mathematics*

FIGURE 9.37

Procedure   Hold a small card next to the response card and say, "See all these. Find one that looks just like this one."

FIGURE 9.38

Record   The number correct out of nine.

2. Vocabulary
   3. *Largest*
      Materials   8½" × 11" card with illustrations as shown in Figure 9.39.

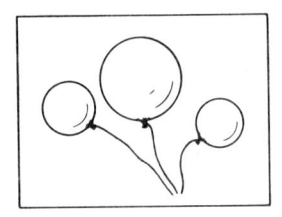

FIGURE 9.39

Procedure   "See these balloons. Which one is the largest?"
Record   Circle the correct response and draw a line through the items missed.

   4. *Highest*
      Materials   8½" × 11" card with illustrations as shown in Figure 9.40.

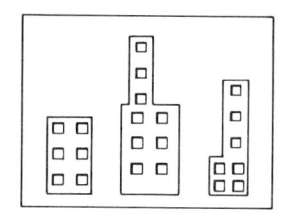

The Evaluation of Pupil Progress in Mathematics 627

FIGURE 9.40

     Procedure "See these buildings. Which one is the highest?"
     Record Circle the correct responses and draw a line through the items missed.

5 & *Check and Sales Slip*
6.   Materials None
    Procedure "What is a check?"
                  "What is a sales slip?"
    Record Circle the correct response and draw a line through missed items.

3. Number Symbols
   7. *Reading Number Words*
      Materials 8½" × 11" card with words printed in large script.

Fifteen

Twenty

Thirty-one

FIGURE 9.41

     Procedure Hold the card so it is within easy vision and say, "Read this word, . . . what does this say . . ."
     Record Circle the correct responses and draw a line through the items missed.

   8. *Counting by Two's*
      Materials None
      Procedure "Here is the way we count by two's. Listen to me! Two . . . four . . . six. Now I want you to count by two's just like I did but go as high as you can. Ready?"

"two . . . (four) . . . (six)" Say the four and six only if the child fails to respond.

Record   Write the highest number to which the child could count by two's correctly.

9. *Place Value for One's and Ten's Place*
   Materials   8½" × 11" card with numbers printed as shown in Figure 9.42.

```
┌─────────────────┐
│ 23        20    │
│                 │
│ 30        45    │
└─────────────────┘
```

FIGURE 9.42

Procedure   Present the card and ask: "See this number. Read it to me. (twenty-three, etc.) How many tens are there in twenty-three? Point to the number that shows how many ones there are in the one's place. (three)"

Repeat for the other numbers.

"How many tens are there in twenty . . . thirty . . . forty-five?"

Record   If the child seems to understand place value, write the word "yes"; if not, "no".

4. Cardinal Numbers
   10. *Multiple Groups of Ten*
       Materials   8½" × 11" cards with groups of ten as shown in Figure 9.43.

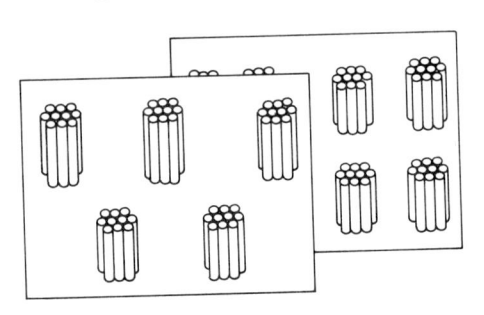

FIGURE 9.43

The Evaluation of Pupil Progress in Mathematics 629

    Procedure "If there are ten sticks in each group, how many are there altogether in this picture?"
    Record Circle the highest group the child counts correctly. Put a line through the number(s) (fifty) or (one hundred) the child counts incorrectly.

11. *Reproducing Sets*
    Materials Twenty counting cubes of same color and size.
    Procedure Place the cubes before the child in a random fashion. Say, "Give me fifteen blocks. Put them right here (pointing)."
    Repeat for nineteen.
    Record Circle the number (s) (fifteen, nineteen) for correct responses and draw a line through the number(s) for incorrect responses.

12. *Fractions*
    Materials 8½" × 11" card with pie fractions as shown in Figure 9.44.

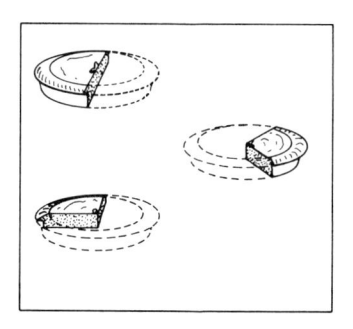

FIGURE 9.44

    Procedure "Look at these pies. Some of each pie has already been eaten. See this pie has only one half left. How much does this pie have left (one-third)? How much is left of this pie (one-fourth)?"
    Record Circle the one-third and one-fourth if identified correctly and draw a line through them if identified incorrectly.

5. Ordinal Numbers
   13. *Which is Tenth*
       Materials 8½" × 11" card with twelve race cars in a row.

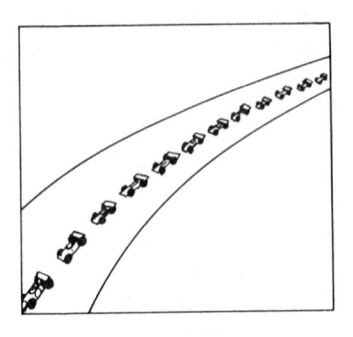

FIGURE 9.45

Procedure "Which is tenth in this row of race cars? Count the cars until you find the tenth one. Which one is it?"

Record Circle "tenth" if correct and draw a line through "tenth" if incorrect.

6. Measurements
    14. *Quart and Gallon*
        Materials None
        Procedure "Which holds more, a quart or a gallon?"
    15. *Teaspoon and Tablespoon*
        Materials None
        Procedure "Which is more, a teaspoon or a tablespoon?"
    16. *Telling Time by the Half Hour*
        Materials 8½" × 11" card with two clocks as shown in Figure 9.46.

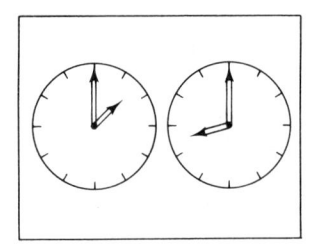

FIGURE 9.46

Procedure "Read this clock. What time does this clock say?"
Record Circle the time(s) read correctly and draw a line through the time(s) read incorrectly.

The Evaluation of Pupil Progress in Mathematics 631

17. *Thermometer*
    Materials   8½" × 11" card with 2 pictures of thermometers.

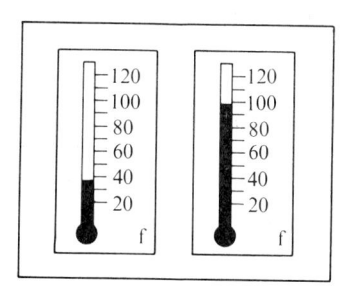

    FIGURE 9.47

    Procedure   "Read this thermometer. What temperature does this thermometer read?"
    Record   Circle the temperature(s) read correctly and draw a line through the temperature(s) read incorrectly.

18. *Inches in a Foot*
    Materials   None
    Procedure   "How many inches in a foot?"
    Record   Place a plus sign in the blank on the record form if the response is correct and a minus sign if the response is incorrect.

19. *Comparison of Foot and Yard*
    Materials   None
    Procedure   "Which is longer, a foot or a yard?"
    Record   Place a plus sign in the blank on the record form if the response is correct and a minus sign if the response is incorrect.

20. *Own Height*
    Materials   None
    Procedure   "How tall are you?"
    Record   Place a plus sign in the blank on the record form if the response is correct and a minus sign if the response is incorrect.

7. Money and Value
    21. *Change*
        Materials   None
        Procedure   "If you bought an ice cream cone for a dime and gave the clerk a quarter, how much change would you get back?"

Record   Place a plus sign in the blank on the record form if the response is correct and a minus sign if the response is incorrect.

22. *Equivalents of Quarter*
    Materials   None
    Procedure   "How many quarters are there in a dollar?"
    Record   Place a plus sign in the blank on the record form if the response is correct and a minus sign if the response is incorrect.

8. Number Operations and Problem Solving
    23. *Computation—Subtraction*
        Materials   A sheet with problems to solve as shown in Figure 9.48.

```
10      12      8
-4      -9      -3

16      128     65
-7      -53     -6

46¢
-33¢
```

FIGURE 9.48

Procedure   "Solve these problems."
Record   Circle or draw lines according to correctness of response.

24. *Computation—Multiplication*
    Materials   8½" × 11" card with problems as shown in Figure 9.49.

```
3 × 2 = ☐

2 × 4 = ☐
```

FIGURE 9.49

Procedure   Show the child the card and ask, how much is 2 × 4 (pointing) . . . 3 × 2?

The Evaluation of Pupil Progress in Mathematics 633

　　　　Record　　Circle or draw lines according to correctness of response.
　25.　*Computation—Division*
　　　　Materials　None
　　　　Procedure　"Two divided into eight equals ____? Three divided into nine equals ____?"
　　　　Record　　Circle or draw lines according to correctness of response.
　26.　*Computation—Addition*
　　　　Materials　None
　　　　Procedure　Present a sheet with problems and say, "Solve these problems."
　27.　*Problem Solving (1)*
　　　　Materials　None
　　　　Procedure　"There are five boys and three girls getting on a school bus. How many children get on the bus?"
　　　　Record　　Circle the correct answers and draw a line through the incorrect responses.
　28.　*Problem Solving (2)*
　　　　Materials　None
　　　　Procedure　"At the first stop of the bus, two boys and one girl get off the bus. Remember you said that ____ children got on the bus. How do you find out how many children are left on the bus? Do you add, subtract, or divide?"
　　　　Record　　Circle or draw lines according to correctness of response.

NUMBER INVENTORY FOR EDUCABLE MENTALLY RETARDED CHILDREN

Junior High Level

Record Blank

Name _____ Date _____
I.Q. and Name of Test_____ _____
Chronological Age _____ Estimated Mental Age _____

1. Form and Perception
　　1. advanced form discrimination II:____
　　2. parquetry designs:____

2. Vocabulary Associated with Mathematics
   3. What do we mean by "luxury"?____
   4. What is a "budget"? ____
   5. What does it mean to "air mail" something? ____
   6. What is a "salary"? ____

3. Number Symbol
   7. read numerals: 672____ 345____ 831____ 999____
   8. read number words: fifty-one   one hundred ____
   9. write numerals: 32   187   728   891 ____
   10. count by 3's: 3   6   9   12   15   18   21   24   27
   11. read money notations: $.05 $1.00 $1.50 $6.73
   12. read roman numerals: II   IV   X   XX

4. Cardinal Numbers
   13. how many tens in: 50   75   100
   14. Fractions: ¾   ⅔

5. Ordinal Numbers
   15. show me the: second in the third row ____ the third in the first row ____

6. Measurement
   16. How many hours in one day? ____
   17. Name the months of the year: Jan Feb Mar Ap My Jn Jly Aug Sept Oct Nov Dec
   18. Which is longer; one month or three weeks? ____
   19. How many feet in a yard?____
   20. Which is more: three quarts or one gallon? ____
   21. Which is more: one ounce or one pound? ____

7. Money
   22. If you bought a model airplane for eighty cents including tax and you gave the clerk one dollar, how much change would you get back?____
   23. How many dimes are there in one dollar? ____
   24. How many nickels are there in a quarter? ____

8. Number Operations and Problem Solving
   25. 21   24   142   11
         6   51   221   26
        __   __   ___   37
        12   433   ___

   26. 25   50 $0.97   692
       −15   −16   − 0.64   −193
       ___   ___   _____   ____

27. 6 × 6 =   3 × 2 =   9 × 9 =   6 × 7 =
28. 27/3   8/2
29. Four boys have 36 marbles altogether. If they divide them equally, how many will each boy have? ____
30. Mary and five of her friends each buy a candy bar which costs six cents. How much do they spend altogether? ____

NUMBER INVENTORY FOR EDUCABLE MENTALLY RETARDED CHILDREN

Junior High Level

DIRECTIONS FOR ADMINISTRATION

This number inventory is designed for educable mentally retarded children of chronological ages thirteen and fourteen with mental ages typically nine and ten years. The average child in such a program can reasonably be expected to achieve skills and concepts in mathematics at a level comparable to that reached by non-handicapped children in the third and fourth grades. This inventory attempts to identify these abilities in order to furnish a definite basis upon which to construct the mathematics curriculum.

The items in this inventory reflect the mathematical categories, objectives, content, and activities outlined in the "Checklist of Mathematics—Junior High Level." This checklist is included in Chapter 6.

This inventory should be administered individually and should be presented as a learning situation rather than as a test. The administration of the items will require approximately twenty-five minutes. The responses to each item are to be indicated on the record blank included with these directions.

No score is yielded by this inventory and no attempt to quantify the results should be made. The items in the inventory reflect the curriculum to such an extent that children who have progressed through the junior high curriculum should respond correctly to eighty or ninety percent of the questions. In this sense, the inventory is a "mastery" test. Those children who perform less well than this should be given the intermediate level inventory or another form of the junior high level. There are relatively few items in each category and the responses to the sub-items in any given category should not cause the teacher to conclude that the child in question has a particular deficit or strength. Further observations should be made. However, the overall performance on the inventory

636   *The Evaluation of Pupil Progress in Mathematics*

will indicate fairly well the child's progress towards the objectives set for the junior high level.

1. Form and Perception
   1. *Advanced Form Discrimination II*
      Materials 8½" × 11" card with 6 forms as shown in Figure 9.50 and four smaller cards with one form each which matches a form on the larger card.

FIGURE 9.50

Procedure "Here is a card with some forms on it. Show me the one like this." Present all four forms.
Record Indicate the number of forms properly matched.

   2. *Parquetry Designs*
      Materials A set of parquetry designs as shown in Figure 9.51.
      Procedure "Watch me." Make the design shown.

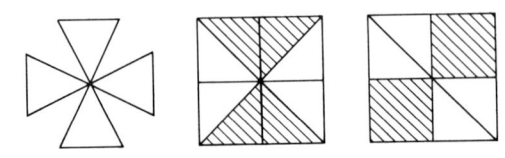

FIGURE 9.51

"Now you make one just like mine." If the child reproduces the design correctly, give him the two designs shown in Figure 9.52, but have him reproduce the designs from the pictures. "Now make one like the one in this picture."

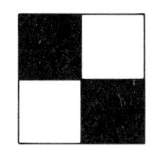

The Evaluation of Pupil Progress in Mathematics 637

FIGURE 9.52

    Record   Place a (+) sign in the blank on the record form if the response to the second two designs is correct and a (−) sign if the response is incorrect.

2. Vocabulary Associated with Mathematics
   3. *Luxury*
      Materials   8½″ × 11″ card with a picture of a luxury item and three essentials.

FIGURE 9.53

    Procedure   "See these. Which is a picture of a luxury?"
    Record   Place a (+) sign in the blank on the record form if the response is correct and a minus sign if the response is incorrect.

  4. *Budget*
     Materials   None
     Procedure   Say, "Budget. Explain what is meant by budget." If the response does not indicate clear understanding say, "Tell me more about it" or "Explain further."
     Record   A plus indicates a correct response and a minus indicates an incorrect response. "A financial statement of estimated income and expenses; a plan

of financing; a plan for spending and saving money; the way you decide to spend your check."

5. *Air Mail*
   Materials   None
   Procedure   "What does it mean to air mail something?"
   Record   Use the plus or minus sign to indicate whether the response was correct or incorrect. The answer should include at least one of these ideas: "The letter goes by airplane; it will get there faster."

6. *Salary*
   Materials   None
   Procedure   "What is a salary?"
   Record   Use the plus or minus sign to indicate whether the response was correct or incorrect. The answer should include the idea of "wage, earnings, payment for services, income, etc."

3. Number Symbols
   7. *Read Three Digit Numerals*
      Materials   8½" × 11" card with the numbers: 672, 345, 182, 831, 999.
      Procedure   "See these numerals. Find 182. Point to 999 . . . 831, etc."
      Record   Use the plus to indicate satisfactory identification of three out of three or four out of five. Use the minus sign to indicate less than four out of five correct identifications.

   8. *Read Number Words*
      Materials   8½" × 11" card with the words fifty-one; one hundred; fifty-four; and one thousand.
      Procedure   "Here is a card with some words on it. Find the word fifty-one. Which one says one hundred?"
      Record   Use a plus to indicate that both words were identified correctly and a minus to indicate that only one or less was identified correctly.

   9. *Write Numerals*
      Materials   8½" × 11" piece of unruled writing paper.
      Procedure   "I am going to say a number, then I want you to write it on your paper. Ready? 32; 187; 728; 891."
      Record   Use a plus to indicate that at least three out of four of the numbers were written correctly and a

The Evaluation of Pupil Progress in Mathematics 639

minus sign to indicate that less than three out of four were written correctly. If the child writes "thirty-two", say "No, just write the number, you do not need to spell the word."

10. *Count by Threes*
    Materials None
    Procedure "I want you to count by three's. Ready? three . . ." The child should pick up the counting and continue six, nine, twelve . . . (and perhaps higher). If the child fails to continue counting or counts incorrectly you may begin again saying: "Now I want you to count by three's. Listen to me then you do it. Three . . . six . . . You try it. Ready? three . . ."
    Record Circle the highest number counted in the sequence.

11. *Read Money Notations*
    Materials 8½" × 11" card with the notations: $.05; $1.00; $1.50; and $6.73.
    Procedure "See this card? Read the amounts of money indicated."
    Record Circle the ones read correctly and draw a line through those incorrectly read.

12. *Read Roman Numerals*
    Materials 8½" × 11" card with the roman numerals: II, IV, X, and XX.
    Procedure "See this card. It has roman numerals on it. This one is two (II). Now read this one: IV . . . X . . . XX."
    Record Circle the ones read correctly and draw a line through those incorrectly read.

4. Cardinal Number
    13. *Tens in a Number*
        Materials None
        Procedure "There are two tens in twenty. How many tens are there in fifty . . . seventy-five . . . one hundred?"
        Record Circle the numbers in which the correct number of tens was identified and put a line through the numbers in which the response was incorrect.
    14. *Fractions*
        Materials 8½" × 11" card with pies illustrating four different fractions.

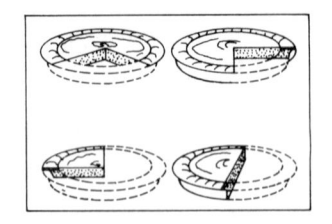

FIGURE 9.54

Procedure   "See these pies. This one has one-half of the pie left. Show me which one has three-fourths of a pie left . . . two-thirds of a pie left."
Record   Circle the fractions correctly identified and draw a line through the ones incorrectly identified.

5. Ordinal Number
    15. *Using Two Ordinals*
        Materials   8½″ × 11″ card with four rows of children, five in each row.

FIGURE 9.55

Procedure   "Point to the second child in the third row. Show me the third child in the first row."
Record   Use a plus sign to indicate that both questions were answered correctly and a minus sign to indicate that one or both were missed.

6. Measurement
    16. *Hours in Day*
        Materials   None
        Procedure   "How many hours in a day?"
        Record   Use a plus to indicate a correct response and a minus to indicate an incorrect response.

17. *Months of the Year*
    Materials   None
    Procedure   "Name of the months of the year."
    Record   Circle the months named.

18. *Months and Weeks*
    Materials   None
    Procedure   "Which is longer? One month or three weeks?"
    Record   Use a plus to indicate a correct response and a minus to indicate an incorrect response.

19. *Feet in a Yard*
    Materials   None
    Procedure   "How many feet are there in one yard?"
    Record   Use a plus to indicate a correct response and a minus to indicate an incorrect response.

20. *Quarts and Gallons*
    Materials   None
    Procedure   "Which is more? Three quarts or one gallon?"
    Record   Use a plus to indicate a correct response and a minus to indicate an incorrect response.

21. *Ounces and Pounds*
    Materials   None
    Procedure   "Which is more? One ounce or one pound?"
    Record   Use a plus to indicate a correct response and a minus to indicate an incorrect response.

7. Money and Value

    22. *Change for a Dollar*
        Materials   None
        Procedure   "If you bought a model airplane for eighty cents including tax and you gave the clerk one dollar, how much change would you get back?"
        Record   Use a plus to indicate a correct response and a minus to indicate an incorrect response.

    23. *Dimes in a Dollar*
        Materials   None
        Procedure   "How many dimes are there in a dollar?"
        Record   Use a plus to indicate a correct response and a minus to indicate an incorrect response.

    24. *Nickels in a Quarter*
        Materials   None

Procedure   "How many nickels are there in a quarter?"
Record   Use a plus to indicate a correct response and a minus to indicate an incorrect response.

8. Number Operations and Problem Solving
   25. *Addition*
       Materials   8½" × 11" paper with these problems:

21	24	142	11
6	51	221	26
	12	433	37

       Procedure   "Here is a paper with some problems of addition. Work them as fast as you can but do not be careless."
       Record   Circle the correct response and place a line through the incorrect ones.

   26. *Subtraction*
       Materials   8½" × 11" paper with these problems:

25	50	$0.97	692
−15	−16	−0.64	−193

       Procedure   "Here is a paper with some problems of subtraction. Work them as fast as you can but do not be careless."
       Record   Circle the correct response and place a line through the incorrect ones.

   27. *Multiplication*
       Materials   8½" × 11" paper with these problems:
       6 × 6 =   2 × 3 =   9 × 9 =
       6 × 7 =

       Procedure   "Here is a paper with some problems of multiplication. Work them as fast as you can but do not be careless."
       Record   Circle the correct response and place a line through the incorrect ones.

   28. *Division*
       Materials   8½" × 11" paper with the following problems:
       $3\overline{)27}$ $2\overline{)8}$

The Evaluation of Pupil Progress in Mathematics 643

    Procedure   "Here is a paper with some problems of division. Work them as fast as you can but do not be careless."
    Record   Circle the correct responses and place a line through the incorrect ones.

29. *Problem of Division*
    Materials   8½″ × 11″ card with the following problem written on it:
    "Four boys have thirty-six marbles altogether. If they divide them equally, how many marbles will each boy have?"
    Procedure   Give the child the card and also read it to him. If necessary, re-read it for him.
    Record   Use a plus to indicate a correct response and a minus to indicate an incorrect response.

30. *Problem of Multiplication*
    Materials   8½″ × 11″ card with the following problem:
    "Mary and five of her friends each buy a candy bar which costs six cents. How much do they spend altogether?"
    Procedure   Hand the card to the child and read it. If necessary, re-read it.
    Record   Use a plus to indicate a correct response and a minus to indicate an incorrect response.

NUMBER INVENTORY FOR EDUCABLE MENTALLY RETARDED CHILDREN

Adultation
Record Blank

Name _____ Date _____
I.Q. and Name of Test_____ _____
Chronological Age _____ Estimated Mental Age _____

1. Form and Perception
    1. Show me the perpendicular line.____
    2. Which is an angle of 90°?____
    3. Draw one like this.____

2. Vocabulary Associated with Mathematics

4. What is Social Security?____
5. What do we mean by insurance?____
6. Why is it better to pay for some purchases with cash than with credit?____
7. What do we mean by a check deduction?____

3. Number Symbols
    8. Read these numerals 1822 12456 1354 43672 1569
    9. Read these words one thousand three hundred two thousand four hundred ____
    10. Write the number 1000 2482 1,295 ____
    11. Read these roman numerals XXX L LX C II V

4. Cardinal Numbers
    12. Show me 1/6 1/8 1/5
    13. How much is 1/2 plus 1/4? 1/2 plus 1/3? ____
    14. Which is more? 1/2 or 3/4? 1/2 or 3/8? 1/2 or 2/6? ____
    15. Which fraction is the same as 1/2? (3/4, 2/4, 1/4, 4/4) ____

5. Ordinal Number
    16. On this calendar, show me the eighteenth day ____; the thirtieth day ____.

6. Measurement
    17. If Bill is driving his car on the highway at 50 miles per hour, how long will it take him to go 250 mi.? ____
    18. How many months make one half of a year? ____
    19. If a man pays his rent once a month, how many times a year will he pay his rent? ____
    20. How many years in a century? ____
    21. At what temperature does water freeze? ____

7. Money
    22. Henry pays his car insurance which is $83.50. He gives the agent a one hundred dollar bill. How much change will he get? ____
    23. Why is it usually cheaper to have your car well maintained than to wait until something goes wrong before you have it repaired? ____

8. Number Operations and Problem Solving
    24.   746   756
          513   4320
         +189   +3679

25. 9282 $90.10
    −3973   −62.96
26. 10 × 9 =   11 × 12 =
27.   85   197
     ×36   ×48
28. 8)5984   12)1248
29. If John has 100 in the bank earning 7% interest, how much money in interest will he receive in one year? ___

NUMBER INVENTORY FOR EDUCABLE MENTALLY RETARDED CHILDREN

Adultation

DIRECTIONS FOR ADMINISTRATION

This number inventory is an illustration of the type of individualized teacher-made test which can be used to measure pupil progress in mathematics. The items are based on the mathematical categories, objectives, content, and activities outlined in the "Checklist of Mathematics—Adultation Level." This checklist is included in Chapter 7.

This number inventory is designed for educable mentally retarded children of chronological ages fifteen, sixteen, seventeen and eighteen with mental ages typically ten to twelve years. The average child in such a program can reasonably be expected to achieve skills and concepts in mathematics at a level comparable to that reached by non-handicapped children in the third, fourth, and in rare cases fifth grade.

The inventory should be administered individually and should be presented in a non-threatening manner. The youngster should be assured that he is not going to be graded on this performance.

No score is yielded by this inventory although pre- and post-test comparisons can be helpful to the teacher. The items in the inventory reflect the curriculum to such an extent that the children who have progressed through the senior high curriculum should respond to eighty to ninety per cent of the questions correctly. In this sense, the inventory is a mastery test. Those children who perform less well than this should be given the junior high inventory or a simpler form of the adultation level. More difficult items should be constructed for those youngsters who answer all of the items correctly.

There are relatively few items in each category and the response to the sub-items in any given category should not cause the teacher to conclude that the youngster has a specific deficit or strength. However, the overall performance on the inventory will indicate fairly well the child's progress towards the objectives set for the senior high school level.

1. Form and Perception
    1. *Perpendicular*
        Materials   8½" × 11" card with four sets of two lines in various relations to each other.

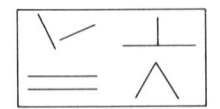

        FIGURE 9.56

        Procedure   "See all these lines? Which lines are perpendicular? Parallel?"
        Record   Use a plus sign on the record blank to indicate correct identification and a minus sign to indicate incorrect identification.
    2. *90°*
        Materials   8½" × 11" card with four different angles.

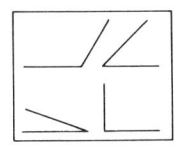

        Procedure   "Look at these lines. They make angles. Which is an angle of 90°?"
        Record   Use a plus sign to indicate correct response and a minus sign to indicate an incorrect identification.
    3. *Reproducing Forms*
        Materials   8½" × 11" card with a form as shown in Figure 9.57. Paper and pencil.

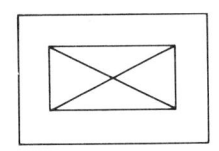

        FIGURE 9.57

Procedure "See this. Draw one like it on your paper."
Record Use a plus or minus to indicate whether the response was satisfactory.

2. Vocabulary Associated with Mathematics
   4. *Social Security*
      Materials None
      Procedure "What is Social Security?"
      Record Use a plus or a minus sign to indicate whether the response was satisfactory. The answer should include at least one of these ideas: "A government program designed to provide for retirement, survivor's insurance, disabled, blind, child welfare, medical care, maternal and child health services."
   5. *Insurance*
      Materials None
      Procedure "You have heard of life insurance, health insurance, car insurance. What is meant by insurance?"
      Record Use a plus or a minus sign to indicate whether the response was satisfactory. The answer should include the idea of protection: "a guarantee against loss by a contingent event, retirement, a kind of savings."
   6. *Credit*
      Materials None
      Procedure "Sometimes we pay for things we buy with cash. Other times we put things on a charge account and pay for it later, usually a small part at a time. For example, we might put a set of tires on our credit card and pay for them at the rate of $20 a month. Why is it better to pay for some purchases with cash rather than to use our credit?"
      Record Use a plus or a minus sign to indicate whether the response was satisfactory. The answer should include the idea of the possibility of an over-extension and that there are interest charges so that the item costs more if bought on credit.
   7. *Check Deduction*
      Materials None
      Procedure "We usually get paid for our work with a check. Our employer will generally withhold some of our pay. This is called a deduction. For example, the employer will probably deduct for social security.

	Give another example of a payroll or check deduction."
Record	Use a plus or a minus sign to indicate whether the response was satisfactory. Among the possible correct answers are: "income tax, savings, retirement."

3. Number Symbols
   8. *Reading Numerals in 1000's*

      Materials   8½" × 11" card with the numbers: 1822, 12,456, 1354, 43,672, 1,569.

      Procedure   "See these numbers. Find 12,456 . . . etc."

      Record   Circle those read correctly and place a line through those read incorrectly.

   9. *Reading Number Words*

      Materials   8½" × 11" card with these words: one thousand, three thousand, two thousand, four thousand.

      Procedure   "See the words on this card. Read this one . . . etc."

      Record   Use a plus sign to indicate that at least two of the words were read correctly.

   10. *Write Numbers*

       Materials   8½" × 11" paper and pencil.

       Procedure   "I am going to say a number then I want you to write it on your paper: 1000   2482   1295."

       Record   Use a plus to indicate two out of three correct. If the child starts to spell the word say, "No, just write the number; you do not need to spell the words."

   11. *Roman Numerals*

       Materials   8½" × 11" card with the roman numerals: XXX   L   LX   C   II   V

       Procedure   "See this card. It has some roman numerals on it. This one is two. Read this one (V). Now read this one XXX . . . etc."

       Record   Circle the ones read correctly and draw a line through those not read correctly.

4. Cardinal Number
   12. *Fractions*

       Materials   8½" × 11" card with pies illustrating four different fractions.

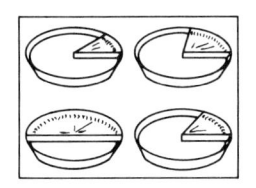

FIGURE 9.58

    Procedure "See these pies. This one has one-half of the pie left. Show me which one has one-sixth . . . one-eighth . . . one-fifth . . . left."
    Record Circle the fractions correctly identified and draw a line through the ones incorrectly identified.

13. *Adding Unlike Fractions*
    Materials 8½" × 11" card with the problems written:
    1/2 + 1/4 =   1/2 + 1/3 =
    Procedure "Here are some problems of adding unlike fractions. Solve them on your paper."
    Record Use a plus if one of the problems is answered correctly and a minus if none are correct.

14. *Comparing Unlike Fractions*
    Materials None
    Procedure "Which is more? 1/2 or 3/4? 1/2 or 3/8? 1/2 or 2/6?"
    Record Record a plus if two are correct and a minus if one or fewer are correct.

15. *Equivalent Fractions*
    Materials 8½" × 11" card with these fractions:
    3/4, 2/4, 1/4, 4/4
    Procedure "Point to the fraction which is the same as one-half."
    Record Record a plus or minus depending on the response.

5. Ordinal Number

    16. *Reading the Calendar with Ordinal Number*
        Materials 8½" × 11" card with a calendar.
        Procedure "Here is a picture of a calendar. Show me the eighteenth day. The thirtieth day."
        Record Record a plus if at least one of the responses is correct.

6. Measurement
    17. *Time En Route*
        Materials   8½" × 11" card with the following problem:
        "If Bill is driving his car on the highway at 50 miles per hour, how long will it take him to go 250 miles?"
        Procedure   Give the card to the youngster, read it to him and re-read if necessary.
        Record   Use a plus or minus depending upon the response.
    18. *Months*
        Materials   None
        Procedure   "How many months make one-half a year?"
        Record   Record a plus or minus depending upon the response.
    19. *Number of Annual Rent Payments*
        Materials   None
        Procedure   "If a man pays his rent once a month, how many times a year will he pay his rent?"
        Record   Record a plus to indicate a correct response and a minus to indicate an incorrect response.
    20. *Years in a Century*
        Materials   None
        Procedure   "How many years in a century?"
        Record   Record a plus or minus depending upon the response.
    21. *Freezing Temperature*
        Materials   None
        Procedure   "At what temperature does water usually freeze?"
        Record   Record a plus or a minus depending upon the response. Of course, assume sea level and standard atmospheric conditions. (59° F)

7. Money and Value
    22. *Change for $100.00*
        Materials   8½" × 11" card with this problem:
        "Henry pays his car insurance which is $83.50. He gives the agent a one hundred dollar bill. How much change will he receive?"
        Procedure   Give the card to the youngster, read it to him and re-read it if necessary.
        Record   Use a plus or minus depending upon the response.
    23. *Maintenance Versus Repair*
        Materials   None

The Evaluation of Pupil Progress in Mathematics 651

      Procedure   "Why is it usually cheaper to have your car well maintained rather than to wait until something goes wrong before you have it repaired?"

8. Number Operations and Problem Solving
   24. *Addition*
       Materials Pencil and sheet of problems including these:

            746   756
            513   4320
          +189   +3679

       Procedure "Here is a paper with some problems. Work them as rapidly as you can without making careless mistakes."
       Record Circle the correct responses and place a line through the incorrect ones.

   25. *Subtraction*
       Materials Pencil and same sheet as #24.

          9282 $90.10
         −3973   −62.96

       Procedure "Here is a paper with some problems. Work them as rapidly as you can without making careless mistakes."
       Record Circle the correct responses and place a line through the incorrect ones.

   26. *Multiplication I*
       Materials Pencil and sheet of problems including these:
          10 × 9 =   11 × 12 =
       Procedure "Here is a paper with some problems. Work them as rapidly as you can without making careless mistakes."
       Record Circle the correct responses and place a line through the incorrect ones.

   27. *Multiplication II*
       Materials Pencil and sheet of problems including these:

           85   197
         ×36   × 48

       Procedure "Here is a paper with some problems. Work them as rapidly as you can without making careless mistakes."
       Record Circle the correct responses and place a line through the incorrect ones.

28. *Division*
    Materials   Pencil and sheet of problems including these:
    $8\overline{)5984}$ $12\overline{)1248}$
    Procedure   "Here is a paper with some problems. Work them as rapidly as you can without making careless mistakes."
    Record   Circle the correct responses and place a line through the incorrect ones.

29. *Figuring Interest*
    Materials   8½" × 11" card with this problem written on it:
    Procedure   "If John has $100.00 in the bank earning 7% interest, how much money in interest will he earn in one year?"
    Record   Record a plus or minus depending upon the response.

Interpretation of the Number Inventory

The number inventory is basically a teacher-made test composed of items of varying difficulty. The items are so constructed that their successful completion gives acceptable evidence of the acquisition of the skills described in the objectives. Since the inventory attempts to survey the curriculum objectives, varying degrees of mastery will be indicated. However, the results should be interpreted with caution because the inventory is subject to all the limitations of teacher constructed instruments. The number inventory should not be interpreted in isolation but should take cognizance of the background and experience of the children. Many of the factors contributing to this background and experience have been elaborated in earlier sections of this chapter.

The examples of number inventories for the educable mentally retarded described in the preceding sections were designed to test for mastery of the curriculum at five different levels. The interpretation of the results of the administration of these or similarly constructed surveys depends on the purpose of the testing. If the purpose were to determine the achievement of the class as a whole when evaluated by the objectives of the intermediate level, the teacher could administer an inventory like the one shown in the preceding section. The results would probably spread over a wide range with a few students failing most of the items, the majority of students passing many items, and a few students passing all of them. Since the purpose of the inventory is to measure mastery of the intermediate level mathematics curriculum, the typical nine-year old child in the special education program would be expected to respond correctly to a minority of the items. Other things being equal, the ten or eleven-year-old child would probably respond correctly to a majority of the items and the twelve-year-old child would probably respond correctly to eighty to ninety percent of the items. This would give the teacher a picture on the status of the class as a whole and also indicate which children might be suited to work together on some topics. If the tests were given early in the fall and readministered in the late spring, it would give some rough indication of the progress of the class as a whole. It would not provide the teacher with the instructional level for each child nor identify specific deficits of particular children. If the purpose of the testing were to determine the progress of a given individual, the teacher could use the same pre-test and post-test procedure. In order to do this, the inventory used would have to have a sufficient range of difficulty so that it would not only assess the child's present level of functioning on the pre-test, but also have enough difficult items to measure the progress made up to the time of the post-test. It is assumed, of course, that the teacher-made inventory reflects proportionately what has been taught. Naturally, the validity of the pre-test and post-test procedure is completely destroyed if the children are "coached" for the test. It is one thing to teach the children so that they will master the material within a given category and a completely different thing to give them practice with specific test items so that progress will be inflated on the post-test.

The number inventories are organized into eight categories which correspond to those presented in the checklists for each of the five levels from preprimary to adultation. Since all of the categories are related it is to be expected that the subtests will show high intercorrelations (Peterson, 1967). The retarded child who is deficient in one category is apt to be deficient in others. Therefore, it is not possible for the teacher to interpret variations in performance from one subtest to another as clear-cut diagnostic signs. It will be rare that the pattern of performance is so uneven that the teacher can indicate with confidence a specific area of difficulty. Furthermore, there are relatively few items in each subtest of the inventory. For example, on the number inventory at the preprimary level the subtest "Form and Perception" consists of three items. It would be practically meaningless to report that a child answered two out of the three correctly. Attempts to quantify the results in this fashion should be avoided. This does not preclude an analysis of the child's performance on the inventory. The results of the number inventory do provide a general, overall assessment of the child's concepts and skills in mathematics. The teacher is likely to pick up some clues and hints about the child's particular assets or liabilities from this broad evaluation. If a child answers all the items in a given category correctly, the teacher will want to construct more difficult items from the appropriate checksheet or move onto the items in the next higher inventory in order to establish a ceiling on performance. If, on the other hand, a child answers all of the items in a given category incorrectly, the teacher will want to construct simpler items from the appropriate checksheet or move down to items on the next lower inventory in order to establish a base of performance. It may likewise be advisable to seek more information about a child who has answered only a small percentage of the items in a given category correctly. Once some range of performance has been established through additional testing and observation the teacher will have a general picture of the child's relative strengths and weaknesses. However, the teacher may want a more detailed picture on the child's achievement pattern in order to uncover specific errors and design a program of remediation.

An Example of Interpretation of a Number Inventory

An example of the interpretation of the number inventory will help the reader visualize the process. The record blank shows the response record for an educable mentally retarded child at the intermediate level. John was able to name three out of four of the forms correctly and he missed on two of the advanced form discrimination. Since he performed so well in this area, the teacher will probably want to prepare some more difficult items such as those at the junior high school level in order to determine just how much strength he has in the area of form and perception. This is also true for the vocabulary section since the only word the meaning of which he did not give correctly was *sales slip*. His answers to problems in the number symbols, ordinal numbers, cardinal numbers, and number operations suggest that he can count well and can solve simple computation problems. These errors in these same categories, however, indicate that he has little understanding of positional notation and that he is not able to apply his computational skills to problem-solving situations. For example, John is able to answer correctly simple subtraction problems (ones that do not call for renaming and regrouping) but is unable to solve a problem of making change for a quarter and fails a word problem that requires him merely to add five and three. Likewise he is unable to tell which processes to use in finding the solution to a simple word problem in subtraction.

NUMBER INVENTORY FOR EDUCABLE MENTALLY
RETARDED CHILDREN

Intermediate Level

Record Blank

Name __John_____ Date __Sept. 5, 1972_____

The Evaluation of Pupil Progress in Mathematics 655

I.Q. and Name of Test __70   Stanford-Binet, 1969__
Chronological Age __10__   Estimated Mental Age __7__

1. Form and Perception
   1. Name forms: (circle) (square) ~~rectangle~~ (triangle)
   2. Advanced form discrimination.
2. Vocabulary Associated with Mathematics   *7 out of 9 correct*
   3. (Largest)
   4. (Highest)
   5. What is a (check?)
   6. What is a ~~sales slip~~?
3. Number Symbols
   7. Fifteen . . . twenty . . . thirty-one
   8. Count by 2's . . . 2,4,6 to 20   *20*
   9. Place value to two places: (a) tens and ones place, (b) how many tens are there in 20? 30? 45?
4. Cardinal Number
   10. If there are ten sticks in each group, how many are on this card? . . . (50) On this card? . . . (100)
   11. From these 20 blocks, give me (15) Then (19)
   12. Which is (1/3) (1/4) (of a pie?)
5. Ordinal Numbers
   13. Which is (tenth) (in a row of 12)?
6. Measurements
   14. Which holds more, a quart or a gallon? *a quart*
   15. Which is more, a teaspoon or a tablespoon? *teaspoon*
   16. Read this clock (2:30) . . . (9:30)
   17. Read this thermometer . . . (show two different pictures)
   18. How many inches in a foot? *12 inches   I don't know*
   19. Which is longer, a foot or a yard? *I don't know*
   20. How tall are you? *10 feet tall*
7. Money and Value
   21. If you bought an ice cream cone for a dime and gave the clerk a quarter, how much change would you get? *10¢*
   22. How many quarters are there in a dollar? *five*
8. Number Operations and Problem Solving
   23. 10−4 = *6*   12−9 = *6*   8−3 = *5*   16−7 = *9*   128−~~35~~ = *65*
       65−6 = *59*   46¢−33¢ = *13¢*
   24. 2×4 = *8*   3×2 = *6*
   25. 2 divided into 8 = *4*   3 divided into 9 = *4*
   26. 9+4 = *13*   2+8 = *10*   1+4+3 = *8*   65+2+2 = *69*   37+~~~~ = *39*
   27. There are five boys and three girls getting on a school bus. How many children get on the bus? *nine*

28. At the first stop of the bus 2 boys and 1 girl get off the bus. How do you find out how many children are left on the bus? Do you add, subtract, or divide?   *I don't know*

John answered only a few of the measurement problems correctly and neither of the money questions. The teacher would probably want to construct in these categories some simpler items like those shown at the primary level.

The results of the inventory cannot stand alone. They need to be supplemented by all possible information about the child's educational background and potential. However, John's performance on the intermediate inventory would probably cause the teacher to form several hypotheses:

1. John may have a relative strength in form perception and vocabulary. Further testing is suggested at a higher level.
2. John has a relative strength in computation but has problems with borrowing and carrying.
3. John does well in counting and naming fractions but appears to have little understanding of positional notation. This may explain in part his problems with renaming and regrouping.
4. John has a relative weakness in the measurement and money categories. Further testing is suggested at a lower level.
5. John is not able to deal very well with word problems involving extraneous material. Perhaps there is some clue in his educational background which will help explain this. It could be that the teacher has not provided sufficient practice in this skill.
6. Even when John is able to give the correct answer, he is unable to identify the process involved in problem solving. Have these processes been properly emphasized by his teacher?

The analysis of the test should suggest to the teacher some relative strengths and weaknesses and some probable causes of the pattern. He will need to seek further information in order to test his hypotheses, but at least he has some idea of the general level of performance and has some possible ideas for modifying his own instruction for John. A consideration of the many variables that affect learning may provide further hints.

The teacher might also want to make some comparison between John's performance and that of the rest of the class. If only a few children are having difficulty with measurement concepts, he might want to provide them with specialized individual attention. However, if a large percentage of the children are experiencing problems with carrying and borrowing, he might want to provide greater emphasis for the entire class on the ideas of renaming and regrouping.

The record of John's performance on the number inventory administered in September should be retained. His teacher may want to readminister it later in the year. This pretest and post-test approach will give him some notation of John's progress during the period in between tests and will also help him judge the effectiveness of the changes he made in his instructional program.

IMPACT OF TEST RESULTS ON CURRICULUM, METHODOLOGY, AND MATERIALS

The results on testing provide the teacher with information about the children in her class. This data should also have an impact on the curriculum, methodology, and instructional aids.

If a significant number of students in a class perform poorly on certain problems in arithmetic reasoning but very well on problems of computation, the teacher might assume that the previous instruction had been insufficient. Among other things, it could be that earlier instruction permitted the development of careless habits, placed emphasis on rote skills, neglected teaching for understanding, or failed to encourage problem-solving skills. The fact that a relatively large percentage of the students did poorly in a given area should cause the teacher to examine the balance and emphasis of the mathematics curriculum. In short, the evaluation of pupil progress is just as much an evaluation of teacher effectiveness and curriculum design. A testing program which does not have implications for teaching is of dubious consequence.

The results of the testing may also suggest modifications in methodology and materials. One explanation of poor performance in problem solving could be that not enough concrete materials were used or that an insufficient variety of instructional aids were used. Perhaps the emphasis in the curriculum is proper and the materials are adequate, but the particular method of teaching does not suit this group. A more frequent use of the unit approach and incidental instruction could be one possible remedy. Underlying problems such as perceptual deficits call for specialized materials and methods with particular children.

The evaluation of pupil progress will have significant impact on classroom instruction and materials. The testing program, then, should promote not only pupil growth but also improvement of the mathematics program.

REPORTING TO PARENTS

All parents are concerned about the growth of their children. Parents look forward to the maturation of their offspring into healthy adults, competent workers, distinguished citizens, and fine persons. They watch for the smallest signs of growth. Much of their information must come from the teacher, since many of the competencies necessary for independent living are developed in schools. Of course, the parent of the handicapped child is especially anxious for signals of progress. It is not an easy thing for any parent to raise a child in this complex technological, computerized society. The parents of a mentally retarded child are alerted to the tremendous obstacles their child will encounter. They desperately need sound information on which to construct their expectancies and build their plans for the future of their child. There are several guidelines which will be helpful to the mathematics teacher in providing the parent with a portion of that information:

1. Let the parents know how the child is doing in comparison to himself.
2. Explain to the parents the obstacles to their child's learning and how they may help.
3. Avoid using grade equivalent standards in explaining the child's progress. Even professional educators become confused about the interpretation of grade equivalents.
4. Do not use letter grades. If the letter grade is used to compare the child to his chronological peers of average intelligence, he will surely be given a "D" or "F" since he is one to three years behind what they are doing. Yet in terms of his capacity, the retarded child might be doing very well. On the other hand, if the retardate is given an "A" or "B" because he is doing well in terms of his own potential there is equal confusion. The parents might call for his return to the regular classroom or wonder why he does so poorly in everyday life when he receives such good grades.
5. Use a parent conference, home visit, or telephone call to explain how the child is progressing.
6. Provide the parents with portfolios of the child's work which actually show the type of work he can and cannot do.
7. Put up room displays of the work of all the children in the class so the parent can form some notion of how the class performs on the whole.
8. Send an occasional letter to the parent detailing progress.
9. Try to be positive and reassuring.

SUMMARY

The purpose of evaluation of pupil progress in mathematics is to provide the teacher with information upon which to base intelligent educational decisions. The determination of whether measured progress is satisfactory depends on a wide range of variables. The teacher can uncover information about these variables through a careful study of the child's educational record, systematic observations, and a well-organized testing program. There are not adequate standardized tests for the mentally retarded so informal number inventories must be constructed. The results of the inventories should be interpreted with caution and will have considerable impact upon the curriculum, methodology, and instructional media. Parents need to have adequate information about the growth of their children in order to make plans for the future.

EVALUATION INSTRUMENTS

It was indicated in this chapter that there are a few arithmetic tests which are useable with the mentally retarded. The tests listed below may prove helpful if cautiously administered and interpreted.

PUBLISHER	TITLE	DESCRIPTION
A-4	*KeyMath Diagnostic Arithmetic Test*	Diagnostic test for preschool through seventh grade with no upper limit for remedial use. Covers content, operations, and applications. Useful with slow learners and educable mentally retarded children.
A-4	*Peabody Individual Achievement Test*	*Mathematics* is one of five subtests of this individually administered test. The items in this subtest sample from such topics as shapes, measurement, time, number symbols, fractions, money, number concepts, operations, and problem solving. Yields grade and age equivalents, percentile ranks and standard scores.
S-2	*SRA Achievement Series*	Subtest of SRA Achievement for grades 2-6. Yields scores on (1) concepts, (2) reasoning,

PUB-LISHER CODE	TITLE	DESCRIPTION
		(3) computation, (4) total. This is an especially useful test since it goes as low as grade one and has guidelines for further diagnostic work.
W-6	*Wide Range Achievement Test*	Tests levels from kindergarten to college. Stresses computation.
C-12	*Diagnostic Arithmetic Tests*	Eight tests: addition, subtraction, multiplication, division, weights, percentage, measures, fractions.
C-12	*Los Angeles Diagnostic Tests*	Two tests available: *Fundamentals of Arithmetic* and *Reasoning in Arithmetic*.
C-12	*California Arithmetic Tests*	Subtest of California Achievement tests. Grades 1-2, 2.5-4.5, 4-6, 7-9. The tests give three scores (1) reasoning, (2) fundamental, (3) total.
H-3	*Metropolitan Achievement Tests*	Subtest of Metropolitan Achievement Tests including grades 3-4, 5-6, 7-9 yielding two scores: (1) computation, (2) problem solving and concepts.
S-4	*Seeing through Arithmetic Tests*	Mainly for use with the Scott, Foresman Series, *Seeing Through Arithmetic*, 1962. However, may have value for some retarded children involved in a modern mathematics program in Grades 3, 4, 5, 6, yielding six scores: (1) problem solving (2) computation (3) selecting equations (4) information (5) concepts (6) total.

PUB-LISHER CODE	TITLE	DESCRIPTION
R-7	*Trainable Mentally Retarded Performance Profile*	Consists of six areas. One of these areas has a sub-test on basic knowledge of numbers. For use with the trainable mentally retarded.
R-7	*YEMR Performance Profile for the Young Moderately and Mildly Retarded*	Consists of ten areas including sections on motor skills, perceptual and intellectual development, and academics.
A-4		American Guidance Service, Inc., Publishers' Building, Circle Pines, Minnesota
B-4	*Fundamental Processes in Arithmetic*	Diagnosis of errors in addition, subtraction, multiplication and division.

REFERENCES

Allen, Robert M. and Allen, Sue P. *Intellectual Evaluation of the Mentally Retarded Child: A Handbook.* Beverly Hills, California: Western Psychological Services, 1967.

Anastasi, Anne. *Psychological Testing.* New York: The MacMillan Company, 1961.

Buros, Oscar Krisen. *The Sixth Mental Measurements Yearbook.* Highland Park, New Jersey: The Gryphon Press, 1965.

Hammit, Helen. "Evaluating and Re-teaching the Slow Learner," *The Arithmetic Teacher,* XIV: No. 1 (January, 1967): 40-41.

Peterson, Daniel L. *Mathematical Knowledge of Young Mental Retardates.* dissertation, University of Missouri, 1967.

Prescott, Daniel. *The Child in the Educative Process.* New York: McGraw-Hill Book Company, Inc., 1957.

Shotwell, A. M., Dingman, H. F. and Tarjan, G. "A Number Test for Mental Defectives." *American Journal of Mental Deficiency* 60: 389, (1956).

Smith, E. M. *Counting, and Measuring.* Toronto: University of Toronto Press, 1961.

Terman, Lewis M. and Merrill, Maud A. *Stanford-Binet Intelligence Scale, Form L-M.* Boston: Houghton Mifflin Company, 1960.

Valett, Robert E. *The Remediation of Learning Disabilities.* Palo Alto, California: Fearon Publishers, 1967.

Wechsler, David. *Wechsler Intelligence Scale for Children.* New York: The Psychological Corporation, 1949.

appendix:

Publishers' Code

A-1 Allyn & Bacon, Inc.
     310 West Polk Street
     Chicago, Illinois 60607

B-2 Benefic Press
     Publishing Division of
     Beckley-Cardy Co.
     10300 W. Roosevelt Road
     Westchester, Illinois 60153

B-3 Benton Review Publishing Co.
     Fowler, Indiana 47944

C-3 Children's Press
     Jackson Boulevard and Racine Avenue
     Chicago, Illinois 60607

C-5 Continental Press
     Elizabethtown, Pennsylvania 17022

C-6 Creative Playthings, Inc.
     Princeton, New Jersey 08540

C-7 Arthur C. Croft, Publishers
     New London, Connecticut 06320

C-9	Cuisenaire Company of America, Inc. 9 Elm Avenue Mount Vernon, New York 10550
C-11	Constructive Playthings 1040 E. 85th Street Kansas City, Missouri 64131
D-6	Doubleday and Company Garden City, New York
D-7	Development Learning Materials 3505 North Ashland Avenue Chicago, Illinois 60657
E-4	Exceptionale Products Corporation P.O. Box 6374 Minneapolis, Minnesota 55423
F-1	Fearon Publishers, Inc. 2165 Park Boulevard Palo Alto, California 94306
F-4	Follett Publishing Company 1010 West Washington Boulevard Chicago, Illinois 60607
F-5	Field Educational Publications, Inc. 117 E. Palatine Road Palatine, Illinois 60067
G-4	Golden Press, Inc. Educational Division 850 Third Avenue New York, New York 10022
H-3	Harcourt, Brace, Jovanovich 7555 Caldwell Avenue Chicago, Illinois 60648
H-4	Harper and Row, Publishers, Inc. 49 East 33 Street New York, New York 10016

Appendix

H-6   Harr Wagner Publishing Company
609 Mission Street
San Francisco, California 94105

H-7   D. C. Heath Company
1815 Prairie Avenue
Chicago, Illinois 60616

H-9   Holt, Rinehart, and Winston, Inc.
283 Madison Avenue
New York, New York 10017

H-10   Houghton-Mifflin Company
110 Tremont Street
Boston, Massachusetts 02107

H-12   Hayes School Publishing Company
321 Pennwood Avenue
Wilkinsburg, Pennsylvania 15221

I-4   Instructo Products
Philadelphia, Pennsylvania 19131

J-1   The Judy Company
310 North Second Street
Minneapolis, Minnesota 55401

K-1   Kenworthy Educational Service, Inc.
Box 3031
Buffalo, New York 14205

L-3   The Learning Center, Inc.
P.O. Box 330
Princeton, New Jersey 08540

M-2   Mafex Associates
Box 519
Johnstown, Pennsylvania 15907

M-6   Melmont Publishers, Inc.
310 South Racine Avenue
Chicago, Illinois 60607

M-10   Milton Bradley Company
Springfield, Massachusetts 01101

N-1	National Education Association 1201 16th Street, N.W. Washington, D.C. 20036
N-5	New York University Press Washington Square New York, New York 10003
O-2	The Oxford Book Company 71 Fifth Avenue New York, New York 10003
P-2	Pierson Trading Company 6109 Burns Way Sacramento, California 95824
P-5	Prentice-Hall, Inc. Englewood Cliffs, New Jersey 07632
R-5	Frank E. Richards 1453 Main Street Phoenix, New York 13135
S-1	Scholastic Book Services 50 West 44th Street New York, New York 10036
S-4	Scott, Foresman and Company 433 East Erie Street Chicago, Illinois 60611
S-11	Stanwix House, Inc. 3020 Chartiers Avenue Pittsburgh, Pennsylvania 15204
S-14	The Steck-Vaughn Company P.O. Box 2028 Austin, Texas 78767
S-16	R. H. Stone Products Box 44 Detroit, Michigan
S-18	Charles Scribner's Sons New York, New York 10017
T-1	Tools for Education Inc. Burlington, Wisconsin 53105

Appendix

T-4   Fern Tripp
2035 East Sierra Valley
Dinuba, California

T-5   Teaching Resources, Inc.
334 Boylston Street
Boston, Massachusetts 02116

V-2   Vanguard Press
424 Madison Avenue
New York, New York 10017

V-3   The Viets Company
986 Rushleigh Road
Cleveland, Ohio 44121

W-5   Welsh Printing Company, Inc.
2785 East Foothill Boulevard
Pasadena, California 91107

S-2   Science Research Associates (SRA)
259 East Erie Street
Chicago, Illinois

C-12   California Test Bureau
McGraw-Hill Book Company
Del Monte Research Park
Monterey, California 93940

E-5   Educational Testing Service
20 Nassau Street
Princeton, N.J. 08540

P-6   Psychological Service
1800 Wilshire Boulevard
Los Angeles, California 90057

W-6   Western Psychological Services
12031 Wilshire Boulevard
Los Angeles, California 90025

R-7   Reporting Service for Children
563 Westview Avenue
Ridgefield, New Jersey 07657

I-5   Ideal School Supply Company
Oak Lawn, Illinois 60451

Index

Index

abacus, 235
ability levels:
  preprimary educable mentally retarded, 53-54
  primary educable mentally retarded, 100-01
  intermediate educable mentally retarded, 195-96
  junior high educable mentally retarded, 299-300
  senior high educable mentally retarded, 377-78
  preprimary trainable mentally retarded, 505
  primary trainable mentally retarded, 510-11
  intermediate trainable mentally retarded, 531
  advanced trainable mentally retarded, 557
abstract problems, 36
acalculia, 5, 37
achievement, obstacles to, 20:
  of educable mentally retarded, 10-12
  of trainable mentally retarded, 12-15
achievement discrepancy, 26
achievement:
  mental age as a guide to achievement and anticipated grade potential, 104-05
Adams, H. W., 29, 49
Adaptations, principles of, 35-37:
  abstract problems, 36
  acalculia, 37
  age tripod, 35
  alternative to alternative, 33
  arithmetic reasoning, 36
  attention span, 37
  carelessness, 36
  concrete rewards, 35
  consistency of reward, 35
  drill, 36
  emphasis on process, 36
  expectancies, 35
  focus on target, 35
  individual differences, 34
  integration, 36
  intermediate step, 33
  motivation, 34
  patience, 32
  practical experience, 38
  pity, 32

adaptations (cont'd)

readiness, 32
regular texts, 37
strategic retreat, 34
success spiral, 36
vocabulary, 34
word problems, 37

addition, 171-77, 235-36, 271-76, 341-46,
552-54, 563, 570-71
addresses, 146, 241
age tripod, 35
algorithms, 273, 280
Allen, A., 292, 367, 487
Allen, R., 661
Allen, S., 661
Anastasi, A., 661
anecdotal records, 589
angles, 312
amentia, 1
American Association on Mental Deficiency, 2
anticipated grade potential (AGP), 21-24
arithmetic reasoning, 36
art activities, 201-204, 207
associative property, 44, 354-57
attention span, 5, 37
auctions, 433
Auger, 14
automobile (*see* car)

balance board, 209
banking, 407
barometer, 389
Barsch, Ray H., 579
base ten, 222
Baumgartner, Bernice B., 579
beadframe, 139
beadline, 236
behavior modification, 32-37;
and rewards 35
and expectancies, 35
Benoitt, Paul E., 49
Bensburg, Gerard, 8, 16, 49

Bijou, 593
bills, 421:
electric, 422
gas, 422
household, 421
laundry, 424
medical, 424
telephone, 421
block design, 307
blockmobile, 111
body image, 59, 76
borrowing, 571
bowling, 427
brain damage, 5-6
Brueckuer, Leo J., 501
budgeting, 270, 412-34
budget sheet, 418
building blocks, 61
Burns, Paul C., 12, 16, 47, 49
Buros, 661
bushels, 397
Bushwell-John Diagnostic Chart, 10
Bushwell Vocabulary Test, 12
buying wisely, 429-34

Cain, L. F., 14, 16, 579
calendar, 159, 246-51, 326, 429, 529
California Achievement Test, 594
Callahan, John J., 296
calorie, 399
can sizes, 399
car (*see also* transportation), 390-95, 434-36
cardinal number, 47, 58, 103, 199, 303, 379:
advanced trainable mentally retarded, 563-64
intermediate educable mentally retarded, 299-300
intermediate trainable mentally retarded, 540
junior high educable mentally retarded, 315-21
preprimary educable mentally retarded, 81-87
preprimary trainable mentally

Index

cardinal numbers (cont'd)
    retarded, 514
    primary educable mentally retarded, 127-43
    primary trainable mentally retarded, 514
    senior high educable mentally retarded, 379
carelessness, 36
catalog, 434
Cawley, John F., 190
Central Time, 403-07
chalkboard training, 208-09
Chaney, C. M., 49
change making (*see also* money and value), 107, 408
characteristics, 67-69
charge accounts, 443
charts, 415-16
checklists of mathematics skills:
    advanced trainable mentally retarded, 558-59
    intermediate educable mentally retarded, 198-200
    intermediate trainable mentally retarded, 532-33
    junior high educable mentally retarded, 302-04
    preprimary, 57
    preprimary trainable mentally retarded, 510-11
    primary educable mentally retarded, 102-04
    primary trainable mentally retarded, 510-11
    senior high educable mentally retarded, 378-40
checks, 410
chronological age, 58
circle, 137, 208
classification of mental retardation, 2
climbing, 62, 63
clock (*see* time and measurement)
clothing, 400-01
coin (*see* money and value)

Coleman, Josephine K., 49
column addition (*see* addition, number operations)
combing (*see* addition)
commutative properties, 44, 288
computational skills (*see* number operations)
conceptual disorders, 6
Conner, Frances, 579
configuration cards, 108
consumer mathematics, 376
cooking:
    measurement in, 395-97
coordination board, 66, 106
correspondence, 85, 128-29, 225, 265, 278, 525, 539
counting, 82, 134, 226, 264-66, 278, 525, 539
Coxford, Arthur F., 47, 49
Crawford, William L., 501
creativity, 7
credit, 439-43
cross, 187, 208, 292, 367
Cruickshank, William M., 10, 11, 16, 21, 49
cubes, 141
cubic measures, 386
cuisenaire materials, 231
cups, 395-96 (see measurement)
curriculum content, 46-48
curriculum construction, 19-50
curriculum and testing, 583-84

date, 247
days of weeks, 247
defeat cycle, 9
deficiency, mental, 1
depositing, 409
developmental sequence of mathematical skills:
    early childhood, 57
    intermediate educable mentally retarded, 197-200
    junior high educable mentally retarded, 301-02
    preprimary educable mentally

developmental sequence of mathematical skills (cont'd)

    retarded, 57
    primary educable mentally retarded, 102-05
    senior high educable mentally retarded, 378-80
directions, 204
distributive property, 45, 354
division, 288-91, 357-67
docking, 450
dot-to-dot, 67
drawing, 132
drill, 36
Dunn, Lloyd M., 11, 16, 21, 49

east, 204
Eastern Time, 403-404
Edwards, Alice D., 49
Erickson, Leland H., 9, 16
Erie School Program, 200, 216
evaluation, 583 (see also inventory)
expectancies, 35-36
experience, 34
eye-hand motor coordination, 201

Fairbanks-Robinson Program, 220
feet, 325
Feingold, Abraham, 190, 297
figure-ground, 6, 211, 212-13
fine motor skills, 517
finger plays, 72, 204
Finley, Carment J., 11, 16
forced responsiveness, 6-7
form, 57, 67, 69, 71, 72, 74, 77, 102, 198, 200-08
form and perception, 46, 57:
    advanced trainable mentally retarded, 558
    intermediate educable mentally retarded, 199
    intermediate trainable mentally retarded, 532
    junior high educable mentally retarded, 305-12

form and perception (cont'd)

    preprimary educable mentally retarded, 58
    preprimary trainable mentally retarded, 510
    primary educable mentally retarded, 105
    primary trainable mentally retarded, 516
    senior high educable mentally retarded, 378-79
fractions, 237, 319-21, 325, 383-85
Frankel, Max G., 578
Frostig, Marianne, 200, 207, 211-214, 296
functional mathematics (see also mathematics), 27
fundamental processes, 594

gallons, 243, 322
garage sales, 433
gas guage, 391
geometric shapes, 202
Goldstein, Herbert, 16
grade potential (see anticipated grade potential)
grades, 583
grouping, 321
gross motor areas, 518
Guenther, R. J., 13, 16, 579

Hammit, Helen, 661
handicap, mental, 1
Headstart, 99
holiday pay, 450
Hommes, Csanyi, 49
Hottel, J. V., 13-14, 16, 579
Hudson, Margaret, 14, 16-17
hyperactivity, 7

identity element 287, 291
incidental instruction, 39
inches (see measurement)
individual differences, 34
insurance, 448-49

Index

integration, 36, 39-40
intermediate mathematics, 193, 531-32
intermediate step, 33
interpersonal relations, 4-5
inventory of mathematics skills:
   administration of, 595
   adult level, 643
   classroom, 596
   intermediate level, 624
   interpretation of, 652
   junior high level, 633
   pre-primary level, 603
   primary level, 611

Jacobs, A. N., 8, 10
job, 449-51
Johnson, G. Orville, 46, 501, 579
Jordan, Laura, 40

Kaleski, Lotte, 49
Kelly, Elizabeth M., 17
Kephart, Newell C., 5, 17, 59, 62, 112, 190, 200, 207, 208-11, 297, 559-60, 579
KeyMath, 593
kinesthetics, 78
Kirk, Samuel A., 46, 49, 50
Klausmeier, H. H., 8, 12, 17
Kolburne, Luma Louis, 504, 579
Kolstoe, Oliver P., 12, 17, 372, 501

language deficiency, 7
language:
   of trainable mentally retarded, 14
learning characteristics, 4-10
left, 204
Lewis, W. D., 22, 50
lotto, 135-36

McDowell, Louis K., 17
map reading, 312, 392-94
Mastain, Richard K., 46, 47, 50
matching, 64-65
materials (*see* teaching aids)
mathematics sentences, 45

mathematics:
   disabilities, 5-7
   early childhood, 53
   for adultation, 375
   for everyday living, 28-32
   for intermediate educable mentally retarded, 193
   for junior high educable mentally retarded, 299
   for preprimary educable mentally retarded, 53
   for preprimary trainable mentally retarded, 508-09
   for primary educable mentally retarded, 99
   for primary trainable mentally retarded, 515
   for senior high educable mentally retarded, 375
   for trainable mentally retarded, 375
   modern, 41-42
   pre-adultation, 299
measurement, 103, 149-61, 242-46, 303:
   and advanced trainable mentally retarded, 564-67
   and intermediate educable mentally retarded, 242-46
   and intermediate trainable mentally retarded, 544
   and junior high educable mentally retarded, 322-32
   and preprimary educable mentally retarded, 88-90
   and preprimary trainable mentally retarded, 513
   and primary educable mentally retarded, 149
   and primary trainable mentally retarded, 545-46
   and senior high educable mentally retarded, 379-80, 385-407
measures:
   linear, 160-61
   liquid, 159
   standard, 242-44

676

Index

measuring areas, 312
memory, 8
mental age, 20-21, 54, 55, 196, 376, 506-07, 515, 531, 557
mental retardation:
  characteristics, 4-10
  classifying, 2-4
  definition, 3
  educable, 3
  trainable, 3
menu, 267
Merrill, Maud A., 12, 17
Metropolitan Achievement Test, 594
Miller, Donald Y., 501
money and value, 47, 58, 304:
  and advanced trainable mentally retarded, 567-70
  and intermediate educable mentally retarded, 263-70
  and intermediate trainable mentally retarded, 546-51
  and junior high educable mentally retarded, 332-40
  and preprimary trainable mentally retarded, 530
  and senior high educable mentally retarded, 407-34
monocular, 210
Montessori, Maria, 114
month, 247
moron, 1
motivation, 5, 9-11, 34
motor skills (*see* form and perception)
Mountain Time, 403
multiple criteria, 25, 26
multiplication, 282-88, 351-57
music, 200, 204

natural numbers, 42-43
neurological disorders, 5-7
Norton, John K., 29, 50
north, 204
Nossoff, 46, 47, 50
notation, 43-44
number blindness, 5
number, cardinal (*see* cardinal number)

number families, 224
number frame, 79
number illustrations, 83-84
number inventory (*see* inventory)
number line, 121, 181, 222, 245, 279, 284, 360
number operations, 44-45, 50:
  and advanced trainable mentally retarded, 570-76
  and intermediate educable mentally retarded, 270-91
  and intermediate trainable mentally retarded, 551-57
  and junior high educable mentally retarded, 341-67
  and preprimary educable mentally retarded, 91-92
  and primary educable mentally retarded, 171-86
  and primary trainable mentally retarded, 530-32
  and senior high educable mentally retarded, 451
number, ordinal (*see* ordinal number)
number patterns, 46
number pockets, 232
number symbols, 47:
  and advanced trainable mmentally retarded, 563
  and intermediate educable mentally retarded, 221
  and intermediate trainable mentally retarded, 537
  and junior high educable mentally retarded, 313-15
  and preprimary educable mentally retarded, 76-81
  and preprimary trainable mentally retarded, 513-14
  and primary educable mentally retarded, 119
  and primary trainable mentally retarded, 521-23
numerals, 43 (*see also* writing numbers)

Index

objectives, 28-32:
  for advanced trainable mentally retarded, 558
  for educable mentally retarded, 31
  for intermediate educable mentally retarded, 196-97
  for intermediate trainable mentally retarded, 532
  for junior high educable mentally retarded, 300-01
  for preprimary educable mentally retarded, 56-57
  for preprimary trainable mentally retarded, 509-10
  for primary educable mentally retarded, 101-02
  for primary trainable mentally retarded, 516
  for senior high educable mentally retarded, 377-78
  for trainable mentally retarded, 558
ocular control, 209
odometer, 391
ordinal number, 47, 58, 103, 143-49, 199, 303, 321-22:
  advanced trainable mentally retarded, 564
  intermediate educable mentally retarded, 239-41
  intermediate trainable mentally retarded, 540-45
  junior high educable mentally retarded, 315
  preprimary educable mentally retarded, 87-88
  preprimary trainable mentally retarded, 514
  primary educable mentally retarded, 143-49
  primary trainable mentally retarded, 528
  senior high educable mentally retarded, 379, 382-84

ounces, 323, 396
oven, 397
overtime, 450

Pacific Time, 403
parents, reporting to, 658
parquetry blocks, 109
pathological fixation, 6
patience, 33
paying bills, 18-26
peck, 395
peg board, 132, 210-11, 519
perception, 46, 57, 58-73, 102, 511, 559-62 (*see also* form and perception)
perceptual constancy, 211, 213
perceptual impairment, 6
perceptual-motor tasks, 59-73
perception of position in space, 211, 213
Perry, Natalie, 505, 506, 580
Peterson, Daniel L., 17, 46, 50, 580, 661
physical education, 200, 204, 207
Piaget, Jean, 46, 50
picture file, 83
pictures, 137, 140, 225-26, 553
pints, 322
pity, 33
place value, 221, 223, 316, 344
positional notation, 221
pounds, 323-24
Prescott, Daniel, 589, 661
principles of adaptation (*see* adaptation)
problem solving, 48
  (*see also* number operations)
psycho-sociological impairments, 194
psychometric reports, 584-86
puzzles, 71, 136, 210, 308

quarts, 243, 322, 395

readiness, 32
records, 249
rectangle, 209

regrouping, 273, 277, 342, 347, 364 (*see also* number operations)
reinforcement, 37
restaurant, 425-27
rewards, 35
rhythms, 113, 124
rhymes, 120
right, 204
Reynolds, M. C., 12, 17
Ring, S. B., 21, 50
Roach, Eugene G., 580
Roman numerals, 314-15, 383
Rosenberg, M. B., 50
Rosenzweig, Louis E., 505, 580
ruler, 245 (*see* measurement)
rummage sales, 433

sales, 429-31
savings, 270, 437-39
savings bonds, 438
seasons, 247
self-control, 7
sensory motor training, 209
seriation, 240, 563
set, 42, 127-28, 135, 175, 234, 541, 543
sewing, 400-01
sex, 8-9
shapes, 306
Shotwell, A. M., 662
Silverstein, A. B., 14, 17
"Simon Says," 65
slow learner, 1
Smith, E. M., 662
Smith, R., 190
Sniff, William F., 372, 501
Social Security, 449
socio-economic background, 9
sorting, 67, 70, 87, 130, 547
south, 204
spatial arrangements, 70
spatial fields, 5, 70
spatial relationships, 213
speedometer, 390-91
spool, 66
square, 208
Stanford-Binet, 22, 585, 586

Stanford Achievement Test, 12
Stephens, T. M., 50
stepping, 65, 66
Stern, Catherine, 296
stick figures, 210
strategic retreat, 34
Strauss, Alfred A., 5, 17, 59
Stutler, Mary S., 46, 47, 50
subtraction, 179-84, 236, 277-81, 346-51, 554-57, 571, 573-77
success spiral, 36

tables, 317-18
tablespoon, 396
Talbot, 578
taxes, 442
teaching aids, 293-96:
   for intermediate educable mentally retarded, 292-95
   for junior high educable mentally retarded, 367-71
   for preprimary educable mentally retarded, 93-95
   for primary educable mentally retarded, 187-90
   for senior high educable mentally retarded, 487-500
   for trainable mentally retarded, 577-78
teaspoon, 396
telephone, 146, 241, 421-22
temperature, 319, 387-89 (*see also* measurement)
Terman, Lewis M., 662
tests (*see* inventories)
texts, 37
test items, 596-99
thermostat, 387
Thurstone, Thelma, 8, 17
time, 149-53, 251-63, 326-32, 401-07, 567-70
trading stamps, 431
traffic signals, 202, 310-11, 381
transportation, 434-36
Trapp, 50
triangle, 209
tunnel crawling, 61

Index

unit method, 40, 451-86
used purchases, 432

Valett, 50, 586, 662
Vigilante, Nicholas J., 296
visual-motor coordination (*see* form and perception)
visual-motor synchronism, 60
visual perception, 5 (*see also* perception)
vocabulary, 75, 34, 46, 58, 73-76, 103:
  of advanced trainable mentally retarded, 561
  of early childhood, 115-19
  of intermediate educable mentally retarded, 198, 221
  of intermediate trainable mentally retarded, 536
  of junior high educable mentally retarded, 312-13
  of primary educable mentally retarded, 115
  of primary trainable mentally retarded, 520-21
  of senior high educable mentally retarded, 379, 381-82
  preprimary, 116
vocational mathematics, 375

walking board, 209
Warren, Sue A., 14, 15, 17
Weaver, J. Fred, 46, 50
weight, 159-60, 244-45 (*see also* measurement)
west, 204
Williams, Alfred H., 46, 47, 50, 580
Wilson, F. T., 11, 17
withholding, 447
WISC, 24, 484, 587
Witty, P. A., 50
word problems, 37, 193
writing numbers, 79-81, 126, 523-24, 537
W-2 Forms, 447

yard, 245, 325-26
YEMR profile, 594

Zigler, Edward, 20, 51